Seventh
Canadian
Edition

# Managing Human Resources

**Monica Belcourt, PhD, FCHRP**

Professor, School of Human Resource Management
York University

**Parbudyal Singh**

Professor, School of Human Resource Management
York University

**George Bohlander**

Professor Emeritus of Management
Arizona State University

**Scott Snell**

Professor of Business Administration
University of Virginia

NELSON / EDUCATION

# NELSON / EDUCATION

**Managing Human Resources, Seventh Canadian Edition**

by Monica Belcourt, Parbudyal Singh, George Bohlander, and Scott Snell

**Vice President, Editorial Higher Education:**
Anne Williams

**Acquisitions Editor:**
Alwynn Pinard

**Marketing Manager:**
Dave Stratton

**Developmental Editor:**
Lacey McMaster

**Photo Researcher and Permissions Coordinator:**
Lynn McLeod

**Content Production Manager:**
Jennifer Hare

**Production Service:**
MPS Limited

**Copy Editor:**
Holly Dickinson

**Proofreader:**
Jennifer McIntyre

**Indexer:**
Dave Luljak

**Manufacturing Manager:**
Joanne McNeil

**Design Director:**
Ken Phipps

**Managing Designer:**
Franca Amore

**Interior Design:**
Sharon Lucas

**Cover Design:**
Sharon Lucas

**Cover Image:**
© Gillian Blease/Getty Images

**Compositor:**
MPS Limited

**Printer:**
RR Donnelley

**Library and Archives Canada Cataloguing in Publication Data**

Managing human resources / Monica Belcourt ... [et al.].—7th Canadian ed.

Includes bibliographical references and index.
ISBN-978-0-17-650690-2

1. Personnel management—Textbooks. 2. Personnel management—Canada—Textbooks. I. Belcourt, Monica

HF5549.M3135 2013
658.3    C2012-906454-8

ISBN-13: 978-0-17-650690-2
ISBN-10: 0-17-650690-X

*To my husband, Michael Belcourt, who brings such adventure into our lives*

*To my wife, Nirmala Singh, and our children, Alysha, Amelia, and Aren,*
*for all their love and support*

*To my wife, Ronnie Bohlander, and to our children, Ryan and Kathryn*

*To my wife, Marybeth Snell, and to our children, Sara, Jack, and Emily*

# FEATURES

## FEATURES

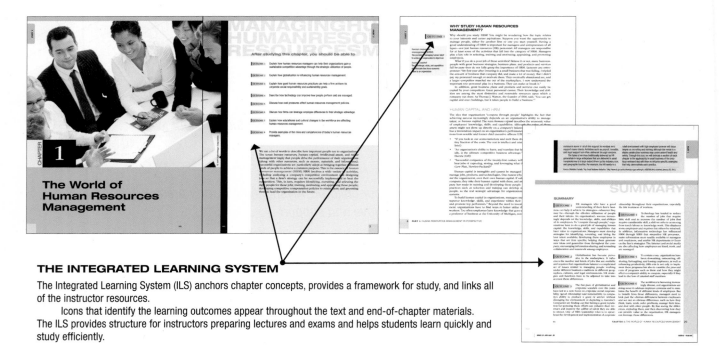

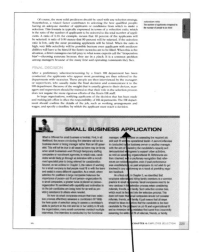

## THE INTEGRATED LEARNING SYSTEM

The Integrated Learning System (ILS) anchors chapter concepts, provides a framework for study, and links all of the instructor resources.

Icons that identify the learning outcomes appear throughout the text and end-of-chapter materials. The ILS provides structure for instructors preparing lectures and exams and helps students learn quickly and study efficiently.

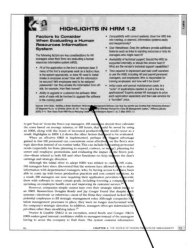

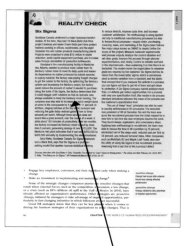

## HIGHLIGHTS IN HRM

This popular boxed feature provides real-world examples of how organizations perform HR functions. The Highlights are introduced in the text discussion and include topics such as small business and international issues.

## SMALL BUSINESS APPLICATION

Small Business Application takes the principles and prescriptions of a functional area, such as recruitment, and demonstrates how these can be applied in a small business setting.

## REALITY CHECK

Reality Check presents an interview with a Canadian expert in the field, illustrating how the material in the chapter is used in the real world.

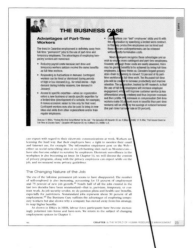

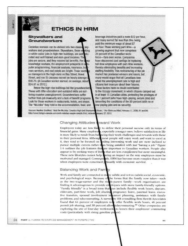

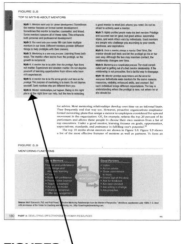

## THE BUSINESS CASE

The Business Case features the business or financial implications of the adoption of HR practices. It also helps students build the skills necessary to recommend practices and projects, based on the projected costs and benefits, to senior management.

## ETHICS IN HRM

Ethics in HRM provokes debate and discussion among students around the often grey areas of human resources management (HRM), including drug testing of employees and electronic surveillance of employees at work.

## FIGURES

Chapters include an abundance of graphic materials and flowcharts, providing a visual, dynamic presentation of concepts and HR activities. All figures are systematically referenced in the text discussion.

## USING THE INTERNET

The Internet is referenced in all chapters, with new government, research, and business Internet links and addresses.

## KEY TERMS IN MARGIN

Key terms appear in boldface and are defined in margin notes next to the text discussion. The key terms are also listed at the end of each chapter and in the glossary at the end of the text.

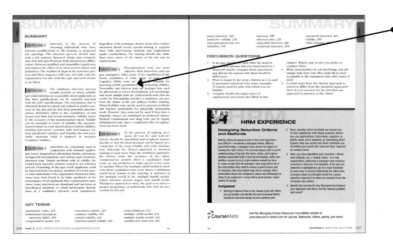

## SUMMARY

At the end of each chapter, a brief description of each learning outcome provides a focused review of the chapter material.

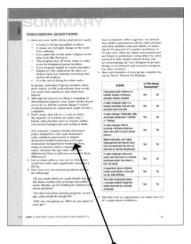

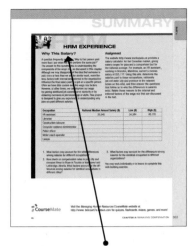

## DISCUSSION QUESTIONS

Discussion questions following the chapter summary offer an opportunity to focus on each of the learning outcomes in the chapter and to stimulate critical thinking. Many of these questions allow for group analysis and class discussion.

## HRM EXPERIENCE EXERCISES

These skill-building exercises help students gain practical experience when dealing with employee/management concerns. Students can work through the exercises on either an individual or a team basis.

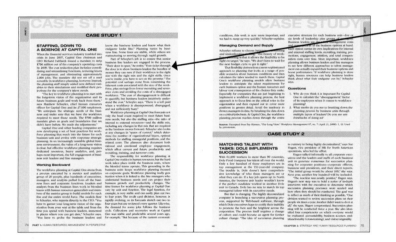

## CASES

Two or more case studies per chapter present current HRM issues in real-life settings that encourage consideration and critical analysis.

Visit the *Managing Human Resources* CourseMate website at www.belcourt7e.nelson.com for quizzes, flashcards, videos, games, and more!

# BRIEF CONTENTS

# CONTENTS

# CONTENTS

# CONTENTS

## CHAPTER 4
## JOB ANALYSIS AND WORK DESIGN   120

# CONTENTS

# CONTENTS

# CONTENTS

# CONTENTS

# CONTENTS

# CONTENTS

# CONTENTS

# CONTENTS

# CONTENTS

## PART 6
## EXPANDING HUMAN RESOURCES MANAGEMENT HORIZONS

# CONTENTS

# PREFACE

The seventh Canadian edition of *Managing Human Resources* will place your students at the forefront in understanding how organizations can gain sustainable competitive advantage through people. The role of human resources (HR) professionals is no longer limited to service functions such as recruiting and selecting employees. Today, HR managers assume an active role in the strategic planning and decision making at their organizations. Those managers who are good at it can have a major impact on the success of their firms. And human resources management (HRM) is not limited to HR staff. The best organizations recognize that managing people is the job of every manager, working in partnership with HR.

Each edition of the book highlights the ways in which the environment for managing human resources is changing somewhat but reveals that the goal of utilizing an organization's talent in the best way possible never changes. The purpose of this book is twofold: (1) to equip students with the tools and practices of HRM and an appreciation for the changes that they can effect by understanding how best to manage people and (2) to present the most current challenges and opportunities graduating students will face when it comes to today's HRM environment. These challenges exist both for those who will become HR managers and those who will become other types of managers.

Toward that end, the first chapter of the book lays out in broad terms the key challenges in HRM today. It includes a discussion of the HR strategies pursued by firms. Other aspects include how social media is affecting HRM and employees' privacy rights and a new discussion on how HR practices can help a firm achieve its corporate social responsibility and sustainability goals, making it an employer of choice. This chapter also discusses the important partnership with line managers and the competencies required of HR management.

Strategy and talent have become such central concerns of HR today that we continue to emphasize these topics in Chapter 2 and Chapter 5. The detailed coverage of these topics solidifies *Managing Human Resources* as perhaps the premier text for thought leadership, especially regarding the global talent pool. Employee diversity and how organizations can leverage all types of differences among their workers to their strategic advantage relate to this central theme of managing talent.

Whether the reader becomes a manager, a supervisor, or an HR specialist or is employed in other areas of the organization, *Managing Human Resources* provides a functional and practical understanding of HR programs to enable readers to see how HR affects all employees, the organization, the community, and the larger society.

Organizations in today's competitive world are discovering that it is how the individual HR functions are combined that makes all the difference. Managers typically do not focus on HR issues such as staffing, training, and compensation in isolation from one another. Each of these HR practices is combined into an overall system to enhance employee involvement and productivity.

## WHAT'S NEW IN THE SEVENTH CANADIAN EDITION

The most exciting change is the addition of a new Canadian author: Professor Parbudyal Singh, Director of the School of Human Resource Management at York University. Dr. Singh is one of the most prolific HR researchers in North America. He has won awards for research excellence and for teaching excellence. We are delighted to welcome him to the team. As you know, for each edition updates are made to laws, regulations, guidelines, and HR practices to reflect current contexts. To help instructors incorporate the new material into their courses, the following is a list of significant chapter-by-chapter changes:

## Chapter 1

- A new discussion on retaining and motivating employees in the face of downsizing and economic downturns and better workforce planning so that layoffs can be avoided in the first place
- A new discussion on nearshoring, which is the process of moving jobs closer to one's home country
- Intergenerational work issues
- A new section on corporate social responsibility

## Chapter 2

- A new discussion on the quality-of-fill metric, which attempts to measure how well new hires are performing so that the company will have enough top performers to propel it toward its strategic objectives
- A new discussion on how HR managers can significantly enhance their worth to their organizations by effectively gathering informal information or competitive intelligence about the strategic and HRM practices of their competitors
- An introduction to values-based hiring

## Chapter 3

- A new Reality Check on the award-winning RBC diversity program

## Chapter 4

- A new discussion on organizational restructuring and reengineering
- A new business case on how Purolator reduced business costs through better job analysis
- A new discussion on the contextual aspect of job analysis
- A new ethics case on job inflation
- A new highlight on flexible work schedules
- A new case study on Fairmont Hotels and Resorts

## Chapter 5

- A new discussion on employee profiling, which involves surveying a firm's top performers about what they like to do, what events they attend, and how they like to be contacted and recruited. Similar candidates can then be recruited using this information.
- A new section on the strategic aspects of recruiting: how the recruiting should reflect a firm's competitive priorities and who should do the recruiting, where, and how
- A new section on employer branding and recruiting using social networks, blogs, and philanthropic activities to improve a company's HR brand
- New information on mobile recruiting, the process of recruiting candidates via their mobile devices using text messages and application for LinkedIn, Twitter, etc.
- New information on job fairs and virtual job fairs
- New information on employee referral software, which makes it easier for current employees to recommend candidates

- New information on rerecruiting and "alumni networks." Rerecruiting is the process of keeping track of and maintaining relationships with former employees in the event that they wish to return to the firm.
- A section on improving the effectiveness of internships

### Chapter 6

- A new section on initial screening résumés and applications and a checklist for doing so
- A new discussion on video résumés
- New discussions on sequential interviews and phone interviews
- The addition of a candidate evaluation form
- A new discussion on making job offers and rejecting candidates

### Chapter 7

- A new section about onboarding
- A strategic perspective on training including the strategic training goals of Canadian organizations
- Web conferencing as a training method

### Chapter 8

- A new introduction explaining the context of appraisals
- A new section on providing ongoing performance feedback as a management tool
- New information on focal performance appraisal and its pros and cons
- New information on calibration as a tool to ensure standardized performance appraisals
- Techniques for giving feedback to Generation Y
- Two new cases

### Chapter 9

- A new discussion on the importance of an organization's compensation and reward systems and the links between the 2008 financial crisis and organizational incentives
- A new discussion on strategic compensation systems, including Google's
- A new discussion on motivational theories and pay systems
- A new ethics case related to unpaid interns
- A new highlight in compensation surveys and pay for HR and accounting professionals
- Revisions to the business case on pay equity
- A new small business application
- A new case study

### Chapter 10

- A new contextual discussion on pay-for-performance systems
- A new highlight/discussion on non-cash compensation
- A new ethics in compensation case
- A new discussion and data on executive compensation
- A new discussion on effective team incentives

- A new case on incentives at WestJet
- A new small business application
- A new case study on compensation for hospital executives

**Chapter 11**

- A new discussion on the context of employee benefits and managing benefits programs
- A new business case on managing the costs of benefits
- A new ethics case on benefits fraud
- A new discussion on a team approach to benefits cost containment
- A new highlight/discussion on childcare benefits and benefits at Business Development Bank of Canada

**Chapter 12**

- A new section on the practice of interviewing applicants for a culture of safety and fitness for duty
- New sections on employee fatigue and distracted driving
- An expanded section on workplace emergencies and emergency action plans
- Some information on Ontario's Bill 168

**Chapter 13**

- Additional information about employee rights with regard to Internet postings, computer use, and the use of social networks

**Chapter 14**

- A new discussion on the unionization process and the role of unions
- A new discussion on unionization at Walmart in Canada
- A new business case on building trust and saving money in union–management relations
- A new discussion on the use of replacement workers and labour disputes, focusing on the tragic Giant Mine case in Yellowknife, Northwest Territories
- A new case study on the unionization of farm workers

**Chapter 15**

- A reorganized chapter starting with a new discussion on the global environment and the similarities and differences across countries
- A new section on business services versus manufacturing from an HR perspective
- A new discussion on integrated technology platforms as a tool for global HR
- A new section on the employee selection process in emerging countries
- A discussion on new research on expatriate management and the importance of cultural understanding
- A discussion on the role of civil society in improving employment conditions in emerging markets, including an introduction to the "dirty" list

## FEATURES OF THE BOOK

We introduce overall text improvements that more accurately reflect HRM in today's business world and help the reader understand HRM issues more effectively.

The seventh Canadian edition reflects the body of knowledge required by students to pass the national knowledge exam, given by the Canadian Council of Human Resource Associations, as one of the steps toward the granting of the HR designation, the CHRP (Certified Human Resources Professional). The lead author, Dr. Monica Belcourt, participated in the development of the standards for the national certification process. This text covers more than 90 percent of the material being tested on the national knowledge exam. As a CHRP herself, Dr. Belcourt is very familiar with the competencies required for the profession and has written the text with these required professional competencies (RPCs) as the foundation for learning about HR.

- **Small Business Application.** Continuing in this edition is the inclusion of a section in each chapter that takes the principles and prescriptions of a functional area, such as recruitment, and demonstrates how these can be applied in a small business, of which there are about 1 million in Canada. This feature was initiated by Angus Duff, a Ph.D. candidate in Human Resources Management at York University and a former manager of HR with extensive experience in small and large businesses, in a previous edition of the text. Revisions to these cases and new cases were added in this edition.

- **HRM Experience.** We build on a popular feature in previous editions of *Managing Human Resources* by including many new experiential exercises to explore significant issues in HR. These skill-building exercises will help students gain practical experience when dealing with employee/management concerns such as pay for performance, effective team building, employee benefits, reducing employee stress, employee rights, balancing competitive challenges and employee concerns, customizing HR for different types of human capital, designing selection criteria and methods, and assessing the strategic fit of high-performance work systems. Students can work through the new exercises on either an individual or a team basis.

- **Human resources information systems (HRIS).** Throughout the text, we have specifically highlighted the use of HRIS to facilitate the managing of employees and the efficient performance of HR functions. For example, the impact of information technology on HR and the role of HRIS in such areas as compensation, recruitment and selection, training, job analysis, and safety are discussed.

- **Diversity.** Because we believe that diversity issues are an integral part of every HRM activity, updated and expanded coverage is included throughout the text.

- **HRM strategy.** The increasingly important role HRM plays in strategic planning is covered in Chapter 2. However, many of the chapters on functional areas such as recruitment, training, and compensation are now approached from a strategic perspective.

- **Coverage of global issues.** Global and international concerns are covered in great detail. This includes issues such as the World Trade Organization, China, and the impact of globalization on HR; multinationals and joint ventures; and global rights issues such as data protection and intellectual property. Although these issues have perhaps been peripheral to HRM in the past, they are increasingly seen as front and centre by many organizations.

- **Up-to-date HRM legislation and court cases.** A complete and thorough review and update of legislation and court cases governing HRM was completely rewritten for the previous edition by Dr. David Doorey, a professor of employment and labour law at the School of Human Resource Management at York University. Dr. Doorey has a B.A. and a Master's degree in Industrial Relations from the University of Toronto; an L.L.M. from the London School of Economics, and an L.L.B. and a Ph.D. from Osgoode Hall Law School.

He practised labour and employment law in British Columbia and Ontario. Check out his blog at http://www.yorku.ca/ddoorey/lawblog for current insights into these issues.

- **Comprehensive cases.** Five comprehensive cases are found on the CourseMate site accompanying the book. This exciting feature includes real cases used in Excalibur, the Canadian University Tournament in Human Resources, whereby university students from across Canada are asked to demonstrate their knowledge of HR to a jury. After students have developed solutions to the problems faced by dynamic companies such as Cirque du Soleil and Aeroplan, the instructor can compare their responses to the one generated by the winning university team and the answer prepared by an HR professor.

- **Updated boxed elements.** Many new Highlights in HRM boxes, Reality Checks, Ethics in HRM boxes, and Business Cases have been added. As a former president of the Human Resources Professionals Association of Ontario (HRPA), Dr. Monica Belcourt is very involved in the HR profession, with access to some of the thought leaders in HR in Canada.

- **Internet.** The ever-growing role of the Internet in HR activities is evident throughout the text. A few examples include social networking and mobile recruiting in Chapter 5, web-based training and e-learning in Chapter 7, and online 360-degree performance appraisal in Chapter 8.

- **End-of-chapter cases.** Most chapters have at least one new end-of-chapter case study highlighting chapter content. These cases have been selected to provide students with both current and practical HR problems and issues.

## ANCILLARY TEACHING AND LEARNING MATERIALS

### FOR INSTRUCTORS

### NETA Products

The **Nelson Education Teaching Advantage (NETA)** program delivers research-based instructor resources that promote student engagement and higher-order thinking to enable the success of Canadian students and educators.

Instructors today face many challenges. Resources are limited, time is scarce, and a new kind of student has emerged: one who is juggling school with work, has gaps in his or her basic knowledge, and is immersed in technology in a way that has led to a completely new style of learning. In response, Nelson Education has gathered a group of dedicated instructors to advise us on the creation of richer and more flexible ancillaries and online learning platforms that respond to the needs of today's teaching environments. Whether your course is offered in-class, online, or both, Nelson is pleased to provide pedagogically driven, research-based resources to support you.

The following members of our editorial advisory board have experience across a variety of disciplines and are recognized for their commitment to teaching:

**Norman Althouse**, Haskayne School of Business, University of Calgary

**Brenda Chant-Smith**, Department of Psychology, Trent University

**Scott Follows**, Manning School of Business Administration, Acadia University

**Jon Houseman**, Department of Biology, University of Ottawa

**Glen Loppnow**, Department of Chemistry, University of Alberta

**Tanya Noel**, Department of Biology, York University

**Gary Poole**, Senior Scholar, Centre for Health Education Scholarship, and Associate Director, School of Population and Public Health, University of British Columbia

**Dan Pratt**, Department of Educational Studies, University of British Columbia

**Mercedes Rowinsky-Geurts**, Department of Languages and Literatures, Wilfrid Laurier University

**David DiBattista**, Department of Psychology, Brock University

**Roger Fisher**, Ph.D.

In consultation with the editorial advisory board, Nelson Education has completely rethought the structure, approaches, and formats of our key textbook ancillaries. We have also increased our investment in editorial support for our ancillary authors. The result is the Nelson Education Teaching Advantage and its key components: *NETA Engagement, NETA Assessment, NETA Presentation,* and *Nelson Digital*. Each component includes one or more ancillaries prepared according to our best practices and may also be accompanied by documentation explaining the theory behind the practices.

*NETA Engagement presents* materials that help instructors deliver engaging content and activities to their classes. Instead of Instructor's Manuals that regurgitate chapter outlines and key terms from the text, NETA Enriched Instructor's Manuals (EIMs) provide genuine assistance to teachers. The EIMs answer questions such as *What should students learn? Why should students care?* and *What are some common student misconceptions and stumbling blocks?* EIMs not only identify the topics that cause students the most difficulty but also describe techniques and resources to help students master these concepts. Dr. Roger Fisher's *Instructor's Guide to Classroom Engagement (IGCE)* accompanies every EIM. (Information about the NETA EIM prepared for *Managing Human Resources* is included in the description of the Instructor's Resource CD [IRCD] below.)

*NETA Assessment* relates to testing materials. Under *NETA Assessment*, Nelson's authors create multiple-choice questions that reflect research-based best practices for constructing effective questions and testing not just recall but also higher-order thinking. Our guidelines were developed by David DiBattista, a 3M National Teaching Fellow whose recent research as a professor of psychology at Brock University has focused on multiple-choice testing. All Test Bank authors receive training at workshops conducted by Prof. DiBattista, as do the copy editors assigned to each Test Bank. A copy of *Multiple Choice Tests: Getting Beyond Remembering,* Prof. DiBattista's guide to writing effective tests, is included with every Nelson Test Bank/ Computerized Test Bank package. (Information about the NETA Test Bank prepared for *Managing Human Resources* is included in the description of the IRCD below.)

*NETA Presentation* has been developed to help instructors make the best use of PowerPoint® in their classrooms. With a clean and uncluttered design developed by Maureen Stone of StoneSoup Consulting, NETA Presentation features slides with improved readability, more multimedia and graphic materials, activities to use in class, and tips for instructors on the Notes page. A copy of *NETA Guidelines for Classroom Presentations* by Maureen Stone is included with each set of PowerPoint® slides. (Information about the NETA PowerPoint® prepared for *Managing Human Resources* is included in the description of the IRCD below.)

*NETA Digital* is a framework based on Arthur Chickering and Zelda Gamson's seminal work "Seven Principles of Good Practice In Undergraduate Education" (AAHE Bulletin, 1987) and the follow-up work by Chickering and Stephen C. Ehrmann, "Implementing the Seven Principles: Technology as Lever" (AAHE Bulletin, 1996). This aspect of the NETA program guides the writing and development of our digital products to ensure that they appropriately reflect the core goals of contact, collaboration, multimodal learning, time on task, prompt feedback, active learning, and high expectations. The resulting focus on pedagogical utility, rather than technological wizardry, ensures that all of our technology supports better outcomes for students.

## Instructor's Resource CD

Key instructor ancillaries are provided on the *Instructor's Resource CD* (ISBN 0176617299), giving instructors the ultimate tool for customizing lectures and presentations. (Downloadable web versions are also available at **http://www.belcourt7e.nelson.com.**) The IRCD includes the following:

- **NETA Engagement.** The **Enriched Instructor's Manual (EIM)** was written by Amanda Shantz, York University. It is organized according to the textbook chapters and addresses key educational concerns, such as why students should be motivated to learn the material and suggestions for student engagement strategies. Other features include suggested answers to discussion and case study questions, as well as recommendations for additional teaching resources.

- **NETA Assessment.** The Test Bank was written by Parbudyal Singh, York University. It includes over 800 multiple-choice questions written according to NETA guidelines for effective construction and development of higher-order questions. Also included are approximately 770 true/false and 52 essay questions. Test Bank files are provided in Word format for easy editing and in PDF format for convenient printing whatever your system.

    The Computerized Test Bank by ExamView® includes all the questions from the Test Bank. The easy-to-use ExamView® software is compatible with Microsoft® Windows® and Mac OS. Create tests by selecting questions from the question bank, modifying these questions as desired, and adding new questions you write yourself. You can administer quizzes online and export tests to WebCT, Blackboard, and other formats.

- **NETA Presentation.** Microsoft® PowerPoint® lecture slides for every chapter have been created by Monica Belcourt, York University. There is an average of 25–30 slides per chapter, many featuring key figures, tables, and photographs from *Managing Human Resources*. NETA principles of clear design and engaging content have been incorporated throughout.

- **Image Library.** This resource consists of digital copies of figures, short tables, and photographs used in the book. Instructors may use these jpegs to create their own PowerPoint® presentations.

- **Day One.** Day One—Prof InClass is a PowerPoint® presentation that you can customize to orient your students to the class and their text at the beginning of the course.

## Additional Resources

- **TurningPoint®.** Another valuable resource for instructors is **TurningPoint® classroom response software** customized for *Managing Human Resources*. Now you can author, deliver, show, access, and grade, all in PowerPoint®—with no toggling back and forth between screens! JoinIn on TurningPoint® is the only classroom response software tool that gives you true PowerPoint® integration. With JoinIn, you are no longer tied to your computer. You can walk about your classroom as you lecture, showing slides

and collecting and displaying responses with ease. There is simply no easier or more effective way to turn your lecture hall into a personal, fully interactive experience for your students. If you can use PowerPoint®, you can use JoinIn on TurningPoint®! (Contact your Nelson publishing representative for details.)

- **CBC Videos** (ISBN 0176541861). CBC videos, organized by part, can be used in class for discussion and activity purposes. Students can also access these videos on the CourseMate website.

- **On the Job Video Cases.** This video collection, also featured on the CourseMate website, features both small and large companies with innovative HR practices, many of which have been recognized for their excellence. Each video is accompanied by a media quiz to reinforce students' knowledge of course concepts.

- **CourseMate.** CourseMate brings course concepts to life with interactive learning and exam preparation tools that integrate with the printed textbook. Students activate their knowledge through quizzes, games, and flashcards, among many other tools.

  CourseMate provides immediate feedback that enables students to connect results to the work they have just produced, increasing their learning efficiency. It encourages contact between students and faculty. You will be able to monitor your students' level of engagement with CourseMate, correlating their efforts to their outcomes. You can even use CourseMate's quizzes to practise "Just in Time" teaching by tracking results in the Engagement Tracker and customizing your lesson plans to address their learning needs.

  Watch student comprehension and engagement soar as your class engages with CourseMate. The website can be found at http://www.belcourt7e.nelson.com. Ask your Nelson representative for a demonstration today.

## FOR STUDENTS

### InfoTrac® College Edition

With InfoTrac®, students can receive anytime, anywhere online access to a database of full-text articles from hundreds of popular and scholarly periodicals, such as *Canadian Business, Canadian Business Review, BusinessWeek, Canadian Labour, HR Magazine,* and HR Professional, among others. Students can use its fast and easy search tools to find relevant news and analytical information among the tens of thousands of articles in the database—updated daily and going back as far as four years—all at a single website. InfoTrac® is a great way to expose students to online research techniques, with the security that the content is academically based and reliable. An InfoTrac® College Edition subscription card is packaged free with all new copies of *Managing Human Resources.*

### CourseMate

The more you study, the better the results. Make the most of your study time by accessing everything you need to succeed in one place. Read your textbook, take notes, review flashcards, watch videos, and take practice quizzes online with CourseMate. View the free preview of these study resources at http://www. belcourt7e.nelson.com; to purchase, go to http://www.nelsonbrain.com.

- **Online study guide to accompany *Managing Human Resources.*** In partnership with Captus Press, Nelson is pleased to offer an online study guide prepared by Dr. Monica Belcourt (to access, visit http://www.belcourt7e.nelson.com). Complete with chapter summaries, multiple-choice questions, short-answer questions, and progress checks, this supplement will enhance your learning experience. Equally important, the study guide provides the opportunity to practise taking multiple-choice tests in preparation for the National Knowledge Examination, given by the Canadian Council of Human Resource Associations (CCHRA), a first step in becoming a CHRP.

- **Internet course.** For students seeking extra help, a full online HRM course is available from Captus Press. Supplement classroom teaching by accessing the Internet server and listening to lectures given by Dr. Monica Belcourt. You can then scroll to areas of interest and access necessary information. Please contact Captus Press directly for information on the cost of these options (http://www.captus.com).

- **Online exam preparation for the National Knowledge Exam.** The CCHRA offers an online preparation course for the National Knowledge Exam, the first exam leading to the designation of CHRP. The course includes a diagnostic test that assesses knowledge of the Required Professional Capabilities (RPCs) and links to appropriate content in this text and others. There are also three practice exams, online multimedia lectures, and quizzes. For more information, contact the CCHRA website (http://www.cchra-ccarh.ca) or Captus Press (http://webclients.captus.com/cchra/).

## ACKNOWLEDGMENTS FOR THE SEVENTH CANADIAN EDITION

In preparing the manuscript for this edition, we have drawn on not only the current literature but also the current practices of organizations that furnished information relating to their HR programs. We are indebted to the leaders in the field who have influenced us through their writings and personal associations. We have also been aided by our present and former students, by our colleagues at the HRPA with whom we have been associated, by HR managers, and by our academic colleagues. We are particularly appreciative of the review of legislation and court cases by Dr. David Doorey. Dr. Doorey also revised Chapter 13, Employee Rights and Discipline. Because of his feedback and contribution, the reader is assured that the "legal content" is accurate and current. We also wish to acknowledge and thank Targol Khoshnevisan and Paulette Burgher, graduate students in the School of Human Resource Management at York University, for their assistance with the literature review and experiential education material for this edition.

As we will see, although the HRM principles outlined in each chapter apply to both large and small organizations, the delivery of HR practices in small organizations is largely by managers and business owners rather than HR practitioners. The Small Business Application feature was initiated by Angus Duff, a Ph.D. candidate in Human Resources Management at York University and a former HR manager. As an HR practitioner, Mr. Duff has provided HR support to organizations as small as 25 employees and as large as 20,000. Using the material discussed in each chapter, Angus outlined how it could be used in a small business, of which there are over 1 million in Canada. Small business represents nearly 50 percent of all private-sector jobs, and we estimate that managers in small businesses are managing over 5 million employees, without the assistance of an HR generalist. Thus, this feature is extremely useful for this segment.

We would like to express our appreciation to the following reviewers who have helped shape the text:

Jules Carrière, University of Ottawa
Gary Gannon, Durham College
Jim Grant, Acadia University

Sean MacDonald, University of Manitoba
Marc Mentzer, University of Saskatchewan
Sandra Rever, Mount Royal University
Jean Taplin, Humber College

We appreciate the efforts of the team at Nelson who helped to develop and produce this text. They include Alwynn Pinard, Acquisitions Editor; Lacey McMaster, Developmental Editor; Jennifer Hare, Content Production Manager; and Holly Dickinson, copy editor, as well as the wonderful sales representatives who have enthusiastically supported the book. We also want to acknowledge the past work of Karina Hope, Developmental Editor for the previous five editions. Since 1998, Karina developed the superb foundation for this text, contributing greatly to its success.

Our greatest indebtedness is to our spouses—Michael Belcourt, D. Comm, Nirmala Singh, Ronnie Bohlander, and Marybeth Snell—who have contributed in so many ways to this book. They are always sources of invaluable guidance and assistance. Furthermore, by their continued enthusiasm and support, they have made the process a more pleasant and rewarding experience. We are most grateful to them for their many contributions to this publication, to our lives, and to our families.

# ABOUT THE AUTHORS

## MONICA BELCOURT

Monica Belcourt is the founding Director of the School of Human Resource Management at York University. Additionally, she is a Full Professor, Human Resources Management, and founding Director of the Graduate Program in HRM at the Atkinson Faculty of Liberal and Professional Studies, York University. She has an extensive and varied background in HRM. After receiving a B.A. in psychology from the University of Manitoba, she joined the Public Service Commission as a recruitment and selection specialist. During her tenure with the federal government, she worked in training, HRM research, job analysis, and HR planning.

Dr. Belcourt alternated working in HRM with graduate school, obtaining an M.A. in psychology from York University, an M.Ed. in adult education from the University of Ottawa, and a Ph.D. in management from York University. Her research is grounded in the experience she gained as Director of Personnel for the 63,000 employees at CP Rail; as Director of Employee Development at the National Film Board; and as a functional HR specialist for the federal government. She has taught HRM at Concordia University, Université du Québec à Montréal, McGill University, and York University, where she founded and managed the largest undergraduate program in HRM in Canada. She created Canada's first degrees in HRM: B.HRM, B.HRM (honours), and a Master's in HRM. A full description of these degrees can be found at http://www.yorku.ca/laps/shrm.

Dr. Belcourt was Director of the International Alliance for Human Resources Research (IAHRR), which was a catalyst for the discovery, dissemination, and application of new knowledge about HRM. This research centre has now been moved to the HRPA, where it is called the Human Resources Research Institute. Her research interests focus on strategic HRM, and she has published more than 100 articles, several of which received best paper awards. Dr. Belcourt is Series Editor for the Nelson Series in Human Resources Management: *Managing Performance through Training and Development; Management of Occupational Health and Safety; Human Resources Management Systems; Recruitment and Selection in Canada; Strategic Compensation in Canada; Strategic Human Resources Planning; Research, Measurement and Evaluation in HRM; The Canadian Labour Market; International Human Resources Management: A Canadian Perspective;* and *Industrial Relations in Canada.*

Active in many professional associations and not-for-profit organizations, Dr. Belcourt was the President of the HRPA of Ontario, served on the national committee for HR certification, and was a board member of CIBC Insurance and the Toronto French School. She is a frequent commentator on HRM issues for Workopolis, CTV, *Canada AM*, CBC, *The Globe and Mail, Canadian HR Reporter*, and other media. She has been recognized as a champion of HR by *Canadian HR Reporter.* In 2009, the HRPA honoured Dr. Belcourt with the award of Right Management HR Academic of the Year—an award given for outstanding contributions to the HR profession and for thoughtful leadership. The following year, the Association recognized her outstanding contribution to the HR profession by awarding her the Fellow designation (FCHRP). Dr. Belcourt is only the fourth person to receive the award since its inception in 1936. The award is given to CHRPs who have promoted best practices in the field, upheld the reputation, and made significant contributions in innovative ideas.

## PARBUDYAL SINGH

Parbudyal Singh is Full Professor and the Director of the School of Human Resource Management at York University. Prior to this, he was the Associate Dean of the School of Business, University of New Haven, Connecticut. He also taught at McMaster University. His Ph.D. studies, completed in 1998 at McMaster University, focused on the effects of organizational strategy on executive compensation.

Dr. Singh has won numerous scholastic awards and national research grants. Among other awards, at York University he won the Atkinson Alumni Teaching Award (2005), the Dean's Award for Excellence in Research (2005), and the Dean's Award for Excellence in Teaching (2007). He has supervised more than 35 graduate students (Ph.D. and Master's).

Dr. Singh's research covers a broad array of management issues, especially those related to the effects of the changing business environment on HRM and industrial relations. He has more than 80 publications, including articles in top refereed journals such as *Industrial Relations, British Journal of Industrial Relations, Human Resource Management, The Leadership Quarterly, Human Resource Management Review, Journal of Labor Research, Management International Review, International Journal of Human Resource Management, Journal of Vocational Behavior, Comparative Labor Law Journal, Canadian Public Administration, Group and Organization Management,* and *Canadian Labour and Employment Law Journal.* He serves on the editorial boards of several journals.

Dr. Singh has worked as an HR manager in a large manufacturing company. He has offered advice to more than 30 of Canada's leading organizations.

## GEORGE BOHLANDER

George Bohlander is Professor Emeritus of Management at Arizona State University (ASU). He received his M.B.A. from the University of Southern California and his Ph.D. from the University of California at Los Angeles. His areas of expertise include employment law, compensation work teams, public policy, and labour relations. He has received the Outstanding Undergraduate Teaching Excellence Award presented by the College of Business at ASU and the prestigious ASU Parents Association Professorship for his contributions to students and teaching.

Dr. Bohlander is an active researcher and author. He has published over 50 articles and monographs in professional and practitioner journals such as *National Productivity Review, HR Magazine, Labor Law Journal,* and *The Journal of Collective Bargaining in the Public Sector,* among others. Dr. Bohlander continues to be a consultant to public and private organizations, including the U.S. Postal Service, BFGoodrich, McDonnell Douglas, Banner Health Services, and Del Webb. He is also an active labour arbitrator.

## SCOTT SNELL

Scott Snell is Professor of Business Administration at the University of Virginia's Darden Graduate School of Business. He teaches in the Leadership and Organization area and specializes in strategic HRM. In recent years, he has worked with companies such as American Express, AstraZeneca, CIGNA, Deutsche Telekom, Heineken, Shell, and the World Bank to address the alignment of HR issues and strategic management. Professor Snell is the author of over 50 publications in professional journals and edited texts and has coauthored four books: *Managing Human Resources; Management: Leading and Collaborating in a Competitive World; M: Management;* and *Managing People and Knowledge in Professional Service Firms.* He has served on the boards of the Society for Human Resource Management Foundation, the Academy of Management's Human Resource Division, the *Human Resource Management Journal,* the *Academy of Management Journal,* and the *Academy of Management Review.*

Prior to joining the Darden faculty in 2007, Dr. Snell was Professor and Director of Executive Education at Cornell University's Center for Advanced Human Resource Studies and Professor of Management in the Smeal College of Business at Pennsylvania State University. He received a B.A. in Psychology from Miami University, as well as M.B.A. and Ph.D. degrees in Business Administration from Michigan State University. Originally from Lodi, Ohio, he now lives in Charlottesville, Virginia, with his wife and three children.

# The World of Human Resources Management

# After studying this chapter, you should be able to

| OUTCOME 1 | Explain how human resources managers can help their organizations gain a sustainable competitive advantage through the strategic utilization of people. |

| OUTCOME 2 | Explain how globalization is influencing human resources management. |

| OUTCOME 3 | Explain how good human resources practices can help a firm achieve its corporate social responsibility and sustainability goals. |

| OUTCOME 4 | Describe how technology can improve how people perform and are managed. |

| OUTCOME 5 | Discuss how cost pressures affect human resources management policies. |

| OUTCOME 6 | Discuss how firms can leverage employee differences to their strategic advantage. |

| OUTCOME 7 | Explain how educational and cultural changes in the workforce are affecting human resources management. |

| OUTCOME 8 | Provide examples of the roles and competencies of today's human resources managers. |

We use a lot of words to describe how important people are to organizations. The terms *human resources, human capital, intellectual assets,* and *talent management* imply that people drive the performance of their organizations (along with other resources, such as money, materials, and information). Successful organizations are particularly adept at bringing together different kinds of people to achieve a common purpose. This is the essence of **human resources management (HRM)**. HRM involves a wide variety of activities, including analyzing a company's competitive environment and designing jobs so that a firm's strategy can be successfully implemented to beat the competition. This, in turn, requires identifying, recruiting, and selecting the right people for those jobs; training, motivating, and appraising these people; developing competitive compensation policies to retain them; and grooming them to lead the organization in the future.

# WHY STUDY HUMAN RESOURCES MANAGEMENT?

**human resources management (HRM)**
The process of managing human talent to achieve an organization's objectives

**human capital**
The knowledge, skills, and capabilities of individuals that have economic value to an organization

Why should you study HRM? You might be wondering how the topic relates to your interests and career aspirations. Suppose you want the opportunity to manage people, either for another firm or one you start yourself. Having a good understanding of HRM is important for managers and entrepreneurs of all types—not just human resources (HR) personnel. All managers are responsible for at least some of the activities that fall into the category of HRM. Managers play a key role in selecting, training and motivating, appraising, and promoting employees.

What if you do a poor job of these activities? Believe it or not, many business-people with great business strategies, business plans, and products and services fail because they do not fully grasp the importance of HRM. Laments one entre-preneur: "My first year after investing in a small business that was failing, I tripled the amount of business that company did, and made a lot of money. But I didn't pay my personnel enough or motivate them. They eventually abandoned me, and a larger competitor muscled me out of the marketplace. I now understand the important role personnel play in a business. They can make or break it."

In addition, great business plans and products and services can easily be copied by your competitors. Great personnel cannot. Their knowledge and abilities are among the most distinctive and renewable resources upon which a company can draw. As Thomas J. Watson, the founder of IBM, said, "You can get capital and erect buildings, but it takes people to build a business."[1]

## HUMAN CAPITAL AND HRM

The idea that organizations "compete through people" highlights the fact that achieving success increasingly depends on an organization's ability to manage talent, or **human capital**. The term *human capital* describes the economic value of employees' knowledge, skills, and capabilities. Although the value of these assets might not show up directly on a company's balance sheet, it nevertheless has a tremendous impact on an organization's performance. The following quota-tions from notable and former chief executive officers (CEOs) illustrate this point:

- "If you look at our semiconductors and melt them down for silicon, that's a tiny fraction of the costs. The rest is intellect and mistakes." (Gordon Moore, Intel)

- "An organization's ability to learn, and translate that learning into action rap-idly, is the ultimate competitive business advantage." (Jack Welch, General Electric [GE])

- "Successful companies of the twenty-first century will be those who do the best jobs of capturing, storing, and leveraging what their employees know." (Lew Platt, Hewlett-Packard)[2]

Human capital is intangible and cannot be managed the way organizations manage jobs, products, and technologies. One reason why is because employees, *not* the organization, own their own human capital. If valued employees leave a company, they take their human capital with them, and any investment the com-pany has made in training and developing these people is lost. However, HRM practices such as selection and training can develop replacements for these people, so the real strategic advantage for organizations is high-quality HRM systems.

To build human capital in organizations, managers must continue to develop superior knowledge, skills, and experience within their workforces and retain and promote top performers.[3] Beyond the need to invest in employee develop-ment, organizations have to find ways to better utilize the knowledge of their workers. Too often employees have knowledge that goes unused. As Dave Ulrich, a professor of business at the University of Michigan, notes: "Learning capability

**FIGURE 1.1**

OVERALL FRAMEWORK FOR HUMAN RESOURCES MANAGEMENT

| COMPETITIVE CHALLENGES | HUMAN RESOURCES | EMPLOYEE CONCERNS |
|---|---|---|
| • Changes in the marketplace and economy<br>• Globalization<br>• Technology<br>• Cost containment<br>• Leveraging employee differences | • Planning<br>• Recruitment<br>• Staffing<br>• Job design<br>• Training/development<br>• Appraisal<br>• Communications<br>• Compensation<br>• Benefits<br>• Labour relations | • Job security<br>• Health care issues<br>• Age and generational work issues<br>• Retirement issues<br>• Gender issues<br>• Educational levels<br>• Employee rights<br>• Privacy issues<br>• Work attitudes<br>• Family concerns |

is *g* times *g*—a business's ability to *generate* new ideas multiplied by its adeptness at *generalizing* them throughout the company."[4]

HRM and programs are often the conduit through which knowledge is developed and transferred among employees. A survey by the Human Resource Planning Society (HRPS) revealed that 65 percent of responding companies believe that their HR groups play a key role in developing human capital. Arvinder Dhesi, the head of talent for the insurance company Aviva, explains that his firm's goal is to treat *everyone* as talent and not just focus on a few. "We talk about the sum of people's experiences as well as their skills," says Dhesi, who notes that Aviva is rolling out new software that will create a "talent profile" of each of the firm's employees worldwide.

Although "competing through people" is a major theme of HRM, on a day-to-day basis, managers of all types have to carry out the specific activities for a company to effectively do so. Figure 1.1 provides an overall framework of these activities. From this figure, we can see that managers have to help blend many aspects of management; at this point, we will simply classify them as either "competitive challenges" or "employee concerns." We will use Figure 1.1 as a basis for our discussion throughout this chapter.

## COMPETITIVE CHALLENGES AND HUMAN RESOURCES MANAGEMENT

Professional organizations such as provincial HR associations and the HRPS conduct ongoing studies of the most pressing competitive issues facing firms. By seeking the input of chief executives and HR managers, these organizations keep a finger on the pulse of major trends. The top trends, or challenges, they name today include those outlined in the sections that follow.

| OUTCOME 2

### CHALLENGE 1: RESPONDING STRATEGICALLY TO CHANGES IN THE MARKETPLACE

Given the pace of commerce, organizations can rarely stand still for long. In today's highly competitive environments, in which competition is global and innovation is continuous, being able to adapt has become the key to capturing opportunities and overcoming obstacles, as well as the very survival of organizations.

**PART 1**

**Six Sigma**
A set of principles and practices whose core ideas include understanding customer needs, doing things right the first time, and striving for continuous improvement

**reengineering**
The fundamental rethinking and radical redesign of business processes to achieve dramatic improvements in cost, quality, service, and speed

**downsizing**
Planned elimination of jobs

**outsourcing**
Contracting out work that was formerly done by employees

**change management**
Change management is a systematic way of bringing about and managing both organizational changes and changes on the individual level

Stockbyte Gold/Getty Images

HR managers understand business operations and strategies.

As one pundit put it, "No change means chance." Successful companies, says Harvard Business School professor Rosabeth Moss Kanter, develop a culture that just keeps moving all the time.[5]

Consider what happened to the parts suppliers for automakers when the bankruptcy of General Motors (GM), Chrysler, and Ford looked imminent in 2008–2009. Most of the suppliers sold exclusively to the three automakers. As a result, they had to rapidly find other markets, products to make for those markets, and ways to sell them—all of which required significant HR changes and challenges.

## HR MANAGERS AND BUSINESS STRATEGY

Ten or 20 years ago, HR personnel were often relegated to conducting administrative tasks. But that has changed. Executives know that HR professionals can help them improve not only a company's bottom line by streamlining employment costs but also the top line by forecasting labour trends, designing new ways to acquire and utilize employees, measuring their effectiveness, and helping managers enter new markets. Says Robin Lissak with the HR consulting arm of Deloitte, "Most business leaders say they want [HR] to focus on the new types of services companies need and want. They include driving mergers and acquisitions and helping companies enter new markets, like expanding to China." Executives at these companies expect their HR personnel to be able to answer questions, such as "What is our entry strategy? Who should we send first? Where should we locate our sales, production, and other personnel, and how do we keep them safe abroad? How do we manage a crisis should it occur?[6]

To answer questions such as these, HR managers need an intimate understanding of their firms' competitive business operations and strategies, whatever they may be. During what is being called the "Great Recession," which began in 2008, many companies pursued cost-cutting strategies, often in part by trimming workers' benefits. Other companies took a different strategy: They improved their benefit programs to attract top talent from other companies and expanded to be ready when the economy began growing again.

Total quality improvement, reengineering, downsizing, and outsourcing are also examples of the means organizations use to modify the way they operate to be more successful. **Six Sigma** is a set of principles and practices whose core ideas include understanding customer needs, doing things right the first time, and striving for continuous improvement.

**Reengineering** has been described as "the fundamental rethinking and radical redesign of business processes to achieve dramatic improvements in cost, quality, service, and speed."[7] **Downsizing** is the planned elimination of jobs, and **outsourcing** simply means hiring someone outside the company to perform business processes that were previously done within the firm.

A common denominator of all of these strategies is that they require companies to engage in **change management**. Change management is a systematic way of bringing about and managing both organizational changes and changes on the individual level. According to a survey by the research institute Roffey Park, two-thirds of firms believe that managing change is their biggest challenge. Although most employees understand that change is continuous—responsibilities, job assignments, and work processes change—people often resist it because it requires them to modify or abandon ways of working that have been successful or at least familiar to them. Successful change rarely occurs naturally or easily.

To manage change, executives and managers, including those in HR, have to envision the future, communicate this vision to employees, set clear expectations for performance, and develop the capability to execute by reorganizing people and reallocating assets. Organizations that have been successful in engineering change

- Link the change to the business strategy
- Show how the change creates quantifiable benefits

# REALITY CHECK

## Six Sigma

Goodyear Canada underwent a major business transformation. At the time, they had 19 Black Belts (full-time project leaders) and seven Green Belts (part-time project leaders) working in offices, warehouses, and the eight Canadian tire and rubber products manufacturing plants. Projects were projected to yield $10 million in waste reduction, avoid capital equipment purchase, and increase sales through elimination of production bottlenecks.

Goodyear's tire manufacturing facility in Medicine Hat, Alberta, needed to produce more rubber from its Banbury rubber mixer to meet its daily quota and lessen its dependence on rubber produced by outside sources. In buying material, the factory was paying freight charges to get the rubber to the factory. By optimizing the Banbury uptime and increasing the Banbury output, the factory could reduce the amount of rubber it needed to purchase. Using the tools of Six Sigma, the factory determined that it could stagger shift rotations so that an operator was always available to keep the Banbury mixer running. The company was also able to increase the batch weight sizes of some of the compounds by 4 percent to 11 percent. In addition, staging batches at the top of the conveyor and reducing the gate delay realized gains of two to three seconds per batch. Although three seconds does not sound like a great amount, over the course of a week, it adds about 150 minutes of productivity. After six months, the factory increased its Banbury mixer output by more than 5 percent, generating savings of over $110,000. The Medicine Hat plant estimates that it can save $250,000 to $400,000 annually by implementing the new procedures.

Gary Blake, Goodyear Canada Six Sigma champion and a Black Belt, says that Six Sigma is a problem-solving model that applies rigorous statistical thinking to reduce defects, improve cycle time, and increase customer satisfaction. The methodology is being applied not only to traditional manufacturing processes but also to transactional processes—supply chain, purchasing, invoicing, sales, and marketing. A Six Sigma team follows five major steps known as DMAIC to clearly Define the scope of the project, Measure customer requirements and process outputs, Analyze the current situation and set clear goals, Improve the process through planned experimentation, and, finally, Control to validate and lock in the improvement—then sustaining it so that there is no backslide. The model moves the organization to whatever goals are required by the customer. Six Sigma derives its name from the Greek letter *sigma*, which is sometimes used to denote variation from a standard, and the statistical concept that if you measure the defects in a process, you can figure out how to get rid of them and get closer to perfection. A Six Sigma company cannot produce more than 3.4 defects per million opportunities. For a process with only one specification limit, this results in six process standard deviations between the mean of the process and the customer's specification limit.

The use of these "lean" principles can also be used to identify deficiencies in HR processes. The associate vice president of HR at Canadian Tire and his team analyzed the recruitment process from the initial request for a new hire to the time the new employee reported for work. They found delays, duplication, and unnecessary steps. Applying lean methodology to recruitment, the team was able to reduce the time to fill a position by 25 percent, eliminated half of the steps used, reduced cost per hire by 34 percent, and reduced turnover rates. Other companies, such as WorkSafe BC and Maple Leaf Foods, also saw the utility of using Six Sigma in the recruitment process, reasoning that a bad hire is like a product defect.

Sources: Interview with Gary Blake; V. Galt, "Canadian Tire Applied Its 'Lean' Ideals to Headquarters," *The Globe and Mail*, February 23, 2012, B21; E. Kelly, "The Skinny on Six Sigma," *HR Professional* (March/April 2010): 26–27.

- Engage key employees, customers, and their suppliers early when making a change
- Make an investment in implementing and sustaining change[8]

Some of the strategic changes companies pursue are **reactive changes** that result when external forces, such as the competition, a recession, a law change, or a crisis (such as BP's offshore oil spill in the Gulf of Mexico in 2010), have already affected an organization's performance. Other strategies are **proactive change**, initiated by managers to take advantage of targeted opportunities, particularly in fast-changing industries in which followers are not successful.

Good HR managers know that they can be key players when it comes to driving the business strategies of their organizations to make changes. That is

**reactive change**
Change that occurs after external forces have already affected performance

**proactive change**
Change initiated to take advantage of targeted opportunities

Many Canadian companies use business process reengineering to improve productivity at their plants.

NORM BETTS/Landov

**globalization**
The trend to opening up foreign markets to international trade and investment

why forward-looking CEOs such as Gregg Saretsky of WestJet, Howard Schultz at Starbucks, and Jeff Immelt at GE make certain that their top HR executives report directly to them and help them address key issues.

A rapidly growing number of companies, including Ford, Intel, and United Technologies, are assigning HR representatives to their core business teams to ensure that they are knowledgeable about core business issues. Companies are increasingly rotating non-HR managers *into* HR positions and vice versa to give them exposure to different areas of the organization. Rather than emphasizing the administrative aspects of HR, forward-thinking companies develop and promote their HR personnel and provide them with key business statistics and numbers they can use to measure the effectiveness of the workforce. We will discuss more about competitive HR strategies and HR in Chapter 2. Meanwhile, keep in mind that HR's role is not all about providing advice to CEOs and supervisors. In addition to serving as strategic partners to management, HR managers are also responsible for listening to and advocating on behalf of employees to make sure their interests are aligned with those of the firm and vice versa. A good deal of evidence suggests that this is one of the toughest parts of an HR manager's job. We will discuss more about this aspect of the job later in the chapter.

## CHALLENGE 2: COMPETING, RECRUITING, AND STAFFING GLOBALLY

The strategies companies are pursing today increasingly involve one or more elements of **globalization**. The integration of world economies and markets has sent businesses abroad to look for opportunities and fend off foreign competitors domestically. Consumers around the world want to be able to buy "anything, anytime, anywhere," and companies are making it possible for them to do so. Want to buy a Coke in Pakistan? No problem. Coca-Cola has an elaborate delivery system designed to transport its products to some of the remotest places on the planet. In fact, the company has long generated more of its revenues abroad than it does in the United States. But globalization is not of interest only to large firms such as Coca-Cola. Although estimates vary widely, approximately 70 to 85 percent of the Canadian economy today is affected by international competition, including small companies.

China could surpass the United States to become the largest economy in the world by 2041, and India could be the third largest. These countries can produce goods and provide services at a fraction of the cost of Canadian workers. As the vice president and chief economist of the Conference Board of Canada stated, "There are billions of people in Asia who want to get to where we are, and they're prepared to work longer and harder. So we have to work smarter."[9]

The manufacturing of cars in Canada provides a good example of the impact of globalization. There is no such thing as a Canadian car. Most parts—up to 85 percent—of cars manufactured in Canada come from other countries. On the other hand, Canadian content represents about 10 percent for cars assembled outside Canada.[10] A recent study suggests that about 37 percent of Canada's workforce will be affected by globalization, with knowledge workers and manufacturing jobs taking the brunt of the impact of the competition by lower wage countries.[11]

Partnerships and mergers are two other ways companies both large and small are globalizing. Coca-Cola has tried to expand in China by partnering with that nation's largest juice maker.

As a result of globalization, the national identities of products are blurring too. BMW has traditionally been a German brand, but now the automaker builds cars in the United States, China, and elsewhere. Likewise, you probably think of Budweiser as an American beer, but would it surprise you to know that the maker of Budweiser (Anheuser-Busch) is owned by a Belgian company called InBev? Like many other companies, Anheuser-Busch InBev is now looking for factories and brands in China to purchase to expand its sales.[12]

Numerous free-trade agreements forged between nations in the last half-century have helped quicken the pace of globalization. The first major trade agreement of the twentieth century was made in 1948, following World War II. Called the General Agreement on Tariffs and Trade (GATT), it established rules and guidelines for global commerce between nations and groups of nations. Although the Great Recession temporarily caused a sharp drop in the amount of world trade, since GATT began, world trade has exploded, increasing nearly 30 times the dollar volume of what it once was. This is three times faster than the world's overall output has grown during the same period. GATT paved the way for the formation of many major trade agreements and institutions, including the European Union (EU) in 1986 and the North American Free Trade Agreement (NAFTA) in 1994, encompassing the United States, Canada, and Mexico. The World Trade Organization (WTO), headquartered in Lausanne, Switzerland, now has more than 153 member countries, and new free-trade agreements seem to be forged annually.[13]

## How Globalization Affects HRM

For all of the opportunities afforded by international business, when managers talk about "going global," they have to balance a complicated set of issues related to different geographies, including different cultures, employment laws, and business practices. HR issues underlie each of these concerns. They include such things as dealing with employees today who, via the Internet, are better informed about global job opportunities and are willing to pursue them, even if it means working for competing companies. Gauging the knowledge and skill base of international workers and figuring out how best to hire and train them, sometimes with materials that must be translated into a number of different languages, are also issues for firms. Relocating managers and other workers to direct the efforts of an international workforce is a challenge as well. HR personnel are frequently responsible for implementing training programs and enhancing their firms' managers' understanding of other cultures and practices, as well as dealing with the culture shock these workers might experience and pay differentials that must be adjusted, depending on the country. The international arena for HRM has become so crucial and so involved that we have devoted an entire chapter (Chapter 15) to discussing its competitive, cultural, and practical implications.

**Using the Internet**

To learn more about the effects NAFTA has had, go to

**http://www.nafta-sec-alena.org**

**CHAPTER 1:** THE WORLD OF HUMAN RESOURCES MANAGEMENT

## CHALLENGE 3: SETTING AND ACHIEVING CORPORATE SOCIAL RESPONSIBILITY AND SUSTAINABILITY GOALS

OUTCOME 3

### Using the Internet

Sources of information about companies and their programs to promote corporate social responsibility can be found on this news service at

**http://www.csrwire.com**

**corporate social responsibility**
The responsibility of the firm to act in the best interests of the people and communities affected by its activities

**collaborative software**
Software that allows workers to interface and share information with one another electronically

Globalization has led to an improvement in people's living standards in the last half-century. As a result of free trade, Canadians are able to buy products made abroad more cheaply. Conversely, people in low-wage countries that make those goods and services are becoming wealthier and are beginning to buy North American–made products. Nonetheless, globalization stirs fierce debate—especially when it comes to jobs. Since the turn of the century, thousands of Canadian jobs—both white and blue collar—have been exported to low-wage nations all around the world. Some people worry that free trade is creating a "have/have not" world economy, in which the people in developing economies and the world's environment are being exploited by companies in richer, more developed countries. This has sparked anti–free trade protests in many nations.

Concerns such as these, coupled with corporate scandals over the years, including the use of sweatshop labour in third-world countries, risky lending tactics that fuelled a worldwide banking crisis, and a class action lawsuit alleging that Walmart discriminated against hundreds of thousands of female employees over the years, have led to a new focus on **corporate social responsibility**, or good citizenship. In a recent survey, the *Chronicle of Philanthropy* found that 16 percent of companies were making more donations of products and services and that 54 percent of companies were encouraging more employees to volunteer their time.[14] Companies are learning (sometimes the hard way) that being socially responsible both domestically and abroad can not only help them avoid lawsuits but also improve their earnings. For example, researchers at the Boston College's Center for Corporate Citizenship found that as a company's reputation improved, so did the percentage increase in the number of people who would recommend that firm. Nearly two-thirds of the members of the 80 million–strong millennial generation (people born in the 1980s and 1990s) consider a company's social reputation when deciding where to shop, and 9 out of 10 of them say they would switch brands based on their perceptions of a company's commitment to social responsibility.[15] Moreover, prospective workers are saying that corporate responsibility is now more important to their job selection.

Sustainability is closely related to corporate social responsibility. Sustainability refers to a company's ability to produce a good or service without damaging the environment or depleting a resource. Achieving complete sustainability is nearly impossible, but companies are making strides to reduce their "carbon footprints." Those that are not are finding themselves under pressure from consumers and groups determined that they do. Consider what happened to Hewlett-Packard (HP). After HP broke a promise to eliminate toxic materials in its computers by 2009, Greenpeace activists painted the words "Hazardous Products" on the roof of the company's headquarters in Palo Alto, California. Meanwhile, a voice-mail message from *Star Trek* actor William Shatner was delivered to all of the phones in the building. "Please ask your leader [CEO Mark Hurd] to make computers that are toxin free like Apple has done," Shatner said in the recording. The stunt and publicity it generated worked. HP got the message and later delivered on its promise.[16] One of HR's leadership roles is to spearhead the development and implementation of corporate citizenship throughout their organizations, especially the fair treatment of workers.[17]

## CHALLENGE 4: ADVANCING HRM WITH TECHNOLOGY

OUTCOME 4

Advancements in information technology have enabled organizations to take advantage of the information explosion. Computer networks and "cloud computing" (Internet computer services and data storage) have made it possible for nearly unlimited amounts of data to be stored, retrieved, and used in a wide variety of ways. **Collaborative software** that allows workers anywhere anytime to interface and share information with one another electronically—wikis, document-sharing platforms such as Google Docs, online chat and instant

# HIGHLIGHTS IN HRM 1.1

## An Economy Based on Brains, Not Brawn

According to experts such as Richard Florida, who teaches at the Rotman School at the University of Toronto; Nick Bontis, who teaches knowledge management at McMaster University; and Canadian futurist Dan Tapscott, the workplace of the future will look like this:

- Workers will be chained to their BlackBerrys and smart phones, not their desks.
- Education will be lifelong; jobs won't.
- You will work with people whom you never meet and create goods and services online.
- Freedom, flexibility, and respect will be valued more than compensation.

- Workers will have to read faster—up to 300 words a minute.
- Learning another language will be essential as five billion more people access the Net from Asia, Africa, and the Middle East.
- Clearing your inbox will be time consuming as you will get emails not just from people but from your car ("need electricity"), your refrigerator ("need cheese"), and your store ("shoes you like just arrived").

Other experts predict that corporations will become mini-states and assume a socially responsible role by identifying workers at 16 and paying for their tuition and housing.

Sources: Adapted from Dianne Rinehart, "When Brains Replaces Brawn," *The Globe and Mail*, October 1, 2007, B12; Shannon Klie, "What Will Working World Look Like in 2020?" *Canadian HR Reporter* (September 22, 2008), vol. 21, iss. 16; 1, 2.

messaging, web and videoconferencing, and electronic calendar systems—have changed how and where people and companies do business. For example, Boeing Satellite Systems has a "lessons learned" site on its intranet where people from all areas of the company can store the knowledge they have and others can access it. Executives at Boeing estimate that the measure has reduced the cost of developing a satellite by as much as $25 million.[18]

The Internet and social media are also having an impact. Social media networking has become the new way to find employees and check them out to see if they are acceptable candidates. Companies are hiring firms such as Social Intelligence, which combs through Facebook, LinkedIn, Twitter, Flickr, YouTube, and "thousands of other sources" to create reports about the "real you"—not the "you" you have presented in your résumé.[19] (Care to change your Facebook page, anyone?) HR managers are also grappling with whether or not to develop blogging and social media policies and whether or not to establish rules about the amount of time employees can spend online or to install software that cuts them off after a certain amount of time.

> **knowledge workers**
> Workers whose responsibilities extend beyond the physical execution of work to include planning, decision making, and problem solving

## From Touch Labour to Knowledge Workers

Advanced technology tends to reduce the number of jobs that require little skill and to increase the number of jobs that require considerable skill. In general, this transformation has been referred to as a shift from "touch labour" to **knowledge workers**, in which employee responsibilities expand to include a richer array of activities, such as planning, decision making, and problem solving.[20]

The workplace of the knowledge worker is described in Highlights in HRM 1.1.

Technology, transportation, communications, and utilities industries tend to spend the most on training. Knowledge-based training has become so important that Manpower Inc., the largest employment agency in the United States, offers free information technology training through its Manpower Training and Development Center (http://www.manpowerdc.com), an online university for its employees in its 4000 offices worldwide. The Manpower site features thousands of hours of online instruction in technology applications, along with professional

**human resources information system (HRIS)**
A computerized system that provides current and accurate data for purposes of control and decision making

development, business skills, and telecommunications courses. In fact, Manpower is so focused on developing technical skills in potential employees that it has set up the system so that some training and career planning information is available to those who simply send the company a résumé. "Just-in-time" learning delivered via the Internet to employees' desktops when and where they need training has become commonplace. "Virtual" learning is taking place as well. IBM, Cisco, Kelly Services, and Manpower are among the companies that have built training facilities, offices, and meeting rooms inside the online reality game Second Life. The spaces these companies build online enable them to do certain things more easily and cheaply than they can in the real world—for example, bringing people from several continents into one room for training.[21]

## Influence of Technology on HRM

Perhaps the most central use of technology in HRM is an organization's **human resources information system (HRIS)**. Because HR affects the entire workforce—everyone who works for the company must be hired, trained, paid, and promoted, usually through HR—the impact of the HRIS has been dramatic. It has become a potent weapon for lowering administrative costs, increasing productivity, speeding up response times, improving decision making, and tracking a company's talent.

The most obvious impact has been operational—that is, automating routine activities, alleviating administrative burdens, reducing costs, and improving productivity internal to the HR function itself. The most frequent uses include automating payroll processing, maintaining employee records, and administering benefits programs. "Self-service"—setting up systems, usually on an intranet—allows managers to access employee records themselves for administrative purposes and to access and change their own benefits and other personal information.

The second way in which information technology is affecting HRM is relational in nature—connecting people with each other and with HR data they need. For example, companies are using software to recruit, screen, and pretest applicants online before hiring them as well as to train, track, and promote employees once they have been hired. The drugmaker Merck's HRIS captures information from job recruiting sites, scans applicants' résumés, and makes the information immediately accessible to managers so that they can search systematically for the people whose skills they want. Managers can search online for internal and external talent by running searches of candidates who have been categorized by skill set.[22]

The third effect of the HRIS is transformational in nature—changing the way HR processes are designed and executed. Corning, Inc. uses HR software, among other things, to set the developmental goals of its employees once they have been hired and to gauge how well they are meeting them. Employees can look online to see their own goals and mark their progress as well as see everyone else's goals in the command chain, from the CEO down to their immediate supervisors. This "cascading" of goals has helped Corning's employees align their personal goals with the organization's overall objectives to reach higher levels. "Like any large company, we tended to get 'silo-ed' and fragmented the more we grew," said one vice president at a company using a system similar to Corning's. "We needed a better way to pull our global team together and get people focused on what the priorities are for our business."[23]

So what sort of system should HR professionals choose among the many options available to them? Prepackaged, or "canned," HR Web-based solutions are as commonly used as custom-designed systems. Generally, companies also have the choice of hosting the applications on their own servers or having software vendors such as IBM or PeopleSoft do it for them. Experts say the first step in choosing an HRIS is for HR personnel to evaluate the biggest "headaches" they experience, or the most time-consuming tasks, and then choose the applications that can have the strongest impact on the firm's financial measures—that is, the ones that get the "biggest bang for the buck." These applications are more likely

# HIGHLIGHTS IN HRM 1.2

## Factors to Consider When Evaluating a Human Resources Information System

The following factors are key considerations for HR managers when their firms are evaluating a human resources information system (HRIS).

- *Fit of the application to the firm's employee base.* If many of the firm's employees work on a factory floor, is the system appropriate, or does HR need to install kiosks in employee areas? How will the information be secured? Will employees need to be assigned passwords? Can they access the information from off-site, for example, from their homes?

- *Ability to upgrade or customize the software.* What sorts of costs will be involved to upgrade the software in the coming years?

- *Compatibility with current systems.* Does the HRIS link into existing, or planned, information systems easily and inexpensively?

- *User friendliness.* Does the software provide additional features such as links to learning resources or help for managers who might need it?

- *Availability of technical support.* Should the HRIS be supported internally, or should the vendor host it? What are the vendor's technical support capabilities?

- *Time required to implement and train staff members to use the HRIS, including HR and payroll personnel, managers, and employees.* Who is responsible for training employees, and how will it be done?

- *Initial costs and annual maintenance costs.* Is a "suite" of applications needed or just a few key applications? Experts advise HR managers to price each application separately and then ask vendors for a "bundled" price.

Sources: Drew Robb, "Building a Better Workforce," 86–92; "How to Implement an Effective Process for a New HR Management System," *HRfocus* (January 2005): 3–4; "New Study Finds HRIS Key to Reducing Costs," *Payroll Managers Report* 7, no. 5 (May 2007): 13.

to get "buy-in" from the firm's top managers. HR managers should then calculate the costs based on average salaries, or HR hours, that could be saved by using an HRIS, along with the hours of increased productivity that would occur as a result. Highlights in HRM 1.2 shows the other factors that need to be evaluated.

When an effective HRIS is implemented, perhaps the biggest advantage gained is that HR personnel can concentrate more effectively on the firm's strategic direction instead of on routine tasks. This can include forecasting personnel needs (especially for firms planning to expand, contract, or merge), planning for career and employee promotions, and evaluating the impact of the firm's policies—those related to both HR and other functions—to help improve the firm's earnings and strategic direction.

Although the initial drive to adopt HRISs was related to cutting HR costs, HR managers have since discovered that the systems have allowed them to share information with departmental managers, who, by having access to it, have been able to come up with better production practices and cost control solutions. As a result, HR managers are now requiring their application providers to provide them with software to meet certain goals, including lowering a company's total spending on employee health care and improving its customer service.[24]

However, companies simply cannot turn over their strategic talent issues to an HRIS. Researchers Douglas Ready and Jay Conger found that despite such systems—electronic or otherwise—most of the firms they examined lacked high-potential employees to fill strategic management roles. Although companies had talent management processes in place, they were no longer synchronized with the company's strategic direction. In addition, managers often get sidetracked by priorities other than identifying talent.[25]

Procter & Gamble (P&G) is an exception, noted Ready and Conger. P&G's HRIS makes good internal candidates visible to managers instead of the managers having to scour the company to find them. The system contains information about its 135,000 employees worldwide for promotion purposes at the country, business category, and regional levels. It contains employees' career histories and capabilities, as well as their education, community affiliations, and development needs, and tracks the diversity of candidates. Perhaps most importantly, managers are evaluated and compensated on their ability to find and groom talented employees. P&G's results are consistent with Ready and Conger's findings that firms do a better job of fostering talent when there is commitment, involvement, and accountability by a company's supervisors to do so rather than when the task is "owned" by the HR department.[25]

## CHALLENGE 5: CONTAINING COSTS WHILE RETAINING TOP TALENT AND MAXIMIZING PRODUCTIVITY

**OUTCOME 5**

For years, most HR managers have been under pressure to cut labour costs. Stretching a company's labour dollars while gaining productivity from workers is a challenge for managers. Organizations take many approaches to lowering labour-related costs, including carefully managing employees' benefits, downsizing, outsourcing, offshoring, furloughing employees, and engaging in employee leasing in an attempt to enhance productivity.

Few jobs come with lifetime guarantees and benefits that will never change. Nonetheless, employees want to work for employers that can provide them with a certain amount of economic security. Layoffs and cuts in employee benefits have heightened these concerns. Some companies, such as Google, are able to hire talented employees by offering them a great deal of job security and very good benefits. However, most companies, especially small ones or ones that are struggling, find it hard to compete with bigger firms such as Google with deluxe benefit packages. What can they do? This is where an HR manager's expertise and creativity come in. Read on to see how firms are handling this challenge.

### Downsizing

Companies are becoming creative about solutions to the need to reduce costs and eliminate jobs. For example, when L.L. Bean saw that sales had fallen, the company undertook a number of efforts to identify what it called "smart cost reductions." Bean's total quality management activities helped the company target quality problems and saved an estimated $30 million. But the cuts were not enough, and, ultimately, Leon Gorman, president of the firm, and Bob Peixotto, vice president of HR and quality, realized that the company needed to eliminate some jobs. Instead of simply laying off people, however, the company started early retirement and "sweetened" voluntary separation programs. Then the company offered employee sabbaticals for continuing education.[26]

These efforts, combined with better employee communication, helped soften the blow of layoffs at L.L. Bean. But the pain of downsizing has been widespread throughout North America. Virtually every major corporation has undergone some cycle of downsizing. Historically, layoffs tended to affect manufacturing firms and line workers in particular, but beginning in the 1990s, the layoffs began to encompass white-collar workers in greater numbers in knowledge-intensive industries. Engineering, accounting, information technology, and architecture have been among the hardest hit professions.[27]

But downsizing is no longer being regarded as a short-term fix when times are tough. It has now become a tool continually used by companies to adjust to changes in technology, globalization, and the firm's business direction. For example, in a study that surveyed 450 senior HR executives at companies that had downsized, only 21 percent said that financial difficulties had spurred the cutbacks. In fact, 34 percent of the executives said the downsizing was done to strengthen their companies' future positions; 21 percent said it was done to achieve fundamental staff realignment; and 17 percent said it was due to a merger or acquisition.

Whatever the reason, whereas some firms improve efficiency (and lower costs) with layoffs, many others do not obtain such benefits.

Advocates of a no-layoff policy often note that layoffs may backfire after taking into account hidden costs such as the following:

- Severance and rehiring costs
- Accrued vacation and sick-day payouts
- Pension and benefit payoffs
- Potential lawsuits from aggrieved workers
- Loss of institutional memory and trust in management
- Lack of staffers when the economy rebounds
- Survivors who are risk averse, paranoid, and political

In contrast, companies that avoid downsizing say they get some important benefits from such policies:

- A fiercely loyal, more productive workforce
- Higher customer satisfaction
- Readiness to snap back with the economy
- A recruiting edge
- Workers who are not afraid to innovate, knowing their jobs are safe[28]

More than one executive has concluded that you do not get dedicated and productive employees if at the first sign of trouble you show them that you think they are expendable.

To approach downsizing more intelligently, some companies have made special efforts to reassign and retrain employees for new positions when their jobs are eliminated. Others, such as Rogers Communications, Inc., offered their employees a four-day work week for reduced pay on a voluntary basis.[29] This is consistent with a philosophy of employees as assets, as intellectual capital.

## Furloughing

An alternative to downsizing is **furloughing**. When a company furloughs employees, it asks them to take time off for either no pay or reduced pay. Some companies are utilizing creative furlough strategies to avoid downsizing and losing talent to competitors. Instead of laying off people, the consulting firm Accenture instituted a voluntary sabbatical program known as "Flexleave." Employees received 20 percent of their salaries and continued benefits for 6 to 12 months, and their stock options remained in place. The workers could take other jobs during their sabbaticals as long as they did not work for a competitor. Cisco Systems offered 8,500 employees an unusual deal as well. Instead of a severance package, they received a third of their salaries, all benefits, and stock option awards while working for one year at a not-for-profit group already associated with the company. Likewise, when Texas Instruments (TI) had to lay off some of its employees, it did not just send them out the door. It found them jobs with its suppliers, with the agreement that the employees would return to TI when business picked up.[30]

Although furloughs might sound preferable to downsizing, they have their drawbacks, too, say some HR experts. Costs are not cut as significantly as they would be with downsizing because employees generally retain their benefits while they are furloughed. Employees who are not furloughed often end up with more work and feel resentful, and product and service quality as well as innovation suffer as a result of the higher workloads. And, as with downsizing, furloughing employees can hurt a company's recruiting efforts when the public discovers it has resorted to such a measure.[31]

More diligent workforce planning is a better solution, says John Sullivan, an HR expert and consultant. Business revenues seldom fall off overnight. Sullivan says the best managers look for warning signs and develop a process

**CHAPTER 1:** THE WORLD OF HUMAN RESOURCES MANAGEMENT

that pinpoints skills the company no longer needs, low-impact jobs, and poor performers in advance of a crisis. Instead, part-time or contract employees can be hired and their hours of service adjusted as needed.[32]

## Outsourcing

Over the past 25 years, the employment relationship between companies and employees has shifted from relationship based to transaction based. Fewer people are working for one employer over the course of their lifetimes, and as we have explained, the Internet has created a workforce that is constantly scanning for new opportunities. In addition, more people are choosing to work on a freelance, or contract, basis or to work part-time, especially women and senior citizens. Outsourcing is evidence of this trend.[33] Companies hire accounting firms to take care of their financial services. They hire advertising firms to handle promotions, software firms to develop data-processing systems, and law firms to handle their legal issues. Maintenance, security, catering, payroll (and, in small companies, sometimes entire HR departments) are outsourced to increase the organization's flexibility and lower its overhead costs.

The interest in outsourcing has been spurred on by executives who want to focus their organization's activities on what they do best. In fact, some management experts predict that companies will one day strip away every function not regarded as crucial. Even now, many firms are outsourcing what would seem to be their core functions. Drug companies such as GlaxoSmithKline are outsourcing their research and development functions to smaller firms that can more cheaply and nimbly create new products for them. P&G outsources a major portion of its product development. Outsourcing has been one of the most prominent HR trends of the last 10 years and will continue to be.[34]

## Offshoring

© Andrew Hollbrooke/Corbis

**Offshoring**, also referred to as "global sourcing," involves shifting work to overseas locations. Almost half of 500 senior finance and HR leaders surveyed said their firms are either offshoring or are considering offshoring in the next three years, according to a study by Hewitt Associates. Spending on offshore services has been rising worldwide.[35] Cost reduction is among the key motivators for these decisions—companies estimate that they can save 40 to 60 percent on labour costs by reallocating work to countries such as India, where highly educated workers can perform the same jobs as Canadian workers at half the price. Other labour markets include the Philippines, Russia, China, Mexico, Brazil, Hungary, and Bosnia.

But hidden costs can sometimes chew up much of the financial gains from offshoring, including those associated with finding foreign vendors, productivity lost during the transition, domestic layoff costs, language difficulties, international regulatory challenges, and political and economic instability that can threaten operations. In Chapter 2, you will learn about the other ways firms can gain a competitive edge besides just cutting labour costs. Nonetheless, offshoring will continue to be a key employment strategy as global economies continue to shift. The key is for top managers, finance departments, and the offshoring consulting firms they hire to begin working in conjunction with their companies' HR departments early in the game.

Another new trend is "nearshoring." **Nearshoring** is the process of moving jobs closer to one's home country. For example, rising labour costs in China are now making it attractive for North American firms to offshore work to Mexico and Central America. Shipping the finished goods made there is also cheaper, and the products get to sellers (and ultimately the buyers who want them) more quickly, which can provide a firm with a competitive advantage. Yet another new way companies are both economizing and bringing jobs back to their domestic markets is by "homeshoring." Call centre jobs are a notable example. When a

Offshoring work to countries that offer a highly educated but lower paid workforce has become a common cost-cutting strategy for organizations.

company homeshores call centre jobs, it outsources the work to domestic independent contractors who work out of their homes.

Offshoring, nearshoring, and homeshoring are going to continue to be key employment strategies as global economies continue to shift. The key is for top managers, finance departments, and the offshoring consulting firms they hire to begin working in conjunction with their companies' HR departments prior to these activities occurring. "Companies can minimize hidden costs and maximize their returns by enabling HR to have a seat at the table early so they can carefully address issues such as the types of jobs that should and should not be outsourced, skill and language requirements, labour costs by market, alternative talent pools, workforce training, retraining, and change management," says Mark Arian, a corporate restructuring executive for the HR consulting group Hewitt.[36] To minimize problems, HR managers have to work together with the firm's other functional groups to define and communicate transition plans, minimize the number of unknowns, and help employees identify their employment options.

## Employee Leasing

As an alternative to downsizing, outsourcing, offshoring, and furloughing, many companies, especially small ones, have decided to sign **employee leasing** agreements with professional employer organizations (PEOs). A PEO—typically a larger company—takes over the management of a smaller company's HR tasks and becomes a coemployer to its employees. The PEO performs all the HR duties of an employer—hiring, payroll, and performance appraisal. Because PEOs can coemploy a large number of people working at many different companies, they can provide employees with benefits that small companies cannot afford, such as vision care plans. In addition, many PEOs offer their employees flextime, job sharing, part-time employment, consulting arrangements, seasonal work, and on-call work. The value of employee leasing lies in the fact that an organization can essentially maintain its working relationships with its employees but shift some employment costs to the PEO, in return for a fee. More details on employee leasing will be discussed in Chapter 5.

## Productivity Enhancements

The results of pure cost-cutting efforts such as downsizing, furloughing, outsourcing, and employee leasing can be disappointing, however, if managers use them as simple solutions to complex performance problems. Overemphasizing labour costs misses the broader issue of improving a firm's productivity. Employee productivity is the result of a combination of employees' abilities, motivation, and work environment and the technology they use to work. Since productivity can be defined as "the output gained from a fixed amount of inputs," organizations can increase their productivity either by reducing their inputs (the cost approach) or by increasing the amount that employees produce by adding more human and/or physical capital to the process (the investment approach). Companies such as Southwest Airlines, Nucor, and Toyota achieve low costs in their industries not because they scrimp on employees but because they are the most productive.

In absolute terms, the United States remains the world's most productive nation, even when it comes to manufacturing. If Canada's labour productivity had been the same as that of the United States, individual Canadians would be wealthier, profits would be higher, and governments would have received more taxes.[37] Apparel and textile manufacturing have decreased, but they have been replaced by industries that rely more on technological precision and brainpower than on low-skilled labour—industries for aircraft, sophisticated machinery, medical devices, and so on. However, the growth in output per worker is now climbing fast in less developed countries such as China that have lacked expertise and technology in the past but are making strides to close the gap. When the investment in faster computers and more efficient machine tools levels off, this limits how much assistance technology can offer employees in terms of their productivity. Any additional productivity will have to come from the enhanced ability of employees, their motivation, and their work environment, which makes the job of the HR manager in the coming years all the more crucial.[38]

Many companies are finding that providing work flexibility is a good way to improve the productivity and motivation of valuable employees, especially when giving them larger benefit packages is not an option. For example, when gasoline prices skyrocketed in 2008, most companies could not afford to automatically increase employees' pay because they were facing higher transportation costs themselves for the goods and services they had to buy. But some companies let employees either telecommute or work 10 hours per day, 4 days a week.

## CHALLENGE 6: RESPONDING TO THE DEMOGRAPHIC AND DIVERSITY CHALLENGES OF THE WORKFORCE

**OUTCOME 6**

Almost half of organizations reported that the biggest investment challenge facing organizations over the next 10 years is obtaining human capital and optimizing their human capital investments.[39] Why is this so? Changes in the demographic makeup of employees, such as their ages, education levels, and ethnicities, are part of the reason.

To forecast trends to support the strategies of their organizations, HR managers frequently analyze the capabilities of different demographic groups and how well each is represented in both fast-growing and slow-growing occupations. To accommodate shifts such as these, find qualified talent, and broaden their customer bases, businesses know it is absolutely vital to increase their efforts to recruit and train a more diverse workforce. And with a more diverse workforce come more diverse expectations on the part of employees for their employers to meet.

### Demographic Changes

Among the most significant challenges to managers are the demographic changes occurring in Canada. Because they affect the workforce of an employer, these changes—in employee background, age, gender, and education—are important topics for discussion.

### The Diversity/Immigration Challenge

Figure 1.2 shows the 2006 composition of the population of Canada (note that new census data will be published in 2013). Minorities in Canada are increasing relative to the population. Between 2001 and 2006, minorities increased by 27.2 percent, compared to a 5.4 percent increase in the population of Canada for the same period. British Columbia and Ontario lead the country in the percentage of their visible minority populations at 24.8 percent and 22.8 percent, respectively.

How a shortage of immigrant labour could undercut competitiveness is not lost on Canadian businesses that need talent on both ends of the spectrum (low-level jobs as well as those requiring high levels of education). To accommodate the shift in demographics, demand, and labour trends, these businesses know it is absolutely vital to increase their efforts to recruit and train a more diverse workforce. They realize that immigrants are not only critical to their very survival but also add to their strength and allow them to better attract and serve a larger customer base. Hotel chain Marriott and Big Four accounting firm Deloitte & Touche are examples.[40]

### Age Distribution of Employees

Canada's population was 35 million in 2012. About five million are 65 or over, and this number is expected to double over the next 10 years.[41]

## FIGURE 1.2

### COMPOSITION OF THE POPULATION OF CANADA (MILLIONS)

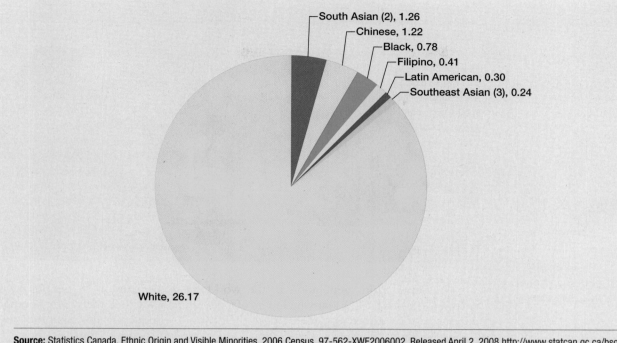

South Asian (2), 1.26
Chinese, 1.22
Black, 0.78
Filipino, 0.41
Latin American, 0.30
Southeast Asian (3), 0.24
White, 26.17

Source: Statistics Canada, Ethnic Origin and Visible Minorities, 2006 Census, 97-562-XWE2006002, Released April 2, 2008 http://www.statcan.gc.ca/bsolc /olc-cel/olc-cel?catno=97-562-X2006002&lang=eng

The echo boom generation in Canada, comprising people born roughly between 1977 and 1997, represents 20 percent of the population of Canada. These workers will be needed to fill the workforce demands created by the retirement of 8.6 million baby boomers.[42]

The imbalance in the age distribution of the labour force is having a significant effect on employers. Companies are finding that large portions of their workforces are nearing retirement. Beyond the sheer number of employees they will have to replace, managers are concerned that the expertise of these employees is likely to be drained too rapidly from the company. As a stopgap measure, employers are making positive efforts to attract older workers, especially those who have taken early retirement. Workers are taking them up on the offer. Many baby boomers say they expect to work past traditional retirement age. Good health and longer life expectancies play the biggest role in extended work lives. But some retirees have returned to the workforce because of economic needs.

Home Depot and McDonald's Canada are among the companies making efforts to attract older workers. Recruiting older workers may sound counterintuitive because they incur higher health care costs. But older workers also have fewer dependants and offer other cost savings. As one HR professional states, "Our over-50 employee turnover is ten times less than those under 30. So when you think about the savings you have in training costs, transitions costs, and recruitment costs, you save a lot more on that for the over-50 workers than you do for others."[43]

The millennial generation, of which you may be a member, is also having an effect on the labour market in Canada. Also known as Generation Y, millennials are generally regarded as having good technological know-how and initiative, especially when it comes to starting their own businesses. (Facebook founder Mark Zuckerberg is a notable example.) They are particularly interested in meaningful work that will improve the world around them. Similar to the trends with baby boomers, those who constitute this new population bulge are experiencing greater competition for advancement from others of approximately the same age.

Three generations work together in this setting.

© Radius Images/Corbis

The other major generation in the workforce is Generation X, people born between 1964 and 1979. Many members of Generation X watched their baby-boomer parents get downsized at some point in their lives. Consequently, now that they are raising children themselves, Generation X-ers value job security. However, they are less likely to think of themselves as being wed to one employer as their parents were. The members of Generation X are also independent. They like challenging rather than repetitive work and dislike supervisors who look over their shoulders.

Managers can find themselves challenged in terms of getting the three generations to work well together. Baby boomers sometimes categorize younger workers as having a poorer work ethic. Some younger workers have the perception that older workers are set in their ways and technologically challenged. The situation can also create supervisory issues. How will a 55-year-old react to being managed by someone in their twenties or thirties? To help companies overcome these obstacles, HR departments and experts are developing programs to help the generations understand one another better so they can capitalize on one another's strengths rather than preying on one another's weaknesses.

Keep in mind that the three generations of workers we have described here are generalizations. Individual employees are vastly different from one another and motivated by different factors, even if they belong to the same generation. It is up to managers to determine what drives each person so as to best utilize his or her talents and to meet the person's employment demands and career aspirations.

## Gender Distribution of the Workforce

### Using the Internet

Learn more about programs that support workplace literacy at **http://abclifeliteracy.ca**

Women make up nearly half of the workforce in Canada, and the educational attainment of women is also increasing relative to men. Today, 61 percent of university graduates are women. Employers wanting to attract the talent that women have to offer are taking measures to ensure they are treated equally in the workplace in terms of their advancement opportunities and compensation. In addition, more companies are accommodating working parents by offering them parental leave, part-time employment, flexible work schedules, job sharing, telecommuting, and childcare and eldercare assistance.

Companies are having trouble finding trained and certified workers such as pipe fitters, motorcycle mechanics, and air traffic controllers. As baby boomers retire, the problem will likely worsen. HR departments will have to offer higher compensation packages to attract qualified candidates, and recruiting and selection systems will have to function much more competitively to identify talent. Given the economic downturn and rise in unemployment Canada has experienced recently, this might sound strange. But demographic shifts can, and will, have a huge impact on HR and society. HR managers are interested in these trends because the economy and job market are critical to HR operations. For example, given that visible minorities and women have increased their share of the labour force, HR managers frequently analyze how each group is represented in both fast-growing and slow-growing occupations—a topic to which we will return in Chapter 3.

As we have suggested, harnessing a company's talent means being aware of characteristics *common* to employees while also managing these employees as *individuals*. It means not just tolerating or accommodating all sorts of differences but also supporting, nurturing, and utilizing these differences to the organization's advantage—in other words, strategically leveraging them rather than simply managing them so that people are treated equitably and "everyone gets along."[44] HR managers have to ask themselves the following question: What is it about the experiences, mindsets, and talents of different groups of people that can be utilized in a strategic way? After all, despite our similarities, *all* of us are different in one way or another, aside from the obvious differences we have outlined in this section. These differences, too, can be the source of organizational strength. Later in the book we will discuss more about the steps firms can take to leverage employee differences.

## CHALLENGE 7: ADAPTING TO EDUCATIONAL AND CULTURAL SHIFTS AFFECTING THE WORKFORCE

### Education of the Workforce

The 2006 Census confirmed that higher education is a gateway to higher earnings, as did all previous censuses. For men and women of all ages, full-time, full-year earners with a university degree earned substantially more than their counterparts who did not have a high school diploma. Figure 1.3 shows the extent to which more years of education result in increased earnings.

> **OUTCOME 7**

Experts estimate that the value of a college or university degree is $1 million over the course of a career, according to the Association of Universities and Colleges of Canada. The unemployment rates of those with only high school education are on average 12 to 20 percent higher than those of degree holders of the same age.[45] It is important to note, however, that whereas the complexity of jobs is increasing significantly, the skills gap is huge and widening. More than three million Canadians (aged 16 to 65) have problems reading printed material. The BHP Ekati Diamond Mine in the Northwest Territories realized that a large number of candidates had not completed high school, so the company hired educators to deliver training in basic math and literacy, using actual workplace documents and manuals as teaching tools. Many employers are using a tool, the Test of Workplace Essential Skills (TOWES), developed at the Bow Valley College in Calgary, Alberta, to assess employee competence in three essential skills: reading text, document use, and numeracy. The test results provide managers with information about the gaps in existing skills sets in employees; managers can then turn to educators or institutions for remedial training. As a result of skills gaps, businesses now spend millions of dollars on basic skills training for their employees.[46]

### Cultural Changes

The attitudes, beliefs, values, and customs of people in a society are an integral part of their culture. Naturally, their culture affects their behaviour on the job and the environment within the organization, influencing their reactions to work assignments, leadership styles, and reward systems. Like the external and internal environments of which it is a part, culture is undergoing continual change. HR policies and procedures therefore must be adjusted to cope with this change.

## FIGURE 1.3

EDUCATION OF THE WORKFORCE

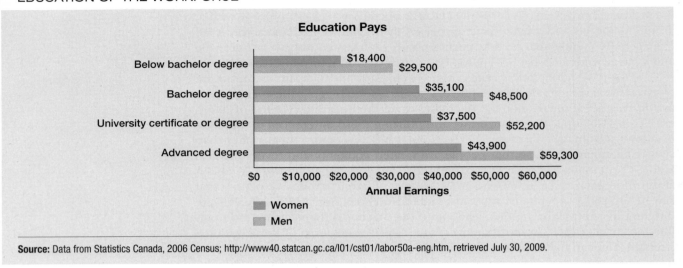

**Education Pays**

| | Women | Men |
|---|---|---|
| Below bachelor degree | $18,400 | $29,500 |
| Bachelor degree | $35,100 | $48,500 |
| University certificate or degree | $37,500 | $52,200 |
| Advanced degree | $43,900 | $59,300 |

Annual Earnings

**Source:** Data from Statistics Canada, 2006 Census; http://www40.statcan.gc.ca/l01/cst01/labor50a-eng.htm, retrieved July 30, 2009.

## Employee Rights

Over the past few decades, federal legislation has radically changed the rules for management of employees by granting them many specific rights. Among these are laws granting employees the right to equal employment opportunity (Chapter 3), union representation if they desire it (Chapter 14), a safe and healthful work environment (Chapter 12), pension plans regulated by the government (Chapter 11), equal pay for men and women performing essentially the same job (Chapter 9), and privacy in the workplace (Chapter 13). An expanded discussion of the specific areas in which rights and responsibilities are of concern to employers and employees will be presented in Chapter 13.

## Concern for Privacy

HR managers and their staffs, as well as line managers in positions of responsibility, generally recognize the importance of discretion in handling all types of information about employees. *The Personal Information Protection and Electronic Documents Act* (PIPEDA) is a federal law that deals with the collection, use, and disclosure of personal information (note that Quebec is the only province with similar laws, although Ontario, British Columbia, and others have draft legislation in place). This law requires federally regulated organizations holding personal information on customers or employees to obtain their consent before they use, collect, or disclose this information. Employer responses to the issue of information privacy vary widely. IBM was one of the first companies to show concern for how personal information about employees was handled. It began restricting the release of information as early as 1965 and in 1971 developed a comprehensive privacy policy. The Royal Bank, the Hudson's Bay Company, and Zero Knowledge Systems in Montreal are among other employers that have developed privacy programs.

Globalization has added another twist to privacy compliance. For example, EU countries prohibit the transfer of personal data to countries with inadequate data protection laws, such as China. In addition to implementing privacy policies, most companies now try to limit the use of social insurance numbers on time sheets, log-in sheets, and other employment forms. Some companies lock up employee files, conduct background checks on employees who have access to others' files, educate employees in fraud prevention, and contract with outside firms specializing in identity theft.[47]

Although the PIPEDA protects people's electronic communications, such as their email, the rules are different when it comes to the privacy that employees

# THE BUSINESS CASE

## Advantages of Part-Time Workers

The trend in Canadian employment is definitely away from full-time "permanent" jobs to the use of part-time and temporary employees. The advantages of employing temporary workers are numerous:

- Reducing payroll costs because part-time and temporary workers seldom receive the same benefits as full-time workers.

- Responding to fluctuations in demand. Contingent workers can be hired or dismissed during periods of high or low demand (e.g., for retail stores—high demand during holiday seasons; low demand in January).

- Access to specific expertise—when an organization enters a new business or needs specific expertise for a limited time (development of a website, for example), it makes economic sense to hire only for that need. Contingent workers may also be used to bring in new ideas and skills from other organizations and/or train regular employees.

- Organizations can "test" employees' skills and fit with the organization by specifying a limited work contract. In this way, productive employees can be hired and those who are underperformers can be released without costly termination costs.

Most employers recognize these advantages and so wish to employ more contingent and part-time employees. However, although these costs are easily assessed, there may be greater benefits to be achieved by hiring full-time employees. Loblaws thinks so. Canada's largest grocery store chain is planning to convert 10 percent of its part-time workforce to full-time work. Ten thousand full-time jobs will be created to increase productivity and improve retention. The assumption, backed by HR research, is that the use of full-time employees will increase employee engagement, which will improve customer service (a key differentiator among retailers) and thus improve revenues and then profits. The increases in compensation (full-time workers make 50 percent more in benefits than part-time workers) will be offset by the savings of reduced turnover (the part-timer turnover rate is 50 percent).

Sources: G. White, "Finding the Best Temp Worker for the Job," *Canadian HR Reporter*, (May 4, 2009), vol 22, Issue 9: 17; S. Klie, "Part-timers Could Go Full Time at Grocery Giant," *Canadian HR Reporter* (March 23, 200) Vol. 22, Iss. 6: 1, 8.

can expect with regard to their electronic communications at work. Workers are learning the hard way that their employers have a right to monitor their email and Internet use, for example. The information employees post on the Web—either on social networking sites or on job-hunting sites such as Monster.com—have also become subject to scrutiny by employers. Electronic surveillance in the workplace is also becoming an issue. In Chapter 13, we will discuss the content of privacy programs, along with the privacy employees can expect while on the job, and recommend some privacy guidelines.

## The Changing Nature of the Job

The era of the full-time permanent job seems to have disappeared. The number of self-employed is also increasing, accounting for 15 percent of employment and 75 percent of new job growth.[48] Nearly half of all the jobs created in the last two decades have been nonstandard—that is, part-time, temporary, or contract work. As job security erodes, so do pension plans and health care benefits, especially for part-timers. Nonstandard jobs represent about 30 percent of all employment.[49] The Business Case outlines the advantages of employing temporary workers but also shows why a company has moved away from this strategy, to reap higher benefits.

As shown in Ethics in HRM, labour force participants have become increasingly polarized into haves and have-nots. We return to the subject of changing employment options in Chapter 4.

# ETHICS IN HRM

## Skywalkers and Groundworkers

Canadian workers can be divided into two classes: sky-walkers and groundworkers. Skywalkers, those working in white-collar jobs in high-rise buildings, are well educated and well trained and earn good incomes. Their jobs are secure, and they receive full benefits. For these knowledge workers, the employment prospects in computer programming, financial analysis, insurance, business services, and real estate are bright. Those working as managers in the high-rises on Bay Street, Howe Street, and rue St-Jacques earned an hourly average of $30.70. (A Canadian worker earned, on average, about $24.81 in 2012.)

Below the high-rise buildings toil the groundworkers. Those with little education and outdated skills are suffering massive unemployment. Groundworkers suffer further from job insecurity and a lack of benefit programs. Look for these workers in restaurants, hotels, and shops. The "McJobs" they hold in the accommodation, food, and beverage industries paid a mere $12 per hour, and many earned far less than this, being paid the minimum wage of about $7 an hour. Those working part-time—a growing segment that now comprises 34 percent of the Canadian workforce—fare even worse. Companies have discovered cost savings by replacing full-time employees with part-time workers, thereby eliminating benefits and increasing staffing flexibility. This restructuring of the job market has produced winners and losers, but many would argue that all Canadians lose when the unemployment rate is high and citizens feel insecure about their futures. These factors have no doubt contributed to the Occupy movement, in which citizens camped out in at least 15 Canadian cities, protesting the privileges of the 1 percent (who have high-paying, secure jobs) and lamenting the conditions of the 99 percent (with no or low-paying jobs and no security).

Sources: Heather Scoffield, "Hold the McJobs: Canada's High End Employment Boom," *The Globe and Mail*, February 17, 2006, B1 and B4; Statistics Canada, Statistics Canada Measures of Weekly Earnings. http://www4.hrsdc.gc.ca/.3ndic.1t.4r@-eng.jsp?iid=18, retrieved May 11, 2009.

## Changing Attitudes toward Work

Employees today are less likely to define their personal success only in terms of financial gains. Many employees, especially younger ones, believe satisfaction in life is more likely to result from balancing their work challenges and rewards with those in their personal lives. Although most people still enjoy work and want to excel at it, they tend to be focused on finding interesting work and are more inclined to pursue multiple careers rather than being satisfied with just "having a job." Figure 1.4 outlines the job features that are important to Canadian workers. People also appear to be seeking ways of living that are less complicated but more meaningful. These new lifestyles cannot help having an impact on the way employees must be motivated and managed. Consequently, HRM has become more complex than it was when employees were concerned primarily with economic survival.

## Balancing Work and Family

Work and family are connected in many subtle and not-so-subtle social, economic, and psychological ways. Because of the forms that the family now takes—such as the two-wage earner and the single-parent family—work organizations are finding it advantageous to provide employees with more family-friendly options. "Family friendly" is a broad term that can include flexible work hours, daycare, eldercare, part-time work, job sharing, pregnancy leave, parental leave, executive transfers, spousal involvement in career planning, assistance with family problems, and telecommuting. A survey by HR consulting firm Hewitt Associates found that 64 percent of employers now offer flexible work hours, 46 percent permit job sharing, and 39 percent allow telecommuting.[50] Other companies are exploring the use of four-day workweeks to lessen their employees' commuting costs (particularly with rising gasoline prices).

## FIGURE 1.4

### WORK IS MORE THAN JUST A PAYCHEQUE

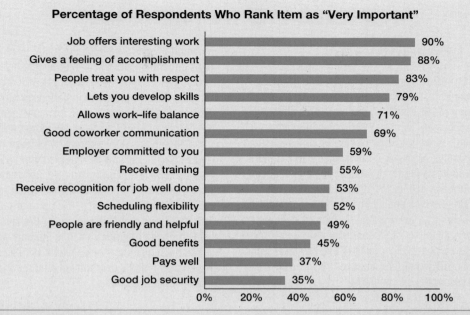

**Percentage of Respondents Who Rank Item as "Very Important"**

| Item | Percentage |
|---|---|
| Job offers interesting work | 90% |
| Gives a feeling of accomplishment | 88% |
| People treat you with respect | 83% |
| Lets you develop skills | 79% |
| Allows work–life balance | 71% |
| Good coworker communication | 69% |
| Employer committed to you | 59% |
| Receive training | 55% |
| Receive recognition for job well done | 53% |
| Scheduling flexibility | 52% |
| People are friendly and helpful | 49% |
| Good benefits | 45% |
| Pays well | 37% |
| Good job security | 35% |

**Source:** http://www.jobquality.ca Online Survey: "What Do You Value in a Job?" *Canadian Policy Research Networks* (2004), http://www.jobquality.ca/surveys/results_8.shtml, retrieved July 26, 2009.

Companies with programs such as these calculate that accommodating their employees' individual needs and circumstances is a powerful way to attract and retain top-calibre people. Aetna Life and Casualty, for example, cut its turnover by 50 percent after it began offering six-month parental leaves, coupled with an option for part-time work when employees return to the job.[51] With that said, family-friendly companies have to balance the benefits they provide to families versus their single employees. The majority of employees have no children under 18. A Conference Board survey of companies with family-friendly programs found that companies acknowledge that childless employees harbour resentment against employees with children who are able to take advantage of these programs.[52]

See Highlights in HRM 1.3 for a discussion with Nora Spinks, an expert in work–life harmony.

> **line managers**
> Non-HR managers who are responsible for overseeing the work of other employees

## THE PARTNERSHIP OF LINE MANAGERS AND HUMAN RESOURCES DEPARTMENTS

We have taken a good deal of time upfront in this book to outline today's competitive and social challenges to reinforce the idea that managing people is not something that occurs in a backroom called the HR department. Managing people is every manager's business, and successful organizations combine the experience of **line managers** with the expertise of HR specialists to develop and utilize the talents of employees to their greatest potential. Addressing HR issues is rarely the exclusive responsibility of HR departments acting alone. Instead, HR managers work side by side with line managers to address the people-related issues of the organization. Although this relationship has not always achieved its ideal, the situation is rapidly improving. HR managers are assuming a greater role in top management planning and decision making, a trend that reflects the growing awareness among executives that HRM can make important contributions to the success of an organization.

Just as there are different types of line managers who specialize in different functions—operations, accounting, marketing, and so forth—there are different types of HR managers who specialize in different HR functions. Some of these

**OUTCOME 8**

# HIGHLIGHTS IN HRM 1.3

## Work–Life Harmony

Nora Spinks, president and CEO of Work–Life Harmony, a consulting company specializing in work–life balance issues, comments on the demographic issues affecting employee behaviour: "Women are in the workplace to stay; they have fewer and shorter career breaks and have more opportunities to make or influence organizational decisions. There is a high proportion of the aging 'boomer' workforce that are asking, 'What is my legacy?' They are rethinking priorities and lifestyles and reducing the number of hours they are working. At the same time, the millenial generation [i.e., the generation born in the 1980s] is entering the workforce and managerial positions with a fresh perspective and different outlook on the work experience. They see work as a means to having a life, not as

life in and of itself. The boomers tend to live to work, the nexus generation work to live. Growing up, they witnessed people give up a life for the sake of a job, only to see them ultimately lose employment in periods of downsizing and restructuring. They don't want the same experience.

"A recent international study of students found that young people about to enter the workforce wanted to have a challenging career with plenty of opportunity to grow personally and professionally, and they wanted to be able to take advantage of those opportunities while achieving work–life balance. It is up to organizations, executives, and managers to create the kinds of environments to make that possible. It is the only way for them to meet increasing customer/client demands, meet the challenges of global competition, and reach their organizational objectives."

Source: Interview with Nora Spinks.

workers specialize in employee training and development, recruitment, or compensation. Other HR employees specialize in studying the effects of industry and occupational trends or concentrate on labour relations and prepare information for managers to use during negotiations with labour unions. By contrast, an HR generalist can be responsible for handling all aspects of HR work depending on his or her employer's needs.[53]

Human Resources and Skills Development Canada is projecting an excess demand for HR managers and professions. Nonetheless, we understand that most readers of this book will be line managers and supervisors rather than HR specialists. The text is, therefore, oriented to *helping people manage people more effectively,* whether they become first-line supervisors or CEOs. Students now preparing for careers in organizations will find that the study of HRM provides a background that will be valuable in managerial and supervisory positions. Becoming familiar with the role HR managers play should help facilitate closer cooperation between the different departments of firms and enable line and executive-level managers to fully utilize the assistance and services offered by their HR groups.

## RESPONSIBILITIES OF THE HR MANAGER

Although line managers and HR managers need to work together, their responsibilities are different, as are their competencies and expertise. The major activities for which an HR manager is typically responsible are as follows:

1. *Advice and counsel.* The HR manager often serves as an in-house consultant to supervisors, managers, and executives. Given their knowledge of internal employment issues (policies, labour agreements, past practices, ethics and corporate governance, and the needs of employees), as well as their awareness of external trends (such as economic and employment data, new legal and regulatory issues), HR managers can be an invaluable resource for making decisions. For example, larger companies have begun appointing "chief ethics officers" to help their employees wade through grey areas when it comes to right and wrong. The firm's top HR manager is in a good position for this job. In smaller companies, however, this task frequently falls on the

shoulders of individual HR managers. HR managers are also being relied on more heavily to advise compensation committees, which are more closely scrutinizing executives' pay than they have in years past.

2. *Service*. HR managers also perform a host of service activities, such as recruiting, selecting, testing, planning and conducting training programs, and hearing employee concerns and complaints. Technical expertise in these areas is essential for HR managers and forms the basis of HR program design and implementation. Moreover, managers must be convinced that HR staff are there to help them increase their productivity rather than to impose obstacles to their goals. This requires not only the ability on the part of the HR executive to consider problems from the viewpoint of line managers and supervisors but also skill in communicating with managers and supervisors.

3. *Policy formulation and implementation*. HR managers generally propose and draft new policies or policy revisions to address recurring problems or to prevent anticipated problems. Ordinarily, these are proposed to the senior executives of the organization, who actually issue the policies. HR managers may monitor performance of line departments and other staff departments to ensure conformity with established HR policies, procedures, and practices. Perhaps more important, they are a resource to whom managers can turn for policy interpretation.

4. *Employee advocacy*. One of the enduring roles of HR managers is to serve as an employee advocate—listening to employees' concerns and representing their needs to managers—to ensure that the interests of employees and the interests of the organization are aligned with one another. Effective employee relations provide a support structure when disruptive changes interfere with workers' normal daily activities.

## COMPETENCIES OF THE HR MANAGER

As top executives expect HR managers to assume a broader role in overall organizational strategy, many of these managers will need to acquire a complementary set of competencies. These competencies are summarized here and shown in Figure 1.5.

1. *Business mastery*. HR professionals need to know the business of their organization thoroughly. This requires an understanding of its economic and financial capabilities so that they can become a key member of the team of business managers to develop the firm's strategic direction. It also requires that HR professionals develop skills at external relations focused on their customers.

2. *HR mastery*. HR professionals are the organization's behavioural science experts. HR professionals should develop expert knowledge in the areas of staffing, development, appraisals, rewards, team building, and communication.

3. *Change mastery*. HR professionals must be able to manage change processes so that their firms' HR activities are effectively merged with the business needs of their organizations. This involves interpersonal and problem-solving skills, as well as innovativeness and creativity.

4. *Personal credibility*. Like other management professionals, HR professionals must establish personal credibility in the eyes of their internal and external customers. Credibility and trust are earned by developing personal relationships with one's customers, demonstrating the values of the firm, standing up for one's own beliefs, and being fair-minded when dealing with others.

Good HR managers help their organizations build a sustained competitive advantage. At lower levels in the organization, a rapidly growing number of companies, including Ford Canada and UPS Canada, are assigning HR representatives to their core business teams to make certain that HR issues are addressed on the job and that their HR representatives, in turn, are knowledgeable about core business issues rather than simply focusing on employee-related administrative functions.

**Using the Internet**

Canadian HR professionals abide by a code of ethics, which can be found on

**http://www.cchra.ca**

The HR-required professional competencies can also be found on this site.

## FIGURE 1.5

## HUMAN RESOURCE COMPETENCY MODEL

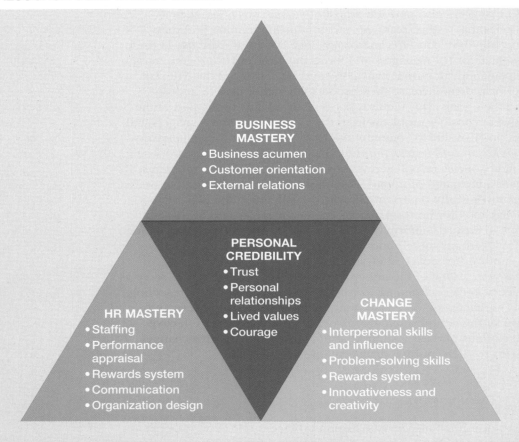

**BUSINESS MASTERY**
- Business acumen
- Customer orientation
- External relations

**PERSONAL CREDIBILITY**
- Trust
- Personal relationships
- Lived values
- Courage

**HR MASTERY**
- Staffing
- Performance appraisal
- Rewards system
- Communication
- Organization design

**CHANGE MASTERY**
- Interpersonal skills and influence
- Problem-solving skills
- Rewards system
- Innovativeness and creativity

**Source:** Arthur Yeung, Wayne Brockbank, and Dave Ulrich, "Lower Cost, Higher Value: Human Resource Function in Transformation." Reprinted with permission from *Human Resource Planning*, Vol. 17, No. 3 (1994). Copyright 1994 by The Human Resource Planning Society, 317 Madison Avenue, Suite 1509, New York, NY 10017. Phone: (212) 490-6387. Fax: (212) 682-6851.

# SMALL BUSINESS APPLICATION

Organizations have a variety of staff-related requirements associated with supporting business operations. These could include hiring, paying, managing, training, or terminating staff. This could also involve work design or staffing strategies and ensuring legal compliance. Traditionally, the role of an HR generalist is a position in medium or large organizations, those with 100 employees or more.

However, as of 2012, 98 percent of businesses in Canada are considered small, and there are one million of these. The vast majority of these would have fewer than 100 employees, which would be too small to justify having an HR generalist on staff. Small business represents 48 percent of private-sector jobs in Canada, employing more workers than either large or medium

enterprises. As a result, small business owners without HR generalists manage over five million employees in Canada. It is apparent that small business owners need the tools and practices employed by HR generalists integrated into a handbook they can refer to as needed.

Who is responsible for the delivery of HR responsibilities in small business depends on a number of contextual factors: the size of the company, the nature of the business, the financial status of the company, the management structure, the structure of support roles, the leadership culture, and the approach to using vendors. HR support may be delivered by business owners themselves for very small companies, by managers for slightly larger companies, and by office managers for larger companies. Small businesses may outsource some or all of this support to vendors who support many clients. Activities such as payroll, benefits, and legal support are often delivered through vendors.

The types of services traditionally delivered by HR generalists in large enterprises that are delivered in small companies are to a large extent driven by the industry, size, and geographic location. For example, the HR needs in a retail environment with high employee turnover will focus largely on recruiting and training, although the needs in a stable construction business may centre around health and safety. Through this text, we will dedicate a section of each chapter to the applicability to small business of the practices reviewed and will draw on industry-specific examples that help demonstrate each practice.

Source: Statistics Canada, "Key Small Business Statistics," July 2007. http://www.ic.gc.ca/eic/site/sbrp-rppe.nsf/vwapj/KSBS_July2007_Eng.pdf/$FILE/KSBS_July2007_Eng.pdf

# SUMMARY

**OUTCOME 1** HR managers who have a good understanding of their firm's business can help it achieve its strategies—whatever they may be—through the effective utilization of people and their talents. An organization's success increasingly depends on the knowledge, skills, and abilities of its employees. To "compete through people," organizations have to do a good job of managing human capital: the knowledge, skills, and capabilities that have value to organizations. Managers must develop strategies for identifying, recruiting, and hiring the best talent available; developing these employees in ways that are firm specific; helping them generate new ideas and generalize them throughout the company; encouraging information sharing; and rewarding collaboration and teamwork among employees.

**OUTCOME 2** Globalization has become pervasive in the marketplace. It influences the number and kinds of jobs that are available and requires that organizations balance a complicated set of issues related to managing people working under different business conditions in different geographies, cultures, and legal environments. HR strategies and functions have to be adjusted to take into account these differences.

**OUTCOME 3** The fast pace of globalization and corporate scandals over the years have led to a new focus on corporate social responsibility (good citizenship) and sustainability (a company's ability to produce a good or service without damaging the environment or depleting a resource). Companies are finding out that having a good reputation for pursuing these efforts can enhance their revenues and improve the calibre of talent they are able to attract. One of HR's leadership roles is to spearhead the development and implementation of corporate citizenship throughout their organizations, especially the fair treatment of workers.

**OUTCOME 4** Technology has tended to reduce the number of jobs that require little skill and to increase the number of jobs that require considerable skill, a shift we refer to as moving from touch labour to knowledge work. This displaces some employees and requires that others be retrained. In addition, information technology has influenced HRM through HRISs that streamline HR processes, make information more readily available to managers and employees, and enable HR departments to focus on the firm's strategies. The Internet and social media are also affecting how employees are hired, work, and are managed.

**OUTCOME 5** To contain costs, organizations have been downsizing, outsourcing, offshoring, furloughing, and leasing employees, as well as enhancing productivity. HR's role is not only to implement these programs but also to consider the pros and cons of programs such as these and how they might affect a company's ability to compete, especially if they lead to the loss of talented staff members.

**OUTCOME 6** The workforce is becoming increasingly diverse, and organizations are doing more to address employee concerns and to maximize the benefit of different kinds of employees. But to benefit from those differences, managers need to look past the obvious differences between employees and see not so obvious differences, such as how they think, learn, work, solve problems, manage their time, and deal with other people. By first seeing the differences, exploring them, and then discovering how they can provide value to the organization, HR managers can leverage those differences.

**OUTCOME 7** HR managers must keep abreast of the educational abilities of the talent available to their organization. Despite the fact that the educational attainment of the labour force has risen in general, many firms are finding it difficult to find workers with the basic skills they need. As baby boomers retire, HR departments may have to offer higher compensation packages to attract qualified candidates, and recruiting and selection systems will have to function much more competitively. Employee rights, privacy concerns, attitudes toward work, and efforts to balance work and family are becoming more important to workers as the cultural dynamics of the labour force shift. Companies are finding that accommodating employees' individual needs as a result of these shifts is a powerful way to attract and retain top-calibre people.

**OUTCOME 8** In working with line managers to address their organization's challenges, HR managers play a number of important roles; they are called on for strategic advice and ethics counsel, various service activities, policy formulation and implementation, and employee advocacy. To perform these roles effectively, HR managers must have a deep understanding of their firm's operational, financial, and personnel capabilities. HR managers who do and are creative and innovative can help shape a firm's strategies so as to respond successfully to changes in the marketplace. Ultimately, managing people is rarely the exclusive responsibility of the HR function. Every manager's job involves managing people. Consequently, successful companies combine the expertise of HR specialists with the experience of line managers and executives to develop and use the talents of employees to their greatest potential.

## KEY TERMS

change management 6
collaborative software 10
corporate social responsibility 10
downsizing 6
employee leasing 17
furloughing 15
globalization 8

human capital 4
human resources information
    system (HRIS) 12
human resources
    management (HRM) 3
knowledge workers 11
line managers 25

nearshoring 16
offshoring 16
outsourcing 6
proactive change 7
reactive change 7
reengineering 6
Six Sigma 6

## DISCUSSION QUESTIONS

1. Are people always an organization's most valuable asset? Why or why not? Name other strategic or valuable assets of organizations.
2. Suppose your boss asked you to summarize the major people-related concerns in opening an office in China. What issues would be on your list?
3. Name a company you hope to work for someday. What is its track record in terms of corporate social responsibility and sustainability? Are these factors important to you? Why or why not?
4. Will technology eliminate the need for HR managers?
5. In groups, debate the proposition: *Employees are an expense, and their numbers should be reduced.*

6. What are the pros and cons of having a more diverse workforce? Is Canada in a better position to compete globally because of its diverse population? Find examples from a school or work project where having a diverse team made a difference and explain that difference.
7. Why do HR managers need to stay abreast of the educational levels and work expectations of people in the workforce?
8. In your opinion, what is the most important role of HR managers? Should HR professionals be the "voice" for employees or the "spokesperson" for managers? Explain your view. Should HR professionals be licensed, like accountants and lawyers?

# HRM EXPERIENCE

## Balancing Competitive Challenges and Employee Concerns

HRM is not just the responsibility of the personnel department. If people are a competitive resource, then line managers play an increasingly important role in managing the workforce. But this is not an either/or situation. Rather than seeing line managers assume the responsibilities of HR managers, we see both groups working together to handle workforce issues. But how exactly do these two groups work together?

### Assignment

1. Working in teams of four to six individuals, identify what role the HR department would play in terms of the following activities and what role line managers would play. Where would overlaps occur, and would there be any likely problems?

   a. Recruiting and selection
   b. Training and development
   c. Compensation
   d. Performance evaluation
   e. Labour relations

2. How would potential problems be resolved?

3. Write the groups' findings on flip charts and post for all to see. One member from each team should explain his or her findings to all class members.

4. Point out the similarities and differences across the teams. Save these points and revisit them—possibly revising them—as you study subsequent chapters in this text.

 Visit the *Managing Human Resources* CourseMate website at http://www. belcourt7e.nelson.com for quizzes, flashcards, videos, games, and more!

## CASE STUDY 1

### NEW HR STRATEGY MAKES LLOYD'S A "BEST COMPANY"

After a mere 320 years in business, the iconic global insurer Lloyd's of London finally set out to establish its first true HR strategy, starting with the hiring of HR Director Suzy Black in 2009. "I was brought in to transform the HR function from one modeled on an old-style personnel office to a function that is more cutting edge, business focused, and value adding," says Black.

Black's first order of business was to evaluate the current state of affairs, particularly how the corporation's senior managers perceived the HR role. With this information in hand, Black and her team began to develop an overarching strategic agenda as well as specific tactics, addressing everything from recruitment, to performance management, to basic policies, to rewards and compensation. Early

on, Black admits, her main priority was simply "getting the basics right," an objective that was made more challenging by the global reach of the company, which demanded flexibility and variation to meet the needs of all Lloyd's employees while still benefitting the company.

Changing long-time employees' perception of HR then took a bit of convincing, but employees quickly began to recognize the value of Black's actions. Through repeated presentations, employees worldwide grew to appreciate Black's insistence on transparency regarding the nature of the employer–employee relationship. Gradually, they could see how the HR strategies were effectively creating conditions in which they could develop in their careers, be successful, and find meaning and value in their work. Today, Lloyd's employees list the company's challenging work environment, healthy incentive programs, and meaningful community outreach programs among the key reasons they enjoy working for the insurance giant.

And Black's efforts are now gaining recognition outside the firm, positioning the company as a desirable place to work. In 2011, Lloyd's landed on the *Sunday Times* Top 100 Best Companies to Work For (in the United Kingdom) list and was hailed as one of the United Kingdom's Top 40 Business Brands by an independent researcher. Black emphasizes that the transformation was a company-wide effort, and Lloyd's CEO Richard Ward adds, "I believe Lloyd's to be an inspiring and rewarding place to work and am pleased that our staff agree. I am extremely proud of the achievements of the corporation over the last 12 months and thank all Lloyd's employees for their continuing dedication, commitment, and professionalism."

Ironically, this leadership position is the first HR position Black has ever held as she rose through the ranks in other arenas in business. But her experience has given her a clear definition of the ideal characteristics of HR professionals of the future. Black says they must be commercial, challenging, and focused on delivery and excellence. "They must understand change and transformation, excel at operations, and balance tactical and strategic thinking and acting." She adds, "They will have to be able to manage and navigate organizational complexity and ambiguities and not be afraid to say no occasionally in order to establish appropriate boundaries with the business."

## Questions

1. What skills does Black think employees need to work successfully in the area of HR?
2. What are some of the outcomes of the company's new HR strategy?
3. What do you think might be some of the challenges of establishing HR policies for a global company?
4. What types of situations do you think might require an HR manager to say "no"?

**Sources:** Helen William, "City Slicker," *Personnel Today* (August 11, 2009): 10–11; Digby Morgan Human Resourcefulness Newsletter, February 2010, http://www.digbymorgannewsletter.com/story04_HR_02_10.htm; company website: http://www.lloyds.com.

# CASE STUDY 2

## INTERGENERATIONAL ISSUES

When Jason Traynor was a junior HR administrator at Peregrine Incorporated, he faced serious challenges with a workforce of different ages. The reason for many of the issues was that GM had recently sold off the fabrication plant as part of its new business strategy to get out of auto parts manufacturing and focus solely on assembling vehicles. With the sale of the plant came the condition that any GM employee would be allowed to return to the main GM autoplex as positions came open through employee attrition. Once a GM employee left, he had to be replaced. More times than not, GM would "call out" (recruit) 30 to 40 employees with only two or three days' notice to Peregrine. With no pool of candidates available, Peregrine had to react quickly so as not to disrupt production at GM.

Due to time constraints, prescreening was minimal. There were often no interviews, reference checks, or selection instruments. On several occasions, people would be selected on Friday night for a Monday morning start. The majority of the new hires were young and right out of high school. These new employees, with limited postsecondary education and little, if any, factory experience, were earning $28 an hour, plus benefits, which equaled approximately $85,000 per year. The job was so lucrative that many opted out of pursuing further education. The biggest challenge came when the 18- to 19-year-olds were thrown into a working environment of preretirement 60-year-old factory workers. There was conflict and complaints about everything from the type of music choice on the shop floor to clothing tastes and inappropriate sexual comments.

One of the greatest challenges began when the senior employees began interacting with the junior employees and the new employees would attempt to "use" the system in the same way that a 25-year employee did. The junior employees learned very quickly how to manipulate the collective agreement to their advantage. Activities such as punch card fraud, not badging in or out, and leaving the facility unauthorized while still on the clock were quickly becoming the norm. According to Jason Traynor, "This is not the kind of behaviour you want in your new hires." Having new employees acting as though they had put in 20 years of service often created conflict between the two generations as many of the senior employees felt that these "kids" had not paid their dues and were simply riding the coattails of the senior membership. Addiction problems were rampant among the new employees—many having never been exposed to the readily available supply of drugs and alcohol. Linked to this were the increasing levels of casual absenteeism. Many new hires were terminated, and a great deal of time and energy was spent with the union, which fought to reinstate these employees.

An independent third-party consulting company was asked to help manage these issues. Self-directed workshops were initiated to teach the workers about teamwork and quality. Employee assistance programs were created to help struggling employees. A labour council was started to deal with conflict on the factory floor. The company adopted aptitude testing and joint interviewing with the union in an attempt to select employees who were more qualified.

In the end, Peregrine eventually failed and went out of business.

## Questions

1. Based on your experiences working with students/colleagues of different ages, do you believe that there are generational differences in attitudes toward work? Do a search to see if there is any evidence for these beliefs.
2. As the demand for autos declined, and GM and Chrysler faced bankruptcy, the benefits given to auto workers were reduced. Check out the compensation packages for new auto workers and decide if the package is attractive enough for young workers to leave school, as these young workers did.

## CASE STUDY 3

# SHELL'S TOP RECRUITER TAKES HIS CUES FROM MARKETING

When Navjot Singh joined Royal Dutch Shell in 2003, the company was facing an extraordinary challenge: the rate at which Shell's engineers were retiring meant the global firm needed to double the number of new recruits it hired from 2,697 in 2005 to 5,440 by 2006 and to nearly 8,000 in 2008. Yet at the time, Shell was not considered an employer of choice. The global oil and gas company needed to project a new image—fast! Says Singh, "In the same way marketers know they need to advertise to be a market leader, HR had to know how to create an employer brand. Marketing is the only way to ensure customers buy products. It was also the only way to ensure Shell got the best people coming to us first."

Wait! Why is Shell's HR guy talking about marketing? As both an HR and a marketing expert, Singh sees a powerful synergy between the two. "I'm 50% a marketer—the rest is HR, communications, and recruitment," says Singh. "But I'm an HR person, really." Singh's official job title, however, is Global Marketing Manager, Recruitment and Global HR Communications Manager, Shell (UK), a title and position like no other. Having come to Shell from DaimlerChrysler, where he served as the marketing director, Singh initially started out as vice president of customer relationship management but quickly joined the HR team when he recognized Shell's emerging need for new talent and the immense potential for him to use classic marketing techniques to help the company achieve its objectives. His vision, skill sets, and experience were a perfect match for the company's situation.

So in Singh's mind, addressing the company's need for new talent meant building a brand as an employer, which in turn meant creating a cohesive message. But Shell's global recruiting approach was anything but cohesive. "At the time we had 1,200 recruitment systems, 35 recruitment companies, and 400 executive search companies working for us," he recalls. "I attended a careers event at Cambridge University where there were three Shell stands beside each other—one from the UK, one from Malaysia, and another from Nigeria. This was a fragmented approach and tough for candidates to understand." Shell needed to create a unified outreach program if it was going to meet its need for numbers while fulfilling its desire for a global talent pool. The company recruits from among 90 different nationalities each year because it recognizes the benefits of cultural diversity.

Singh and his team set about applying various marketing techniques to the recruitment process, which have since resulted in an 80 percent cut in recruitment costs, a 20 percent reduction in the time to hire new staff, and a very real claim to being the top employer in its market segment. In fact, Shell has won 80 awards for its unique HR strategy. "I think it's important to make sure that employer branding activities are efficient and effective and that you have the right tools and processes, but also that it's competitively positioned from a cost perspective," notes Singh. "I also think you need to look at it in terms of satisfaction, with the employer value proposition which you create. You need to ensure that there is a high satisfaction level amongst your staff, that they are motivated and have pride in working for your company."

Having come so close to putting itself in danger of not attracting enough skilled candidates, Shell intends to continue running its recruitment program just like any other branding effort, thus ensuring it has the right human resources to deliver on its promises and achieve worldwide success. Singh believes Shell is typical of many firms, noting, "In the future, companies will have to apply for skilled people to work for them rather than candidates applying to work at an organization. HR must still realize the strategic value it can bring."

## Questions

1. What functions of HRM are similar to marketing functions? How can thinking about "marketing" a company's jobs improve the strategic focus of HR personnel?

2. If you were planning to use marketing strategies to "brand" a company as an employer of choice, what are some of the factors you would consider?

3. Do you agree with Singh's statement that in the future, companies will have to apply for skilled people to work for them rather than candidates applying to work at an organization? Why or why not?

**Sources:** Excerpted from Don Wood, "Lateral Thinking," *Human Resources* (January 2010): 12–13; Christopher Van Mossevelde, "Views from the Top," *Employer Branding Today* (April 16, 2009), http://www.employerbrandingtoday .com; Peter Crush, "Shell UK Combines HR and Marketing to Sell the Brand," *HR Magazine* (August 25, 2009), http://www.hrmagazine.co.uk.

## NOTES AND REFERENCES

1. T. J. Watson, Jr., *A Business and Its Beliefs: The Ideas That Helped Build IBM* (New York: McGraw-Hill, 1963).

2. Donald C. Busi, "Assignment Reviews (ARs): Moving toward Measuring Your Most Valuable Asset," *Supervision* 66, no. 1 (January 2005): 3–7.

3. David Lepak and Scott Snell, "Managing the Human Resource Architecture for Knowledge-Based Competition," in S. Jackson, M. Hitt, and A. DeNisi (eds.), *Managing Knowledge for Sustained Competitive Advantage: Designing Strategies for Effective Human Resource Management.* (SIOP Scientific Frontiers Series, 2003): 127–154); David Lepak and Scott Snell, "Examining the Human Resource Architecture: The Relationship among Human Capital, Employment, and Human Resource Configurations," *Journal of Management* 28, no. 4 (2002): 517–543; Steve Bates, "Study Links HR Practices with the Bottom Line," *HR Magazine* 46, no. 12 (December 2001): 14; Ann Pomeroy, "Cooking Up Innovation: When It Comes to Helping Employees Create New Products and Services, HR's Efforts Are a Key Ingredient," *HR Magazine* 49, no. 11 (November 2004): 46–54.

4. Dave Ulrich, Steve Kerr, and Ron Ashkenas, *The GE Work-Out: How to Implement GE's Revolutionary Method for Busting Bureaucracy & Attacking Organizational Problems* (New York: McGraw-Hill Professional Publishing, 2002).

5. John P. Kotter, "Ten Observations," *Executive Excellence* 16, no. 8 (1999): 15–16.

6. HR Success Increasingly Tied to Showing of Strong Business Acumen," *HRfocus* (December 2010): 1–5.

7. M. Hammer and J. Champy, *Reengineering the Corporation* (New York: HarperCollins, 1994). See also Michael Hammer, *Beyond Reengineering: How the Process-Centered Organization Is Changing Our Work and Our Lives* (New York: HarperBusiness, 1996); William M. James, "Best HR Practices for Today's Innovation Management," *Research-Technology Management* 45, no. 1 (January–February 2002): 57–61.

8. Lee G. Bolman and Terry E. Deal, "Four Steps to Keeping Change Efforts Heading in the Right Direction," *Journal of Quality and Participation* 22, no. 3 (May/June 1999): 6–11; "Coaching Employees through the Six Stages of Change," *HRfocus* 79, no. 5 (May 2002): 9; Stefan Stern, "Forever Changing," *Management Today* (February 7, 2005): 40; Dennis Smillie, "Managing Change, Maximizing Technology," *Multi-Housing News* 40, no. 1 (January 2005): 4.

9. Jennifer Rivkin, "The New Rules of Growth," *Profit* 24, no. 5, 2005: 58.

10. Helmar Drost and Richard Hird, *An Introduction to the Canadian Labour Market*, 2nd edition (Thomson Nelson, 2006).

11. HRPAO, "Globalization of Knowledge Work Threatens 2.4 Million Canadian Jobs," http://www.hrpao.org/hrpao/knowledgecentre, retrieved December 19, 2005.

12. Beermaker Eyes Chinese Factories," *Fort Worth Star-Telegram* (December 28, 2010): 3C; Susan Meisinger, "Going Global: A Smart Move for HR Professionals," *HR Magazine* 49, no. 3 (March 2004): 6.

13. World Trade Organization, *World Trade Report*, 2010 (Geneva: WTO Publications): 20; "One Ninth of All U.S. Production Is for Export," *PPI Trade Fact of the Week* (March 19, 2008).

14. Laura McKnight, "For Companies, Doing Good Is Good Business," *Kansas City Star* (December 26, 2010), http://www.kansascity.com.

15. Ibid.

16. Jeff Tanner and Mary Anne Raymond, *Principles of Marketing* (Nyack, NY: FlatWorld Knowledge, 2010): Chapter 10.

17. Nancy R. Lockwood, "Corporate Social Responsibility: HR's Leadership Role," *HR Magazine* 49, no. 2 (December 2004): S1–11.

18. Benoit Guay, "Knowledge Management Is a Team Sport," *Computing Canada* 27, no. 3 (July 13, 2001): 23; Pimm Fox, "Making Support Pay," *Computerworld* 36, no. 11 (March 11, 2002): 28; "Visions of the Future," *Human Resources* (January 2008): 22.

19. Carol Carter, *Keys to Business Communication* (Upper Saddle River, NJ: Pearson, 2012): 414.

20. China Engineers Next Great Leap with Wave of 'Knowledge Workers,'" *Milwaukee Journal Sentinel* (via Knight-Ridder/Tribune News Service), December 31, 2003; "Edward Yourdon's New Book Helps 'Knowledge Workers' Put Emotion Aside to Look at the Facts of the New Economic Reality," *PR Newswire* (October 4, 2004); Marshall

Goldsmith, "Supervisors of the Smart," *BRW* 30, no. 20 (May 22, 2008): 57.

21. Ben Worthen, "Measuring the ROI of Training," *CIO* 14, no. 9 (February 15, 2001): 128–136; Hashi Syedain, "Out of this World," *People Management* 14, no. 8 (April 17, 2008): 20–24.

22. Scott A. Snell, Donna Stueber, and David P. Lepak, "Virtual HR Departments: Getting Out of the Middle," in R. L. Heneman and D. B. Greenberger (eds.), *Human Resource Management in Virtual Organizations* (Columbus, OH: Information Age Publishing, 2002); Samuel Greengard, "How to Fulfill Technology's Promise," *Workforce* (February 1999): *HR Software Insights* supplement, 10–18.

23. Drew Robb, "Building a Better Workforce: Performance Management Software Can Help You Identify and Develop High-Performing Workers," *HR Magazine* 49, no. 10 (October 2004): 86–92.

24. Bruce Shutan, "HRMS Flexibility Unlocks Secret to Success," *Employee Benefits* (August 1, 2004); "New Study Finds HRIS Key to Reducing Costs," *Payroll Managers Report* 7, no. 5 (May 2007): 13.

25. Douglas A. Ready and Jay A Conger, "Make Your Company a Talent Factory," *Harvard Business Review* (June 2007): 1.

26. "Up to Speed: L.L. Bean Moves Employees as Workloads Shift," *Chief Executive* (July–August 1996): 15; Darrell Rigby, "Look Before You Lay Off," *Harvard Business Review* 80, no. 4 (April 2002): 20–21.

27. "WorldatWork Finds One-Third of Companies Downsized after 9/11," *Report on Salary Surveys* (December 2002): 2; Jeanne Whalen, "Glaxo Is Eliminating R&D Jobs as Part of Cost-Cutting Plan," *The Wall Street Journal* 251, no. 137 (June 12, 2008).

28. Stephanie Armour, "Some Companies Choose No-Layoff Policy," *USA Today,* December 17, 2001, B-1; Gene Koretz, "Hire Math: Fire 3, Add 5," *BusinessWeek Online* (March 13, 2000); Michelle Conlin, "Where Layoffs Are a Last Resort," *BusinessWeek Online* (October 8, 2001); Lynn Miller, "Downsizing Trend Brings New Change to HR Directors," *HR Magazine* 45, no. 1 (January 2001); Norman E. Amundson, William A. Borgen, Sharalyn Jordan, and Anne C. Erlebach, "Survivors of Downsizing: Helpful and Hindering Experiences," *Career Development Quarterly* 52, no. 3 (March 2004): 256–272.

29. Tavia Grant "Not a Cure-all, But Creativity Is Saving Some Jobs," *The Globe and Mail,* January 24, 2009, B15.

30. Ruth Morss, "Creative Approaches to Layoffs," http://www.salary.com, retrieved December 29, 2010.

31. Ibid.

32. John Sullivan, "Employee Furloughs Can Be a Bad Alternative to Layoffs," http://www.ere.net, February 9, 2009.

33. Gubman, "HR Strategy and Planning," 13–21.

34. Gubman, "HR Strategy and Planning," 13–21; Thomas W. Gainey, Brian S. Klaas, and Darla Moore, "Outsourcing the Training Function: Results from the Field," *Human Resource Planning* 25, no. 1 (2002): 16–23, 873, 881; Denise Pelham, "Is It Time to Outsource HR?" *Training* 39, no. 4 (April 2002): 50–52; Tom Anderson, "HR Outsourcing Expected to Surge This Year," *Employee Benefit News* (February 1, 2005); Jessica Marquez, "More Piecemeal Approach to HRO Emerging," *Workforce Management*, 87, no. 8 (May 5, 2008): 10.

35. Karyn Siobhan Robinson, "HR Needs Large Role in Offshoring," *HR Magazine* 590, no. 45 (May 2004): 30–32; Nick Heath, "Global Outsourcing to Grow in 2008," *BusinessWeek* (January 10, 2008).

36. Pam Babcock, "America's Newest Export: White-Collar Jobs," *HR Magazine* 49, no. 4 (April 2004): 50–54.

37. Eric Lam, "What If Canada Were as Productive as the US? *The Financial Post*, November 17, 2011, 2.

38. Patrick Barta and Andrew Caffrey, "Productivity Leap Shows Potential of U.S. Economy—Rise at 8.6 Percent Pace, Positive for Profits, Doesn't Bode Very Well for Employment," *The Wall Street Journal*, May 8, 2002, A1; Jon E. Hilsenrath, "The Economy: Big U.S. Service Sectors Boosted Late 1990s Surge in Productivity," *The Wall Street Journal*, April 22, 2002, A2; Karen Lowry Miller, "Economy: Out of Steam—A Dip in U.S. Productivity Provokes Anxious Questions," *Newsweek International* (February 21, 2005): 34; Milan Yager, "Outsource to Gain Human Resources Expertise," *Hotel & Motel Management* 223, no. 7 (April 21, 2008): 14.

39. "Poll Identifies Top Challenges for HR during Next 10 Years," *HR Magazine* 55, no. 11 (November 2010): 80.

40. Irwin Speizer, "Diversity on the Menu: Rachelle Hood, Denny's Chief Diversity Officer, Has Boosted the Company's Image. But That Hasn't Sold More Breakfasts," *Workforce Management* 83, no. 12 (November 1, 2004): 41; Patrick Purcell, "Older Workers: Employment and Retirement Trends," *Journal of Pension Planning & Compliance* 34, no. 1 (Spring 2008): 32–48.

41. Statistics Canada, "Canada's Changing Labour Force, 2006 Census: Overview of Canada's Changing Labour Force," June 29, 2009, http://www12.statcan.ca /census-recensement/2006/as-sa/97-559/p2-eng.cfm, retrieved August 5, 2009.

42. Ibid.

43. "Work Force Reflects How Much Gray Matters," *The Kansas City Star* (via Knight Ridder/Tribune Business News), March 6, 2005; Kevin G. Hall, "Age-Old Dilemma," *Fort Worth Star-Telegram* (via Knight Ridder/Tribune News Service), March 7, 2005, C3–C4; Milan Yager, "A Workforce That Doesn't Retire," *Accounting Today* 22, no. 6 (March 31, 2008): 26–27; Mark L. Alch, "Get Ready for a New Type of Worker in the Workplace: The Net Generation," *Supervision* 69, no. 6 (June 2008): 18–21.

44. Kathleen Iverson, "Managing for Effective Workforce Diversity," *Cornell Hotel and Restaurant Administration Quarterly* 41, no. 2 (April 2000): 31–38; Gail Johnson, "Time to Broaden Diversity Training," *Training* 41, no. 9 (September 2004): 16.

45. Wallace Imen, "The Value of a Degree: A Million Bucks," *The Globe and Mail*, May 24, 2005, C1.

46. Uyen Yu, "Northern Mine Develops Essential Skills in Its Workforce," *Canadian HR Reporter*, July 18, 2005: 8; David Hayes, "Canadian Organizations Move to Develop Workplace Literacy and Numerical Skills," *Canadian HR Reporter*, July 18, 2005: 7; Conrad Murphy, "Assessing Essential Skills to Recruit and Train," *Canadian HR Reporter*, July 18, 2005: 11.

47. "Avoiding Identity Theft," *Aftermarket Business* 114, no. 12 (December 2004): 10.

48. "Small Business Statistics," http://www.ic.gc.ca/eic /site/sbrp-rppe.nsf/eng/rd02610.html, retrieved January 22, 2012.

49. Personal correspondence with Leah F. Vosko, Canada Research Chair in Feminist Political Economy, York University, who studies precarious (i.e., nonstandard) employment.

50. Hewitt Canada, "Employers Missing Opportunity to Boost Employee Attraction and Retention" (August 14, 2008), http://www.hewittassociates.com/Intl /NA /en-CA/AboutHewitt/Newsroom/PressReleaseDetail. aspx?cid=5486, retrieved July 26, 2009.

51. Todd Raphael, "The Drive to Downshifting," *Workforce* 80, no. 10 (October 2001): 23; Jim Olsztynski, "Flexible Work Schedules May Make More Sense: One in Six Americans Qualifies as a Caregiver

Who May Benefit from Flextime," *National Driller* 26, no. 2 (February 2005): 16–19; Karen Springen, "Cutting Back Your Hours," *Newsweek* 151, no. 19 (May 12, 2008): 60.

52. Leah Carlson, "Flextime Elevated to National Issue," *Employee Benefit News* (September 15, 2004).

53. U.S. Bureau of Labor Statistics, "Human Resources, Training, and Labor Relations Managers and Specialists, *Occupational Outlook Handbook,* 2010–11, http://www.bls.gov/, retrieved January 20, 2011.

# Strategy and Human Resources Planning

MANAGING HUMAN RESOURCES

## After studying this chapter, you should be able to

| | |
|---|---|
| OUTCOME 1 | Identify the advantages of integrating human resources planning and strategic planning. |
| OUTCOME 2 | Understand how an organization's competitive environment influences its strategic planning. |
| OUTCOME 3 | Understand why it is important for an organization to do an internal resource analysis. |
| OUTCOME 4 | Describe the basic tools used for human resources forecasting. |
| OUTCOME 5 | Explain the linkages between competitive strategies and human resources. |
| OUTCOME 6 | Understand what is required for a firm to successfully implement a strategy. |
| OUTCOME 7 | Recognize the methods for assessing and measuring the effectiveness of a firm's strategy |

One of the clichés about the annual reports of companies is that they often claim that "people are our most important asset." Although we might believe this to be true, the fact is that, historically, managers often have not acted as though they believed it. In the past, executives often tried to remove human capital from the strategy equation by substituting capital for labour where possible or by creating hierarchical structures that separated those who think from those who actually do the work. But much is changing today.

Surveys show that 92 percent of chief financial officers now believe human capital affects an organization's customer service, 82 percent believe it affects profitability, and 72 percent believe it affects innovation.[1] And in a survey by the consulting firm Deloitte, nearly 80 percent of corporate executives said the importance of HRM in their firms has grown substantially over the years, and two-thirds said that HR expenditures are now viewed as a strategic investment rather than simply a cost to be minimized. Indeed, research shows that strategically designed and implemented HR systems increase the value of firms, something executives are keenly interested in accomplishing. They are also demanding that their HR groups push past short-term projections and provide detailed forecasts for needs and the associated costs over a two- to three-year horizon. Even small companies are realizing that their employees are the key to ensuring their ability to compete and survive. As General Electric's legendary ex-CEO Jack Welch puts it: "We live in a global economy. To have a fighting chance, every company needs to get every employee, with every idea in their heads and every morsel of energy in their bodies, into the game."[2]

# STRATEGIC PLANNING AND HUMAN RESOURCES

| OUTCOME 1 |

**strategic planning**
Procedures for making decisions about the organization's long-term goals and strategies

**human resources planning (HRP)**
The process of anticipating and providing for the movement of people into, within, and out of an organization

**strategic human resources management (SHRM)**
The pattern of human resources deployments and activities that enable an organization to achieve its strategic goals

As we explained in Chapter 1, "competing through people" is the theme for this book. But the idea remains only a premise for action until we put it into practice. To deliver on this promise, we need to understand some of the systems and processes in organizations that link HRM and strategic management. A few definitions may be helpful upfront.

**Strategic planning** involves a set of procedures for making decisions about the organization's long-term goals and strategies. In this chapter, we discuss strategic plans as having a strong external orientation that covers major portions of the organization. The plans especially focus on how the organization will position itself relative to its competitors to ensure its long-term survival, create value, and grow. **Human resources planning (HRP)**, by comparison, is the process of anticipating and providing for the movement of people into, within, and out of an organization. Overall, its purpose is to help managers deploy their human resources as effectively as possible, where and when they are needed, to accomplish the organization's goals. **Strategic human resources management (SHRM)** combines strategic planning and HR planning. It can be thought of as the pattern of human resources deployments and activities that enable an organization to achieve its strategic goals.

HR planning is an essential activity of organizations. Consider CNA Financial Corp., an insurance company, for example. CNA Financial discovered via HR planning that it would run short of underwriters—a key skill pool in the company—in just two years if its turnover rate continued at the current pace. The global strategies firms are increasingly pursuing, such as mergers, joint ventures, offshoring, the relocation of plants, product innovation plans, and downsizing, are also making HRP more critical and more complex for managers. The good news, according to the president and CEO of the HRPS, is that increased global competitiveness, which in many industries has led to the commoditization of products based on price, is making talent the "great differentiator" among firms. After all, it is relatively easy for a competitor to copy your product and make it more cheaply. But duplicating the talents of your employees will prove much more difficult.[3] The dramatic shifts in the composition of the labour force that are occurring also require that HR managers become more involved in planning because these changes affect the full range of a company's HR practices (such as employee recruitment, selection, training, compensation, and motivation).

## STRATEGIC PLANNING AND HR PLANNING: LINKING THE PROCESSES

As organizations plan for their future, HR managers must be concerned with meshing HRP and strategic planning for the organization as a whole. HRP relates to strategic planning in several ways, but at a fundamental level, we can focus on two issues: strategy formulation and strategy implementation. HRP provides a set of inputs into the strategic *formulation* process in terms of what is possible, that is, whether a firm has the types and numbers of people available to pursue a given strategy. For example, when Indigo executives contemplated the move into Web-based commerce to compete with Amazon.com, one of the issues they had to address was whether they had the talent needed to succeed in that arena.

In addition to strategy formulation, HRP is important in terms of strategy *implementation*. In other words, once the firm has devised its strategy, the company's executives must make resource allocation decisions to implement that strategy, including decisions related to the firm's structure, processes, and human capital.[4] Companies such as GE and IBM have taken strides to combine these two aspects of strategic management.[5] All the available evidence suggests that the integration of HRP and strategic planning tends to be most effective when there is a reciprocal relationship between the two processes. When this occurs, a firm's top management team recognizes that strategic planning decisions

**FIGURE 2.1**

PART 1

LINKING STRATEGIC PLANNING AND HUMAN RESOURCES

| | **BUSINESS/CORPORATE** | **HUMAN RESOURCES** |
|---|---|---|
| **Mission, Vision, and Values** | • Identify purpose and scope<br>• Clarify long-term direction<br>• Establish enduring beliefs and principles | • Capture underlying philosophy<br>• Establish foundation of culture<br>• Guide ethical codes of conduct |
| **External Analysis** (SWOT Analysis) | • Opportunities and threats (OT)<br>• Environmental scanning (legal, etc.)<br>• Industry/competitor analysis | • Demographic trends<br>• External supply of labour<br>• Competitor benchmarking |
| **Internal Analysis** (SWOT Analysis) | • Strengths and weaknesses (SW)<br>• Core competencies<br>• Resources: People, process, systems | • Culture, competencies, composition<br>• Forecast demand for employees<br>• Forecast supply of employees |
| **Strategy Formulation** | • Corporate strategy<br>• Business strategy<br>• Functional strategy: alignment | • Productivity and efficiency<br>• Quality, service, speed, innovation<br>• External fit/alignment and internal fit |
| **Strategy Implementation** | • Design structure, systems, etc.<br>• Allocate resources<br>• Leadership, communication, and change | • Reconcile supply and demand<br>• Downsizing, layoffs, etc.<br>• HR practice: staffing, training, rewards, etc. |
| **Evaluation** | • Assessment and benchmarking<br>• Ensuring alignment<br>• Agility and flexibility | • Human capital metrics<br>• Balanced scorecard |

affect—and are affected by—HR concerns. Figure 2.1 shows how companies align their HRP and strategic planning in this way. As James Walker, a noted HRP expert, puts it, "Today, virtually *all* business issues have people implications; *all* human resource issues have business implications."[6] HR managers, along with the other top executives of their firms, are therefore important facilitators and strategic partners of the planning process.[7] That is why, in this chapter, we lay out a step-by-step process to show how a firm's HRP and strategy efforts can be integrated.

**mission**
The basic purpose of the organization as well as its scope of operations

**strategic vision**
A statement about where the company is going and what it can become in the future; clarifies the long-term direction of the company and its strategic intent

## STEP 1: MISSION, VISION, AND VALUES

The first step in strategic planning is establishing a mission, vision, and values for the organization. The **mission** is the basic purpose of the organization, as well as its scope of operations. It is a statement of the organization's reason for existing. The mission often is written in terms of general clients the organization services. Depending on the scope of the organization, the mission may be broad or narrow. For example, the mission of Google is "to organize the world's information and make it universally accessible and useful."[8] The **strategic vision** of the organization moves beyond the mission statement to provide a perspective

# HIGHLIGHTS IN HRM 2.1

## Air Canada: Mission, Vision, and Values

**Our Mission**
Connecting Canada and the World.

**Our Vision**
Building loyalty through passion and innovation.

**Our Values**
Underpinning our Mission and Vision are core Values that inform all we do as individuals and collectively at Air Canada. These values serve as touchstones to guide out actions.

**Safety First and Last**
100%. All the time.

**Make every Customer feel Valued**
With our words. With our actions. With our products and services.

**Working Together**
With Colleagues, Customers and Community.

**Act with Integrity**
We are accountable. We foster an environment of trust. We communicate openly and in a timely manner.

**All Employees are Valued**
We respect. We listen. We act.

**Drive for Excellence**
Personally. Corporately. Ever reaching for the next level of innovation, quality and service.

Source: Reproduced with the permission of Air Canada

---

**core values**
The strong and enduring beliefs and principles that the company uses as a foundation for its decisions

on where the company is headed and what the organization can become in the future. The mission and vision of Tim Hortons is as follows:

> Our guiding mission is to deliver superior quality products and services for our customers and communities through leadership, innovation and partnerships. Our vision is to be the quality leader in everything we do.

Although the terms *mission* and *vision* are often used interchangeably, the vision statement ideally clarifies the long-term direction of the company and its strategic intent.

Organizational **core values** are the strong, enduring beliefs and principles that the company uses as a foundation for its decisions. These are the underlying parameters for how the company will act toward customers, employees, and the public in general. In many cases, the values capture the underlying philosophy of the company culture and give direction to its employees. The values also place limits on what behaviour is seen as ethical and acceptable. Highlights in HRM 2.1 shows the mission, vision, and values of Air Canada.

## STEP 2: ENVIRONMENTAL ANALYSIS

OUTCOME 2

The mission, vision, and values drive the second component of the strategic management process: analysis of external opportunities and threats. Changes in the external environment have a direct impact on the way organizations are run and people are managed. Some of these changes represent opportunities, and some of them represent threats to the organization. Because of this, successful strategic management depends on an accurate and thorough evaluation of the environment. **Environmental scanning** is the systematic monitoring of the major external forces influencing the organization.[9] Managers attend to a variety of external issues; however, the following six are monitored most frequently:

environmental scanning
Systematic monitoring of the major external forces influencing the organization

1. Economic factors and development information, including general, regional, and global conditions
2. Industry and competitive trends, including new processes, services, and innovations
3. Technological changes, including information technology, innovations, and automation
4. Government and legislative issues, including laws and administrative rulings
5. Social concerns, including childcare, eldercare, the environment, and educational priorities
6. Demographic and labour market trends, including the age, composition, and literacy of the labour market and immigration

By continuously scanning the environment for changes that will likely affect an organization, managers can anticipate their impact and make adjustments early.

## COMPETITIVE ENVIRONMENT

Many factors in the general environment—factors a firm cannot directly control—can affect its strategic decisions. This is why analyzing the firm's competitive environment is central to strategic planning. The competitive environment includes the specific organizations with which the firm interacts. As Figure 2.2 shows, the competitive environment includes the firm's customers, rival firms, new entrants, substitutes, and suppliers. A general rule of thumb about this analysis is that the more power each of these forces has, the less profitable (and therefore attractive) the industry will be. Let us look at each of the five forces.

### Customers

One of the most important assessments a firm can make is identifying the needs of its customers. At a fundamental level, a firm's strategy should focus on creating customer value—and different customers often want different things. For example,

**FIGURE 2.2**

FIVE FORCES FRAMEWORK

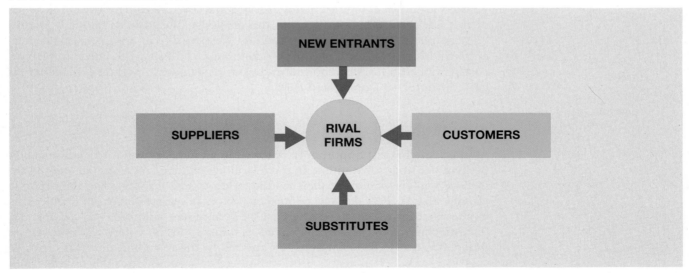

in the hotel industry, business travellers may want convenient locations with meeting facilities. Vacationers may want resort locations with swimming pools, golf courses, and luxury spas. Other travellers may just want an inexpensive room next to the highway. The point is that, increasingly, "one size does not fit all," and organizations need to know how they will provide value to customers. That is the foundation for strategy, and it influences the kind of skills and behaviour that will be needed from employees. For example, actions and attitudes that lead to excellent customer service can include the following:

- Speed of delivering normal orders
- Willingness to meet extraordinary needs
- Merchandise delivered in good condition
- Readiness to take back defective goods and resupply new goods quickly
- Availability of installation and repair services and parts

## Rival Firms

In addition to customer analysis, perhaps the most obvious element of industry analysis is examining the nature of competition. The first question to consider is: Who is the competition? Often the answer is clear to everyone, but sometimes it is not. For example, for many years, Toys "R" Us viewed its main competitors to be other toy stores such as FAO Schwarz or KB Toys. However, other retailers, such as Zellers and Walmart, soon moved into this space very successfully. This had a direct effect on HRP for Toys "R" Us. Although in the past, Toys "R" Us had been successful with a volume-based approach (that is, "stack it high, and let it fly"), bigger retailers soon gained an advantage—who can beat Walmart's volume and cost advantage? As a consequence, Toys "R" Us had to modify its strategy to compete more on customer service and the expertise of its employees. But did Toys "R" Us have the number and kind of employees required to compete in this way? Were its staffing, training, performance management, and compensation practices aligned with this strategy?

## New Entrants

As we suggested previously, new companies can sometimes enter an industry and compete well against established firms, and sometimes they cannot. To protect their position, companies often try to establish entry barriers to keep new firms out of the industry. However, when new firms do enter an industry, it is often because they have a different—and perhaps better—way to provide value to customers. For example, when WestJet entered the airline business, it distinguished itself by providing friendly service and low prices. The HR implications of this are clear. When we look at the challenges faced by traditional airlines because of the threat of carriers such as WestJet, we can clearly see that new entrants can change the "rules of the game" in an industry. The impact on labour costs, productivity, skills required, and work design are important considerations in both strategic planning and HRP.

## Substitutes

At times, the biggest opportunity or threat in an industry is not from direct competition but from substitution. In the telephone industry, for example, people are increasingly disconnecting their landline phones and instead using their mobile phones and VoIP (Voice Over Internet Protocol) services, such as Skype. This implies that firms may need to adjust their employee skill bases to support different technologies, or they may need to think about how they will compete in different ways. As an example, think about how the travel business has changed over the years. Travel agents used to be the key resource for flights, hotels, and rental cars. The focus was almost exclusively on transactions. However, with the advent of online reservation systems, travel agents have had to adapt their approach. Today, they are as likely to compete based on the service they provide and the expertise they have about particular locations.

## Suppliers

Organizations rarely create everything on their own but instead have suppliers that provide them with key inputs. These inputs can include raw materials for production, money (from banks and stockholders), information, and people. This last factor—people, or labour, as it is historically called—has direct implications for strategic planning and HRP. Because of its central role in both strategic planning and HRP, we explore it next in much more detail.

## EXTERNAL SUPPLY OF LABOUR

Many factors influence the labour supply, including demographic changes in the population, national and regional economics, education level of the workforce, demand for specific employee skills, population mobility, and governmental policies.

Consider these labour force statistics:

- About 18 million people are in the workforce—a participation rate of 67 percent. This rate will decline in the coming decades because of aging baby boomers and declining fertility rates.

- The largest gains in employment are in the service sector. The beneficiaries of this gain are women, who tend to be overrepresented in this sector; as a result, their participation rate in the labour force is increasing more rapidly than that of men.

- In 2007, about one in five workers was employed part-time, a rate that has doubled over the last three decades. A quarter of these part-time workers would prefer full-time work.

- The number of hours that Canadians work per week has been trending downward and now hovers around 33 per week.

- The vast majority (81 percent) of Canadians held permanent jobs (i.e., jobs that did not have a specified end date). The holders of these jobs were paid on average $21 an hour, compared to $16 an hour for those in temporary jobs. The number of Canadians holding two or more jobs has tripled over the last three decades and accounts for 5 percent of all workers.

- One in three Canadians will be 55 or older by 2027. The median age of retirement is 61.

- The number of immigrants to Canada averages 225,000 annually, and about 70 percent of these locate in Toronto, Vancouver, and Montreal (cities that are home to only 34 percent of Canada's population).[10]

These labour force trends illustrate the importance of monitoring demographic changes as a part of environmental scanning. Fortunately, labour market analysis is aided by various published documents. Statistics Canada and Human Resources and Skills Development Canada publish many studies on the labour force, as do various provincial governments. In addition, local chambers of commerce and city planning departments can assist both large organizations and new business ventures by providing them with a labour market analysis of their areas. Offshore consulting firms such as IBM and Accenture can be a good source for information about labour trends in other countries.

These sources of information are invaluable; in a rapidly changing environment, it is extremely risky to be caught off-guard. Such changes are important for many reasons, some related to operational issues and some to strategic issues. HRP has to focus on both. At an operational level, the change in labour supply

# REALITY CHECK

## Spotting Trends in the Global Economy

Every HR professional recognizes that anticipating trends is an important part of the job. Furthermore, senior HR professionals want to influence strategy, not just respond to strategies determined by the "real players" at the boardroom table.

David Foot, a famous Canadian economist and demographer at the University of Toronto, says that HR professionals are often ill-equipped to contribute to their organization's strategy. He contends that HR people are experienced in dealing with micro issues but often lack the big-picture or macro perspective that is necessary to deal with corporate or strategic issues.

Having worked with executives and boards of directors, he is very familiar with the issues facing them and with the inability of HR managers to advance the HR view of the implications of strategic decisions. He offers this example: A company is thinking about going global—say, by expanding into Mexico. The HR person has very little knowledge about the labour market of that country (where there are many young people but relatively few seniors). Furthermore, he or she is likely to be preoccupied with important micro issues, such as how to hire employees and what the local health and safety rules are, when he or she ought to be considering, for example, Mexico's

regional unemployment and education rates by region to determine plant location.

Other executives can think strategically when faced with changes in the environment. Foot asks: "How many HR professionals could answer the question, 'How does the exchange rate impact HRP?'" Those with a macro perspective would immediately determine (1) How much business is internal/external? (2) Have the financial people bought insurance against exchange rate fluctuations? (3) If the Canadian dollar depreciates, and there will be more demand for our products, what are the opportunities to access labour in external markets such as Poland or Mexico? How can we recruit these people faster than other companies? This mindset is crucial to being at the boardroom table.

"Let me give you another example of reactionary micro thinking," says Foot. "Low unemployment rates traditionally result in demands from business for higher immigration levels to ease labour shortages. But this traditional HR response will become increasingly inappropriate in the new millennium because more immigrants will only compete with the children of boomers who will be entering the labour force. A proactionary macro-thinking HR person will, therefore, be able to advise the CEO that this is likely to be a short-term, not a long-term, labour shortage and to think internally rather than externally for new workers. This information could be crucial in influencing the company's strategic planning for the next five years."

Source: Interview with David Foot.

directly influences hiring plans that must take into account the demographic composition of the population in the area in which the organization is located or plans to locate. Similarly, with a "maturing" workforce, HRP must consider the implications for recruitment and replacement policies.

From a strategic standpoint, changes in the labour supply can limit the strategies available to firms. High-growth companies in particular may find it difficult to find the talent they need to expand their businesses. Although unemployment rates vary by sector, the shortage of talent in high-skill jobs continues to create challenges for firms.

In Reality Check, David Foot, a demographer at the University of Toronto, explains why HR professionals must become aware of the need to scan.

## STEP 3: INTERNAL ANALYSIS

OUTCOME 3

As organizations conduct external analyses of environmental opportunities and threats, they also analyze their internal strengths and weaknesses. Internal analysis provides strategic decision makers with an inventory of organizational skills and resources as well as performance levels.

To be sure, many resources combine to give organizations a competitive advantage. But in contrast to the past, the advantages due to physical assets are being supplanted by intangible assets, including people. As James Brian Quinn noted,

"With rare exceptions, the economic and producing power of firms lies more in its intellectual and service capabilities than in its hard assets—land, plant, and equipment."[11]

**core capabilities**
Integrated knowledge sets within an organization that distinguish it from its competitors and deliver value to customers

## THE THREE Cs: CAPABILITIES, COMPOSITION, AND CULTURE

In the context of HRP, internal analysis focuses especially on "the three Cs": capabilities, composition, and culture.

### Capabilities: People as a Strategic Resource

A growing number of experts now argue that the key to a firm's success is based on establishing a set of **core capabilities**—bundles of people, processes, and systems that distinguish an organization from its competitors and deliver value to customers. McDonald's, for example, has developed core capabilities in management efficiency and training. FedEx has core capabilities in package routing, delivery, and employee relations. Royal Dutch Shell has core capabilities in oil exploration and production.[12] Core capabilities tend to be limited in number, but they provide a long-term basis for technology innovation, product development, and service delivery.

In many cases, people are a key resource that underlies a firm's core capabilities. Particularly in knowledge-based industries such as the software and information services industries, success depends on "people-embodied know-how." This includes the knowledge, skills, and abilities of employees. As a result, a number of companies that previously relied on standard plans for recruiting and managing their employees are designing more tailored plans for them. These personalized plans are designed to address the individual needs of employees so they will be in a better position to help implement their firms' strategies. Microsoft goes so far as to ask certain types of employees to design their own career paths. For example, the company offers software engineers both a management-focused and a technical specialist career track and allows them to move back and forth between the two.

Organizations can achieve a sustained competitive advantage through people if they are able to meet the following criteria[13]:

1. *The resources must be valuable.* People are a source of competitive advantage when they improve the efficiency or effectiveness of the company. Value is increased when employees find ways to decrease costs, provide something unique to customers, or some combination of the two. To improve the bottom line, RBC and Enbridge are among the companies that utilize employee empowerment programs, total quality and continuous improvement efforts, and flexible work arrangements to motivate and spark the creativity of their workers.
2. *The resources must be rare.* People are a source of competitive advantage when their knowledge, skills, and abilities are not equally available to competitors. Companies such as Microsoft and Four Seasons Hotels therefore invest a great deal to hire and train the best and the brightest employees to gain an advantage over their competitors.
3. *The resources must be difficult to imitate.* People are a source of competitive advantage when the capabilities and contributions of a firm's employees cannot be copied by others. Disney, Southwest Airlines, and Starbucks are each known for creating unique cultures that get the most from employees (through teamwork) and are difficult to imitate.
4. *The resources must be organized.* People are a source of competitive advantage when their talents can be combined and deployed to work on new assignments at a moment's notice. Companies such as IBM and GE have invested in information technology to help allocate and track employee assignments to temporary projects. Teamwork and cooperation are two other pervasive methods for ensuring an organized workforce.

These four criteria highlight the importance of people and show the closeness of HRM to strategic management.

## Composition: The Human Capital Architecture

A related element of internal analysis for organizations that compete on capabilities is determining the composition of the workforce. That is, managers need to determine whether people are available, internally or externally, to execute an organization's strategy. Managers have to make tough decisions about whom to employ internally, whom to contract externally, and how to manage different types of employees with different skills who contribute in different ways to the organization. The Province of British Columbia recognizes the value of human capital as described in Highlights in HRM 2.2.

Figure 2.3 shows that different skill groups in any given organization can be classified according to the degree to which they create strategic value and are unique to the organization. This figure shows the departments for an Australian biotechnology firm and the quadrants those groups fall into as well as their gradual migration given a strategic organizational shift to one that focuses on customer service. As a general rule, managers often consider contracting externally (or outsourcing) skill areas that are not central to the firm's core competence.

# HIGHLIGHTS IN HRM 2.2

## The Measurement of Human Capital

The Office of the Auditor General of British Columbia recognized that human capital is critically important to the delivery of high-quality service to the province's citizens. So it set out to measure whether training and development (T&D) were being used to increase human capital in the B.C. public service. As a first step, it defined human capital as the collective brainpower in an organization. This brainpower consists of

- *facts* acquired through informal and formal education
- *skills* gained through training and practice
- *experience* gained through reflection on past successes and mistakes
- *value judgments* based on individual perceptions
- *social networks* developed through relationships with coworkers, colleagues, and customers

The audit took several measures, including a large-scale survey of a random sample of full-time employees and an in-depth audit of three ministries. Some of the data generated by this audit are the following:

- Thirty-six percent of government employees had received no formal training.

- The average B.C. government employee received 17 hours of training (compared to a Canadian benchmark of 29 hours).
- Less than 1 percent of payroll was spent on training (compared to the 4 percent that the best employers spend).
- Forty percent of employees had had their jobs redefined.
- Forty-three percent of senior managers would reach age 55 in the next five years and be eligible to retire.
- Thirty-three percent of employees with less than one year of employment did not feel they had been trained properly to carry out their duties.

The audit revealed that most T&D decisions were based on requests made from individual employees and that most programs they attended consisted of one- and two-day courses outside the organization. It had never been ascertained whether these courses increased employees' skills or helped the organization achieve its goals. There was no way of knowing how effective this training was, nor was there any accounting for T&D expenditures.

Government employees generally believed that training was of great value to them and their organizations. Paradoxically, they also believed that they were not being supported in their work, and only half thought they had the tools and resources they needed to do their jobs.

Source: Adapted from J. McCannel and L. McAdams, "The Learning Culture in Public Service," *Public Sector Management* 11, no. 1 (2000); http://www.ipac-iapc.ca. Used by permission.

## FIGURE 2.3

## MAPPING HUMAN CAPITAL

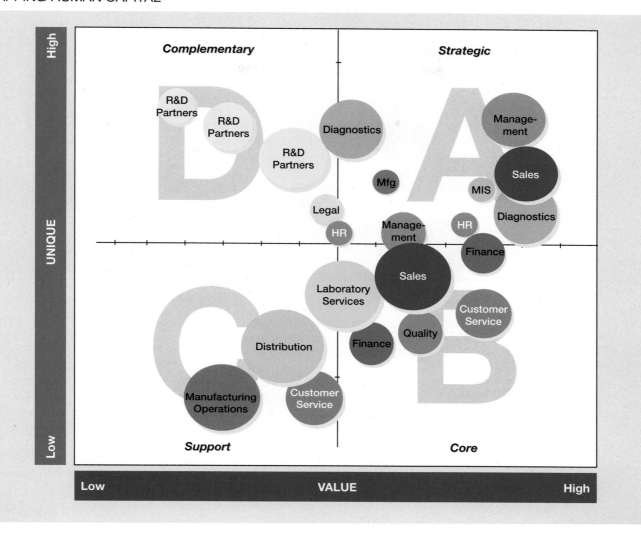

HRP plays an important role in helping managers weigh the costs and benefits of using one approach to employment versus another.

Evidence from research suggests that employment relationships and HR practices for different employees vary according to which segment they occupy in this matrix. Here are some general trends:

*Strategic knowledge workers.* This group of employees tends to have unique skills that are directly linked to the company's strategy and are difficult to replace (such as R&D scientists in pharmaceuticals company or computer scientists in a software development company). These employees typically are engaged in knowledge work that involves considerable autonomy and discretion. Companies tend to make long-term commitments to these employees, investing in their continuous training and development and perhaps giving them an equity stake in the organization.

*Core employees.* This group of employees has skills that are quite valuable to a company but are not particularly unique or difficult to replace (such as salespeople in a department store or truck drivers for a courier service). These employees tend to be employed in traditional types of jobs. Because their skills are transferable, it is quite possible that they could leave to go to another firm. As a consequence, managers frequently make less investment in training and development and tend to focus more on paying for short-term performance achievements.

Package handlers are core employees of the human capital architecture at FedEx.

AP/Wide World Photos

*Supporting workers.* This group of employees typically has skills that are of less strategic value to the firm and are generally available in the labour market (such as clerical workers, maintenance workers, and staff workers in accounting and HR). Individuals in these jobs are increasingly hired from external agencies on a contract basis to support the strategic knowledge workers and core employees. The scope of their duties tends to be limited, and their employment relationships tend to be transaction based, focused on rules and procedures, with less investment in development. Ethics in HRM describes some issues associated with contract employees. The Business Case outlines the advantages to the employer of hiring contract labour.

*Partners and complementary skills.* This group of individuals has skills that are unique but frequently are not directly related to a company's core strategy

## ETHICS IN HRM

### The Employment Contract

The number of organizations substituting part-time workers for full-time employees is growing. Employees— even those with excellent track records and many years of service—are considered expendable as organizations revise their strategies to become more competitive and more profitable. When yet another reorganization occurs, management reveals the new plan with excitement. However, although management thinks it is telling employees, "We will provide you with meaningful, challenging, and skill-building work that will be good for your résumé—you are responsible for your own employment," employees are hearing, "We will work you to the bone, pay you enough to prevent you from quitting, and fire you when we no longer need you. Oh, and by the way, you are our most valuable resource."

Some employment contracts are extremely one-sided, with employers determining when to hire and when to fire, without obligation or guilt. This kind of contract works when people need jobs more than organizations need employees. However, as some sectors continue to experience rapid growth, and as the labour market for certain skills becomes tighter, employees are making contractual demands that place them in the driver's seat. They are demanding signing bonuses, stock equity, retention bonuses, and sufficient notification with predetermined buyouts for termination. Furthermore, the courts are ruling that if an employee is retained for a series of uninterrupted contracts, then that contract worker is de facto an employee.

# THE BUSINESS CASE

## Hiring Contract Workers Pays

As you can see, the employer can save a lot of money by hiring only contract employees. The use of contract workers has the additional benefits of functional flexibility (employers can hire the workers with the exact skills needed) and numerical flexibility (workers can be added or discharged as work demand fluctuates). Contract workers (also called temporary workers or "temps") are defined as paid workers with a specified end date for their job or completion of a task or project. In 2007, about 10 percent of all Canadian workers were temporary or permanent part-time workers.

Employers want to hire people on contract for several reasons, including the following:

- The ability to terminate their contracts easily
- No obligation to pay benefits

- Reduced need for training and development investments
- Less pay is required because contract workers rarely benefit from seniority provisions
- Typically, contract workers are not entitled to paid sick leave or vacation pay
- No obligation on the part of the employer to pay into a pension plan
- Typically, contract employees do not participate in company incentive compensation programs that award merit pay or bonuses.

A growing organization must decide whether to hire full-time or part-time employees, and the chart below will assist in this decision.

### ADVANTAGES AND LIMITATIONS OF PART-TIME EMPLOYMENT

| Advantages for the Employer | Advantages for the Employee |
| --- | --- |
| Work scheduling flexibility | Control over personal time |
| Reduced compensation costs | More variety in jobs |
| Increased ability to add/reduce programs | Home office tax advantages |

| Limitations for the Employer | Limitations for the Employee |
| --- | --- |
| No organizational loyalty | No job security |
| Costs of continuous replacement | Limited benefits |
| Costs of continual training | Stresses of continuous learning |
| Strategic competencies can quit | Lack of training and career progression |

Sources: Adapted from Helmar Drost and H. Richard Hird, *An Introduction to the Canadian Labour Market*, 2nd edition, Thomson Nelson, 2006; Barbara Moses, "Loss of Loyalty Cuts Both Ways," *The Globe and Mail*, November 6, 1997, B17; R. S. Echlin, "Courts Apply Smell Test in Judging Contract Workers as Long Term Employees," *The Globe and Mail*, November 22, 1999, B1.

(such as lawyers, consultants, and research lab scientists). Although companies perhaps cannot justify their internal employment, given their indirect link to strategy, these individuals have skills that are specialized and not readily available to all firms. As a consequence, companies tend to establish longer-term alliances and partnerships with them and nurture an ongoing relationship focused on mutual learning. Considerable investment is made in the exchange of information and knowledge.[14]

**cultural audits**
Audits of the culture and quality of work life in an organization

## Culture: Values, Assumptions, Beliefs, and Expectations (VABEs)

Think about our initial discussion (in Step 1) of mission, vision, and values. Because managers increasingly understand that their employees are critical to their success, they often conduct **cultural audits** to examine the values, assumptions, beliefs, and expectations (VABEs) of their workforces as well. Cultural audits can consist of surveys and interviews to measure how employees feel on a number of critical issues.

**values-based hiring**
The process of outlining the behaviours that exemplify a firm's corporate culture and then hiring people who are a fit for them

According to author James Clawson, leaders who target employees' values, attitudes, beliefs, and expectations are more effective than those who simply focus on workers' behaviours or thought processes.[15] This makes sense. Recall from Chapter 1 the story about the entrepreneur who tripled his sales but, because he took his staff for granted, was then muscled out of the market by a competitor. If a firm lacks a clear idea of how employees view the organization, no matter how great the organization's plans are, those plans might never be successfully executed and sustained.

However, these audits can go much deeper. Sears, for example, found that positive employee attitudes on 10 essential factors—including workload and treatment by bosses—are directly linked to customer satisfaction and revenue increases.[16]

To prevent legal and ethical breaches, some firms conduct cultural audits that ask employees questions about the degree of fear associated with meeting their firms' revenue goals and incentive plans that could encourage unethical or illegal behaviour.[17] Cultural audits can also be used to determine whether there are different groups, or subcultures, within the organization that have distinctly different views about the nature of the work and how it should be done.

Knowing that a company's corporate culture is a source of competitive advantage, firms are also beginning to engage in what is called **values-based hiring**, which involves outlining the behaviours that exemplify a firm's corporate culture and then hiring people who are a fit for them.

## FORECASTING: A CRITICAL ELEMENT OF PLANNING

| OUTCOME 4 |

Although internal analysis of the three Cs (capabilities, composition, and culture) may reveal a great deal about where the organization is today, things change. In an important sense, strategic planning is about managing that change. Managers must continually forecast both the needs and the capabilities of the firm for the future to do an effective job at strategic planning. As shown in Figure 2.4, managers focus on (at least) three key elements: (1) forecasting the demand for labour, (2) forecasting the supply of labour, and (3) balancing supply and demand considerations. Careful attention to each factor helps top managers meet their HR requirements.

### FIGURE 2.4

MODEL OF HR FORECASTING

**FORECASTING DEMAND**

**Considerations**
- Product/service demand
- Economics
- Technology
- Financial resources
- Absenteeism/turnover
- Organizational growth
- Management philosophy

**Techniques**
- Trend analysis
- Managerial estimates
- Delphi technique

**BALANCING SUPPLY AND DEMAND**

(Shortage) Recruitment
- Full-time
- Part-time
- Recalls

**Techniques**
- Staffing tables
- Markov analysis
- Skills inventories
- Management inventories
- Replacement charts
- Succession planning

**External Considerations**
- Demographic changes
- Education of workforce
- Labour mobility
- Government policies
- Unemployment rate

(Surplus) Reductions
- Layoff
- Attrition
- Termination

**FORECASTING SUPPLY**

## HIGHLIGHTS IN HRM 2.3

### HR Planning for Registered Nurses

The Canadian Nurses Association released a study that showed that Canada could have a shortfall of 60,000 registered nurses by 2022. There are currently 217,000 registered nurses (RNs) in Canada, the single largest group of health care workers. The majority of these work in acute care hospitals.

Proposed solutions:

- Faster processing by the federal government would allow temporary foreign workers into Canada.

- Reduced absenteeism (which is currently 14 days a year, almost double that of the average Canadian worker) would result in the equivalent of an additional 7,000 RNs.

- Increase enrollment in nursing schools by adding about 1,000 new spaces a year. Couple this with reducing the attrition rate in the nursing school. About one in four nurses do not complete their studies or do not practise after graduating.

Sources: A. Picard, "Six Steps Urged to Reverse RN Shortfall," *The Globe and Mail*, May 12, 2009, L1; D. Harder, "Rules Eased in B.C., Alberta for Temp Foreign Workers," *Canadian HR Reporter* (November 5, 2007): 1.

Consider for a moment the high costs of not forecasting—or forecasting poorly. If job vacancies are left unfilled, the resulting loss in efficiency can be very costly, particularly when you consider the amount of time it takes to hire and train replacement employees. As pointless as it may sound, we have seen situations in which employees are laid off in one department while applicants are hired for similar jobs in another department. Poor forecasting that leads to unnecessary layoffs also makes it difficult for employees to accurately assess their own career prospects and development. When this happens, some of a firm's more competent and ambitious workers will be inclined to seek other employment where they feel they will have better career opportunities.[18]

On the plus side, accurate forecasting provides the kind of information managers need to make sound decisions. It can help them ensure that they have the right number and right kinds of people in the right places at the right times, doing things that provide value to both the organization and the employees.

Highlights in HRM 2.3 describes the labour market forecasts for nurses and provides some solutions for the anticipated shortages.

> **trend analysis**
> A quantitative approach to forecasting labour demand based on an organizational index such as sales

## Forecasting a Firm's Demand for Employees

If a key component of forecasting is predicting the number and types of people an organization needs to meet its objectives, the question remains: "How can this be done?" A variety of factors, including a firm's competitive strategy, technology, structure, and productivity, can affect the demand for labour. External factors such as business cycles—economic and seasonal trends—can also play a role. For example, retailers such as The Bay and Canadian Tire rely heavily on temporary employees between November and January. There are two approaches to HR forecasting: quantitative and qualitative, which we discuss next. An organization's demands will ultimately determine which technique is used. Regardless of the method, however, forecasting should not be neglected, even in relatively small organizations.

*Quantitative approaches.* Quantitative approaches to forecasting involve the use of statistical or mathematical techniques. One example is **trend analysis**, whereby a firm's employment requirements are forecasted on the basis of some organizational index. Trend analysis is one of the most commonly used approaches for projecting HR demand and is typically done in several stages.

External factors such as business cycles—economic and seasonal trends—can play a role in forecasting the demand for and supply of employees.

Lana Slezic/GetStock.com

First, select an appropriate business factor. This should be the best available predictor of HR needs. Frequently, sales or value added (the selling price of the firm's products minus the costs of the materials and supplies used to make them) is used as a predictor in trend analysis. Second, plot a historical trend of the business factor in relation to the number of employees. The ratio of employees to the business factor will provide a labour productivity ratio (e.g., sales per employee). Third, compute the productivity ratio for at least the past five years. Fourth, calculate HR demand by multiplying the business factor by the productivity ratio. Finally, project the firm's HR demand out to the target year. This procedure is illustrated in Figure 2.5 for a hypothetical building contractor.

Other, more sophisticated statistical planning methods include modelling or multiple predictive techniques. Whereas trend analysis relies on a single factor

## FIGURE 2.5

### EXAMPLE OF TREND ANALYSIS OF HR DEMAND

| Year | Business Factor (Sales in Thousands) | Labour Productivity (Sales/Employee) | HR Demand (Number of Employees) |
|------|------|------|------|
| 2006 | $2,351 | 14.33 | 164 |
| 2007 | $2,613 | 11.12 | 235 |
| 2008 | $2,935 | 8.34 | 352 |
| 2009 | $3,306 | 10.02 | 330 |
| 2010 | $3,613 | 11.12 | 325 |
| 2011 | $3,748 | 11.12 | 337 |
| 2012 | $3,880 | 12.52 | 310 |
| 2013* | $4,095 | 12.52 | 327 |
| 2014* | $4,283 | 12.52 | 342 |
| 2015* | $4,446 | 12.52 | 355 |

*Projected figures

(such as sales) to predict employment needs, the more advanced methods combine several factors, such as interest rates, gross national product, disposable income, and sales, to predict employment levels. Forecasting methods such as these are usually used by larger companies with the help of analysts and statisticians. However, advances in data collection technology and computer software are making it easier and more affordable for smaller businesses to use more sophisticated forecasting techniques.

*Qualitative approaches.* Admittedly, forecasting is frequently more an art than a science, providing inexact approximations rather than absolute results. The ever-changing environment in which an organization operates contributes to this situation. For example, estimating changes in the demand for a firm's products or services is a basic forecasting concern, as is anticipating changes in national or regional economics. A firm's internal changes are critical, too. For example, a community hospital anticipating internal changes in its technology or how the facility is organized or managed must consider these factors when it forecasts its staffing needs. Also, the forecasted staffing needs must be in line with the organization's financial resources.

In contrast to quantitative approaches, qualitative approaches to forecasting are less statistical. **Management forecasts** are the opinions (judgments) of supervisors, department managers, experts, or others knowledgeable about the organization's future employment needs. Another qualitative forecasting method, the Delphi technique, attempts to decrease the subjectivity of forecasts by soliciting and summarizing the judgments of a preselected group of individuals. HR personnel can do this by developing a list of questions to ask the managers in their companies. Highlights in HRM 2.4 contains a list of good questions to ask. The final forecast thus becomes a collective, or group, judgment. Ideally, forecasting should include the use of both quantitative and qualitative approaches. Numbers without context—including the context supplied by skilled HR professionals who understand the business and can analyze and interpret the data—are less useful. "The most important software is the one running between your ears," explains Matthew C. Brush, the director of human capital planning at Corning, Inc. Indeed, in small organizations, forecasting may be as informal as having one person who knows the organization and anticipates its future HR requirements.[19]

**management forecasts**
The opinions (judgments) of supervisors, department managers, experts, or others knowledgeable about the organization's future employment needs

# HIGHLIGHTS IN HRM 2.4

## HRP and Strategy Questions to Ask Business Managers

Workforce planning requires that HR leaders periodically interview their managers to gauge future workforce needs. Here are some sample questions to ask:

- What are your mission, vision, and values?

- What are your current pressing business issues?

- What are our organizational strengths?

- What are our competitors' organizational strengths? How do we compare?

- What core capabilities do we need to win in our markets?

- What are the required knowledge, skills, and abilities we need to execute the winning strategy?

- What are the barriers to optimally achieving the strategy?

- What types of skills and positions will be required or no longer required?

- Which skills should we have internally versus contract with outside providers?

- What actions need to be taken to align our resources with strategy priorities?

- What recognition and rewards are needed to attract, motivate, and retain the employees we need?

- How will we know if we are effectively executing our workforce plan and staying on track?

Source: Adapted from Agilent Technologies for The Conference Board and the Society for Human Resource Management.

## Forecasting the Supply of Employees

**staffing tables**
Graphic representations of all organizational jobs, along with the numbers of employees currently occupying those jobs and future (monthly or yearly) employment requirements

**Markov analysis**
A method for tracking the pattern of employee movements through various jobs

**quality of fill**
A metric designed to assess how well new hires are performing on the job

**skill inventories**
Files of personnel education, experience, interests, and skills that allow managers to quickly match job openings with employee backgrounds

Just as an organization must forecast its future requirements for employees, it must also determine whether sufficient numbers and types of employees are available to staff the openings it anticipates having. As with demand forecasts, the process involves both tracking current employee levels and making future projections about those levels.

*Staffing tables and Markov analysis.* An internal supply analysis can begin with the preparation of staffing tables. **Staffing tables** are graphic representations of all organizational jobs, along with the numbers of employees currently occupying those jobs (and perhaps also future employment requirements derived from demand forecasts). Another technique, called a **Markov analysis**, shows the percentage (and actual number) of employees who remain in each of a firm's jobs from one year to the next, as well as the proportions of those who are promoted, demoted, or transferred or exit the organization. As Figure 2.6 shows, a Markov analysis can be used to track the pattern of employee movements through various jobs and to develop a transition matrix for forecasting labour supply.

Forecasting the supply of human resources available to a firm requires that its managers have a good understanding of employee turnover and absenteeism. We have included formulas for computing turnover and absenteeism rates in an appendix to this chapter. Also included in the appendix is a formula for calculating a new metric called **quality of fill**. It was developed because managers understand that simply having "bodies" in place is not enough. The quality-of-fill metric attempts to measure how well new hires are performing so the company will have enough top performers to propel it toward its strategic objectives. We will show you how it is calculated in Chapter 5 when we discuss recruiting metrics.

*Skill inventories and management inventories.* Staffing tables, a Markov analysis, and turnover rates tend to focus on the *number* of employees in particular jobs. Other techniques are more oriented toward the *types* of employees and their skills, knowledge, and experiences. **Skill inventories** can also be prepared that list each employee's education, past work experience, vocational interests, specific abilities and skills, compensation history, and job tenure. Of course, confidentiality is a vital concern in setting up any such inventory. Nevertheless, well-prepared and up-to-date skill inventories allow an organization to quickly match forthcoming job openings with employee backgrounds. When data are gathered on managers, these inventories are called *management inventories*. All of this analysis is made simpler

### FIGURE 2.6

HYPOTHETICAL MARKOV ANALYSIS FOR A RETAIL COMPANY

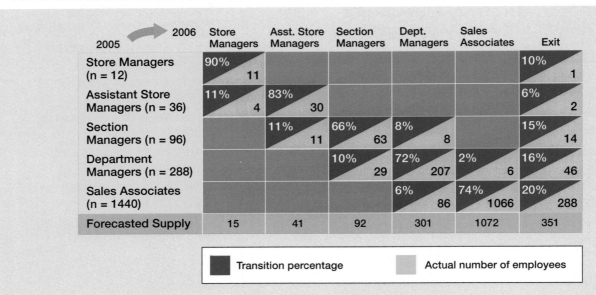

| 2005 \ 2006 | Store Managers | Asst. Store Managers | Section Managers | Dept. Managers | Sales Associates | Exit |
|---|---|---|---|---|---|---|
| Store Managers (n = 12) | 90% / 11 | | | | | 10% / 1 |
| Assistant Store Managers (n = 36) | 11% / 4 | 83% / 30 | | | | 6% / 2 |
| Section Managers (n = 96) | | 11% / 11 | 66% / 63 | 8% / 8 | | 15% / 14 |
| Department Managers (n = 288) | | | 10% / 29 | 72% / 207 | 2% / 6 | 16% / 46 |
| Sales Associates (n = 1440) | | | | 6% / 86 | 74% / 1066 | 20% / 288 |
| **Forecasted Supply** | 15 | 41 | 92 | 301 | 1072 | 351 |

■ Transition percentage　　■ Actual number of employees

## FIGURE 2.7

PART 1

AN EXECUTIVE REPLACEMENT CHART

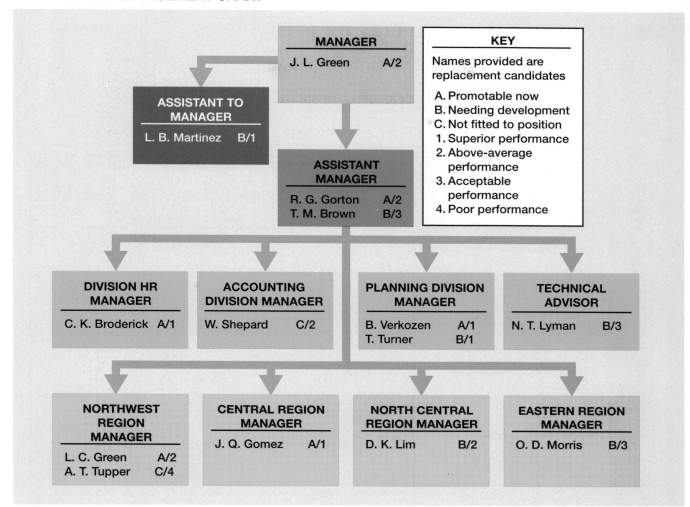

these days through the use of HR information systems and enterprise systems provided by companies such as Oracle-PeopleSoft and SAP.

*Replacement charts and succession planning.* Both skill and management inventories—broadly referred to as talent inventories—can be used to develop employee **replacement charts**, which list current jobholders and identify possible replacements should openings occur. Figure 2.7 shows an example of how an organization might develop a replacement chart for the managers in one of its divisions. Note that this chart provides information on the current job performance and promotability of possible replacements. As such, it can be used side by side with other pieces of information for **succession planning**—the process of identifying, developing, and tracking talented individuals so that they can eventually assume top-level positions.

In a study conducted by the Society for Human Resource Management, three out of four chief executives said succession planning was their most significant challenge for the future. Software developers are responding to this need with new succession planning and talent management software. Software developer Taleo, for example, offers an application based on a firm's organizational chart and baseball card–like representations of its employees. Clicking on the cards flips them over to show statistics about the employees such as their individual performance review data, career information, and succession data. Similarly, the consulting firm Accenture developed a Facebook-like application listing its employees, where they are based, and their individual areas of expertise. The

**replacement charts**
Listings of current jobholders and people who are potential replacements if an opening occurs

**succession planning**
The process of identifying, developing, and tracking key individuals for executive positions

# HIGHLIGHTS IN HRM 2.5

## Succession-Planning Checklist

### RATE THE SUCCESS OF YOUR SUCCESSION PLANNING

For each characteristic of a best-practice succession-planning and management program appearing in the left column below, enter a number to the right to indicate how well you believe your organization manages that characteristic. Ask other decision makers in your organization to complete this form individually. Then compile the scores and compare notes.

| Characteristics of a Best-Practice Succession-Planning and Management Program | How Would You Rate Your Organization's Succession Planning and Management Program on the Characteristic? | | | | |
|---|---|---|---|---|---|
| Your organization has successfully... | Very Poor (1) | Poor (2) | Neither Poor Nor Good (3) | Good (4) | Very Good (5) |
| **1** Clarified the purpose and desired results of the succession-planning and management program. | | | | | |
| **2** Determined what performance is required now for all job categories in the organization by establishing competency models. | | | | | |
| **3** Established a means to measure individual performance that is aligned with the competencies currently demonstrated by successful performers. | | | | | |
| **4** Determined what performance is needed in the future by establishing future competency models for all job categories. | | | | | |
| **5** Created an ongoing means by which to assess individual potential against future competency models. | | | | | |
| **6** Established a means by which to narrow gaps through the use of individual development plans (IDPs). | | | | | |
| **7** Created a means to follow up and hold people accountable. | | | | | |
| **8** Created a means by which to document competence and find organizational talent quickly when needed. | | | | | |
| **9** Created and sustained rewards for developing people. | | | | | |
| **10** Established a means by which to evaluate the results of the succession planning and management program. | | | | | |

Total (add up the scores for items 1–10 and place in the box on the right)

### SCORES

**50–40** Congratulations. The succession-planning and management program in your organization conforms with best practices.

**29–20** Okay. While your organization could make improvements, you appear to have some of the major pieces in place for a succession-planning and management program.

**39–30** Pretty good. Your organization is on the way toward establishing a first-rate succession-planning and management program.

**19–10** Not good at all. Your organization is probably filling positions on an as-needed basis.

**9–0** Give yourself a failing grade. You need to take steps immediately to improve the succession-planning and management practices of your organization.

Source: From William J. Rothwell, "Putting Success into Your Succession Planning," *The Journal of Business Strategy* 23, no. 3 (May/June 2002): 32–37. Emerald Group Publishing

application helps managers with deployment decisions and makes it easier for Accenture's employees who do not necessarily know each other or work together to collaborate with one another.

With or without software, however, more companies will need to engage in succession planning. Highlights in HRM 2.5 shows a checklist for evaluating the "success" of succession planning.[20]

## ASSESSING A FIRM'S HUMAN CAPITAL READINESS: GAP ANALYSIS

Once a company has assessed both the supply and the demand for employee skills, talent, and know-how, it can begin to understand its **human capital readiness**. Any difference between the quantity and quality of employees required versus the quantity and quality of employees available represents a gap that needs to be closed. Figure 2.8 shows how Chemico, a specialty chemical manufacturing company, approaches its assessment of human capital readiness. Similar to our

## FIGURE 2.8

ASSESSING A FIRM'S HUMAN CAPITAL

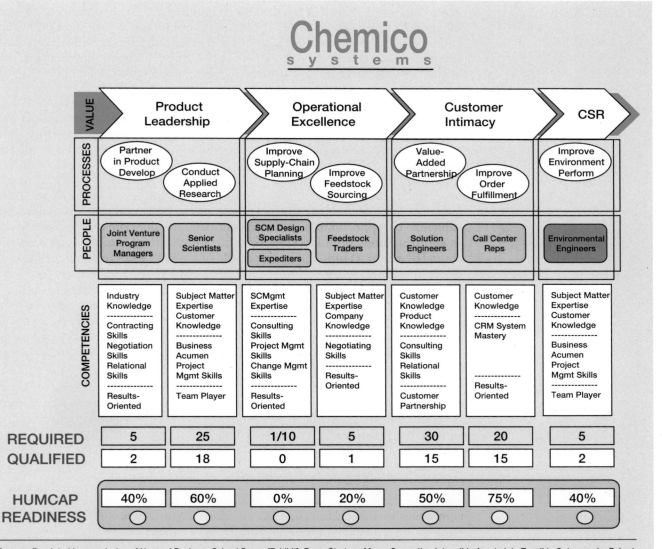

discussion in the preceding sections, managers begin by identifying a company's core capabilities and the key people and processes that are critical to those capabilities. Chemico's executive team identified eight key job "families" that comprise about 100 employees of the firm's 1500-member staff (in other words, less than 10 percent of its workforce). For each of these critical job families, managers identified the critical knowledge, skills, and behaviours necessary to build the core capabilities. They then determined the number of people required for these positions, as well as the number who are currently qualified.

As the lower portion of the figure shows, the company's human readiness ranged between 0 percent for supply chain management design specialists and 75 percent for call centre representatives.

Once the assessment of the firm's human capital readiness is complete, managers have a much better foundation for establishing their strategy going forward and the specific requirements for developing the talent needed to implement the strategy.[21]

## STEP 4: FORMULATING STRATEGY

**OUTCOME 5**

The forecasting techniques discussed previously provide critical information for strategic planning. Recall that we noted at the beginning of the chapter that HR analysis is an input to strategy formulation. However, a word of caution is needed here. Because HR forecasting techniques take us deep into the specifics of labour supply and demand, we need to be careful not to lose sight of the larger strategic picture. One of the biggest concerns among executives is that (at times) HR managers cannot "see the forest for the trees" because they become mired in the administrative details of their planning models. SWOT analysis, discussed below, helps managers combine various sources of information into a broader framework for analysis.

After managers have analyzed the internal strengths and weaknesses of the firm, as well as external opportunities and threats, they have the information they need to formulate corporate, business, and HR strategies for the organization. A comparison of *strengths*, *weaknesses*, *opportunities*, and *threats* is normally referred to as a **SWOT analysis**. SWOT analysis helps executives summarize the major facts and forecasts derived from external and internal analyses. Strategy formulation builds on SWOT analysis to use the strengths of the organization to capitalize on opportunities, counteract threats, and alleviate internal weaknesses. In short, strategy formulation moves from simple analysis to devising a coherent course of action. Figure 2.9 is an example of a SWOT analysis done for the online digital music service Napster.

## CORPORATE STRATEGY

In any industry, firms decide where and how they will compete. Corporate strategy focuses on domain selection, that is, the markets in which they will compete. Some firms choose a concentration strategy that focuses on only a limited portion of the industry. For example, Visteon Corporation specializes in electronics, climate, and power train technologies for the automotive industry. In contrast, Henry Ford at one time had fully integrated his company from the ore mines needed to make steel all the way to the showrooms where his cars were sold.

### Growth and Diversification

Emerging and growing companies execute their strategies differently than mature companies or those in decline. As companies grow, their strategic choices tend to focus on geographic, volume, and product expansion. HRP is a vital input to these decisions. Growth hinges on three related elements: (1) increased employee productivity, (2) a greater number of employees, and (3) employees developing or acquiring new skills. Thus, a firm's staffing, training, and employee motivation efforts can either enable the company to grow or limit its potential.

**FIGURE 2.9**

AN EXAMPLE OF A SWOT ANALYSIS FOR NAPSTER

| Strengths | Weaknesses |
| --- | --- |
| Installed base | Lack of critical complementary assets |
| Strong contagion effects | File selection greatly reduced |
| High market profile | Antagonistic relationship with record labels |
| Powerful design features | Consumer-to-consumer computing |
|  | Transition from a free to a pay model |
| **Opportunities** | **Threats** |
| Best Buy acquisition | Large number of competitors |
| Online entertainment trends | Entry of record labels |
| Potential for alliances with record labels | Advertisement-based models |
| No focused strategy for record labels | Laws/regulation |

**Source:** "E-Commerce: Napster SWOT Analysis," WikiSWOT, http://www.wikiswot.com.

As companies diversify into new businesses, managers are inevitably faced with a "make or buy" decision. That is, should they develop the capabilities in-house or contract externally? For example, when IBM entered the personal computer market in the early 1980s, it contracted with (start-up companies) Intel and Microsoft to make the hardware and operating systems for its personal computer (PC). The decision did not rest solely on HR issues, but they were an important part of the equation. Interestingly, IBM got out of the PC business altogether in 2005 by selling its PC product lineup to Chinese computer manufacturer Lenovo. Instead, IBM is focusing on developing custom technology services for businesses, which it believes will be more profitable in the long run and a harder product for competitors to imitate. To help accomplish this new strategy, the company spent the first part of the decade buying up dozens of business service–related companies and their talent.

Some companies diversify far beyond their core businesses. GE, for example, has diversified from its original base in electrical and home appliance products to such wide-ranging industries as health, finance, insurance, truck and air transportation, and even media with its ownership of NBC. To manage such a diverse portfolio, GE has invested heavily in the development of general management skills and leadership ability. CEO Jeffrey Immelt has stated that GE's future depends on pursuing businesses that leverage human capital (in contrast to its traditional focus on manufacturing). This new strategy is strongly linked to HR. In fact, the strategy is viable only because the company has done such an enviable job developing talent over the years.

## Mergers and Acquisitions

In addition to strategies of growth and diversification, corporate Canada has seen a host of mergers and acquisitions in recent years.

Although there are some important competitive reasons for mergers such as these, it is unfortunate to note that many of them have not gone well. Not surprisingly, perhaps, the failure rate among firms is very high. Some estimates suggest that only about 15 percent of all mergers achieve their objectives (e.g., measured by return on investment, shareholder value). Often the failure is due to cultural inconsistencies, as well as conflicts among the managers of each firm.

**value creation**
What the firm adds to a product or service by virtue of making it; the amount of benefits provided by the product or service once the costs of making it are subtracted

The failure of the merger between the German firm Daimler-Benz (the manufacturer of Mercedes-Benz vehicles) and Chrysler is an example. Although the German portion of the firm had superior technology, reportedly, it was less than eager to share its know-how with its American counterparts. Problems such as this point directly to the importance of effective HR planning prior to—and during—the merger process.

## Strategic Alliances and Joint Ventures

Sometimes firms do not acquire or merge with another firm but instead pursue cooperative strategies such as a strategic alliance or joint venture. Especially when firms enter into international joint ventures, the issues of culture (both company culture and national culture) become paramount. On the front end, HR plays a vital role in assessing the compatibility of cultures and potential problems. As the alliance is formed, HR helps select key executives and develops teamwork across the respective workforces. In addition, HR is typically involved in the design of performance assessment and mutual incentives for the alliance. Of course, one of the controversial issues related to such alliances is the inevitable issue of outsourcing or offshoring work to other locations.

## BUSINESS STRATEGY

Although we think about corporate strategy as domain selection, business strategy is viewed in terms of domain navigation. It is more focused on how the company will compete against rival firms to create value for customers. We can think of **value creation** in a cost/benefit scenario (i.e., value = benefits – costs). Companies can increase the value they offer customers by decreasing the costs of their goods and services or by increasing the benefits their products provide (or some combination of the two). Their business strategies reflect these choices.

## Low-Cost Strategy: Compete on Productivity and Efficiency

A low-cost strategy means keeping your costs low enough so that you can offer an attractive price to customers (relative to competitors). Organizations such as McDonald's have been very successful at using a low-cost strategy. Critical success factors for this strategy focus on efficiency, productivity, and minimizing waste. These types of companies often are large and try to exploit economies of scale in production and distribution. In many cases, their large size allows them to sell their products and services at a lower price, which leads to higher market share, volume, and (it is hoped) profits. However, even a low-cost leader must offer a product or service that customers find valuable. As Gordon Bethune, the former CEO of Continental Airlines, put it, "You can make a pizza so cheap that no one will buy it."[22] Ultimately, organizations need to use a cost strategy to increase value to customers rather than take it away.

A low-cost strategy has several links to HRP. The first has to do with productivity. A common misconception about low-cost strategies is that they inevitably require cutting labour costs. On the contrary, there are several good examples of companies that pay their employees "top dollar" but gain back cost advantages because of excellent productivity. That is, they get a terrific "bang for the buck." Either they produce more from the workforce they have, or they can produce the same amount with a smaller workforce.

According to Peter Cappelli, who heads the Center for Human Resources at the Wharton School at the University of Pennsylvania, the productivity of the best-performing staffs can be 5 to 20 *times* higher than the productivity of the worst-performing staffs, depending on the industry. Billy Beane, the general manager of the Oakland A's, became famous for making the most of the team's small payroll. Beane did so by carefully choosing and developing players and using them more strategically than other major league teams with bigger payroll budgets. The movie *Moneyball* tells this story and provides some interesting examples of HR strategy and practices.

The second way that low-cost strategies are linked to HR pertains to outsourcing. In some cases, companies seeking low cost may consider contracting with an external partner that can perform particular activities or services as well (or better) at a lower cost. This decision directly links strategic planning to HRP. Decisions such as these often result in layoffs, transfers, and the like. As noted previously, organizations need to have a clear understanding of their core processes and skills to make these decisions. Too often, firms approach outsourcing decisions based on costs alone, but this can lead to detrimental effects in the long run if the skills base of their employees suffers and their core capabilities are subsequently eroded.

## Differentiation Strategy: Compete on Value Added

Although decreasing costs is one important way to enhance customer value, another involves providing something unique and distinctive to customers. A differentiation strategy is often based on high product quality, innovative features, speed to market, or superior service. Four Seasons Hotels' commitment to quality and luxury, FedEx's focus on speed and flexible delivery, Holt Renfrew's commitment to fashion and customer service, and Apple's emphasis on innovation and product development are all easily identifiable examples of differentiation strategies.

Each of these strategies is rooted in the management of human resources. Companies that focus on service, for example, need to identify and support ways to empower employees to serve customers better. In contrast to the company that emphasizes low cost and efficiencies, you may find that differentiating companies will bend the rules a bit more, allow more flexibility to let you "have it your way," and customize products and services around the customer's particular needs. In place of rigid rules, service-oriented companies often try to embed their values in the cultural values of the company. Nordstrom's employee handbook consists of just a single five- by eight-inch card that reads: "Welcome to Nordstrom. Rule #1. Use your good judgment in all situations. There will be no additional rules."

The use of part-time employees helps contain labour costs at fast-food restaurants.

© Richard Levine/Alamy

In addition to formulating corporate and business-level strategies, managers also need to "translate" strategic priorities into functional areas of the organization (such as marketing, manufacturing, and HR). This involves all aspects of the business, but in particular there needs to be a clear alignment between HR and the requirements of an organization's strategy. In this regard, HR policies and practices need to achieve two types of fit: vertical and horizontal.[23]

## Vertical Fit/Alignment

*Vertical fit* (or *alignment*) focuses on the connection between the business objectives and the major initiatives in HR. For example, as we noted earlier, if a company's strategy focuses on achieving low cost, its HR policies and practices need to reinforce this idea by reinforcing efficient and reliable behaviour on the part of employees and enhanced productivity. On the other hand, if the organization competes through innovation and new product development, then its HR policies and practices would be more aligned with the notion of fostering creativity and flexibility.

## Horizontal Fit/Alignment

In addition to horizontal fit or alignment, managers need to ensure that their HR practices are all aligned with one another internally to establish a configuration that is mutually reinforcing. The entire range of the firm's HR practices—from its job design, staffing, training, performance appraisal, and compensation—needs to focus on the same workforce objectives. Unfortunately, often one HR practice, such as training, might be focused on teamwork and sharing, whereas another HR practice, such as the firm's appraisal and compensation programs, reinforces the ideas of individual achievement. Charles Schwab and Company faced this very situation. The company has a reputation in the financial services industry for developing a culture of teamwork that has been important to its strategy. However, when it changed its compensation strategy to provide more rewards to its high-performing brokers, the firm sent mixed signals to its employees. Which is more important: teamwork or individual high flyers?[24]

## STEP 5: STRATEGY IMPLEMENTATION

OUTCOME 6

As the old saying goes, "well begun is half done"—but only half. Like any plan, formulating the appropriate strategy is not enough. Managers must also ensure that the new plans are implemented effectively. This is easier said than done. One survey revealed that about half of managers say there is a gap between their organization's ability to develop a vision and strategy and to execute it. Recently, organizations have been paying more attention to implementation and execution.[25]

Figure 2.10 shows the now classic 7-S framework and reveals that HRM is instrumental to almost every aspect of strategy implementation, whether it pertains to structure, systems, style, skills, staff, or shared values. Whereas *strategy* lays out the route that the organization will take in the future, organizational *structure* is the framework in which activities of the organization members are coordinated. If the strategy requires employees to be reorganized or redeployed, HR will be intimately involved. Closely related to structure are *systems* and processes. These include formal and informal procedures that govern the everyday activities of a firm. As organizations consider reengineering and redesign their processes to implement their strategies, HR helps ensure that the best workflow models are in place and—importantly—that employees are involved in sharing their advice, too.

*Shared values* were discussed earlier in the chapter as a guiding parameter for strategic planning. They arise again as an important issue in implementation as well.

## FIGURE 2.10

### THE 7-S MODEL

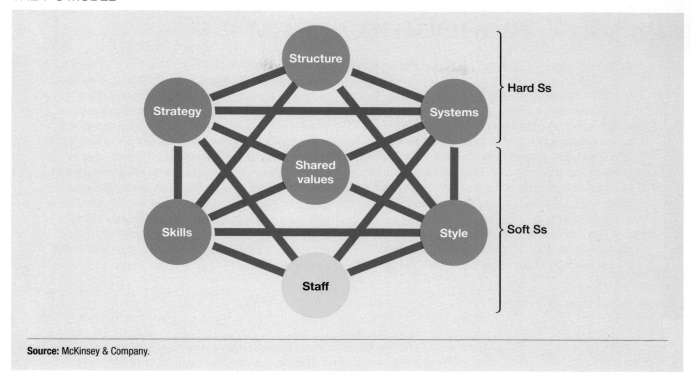

**Source:** McKinsey & Company.

Strategic change often requires employees and managers to modify, or abandon, their old ways of doing things. HR managers play a central role as guardians of the corporate culture—the principles on which the company is founded and the fundamental ideas around which the business is built. This is tightly connected to the issue of *style*, which refers not only to the leadership approach of top managers but also the way in which employees present themselves to the outside world (e.g., to suppliers, customers).

*Skills* and *staff* relate directly to the concerns of HRM and point to the critical role that HR plays in strategy implementation. At a fundamental level, HR's role in strategy implementation focuses on reconciling the (1) human resources demanded and (2) human resources available.

## TAKING ACTION: RECONCILING SUPPLY AND DEMAND

Through HRP, organizations strive for a proper balance between demand considerations and supply considerations. Demand considerations are based on forecasted trends in business activity. Supply considerations involve determining where and how candidates with the required qualifications can be found to fill a firm's vacancies. Because of the difficulty in locating applicants for the increasing number of jobs that require advanced training, this aspect of planning has been receiving much more attention. Greater planning effort is also needed to recruit members of designated groups for managerial jobs and technical jobs that require advanced levels of education.

In an effort to meet their HR demands, organizations have many staffing options, including hiring full-time employees, having current employees work overtime, recalling laid-off workers, using temporary or contract employees, and outsourcing or offshoring some of their business processes. Highlights in HRM 2.6 outlines how one Nova Scotia company dealt with a projected labour shortage.

However, when forecasts show a surplus of employees, organizations often restrict their hiring, reduce their employees' work hours, and consider layoffs,

# HIGHLIGHTS IN HRM 2.6

## Managing Labour Shortages

Dexter, a construction company based in Bedford, Nova Scotia, was facing a skills gap in its labour market. The demands in this sector have changed, and there is less need for manual labourers and a greater demand for technicians with computer literacy skills. For example, a heavy equipment operator or surveyor used to operate by observing and using pen and paper; now much of this work is dictated by GPS (Global Positioning Systems) and integrated software.

Ron Hyson, director of HR for Dexter, decided to partner with the Nova Scotia Community College to recruit, select, and train employees in the required skills.

About 350 candidates applied for the two-year training program, were tested, and then interviewed. A final group of 30 was selected to receive training in all fields of construction. They were cross-trained in surveying and heavy equipment operations and were given courses in management development, job costing, and safety. The training methods were varied. About 40 percent of the time, trainees were in the classroom. The remaining time was spent in the field in six to eight functional areas, such as surveying. Work terms of six months, consisting of rotations in each area for four weeks, were used to help the students determine their interests and abilities. At the end of the program, the trainees were guaranteed employment.

Source: Interview with Ron Hyson.

demotions, and/or terminations. Some organizations try to reduce their workforces by relying on attrition, which is a gradual reduction of employees through resignations, retirements, and deaths. Over the past few decades, early retirements have become a more and more common means for organizations to reduce their excess labour supply. Organizations sometimes encourage employees to accept early retirement by offering "sweetened" retirement benefits. The various types of benefits are discussed in Chapter 11.

## Dealing with Surplus Employees

Several options are available to employers when it comes to dealing with surplus employees: layoffs, attrition, and termination.

### Layoff Strategies

Employee layoff decisions are usually based on seniority and/or ability. With unionized organizations, the criteria for determining an employee's eligibility for layoff are typically set forth in the collective agreement. Similar provisions in the collective agreement provide for the right of employees to be recalled for jobs they are still qualified to perform.

Although it has become customary for employers to recognize seniority in unionized employees, nonunion employees are not always given the same consideration. Due to the demand for a technically skilled workforce, the ability of employees to change jobs and learn new skills, as well as their performance and competencies, is given a great deal of weight in layoff decisions. The most important reason for using seniority as a basis for layoffs is the objective nature of the decision: number of years of work, not perception of ability, is the basis for the decision. The system is fair, and employees themselves can calculate their own probability of being employed.

One of the major disadvantages of overemphasizing seniority is that less competent employees receive the same rewards and security as more competent ones; the seniority system ignores talent and effort. The payroll is also higher than under other systems because more experienced workers tend to earn more money. Also, the practice of using seniority as the basis for deciding which workers to lay off may well have a disproportionate impact on women and visible minority workers, who often have less seniority than other groups.

Under the umbrella of layoff strategies are several work reduction options: reduced workweek, reduced shifts, and transfers to related companies. Under the reduced workweek, employees work about 20 to 30 hours per week. This option allows the organization to retain a skilled workforce and lessens the financial and emotional impact of a full layoff, and at the same time reduces the costs of production. Reduced shift work is based on a similar concept of reducing costs by reducing the number of hours worked. Some plants operate three shifts a day and may shut down the midnight to 8:00 a.m. shift to save money. In some rare cases, organizations can transfer laid-off employees to a sister company. Layoffs are the fastest way to achieve workforce reduction; attrition is the slowest.

## Attrition

**Attrition** refers to the "natural" departure of employees through quits, retirements, and deaths. The turnover rates of an organization vary greatly by industry and by occupation. For example, university professors rarely quit, whereas turnover among fast-food workers can reach 300 percent a year. Most organizations can easily estimate how many people will leave the organization and so can slowly reduce the workforce through natural means.

Attrition must be supplemented by other practices. Hiring freezes are usually implemented at the same time as the organization adopts a strategy of workforce reduction through attrition. A **hiring freeze** means that organizations will not hire new workers as planned or will hire only in areas critical to the success of the organization.

Some organizations attempt to accelerate attrition by offering incentives to employees to leave. These incentives include cash bonuses for people to leave during a specified time, accelerated or early retirement benefits, and free outplacement services. However, the buyout process must be carefully managed. Employees with valuable skills who can easily find another job may be the first to cash in.

If the surplus of employees is deemed to be permanent, terminations may be the only option.

## Termination Strategies

**Termination** is a practice initiated by an employer to separate an employee from the organization permanently. Termination is different from firing, in which an employee is released for such causes as poor performance, high absenteeism, or unethical behaviour. The purpose of termination is to reduce the size of the workforce and thereby save money.

A termination strategy begins with the identification of employees who are in positions that are no longer considered useful or critical to the company's effectiveness. Employers cannot terminate without some form of compensation to the employee. **Severance pay**, a lump-sum payment given to terminated employees, is calculated on the basis of years of service and salary. Every province has legislation such as the *Employment Standards Act*, which establishes minimum standards for termination and severance pay.

# STEP 6: EVALUATION AND ASSESSMENT

At one level, it might seem that assessing a firm's effectiveness is the final step in the planning process. That is true. But it is also the first step. Planning is cyclical, of course, and although we have somewhat conveniently placed evaluation at the end of this chapter, it actually provides the inputs to the next cycle in the planning process.

## EVALUATION AND ASSESSMENT ISSUES

To evaluate their performance, firms need to establish a set of parameters that focus on the "desired outcomes" of their strategic planning, as well as the metrics they will use to monitor how well the organization delivers against those

**attrition**
A natural departure of employees from organizations through quits, retirements, and deaths

**hiring freeze**
A practice whereby new workers are not hired as planned or workers who have left the organization are not replaced

**termination**
Practice initiated by an employer to separate an employee from the organization permanently

**severance pay**
A lump-sum payment given to terminated employees

PART 1

OUTCOME 7

**benchmarking**
The process of comparing the organization's processes and practices to those of other companies

PART 1

outcomes. Because strategic management is ultimately aimed at creating a competitive advantage, many firms evaluate their performance against other firms. **Benchmarking** is the process of identifying "best practices" in a given area—for example, productivity, logistics, brand management, and training—and then comparing your practices and performance to those of other companies. To accomplish this, a benchmarking team would collect information on its own company's operations and those of other firms to uncover any gaps. The gaps help determine the causes of performance differences, and, ultimately, the team would map out a set of best practices that lead to world-class performance. Interestingly, the target company for benchmarking does not need to be a competitor. For example, when Xerox wanted to learn about excellent customer service, it benchmarked L.L. Bean. By working with a noncompeting company, Xerox was able to get access to information a competitor would not divulge.

The metrics fall into two basic categories: human capital metrics and HR metrics. Human capital metrics assess aspects of the workforce, whereas HR metrics assess the performance of the HR function itself.

Most larger companies use software to track their HR metrics over time. Figure 2.11 shows an example of an HR "dashboard," which is software that tracks and graphically displays HR statistics so they can be viewed by managers at a glance (as you do your dashboard readings when you are driving).

Smart HR managers can significantly enhance their worth to their organizations if they go a step further by gathering informal information, or "intelligence," about the strategic and HRM practices of their competitors. This can be done by legal means, such as by reading industry blogs, checking competitors' press releases, and signing up for their news feeds, if they provide them, as well as signing up for Google email alerts that are triggered when competing firms' names appear in the news. Attending industry conventions and talking to your company's suppliers about business and employment trends are other good ways of gathering competitive intelligence. So are interviews with job candidates. Simply asking candidates who turned down job offers at other companies why they did so can yield a great deal of information.

With that said, benchmarking alone will not give a firm a competitive advantage. According to Brian Becker and Mark Huselid, a competitive advantage is based on the unique combination of a company's human capital, strategy, and core capabilities—which differ from firm to firm. This means that HR managers

## FIGURE 2.11

### AN EXAMPLE OF AN HR DASHBOARD

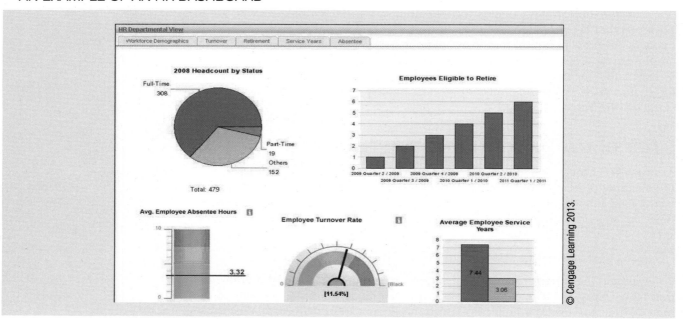

© Cengage Learning 2013.

cannot simply rely on the benchmarks and strategies of other firms. Instead, they must develop their own. If they can successfully do so and implement them, they can achieve a sustained competitive advantage.[26]

## MEASURING A FIRM'S STRATEGIC ALIGNMENT

Earlier in the chapter, we discussed the importance of strategic alignment and fit as an element of strategy formulation and implementation. As an element of evaluation, some very useful techniques help managers assess the extent to which they have achieved these objectives.

### Strategy Mapping and the Balanced Scorecard

One of the tools for mapping a firm's strategy to ensure strategic alignment is the **balanced scorecard (BSC)**. Developed by Harvard professors Robert Kaplan and David Norton, the BSC is a framework that helps managers translate their firms' strategic goals into operational objectives. The model has four related cells: (1) financial, (2) customer, (3) processes, and (4) learning.[27] The logic of the BSC is firmly rooted in HRM. People management and learning help organizations improve their internal processes and provide excellent customer service. Internal processes—product development, service, and the like—are critical for creating customer satisfaction and loyalty; they are also important for ensuring productivity to contain costs for better financial performance. Customer value creation, in turn, drives up revenues, which enhances profitability.

Figure 2.12 shows how this might work at Starbucks. In each cell, Starbucks would identify the key metrics that help translate strategic goals to operational imperatives. For example, under customer metrics, Starbucks might look at the percentage of repeat customers, the number of new customers, and growth rate. Under people metrics, managers might measure the numbers of

PART 1

## FIGURE 2.12

### BUILDING THE METRICS MODEL

| Strategic Theme: "The Third Place" | Objectives | Measures | Targets | Initiatives |
|---|---|---|---|---|
| **Financial**<br>Long-Term Shareholder Value<br>Grow Revenues / Asset Utilization | • Profitability<br>• Grow revenues<br>• Improve cost structure | • Market value<br>• Revenue<br>• General and administrative costs as % of sales | • 20% Compound annual growth rate (CAGR)<br>• 30% CAGR<br>• 5% CAGR | • Intl. growth<br>• Cdn. growth<br>• Corp. layoffs |
| **Customer**<br>Attract & Retain Customers<br>Premium Coffee / The "Third" Place | • New customers<br>• More value to current (now) customers | • # Customers<br>• New stores<br>• Repeat customers<br>• Same store sales | • 20 mill/week<br>• 1,500/yr<br>• 15% 2/wk<br>• 13% growth | • Store develop<br>• New products<br>• Customer loyalty program<br>• New partners |
| **Internal**<br>Engage Cust. / Fill Orders | • Friendly service<br>• Accurate orders<br>• Fast fulfillment | • Customer feedback<br>• First time right<br>• Order fulfillment | • 90+ satisfaction<br>• 99+% accurate<br>• <3 minutes | • Customer engagement<br>• Automation<br>• Cycle time opt. |
| **People**<br>Baristas / Store Manager | • Store manager stability<br>• Barista engagement | • Average tenure<br>• Voluntary turnover<br>• Engagement survey | • Mgr >3 yrs<br>• Barista 80%<br>• 85% rating | • 40 hrs. training<br>• MUG awards<br>• Beanstock |

suggestions provided by employees, participation in Starbucks' stock-sharing program, employee turnover, and training hours spent. Each of these cells links vertically. People management issues such as rewards, training, and suggestions can be linked to efficient processes (e.g., brewing the perfect cup, delivering top-notch customer service). These processes then lead to better customer loyalty and growth. Growth and customer loyalty in turn lead to higher profitability and market value.

## Measuring Horizontal Fit

Recall that horizontal fit means that HR practices are all aligned with one another to establish a configuration that is mutually reinforcing. Figure 2.13 shows an example of how organizations can assess the horizontal fit of their HR practices. There are essentially three steps. First, managers need to identify the key workforce objectives they hope to achieve. Often this information can come from the people/learning cell of the BSC and might include loyalty, customer service, productivity, and creativity. Second, managers would identify each of the HR practices used to elicit or reinforce those workforce objectives (e.g., job design, staffing, training, appraisal, compensation). Third, managers would evaluate each HR practice on a scale of −5 (not supportive) to 5 (supportive). By tallying up the ratings across managers, organizations can get a very clear idea of which HR practices are working together to achieve the workforce objectives and which are not.

**FIGURE 2.13**

ASSESSING HORIZONTAL FIT

*WORKFORCE OBJECTIVES*

| | Sales Productivity | Customer Service | Merchandise Information | Stock Maintenance | Total |
|---|---|---|---|---|---|
| **Structure/Workflow** | | | | | |
| • Cross-functional teams | 3 | 2 | 0 | −1 | 4 |
| • Rotation (Depts.) | 3 | 3 | −1 | −1 | 4 |
| **Staffing** | | | | | |
| • Test battery | 2 | 2 | 1 | 1 | 6 |
| • Select for experience | 5 | 3 | 2 | 2 | 12 |
| **Training** | | | | | |
| • Retail selling skills | 4 | 5 | 1 | 1 | 11 |
| **Rewards** | | | | | |
| • Results appraisal | 5 | −4 | −2 | −5 | −6 |
| • Individual incentives | 5 | −5 | −3 | −5 | −8 |
| **Leadership** | | | | | |
| • Corporate | 3 | 3 | 1 | 0 | 7 |
| • Store manager | 4 | 2 | 2 | 2 | 10 |
| **Technologies** | | | | | |
| • Merchandise IS | 5 | 2 | 5 | 1 | 13 |
| • Daily postings | 4 | −3 | 4 | −1 | 4 |
| | 43/55 | 10/55 | 10/55 | 26/55 | 57/220 |

*SYSTEM COHERENCE*

+5 = strongly supports the priority;
  0 = neutral;
−5 = strongly counterproductive.

*ORGANIZATION* (left vertical label)

*FUNCTIONAL COHESION* (right vertical label)

An important caveat to this analysis is that internal fit is a necessary, but insufficient, cause of strategic alignment. A company could have nearly perfect alignment among its HR practices, and they still might not be aligned with the competitive strategy. For that reason, it is important for managers to assess both internal fit and external alignment.

## ENSURING STRATEGIC FLEXIBILITY FOR THE FUTURE

Apart from the need to establish and measure fit between HR and strategy, HR is also focused on ensuring flexibility and agility when the environment changes. Ultimately, successful HRP helps increase **organizational capability**—the capacity of the organization to continuously act and change in pursuit of sustainable competitive advantage.[28]

Flexibility can be achieved in two primary ways: coordination flexibility and resource flexibility. *Coordination flexibility* occurs through rapid reallocation of resources to new or changing needs. Through HRP, managers can anticipate upcoming events, keep abreast of changes in legal regulations, forecast economic trends, and recognize competitor moves. With advance notice, managers can move people into and out of jobs, retrain them for new skill requirements, and modify the kinds of incentives they use. Use of a contingency workforce composed of part-timers, temporary employees, and external partners also helps achieve coordination flexibility.[29] *Resource flexibility*, on the other hand, results from having people who can do many different things in different ways. Cross-training, job rotations, and team-based work modes are all focused on establishing a flexible workforce.

We will draw on these ideas throughout this text. But at this point, we want to close the chapter by emphasizing that strategic planning is a process designed to ensure superior performance today, as well as establishing the capability and agility to respond tomorrow. As the great hockey player Wayne Gretzky used to say, "I don't skate to where the puck is. I skate to where the puck is going to be."

# SMALL BUSINESS APPLICATION

Small businesses, by their size, provide for a much closer alignment between organizational and people strategies. What is different for small business is threefold: (1) access to resources to analyze the competitive landscape and market opportunities, (2) access to internal and available talent to pursue markets or opportunities, and (3) being less constrained by existing internal processes or structures in the pursuit of new strategies.

As we have seen, the development and integration of HR in the strategic planning process require a scan of market opportunities and the competitive landscape. This research requires time, money, and expertise that may not be readily available in small companies. So how do small companies develop and pursue strategy? Typically, small companies grow around a core competency, a single business activity that has been established to address a specific market need or specific large client requirement. From that centre, all research regarding market opportunities and threats is focused on identifying opportunities that are aligned with this core competency and guarding potential threats to the core business.

Let's use a small printing company with 50 employees as an example. This company has been created out of a need to provide printing services to a packaged-goods company. From this, the company has grown to take on additional clients. However, the packaged-goods company still accounts for 40 percent of the revenue and profitability for the company. With this in mind, the strategic planning exercise focuses on the following: (1) What does the company need to do to grow the business with the existing clients and identify new clients? (2) What risks are there of client or profitability erosion from the existing client base? (3) What changes, if any, are required in the talent the company has in place to sell and deliver printing services to meet these needs?

The challenge for small business is that by the very nature of size, the range of talent available within the existing organization will be constrained. As a result, any change in strategic direction may require retraining or recruitment of talent, both of which will take time and money and will depend on the availability of training services or talent available to hire. These factors will need to be considered in the development of strategy.

# SUMMARY

**OUTCOME 1** SHRM integrates strategic planning and HRP. HRP and strategies become especially critical when organizations consider global strategies, including mergers, joint ventures, offshoring, the relocation of plants, product innovations, and downsizing or when dramatic shifts occur in the composition of the labour and type of people needed to meet organizational objectives.

**OUTCOME 2** Analyzing the firm's competitive environment is central to strategic planning. The competitive environment includes the specific organizations with which the firm interacts. Firms analyze the competitive environment to adapt to or influence the nature of competition.

**OUTCOME 3** Conducting an internal analysis to gauge the firm's strengths and weaknesses involves looking at a firm's "three Cs"—its capabilities, composition, and culture. An internal analysis enables strategic decision makers to inventory the organization's skills and resources as well as employees' performance levels. An organization's success increasingly depends on the knowledge, skills, and abilities of employees, particularly as they help establish a set of core capabilities that distinguish an organization from its competitors. When employees' talents are valuable, rare, difficult to imitate, and organized, a firm can achieve a sustained competitive advantage through its people.

**OUTCOME 4** HRP is a systematic process that involves forecasting the demand for labour, performing supply analysis, and balancing supply and demand considerations. Forecasting demand requires using either quantitative or qualitative methods to identify the number by HR functions. (Supply analysis involves determining whether sufficient employees are available within the organization to meet demand and whether potential employees are available on the job market.)

**OUTCOME 5** As organizations plan for their future, top management and strategic planners must recognize that strategic planning decisions affect—and are affected by—HR functions. On the one hand, HRP plays a reactive role in ensuring that the right number and type of employees are available to implement a chosen business plan. On the other hand, HRP can proactively identify and initiate programs needed to develop organizational capabilities on which future strategies can be built. HRP and strategic planning tend to be most effective when there is a reciprocal relationship between the two processes.

**OUTCOME 6** Formulating a HR strategy is only half of the HR battle; the strategy must also be implemented. Employment forecasts must be reconciled against the internal and the external supplies of labour the firm faces. This can include having current employees work overtime or hiring full-time, part-time, or contract employees. If there is an employee surplus, the organization can consider layoffs, attrition, and termination strategies.

**OUTCOME 7** Firms need to establish a set of parameters that focus on the "desired outcomes" of strategic planning, as well as the metrics they will use to monitor how well the firm delivers against those outcomes. Issues of measurement, benchmarking, alignment, fit, and flexibility are central to the evaluation process. Firms use benchmarking, strategy mapping, and the BSC as tools to gauge their outcomes.

# KEY TERMS

attrition, 67

balanced scorecard (BSC), 69

benchmarking, 68

core capabilities, 47

core values, 42

cultural audits, 51

environmental scanning, 43

hiring freeze, 67

human capital readiness, 59

human resources planning (HRP), 40

management forecasts, 55

Markov analysis, 56

mission, 41

organizational capability, 71

quality of fill, 56

replacement charts, 57

severance pay, 67

skill inventories, 56

staffing tables, 56

strategic human resources management (SHRM), 40

strategic planning, 40

strategic vision, 41

succession planning, 57

SWOT analysis, 60

termination, 67

trend analysis, 53

value creation, 62

values-based hiring, 52

## DISCUSSION QUESTIONS

1. Identify the three key elements of the HRP model and discuss the relationships among them.
2. What environmental forces influence the future of community colleges and universities? List these and discuss the implications for the demand for faculty.
3. Think about an organization that you know well. Place the employees of this organization into the following categories: strategic knowledge workers, core employees, supporting workers and partners, and complementary skills workers.
4. Which approach do you think should be relied on more heavily for strategy formulation—the quantitative or the qualitative approach?
5. Research In Motion (RIM) is an interesting Canadian business story. From its website and news articles, try to articulate its corporate strategy. Compare it to the corporate strategy of Tim Hortons.
6. During this course, there will be news about an organization needing to reduce the workforce by thousands of employees. What are the options? What are the advantages and disadvantages of each option?
7. Imagine that you are president of the HR student association at your school. You want to measure the success of the association during your term. What metrics would you use? What benchmarks would you use?

# HRM EXPERIENCE

## Customizing HR for Different Types of Human Capital

Part of strategic planning in HR is mapping an organization's human capital. When we look at the strategic value of a person's skills and their uniqueness, we soon discover that organizations comprise different kinds of workers who have very different kinds of skills. Some are core knowledge workers, some are more traditional job-based employees, some are contract workers, and some are external partners. In this context, it is unlikely that we would manage all of these employees in the same way (as much as we might want to for fairness). There are differences in HR practices for different groups. This is not bad, but it makes the job of HR managers more difficult.

### Assignment

The following are descriptions of three different employees. How would you characterize each worker? What role does each play when it comes to the organization's strategy?

*Andrea Bascomb* is a highly talented computer programmer for MiniFluff, Inc. She is among the elite set of engineers in the computer industry that is doing leading-edge work on advanced computer modelling.

In truth, CEO Bill Ding believes that the future of the company rests on the innovative work that Andrea and her team are doing. He worries that someone might lure Andrea away to work for them. So he wants to give her all the room she needs to grow and stay committed to MiniFluff.

*Calvin Duff* is a salesperson on the retail side of MiniFluff. He has daily contact with customers and is responsible for making sales and communicating with service personnel. Make no mistake: to many customers, Calvin and his coworkers are the "face" of MiniFluff. Always on the lookout for a better situation, Calvin has thought about working for PeachTree Computing, MiniFluff's main competitor. In truth, other salespeople have found that they can leave MiniFluff and get "up to speed" easily at other firms. Their skills are very transferable, and the transition is not difficult. Bill Ding and other managers at MiniFluff recognize this fact, so they try to keep salespeople loyal and productive, recognizing that many of them do eventually leave.

*Evelyn Frank* is a part-time secretary for MiniFluff. She handles routine typing and filing work for the company, particularly in peak periods in the summer and around the holidays. She usually works for a few weeks at a time and then takes time off. The executives at MiniFluff have considered either outsourcing the job to an agency or automating it through a new computer system. But for now things are steady.

Visit the *Managing Human Resources* CourseMate website at http://www.belcourt7e.nelson.com for quizzes, flashcards, videos, games, and more!

# STAFFING, DOWN TO A SCIENCE AT CAPITAL ONE

When the financial services industry tumbled into crisis in June 2007, Capital One chairman and CEO Richard Fairbank issued a mandate to strip $700 million out of the company's operating costs by 2009. The cost reduction plan includes consolidating and streamlining functions, reducing layers of management, and eliminating approximately 2,000 jobs. The mandate did not set off a mad scramble in workforce planning, however. Instead, the planning staff simply added new defined variables to their simulations and modified their projections for the company's talent needs.

"The key to workforce planning is to start with the long-term vision of the organization and its future business goals and work back from there," says Matthew Schuyler, chief human resources officer for Capital One and its 27,000 employees. "We anticipate the strategic needs of the business and make sure that we have the workforce required to meet those needs. The $700 million mandate gives us goals and boundaries that we didn't have before. We made the adjustments."

Capital One and other leading companies are now developing a set of best practices for workforce planning that reach into the future for each business unit and evolve with corporate strategic planning. In an increasingly unstable global business environment, the value of a long-term vision is clear, but effective workforce planning requires dedicated resources, heavy analytics, and, perhaps most important, the full engagement of business unit leaders and line managers.

## Working Backward

The workforce planning at Capital One stems from a process executed by a metrics and analytics group of 20 people, plus hundreds of executives, managers, and analysts pulled from all the business lines and corporate functions. Leaders and analysts from the business lines work in blended teams with human resources generalists and members of the metrics group to build models for each line and the entire world force. The models flow to Schuyler, who reports directly to the CEO. "You have to garner your long-term vision of the organization from your seat at the table and from the time you spend with business leaders, immersed in places where you can get data," Schuyler says. "You have to probe the business leaders and know the business leaders and know what their endgame looks like." Planning varies by business line. Some lines are stable, while others are restructuring or moving through rapid growth.

Part of Schuyler's job is to ensure that senior business line leaders are engaged in the process. "Their door is open," he notes. "Your ticket through the door is to show business leaders the bundles of money they can save if their workforce is the right size with the right mix and the right skills. Once you're inside, you have to act on the promise." The potential cost savings come from minimizing the inherent costs associated with the size of the workforce, plus savings from lower recruiting and severance costs and avoiding the costs of a disengaged workforce. "The cost of disengagement is difficult to quantify, but business leaders intuitively understand the cost," Schuyler says. "There is a toll paid when a workforce is disempowered, disengaged, and not sufficiently busy."

Workforce planning at Capital One forecasts not only the head count required to meet future business needs, but also the staffing mix—the ratio of internal to external resources—and the skills mix, including any changes in that mix that are required as the business moves forward. Schuyler also looks at any changes in "spans of control," which determine the number of organizational layers, optimal methods for staffing managerial positions, and the related costs. The planners also document both rational and emotional employee engagement, which affect current and future productivity and recruiting, training, and turnover costs.

The responsibility for workforce planning at Capital One resides in human resources, but the hard work takes place inside the business units, where the blended teams operate. This grounding in the business units keeps workforce planning focused on corporate goals. Workforce planning really gets traction when it is linked to the line managers who understand business needs and can project their business growth and productivity changes. The time frames for workforce planning at Capital One vary by unit and function. The legal function, for example, is very stable and can easily plan out two to four years. The credit card division, however, is rapidly evolving, so its forecasts stretch out two to four years but are reviewed every quarter. Likewise, the demand for some jobs follows the business cycle. Collections and recoveries work at Capital One was stable and predictable several years ago, for example. "But because of the current economic conditions, this work is now more important, and we had to ramp up very quickly," Schuyler explains.

PART 1

## Managing Demand and Supply

Schuyler refuses to choose between overshooting and undershooting staffing. "The beauty of workforce planning is that it allows the flexibility to be right on target," he says. "We don't have to wait for the next budget cycle to get it right."

That flexibility derives from a more sophisticated approach to planning that looks at a range of possible scenarios about business conditions and then calculates the labor needed to match them. Capital One's workforce planning models allow business leaders to anticipate the talent requirements for each business option and the human resources and labour cost consequences of the choices they make. Especially for companies that are just beginning to implement a workforce planning process, the best approach is to focus first on the critical roles in the organization and then expand out to cover more positions in greater detail. Avoid the tendency to drown managers in data, by breaking the data down on a critical-jobs basis. At Capital One, the workforce planning process reaches down through the entire executive structure for each business unit—five or six levels of leadership plus groups of managers. Business leaders see the talent management costs and consequences of the business options at hand. Each option carries its own implications for internal and external staffing levels, recruiting, training, promotions, engagement, attrition, and total compensation costs over time. More important, workforce planning allows business leaders and line managers to see how different approaches to talent management can actually expand their business options and boost performance. "If workforce planning is done right, human resources can help business leaders think about what their endgame can be," Schuyler says.

## Questions

1. Why do you think it is important for Capital One to calculate the "disengagement" factor of its employees when it comes to workforce planning?
2. What merits do you see to breaking down the planning process by business units through multiple layers of leaders? Do you see any drawbacks of doing so?

**Source:** Excerpted from Fay Hansen, "The Long View," *Workforce Management* 87, no. 7 (April 21, 2008): 1, 19. Used by permission.

---

## CASE STUDY 2

### MATCHING TALENT WITH TASKS: DOLE IMPLEMENTS SUCCESSION

With 61,000 workers in more than 90 countries, Dole Food Company has talent all over the world. Only a few hundred of those employees are in top management at the 151-year-old company. The trouble is, Dole doesn't have comprehensive knowledge of who these managers are or what they can do. If a key job opens up in North America, the business unit leader wouldn't know if the perfect candidate worked in another Dole unit in Canada. Dole has no way to match its top managerial talent with its executive needs.

But that is changing. The highly decentralized company is launching a succession planning process, supported by Web-based software, through which Dole executives hope to rectify their inability to promote the best and the brightest across the corporation. The process itself requires a change of culture and could become an agent for further culture change. "The idea of succession planning is contrary to being highly decentralized," says Sue Hagen, vice president of HR for North American operations, who led the effort.

Hagen talked informally to all corporate executives and the leaders and staffs of each business unit to generate consensus for succession planning for corporate positions—corporate officers, business unit presidents, and their direct reports. "The initial group would be about 100," she says. Next year, another few hundred will be included.

"The reaction was mostly positive," Hagen says. Hagen's next step was to hold a series of in-depth interviews with the executives to determine which succession planning processes were needed and how often they should be conducted. The goal was to reflect as much of their thinking as possible. "One division wanted to review succession plans on their people six times a year. Another didn't want to do it at all," she says. Hagen compromised. Succession planning will be conducted twice a year. She also identified four competencies on which everyone would be evaluated: accountability, business acumen, multifunctionality (cross-training), and vision/originality.

Many human resource management system (HRMS) software suites have an optional succession planning module, but neither Dole nor its business

**CHAPTER 2:** STRATEGY AND HUMAN RESOURCES PLANNING

units have a HRMS. "Since most employees are farm or factory workers, there is not much need for the detailed information a HRMS provides," says Hagen. "It would be overkill. In a way, the succession planning software Dole adopted will become a mini HRMS for top personnel," she adds.

Hagen also wanted an application service provider (ASP) model. Outsourcing, including payroll, is common at Dole. Hagen didn't want to own and support technology, and she didn't want the small corporate information technology staff to have to work on it.

The users of the system—top managers—access the program from the Web with a password. They fill out a résumé, including career interests, and note any mobility restrictions. They assess themselves on the four competencies. When they are done, the system automatically notifies their manager, who does an assessment and indicates whether he or she thinks the individual could be promoted. The manager also assesses overall potential and the risk of losing the user. This assessment then goes automatically to the division head, then to the divisional HR director, and then to Hagen. Hagen will use the information to create a career development plan for each individual, including seminars she'll organize. She'll also direct business unit leaders to potential candidates in other units when they have appropriate openings. "The beauty is, for the first time we'll have a database that ties together these talent metrics and can serve as a clearinghouse for people available for opportunities," Hagen says. "Dole's corporate management hopes all business units will eventually adopt similar succession planning processes and software," Hagen says. "I view this as a pilot, a very visible pilot," she says. "To get the buy-in of individual business units, we'll show them that this was adopted by their senior management and that it works."

## Questions

1. Why do you think companies like Dole need succession planning?
2. Do you see any disadvantage of "automating" succession planning?

---

**Sources:** Excerpted from Bill Roberts, "Matching Talent with Tasks: Dole Implements Succession Planning to Get Ready for Changes at the Top," *HR Magazine* 47, no. 11 (November 2002): 91–95. Reprinted with permission of *HR Magazine*. Published by the Society for Human Resource Management, Alexandria, VA.

## NOTES AND REFERENCES

1. Chistopher Rees, Hasanah Johari, "Senior Managers' Perceptions of the *HRM* Function during Times of Strategic Organizational Change," *Journal of Organizational Change Management* 23, no 2. (2010): 517.

2. "The Importance of HR," *HRfocus* 73, no. 3 (March 1996): 14; "Retiring Workforce, Widening Skills Gap, Exodus of 'Critical Talent' Threaten Companies: Deloitte Survey," *Canadian Corporate News* (February 15, 2005); Brian E. Becker and Mark A. Huselid, "Strategic Human Resources Management: Where Do We Go From Here?" *Journal of Management* 32, no. 6 (January 2006): 898–925; Jack Welch, "The 'But' Economy," *Wall Street Journal* (October 30, 2003).

3. Scott A. Snell, Mark Shadur, and Patrick M. Wright, "Human Resources Strategy: The Era of Our Ways," in M. A. Hitt, R. E. Freeman, and J. S. Harrison (eds.), *Handbook of Strategic Management* (Oxford, UK: Blackwell, 2002), 627–649; Patrick M. Wright, Benjamin Dunford, and Scott A. Snell, "Human Resources and the Resource-Based View of the Firm," *Journal of Management* 27, no. 6 (2002): 701–721; "What's Affecting HR Operations? Globalization, Sustainability, and Talent," *HRfocus* 84, no. 8 (August 2007): 8; Doris Sims, "Do You Know Where Your Talent Is?" *Training* 45, no. 1 (January 2008): 42–46.

4. "The Importance of HR," 14. For data from a similar survey conducted in Canada, see David Brown, "HR's Role in Business Strategy: Still a Lot of Work to Be Done," *Canadian HR Reporter* 14, no. 19 (November 5, 2001): 1–20; "How Should the HR Dept. of 2004 Be Structured?" *Human Resource Department Management Report*, no. 3 (November 2003): 1.

5. T. J. Watson, Jr., *A Business and Its Beliefs: The Ideas That Helped Build IBM* (New York: McGraw-Hill, 1963).

6. James W. Walker, "Integrating the Human Resource Function with the Business," *Human Resource Planning* 14, no. 2 (1996): 59–77; James W. Walker, "Perspectives," *Human Resource Planning* 25, no. 1 (2002): 12–14.

7. Patrick Wright, Gary McMahan, Scott Snell, and Barry Gerhart, "Comparing Line and HR Executives' Perceptions of HR Effectiveness: Services, Roles, and Contributions," *Human Resource Management* 40, no. 2 (2001): 111–123; Ryan Langlois, "Fairmont Hotels: Business Strategy Starts with People," *Canadian HR Reporter* 14, no. 19 (November 5, 2001): 19–25.

8. Bala Iyer, "Deconstructing Google," *Computerworld* 42, no. 15 (April 7, 2008): 32–33.

9. Jay J. Jamrog and Miles H. Overholt, "Building a Strategic HR Function: Continuing the Evolution,"

*Human Resource Planning* 27, no. 1 (March 2004): 51; Gary L. Nielson, Karla L. Martin, and Elizabeth Powers, "The Secrets to Successful Strategy Execution," *Harvard Business Review* 86, no. 6 (June 2008): 60–70.

10. For example, see U.S. Department of Labor, Bureau of Labor Statistics, Geographic Profiles of Employment and Unemployment. The data and information are accessible via the Office of Employment Projections home page at http://www.bls.gov/emp.

11. J. B. Quinn, "The Intelligent Enterprise: A New Paradigm," *Academy of Management Executive* 6, no. 4 (2002): 48–63.

12. For more information on methods to identify a firm's core capabilities, see Khalid Hafeez, YanBing Zhang, and Naila Malak, "Core Competence for Sustainable Competitive Advantage: A Structured Methodology for Identifying Core Competence," *IEEE Transactions on Engineering Management* 49, no. 1 (February 2002): 28–35; Quinn, "The Intelligent Enterprise," 48–63; Jane Wollman Rusoff, "Outsourced Solutions: Brokerage Firms Looking to Focus on Their Core Competencies Find the Most Value in a Resource-Rich Clearing Partner," *Research* 27, no. 11 (November 2004): 37–40.

13. Snell, Shadur, and Wright," Human Resources Strategy," 627–649; Wright, Dunford, and Snell, "Human Resources and the Resource-Based View of the Firm," 701–721; David Collis and Cynthia Montgomery, "Competing on Resources," *Harvard Business Review* 86, no. 7/8 (July–August 2008): 140–150; Susan Cantrell, "The Work Force of One," *The Wall Street Journal* 249, no. 140 (June 16, 2007): R10.

14. D. P. Lepak and S. A. Snell, "The Human Resource Architecture: Toward a Theory of Human Capital Development and Allocation," *Academy of Management Review* 24, no. 1 (1999): 31–48; David Lepak and Scott Snell, "Examining the Human Resource Architecture: The Relationship among Human Capital, Employment, and Human Resource Configurations," *Journal of Management* 24, no. 1 (January 1999): 31; Mike Berry, "HR Must Push for Change to Drive Human Capital Strategy," *Personnel Today* (April 6, 2004): 4; Brian E. Becker and Mark A. Huselid, "A Players or A Positions? The Strategic Logic of Workforce Management," *Harvard Business Review* 83, no. 12 (December 2005): 110–117.

15. James Clawson, *Level Three Leadership: Betting Below the Surface*, 4th ed. (Upper Saddle River, NJ: Prentice Hall, 2008).

16. Jennifer Laabs, "The HR Side of Sears' Comeback," *Workforce* 78, no. 3 (March 1999): 24–29.

17. Joseph F. Castellan and Susan S. Lightle, "Using Cultural Audits to Assess Tone at the Top," *CPA Journal* 75, no. 2 (February 2005): 6–11.

18. Stephenie Overman, "Gearing Up for Tomorrow's Workforce," *HRfocus* 76, no. 2 (February 1999): 1, 15;

Kathryn Tyler, "Evaluate Your Next Move," *HR Magazine* 46, no. 11 (November 2001): 66–71; Bill Leonard, "Turnover at the Top," *HR Magazine* 46, no. 5 (May 2001): 46–52.

19. Carolyn Hirschman, "Putting Forecasting in Focus," *HR Magazine* 52, no. 3 (March 2007): 44–49.

20. "Talent Management: Now It's the Top Priority for CEOs & Their Organizations," *HRfocus* 85, no. 2 (February 2008): 8–9; "Finding Top Talent," *Community Banker* 17, no. 4 (April 2008): 15; Paul Bernthal and Richard Wellins, "Trends in Leader Development and Succession," *Human Resource Planning* 29, no. 2 (2006): 31–40; Sarah Needleman, "Demand Rises for Talent-Management Software," *The Wall Street Journal* 251, no. 12 (January 15, 2008): B8.

21. Robert Kaplan and David Norton, *Strategy Maps: Converting Intangible Assets into Tangible Outcomes* (Boston: Harvard Business School Press, 2006): Chapter 8.

22. John Huey, "Outlaw Flyboy CEOs," *Fortune* 142, no. 11 (November 13, 2000): 237–250; "Visions of the Future," *Human Resources* (January 2008): special section, 22.

23. Brian Becker, Mark Huselid, and Dave Ulrich. *The HR Scorecard: Linking People, Strategy and Performance* (Cambridge, MA: Harvard Business School Press, 2001). See also Shari Caudron, "How HR Drives Profits," *Workforce* 90, no. 12 (December 2001): 26–31.

24. "A Singular Sensation for Schwab Brokers," *BusinessWeek Online* (January 24, 2002).

25. Larry Bossidy, Ram Charan, and Charles Burck, *Execution: The Art of Getting Things Done* (New York: Crown Business, 2002); Stacey L. Kaplan, "Business Strategy, People Strategy and Total Rewards—Connecting the Dots," *Benefits & Compensation Digest* 44, no. 9 (September 2007): 1–19; Gary L. Neilson, Karla L. Martin, and Elizabeth Power, "The Secrets to Successful Strategy," *Harvard Business Review* 86, no. 6 (June 2008): 60–70; Mark Vickers, "HR Growing Pains: Getting from Awkward to Accomplished," *Human Resource Planning* 30, no. 4 (2007): 20–24.

26. Becker and Huselid, "Strategic Human Resources Management."

27. Kaplan and Norton, *Strategy Maps*.

28. P. M. Wright and S. A. Snell, "Toward a Unifying Framework for Exploring Fit and Flexibility in Strategic Human Resource Management," *Academy of Management Review* 22, no. 4 (1998): 756–772; Snell, Shadur, and Wright, "Human Resources Strategy," 627–649; Wright, Dunford, and Snell, "Human Resources and the Resource-Based View of the Firm," 701–721.

29. R. Sanchez, "Strategic Flexibility in Product Competition," *Strategic Management Journal* 16 (1995): 135–159; Wright and Snell, "Toward a Unifying Framework," 756–772.

# APPENDIX
# Calculating Turnover and Absenteeism

Throughout this chapter, we have emphasized that HRP depends on having an accurate picture of both the supply of and the demand for employees. Two factors, employee turnover and absenteeism, have a direct impact on HRP strategy and recruitment processes. In this appendix, we provide a detailed discussion of turnover and absenteeism, methods for measuring them, and suggestions for managing their impact.

## EMPLOYEE TURNOVER RATES

*Employee turnover* refers simply to the movement of employees out of an organization. It is often cited as one of the factors behind the failure of Canadian employee productivity rates to keep pace with those of foreign competitors. It is also one of the chief determinants of labour supply. Even if everything else about an organization stays the same, as employees turn over, its supply of labour goes down. This involves both direct and indirect costs to the organization.

### COMPUTING THE TURNOVER RATE

The following formula for computing turnover rates is often used:

$$\frac{\text{Number of separations during the month}}{\text{Total number of employees at mid-month}} \times 100$$

Thus, if there were 25 separations during a month and the total number of employees at mid-month was 500, the turnover rate would be

$$\frac{25}{500} \times 100 = 5 \text{ percent}$$

Turnover rates are computed on a regular basis to compare specific units such as departments, divisions, and work groups. Another method of computing the turnover rate is one that reflects only the avoidable separations (S). This rate is computed by subtracting unavoidable separations (US)—for example, due to childbirth, return to school, death, or marriage—from all separations. The formula for this method is as follows:

$$\frac{S - US}{M} \times 100 = T \text{ (turnover rate)}$$

where M represents the total number of employees at mid-month. For example, if there were 25 separations during a month, 5 of which were US, and the total number of employees at mid-month (M) was 500, the turnover rate would be

$$\frac{25 - 5}{500} \times 100 = 4 \text{ percent}$$

In looking at the impact of turnover on HRP and recruitment, it is vitally important to recognize that quantitative rates of turnover are not the only factor to be considered. The *quality* of employees who leave an organization is equally important. If poor employees leave, what experts refer to as "functional turnover," this can prove to be beneficial to the organization. The costs of keeping unproductive workers may be far more than the costs to recruit and train a new, more effective performer.

## DETERMINING THE COSTS OF TURNOVER

Replacing an employee is time consuming and expensive. Costs can generally be broken down into three categories: separation costs for the departing employee, replacement costs, and training costs for the new employee. These costs are conservatively estimated at two to three times the monthly salary of the departing employee and do not include indirect costs such as low productivity prior to quitting and lower morale and overtime for other employees because of the vacated job. Consequently, reducing turnover could result in significant savings to an organization. Highlights in HRM 2.A1 details one organization's costs associated with the turnover of a single computer programmer. Note that the major expense is the cost involved in training a replacement.

# EMPLOYEE ABSENTEEISM RATES

How frequently employees are absent from their work—the absenteeism rate—is also directly related to HRP and recruitment. When employees miss work, the organization incurs direct costs of lost wages and decreased productivity. It is not uncommon for organizations to hire extra workers just to make up for the number of absences totalled across all employees. In addition to these direct costs, indirect costs may underlie excessive absenteeism. A certain amount of absenteeism is, of course, unavoidable. There will always be some who must be absent from work because of sickness, accidents, serious family problems, or other legitimate reasons. However, chronic absenteeism may signal deeper problems in the work environment.

## COMPUTING ABSENTEEISM RATES

Managers should determine the extent of the absenteeism problem, if any, by maintaining individual and departmental attendance records and by computing absenteeism rates. Although there is no universally accepted definition of "absence" or a standard formula for computing absenteeism rates, one frequently used method is

$$\frac{\text{Number of worker-days lost through job absence during period}}{\text{Average number of employees} \times \text{number of workdays}} \times 100$$

If 300 worker-days are lost through job absence during a month having 25 scheduled working days at an organization that employs 500 workers, the absenteeism rate for that month is

$$\frac{300}{500 \times 25} \times 100 = 2.4 \text{ percent}$$

Job absence can be defined as the failure of employees to report to work when their schedules require it, whether or not such failure to report is excused. Scheduled vacations, holidays, and prearranged leaves of absence are not counted as job absence.

# HIGHLIGHTS IN HRM 2.A1

## Costs Associated with the Turnover of One Computer Programmer

Turnover costs = Separation costs + Replacement costs + Training costs

### Separation costs

1. Exit interview = cost for salary and benefits of both interviewer and departing employee during the exit interview = $30 + $30 = $60

2. Administrative and record-keeping action = $30 separation costs = $60 + $30 = $90

### Replacement costs

1. Advertising for job opening = $2,500

2. Preemployment administrative functions and record-keeping action = $100

3. Selection interview = $250

4. Employment tests = $40

5. Meetings to discuss candidates (salary and benefits of managers while participating in meetings) = $250

Replacement costs = $2,500 + $100 + $250 + $40 + $250 = $3,140

### Training costs

1. Booklets, manuals, and reports = $50

2. Education = $240/day for new employee's salary and benefits × 10 days of workshops, seminars, or courses = $2,400

3. One-to-one coaching = ($240/day per new employee + $240/day per staff coach or job expert) × 20 days of one-to-one coaching = $9,600

4. Salary and benefits of new employee until he or she gets "up to par" = $240/day for salary and benefits × 20 days = $4,800

Training costs = $50 + $2,400 + $9,600 + $4,800 = $16,850

Total turnover costs = $90 + $3,140 + $16,850 = $20,080

Source: Adapted from the book *Turning Your Human Resources Department into a Profit Center*™ by Michael Mercer, PhD (Barrington, IL: Castlegate Publishers, Inc.). Copyright 2002, 2012 Michael Mercer, PhD.

## COSTS OF ABSENTEEISM

Traditional accounting and information systems often do not generate data that reflect the costs of absenteeism. Consequently, their usefulness in HRP is often limited. To accentuate the impact of absenteeism on organizational performance, managers should translate the data into dollar costs. A system for computing absenteeism costs for an individual organization is available. Organizations with computerized absence reporting systems should find this additional information easy and inexpensive to generate. The cost of each person hour lost to absenteeism is based on the hourly weighted average salary, costs of employee benefits, supervisory costs, and incidental costs.

For example, XYZ Company, with 1200 employees, has 78,000 person hours lost to absenteeism; the total absence cost is $560,886. When this figure is divided by 1,200 employees, the cost per employee is $467.41. (In this example, we are assuming the absent workers are paid. If absent workers are not paid, their salary figures are omitted from the computation.)

# HIGHLIGHTS IN HRM 3.1

## Retention Strategies

**What can companies do to retain women? Here are seven strategies:**

1. *Equal pay*—People talk about pay, and it is important that women know that they are receiving equal pay for work of equal value.

2. *Flex schedules*—Accommodate women with childcare and eldercare responsibilities by offering them four 10-hour days, half-days, or flexible arrival times.

3. *Forty-hour workweeks*—Many professionals are willing to work and accomplish but unwilling to put in 80-hour weeks.

4. *Part-time and job sharing*—This is an ideal solution for new mothers.

5. *Mentoring*—Pair a promising woman professional with a senior manager to help her develop a career strategy.

6. *Focus on the family*—Allow women to get the work done but on a schedule that accommodates their family responsibilities.

7. *Offer opportunities*—All employees will stay in jobs if they are learning.

Sources: D. De Marco, "Retaining Gen X Women Becoming Crucial," *Canadian HR Reporter* (December 3, 2007), vol. 20, iss. 31: 31; A. Tomlinson, "Wall Street Rougher than Bay Street," *Canadian HR Reporter* 15, no. 5 (March 11, 2002): 1, 14.

---

men. The census found that women working full-time earned 85 cents for every dollar earned by men in 2005. (StatsCan did find that in cases of identical education, experience, and occupation, men and women earn the same.[3])

Several strategies for the retention of women can be found in Highlights in HRM 3.1.

According to the 2006 Census, over 1 million people self-identify as Aboriginal in Canada, approximately 3.8 percent of the total Canadian population. Among people who identify themselves as Aboriginal, 60 percent are First Nations, 33 percent are Métis, and 4 percent are Inuit. Their unemployment rate is higher than the national unemployment rate. In 2006, 45 percent of Aboriginal people aged 25 to 54 were postsecondary graduates, 14 percent had a trade credential, 19 percent had a college diploma, and 8 percent had a university degree. Employment rates tend to rise with higher educational attainment.[4] The median income for the Canadian population is $29,000, whereas the median for Aboriginal people is $18,000. In western Canada, they will account for a substantial portion of labour market growth. However, many Aboriginal people face major barriers to employment, which are often compounded by low educational achievement and lack of job experience, as well as by language and cultural barriers. In urban centres, many Aboriginal workers are concentrated in low-paying, unstable employment. Economic self-sufficiency and participation in the economy are seen as essential to Aboriginal development. Interestingly, Aboriginal values such as cooperation and consensus decision making have become more closely aligned with management approaches.[5] A study in one Canadian company showed that the creation of an Aboriginal networking group, based on cultural concepts such as talking circles and collective decision making, resulted in Aboriginal people with strong feelings of belonging and a sense of professional purpose, and this in turn made them willing to help recruit other Aboriginal people.[6]

It is estimated that one in seven Canadians has a disability. This rate increases with age, with about 5 percent of those between 15 and 24 and 18 percent of those aged 45 to 64 having a disability. People with disabilities represent 14 percent of Canada's population, but, again, their workforce representation is low at 1.6 percent.[7] About one-third of those with disabilities became disabled as adults,

# HIGHLIGHTS IN HRM 3.2

## Accessibility

A candidate comes to your office for an employment interview. Because of a vision impairment, she uses a long white cane to navigate. You approach her to guide her to the interview room. Do you

a) take her arm and guide her to the room?

b) suggest that she follow your voice?

c) ask her if she needs assistance?

If you don't know the answer (it's c), training is available through Ontario's new mandatory accessibility standard, which came into force for private organizations in 2012. The customer service training program teaches how to deal with people with disabilities, what a disability is, and the different types of disabilities. It also teaches how to accommodate employees with disabilities that conflict (a person with a service animal seated next to someone who is allergic to animals). It means rethinking general rules that discriminate against an individual. For example, some professors do not allow laptops in the classroom, but a person with hearing disabilities may require one to participate. The professor is encouraged to allow everyone to have a laptop rather than make an exception for one individual.

Source: Anonymous "Accessibility" *HR Professional*, May /June 2010, page 24–27. Canadian Council in Social Development and Accessibility for Ontarians with disabilities, Act 2005

resulting in 70 percent of them being forced to make career changes. People with disabilities face attitudinal barriers, physical demands that are unrelated to actual job requirements, and inadequate access to the technical and human support systems that would make productive employment possible. Seventy percent of those with disabilities need some kind of workplace accommodation, and in 80 percent of the cases, the cost is less than $500.[8] Employers can seek to redress attitudinal barriers by focusing on abilities, not disabilities. Highlights in HRM 3.2 provides an example of accommodation.

The visible minority population in Canada has experienced a growth rate of 27.2 percent since the 2001 Census, compared to an overall population growth of 5.4 percent. Visible minorities represent about 16.2 percent of Canadians and 15.4 percent of the labour force. Visible minority groups vary in their labour force profiles and in their regional distributions. Studies have shown that Latin Americans and Southeast Asians experience lower-than-average incomes, higher rates of unemployment, and reduced access to job interviews, even when they have the same qualifications as other candidates. See Highlights in HRM 3.3 for a study documenting this. Systemic barriers that negatively affect employment for visible minorities include culturally biased aptitude tests, a lack of recognition of foreign credentials, and excessively high language requirements. Recent statistics indicate that although visible minorities—73 percent of recent immigrants are visible minorities—tend to be better educated, they also have the highest unemployment rates.[9] The unemployment rate of recent immigrants (12.1 percent) was still nearly twice that of the Canadian-born population (6.4 percent).[10] As such, there are targeted efforts to recruit them to ensure representation.

Figure 3.1 shows the workforce representation of the designated groups in the Canadian population. Ethics in HRM describes some of the issues in employment equity.

## BENEFITS OF EMPLOYMENT EQUITY

Employment equity makes good business sense. It contributes to the bottom line by broadening the base of qualified individuals for employment, training, and promotions and by helping employers avoid costly human rights complaints. Employment equity enhances an organization's ability to attract and keep the

### Using the Internet

WorkAble Solutions provides job seekers and employers with information on the benefits of hiring persons with disabilities

http://www.workablesolutionsbc.ca

# HIGHLIGHTS IN HRM 3.3

## What's in a Name?

Metropolis, an immigration and diversity research network, sent out 6,000 résumés tailored to the job requirements of 2,000 online postings from employers across 20 occupational categories. These included administrative, financial, marketing, programming, and retail. All résumés included a university degree and two to four years' experience. The only difference on these résumés was the name of the applicant. Some had names like Tara Singh, and others had names like Emily Brown. The results were a wake-up call for Canadians who pride themselves on being less biased than other nationalities. Those with English names received callbacks 16 percent of the time, compared to 11 percent for applicants with Pakistani, Indian, and Chinese names who had the same level of education and experience. According to the study's author, UBC Economics Professor Oeropoulos, "The findings suggest that a distinct foreign-sounding name may be a

significant disadvantage on the job market—even if you are a second- or third-generation citizen." He adds: "In cases where the employer requires the hire to be very good at English, then consciously or unconsciously, they may have a concern when looking at their résumé. The other possibility is preference-based discrimination: the employer, consciously or unconsciously, prefers to have applicants of the same ethnicity working for them."

Those who had been educated outside Canada received callbacks 8 percent of the time and those who had no Canadian work experience only 5 percent, confirming that Canadian work experience is very important to employers. Whereas immigrants had unemployment rates of 11.5 percent in 2006 (compared to 4.9 percent for the Canadian-born population), second-generation immigrants of Chinese and Indian origin have statistically above-average incomes and educations. A new online tool, Roadmap, from the Toronto Region Immigrant Employment Council, will help employers hire, integrate, and retain skilled immigrants. For more information, visit http://www.hireimmigrants.ca/roadmap.

Sources: M. Jimenez, "Right Resume, Wrong Name," *The Globe and Mail*, May 21, 2009, I1; University of British Columbia, "Employers Discriminate Against Applicants with Non-English Names, UBC Study Suggests," *NewsRx Health & Science* (June 21, 2009), 198; D. Karp, "Job Seekers with Asian Names Face Discrimination; Canadians with English Names Are Called Back More Often for Job Interviews, UBC Study Finds," *The Vancouver Sun*, May 21, 2009, A1.

best-qualified employees, which results in greater access to a broader base of skills. It also enhances employee morale by offering special measures such as flexible work schedules and work sharing. Finally, it improves the organization's image in the community.[11]

The *Canadian Charter of Rights and Freedoms,* the federal Canadian *Human Rights Act,* and pay equity and employment equity acts are the governing pieces of legislation dealing with employment equity.

## FIGURE 3.1

REPRESENTATION OF DESIGNATED GROUPS IN THE LABOUR FORCE

|  | Representation in the Canadian Population (%) | Representation in the Workforce (%) |
| --- | --- | --- |
| *Women* | 50.9 | 43.0 |
| *Aboriginal people* | 3.8 | 2.6 |
| *People with disabilities* | 14.3 | 1.6 |
| *Members of visible minorities* | 16.2 | 15.4 |

**Source:** Adapted from 97-562-XCB2006017, referring to "Labour Force Activity (8), Visible Minority Groups (15), Immigrant Status and Period of Immigration (9), Highest Certificate, Diploma or Degree (7), Age Groups (9) and Sex (3) for the Population 15 Years and Over of Canada, Provinces, Territories, Census Metropolitan Areas and Census Agglomerations, 2006 Census-20% Sample Data (table). Topic-based tabulation. 2006 Census of Population." 89-628-XIE, referring to "Participation and Activity Limitation Survey 2006: Tables. Ottawa: Statistics Canada, 2007" 97-558-XIE2006001, referring to "Aboriginal Peoples in Canada in 2006: Inuit, Métis and First Nations, 2006 Census: Findings"

# ETHICS IN HRM

## Ethics: Equality or Equity

The Public Works department of the federal government sent its managers an email telling them that persons recruited externally must be from designated groups. The federal Department of Fisheries ran an ad on the government's website that stated explicitly that those who can apply are "persons working or residing in Canada and Canadian citizens living abroad, who are members of the visible minority groups." *The Employment Equity Act* defines visible minorities as being persons, other than Aboriginal people, who are non-Caucasian in race or non-white in colour. The decision to restrict applicants to visible minorities is part of the government's efforts to have its employees look more like the Canadian population. About 16.2 percent of Canadians identify themselves as visible minorities, and they represent about 15.4 percent of the labour market. However, in 2006, only 7.3 percent worked in the public service. Therefore, the government decreed that about 3 percent of job postings would be restricted to visible minorities.

Unlike the United States, quotas are not in place. But words such as *benchmarks*, *targets*, and *goals* have the same impact. Critics argue that candidates should be judged on merit, not colour, and that other programs to increase minority candidates would be better: provide more education and training for minorities or create an office culture that values diversity. The public service has a good track record in increasing the number of francophones and women, and restricted competitions may not be the best route. But the commissioner of the public service counters that treating all people the same way does not always lead to equitable results, and special measures are necessary.

Sources: T. Blackwell, "White Males Need Not Apply," *The National Post*, November 19, 2005: A1; E. Greenspon, "Don't Apply," *The Globe and Mail*, May 30, 2003: A16; M. Wente, "Whites Need Not Apply," *The Globe and Mail*, May 29, 2003: A21.

## THE LEGAL FRAMEWORK

### THE *CANADIAN CHARTER OF RIGHTS AND FREEDOMS*

OUTCOME 2

The *Constitution Act* of 1982, which contains the *Canadian Charter of Rights and Freedoms,* is the cornerstone of equity legislation. The *Charter* guarantees some fundamental rights to every Canadian, including

- Fundamental freedoms (s. 2) that comprise the standard rights of freedom of speech, press, assembly, association, and religion
- Democratic rights (ss. 3 to 5), covering franchise rights
- Mobility rights (s. 6), concerning the right to move freely from province to province for the purposes of residence and/or employment
- Legal rights (ss. 7 to 14), conferring standard procedural rights in criminal proceedings
- Equality rights (s. 15), guaranteeing no discrimination by law on the grounds of race, ethnic origin, colour, religion, sex, age, sexual orientation, marital status, citizenship, Aboriginal residence, or mental and physical ability
- Language rights (ss. 16 to 23)[12]

Although the *Charter* has offered many Canadians opportunities with regard to their own individual rights and responsibilities, it has also been a source of disappointment. The enactment of the *Charter* created high expectations on the part of various groups, especially unions, which believed that under Section 2, all employees would have a fundamental right to associate, to bargain collectively, and to strike. However, in 1987, the Supreme Court of Canada, in ruling on a challenge to federal public-sector laws relating to compulsory arbitration, back-to-work legislation, and wage restraint legislation,

Lisa S./Shutterstock

declared that Section 2 of the *Charter* does not include the right to bargain collectively and to strike. In the Court's view, these were not fundamental freedoms but rather statutory rights created and regulated by legislation. As a result of this ruling, governments can weaken the collective bargaining process by limiting salary increases, legislating strikers back to work, and imposing compulsory arbitration. However, a 2007 case in British Columbia ruled that the *Charter* does protect the right to bargain collectively. It is important to note that the *Charter* protects only the right of government and public-sector employees, not private-sector employees.

## THE *CANADIAN HUMAN RIGHTS ACT* (CHRA)

The *Canadian Human Rights Act* (CHRA) was passed by Parliament on July 14, 1977, and became effective in March 1978. This act proclaims that every individual should have an equal opportunity with other individuals to make for himself or herself the life that he or she is able and wishes to have, consistent with his or her duties and obligations as a member of society, without being hindered in or prevented from doing so by discriminatory practices based on race, national or ethnic origin, colour, religion, age, sex or marital status, or convictions for an offence for which a pardon has been granted or by discriminatory employment practices based on physical handicap.[13] The act applies to all federal government departments and agencies, to Crown corporations, and to other businesses and industries under federal jurisdiction, such as banks, airlines, railway companies, and insurance and communications companies.

For those areas not under federal jurisdiction (the vast majority of workplaces), protection may be available under provincial human rights laws. Provincial laws, although very similar to federal ones, differ from province to province. Every province and territory has a human rights act (or code), and each has jurisdiction prohibiting discrimination in the workplace.

When looking for employees,
employers need to assess abilities.

**bona fide occupational qualification (BFOQ)**
A justifiable reason for discrimination based on business reasons of safety or effectiveness

The prohibited grounds of discrimination in employment include race, religion, sex, age, national or ethnic origin, physical handicap, and marital status (see Figure 3.2 for a complete listing). Employers are permitted to discriminate if employment preferences are based on a **bona fide occupational qualification (BFOQ)** or BFOR (bona fide occupational requirement), and it is not possible to accommodate the employee without causing undue hardship. A BFOQ is justified

## FIGURE 3.2

### PROHIBITED GROUNDS OF DISCRIMINATION IN CANADA

This document provides comparative information on the grounds of discrimination covered by federal, provincial, and territorial human rights legislation in Canada. In some instances, prohibited grounds for employment differ from those for the provision of services.

| Prohibited Ground | Jurisdiction | Comments |
|---|---|---|
| **Race or colour** | | |
| Employment | All jurisdictions | |
| Provision of Service | All jurisdictions | |
| **Religion** | | |
| Employment | All jurisdictions | Yukon's Act reads "religion or creed, or religious belief, religious association or religious activity" |
| Provision of Service | All jurisdictions | Yukon's Act reads "religion or creed, or religious belief, religious association or religious activity" |
| **Physical or mental disability** | | |
| Employment | All jurisdictions | Quebec uses the phrase "handicap or use of any means to palliate a handicap" |
| Provision of Service | All jurisdictions | Quebec uses the phrase "handicap or use of any means to palliate a handicap" |

| Prohibited Ground | Jurisdiction | Comments |
|---|---|---|
| **Dependence on alcohol or drugs** | | |
| Employment | All except Yukon and Northwest Territories | Policy to accept complaints in British Columbia, Alberta, Saskatchewan, Manitoba, Ontario, New Brunswick, and Prince Edward Island<br>Included in "handicap" ground in Quebec<br>Previous dependence only in New Brunswick and Nova Scotia |
| Provision of Service | All except Yukon, Northwest Territories, and Quebec | Previous dependence only in New Brunswick and Nova Scotia<br>Included in "handicap" ground in Quebec |
| **Age** | | |
| Employment | All jurisdictions | British Columbia: 19–65<br>Alberta: 18+<br>Saskatchewan: 18–64<br>Ontario: 18–65<br>Newfoundland: 19–65<br>Quebec: except as provided for by law |
| Provision of Service | All except British Columbia, Alberta, and Newfoundland | For tenancy only in British Columbia; Saskatchewan does not include accommodation<br>In Ontario, applies to those 18 years and older, although 16- and 17-year-olds who have left the care of parents or guardians are protected regarding accommodation<br>In Quebec, except as provided for by law |
| **Sex (includes pregnancy and childbirth)** | | |
| Employment | All jurisdictions | British Columbia includes breast feeding<br>Alberta uses the term "gender"<br>Manitoba includes gender-determined characteristics<br>Ontario recognizes the protection of transgendered persons and accepts complaints related to "gender identity";<br>Ontario accepts complaints related to female genital mutilation<br>In Quebec, pregnancy as such is considered a ground of discrimination |
| Provision of Service | All jurisdictions | Alberta uses the term "gender"<br>Manitoba includes gender-determined characteristics<br>Ontario recognizes the protection of transgendered persons and accepts complaints related to "gender identity";<br>Ontario accepts complaints related to female genital mutilation<br>In Quebec, pregnancy as such is considered a ground of discrimination |
| **Marital status** | | |
| Employment | All jurisdictions | Quebec uses the term "civil status" |
| Provision of Service | All jurisdictions | Quebec uses the term "civil status" |

*continued*

| Prohibited Ground | Jurisdiction | Comments |
|---|---|---|
| **Family status** | | |
| Employment | All except New Brunswick and Newfoundland | Saskatchewan defines being in a parent–child relationship<br>Quebec uses the term "civil status" |
| Provision of Service | All except New Brunswick and Newfoundland | Saskatchewan defines as being in a parent–child relationship<br>Quebec uses the term "civil status" |
| **Sexual orientation** | | |
| Employment | All jurisdictions | The Supreme Court of Canada read sexual orientation into the *Alberta Human Rights, Citizenship, and Multiculturalism Act* in 1998 |
| Provision of Service | All jurisdictions | The Supreme Court of Canada read sexual orientation into the *Alberta Human Rights, Citizenship, and Multiculturalism Act* in 1998 |
| **National or ethnic origin (including linguistic background)** | | |
| Employment | All except British Columbia and Alberta | Saskatchewan and Northwest Territories use the term "nationality"<br>Ontario's Code includes both "ethnic origin" and "citizenship" |
| Provision of Service | All except British Columbia and Alberta | Saskatchewan and Northwest Territories use the term "nationality"<br>Ontario's Code includes both "ethnic origin" and "citizenship" |
| **Ancestry or place of origin** | | |
| Employment | Yukon, British Columbia, Alberta, Saskatchewan, Manitoba, Northwest Territories, Ontario, and New Brunswick | |
| Provision of Service | Yukon, British Columbia, Alberta, Saskatchewan, Manitoba, Northwest Territories, Ontario, and New Brunswick | |
| **Language** | | |
| Employment | Yukon, Ontario, and Quebec | Ontario accepts complaints on the grounds of ancestry, ethnic origin, place of origin, and race<br>New Brunswick will accept language-related complaints filed on the basis of ancestry, although not an enumerated ground |
| Provision of Service | Yukon, Ontario, and Quebec | Ontario accepts complaints on the grounds of ancestry, ethnic origin, place of origin, and race<br>New Brunswick will accept language-related complaints filed on the basis of ancestry, although not an enumerated ground |
| **Social condition or origin** | | |
| Employment | Quebec, Northwest Territories | New Brunswick and Newfoundland |

| Prohibited Ground | Jurisdiction | Comments |
|---|---|---|
| Provision of Service | Quebec, Northwest Territories, New Brunswick and Newfoundland | |
| **Source of income** | | |
| Employment | Alberta, Saskatchewan, Manitoba, Quebec, Prince Edward Island, and Nova Scotia | Defined as "receipt of public assistance" in Saskatchewan <br> Included under social condition in Quebec |
| Provision of Service | British Columbia, Alberta, Saskatchewan, Manitoba, Ontario, Prince Edward Island, and Nova Scotia | Applies to tenancy only (not public services or facilities) in British Columbia <br> Defined as "receipt of social assistance" in Saskatchewan <br> Ontario bans discrimination in accommodation on the grounds of receipt of public assistance <br> Included under social condition in Quebec <br> Applies to occupancy or accommodation only in Nova Scotia |
| **Assignment, attachment, or seizure of pay** | | |
| Employment | Newfoundland | Included under social condition in Quebec |
| Provision of Service | Newfoundland | Included under social condition in Quebec |
| **Based on association** | | |
| Employment | Yukon, Manitoba, Ontario, New Brunswick, Nova Scotia, Northwest Territories, and Prince Edward Island | Northwest Territories has prohibition on basis of "political association" |
| Provision of Service | Yukon, Manitoba, Ontario, New Brunswick, Nova Scotia, Northwest Territories, and Prince Edward Island | Northwest Territories has prohibition on basis of "political association" |
| **Political belief** | | |
| Employment | Yukon, British Columbia, Manitoba, Quebec, Nova Scotia, Prince Edward Island, New Brunswick, and Newfoundland | Newfoundland has prohibition on basis of "political opinion" |
| Provision of Service | Yukon, Manitoba, Quebec, Nova Scotia, Prince Edward Island, New Brunswick, and Newfoundland | Yukon includes political activity and political association <br> Newfoundland has prohibition on basis of "political opinion" |
| **Record of criminal conviction** | | |
| Employment | Yukon and Quebec | Yukon's Act reads "criminal charges or criminal record" |
| Provision of Service | Yukon, British Columbia, Quebec, and Prince Edward Island | Yukon's Act reads "criminal charges or criminal record" |
| **Pardoned conviction** | | |
| Employment | Federal, Yukon, and Northwest Territories | |
| Provision of Service | Federal, Yukon, and Northwest Territories | |

**Source:** Prohibited grounds of discrimination in Canada 2006 http://www.chrc-ccdp.ca/publications/pgd_mdi-eng.aspx Canadian Human Rights Commission. Reproduced with the permission of the Minister of Public Works and Government Services, 2012.

**Using the Internet**

The Canadian Human Rights Commission deals with complaints concerning discriminatory practices covered by legislation. This site includes a summary of the duty to accommodate

**http://www.chrc-ccdp.ca /preventing_discrimination /toc_tdm-en.asp**

if the employer can establish necessity for business operations. In other words, differential treatment is not discrimination if there is a justifiable reason. For example, according to Ontario provincial legislation, adherence to the tenets of the Roman Catholic Church was deemed a BFOQ for employment as a teacher in a Roman Catholic school.[14] Business necessity also relates to the safe and efficient operation of an organization. There is an ongoing debate as to whether male guards should be allowed to work in women's prisons and whether members of the Sikh religion, whose religion mandates the wearing of turbans, must wear hard hats at construction sites. The duty to accommodate is an important part of human rights legislation and is discussed more thoroughly later in the chapter, under special measures and reasonable accommodation.

## Enforcement of the *Canadian Human Rights Act*

The Canadian Human Rights Commission (CHRC) deals with complaints concerning discriminatory practices covered by the *Canadian Human Rights Act*. The CHRC may choose to act on its own if it believes that sufficient grounds exist for a finding of discrimination. It also has the power to issue guidelines interpreting the act.

Individuals have a right to file a complaint if they feel they have been discriminated against. (The CHRC may refuse to accept a complaint if it has not been filed within a prescribed period of time, if it is deemed trivial, or if it was filed in bad faith.) The complainant must first complete a written report describing the discriminatory action. A CHRC representative reviews the facts and determines whether the claim is legitimate. Once a complaint has been accepted by the CHRC, an investigator is assigned the task of gathering more facts from both the complainant and the accused. The investigator then submits a report to the CHRC recommending a finding of either substantiation or nonsubstantiation of the allegation. If the allegation is substantiated, a settlement may be arranged in the course of the investigation. If the parties are unable to reach agreement, a human rights tribunal consisting of up to three members may be appointed to further investigate the complaint. If the tribunal finds that a discriminatory practice did take place or that the victim's feelings or self-respect have suffered as a result of the practice, it may order the person or organization responsible to compensate the victim. Former employees of Majestic Electronics received $300,000 in compensation because they were harassed after they refused to obey the racist and sexist orders of the company president.[15]

Any person who obstructs an investigation or a tribunal, or who fails to comply with the terms of a settlement, can be found guilty of an offence, which may be punishable by a fine and/or jail sentence. If the guilty party is an employer or an employee organization, the fine can be as high as $50,000.[16]

## THE ENFORCEMENT OF PROVINCIAL HUMAN RIGHTS LAWS

Provincial human rights laws are enforced in a manner very similar to that of the federal system. At the provincial level, employers tend to be small and medium-sized businesses, many of which lack an HR professional who is knowledgeable about human rights legislation. Employers and employees alike may have little experience in matters of discrimination. The Ontario legislation now permits employees to file complaints directly to the Human Rights Tribunal.

The majority of cases are resolved at the investigation stage. If no agreement can be reached, the case is presented to the province's human rights commission. The members of the commission study the evidence and then submit a report to the minister in charge of administering human rights legislation. The minister may appoint an independent board of inquiry, which has powers similar to those of a tribunal at the federal level. Failure to comply with the remedies prescribed by the board of inquiry may result in prosecution in provincial court. Individuals may be fined between $500 and $1,000 and organizations or groups between $1,000 and $10,000. These levies vary from province to province.

## PAY EQUITY

As a result of a 1978 amendment to the *Canadian Human Rights Act,* pay equity became enacted as law in the federal jurisdiction. Pay equity law makes it illegal for employers to discriminate against individuals on the basis of job content. The goal of pay equity is to eliminate the historical wage gap between men and women and to ensure that salary ranges reflect the value of the work performed. In 2010, women aged 15 and over who had employment income made 85 cents for every $1 earned by their male counterparts (the gap was smaller for younger women).[17]

OUTCOME 3

By definition, pay equity means equal pay for work of equal value. It is based on two principles. The *first* is equal pay for equal work—pay equality.[18] Male and female workers must be paid the same wage rate for doing identical work. The *second* is equal pay for similar or substantially similar work (equal pay for work of comparable worth). This means that male and female workers must be paid the same wage rate for jobs of a similar nature that may have different titles (e.g., "nurse's aide" and "orderly"). Professor Marc Mentzer at the Edwards School of Business at the University of Saskatchewan suggests that these key points help in understanding the differences between pay equality and pay equity:

- Pay equality (in which employers are required to pay women the same as men doing the same job) is required by law in every jurisdiction in Canada. Pay equality is about fair pay for individual women employees. For example, a female electrician must be paid the same as a male electrician.

- Pay equity is about fair pay for entire occupations, which are dissimilar, within an organization, such as comparing nurses (as a group) to electricians. Pay equity is required of all federally regulated employers, both private and public sectors. Provincially, it varies from Ontario and Quebec adopting pay equity legislation that applies to both private-sector and public-sector employees to other provinces, such as Saskatchewan, that have no pay equity legislation at all.

Implementation of pay equity is based on comparing the work of female-dominated job classes to the value of work performed in male-dominated jobs by males. Comparisons require the use of a gender-neutral, unbiased comparison system to evaluate the jobs in an establishment.[19] Comparisons must be based on the amount and type of skill, effort, and responsibility needed to perform the job and on the working conditions where it is performed. The comparison must be done in such a way that the characteristics of "male" jobs, such as heavy lifting and "dirty" working conditions, are valued fairly in comparison with the characteristics of "female" jobs, such as manual dexterity and caring for others.[20]

The federal pay equity legislation applies to that section of the workforce under its jurisdiction and covers all organizations regardless of the number of employees. The federal pay equity system is complaint based, meaning that complaints can be raised by an employee, a group of employees, or a bargaining agent.[21] Some recent decisions included compensating high school secretaries at rates similar to the male job class of audiovisual technicians and comparing a female job class of law clerk to that of the male job class of investigator.[22] However, at the time of publication, there are plans to replace this system with a proactive model, such as the one used in Ontario, where employers take the initiative to ensure that jobs of equal value receive equal pay. A more comprehensive review of pay equity is provided in Chapter 9.

# THE *EMPLOYMENT EQUITY ACT* (1995)

| OUTCOME 4 | Employers and Crown corporations that have 100 employees or more and that are regulated under the *Canada Labour Code* must implement employment equity and report on their results. Under the act, the employer is required to |

- Provide its employees with a questionnaire that allows them to indicate whether they belong to one of the four designated groups
- Identify jobs in which the percentage of members of designated groups falls below their availability in the labour market
- Communicate information on employment equity to its employees and consult and collaborate with employee representatives
- Identify possible barriers in existing employment systems that may be limiting the employment opportunities of members of designated groups
- Develop an employment equity plan aimed at promoting an equitable workplace
- Make all reasonable efforts to implement its plan
- Monitor, review, and revise its plan from time to time
- Prepare an annual report on its employment equity data and activities[23]

The concept of employment equity is rooted in the wording of federal and provincial employment standards legislation, human rights codes, and the *Charter*. Employment equity involves identifying and removing systemic barriers to employment opportunities that adversely affect women, visible minorities, Aboriginal people, and people with disabilities. Employment equity also involves implementing special measures and making reasonable accommodation.[24]

Under the Federal Contractors Program (FCP), contractors who bid for goods and services contracts with the federal government valued at $200,000 or more and that employ 100 people or more, as are required to implement an employment equity program. This is not a law, but contractors that do not cooperate may not be allowed to bid. (For a list of this program's implementation criteria, see Highlights in HRM 3.4.) To assist in the process, the federal government provides professional consulting services to employers throughout Canada regarding how to implement employment equity. Federally regulated employers must conduct a workforce analysis to identify underrepresentation of members of designated groups; review their employment systems, policies, and practices to identify employment barriers; and prepare a plan outlining the steps they will take to remove any identified barriers. Most provinces have similar legislation governing employment equity.

Winners of merit awards for initiatives in employment equity include Scotiabank, for increasing the number of visible minorities in its workforce to 19 percent, and the Saskatchewan Wheat Pool, for its partnerships with the Aboriginal community—particularly its investment in an MBA program in Aboriginal business. In the face of threats to employment equity legislation, employers are showing willingness to keep the practice alive. As Robert Rochon, director of employment equity for National Grocer Co., puts it: "Regardless of any legislative requirement, [employment equity] is a good business decision for us. When you consider the changing face of Canada, it just makes good business sense to reflect the customers that you serve."[25]

## ADMINISTRATION AND ENFORCEMENT OF THE *EMPLOYMENT EQUITY ACT*

Human Resources Development Canada is responsible for administering the FCP. The CHRC is mandated under the *Canadian Human Rights Act*[26] to prohibit discrimination in the establishments of federally regulated businesses.[27]

The CHRC is authorized to conduct on-site compliance reviews. Failure to comply may result in fines ranging from $10,000 for first offenders to $50,000 for repeat offenders.

# HIGHLIGHTS IN HRM 3.4

## Requirements for the Federal Contractors Program

By signing a Certificate of Commitment, Federal Contractors Program employers agree to carry out and keep an employment equity program in their workplace. Here are the Federal Contractors Program requirements:

1. Adopt accountability mechanisms for employment equity and assign a senior official.

2. Communicate to employees regarding employment equity.

3. Consult and collaborate with bargaining agents and/or employee representatives.

4. Collect workforce information.

5. Complete a workforce analysis.

6. Complete an employment systems review.

7. Establish short-term and long-term goals.

8. Adopt measures to remove barriers.

9. Adopt special measures, positive policies and practices, and reasonable accommodation measures.

10. Adopt monitoring procedures.

11. Make reasonable efforts and achieve reasonable progress.

12. Review and revise the employment equity plan.

These 12 requirements specify a number of ongoing activities to do in addition to the need to keep files that provide evidence of completion. Employers who do not fulfill the requirements will be found in noncompliance with the program and may be placed on the List of Ineligible Contractors and be subject to sanctions. By going to the link below, you can click on each of the 12 criteria for more information about the requirements.

Source: Federal Contractors Program 2012 http://www.hrsdc.gc.ca/eng/labour/equality/fcp/requirement.shtml Human Resources and Skills Development Canada. Reproduced with the permission of the Minister of Public Works and Government Services Canada, 2012.

## THE IMPLEMENTATION OF EMPLOYMENT EQUITY IN ORGANIZATIONS

The implementation of employment equity in an organization follows the precepts of any change management program. Thus, successful implementation must employ strategic planning, which must be incorporated into an overall business strategy. The FCP outlined in Highlights in HRM 3.4 provides a good overview of what a plan should incorporate. The process involves six main steps: senior management commitment, data collection and analysis, employment systems review, establishment of a workplan, implementation, and a follow-up process that includes evaluation, monitoring, and revision.

**OUTCOME 5**

### STEP 1: SENIOR MANAGEMENT COMMITMENT

Commitment to an employment equity plan necessitates a top-down strategy. A more supportive culture is created when the CEO or owner–operator publicly introduces written policy describing the organization's commitment to employment equity. This policy must be strategically posted throughout the organization and sent to each employee. For example, the CEO, all members of the board of directors, and staff at the Law Society of Upper Canada are fully committed, and all have received equity and human rights training. The world's largest food service company, Compass Group, has employment equity as a top priority by making it a topic at every board meeting, where workforce data are reviewed and built into the performance scorecard of all managers.[28]

An employment equity policy statement may raise many questions, so it is important to be thorough in this process to keep concerns to a minimum. The policy statement should be supplemented with a communiqué explaining what employment equity is, the rationale for the program, and its implications for current and future employees. Assurances must be given at this time that all information provided will be treated confidentially and will not be used to identify individuals other than for the purpose of employment equity program activities. The communiqué should also list the names of individuals responsible for administering the program and outline any planned activities the employer may deem necessary to establish the program (e.g., analysis of the workforce or of policies and procedures).

This commitment to employees and candidates for employment applies to all aspects of the employment relationship, including recruitment, work assignment, training opportunities, compensation, promotions, transfers, and terminations.

Communication tools may include periodic information sessions, workplace posters, departmental or small-group meetings conducted by line management, orientation and training programs, newsletters, and vehicles such as videos, brochures, employee handbooks, and memos from the union. An innovative approach to communications was taken at the Centre de recherche industrielle du Québec (CRIQ), where employees decided to create a video to demonstrate that seemingly harmless comments and attitudes can have devastating consequences for members of designated groups. Their goal was to sensitize people without lecturing or pointing fingers. The employees acted in the video, selected its music, and directed and produced it. Its title was *Moi . . . des préjugés? (Me . . . prejudiced?)*. The video depicts the experiences of a black man, a person who is deaf, and a woman, all of whom are seeking employment with a company and who are confronted with opinions and attitudes that have everything to do with prejudice and nothing to do with the requirements of the job.[29]

## Assignment of Accountable Senior Staff

Senior management must place the responsibility for employment equity in the hands of a senior manager, a joint labour–management committee, and an employment equity advisory committee with mechanisms for union consultation (or, in nonunionized settings, for consultation with designated employee representatives). Senior management must designate line management responsibility and accountability. Anyone given responsibility for employment equity must be knowledgeable about the problems and concerns of designated groups; have the status and ability needed to gain the cooperation of employees at all levels in the organization; have access to financial and human resources required to conduct planning and implementation functions; have sufficient time to devote to employment equity issues; monitor and be in a position to report to the CEO on the results of employment equity measures; and be prepared to serve as the employment equity contact person with federal and provincial government agencies.

Among the employment areas committee members may be required to review are employment practices, advertising and recruitment policies, company-sponsored training, the organization of work schedules and facilities, and systems for promotion to management positions. Although committees are usually given responsibility for making recommendations and reporting on issues, ultimate authority generally rests with senior management.

Employers covered by the *Employment Equity Act* are legally obligated to consult with designated employee representatives or, in unionized settings, with bargaining agents. Consultation means that the employer must supply sufficient information and opportunity to employee representatives or bargaining agents to enable them to ask questions and submit advice on the implementation of employment equity.

The labour movement in Canada generally supports the concept of employment equity, as long as unions are fully informed and involved from the beginning with respect to an employer's planning process. This makes sense considering that unions are the legitimate representatives of employee interests in unionized settings. Supportive mechanisms for achieving employment equity have been reported by Human Resources Development Canada.[30] Many employers and unions have successfully negotiated family-friendly policies such as parental leave, childcare provisions, and flexible hours.

First Nations University is a unique university in Canada that caters to the advanced education needs of Aboriginal people.

Courtesy of First Nations University of Canada

# STEP 2: DATA COLLECTION AND ANALYSIS

The development of an internal workforce profile is an important tool in employment equity planning. Without this information, an organization would not be able to determine where it stands relative to the internal and external workforce. Profiles must be based on both stock data and flow data. **Stock data** provide a snapshot of the organization. They show where members of designated groups are employed in the organization, at what salaries and status, and in what occupations on a particular date. **Flow data** refer to the distribution of designated groups in applications, interviews, hiring decisions, training and promotion opportunities, and terminations. They provide information on the movement of employees into and through the organization. Computerized reporting systems and tracking software are available from Human Resources Development Canada to assist employers in gathering, reporting, and analyzing their internal workforce data.

Most of the information necessary for equity planning (e.g., salary, sex, access to benefits, seniority status, and occupational and career history within the organization) is contained in existing personnel files. Information pertaining to the distribution of members of designated groups in the employer's organization must be accumulated by the employer through a self-identification process. Under the *Employment Equity Act*, employers may gather data on members of designated groups as long as employees voluntarily agree to be identified or identify themselves as members of designated groups and as long as the data are used only for employment equity planning or reporting purposes.

Creating a climate of trust in the management of the program is a major challenge. Employers can encourage participation and confidence in the program by providing focused employment equity training to managers and by providing opportunities for managers to be recognized for their contributions to the development and administration of effective employment equity strategies. Companies such as Pratt & Whitney have introduced equity and diversity training for their supervisors. Cameco Corporation in northern Saskatchewan has committed to improving the job prospects of Aboriginal people as part of its long-term employment strategy, based on economics, not just a keen sense of social responsibility. Mentoring, basic training, educational support, and family assistance programs mean a lot to those employees, who may be the first in their families to have full-time paid employment.[31]

If an employer administers a self-identification questionnaire, confidentiality and a clear commitment at senior levels to the concept of employment equity should be communicated. Having employees self-identify is crucial to the success of the program, but problems may arise with self-identification. Under some provincial employment equity acts, terms such as *Aboriginal* and *racial minority* are not defined. Some employees, who have "hidden" disabilities such as epilepsy or partial deafness, may not wish to label themselves for fear of future discriminatory treatment. Some minorities, such as Aboriginal people, have never disclosed their ethnic origins for similar reasons.

If too many employees with nonvisible disabilities do not identify themselves as disabled, the program could end up being designed to recruit more employees with disabilities, leaving another segment of the employee population underrepresented. Thus, because inaccurate data were accumulated on one group, the other group will not benefit from the employment equity efforts. An additional concern is that individuals with disabilities may need some form of accommodation to help them perform their jobs better. If they do not self-identify, they have denied themselves certain basic rights. Highlights in HRM 3.5 outlines words and actions that are appropriate in dealing with persons with disabilities. A self-identification form should contain the following:

- An explanation of the employer's employment equity policy, the purpose of the employment equity program, and the need for the information requested

- An indication that the information supplied will be confidential and will be used only for employment equity purposes by those individuals identified as responsible for the program

**stock data**
Data showing the status of designated groups in occupational categories and compensation levels

**flow data**
Data that provide a profile of the employment decisions affecting designated groups

# HIGHLIGHTS IN HRM 3.5

## Suggestions for Inclusion

**Person who is blind or person with a visual impairment**

Identify yourself and anyone with you; if you have met before, explain the context of the meeting; speak in a normal tone of voice and indicate to whom you are speaking if in a group; remove obstacles; describe the surroundings ("There is a door on your right"); if offering to guide, ask the person to take your arm above the elbow and walk about a half-step ahead; plan ahead to obtain material in audio cassettes or Braille.

**Person with a physical disability or person with a mobility impairment**

Rearrange furniture or objects to accommodate a wheelchair or other mobility aid; avoid leaning on a mobility aid; push someone in a wheelchair only when asked; give directions that include distance and physical objects such as curbs.

**Person who is deaf or deafened or person with a hearing impairment**

Speak clearly and at a pace that allows the sign language interpreter to interpret and to allow for questions; write notes or use gestures for one-on-one discussions; face the person to facilitate lip reading; speak clearly, slowly, and directly to the person, not the interpreter; reduce or eliminate background noise.

**Person who is unable to speak or person with a speech impairment; person with a learning, developmental, or psychiatric disability**

When needed, offer assistance and provide guidance; repeat information when necessary; speak directly to the person and listen actively.

Sources: Treasury Board of Canada Secretariat, *Creating a Welcoming Workplace for Employees with Disabilities*; David Brown, "Focus on Ability Not Disability," *Canadian HR Reporter* 13, no. 22 (December 18, 2000): 12.

---

**underutilization**
Term applied to designated groups that are not utilized or represented in the employer's workforce proportional to their numbers in the labour market

**concentration**
Term applied to designated groups whose numbers in a particular occupation or level are high relative to their numbers in the labour market

- The categories for self-identification, with brief explanations and examples
- An indication that the form has been reviewed by the relevant human rights agency
- Space for comments and suggestions
- The name of the contact person for information and suggestions[32]

Once the personal information forms have been completed, all occupations within the organization must be cross-referenced to the National Occupational Classification (NOC). This manual was created by Statistics Canada for use in statistical surveys and for other purposes. Personal data are organized under the four-digit NOC classifications. When building a workforce profile, employers should first refer to the four-digit unit groups and then determine in which one each job belongs. For example, secretaries and stenographers are classified in unit group 4111, which in turn can be assigned to the "clerical workers" group.

A full workforce analysis can be generated once all the information has been loaded and the reports are complete. This utilization analysis will include a distribution of members of designated groups according to occupations and salary levels throughout the organization. Comparisons will show which designated groups exhibit **underutilization** and which groups exhibit **concentration** in specific occupations or levels, in proportion to their numbers in the labour market.[33]

## STEP 3: EMPLOYMENT SYSTEMS REVIEW

"Employment systems" or "employment practices" are the means by which employers carry out personnel activities such as recruitment, hiring, training and development, promotion, job classification, discipline, and termination. Some of these practices are found in personnel manuals and collective agreements, whereas others remain more informal and based on traditional practices.

An important legal principle is that employers are accountable even when discrimination is the unintended result of employment systems that block the progress of particular groups of employees or potential employees for reasons unrelated to qualifications, merit, or business requirements. This unintentional discrimination is referred to as systemic discrimination.

**systemic discrimination**
The exclusion of members of certain groups through the application of employment policies or practices based on criteria that are not job related

## Systemic Barriers in Employment Practices

**Systemic discrimination** refers to the exclusion of members of certain groups through the application of employment policies or practices based on criteria that are neither job related nor required for the safe and efficient operation of the business. Systemic discrimination can create legal concerns for an organization. Many employment barriers are hidden, unintentionally, in the rules, procedures, and even facilities that employers provide to manage their human resources. (See Figure 3.3 for examples of systemic barriers, along with possible solutions.) Inequity can result if these barriers encourage or discourage individuals based on their membership in certain groups rather than on their ability to do a job that the employer needs done. In one case, the Supreme Court of Canada ruled that a physical fitness test discriminated against women and required the employer to reinstate the woman as a firefighter.[34]

Another example of systemic discrimination occurs when an employer's workforce represents one group in our society and the company recruits new employees by posting job vacancies within the company or by word of mouth among the employees. This recruitment strategy is likely to generate candidates similar to those in the current workforce, thereby unintentionally discriminating against other groups of workers in the labour market. A better approach might be to vary recruitment methods by contacting outside agencies and organizations. The Toronto Police Force has established an eight-member recruitment task force to boost its community representation, in part by educating visible minority groups about career opportunities in the force.[35]

The following employment practices and issues may need to be reviewed: job classifications and descriptions, recruitment processes, training and development, performance evaluation systems, promotions and upward mobility, levels of compensation, access to benefits, termination processes, discipline procedures, facilities (e.g., building design, barrier-free access), and access to assistance.

## FIGURE 3.3

EMPLOYMENT PRACTICES

### Examples of Systemic Barriers

1. Recruitment practices that limit applications from designated groups, e.g., word of mouth, internal hiring policies.

2. Physical access that restricts those who are mobility impaired, e.g., no ramps, heavy doors, narrow passageways.

3. Job descriptions and job evaluation systems that undervalue the work of positions traditionally held by women.

4. A workplace environment that does not expressly discourage sexual or racial harassment.

### Examples of Possible Solutions

1. Word of mouth could be supplemented by calls to community organizations representing designated groups or to the local Service Canada centre.

2. Facility upgrading.

3. Rewrite job descriptions, rationalize evaluation systems, provide special training for supervisors.

4. Issue a company policy against these practices, with guidelines and follow-up through appraisal and discipline procedures, and develop complaint and problem-solving mechanisms for an employee to use.

**Source:** Employment Equity: A Guide for Employers, Employment and Immigration Canada. P.19 Cat. No. 143-5-91, May 1991 Human Resources and Skills Development Canada. Reproduced with the permission of the Minister of Public Works and Government Services Canada, 2012.

The usual test for identifying systemic barriers involves using the following criteria to assess the policy:

- Is it job related?
- Is it valid? (i.e., does it, or the required qualification, have a direct relationship to job performance?)
- Is it consistently applied?
- Does it have an adverse impact? (i.e., does it affect members of designated groups more than those of dominant groups?)
- Is it a business necessity?
- Does it conform to human rights and employment standards legislation?[36]

# HIGHLIGHTS IN HRM 3.6

## Participation in the Federal Public Service

The goals of the Employment Equity (EE) program in the federal government are to

- Establish a workforce of qualified employees that reflects the diversity of the Canadian population that they serve
- Ensure equal access to job opportunities
- Correct conditions that have historically impeded the full participation of designated groups

Discussions with Aloma Lawrence, Chief Employment Equity Advisor of the Public Service Commission, indicated that although visible minorities represented 8.7 percent of the labour force, they represented only 6.8 percent of the federal employee population. To accomplish the EE goals, the Public Service Commission (PSC) has established a number of special measures, which include the following:

- *Outreach.* The recruiting teams of the federal government have established a visible presence within the visible minority communities. Through contacts with visible minority associations, such as the Association of Black Law Enforcers, recruiters make presentations and hold information sessions about the recruitment processes used by the federal government to fill jobs. Recruiters talk about the structured interviews and tests, procedures that may be unfamiliar to visible minority candidates.
- *Creation of specific tool.* The brochure "So You're Thinking of Working for the Federal Government" was developed specifically for visible minority communities. Workshops that explain the types of tests used, such as the managerial in-basket or the written

communications test, are held within these communities. The PSC has also introduced tools for use by managers and HR professionals in developing and implementing employment equity strategies and approaches. New tools include "Improving Employment Equity Representation: Tips and Tools," "Guidelines for Assessing Persons with Disabilities," and "Guidelines for Fair Assessment in a Diverse Workplace."

- *Composition of recruitment teams.* An effort was made to place visible minorities on the recruitment teams, particularly because selection decisions could be made on perceptions of "fit," and culture plays a large role in this. In 2002, the PSC established an inventory of 100 visible minorities, trained in interviewing processes, who were invited by managers to sit on selection boards. The federal government, like other public-sector employers, has been finding it difficult to recruit visible minorities in areas of law enforcement, such as correctional officers. However, building relationships with visible minority communities is beginning to result in greater interest in federal government jobs.

Is the process working? Yes; the number of visible minorities working in the federal public service increased from 5.9 percent in 2001 to 7.3 percent in 2006. Career development is vital to the retention of good employees, and in 2001, the PSC launched a career assignment program for visible minorities. Because visible minorities represent only 4.1 percent of the executive group, for example, the Career Assignment Program develops participants for executive-level positions. The ultimate goal is to match participation rates in the labour market. However, with the special measures adopted by the PSC, progress is slow but certain.

Source: Interview with Aloma Lawrence, 2006.

If the employee profiles indicate that certain types of people are underrepresented, then special measures may be undertaken to correct this imbalance.

## Special Measures and Reasonable Accommodation

Special measures are initiatives designed to accelerate the entry, development, and promotion of members of designated groups from among the interested and qualified workforce. For example, some special measures may include targeted recruitment or special training initiatives aimed mainly at correcting, over a specified period of time, employment inequities stemming from past discrimination. These measures are intended to hasten the achievement of fair representation of the four designated groups in an employer's workforce. Highlights in HRM 3.6 describes the special measures used by the federal government.

**Reasonable accommodation** involves adjusting employment policies and practices so that no individual is denied benefits, disadvantaged with respect to employment opportunities, or blocked from carrying out the essential components of a job because of race, colour, sex, or disability. Human rights tribunals across Canada have placed employers under a duty to demonstrate a degree of flexibility in meeting the reasonable needs of employees. It is no longer acceptable for employers to simply assume that all employees will "fit in" no matter what their special needs. Employers must find the means to alter systems to meet the needs of their employees as long as this does not cause "undue hardship to the employer." Reasonable accommodation may include redesigning job duties; adjusting work schedules; providing technical, financial, and human support services; and upgrading facilities. The City of Toronto developed award-winning facilities in its barrier-free access program, which was designed to allow people with disabilities accessible passage throughout city facilities. The Canadian military has adopted a policy that allows Aboriginal servicemen to wear their hair in traditional braids.

Reasonable accommodation benefits all employees. When a company provides compensation for childcare expenses for employees taking company-sponsored courses, it does more than remove a barrier to women; it also assists any employee with sole-parenting responsibilities. The flexible work schedules adopted by some companies in northern Canada benefit Aboriginal employees, who are prepared to work atypical hours in exchange for significant breaks away from the work site to take part in traditional hunting and fishing activities. Many other employees also benefit from these flexible work schedules. Highlights in HRM 3.7 recounts two court cases on accommodation.

> **reasonable accommodation**
> Attempt by employers to adjust the working conditions or schedules of employees with disabilities or religious preferences

---

# HIGHLIGHTS IN HRM 3.7

## The Duty to Accommodate

- Two employees of the Ford Motor Company of Oakville, Ontario, became members of a religious group that observed its Sabbath from Friday sunset to Saturday sunset. Both employees were required to work two Friday nights out of four, which they refused to do. They tried, but failed, to make alternative arrangements with other workers. They were disciplined and ultimately terminated for unauthorized absenteeism. After a 71-day hearing, the Human Rights Commission decided it would constitute undue hardship on

Ford to accommodate the religious absences of these employees.

- The Ontario Human Rights Commission found that the City of Ancaster, Ontario, had discriminated against a part-time firefighter when they turned him down for a full-time job because he had partial vision in one eye. As such, he was unable to obtain a class F driver's licence, a job requirement for driving ambulances that are driven by firefighters. The tribunal felt that the city should have accommodated him by assigning him to firefighter duties exclusively.

Source: Laura Cassiani, "Law Takes Tough Stand on Accommodation" *Canadian HR Reporter*, Feb. 26, 2001 issue, pages 1 and 5.

Special arrangements should be made to accommodate people who are visually impaired, illiterate, or unfamiliar with the English language by using tools such as Braille forms, confidential interviews, or translation. Leah Levy, the founder of the Gulf Islands Dog Biscuit Company, found it easy to accommodate deaf employees by installing a white board for messages and a light indicating when the doorbell rang.[37]

## STEP 4: ESTABLISHMENT OF A WORKPLAN

The workforce analysis and the review of employment systems will provide the employer with a useful base from which to develop a workplan with realistic goals and timetables. A narrative statement or summary of the conclusions drawn from the examination of the workforce analysis forms part of the employment equity workplan. The summary should include any restrictions faced in hiring due to collective agreements, staff movements, or the need for specialized skills in a particular profession. The identification of restrictions helps form an overall employment equity strategy.

The plan should be considered a working tool designed to achieve results. It is a document that describes how proposed actions are to be achieved. The plan should be an integral part of the organization's overall operational plans and must include

- Numerical goals with time frames (numerical goals can be expressed in numbers—for example, 42 *percent of our personnel should be women*)
- Explanations about the proposed improvement in the hiring, training, and promotion of the four designated groups to increase their representation and improve their distribution throughout the organization
- Descriptions of specific activities to achieve the numerical goals
- An outline of monitoring and evaluation procedures to follow program implementation

Numerical goals must be realistic numbers related to the workforce analysis. The goals must catalogue opportunities for hiring, training, and promotion and must demonstrate a valid effort to correct underrepresentation or concentration of all designated groups in specific occupations or occupational categories. Non-numerical goals include activities such as implementation of barrier-free design, targeted recruitment and advertising, modification of employment policies or practices, and provision of developmental training.

The overall goal for an organization is to achieve a representative workforce. An organization's workforce is representative when it reflects the demographic composition of the external workforce. A nonrepresentative workforce is an indicator of the need for evaluation and action to remove the barriers that block or discourage certain groups from employment and advancement. Workplan initiatives in conjunction with special measures and reasonable accommodation should contribute to the overall success of this goal.

## STEP 5: IMPLEMENTATION

The implementation of employment equity is idiosyncratic in that no two plans will be the same. Each strategy should be designed to meet the needs of the particular organization. The success of plan implementation depends on senior management's commitment to the process, how the roles and responsibilities are defined, the resources available, the effectiveness of the communications strategy, the acceptance of plan initiatives and objectives, and the availability of training. The plan, in essence a living document, will be affected by the changes in the internal and external environment throughout the implementation period. Therefore, its strategies may be modified or eliminated when results are not achieved or if resource restraints or economic conditions necessitate a different strategy. The implementation is guided and monitored by those responsible and accountable for its outcome.

By monitoring progress, the employer will be able to evaluate the overall success of the equity initiatives used to achieve a representative workforce, as well as respond to organizational and environmental changes. Annual progress reports provided to all employees communicate initiatives and achievements. Interim reports on special projects heighten program visibility and acceptance; they also promote management commitment and accountability. Research suggests that the wage gaps between white men and the designated groups are closing more rapidly in organizations with formal employment equity programs than in organizations without such programs.[38]

The monitoring activity is an essential component in the planning cycle. Only through monitoring can an employer determine whether goals are being attained and problems resolved, whether new programs are succeeding, and whether strategies have been effective. If the employer finds, on review of the program, that there are negative results, alterations to the existing plan will have to be made with new goals. In this regard, the planning process is evolutionary in that the achievement of employment equity involves organizational changes and builds on experience.

## SEXUAL HARASSMENT

Please note that although this section deals only with sexual harassment, many of the prescriptions apply equally to other forms of harassment based on, for example, race or religion. The two main sources of the employer's duty to prevent harassment in the workplace are

1. Human rights legislation, which prevents harassment only on the basis of the designated grounds in the legislation (e.g., sex, race, religion)
2. Common law obligation to treat workers with decency and respect. This is a fairly new development in the common law. However, it applies to all forms of harassment that make the workplace intolerable to the worker. If the employer fails to stop the harassment, it is in breach of the employment contract. The employee could quit and sue for constructive dismissal ("reasonable notice").[39]

Sexual situations in the work environment are not new to organizational life. Sexual feelings are a part of group dynamics, and people who work together may come to develop these kinds of feelings for one another. Unfortunately, however, often these encounters are unpleasant and unwelcome, as witnessed by the many reported instances of sexual harassment.[40]

According to one study, only 4 of every 10 Canadian women who suffer **sexual harassment** at work take any formal action, and only one out of every two women believes that a complaint would be taken seriously in her workplace.[41] This belief is reinforced by cases such as the one involving a female Sears employee who was shot to death by her manager. Fifteen months earlier, she had complained to her employer that she was being sexually harassed by her manager. The company maintained that his behaviour did not constitute sexual harassment and that he was merely a "persistent pursuer." In keeping with this position, Sears made no effort to stop the manager's behaviour.[42] The City of Richmond has only four women among the more than 200 firefighters, and none of them are on active duty. At least one has complained of harassment, saying that she found obscenities on her locker and feces in her boots and that her water pressure was not turned on during a fire inside a building.[43] Sexual harassment costs, as Highlights in HRM 3.8 shows.

Many organizations are developing policies to deal with sexual harassment in the workplace. Such policies are intended as preventive measures against not only damage to reputation and employee morale but also the kind of litigation that Magna International faced when it was sued on the grounds that Magna employees had attempted to win contracts from purchasing officers for the Big

**sexual harassment**
Unwelcome advances, requests for sexual favours, and other verbal or physical conduct of a sexual nature in the working environment

PART 2

| OUTCOME 6

# HIGHLIGHTS IN HRM 3.8

## The Cost of Sexual Harassment

In 2002, sexual harassment complaints topped the list of complaints heard by provincial human rights commissions; 64 percent of working women say they have experienced some form of sexual harassment throughout their careers (up from 48 percent in the previous year). Harassment affects productivity, retention, morale, turnover, and absenteeism rates. It also affects an employee's self-esteem, home life, and stress levels. Some 48 percent of women executives say they left a job because of inhospitable organizational culture and harassment.

An employee at the Victoria Tea Company in Ontario was found guilty of sexual harassment and ordered to pay the victim $50,600. A supervisor at SkyCable in Brandon, Manitoba, was ordered to pay $100,000 in damages for creating a poisoned work atmosphere. The four women employees testified that the supervisor had made inappropriate remarks, sexual advances, and derogatory comments on an ongoing basis. The poisoned work environment generated by his conduct took a toll on

their psychological and physical health and caused them significant pain and suffering. The supervisor's remarks were clearly persistent, repetitious, and serious enough to create a hostile work environment for all the complainants. The Canadian Human Rights Tribunal ruled that the supervisor must compensate the four women for lost wages, hurt feelings, and legal costs. But what exactly is sexual harassment? According to Canadian legal cases, the following behaviours define sexual harassment:

- Sexually degrading words or remarks used to describe an individual or group
- Inquiries or comments about an individual's sex life
- Sexual flirtations, advances, and propositions
- Demands for sexual favours
- Verbal threats or abuse
- Leering
- Unwanted gestures
- Display of sexually offensive material
- Sexual assault

Sources: "Sexual Harassment Endangered Health," *Tribunal OH & S Canada* 18, no. 6 (September 2002): 10; Laura Cassiani, "Sexual Harassment Persists Despite Workplace Fallout," *Canadian HR Reporter* 14, no. 7 (April 9, 2001): 1.

---

Three automakers by wooing them with gifts and entertainment, including trips to topless bars.[44] Some organizations have put policies in place to attempt to deal with the issue. For example, the sexual harassment policy at B.C. Hydro focuses on avoidance and resolution rather than punishment after the fact. In another organization, the Canadian Armed Forces, 90,000 members have been trained to recognize and avoid harassment of all kinds.

The Ontario *Human Rights Code* identifies three kinds of sexual harassment:

1. When someone says or does things to you of a sexual nature and you do not want or welcome it. This includes behaviour that a person should know you do not want or welcome (e.g., your supervisor makes you feel uncomfortable by talking about sex all the time). *The Human Rights Code* says that when you show that you do not welcome or want the remarks or actions, the person must stop doing those things right away.
2. A person who has authority or power to deny you something, such as a promotion or a raise, makes sexual suggestions or requests that you do not want or welcome (e.g., your teacher says you must have sex with him or her or you will not pass the course). Even if you do not complain about a sexual suggestion or request, it can still be sexual harassment unless it is clear that you welcome or want it.
3. A person with authority or the power to deny you something important punishes you or threatens to do something to you for refusing a sexual request (e.g., your employer fires you, or threatens to fire you, because you refuse to go on a date).

For sexual harassment policies to succeed, confidentiality is necessary, and so is a method for filing complaints. Without organizational commitment to zero tolerance

Sexual harassment encounters are unpleasant, causing personal and organizational hardships.

# HIGHLIGHTS IN HRM 3.9

## Basic Components of an Effective Sexual Harassment Policy

1. Develop a comprehensive organization-wide policy on sexual harassment and present it to all current and new employees. Stress that sexual harassment will not be tolerated under any circumstances. Emphasis is best achieved when the policy is publicized and supported by top management.

2. Hold training sessions with supervisors to explain their role in providing an environment free of sexual harassment and institute proper investigative procedures when charges occur.

3. Establish a formal complaint procedure whereby employees can discuss problems without fear of retaliation. The complaint procedure should spell out how charges will be investigated and resolved.

4. Act immediately when employees complain of sexual harassment. Communicate widely that investigations will be conducted objectively and with appreciation for the sensitivity of the issue.

5. When an investigation supports employee charges, discipline the offender at once. For extremely serious offences, discipline should include penalties up to and including discharge. Discipline should be applied consistently across similar cases and among managers and hourly employees alike.

6. Follow up on all cases to ensure a satisfactory resolution of the problem.

with respect to harassment, any such policy will be meaningless. Highlights in HRM 3.9 presents some suggestions for an effective sexual harassment policy.[45]

The concepts of harassment in the workplace are being broadened to include psychological harassment, such as bullying. Laws in Quebec and Saskatchewan ban psychological harassment, which is defined as any repeated, hostile, or unwanted conduct; verbal comments; actions; or gestures that affect an employee's dignity or psychological or physical integrity. This protection requires employers to create policies to prevent this type of harassment.[46] Ontario introduced a law requiring employers to develop and post a harassment policy in the workplace and to develop a system through which employees can report incidents of harassment.

 **Using the Internet**

For more information on the law requiring Ontario employers to have a harassment policy, go to

**http://www.yorku.ca/ddoorey /lawblog/?p=1042**

## MANAGING DIVERSITY

Managing diversity goes beyond Canadian employment equity legislation's four designated groups in addressing the need to create a fair work environment. The terms *diversity management* and employment equity are often used interchangeably, but there are differences. **Diversity management** is voluntary; employment equity is not. Managing diversity is a broader, more inclusive concept encompassing factors such as religion, personality, lifestyle, and education. By managing diversity, organizations hope to gain a strategic and competitive advantage by helping all employees perform to their full potential.[47]

The City of Toronto led by example when it recognized "non-Christian City of Toronto staff" by giving them two days of paid time off for religious holidays if they agreed to work Christmas Day and Good Friday (Christian holidays) at straight time.[48] Also, McDonald's Restaurants of Canada used multiage teams and found the diversity of ages led to a remarkable synergy.[49]

Organizations such as CN, the Bank of Montreal, and Warner-Lambert are pioneers in the diversity movement. According to Marie Tellier, CN's assistant vice president of employment equity, the hiring, development, and good management of a diverse workforce whose values and expectations are different from their managers are no longer an option—they are an economic necessity. In the context of an increasingly diverse labour force, diversity management is not only a legal obligation but also a necessity imposed by market laws, competition, and the need to be the best to survive.[50]

**OUTCOME 7**

**diversity management**
The optimization of an organization's multicultural workforce to reach business objectives

Statistics show that the ethnocultural profile of Canada has been changing since the 1960s and will continue to change dramatically over the next 20 years. European immigrants who led the first wave of immigrants in the early years of the 20th century have been surpassed by immigrants from Asia, including the Middle East.[51] A study by Statistics Canada has found that an immigrant's country of origin and arrival date in Canada are strongly correlated with his or her chances of finding a job. Immigrants born in Southeast Asia and aged 25 to 54 had employment levels close to or better than those of their Canadian-born counterparts, regardless of when they arrived in Canada.[52] The goal of diversity management is to have the workforce at all levels resemble the population.

CEOs in Canada recognize that ethnic groups possess expertise such as language skills, knowledge of foreign cultures and business practices, and natural trade links with overseas markets that can be used to capture market share in emerging economies and new Canadian markets. Ebco, a manufacturing company in Richmond, British Columbia, which has won awards for excellence in race relations, is doing business in Germany and Taiwan because it was able to tap the networks and skills of its employees, who trace their origins to 48 different countries. The spending power of these groups is another motivating factor to incorporate them into all levels of the workforce.[53] According to Edgar Ware, ethnocultural business manager at Digital Equipment of Canada, "We have an obligation to the

# THE BUSINESS CASE

## The Economic Values of Diversity

Although employment equity and its partner, employment diversity, were launched on moral grounds, increasingly, these initiatives are sustained on business grounds. The first principle to understand is that members of the designated groups are consumers, not just potential employees. For example, the purchasing power of people with disabilities is estimated to be $120 billion. Racial minorities control more than $76 billion of combined purchasing power. Women control 80 percent of the consumer dollars spent in North America. People with disabilities account for about $50 billion annually in spending power.

The second business fundamental is that employees who are members of the designated groups represent an organizational resource that facilitates the understanding and linkages to these markets by helping various departments to understand the lifestyles, consumption needs and wants, purchasing preferences, media usage habits, and brand loyalty of these groups. For example, Phoenix Geophysics Ltd, based in Toronto, credits its newest biggest market (Africa) for its geophysical instruments to its Eritrean-born employee, who

speaks five languages. For reasons such as this, one in five businesses has hired an immigrant to help diversify its global client base. Business is increasingly international, and employees who speak other languages and understand other cultures are a valuable resource. A Conference Board of Canada study found that every 1 percent increase in the number of immigrants to Canada increased the value of imports by 0.21 percent and the value of exports by 0.11 percent.

A study of nearly 1,000 companies operating in the European Union reported that a diverse workforce brings these benefits to business (in rank order):

- Access to a new labour pool
- Benefits related to a company's reputation
- Commitment to equality and diversity as company values
- Innovation and creativity
- Compliance with laws
- Competitive advantage
- Economic effectiveness
- Marketing opportunities
- Enhanced customer satisfactionrs

Sources: T. Grant, "Tapping Canada's Immigrant Capital," *The Globe and Mail*, May 11, 2011, B7; Terrence Belford, "Hire Local, Think Global," *The Globe and Mail*, January 26, 2009, E1; European Commission, "Business Case for Diversity," Directorate-General for Employment, Social Affairs, and Equal Opportunity, Luxembourg, 2005; Aparita Bhandari, "Ethnic Marketing—It's More Than Skin Deep," *The Globe and Mail*, September 7, 2005, B3; B. Siu, "Beyond Quotas: The Business Case for Employment Equity," *Canadian HR Reporter* (June 4, 2001): 20.

cultural fabric. We want to look like the people we sell to."[54] Digital's goal is to balance a diversity strategy with the organization's business plan.

Besides the moral issues surrounding diversity, there is a critical economic need for Canada to increase its share of world trade and expand its trade portfolio (see the Business Case). Our export market is dominated by the United States, Japan, and the United Kingdom. If Canadian business continues to rely heavily on these markets, our export growth and standard of living may not keep pace with other international markets.[55] Developing countries in emerging markets will require new investments in infrastructure, public systems, and productive capital. Given the multicultural background of many of its workers, Canada is in an excellent position to provide these services.[56] Canadian companies such as Nortel and SNC-Lavalin have already begun to tap the potential of these emerging markets.

## CREATING AN ENVIRONMENT FOR SUCCESS

Transforming an organizational culture into a culture that embraces diversity can be a complex and lengthy process. Diversity initiatives should be taken slowly so that everyone can understand that this change is an evolutionary process and that expectations should be realistic. Individuals must fully understand the time, effort, commitment, and risk involved and the need for a systematic approach.[57]

Leadership is one of the most important variables in an organization's ability to successfully incorporate diversity into its business strategy. In a Conference Board of Canada survey, 86 percent of respondents indicated that responsibility rested with HR.[58] The initiative should not be perceived as an HR program or policy but rather as a business imperative. In the words of Prem Benimadhu, vice president of HR research for the Conference Board, "Building a racially and culturally diverse workforce has been perceived as a human resources issue. But as long as it is, it's not going to be in the mission statement of organizations."[59] Only 6 percent of firms surveyed by the Conference Board study mentioned ethnic and cultural diversity in their mission statements.

Diversity initiatives should be linked directly to the business objectives and goals of the most senior levels of management. Reality Check demonstrates how RBC manages a wide range of diversity initiatives.

Organizations seeking to incorporate the value of diversity into their corporate philosophy must make use of appropriate internally and externally focused communications. For example, the National Bank of Canada participates annually in Montreal's La semaine des communautés culturelles, a week dedicated to the celebration of Montreal's multiculturalism. The bank believes that

## REALITY CHECK

### Diversity Management Achievements at RBC

RBC won the 2010 Catalyst award given to companies with an exceptional track record of diversity and inclusion practices. According to Zabeen Hirji, chief HR officer at RBC, to create and sustain a diverse, inclusive, and collaborative work environment, people at all levels must be engaged in the effort, starting with

the leadership. The RBC Diversity Leadership Council is chaired by the president and CEO, Gordon Nixon. This group developed a three-year plan to advance and support diversity and inclusion in the workplace, marketplace, and community. As Gord Nixon often state: "While diversity is the right thing to do, it is the smart thing to do and it makes good business sense." Indeed, *diversity for growth and innovation* is one of RBC's core values.

*continued*

Looking only at the diversity issues for employees, the Blueprint for Talent and Workplace states that the goal is to increase the diversity and inclusion of the workforce globally, with a focus on representation of women and minorities at senior management levels. RBC offers a wide range of programs to achieve these goals, including

- Diversity dialogues reciprocal mentoring program for more than 400 participants
- Create Connections, a recruitment road map to attract experienced women financial consultants
- The establishment of the Royal Eagles National Leadership Committee to raise awareness of Aboriginal culture within RBC
- A webcast, "Building Cultural Dexterity for High Performance"
- A webcast, "Creating an Inclusive Workplace for Employees with Disabilities"
- An Aboriginal social network called One Heart

The diversity council issues an annual diversity progress report, an annual employment equity report, and an annual corporate social responsibility report.

Here are some Canadian statistics that show that these programs are working, keeping in mind that diversity efforts can take several years to show progress:

|  | 2010 | 2000 |
|---|---|---|
| Women in management | 67% | 74% |
| Women in executive roles | 54% | 58% |
| Visible minorities in management | 27% | 14% |
| Visible minorities in executive roles | 14% | 6% |
| People with disabilities | 3.5% | 2.7% |
| Aboriginal peoples | 1.6% | 1.1% |

Read the interview with Zabeen Hirji on http://www.jobquality.ca/interviews/interview_rbc.shtml.

Source: RBC 2010 Diversity Progress Report, Anonymous "Commitment to diversity" *National Post*, February 3, 2012. JV 10.

its visible demonstrations of commitment to ethnocultural diversity in the community it serves help raise the bank's profile.[60]

Cross-functional teams established to promote the diversity initiative are used successfully as communication vehicles by many leading-edge organizations. Toronto's Sunnybrook Health Sciences Centre has implemented the Patient Diversity Task Force to examine and report on the barriers faced by its patients, residents, and families.[61] Other organizations seek to raise the awareness of ethnocultural diversity.

Training is essential to the success of diversity implementation. A number of companies, including Imperial Oil and Connaught Laboratories, have incorporated diversity training. Cultural etiquette is an important aspect of diversity training that aims to explain the differences, or diversity, in people.

The Department of National Defence includes diversity training in its basic officer training course.[62] A consortium of European and North American businesses is attempting to develop a global diversity standard, by which companies will be able to use software to rate the success of their diversity programs.[63]

Figure 3.4 outlines some of the key factors in a diversity management strategy. Of even greater importance than training is the need to incorporate elements of diversity into all core training programs and to tailor those elements to meet the needs of specific business units or groups of employees.[64]

An added advantage of implementing a diversity initiative relates to its impact on employee retention. Retention of well-qualified and skilled employees is an important goal, considering the amount of resources—in both time and money—spent on recruiting and hiring new employees. Canadian organizations spend an average of 28 hours recruiting a new management or professional employee, 42 hours recruiting a new executive, and 20 hours recruiting a new technical/supervisory employee.[65] Maintaining a balanced and diversified workforce during periods of downsizing continues to be a major challenge. See Figure 3.5 for a summary of the benefits of diversity management.

## FIGURE 3.4

MODEL OF DIVERSITY MANAGEMENT STRATEGY

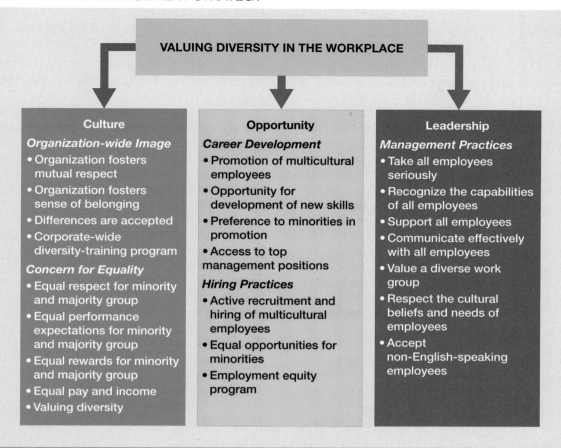

**Source:** Kathleen Iverson, *The Cornell Hotel and Restaurant Administration Quarterly* (41, no 2), "Managing for Effective Workforce Diversity" pp. 31–38, © 2000 SAGE Publications. Reproduced by permission of SAGE Publications.

## FIGURE 3.5

WHY DIVERSITY?

**Source:** Survey data from Gail Robinson and Kathleen Dechant, "Building a Business Case for Diversity," *Academy of Management Executive* 11, no. 3 (August 1997): 21–31.

# SMALL BUSINESS APPLICATION

As we have already said, small businesses are bound to the same legislation regarding workplace standards as are large companies. Although there are some exclusions, such as for employers of less than 100 employees being excluded from the *Employment Equity Act*, small business needs to ensure that practices applying to recruitment, pay, and workplace standards treat all Canadians fairly and equitably and in accordance with the *Canadian Charter of Rights and Freedoms*. In addition to legal compliance, equitable treatment of staff is good business.

But how does small business achieve this? Through the operation of three principles: (1) diverse and inclusive recruitment, (2) equal pay for work of equal value, and (3) maintaining an harassment-free workplace.

To illustrate how this plays out in small companies, let's use an example of a retail store in Surrey, British Columbia. Retail business relies on the local community as the primary source of customers, as well as employees. Part of successfully being able to serve clients comes as a result of understanding the needs of customers and providing an environment sensitive to their specific needs. As such, to serve the diverse population of Surrey, this store is well served by hiring staff that reflects this diverse population. The same is true for gender and people with disabilities. Given equivalent qualifications, many organizations will hire candidates from the designated groups to ensure that their organizations' employees are representative of the Canadian population.

So what strategies can this small business employ to maintain a diverse workforce? First, management can ensure that all people involved in the selection and support of employees recognize the value of maintaining a diverse representative workforce. Second, they can employ simple attraction strategies such as placing an "Employee Wanted" sign in the window of the store to draw from the diverse local community. Lastly, they can take measures to ensure the management of an inclusive workplace. This can include ensuring equitable

wage treatment of staff based on position and performance, as well as providing workplaces that are supportive to all employees.

Although equal pay for equal work is quite complex in large organizations, in small companies, often the exercise is quite easy. In our retail store in Surrey, we could set salary ranges for retail staff based on the regional norms for this work and then set guidelines within that range based on work experience and performance history.

Finally, harassment in the workplace, whether sexual or bullying in nature, is both illegal and destructive. Employers have the obligation to provide a safe work environment, free from such activity. Small employers are bound to the same legal requirements as large companies in this regard. In addition to legal compliance, protecting workplaces from such behaviour guards employers from productivity decreases in the form of absenteeism, turnover, and decreased work performance.

Ensuring a harassment-free workplace requires a leadership commitment to this priority, a monitoring of the environment to ensure that harassment is not taking place, and immediate and effective actions to address harassment in the workplace if it is discovered. In the case of our retail store in Surrey, the store manager is responsible for both hiring and ensuring that the workplace is harassment-free. Recognizing that they would not have an HR generalist to support them, this store could employ a three-pronged approach to ensuring an inclusive workplace. First, the store manager could participate in diversity and harassment training offered by many third-party training providers. Second, the store can seek to eliminate bias in hiring selection by involving someone other than the store manager in the selection process. Lastly, the store can measure turnover and conduct exit interviews to assist in the identification of problems needing resolution.

---

Much the same as is required under employment equity, an overall review of policies and employment practices must be considered. In this regard, the use of an employee attitude survey may prove beneficial in finding areas of systemic or perceived discrimination. The evaluation criteria used most often by Canadian organizations are staff attitudes, increases in promotions for minority employees, a reduction in the turnover of minority employees, a reduction in the number of harassment suits, recruitment statistics for minorities, and improvements in productivity.[66]

A final element in achieving success is monitoring progress and providing qualitative and quantitative evidence of change. For example, during their performance appraisals, all salaried employees at Levi Strauss & Co. (Canada) are evaluated on their ability to meet both business and aspirational goals. Aspirational goals are based on the company's core values, which include valuing diversity, following ethical management practices, and encouraging new behaviours, recognition, communications, and empowerment. These aspirations are the shared values and behaviours that will drive the company toward its mission of "sustained responsible commercial success."[67] When management measures performance as a function of diversity initiatives, values are instilled in the minds of all employees, and it is demonstrated that change and diversity are part of day-to-day business. To achieve success in diversity, it is vital to set an example and to create an atmosphere that respects and values differences. Canadian organizations have recognized the competitive advantage of embracing diversity in their business strategies.

# SUMMARY

**OUTCOME 1** Employment equity refers to the employment of individuals in a fair and nonbiased manner. Four groups in Canada—women, visible minorities, Aboriginal people, and persons with disabilities—tend to be concentrated in a few occupations that are accorded lower status and pay.

**OUTCOME 2** *The Canadian Human Rights Act* applies to all federally governed departments and agencies and all organizations incorporated under federal jurisdiction. The act prohibits discrimination on the basis of grounds such as race, religion, sex, age, national or ethnic origin, physical handicap, and marital status. *The Charter of Rights and Freedoms* guarantees some fundamental rights to every Canadian, including freedom from discrimination. The Canadian Human Rights Commission (CHRC) enforces the act through a formal complaint procedure.

**OUTCOME 3** Pay equity is an amendment to the *Canadian Human Rights Act* that makes it illegal for employers to discriminate against individuals on the basis of job content. By definition, pay equity means equal pay for work of equal value.

**OUTCOME 4** The *Employment Equity Act* requires all federally regulated employers to prepare an employment equity plan that identifies areas in which members of the designated groups are over- or underrepresented and establishes plans to promote an equitable workplace.

**OUTCOME 5** The implementation of employment equity involves six steps: senior management support, data collection and analysis, an employment systems review, establishment of a workplan, implementation, and a follow-up process that includes monitoring, reviewing, and revision.

**OUTCOME 6** Sexual harassment is an employment equity issue undergoing continued debate.

**OUTCOME 7** Managing diversity does more than incorporate employment equity. The goal of diversity management is to optimize the utilization of an organization's multicultural workforce with the goal of realizing strategic advantage.

# KEY TERMS

bona fide occupational qualification (BFOQ), 90
concentration, 100
designated groups, 84

diversity management, 107
employment equity, 84
flow data, 99
reasonable accommodation, 103

sexual harassment, 105
stock data, 99
systemic discrimination, 101
underutilization, 100

# SUMMARY

## DISCUSSION QUESTIONS

1. Here are some myths about employment equity:

   - It leads to hiring unqualified workers.
   - It causes an overnight change in the workforce makeup.
   - It is a plan that would make Calgary's workforce look like Toronto's.
   - This program lays off white males to make room for designated group members.
   - It is a program mainly for racial minorities.
   - Employers who implement the plan can destroy hard-won seniority provisions that protect all workers.
   - It is the end of hiring for white males.

   In groups, determine if group members share these beliefs. As HR professionals, how would you work with employees who hold these beliefs?

2. Although the process for filing a complaint of discrimination appears clear, many would choose not to do so. List the reasons alleged "victims" of discrimination in employment might not file a complaint.

3. Find a male class job (i.e., a job in which the majority of workers are male) and a female class job that seem to require similar educational background and technical skills. (For example, compare female-dominated police dispatchers with male-dominated radio technical supervisors or female-dominated health technicians with male-dominated transportation workers.) Then, using an Internet salary compensation index, calculate the pay rates. Are there differences? How would you account for these differences?

4. List as many jobs as you can in which you could hire only male applicants, based on a BFOQ.

5. Have you ever encountered questions such as the following?

   *"Do you really think you could handle this job? You know it takes a lot of energy and enthusiasm. Besides, we are looking for someone with career potential."*

   *"You don't need this training program. At your age, what would the benefit be?"*

   *"Well, you are getting on. What do you expect at your age?"*

Such comments reflect ageism—an attitude that makes assumptions about older persons and their abilities and puts labels on them. About 15 percent of Canada's workforce is 55 and over. They are often stereotyped and not hired or promoted. Using what you have learned in this chapter about hiring and accommodating the four designated groups, design a recruitment and retention program for older workers.

6. Have each member of your group complete the survey below. Discuss the findings.

| Activity | Is This Sexual Harassment? | |
|---|---|---|
| Employees post cartoons on bulletin boards containing sexually related material. | Yes | No |
| A male employee says to a female employee that she has beautiful eyes and hair. | Yes | No |
| A male manager habitually calls all female employees "sweetie" or "darling." | Yes | No |
| A male manager fails to promote a female employee when she will not grant sexual favours. | Yes | No |
| Male employees use vulgar language and tell sexual jokes that are overheard by, but not directed at, female employees. | Yes | No |
| A male employee leans and peers over the back of a female employee when she wears a low-cut dress. | Yes | No |
| A supervisor gives a female (male) subordinate a nice gift on her (his) birthday. | Yes | No |
| Two male employees share a sexually explicit magazine while observed by a female employee. | Yes | No |

7. Describe how an organization can make best use of a multicultural workforce.

# HRM EXPERIENCE

## Your Opinions about Employment Equity

First, complete the survey below. Then discuss your answers with members of a study group. Try to determine which statement is a myth and which represents reality.

To what extent do you agree with the following statements, on a scale of 1–5?

| 1 | 2 | 3 | 4 | 5 |
|---|---|---|---|---|
| Strongly disagree | disagree | ambivalent | agree | strongly agree |

1. Employment equity means that everyone must be treated the same way. ____

2. Employment equity results in "reverse discrimination." ____

3. Employment equity is a matter of quotas. ____

4. Employment equity means that unqualified people must be recruited. ____

5. Employment equity threatens the principle of seniority. ____

6. Employment equity is equivalent to lowering employment standards. ____

7. It is too difficult and too costly to adapt the workplace to meet the needs of persons with disabilities. ____

8. Employment equity is only achievable in a prosperous economy. ____

Source: Reproduced with the permission of Air Canada.

**CourseMate**

Visit the *Managing Human Resources* CourseMate website at http://www.belcourt7e.nelson.com for quizzes, flashcards, videos, games, and more!

## CASE STUDY 1

### FIGHTING FIRES

In British Columbia, the competition for fire-fighting jobs is fierce, with more than 1,600 people applying for about 60 jobs. At one time, the provincial Ministry of Forests required all job applicants to pass this physical fitness test:

- Lift a 23-kilogram bar in an upright rowing motion 18 times

- Carry pumps and hoses, weighing as much as 50 kilograms, over a timed distance

- Perform a shuttle run, which involves darting back and forth at an increasingly faster pace between cones situated 20 metres apart

The B.C. Government and Service Employees Union argued that the average man, with training, could easily pass the test, whereas the average woman, even with training, could not. Only 35 percent of women who applied for the firefighter's job passed the test; about 70 percent of the men did.

The University of Victoria scientists who designed the tests argued that most women could reach the standard, although they would have to work harder than most men to do so. Female firefighters said they had to train year-round to pass the test, but they took this as a personal responsibility and as the cost of qualifying for the job. Their safety, as well as that of their colleagues and the public, depends on their strength and endurance. The B.C. Ministry of Forests spokeswoman suggested that lowering the standards would be a mistake: "Already male firefighters are asking if blazes will be designated as 'guy' fires and 'girl' fires. We want the fittest people."

## Questions

1. Did the standards result in safer and more effective firefighting crews, or were they inadvertently keeping women out of a traditionally male job?

2. Was this a BFOQ? The ministry was challenged on the basis of sex discrimination.

What did the Supreme Court rule, and what was its reasoning?

3. Female applicants had the chance to train and try the test at B.C. university campuses. Was this special preparation discriminatory?

4. Did the changes made fix the underlying problems? Explain.

**Sources:** "New Test for Reasonable Accommodation," *Canadian HR Reporter*, http://www.cdn-hr-reporter.ca/hr_topics /systemic-discrimination/new-test-reasonable-accommodation, retrieved July 9, 2012; Lesley Young, "Employers Need to Scrutinize All Job Testing for Human Rights Violations, Supreme Court Rules," *Canadian HR Reporter* 12, no. 17 (October 4, 1999): 3.

# CASE STUDY 2

## OUTREACH EFFORTS

Human Resources Development Canada awarded Manitoba Hydro its Vision award for creativity and innovation in its employment equity programs. Currently, Aboriginal people make up 8.3 percent of Manitoba Hydro's workforce. In northern Manitoba, where there is a greater concentration of Aboriginal people, 27.4 percent of the corporation's workforce is Aboriginal. The goal is to get the overall corporate representation of Aboriginal people up to 10 percent and up to 33 percent in the north. The creative ways in which these goals are being reached include the following:

- A zero-tolerance policy of workplace harassment and discrimination

- An outreach and partnership program with Aboriginal organizations to provide information about employment and training opportunities

- Partnerships with postsecondary institutions to provide educational programs and career information and to brand Manitoba Hydro as an employer of choice

- A review of training programs to ensure that there are no systemic barriers

- Systematic recruitment efforts to introduce Aboriginal people by means of internships, co-op placements, summer employment, and part-time work

The most successful program is the preemployment training designed to facilitate the entry of Aboriginal people into Manitoba Hydro's training programs, which are more like apprenticeship programs. The preemployment training provides academic upgrading, a rotation through three trades to familiarize candidates with these jobs, and workshops to deal with the concerns and issues about being away from home. A recent addition to the program is the utility's "Building the Circle Camp," which introduces girls in northern Manitoba to opportunities in engineering, technology, and trades.

SaskTel is a Crown corporation providing cellular, phone, Internet, and multimedia services to 13 cities and more than 500 remote communities in Saskatchewan, many of them inhabited by First Nation and Métis people. SaskTel cares about the Aboriginal population both as customers and employees (8 percent of SaskTel's workforce is Aboriginal, and the company has a target of 13.5 percent, the provincial labour force rate). The company's call centre can offer service in three different First Nation languages. Potash is another large Saskatchewan employer looking to hire more than 800 workers in the next two years. This company has developed a pilot project to introduce Aboriginal people to the world of mining. The rationale is not just social justice or corporate responsability but an economic growth strategy.

First Nation people are participating in the drive to hire and retain more Aboriginal workers and have produced a two-day workshop. The goals are to support the business case for creating a workforce inclusive of Aboriginal people, to become an employer of choice for Aboriginal people, and to develop strategies to recruit, train, and advance Aboriginal workers.

## Questions

1. What are the reasons cited by the companies for wanting to hire Aboriginal people?

2. Of the three initiatives described, which do you think will be most successful to achieve these objectives? Why?

**Sources:** Dianne Jermyn, "A Bridge between Two Worlds," *The Globe and Mail*, May 18, 2011, E3; "Diversity: Mastering Aboriginal Inclusion," *HR Professional*, June/July 2009, 13; Shannon Klie, "Short Circuiting the Labour Supply," *Canadian HR Reporter* 21, no. 22 (December 15, 2008): 6; Laura Bogomolny, Peter Evans, Andy Holloway, Zena Olijnyk, Erin Pooley, and Andrew Wahl, "The Best Workplaces in Canada," *Canadian Business* (April 10–23, 2006): 74; Cheryl Petten, "Manitoba Hydro Recognized for Employment Equity Efforts," *Windspeaker* 20, no. 4 (August 2002): 31.

## WOMEN ON THE RIGHT TRACK AT CP RAIL

Women comprise nearly half of Canada's workforce, but over the last two decades, they have made no progress in obtaining senior management roles. This lack of success may deter younger women from entering certain professions and from learning from role models. Furthermore, research shows that a lack of diversity can affect retention, productivity, and innovation. Companies with more female senior managers have a higher return on equity than those with lower rates of female senior managers. With this research in mind, CP Rail undertook three initiatives to increase the number of women managers:

- Each department must have diversity goals.
- Mentoring programs for females have been established.

- Senior women discuss their careers in forums.
- Women on Track offers networking opportunities.

To date, the program has been successful, with the number of women in senior management doubling over 5 years.

### Questions

1. Compare CP Rail's initiatives to advance women with the recommended six-step program for the implementation of employment equity.
2. Review the list in Highlights in HRM 3.1 (retention strategies). What more could CP Rail undertake?

**Source:** Tavia Grant, "How CP Put Women on the Executive Track," *The Globe and Mail*, September 1, 2011, B1.

## NOTES AND REFERENCES

1. 2006 Census: Immigration in Canada, http://www12. statcan.ca/census-recensement/2006/as-sa/97-557/ index-eng.cfm, retrieved July 29, 2009.

2. Human Resources Development Canada, "Annual Report, Analysis of Employers' Reports," http://www.hrdc-drhc.gc.ca/LEEP/Annual _Reports/03; http://www.hrsdc.gc.ca/eng /lp/lo/lswe/we/ee_tools/reports/annual /index-we.shtml, retrieved July 30, 2009.

3. Statistics Canada, Labour Force Survey 2006; Human Resources Development Canada, *Annual Report, Employment Equity Act,* 2003, Labour Standards and Workplace Equity, Cat. No. MP31-5/2002; http://www12. statcan.ca/english/census06/reference/consultation /92-135/labourforce.cfm.

4. Human Resources Development Canada, "Workplace Equity," http://info.load-otea.hrdc-drhc.gc.ca/ workplace_equity/leep/annual/2002/, retrieved August 4, 2009; http://www.hrsdc.gc.ca/eng/lp/lo/ lswe/we/information/overview.shtml, retrieved July 30, 2009; Shannon Kie, "Feds Pledge Big Money but No Plan to Tackle Aboriginal Unemployment," *Canadian HR Reporter* (January 30, 2006): 3.

5. L. Redpath and M. O. Nielsen, "A Comparison of Native Culture, Non-Native Culture and New Management Ideology," *Canadian Journal of Administrative Studies* 14, no. 3 (1996): 327–339.

6. Deborah Zinni, Barry Wright, and Mark Julien, "Want to Retain Aboriginal Employees?" *HR Professional* (August/September 2005).

7. Alar Prost and David Redmond, "Employers Need Help with Integration," *Canadian HR Reporter* (December 19, 2005): 7.

8. Ibid.

9. Statistics Canada, 2006 Census Ethnic and Visible Minorities, http://www.statcan.gc.ca/daily-quotidien /080402/dq080402a-eng.htm, retrieved July 30, 2009.

10. Ibid.

11. *Employment Equity: A Guide for Employers,* Employment and Immigration Canada, Cat. No. LM-143-5-91, May 1991, 9.

12. Victor S. Mackinnon, "The Canadian Charter of Rights and Freedoms," *Public Administration: Canadian Materials* (North York, ON: Captus Press, 1993): 179–180.

13. *Canadian Human Rights Act*, Canadian Human Rights Commission, 1978, Paragraph 2, Subsection (a).

14. A. P. Aggarwal, *Sex Discrimination: Employment Law and Practices* (Toronto: Butterworths Canada, 1994).

15. "Firm Pays $300,000 in Racial Harassment Settlements," *Human Resources Management in Canada,* Report Bulletin No. 72 (February 1989) (Scarborough, ON: Prentice-Hall Canada): 1–2.

16. *Canadian Human Rights Act*, Paragraph 60, Section 2(a), (b).

17. *Wage Gap between Men and Women*, http://www.parl.gc.ca/Content/LOP/ResearchPublications/2010-30-e.htm#a1, retrieved April 2, 2012.

18. Russel J. G. Juriansz, *Equal Pay Legislation and Ontario's New Pay Equity Act* (Toronto: Blake, Cassels & Graydon, 1995): 3–5.

19. Susan Riggs, "Comparing Apples and Oranges: Job Evaluations," *Worklife* 8, no. 1 (1991): 7–10

20. "Achieving Pay Equity First Goal, But through Co-operation: Commissioner," *Pay Equity Commission Report* 1, no. 1 (March 1988): 6.

21. Morley Gunderson and Roberta Edgecombe Robb, "Equal Pay for Work of Equal Value: Canada's Experience," *Advances in Industrial and Labour Relations* 5 (1991): 151–168. See also John G. Kelly, *Pay Equity Management* (Toronto: CCH Canadian, 1988): 45–54.

22. David Brown, New Rules Proposed for Pay Equity," *Canadian HR Reporter* (May 31, 2004): 1, 2.

23. *Introduction to Employment Equity* (Ottawa: Human Resources Development Canada, 1996).

24. *Employment Equity Act*, http://laws.justice.gc.ca/en/E-5.401/48928.html, retrieved July 30, 2009.

25. Kelly Toughill, "Firms Back Equity: To Some It's 'Good Business' despite Harris's Vow to Scrap It," *Toronto Star*, June 21, 1995, A2.

26. *Canadian Human Rights Act*, S.C. 1976–77, c. as amended.

27. R. G. L. Fairweather, Canadian Human Rights Commission, *The Standing Committee on Legal and Constitutional Affairs*, May 29, 1986, 10.

28. Shenaz Mode, "Employment Equity: An Important Piece in the Human Rights Puzzle," *HR Professional* (April/May 2005): 26.

29. *Towards Equity: 1993 Merit Awards*, Employment Equity Branch, Human Resources Development Canada (June 1994): 17–18.

30. *Workplace Innovations Overview—1996*, Bureau of Labour Information, Human Resources Development Canada: 1–84.

31. *Towards Equity: 1993 Merit Awards*: 11–12; Laura Cassiani, "Canada's Quiet Labour Crisis," *Canadian HR Reporter* 14, no. 3 (February 12, 2001): 1, 8.

32. L. Young, "Employers Need to Scrutinize All Job Testing for Human Rights Violations, Supreme Court Rules," *Canadian HR Reporter* (October 4, 1999): 3.

33. Ibid., 18.

34. Aggarwal, Sex Discrimination.

35. Nicholas Keung, "Police Recruit Ethnic Officers to Boost Force," *Toronto Star*, July 25, 1997, A7.

36. *Employment Equity: A Guide for Employers:* 1995, c4.

37. Wendy Stueck, "Business Taps Talents of Disabled Workers," *The Globe and Mail*, May 18, 2004, B4.

38. Joanne Leck, Sylvie St. Onge, and Isabelle La Lancettee, "Wage Gap Changes among Organizations Subject to the Employment Equity Act," *Canadian Public Policy 21*, no. 44 (December 1995): 387–400.

39. David Doorey, "Employer Bullying: Implied Duties of Fair Dealing in Canadian Employment Contracts" (2005), *Queen's Law Journal* 30 (2005): 500.

40. Seymour Moskowitz, "Adolescent Workers and Sexual Harassment," *Labor Law Journal* 51, no. 3 (Fall 2000): 78–84. For an excellent reference guide on sexual harassment, see William Petrocelli and Barbara Kate Repa, *Sexual Harassment on the Job: What It Is and How to Stop It* (Berkeley, CA: Nolo Press, 1998).

41. "Sexual Harassment," *CACSW Fact Sheet*, Canadian Advisory Council on the Status of Women, March 1993.

42. "Inquest Probes Murder-Suicide Involving Harassment Victim," *Sexual Harassment, Workplace Diversity Update* 5, no. 3 (March 1997): 4.

43. Shannon Kari, "B.C. Fire Chief Vows Policy to Combat Sexual Harassment," *The Globe and Mail*, May 31, 2005, A1.

44. Malcolm McKillop, "A Manager's Guide to Sexual Impropriety," *The Globe and Mail*, October 7, 1997, B23.

45. For a good review of sexual harassment policy, see Dana S. Connell, "Effective Sexual Harassment Policies: Unexpected Lessons from Jacksonville Shipyards," *Employee Relations Law Journal* 17, no. 2 (Autumn 1991): 191–205.

46. Katherine Harding, "Taking Aim at Bullies," *The Globe and Mail*, March 19, 2003, C1.

47. Christine L. Taylor, "Dimensions of Diversity in Canadian Business: Building a Business Case for Valuing Ethnocultural Diversity," *Conference Board of Canada Report* (April 1995): 143–195.

48. Paul Moloney, "Toronto Okays Non-Christian Holidays for Staffers," *Toronto Star*, May 17, 1995, A6.

49. S. Hood, "Generational Diversity," *HR Professional* (June–July 2000): 19.

50. Jennie Constantinides, "Diversity Management: At CN, the 'Token' Will Be Broken," *Human Resources Professional* 7, no. 4 (April 1991): 29–30.

51. Statistics Canada, *Canada's Ethnocultural Portrait: The Changing Mosaic*, http://www12.statcan.ca /english/census01/products/analytic/companion /etoimm/pdf/96F0030XIE2001008.pdf; Erin Anderson, "Immigration Shifts Population Kaleidoscope," The *Globe and Mail*, January 22, 2003, A6.

52. Statistics Canada, *Canada's Ethnocultural Portrait*.

53. Jana Schilder, "The Rainbow Connection: Employers Who Promote Diversity May Discover a Pot of Gold," *HR Professional* 11, no. 3 (April 1994): 13–15.

54. Ibid.

55. Doug Nevison, "Profiting in the Pacific Rim: Can Canada Capture Its Share?" *Conference Board of Canada Report*, 1994: 117–194.

56. World Bank, 1993.

57. R. Roosevelt Thomas, Jr., "Beyond Race and Gender," *AMACOM*, 1991: 34.

58. Taylor, "Dimensions of Diversity in Canadian Business," 13.

59. John Spears, "The Many Colours of Money: Diversity Boosts Profit, Firms Told," *Toronto Star*, May 9, 1995.

60. Taylor, "Dimensions of Diversity in Canadian Business," 15.

61. *Continuing In-patient Focused Care Excellence*, Sunnybrook Community and Public Affairs, Sunnybrook Health Sciences Centre, Toronto, April 1995.

62. P. Lungen, "Military Addresses Racism Issue," *Canadian Jewish News* 30, no. 7 (February 17, 2000), 6.

63. Leslie Young, "Global Diversity Standard in Works," *Canadian HR Reporter* (April 5, 1999): 1.

64. Claudine Kapel, "Variation Is the Theme: Organizations That Value Diversity Glimpse Profits in Improved Productivity," *HR Professional* 1, no. 3 (April 1994): 9–12.

65. Taylor, "Dimensions of Diversity in Canadian Business."

66. Ibid, 18.

67. Young, "Global Diversity Standard in Works," *Canadian HR Reporter* (April 5, 1999): 1

CHAPTER

# 4

# Job Analysis and Work Design

MANAGINGHU
HUMANRESOU
RESOURCESM

# After studying this chapter, you should be able to

| OUTCOME 1 | Discuss the relationship between job requirements and HRM functions. |

| OUTCOME 2 | Indicate the methods by which job analysis typically is completed. |

| OUTCOME 3 | Identify and explain the various sections of job descriptions. |

| OUTCOME 4 | Provide examples illustrating the various factors that must be taken into account in designing a job. |

| OUTCOME 5 | Discuss the various job characteristics that motivate employees. |

| OUTCOME 6 | Describe the different group techniques used to maximize employee contributions. |

| OUTCOME 7 | Differentiate and explain the different adjustments in work schedules. |

The business environment is becoming more complex and increasingly competitive. New technology, changing demographics, and a globalized business environment, among other drivers of change, are forcing organizations to "reengineer" themselves to gain competitive advantage and profitability.[1] The goal is to become more efficient and effective. There is emphasis on smaller scale, less hierarchy, fewer layers, and more decentralized work units.[2] As organizational reshaping takes place, managers want employees to operate more independently and flexibly to meet customer demands. To do this, they require that decisions be made by the people who are closest to the information and who are directly involved in the product or service delivered.[3] The objective is to develop jobs and basic work units that are adaptable enough to thrive in a world of high-velocity change.

In this chapter, we will discuss how jobs can be designed so as to best contribute to the objectives of the organization and at the same time satisfy the needs of the employees who are to perform them. Clearly, the duties and responsibilities present in jobs greatly influence employee productivity, job satisfaction, and employment retention.[4] Therefore, the value of job analysis, which defines clearly and precisely the requirements of each job, will be stressed. Importantly, we will emphasize that these job requirements provide the foundation for making objective and legally defensible decisions in managing HR. The chapter concludes by reviewing several innovative job design and employee contribution techniques that increase job satisfaction while improving organizational performance. Teamwork and the characteristics of successful teams are highlighted.

# RELATIONSHIP OF JOB REQUIREMENTS AND HRM FUNCTIONS

OUTCOME 1

**job**
A group of related activities and duties

**position**
The different duties and responsibilities performed by only one employee

**job family**
A group of individual jobs with similar characteristics

**job specification**
A statement of the needed knowledge, skills, and abilities of the person who is to perform the job

**job description**
A statement of the tasks, duties, and responsibilities of a job to be performed

A **job** consists of a group of related activities and duties. Ideally, the duties of a job should consist of natural units of work that are similar and related. They should be clear and distinct from those of other jobs to minimize misunderstanding and conflict among employees and to enable employees to recognize what is expected of them. For some jobs, several employees may be required, each of whom will occupy a separate position. A **position** consists of different duties and responsibilities performed by only one employee. In a city library, for example, four employees (four positions) may be involved in reference work, but all of them have only one job (reference librarian). Where different jobs have similar duties and responsibilities, they may be grouped into a **job family** for the purposes of recruitment, training, compensation, or advancement opportunities.

The information collected for jobs is useful for almost all HRM functions, including strategic HR planning, recruitment, selection, training and development, performance appraisals, compensation management, and legal compliance. This is why job analysis is usually referred to as the "bedrock" for HRM.

## STRATEGIC HR PLANNING

Information on jobs is used to examine a company's organizational structure and strategically position it for the future. Does the firm have the right numbers and types of jobs needed to cover the scope of its activities? What jobs need to be created? What skills do they require? Are those skills different from the skills required by the company's current jobs?

## RECRUITMENT

Before they can find capable employees for an organization, recruiters need to know the job specifications for the positions they are to fill. A **job specification** is a statement of the knowledge, skills, and abilities required of the person performing the job. See Highlights in HRM 4.1 for examples of job specifications.

Because job specifications establish the qualifications required of applicants for a job opening, they serve an essential role in the recruiting function. These qualifications are typically contained in the notices of job openings. Whether posted on organizational bulletin boards or human resource information system (HRIS) Internet sites or included in help wanted advertisements or employment agency listings, job specifications provide a basis for attracting qualified applicants and discouraging unqualified ones.

## SELECTION

In addition to job specifications, managers and supervisors use **job descriptions** to select employees and orient them to jobs. A job description is a statement of the tasks, duties, and responsibilities of a job. (See "Job Descriptions" later in this chapter.)

In the past, job specifications used as a basis for selection sometimes bore little relation to the duties to be performed under the job description. Examples of such non–job-related specifications abounded. Applicants for the job of labourer were required to have a high school diploma. Firefighters were required to be at least six feet tall, and applicants for skilled craft positions—plumbers, electricians, machinists—were required to be male. These kinds of job specifications discriminated against members of designated groups, many of whom were excluded from these jobs.

## TRAINING AND DEVELOPMENT

Any discrepancies between the knowledge, skills, and abilities (often referred to as KSAs) demonstrated by a jobholder and the requirements contained in the description and specification for that job provide clues to training needs. Also, career development as part of the training function is concerned with preparing employees for advancement to jobs where their capacities can be utilized to the fullest extent possible. The formal qualification requirements set forth in high-level jobs indicate how much more training and development are needed for employees to advance to those jobs.

## PERFORMANCE APPRAISAL

The requirements contained in the description of a job provide the criteria for evaluating the performance of the holder of that job. The results of performance appraisal may reveal, however, that certain requirements established for a job are not completely valid. As we have already stressed, these criteria must be specific and job related. If the criteria used to evaluate employee performance are vague and not job related, employers may find themselves being charged with unfair discrimination.

## COMPENSATION MANAGEMENT

In determining the rate to be paid for performing a job, the relative worth of the job is one of the most important factors. This worth is based on what the job demands of an employee in terms of skill, effort, and responsibility, as well as the conditions and hazards under which the work is performed. The systems of job evaluation by which this worth may be measured are discussed in Chapter 9. As the Business Case outlines, job analysis has financial implications and could cause workplace problems if handled poorly.

## LEGAL COMPLIANCE

A systematic collection of job data ensures that a job's duties match its job description. If the criteria used to hire and evaluate employees are vague and not job related, employers are more likely to find themselves being accused of discrimination. In fact, before firms recognized the importance of regularly engaging in the job analysis process, examples of non–job-related criteria were prevalent: job applicants for labourer positions were required to have high school diplomas; applicants for skilled craft positions—plumbers, electricians, machinists—were sometimes required to be male. These kinds of job specifications are discriminatory.

# THE BUSINESS CASE

## Purolator Reduces Skyrocketing Costs

Purolator has been delivering parcels across Canada (and globally) for over 50 years. A few years ago, it decided to grapple with the skyrocketing costs incurred through workers' compensation claims. In 2005, with 2,130 claims filed, the workers' compensation premiums for the company were $13 million. The firm was able to trace 90 percent of the claims to two occupations: couriers and sorters. These jobs required workers to haul, lift, push, and pull on a daily basis; thus, it is not difficult to understand why injuries are common. As part of its strategy to deal with this issue, Purolator implemented a proactive-approach return-to-work program that encouraged workers to return earlier to their jobs. To do so, the company conducted a job analysis of the 25 jobs in the operations area, where most of the injuries occurred. They were able to identify the physical demands of the jobs; this helped coordinators identify suitable jobs for those returning to work and helped convince union representatives and doctors that workers were not at further risk if they returned earlier to the jobs. This helped saved Purolator significant costs in terms of days lost to injuries.

Source: Uyen Vu, "How Purolator Dealt with Skyrocketing Costs," *Canadian HR Reporter* 19, no. 5 (March 13, 2006): 9–10.

# JOB ANALYSIS

**job analysis**
The process of obtaining information about jobs by determining the duties, tasks, or activities of jobs

Organizations exist because people can accomplish more together than they can on their own. However, the actions of an organization need to be coordinated, and each person within it needs to do those things he or she does best. The division of labour allows for efficiency and specialization and potentially greater organizational effectiveness. The question is, how should the work be divided, and which people should do which tasks? It is a question that businesspeople such as Henry Ford and scientific management researchers such as Frederick Winslow Taylor sought to answer at least a century ago, one that managers still deal with today. Their focus was on how best to organize work so as to make it more efficient. To do so, they had to analyze, among other things, the jobs themselves.

Job analysis is sometimes called the cornerstone of HRM because the information it collects serves so many HRM functions. **Job analysis** is the process of obtaining information about jobs by determining the duties, tasks, or activities of those jobs.[5] The procedure involves systematically investigating jobs by following a number of predetermined steps specified in advance of the study.[6] When completed, job analysis results in a written report summarizing the information obtained from the analysis of 20 or 30 individual job tasks or activities. HR managers use these data to develop job descriptions and job specifications. These documents, in turn, are used to perform and enhance the different HR functions such as the development of performance appraisal criteria or the content of training classes. The ultimate purpose of job analysis is to improve organizational performance and productivity. Figure 4.1 illustrates how job analysis is performed, including the functions for which it is used. In contrast to job design, which reflects subjective opinions about the ideal requirements of a job, job analysis is concerned with objective and verifiable information about the actual

**FIGURE 4.1**

THE PROCESS OF JOB ANALYSIS

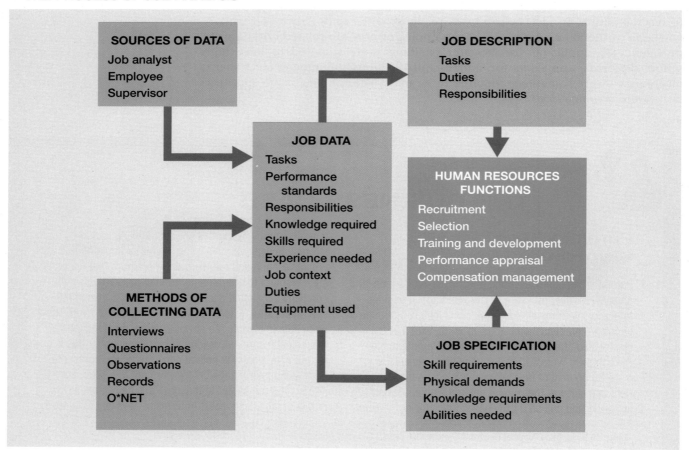

requirements of a job. The job descriptions and job specifications developed through job analysis should be as accurate as possible if they are to be of value to those who make HRM decisions. These decisions may involve any of the HR functions—from recruitment to termination of employees.

## GATHERING JOB INFORMATION

Job data may be obtained in several ways. The more common methods of analyzing jobs are through interviews, questionnaires, observation, and diaries.

- *Interviews.* The job analyst may question individual employees and managers about the job under review.

- *Questionnaires.* The job analyst may circulate carefully prepared questionnaires to be filled out individually by jobholders and managers. These forms will be used to obtain data in the areas of job duties and tasks performed, purpose of the job, physical setting, requirements for performing the job (skill, education, experience, physical and mental demands), equipment and materials used, and special health and safety concerns.

- *Observation.* The job analyst may learn about the jobs by observing and recording on a standardized form the activities of jobholders. Videotaping jobs for later study is an approach used by some organizations.

- *Diaries.* Jobholders themselves may be asked to keep a diary of their work activities during an entire work cycle. Diaries are normally filled out at specific times of the work shift (such as every half-hour or hour) and maintained for a two- to four-week period.

Although HR specialists, called job analysts, are the personnel primarily responsible for the job analysis program, they usually enlist the cooperation of the employees and managers in the departments where jobs are being analyzed (see the Reality Check).

# REALITY CHECK

## Job Analysis at EDS Canada Inc.

As the senior HR specialist at EDS Canada Inc., Don Weatherbee is responsible for conducting job analyses. Although new job codes and classifications are normally developed by head office in Texas, there are three cases that warrant job analysis in Canada. The first is to comply with pay equity legislation that states that men and women should be paid equally for performing work of equal value. To comply with pay equity, jobs are analyzed and weighted for specialized knowledge, effort, responsibility, and the working environment. Salary survey companies are often retained to do this type of analysis because they are the experts in ensuring that the pay grades are in compliance with the *Pay Equity Act* of Ontario.

The second occasion is when new jobs are created, which need to be classified and their compensation rates assessed. In one example, EDS Canada Inc. did not have an entry-level position in HR, so the task force developed an HR administrator position. On another occasion, a business services consultant position needed to be developed at the top end of the business analyst family. Because these positions were new to EDS Canada Inc., the full range of duties needed to be assessed and coded.

The third occasion occurs when, through acquisitions and transitioning people to EDS Canada Inc., job analysis is needed to verify what the employees do because job titles are frequently poor indicators of what a person actually does. For example, when EDS Canada Inc. won a contract bid to do information technology outsourcing for a land registry company, a job analysis was needed to create new job codes for the employees who were transitioning to the company.

Information for both the employees and their supervisors is gathered on a job summary questionnaire (JSQ). This is done to ensure that there is no artificial inflation of job duties. There is one form for management and another form for professional, technical, clerical, trades, and services employees. The management questionnaire is more detailed as it includes areas of responsibilities, supervision given to direct reports, and previous work history that explains how it relates to the present job. Each questionnaire is designed to determine the percentage of time spent on each task, what that task is, for whom the task is done, how it is accomplished, and why it is done.

**CHAPTER 4:** JOB ANALYSIS AND WORK DESIGN

These managers and employees are the sources of much of the information about the jobs and may be asked to prepare rough drafts of the job descriptions and specifications the job analysts need.

## CONTROLLING THE ACCURACY OF JOB INFORMATION

If job analysis is to accomplish its intended purpose, the job data collected must be accurate. Care must be taken to ensure that all important facts are included. A job analyst should be alert for employees who tend to exaggerate the difficulty of their jobs to inflate their egos and their paycheques (see Ethics in HRM).[7] When interviewing employees or reviewing their questionnaires, the job analyst must look for any responses that do not agree with other facts or impressions the analyst has received. One job analyst noted, "When in doubt about the accuracy of employee responses, always double-check the data with others."[8] Furthermore, when job information is collected from employees, a representative group of individuals should be surveyed.

A job analyst who doubts the accuracy of information provided by employees should obtain additional information from them, their managers, or other individuals who are familiar with or perform the same job. It is common practice to have the descriptions for each job reviewed by the jobholders and their managers.

### The NOC and Job Analysis

Commonly referred to as the NOC, the National Occupational Classification is compiled by the federal government. The purpose of the NOC is to compile, analyze, and communicate information about occupations. This information can be used for employment equity, HR planning, and occupational supply-and-demand forecasts and analyses.

The NOC is a composite of the Canadian labour market and has helped bring about a greater degree of uniformity in the job titles and descriptions used by employers in different parts of the country. This uniformity has facilitated the movement of workers from regions that may be experiencing widespread unemployment to areas where employment opportunities are greater. Also, the NOC code numbers facilitate the exchange of statistical information about jobs and are useful in reporting research in the HR area, in vocational counselling, and in

---

# ETHICS IN HRM

## Job Inflation

Many organizations update their job descriptions at regular intervals. This is because, among other reasons, jobs change; others may become obsolete, and some may be new. During this process, a job analysis will most likely be done and employees may be asked, through interviews or surveys, for instance, to describe their jobs, including the tasks they perform and their responsibilities. They may sense that this is an opportunity to inflate their jobs so as to make it appear more important. They may perceive that by inflating their jobs, they will become entitled to better compensation and benefits. Or it may just satisfy their egos. Even managers and supervisors may be tempted to inflate the jobs of their subordinates.

This would make their own roles appear to be more complex, thus providing the possibility of increased pay and promotions. Some firms give fancy titles to reflect these outcomes—a senior teller at a bank becomes a senior customer service coordinator or a supervisor at a call centre becomes a second vice president. Night clerks in hotels become auditors, and receptionists become administrators. Although some of these new titles offer a fleeting boost to the egos of the jobholders, there are questions on the ethics of the process, especially when the hope of increased pay may be tied to the outcomes.

charting career paths through job transfers and/or advancements. Some professional associations provide a job classification system that is intended to be more current than the NOC.[9]

## APPROACHES TO JOB ANALYSIS

The systematic and quantitative definition of job content that job analysis provides is the foundation of many HRM practices. Specifically, the job analysis serves to justify job descriptions and other HRM selection procedures. Several different job analysis approaches are used to gather data, each with specific advantages and disadvantages.[10] Four of the more popular methods are the position analysis questionnaire, critical incident method, task inventory analysis, and competency-based analysis.

### The Position Analysis Questionnaire System

The **position analysis questionnaire (PAQ)** is a quantifiable data collection method covering 194 different worker-oriented tasks. Using a five-point scale, the PAQ seeks to determine the degree, if any, to which the different tasks, or job elements, are involved in performing a particular job.

A sample page from the PAQ covering 11 elements of the Information Input Division is shown in Figure 4.2. The person conducting an analysis with this questionnaire would rate each of the elements using the five-point scale shown in the upper right-hand corner of the sample page. The results obtained with the PAQ are quantitative and can be subjected to statistical analysis. The PAQ also permits dimensions of behaviour to be compared across a number of jobs and permits jobs to be grouped on the basis of common characteristics.

### The Critical Incident Method

The objective of the **critical incident method** is to identify critical job tasks. Critical job tasks are those important duties and job responsibilities performed by the jobholder that lead to job success. Information about critical job tasks can be collected through interviews with employees or managers or through self-report statements written by employees.

Suppose, for example, that the job analyst is studying the job of reference librarian. The interviewer will ask the employee to describe the job on the basis of what is done, how the job is performed, and what tools and equipment are used. The reference librarian may describe the job as follows:

> I assist clients by answering their questions related to finding books, periodicals, or other library materials. I also give them directions to help them find materials within the building. To perform my job, I may have to look up materials myself or refer patrons to someone who can directly assist them. Some individuals may need training in how to use reference materials or special library facilities. I also give library tours to new patrons. I use computers and a variety of reference books to carry out my job.

After the job data are collected, the analyst then writes separate task statements that represent important job activities. For the reference librarian, one task statement might be, "Listens to clients and answers their questions related to locating library materials." Typically, the job analyst writes 5 to 10 important task statements for each job under study. The final product comprises written task statements that are clear, complete, and easily understood by those unfamiliar with the job. The critical incident method is an important job analysis method because it teaches the analyst to focus on employee behaviours critical to job success.

**position analysis questionnaire (PAQ)**
A questionnaire covering 194 different tasks that, by means of a five-point scale, seeks to determine the degree to which different tasks are involved in performing a particular job

**critical incident method**
A job analysis method by which important job tasks are identified for job success

**Using the Internet**

For additional information on various job analytic techniques, see

**http://www.humanresources.hrvinet.com/18-methods-of-job-analysis/**

## FIGURE 4.2

### A SAMPLE PAGE FROM THE PAQ

# INFORMATION INPUT

**1 INFORMATION INPUT**

*1.1 Sources of Job Information*

| Extent of Use (U) | |
|---|---|
| NA | Does not apply |
| 1 | Nominal/very infequent |
| 2 | Occasional |
| 3 | Moderate |
| 4 | Considerable |
| 5 | Very substantial |

Rate each of the following items in terms of the extent to which it is used by the worker as a source of information in performing his job.

**1.1.1**     Visual Sources of Job Information

**01 U**     Written materials (books, reports, office notes, articles, job instructions, signs, etc.)

**02 U**     Quantitative materials (materials which deal with quantities or amounts, such as graphs, accounts, specifications, tables of numbers, etc.)

**03 U**     Pictorial materials (pictures or picturelike materials used as sources of information, for example, drawings, blueprints, diagrams, maps, tracings, photographic films, x-ray films, TV pictures, etc.)

**04 U**     Patterns/related devices (templates, stencils, patterns, etc., used as sources of information when observed during use; do not include here materials described in item 3 above)

**05 U**     Visual displays (dials, gauges, signal lights, radarscopes, speedometers, clocks, etc.)

**06 U**     Measuring devices (rulers, calipers, tire pressure gauges, scales, thickness gauges, pipettes, thermometers, protractors, etc., used to obtain visual information about physical measurements; do not include here devices described in item 5 above)

**07 U**     Mechanical devices (tools, equipment, machinery, and other mechanical devices which are sources of information when observed during use or operation)

**08 U**     Materials in process (parts, materials, objects, etc., which are sources of information when being modified, worked on, or otherwise processed, such as bread dough being mixed, workpiece being turned in a lathe, fabric being cut, shoe being resoled, etc.)

**09 U**     Materials not in process (parts, materials, objects, etc., not in the process of being changed or modified, which are sources of information when being inspected, handled, packaged, distributed, or selected, etc., such as items or materials in inventory, storage, or distribution channels, items being inspected, etc.)

**10 U**     Features of nature (landscapes, fields, geological samples, vegetation, cloud formations, and other features of nature which are observed or inspected to provide information)

**11 U**     Man-made features of environment (structures, buildings, dams, highways, bridges, docks, railroads, and other "man-made" or altered aspects of the indoor or outdoor environment which are observed or inspected to provide job information; do not consider equipment, machines, etc., that an individual uses in his work, as covered by item 7)

**Source:** Position Analysis Questionnaire, copyright 1969, 1989 by Purdue Research Foundation, West Lafayette, IN 47907. Reprinted with permission.

## Task Inventory Analysis

The **task inventory analysis** method can be considered a job-oriented type of job analysis. The technique was pioneered by the U.S. Air Force to analyze jobs held by Air Force specialists. Unlike the PAQ, which uses a standardized form to analyze jobs in different organizations, a task inventory questionnaire can be tailor-made to a specific organization.

The technique is developed by identifying—with the help of employees and managers—a list of tasks and their descriptions that are components of different jobs. The goal is to produce a comprehensive list of task statements that are applicable to all jobs. Task statements are then listed on a task inventory survey form to be completed by the person analyzing the job under review. A task statement might be, "Inventories current supplies to maintain stock levels." The job analysis would also note the importance and frequency of use of the task to the successful completion of the job.

**task inventory analysis**
An organization-specific list of tasks and their descriptions used as a basis to identify components of jobs

## Competency-Based Analysis

The traditional approach to job analysis assumes a static job environment in which jobs remain relatively stable apart from incumbents who might hold these jobs. Here, jobs can be meaningfully defined in terms of tasks, duties, processes, and skills necessary for job success. This assumption, unfortunately, discounts technological advances that are often so accelerated that jobs, as they are defined today, may be obsolete tomorrow. Furthermore, the need to respond to global change can alter the nature of jobs and the requirement of individuals needed to perform them successfully. Therefore, in a dynamic environment where job demands rapidly change, obsolete job analysis information simply hinders an organization's ability to adapt to change.

When organizations operate in a fast-moving environment, managers may adopt a competency-based approach to job analysis.[11] This job analysis method relies on building job profiles that look at the responsibilities and activities of jobs and the worker competencies necessary to accomplish them. The objective is to identify "key" competencies for organizational success. Competencies can be identified through focus groups, surveys, or interviews and might include such things as interpersonal communication skills, decision-making ability, conflict resolution skills, adaptability, or self-motivation. An organization's job descriptions, recruitment requirements, and performance evaluation system will reflect the competencies needed by employees.

Task inventory analysis uses employees to develop lists of job tasks and descriptions common to all jobs.

## HRIS and Job Analysis

HRISs have greatly facilitated the job analysis process. Available today are various software programs designed specifically to analyze jobs and to write job descriptions and job specifications based on those analyses. These programs normally contain generalized task statements that can apply to many different jobs. Managers and employees select those statements that best describe the job under review, indicating the importance of the task to the total job where appropriate. Advanced computer applications of job analysis combine job analysis with job evaluation (see Chapter 9) and the pricing of organizational jobs. Computerized job analysis systems can be expensive to initiate, but where the organization has many jobs to analyze, the cost per job may be low. HR publications such as *Canadian HR Reporter* contain advertisements from numerous software companies offering HRIS job analysis packages.

## JOB DESCRIPTIONS

**OUTCOME 3**

As previously noted, a job description is a written description of a job and the types of duties it includes. Since there is no standard format for job descriptions, they tend to vary in appearance and content from one organization to another. However, most job descriptions will contain at least three parts: a job title, a job identification section, and a job duties section. If the job specifications are not prepared as a separate document, they are usually stated in the concluding section of the job description. Highlights in HRM 4.1 shows a job description for an HR employment assistant. This sample job description includes both job duties and job specifications and should satisfy most of the job information needs of managers who must recruit, interview, and orient a new employee.[12]

Job descriptions are of value to both the employees and the employer. From the employees' standpoint, job descriptions can be used to help them learn their job duties and to remind them of the results they are expected to achieve. From the employer's standpoint, written job descriptions can serve as a basis for minimizing the misunderstandings that occur between managers and their subordinates concerning job requirements. They also establish management's right to take corrective action when the duties covered by the job description are not performed as required.

### Job Title

Selection of a job title is important for several reasons. First, the job title is of psychological importance, providing status to the employee. For instance, "sanitation engineer" is a more appealing title than "garbage collector." Second, if possible, the title should provide some indication of what the duties of the job entail. Titles such as *meat inspector, electronics assembler, salesperson,* and *engineer* obviously hint at the nature of the duties of these jobs. The job title also should indicate the relative level occupied by its holder in the organizational hierarchy. For example, the title *junior engineer* implies that this job occupies a lower level than that of *senior engineer.*

### Job Identification Section

The job identification section of a job description usually follows the job title. It includes items such as the departmental location of the job, the person to whom the jobholder reports, and the date the job description was last revised. "Job Statement" usually appears at the bottom of this section and distinguishes the job from other jobs—something the job title may fail to do.

### Job Duties, or Essential Functions, Section

Statements covering job duties are typically arranged in order of importance. These statements should indicate the weight, or value, of each duty. Usually, but not always, the weight of a duty can be gauged by the percentage of time

# HIGHLIGHTS IN HRM 4.1

## Job Description for an HR Employment Assistant

**Job Identification**

### JOB TITLE: Employment Assistant

| | |
|---|---|
| Division: | Western Region |
| Department: | Human Resources Management |
| Job Analyst: | Virginia Sasaki |
| Date Analyzed: | 12/3/11 |
| Report to: | HR Manager Job Code: 11–17 |
| Date Verified: | 12/17/11 |

**Brief Listing of Major Duties**

### Job Statement

Performs professional human resources work in the areas of employee recruitment and selection, testing, orientation, transfers, and maintenance of employee human resources files. May handle special assignments and projects in employment equity, employee grievances, training, or classification and compensation. Works under general supervision. Incumbent exercises initiative and independent judgment in the performance of assigned tasks.

**Essential Functions and Responsibilities**

### Essential Functions

1. Prepares recruitment literature and job advertisements for applicant placement.

2. Schedules and conducts personal interviews to determine applicant suitability for employment. Includes reviewing mailed applications and résumés for qualified personnel.

3. Supervises administration of testing program. Responsible for developing or improving testing instruments and procedures.

4. Presents orientation program to all new employees. Reviews and develops all materials and procedures for orientation program.

5. Coordinates division job posting and transfer program. Establishes job-posting procedures. Responsible for reviewing transfer applications, arranging transfer interviews, and determining effective transfer dates.

6. Maintains a daily working relationship with division managers on human resources matters, including recruitment concerns, retention or release of probationary employees, and discipline or discharge of permanent employees.

7. Distributes new or revised human resources policies and procedures to all employees and managers through bulletins, meetings, memorandums, and/or personal contact.

8. Performs related duties as assigned by the human resources manager.

**Job Specifications and Requirements**

### Job Specifications

1. Four-year college or university degree with major course work in human resources management, business administration, or industrial psychology OR a combination of experience, education, and training equivalent to a four-year degree in human resources management.

2. Considerable knowledge of principles of employee selection and assignment of personnel.

3. Ability to express ideas clearly in both written and oral communications.

4. Ability to independently plan and organize one's own activities.

5. Knowledge of human resources computer applications desirable.

devoted to it. The statements should stress the responsibilities all the duties entail and the results they are to accomplish. It is also general practice to indicate the tools and equipment used by the employee in performing the job. Remember, the job duties section must list only the essential functions of the job to be performed.

## Job Specification Section

As stated earlier, the personal qualifications an individual must possess to perform the duties and responsibilities contained in a job description are compiled in the job specification. Typically, this section covers two areas: (1) the skill required to perform the job and (2) the physical demands the job places on the employee performing it.

Skills relevant to a job include education or experience, specialized training, personal traits or abilities, and manual dexterities. The physical demands of a job refer to how much walking, standing, reaching, lifting, or talking must be done on the job. The condition of the physical work environment and the hazards employees may encounter are also among the physical demands of a job.

Job specifications should also include interpersonal skills or key competencies necessary for job success. For example, behavioural competencies might include the ability to make decisions on imperfect information, decisiveness, the ability to handle multiple tasks, and conflict resolution skills. Behavioural competencies can be assessed by asking applicants situational interview questions (see Chapter 6). For example, a manager could ask an applicant about a time when he or she had to make a critical decision quickly.

## PROBLEMS WITH JOB DESCRIPTIONS

Managers consider job descriptions a valuable tool for performing HRM functions. Nevertheless, several problems are frequently associated with these documents, including the following:

1. If they are poorly written, using vague rather than specific terms, they provide little guidance to the jobholder.
2. They are sometimes not updated as job duties or specifications change.
3. They may violate the law by containing specifications not related to job success.
4. They can limit the scope of activities of the jobholder, reducing organizational flexibility.

## Writing Clear and Specific Job Descriptions

When writing a job description, it is essential to use statements that are terse, direct, and simply worded. Unnecessary words or phrases should be eliminated. Typically, the sentences that describe job duties begin with a present-tense verb, with the implied subject of the sentence being the employee performing the job. The term *occasionally* is used to describe duties that are performed once in a while. The term *may* is used in connection with duties performed only by some workers on the job.

Managers may find that writing job descriptions is a tedious process that distracts from other supervisory responsibilities. Fortunately, software packages are available to simplify this time-consuming yet necessary task. One program provides an initial library of more than 2,500 prewritten job descriptions. Since the program works much like a word processor, text can be easily deleted, inserted, or modified to user demands.

# JOB DESIGN

It is not uncommon for managers and supervisors to confuse the processes of job analysis and job design. Job analysis is the study of jobs as currently performed by employees. It helps with the job description, which identifies job duties and the requirements needed to perform the work successfully. **Job design**, which is an outgrowth of job analysis, is concerned with structuring jobs to improve organization efficiency and employee job satisfaction. Job design is concerned with changing, modifying, and enriching jobs to capture the talents of employees while improving organizational performance.[13] Job design should facilitate the achievement of organizational objectives. At the same time, the design should recognize the capabilities and needs of those who are to perform the job.

As Figure 4.3 illustrates, job design is a combination of four basic considerations: (1) the organizational objectives the job was created to fulfill; (2) behavioural concerns that influence an employee's job satisfaction; (3) industrial engineering considerations, including ways to make the job technologically efficient; and (4) ergonomic concerns, including workers' physical and mental capabilities.[14] We have already briefly discussed the organizational objective considerations of job design—for example, to improve efficiency and employee job satisfaction. We will now look more closely at the other three considerations.

**job design**
An outgrowth of job analysis that improves jobs through technological and human considerations to enhance organization efficiency and employee job satisfaction

## BEHAVIOURAL CONCERNS

Would you like it if your supervisor timed down to the minute each task associated with your job and then asked you to adhere to those times? Would you find this motivating? Probably not. In an effort to counter the motivational problems that occur when workers do standardized, repetitive tasks, researchers began proposing theories they believed could improve simultaneously the efficiency of organizations and the job satisfaction of employees. Job design methods seek to incorporate the behavioural needs of employees as they perform their individual jobs. The two methods discussed below strive to satisfy the intrinsic needs of employees and motivate them in their work environments. The job enrichment model and the job characteristics model have long been popular with researchers and practitioners as ways to increase the job satisfaction of employees.

**FIGURE 4.3**

BASIS FOR JOB DESIGN

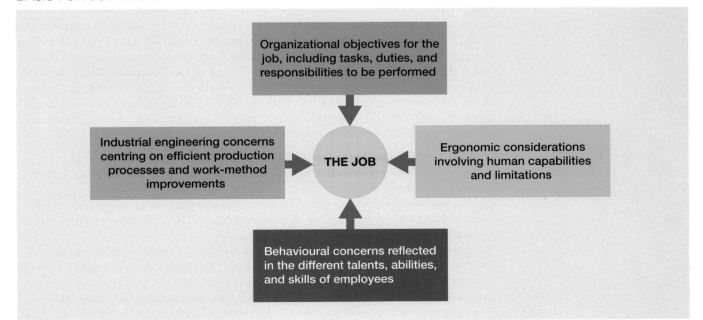

**job enrichment**
Enhancing a job by adding more meaningful tasks and duties to make the work more rewarding or satisfying

**job characteristics model**
A job design theory that purports that three psychological states (experiencing meaningfulness of the work performed, responsibility for work outcomes, and knowledge of the results of the work performed) of a jobholder result in improved work performance, internal motivation, and lower absenteeism and turnover

## Job Enrichment

Any effort that makes work more rewarding or satisfying by adding more meaningful tasks to an employee's job is called **job enrichment**. Originally popularized by Frederick Herzberg, job enrichment is touted as fulfilling the high motivational needs of employees, such as self-fulfillment and self-esteem, while achieving long-term job satisfaction and performance goals.[15] Job enrichment, or the vertical expansion of jobs, may be accomplished by increasing the autonomy and responsibility of employees. Herzberg discusses five factors for enriching jobs and thereby motivating employees: achievement, recognition, growth, responsibility, and performance of the whole job versus only parts of the job. For example, managers can use these five factors to enrich the jobs of employees by

- Increasing the level of difficulty and responsibility of the job
- Allowing employees to retain more authority and control over work outcomes
- Providing unit or individual job performance reports directly to employees
- Adding new tasks to the job that require training and growth
- Assigning individuals specific tasks, enabling them to use their particular competencies or skills

These factors allow employees to assume a greater role in the decision-making process and become more involved in planning, organizing, directing, and controlling their own work. Vertical job enrichment can also be accomplished by organizing workers into teams and giving these teams greater authority for self-management.

In spite of the benefits to be achieved through job enrichment, it must not be considered a panacea for overcoming production problems and employee discontent. Job enrichment programs are more likely to succeed in some jobs and work situations than in others. They are not the solution to problems such as dissatisfaction with pay, employee benefits, or employment security. Moreover, not all employees object to the mechanical pacing of an assembly line, nor do all employees seek additional responsibility or challenge. Some prefer routine jobs because these jobs are predictable and concise.

## Job Characteristics

**OUTCOME 5**

Job design studies explored a new field when behavioural scientists focused on identifying various job dimensions that would improve simultaneously the efficiency of organizations and the job satisfaction of employees. Perhaps the theory that best exemplifies this research is the one advanced by Richard Hackman and Greg Oldham.[16] Their **job characteristics model** proposes that three psychological states of a jobholder result in improved work performance, internal motivation, and lower absenteeism and turnover.[17] A motivated, satisfied, and productive employee (1) experiences *meaningfulness* of the work performed, (2) experiences *responsibility* for work outcomes, and (3) has *knowledge of the results* of the work performed. Hackman and Oldham believe that five core job dimensions produce the three psychological states. The five job characteristics are as follows:

1. *Skill variety:* the degree to which a job entails a variety of different activities, which demand the use of a number of different skills and talents by the jobholder
2. *Task identity:* the degree to which the job requires completion of a whole and identifiable piece of work, that is, doing a job from beginning to end with a visible outcome
3. *Task significance:* the degree to which the job has a substantial impact on the lives or work of other people, whether in the immediate organization or in the external environment
4. *Autonomy:* the degree to which the job provides substantial freedom, independence, and discretion to the individual in scheduling the work and in determining the procedures to be used in carrying it out

5. *Feedback:* the degree to which carrying out the work activities required by the job results in the individual being given direct and clear information about the effectiveness of his or her performance

**employee empowerment**
Granting employees power to initiate change, thereby encouraging them to take charge of what they do

The job characteristics model appears to work best when certain conditions are met. One of these conditions is that employees must have the psychological desire for the autonomy, variety, responsibility, and challenge of enriched jobs. When this personal characteristic is absent, employees may resist the job redesign effort. In addition, job redesign efforts almost always fail when employees lack the physical or mental skills, abilities, or education needed to perform the job. Forcing enriched jobs on individuals lacking these traits can result in frustrated employees.

## Employee Empowerment

Job enrichment and job characteristics are specific programs by which managers or supervisors can formally change the jobs of employees. A less structured method is to allow employees to initiate their own job changes through the concept of empowerment. **Employee empowerment** is a technique of involving employees in their work through the process of inclusion. Empowerment encourages employees to become innovators and managers of their own work and involves them in their jobs in ways that give them more control and autonomous decision-making capabilities (see Highlights in HRM 4.2).

# HIGHLIGHTS IN HRM 4.2

## Empowered Employees Achieve Results

In today's highly competitive and dynamic business environment, employers as diverse as Home Depot and RBC have turned to their employees to improve organizational performance. Empowered employees have made improvements in product or service quality; reduced costs; and modified or, in some cases, designed products.

- At Kraft Foods, employees participated in work redesign changes and team building that increased productivity, reduced overhead, and cut assembly time.

- At a Ford factory, one group of employees made a suggestion that resulted in savings of $115,000 annually on the purchase of gloves used to protect workers who handle sheet metal and glass. The group figured out how to have the gloves washed so that they could be used more than once.

- Home Depot's Special Project Support Teams (SPST) work to improve the organization's business and information services. Employees with a wide range of backgrounds and skills collaborate to address a wide range of strategic and tactical business needs.

- American Airlines' "Rainbow Team" of gay employees brought in $192 million in annual revenue by targeting the gay community.

Although defining empowerment can become the first step to achieving it, for empowerment to grow and thrive, organizations must encourage these conditions:

- *Participation.* Employees must be encouraged to take control of their work tasks. Employees, in turn, must care about improving their work process and interpersonal work relationships.

- *Innovation.* The environment must be receptive to people with innovative ideas and encourage people to explore new paths and to take reasonable risks at reasonable costs. An empowered environment is created when curiosity is as highly regarded as is technical expertise.

- *Access to information.* Employees must have access to a wide range of information. Involved individuals decide what kind of information they need for performing their jobs.

- *Accountability.* Empowerment does not involve being able to do whatever you want. Empowered employees should be held accountable for their behaviour toward others, producing agreed-on results, achieving credibility, and operating with a positive approach.

**industrial engineering**
A field of study concerned with analyzing work methods and establishing time standards

**ergonomics**
An interdisciplinary approach to designing equipment and systems that can be easily and efficiently used by human beings

Additionally, employee empowerment succeeds when the culture of the organization is open and receptive to change.[18]

## INDUSTRIAL ENGINEERING CONSIDERATIONS

The study of work is an important contribution of the scientific management movement. **Industrial engineering**, which evolved with this movement, is concerned with analyzing work methods and establishing time standards.[19] Specifically, it involves the study of work cycles to determine which, if any, elements can be modified, combined, rearranged, or eliminated to reduce the time needed to complete the cycle. Next, time standards are established by recording the time required to complete each element in the work cycle, using a stopwatch or work-sampling technique. By combining the times for each element, observers can determine the total time required. This time is subsequently adjusted to allow for the skill and effort demonstrated by the observed worker and for interruptions that may occur in performing the work. The adjusted time becomes the time standard for that particular work cycle.

Industrial engineering constitutes a disciplined and objective approach to job design. Unfortunately, the concern of industrial engineering for improving efficiency and simplifying work methods may cause the behavioural considerations in job design to be neglected. What may be improvements in job design and efficiency from an engineering standpoint can sometimes prove psychologically unsound. For example, the assembly line, with its simplified and repetitive tasks, embodies sound principles of industrial engineering, but these tasks are often not psychologically rewarding for those who must perform them. Thus, to be effective, job design must also provide for the satisfaction of behavioural needs.

## ERGONOMIC CONSIDERATIONS

Consider this statistic. In North America, millions of workplace injuries occur yearly from motions such as lifting, bending, and typing. These injuries cost employers through lost productivity, medical benefits, and lost time payments. Therefore, ergonomics is an important element of job design.

**Ergonomics** is the study of people at work and the practice of matching the features of products and jobs to human capabilities, preference, and the limitations of those who are to perform a job. Ergonomics focuses on ensuring that jobs are designed for safe and efficient work while improving the safety, comfort, and performance of users. In short, it seeks to fit the job to the person rather than the person to the job. Additionally, ergonomics attempts to minimize the harmful effects of carelessness, negligence, and other human fallibilities that otherwise may cause product defects, damage to equipment, or even the injury or death of employees.[20] Alan Hedge, professor of ergonomics at Cornell University, notes, "The goal of sound ergonomics is to boost employee performance while reducing injuries and errors."[21]

Equipment design must consider the physical abilities of operators to use the equipment and to react through vision, hearing, and touch to the way the equipment operates. For example, there is substantial variation in the way individuals move depending on their physical size, gender, age, and other factors. Designing equipment controls to be compatible with both the physical characteristics and the reaction capabilities of the people who must operate them and the environment in which they work is critically important.

Ergonomics improves productivity and morale and yields a positive return on investment (ROI). Ergonomics has proven cost-effective at organizations such as Compaq Computer and Pratt & Whitney. Ergonomics has recently focused on the elimination, or at least reduction, of many repetitive-motion injuries, particularly those related to the back and wrist. For example, with the increased use

**FIGURE 4.4**

PART 2

COMPUTER WORKSTATION ERGONOMICS CHECKLIST

Use the following list to identify potential problem areas that should receive further investigation. Any "no" response may point to a problem.

1. Does the workstation ensure proper worker posture, such as
   - Thighs in the horizontal position?
   - Lower legs in the vertical position?
   - Feet flat on the floor or on a footrest?
   - Wrists straight and relaxed?

2. Does the chair
   - Adjust easily?
   - Have a padded seat with a rounded front?
   - Have an adjustable backrest?
   - Provide lumbar support?
   - Have casters?

3. Are the height and tilt of the work surface on which the keyboard is located adjustable?
4. Is the keyboard detachable?
5. Do keying actions require minimal force?
6. Is there an adjustable document holder?
7. Are armrests provided where needed?
8. Are glare and reflections minimized?
9. Does the monitor have brightness and contrast controls?
10. Is there sufficient space for knees and feet?
11. Can the workstation be used for either right- or left-handed activity?

**Source:** The National Institute of Occupational Safety and Health (NIOSH), *Elements of Ergonomics Programs: A Primer Based on Workplace Evaluations of Musculoskeletal Disorders* (Washington, DC: U.S. Government Printing Office, March 1997).

of computers, ergonomics has particular application at employee workstations. Figure 4.4 provides a checklist of potential repetitive-motion problem areas for employees using computers.

## DESIGNING WORK FOR GROUPS AND TEAMS

Although a variety of group techniques have been developed to involve employees more fully in their organizations, all of these techniques have two characteristics in common: enhancing collaboration and increasing synergy. In increasing the degree of collaboration in the work environment, these techniques can improve work processes and organizational decision making. In increasing group synergy, the techniques underline the adage that the contributions of two or more employees are greater than the sum of their

| OUTCOME 6

Many companies willingly invest in ergonomically designed workstations because they protect the health and productivity of employees.

Valeriy Lebedev/Shuttershock.com

**employee involvement groups (EIs)**
Groups of employees who meet to resolve problems or offer suggestions for organizational improvement

individual efforts. Furthermore, research has shown that working in a group setting strengthens employee commitment to the organization's goals, increases employee acceptance of decisions, and encourages a cooperative approach to workplace tasks.[22] Two collaborative techniques are discussed here: employee involvement groups and employee teams.

## Employee Involvement Groups

Groups of 5 to 10 employees doing similar or related work who meet regularly to identify, analyze, and suggest solutions to shared problems are often referred to as **employee involvement groups (EIs)**. Also known as *quality circles (QCs)*, EIs are used principally as a means of involving employees in the larger goals of the organization through their suggestions for improving product or service quality and cutting costs.[23] Generally, EIs recommend their solutions to management, which decides whether to implement them.

The EI process, illustrated in Figure 4.5, begins with EI members brainstorming job-related problems or concerns and gathering data about these issues. The process continues through the generation of solutions and recommendations that are then communicated to management. If the solutions are implemented, the results are measured, and the EI and its members are usually recognized for the contributions they have made. EIs typically meet four or more hours per month, and the meetings are chaired by a leader chosen from the group. The leader does not hold an authority position but instead serves as a discussion facilitator.

Although EIs have become an important employee contribution system, they are not without their problems and their critics. First, to achieve the results desired, those participating in EIs must receive comprehensive training in problem identification, problem analysis, and various decision-making tools, such as statistical analysis and cause-and-effect diagrams. Comprehensive training for EIs is often cited as the most important factor leading to their

## FIGURE 4.5

### THE DYNAMICS OF EMPLOYEE INVOLVEMENT GROUPS

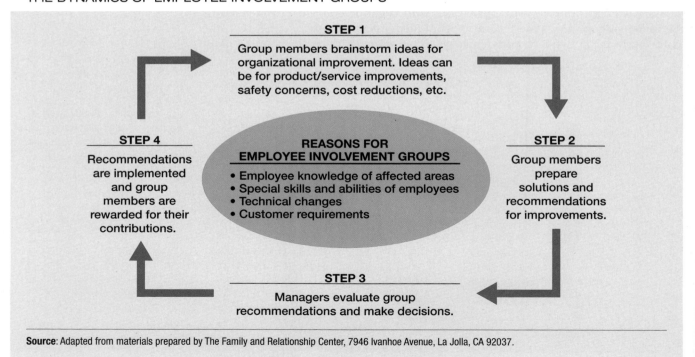

**STEP 1**
Group members brainstorm ideas for organizational improvement. Ideas can be for product/service improvements, safety concerns, cost reductions, etc.

**STEP 2**
Group members prepare solutions and recommendations for improvements.

**STEP 3**
Managers evaluate group recommendations and make decisions.

**STEP 4**
Recommendations are implemented and group members are rewarded for their contributions.

**REASONS FOR EMPLOYEE INVOLVEMENT GROUPS**
- Employee knowledge of affected areas
- Special skills and abilities of employees
- Technical changes
- Customer requirements

**Source**: Adapted from materials prepared by The Family and Relationship Center, 7946 Ivanhoe Avenue, La Jolla, CA 92037.

success. Second, managers should recognize the group when a recommendation is made, regardless of whether the recommendation is adopted. This approach encourages the group to continue coming up with ideas even when they are not all implemented by management. Third, some organizations have found that EIs run out of ideas, and management must feed them ideas to keep the process going. Finally, and most important, managers and supervisors must exhibit a participative/democratic leadership style in which employees are encouraged to work collaboratively with management to improve organizational performance.

## Employee Teams

During the past decade, perhaps one of the more radical changes to how work is done is the introduction of organizational teams. Jim Barksdale, president and chief executive officer (CEO) of Netscape Communications, states, "These days it seems as if every time a task needs to be accomplished within an organization, a team is formed to do it." This statement simply emphasizes the increasing importance of teams to organizational success in an ever-dynamic business climate. At such diverse organizations as FedEx, Hewlett-Packard, and LucasFilm, producer of the *Star Wars* and *Indiana Jones* films, the benefits of employee teams have included more integration of individual skills, better performance in terms of quality and quantity, solutions to unique and complex problems, reduced delivery time, reduced turnover and absenteeism, and accomplishments among team members.[24]

**Employee teams** are a logical outgrowth of employee involvement and the philosophy of empowerment. Although many definitions of teams exist, we define a work team as a group of individuals working together toward a common purpose, in which members have complementary skills, members' work is mutually dependent, and the group has discretion over tasks performed. Furthermore, teams seek to make members of the work group share responsibility and accountability for their group's performance. Inherent in the concept of employee teams is that employees, not managers, are in the best position to contribute to workplace performance. With work teams, managers accept the notion that the group is the logical work unit for applying resources to resolve organizational problems and concerns.[25]

Teamwork also embraces the concept of *synergy*. Synergy occurs when the interaction and outcome of team members are greater than the sum of their

**employee teams**
An employee contributions technique whereby work functions are structured for groups rather than for individuals and team members are given discretion in matters traditionally considered management prerogatives, such as process improvements, product or service development, and individual work assignments

 **Using the Internet**

The Employee Involvement Association has interesting content on this issue at
**http://www.eianet.org**

Teams create synergy through the integration of their members' knowledge, skills, and abilities and the acceptance of individual diversities.

Vadym Drobot/Shutterstock

## FIGURE 4.6

### SYNERGISTIC TEAM CHARACTERISTICS

Team synergy is heightened when team members engage in these positive behaviours.

- *Support.* The team exhibits an atmosphere of inclusion. All team members speak up and feel free to offer constructive comments.
- *Listening and clarification.* Active listening is practised. Members honestly listen to others and seek clarification on discussion points. Team members summarize discussions held.
- *Disagreement.* Disagreement is seen as natural and is expected. Member comments are nonjudgmental and focus on factual issues rather than personality conflicts.

- *Consensus.* Team members reach agreements through consensus decision making. Consensus decisions require finding a proposal that is acceptable to all team members, even if not the first choice of individual members. Common ground among ideas is sought.
- *Acceptance.* Team members are valued as individuals, recognizing that each person brings a valuable mix of skills and abilities to team operations.
- *Quality.* Each team member is committed to excellent performance. There is emphasis on continuous improvement and attention to detail.

individual efforts.[26] Unfortunately, synergy may not automatically happen; rather, it must be nurtured within the team environment.[27] Figure 4.6 lists the factors contributing to a synergistic team setting.

Teams can operate in a variety of structures, each with different strategic purposes or functional activities. Figure 4.7 describes common team forms. One form, self-directed teams, is often championed as being the highest form of team structure. Self-directed teams, also called *autonomous work groups*, *self-managed teams*, or *high-performance teams*, are groups of employees who are accountable for a "whole" work process or segment that delivers a product or service to an internal or external customer. For example, in a manufacturing environment, a team might be responsible for a whole product (e.g., a computer screen) or a clearly defined segment of the production process, such as the building of an engine for a passenger car. Similarly, in a service environment, a team is usually responsible for entire groupings of products and services, often serving clients in a designated geographic area. Typical team functions include setting work schedules, dealing directly with external customers, training team members, setting performance targets, budgeting, managing inventory, and purchasing equipment or services. To operate efficiently, team members acquire multiple skills, enabling them to perform a variety of job tasks.

## FIGURE 4.7

### FORMS OF EMPLOYEE TEAMS

- *Cross-functional teams:* a group staffed with a mix of specialists (e.g., marketing, production, engineering) and formed to accomplish a specific objective. Cross-functional teams are based on assigned rather than voluntary membership.
- *Project teams:* a group formed specifically to design a new product or service. Members are assigned by management on the basis of their ability to contribute to success. The group normally disbands after task completion.
- *Self-directed teams:* groups of highly trained individuals performing a set of interdependent job tasks within a natural work unit. Team members use consensus decision

making to perform work duties, solve problems, or deal with internal or external customers.
- *Task force teams:* a task force is formed by management to immediately resolve a major problem. The group is responsible for developing a long-term plan for problem resolution that may include a charge for implementing the solution proposed.
- *Process improvement teams:* a group made up of experienced people from different departments or functions and charged with improving quality, decreasing waste, or enhancing productivity in processes that affect all departments or functions involved. Team members are normally appointed by management.

To compete in today's national and international markets, managers increasingly form virtual teams. **Virtual teams** use advanced computer and telecommunications technology to link team members who are geographically dispersed, often worldwide. Management may form a project team (see Figure 4.7) to develop a new pharmaceutical drug and have the team operate in a virtual environment to achieve its goal. For a major telecommunications client, IBM used a global team to develop a Web-based tool for launching new services. The team included members from Japan, Brazil, and Britain and delivered a finished product in two months—a considerable reduction in product delivery time.[28] Although virtual teams have many benefits, they are not without problems.[29] Paulette Tichenor, president of Organizational Renaissance, a team-training organization, notes these concerns with virtual teams: language and cultural barriers, unclear objectives, time conflicts due to diverse geographic locations, and selecting people who can work in a collaborative setting.[30]

People can also lose the intimacy of physically meeting, for instance, in the workplaces and cafeterias. To reduce this problem, companies such as Nokia are careful to select people who have a collaborative mindset. At Nokia, team members are encouraged to network online and to share their pictures and personal biographies. In another example, Accenture, a worldwide consulting organization, yearly involves 400 managers in virtual team leadership training. The goal is to create team effectiveness and to promote understanding of cross-cultural differences.

Regardless of the structure or purpose of the team, the following characteristics have been identified with successful teams:

- Commitment to shared goals and objectives
- Motivated and energetic team members
- Open and honest communication
- Shared leadership
- Clear role assignments
- Climate of cooperation, collaboration, trust, and accountability
- Recognition of conflict and its positive resolution

Unfortunately, not all teams succeed or operate to their full potential. Therefore, in adopting the work team concept, organizations must address several issues that could present obstacles to effective team function, including overly high expectations, group compensation, specialized team training, career movement, and conflict resolution. For example, new team members must be retrained to work outside their primary functional areas, and compensation systems must be constructed to reward individuals for team accomplishments. Importantly, research shows that teams achieve greater effectiveness when team members initially establish team ground rules, or team norms, for operational and behavioural success. HRM Experience, at the end of the chapter, presents an exercise to set team ground rules.

Another difficulty with work teams is that they alter the traditional manager–employee relationship. Managers often find it hard to adapt to the role of leader rather than supervisor and sometimes feel threatened by the growing power of the team and the reduced power of management. Furthermore, some employees may also have difficulty adapting to a role that includes traditional supervisory responsibilities. Therefore, from our experience in working with teams, extensive attention must be given to training team members as they move through the four stages of team development: forming, storming, norming, and performing.[31]

## FLEXIBLE WORK SCHEDULES

Flexible work schedules are not a true part of job design because job tasks and responsibilities are not changed. Nevertheless, we discuss adjustments in work schedules here because they alter the normal workweek of five eight-hour days

**virtual team**
A team with widely dispersed members linked together through computer and telecommunications technology

PART 2

© Cultura Creative/Alamy

Online services such as Skype and iMeet allow virtual workers to get acquainted with one another and have face-to-face conversations across any distance

**OUTCOME 7**

# HIGHLIGHTS IN HRM 4.3

## How to Request a Flexible Work Schedule

You might be thinking, "My manager would never agree to a flexible work schedule." But that is not necessarily so. When valued employees make reasonable scheduling requests, managers often try to accommodate employee proposals. Many students who work full- or even part-time can benefit from flexible work schedules as this would offer them more opportunities to match their college and university schedules. Many Canadian organizations offer flexible work schedules. Here are some proven strategies for securing different types of flexible work-hour arrangements.

- *Investigate.* Look into similar arrangements others have made within your company or industry. Research your company's policy on flexible schedules. Be realistic by providing a schedule that will fit the demands of your organization.

- *Be professional.* Treat your request as a business proposal. Be positive and assume a "can do" attitude.

Be serious and present the proposal as a benefit to both you and your company. Present your idea as a "win-win" arrangement.

- *Write it out.* Submit your request for a flexible work-hour arrangement in a well-organized, detailed, written proposal.

- *Promote yourself.* Explain your value to your organization. Have others speak to your abilities—especially those in authority. Ask to be evaluated based on your quantity and quality of work rather than on the hours you actually spend on the job.

- *Anticipate questions.* Be prepared for potential problems and have specific answers on how to deal with these issues, for example, how you will communicate or coordinate with other employees.

- *Propose a review.* Propose review dates to evaluate your new flexible schedule. Continually assess how you work with others and your manager.

Sources: Adapted from Julie Shields, "Showing How to Flex It," *Incentive* 178, no. 3 (March 2004): 47; Sonya Felix, "A Flexible Workplace," *Benefits Canada* 31, no. 6 (June 2007): 16–18, 20.

---

in which all employees begin and end their workday at the same time. Employers may depart from the traditional workday or workweek in their attempt to improve organizational productivity and morale by giving employees increased control over the hours they work.[32]

Speaking on the importance of flexible work schedules, Lois Brakon, co-director of the Families and Work Institute, notes, "Flexible schedules are going to be the way good, competitive businesses work." Flexible work schedules may be assigned by the organization or requested by individual employees—and are particularly valuable to students (see Highlights in HRM 4.3). The more common flexible work schedules are the compressed workweek, flextime, job sharing, and telecommuting.

## Compressed Workweek

Under the compressed workweek, the number of days in the workweek is shortened by lengthening the number of hours worked per day. This schedule is best illustrated by the 4-day, 40-hour week, generally referred to as 4/10 or 4/40. Employees working a 4-day workweek might work 10 hours a day, Monday through Thursday. Although the 4/10 schedule is probably the best known, other compressed arrangements include reducing weekly hours to 38 or 36 hours or scheduling 80 hours over 9 days (9/80), taking one day off every other week. Managers cite the following reasons for implementing compressed workweek schedules:

- Recruitment and retention of employees[33]

- Coordinating employee work schedules with production schedules

- Accommodating the leisure-time activities of employees while facilitating employee personal appointments (medical, dental, financial)
- Improvements in employee job satisfaction and morale[34]

## Flextime

**Flextime**, or flexible working hours, permits employees the option of choosing daily starting and quitting times provided that they work a certain number of hours per day or week. With flextime, employees are given considerable latitude in scheduling their work. However, there is a "core period" during the morning and afternoon when all employees are required to be on the job. Flexible working hours are most common in service-type organizations—financial institutions, government agencies, and other organizations with large clerical operations.

Flextime provides both employees and employers with several advantages. By allowing employees greater flexibility in work scheduling, employers can reduce some of the traditional causes of tardiness and absenteeism.[35] Employees can adjust their work to accommodate their particular lifestyles and, in doing so, gain greater job satisfaction. Employees can also schedule their working hours for the time of day when they are most productive. In addition, variations in arrival and departure times can help reduce traffic congestion at the peak commuting hours. In some cases, employees require less time to commute, and the pressures of meeting a rigid schedule are reduced.

From the employer's standpoint, flextime can be most helpful in recruiting and meeting the challenges of age diversity in the workforce.[36] It has proved invaluable to organizations wishing to improve service to customers or clients by extending operating hours. Qwest, a telecommunications company, uses flextime to keep its business offices open for customers who cannot get there during the day. Research demonstrates that flextime can have a positive impact on the performance measures of reliability, quality, and quantity of employee work.

There are, of course, several disadvantages to flextime. First, it is not suited to some jobs. It is not feasible, for example, where specific workstations must be staffed at all times. Second, it can create problems for managers in communicating with and instructing employees. Flextime schedules may also force these managers to extend their workweek if they are to exercise control over their subordinates.

## Job Sharing

The arrangement whereby two part-time employees perform a job that otherwise would be held by one full-time employee is called **job sharing**. Job sharers usually work three days a week, "creating an overlap day for extended face-to-face conferencing." Their pay is three-fifths of a regular salary. Employers note that without job sharing, two good employees might otherwise be lost.

Job sharing is suited to the needs of families in which one or both spouses desire to work only part-time.[37] It is also suited to the needs of older workers who want to phase into retirement by shortening their workweek. For the employer, the work of part-time employees can be scheduled to conform to peaks in the daily workload. Job sharing can also limit layoffs in hard economic times. A final benefit is that employees engaged in job sharing have time off during the week to accommodate personal needs, so they are less likely to be absent.

Job sharing does have several problems, however. Employers may not want to employ two people to do the work of one because the time required to orient and train a second employee constitutes an added burden. Additionally, managers may find it more difficult to supervise two employees, particularly when one job sharer is not dependable, job sharers cannot effectively work together, or they simply distrust one another.[38] The key to making job sharing work is good communication between partners, who can use a number of ways to stay in contact—phone calls, written updates, email, and voice mail.

**telecommuting**
Use of personal computers, networks, and other communications technology to do work in the home that is traditionally done in the workplace

## Telecommuting

**Telecommuting** is the use of personal computers, networks, and other communications technology to do work in the home that is traditionally done in the workplace. A variant of telecommuting is the *virtual office*, where employees are in the field helping customers or are stationed at other remote locations working as if they were in the home office.[39] Telecommuting has several advantages:

- Increased flexibility for employees—better work–life balance
- Reduced absenteeism
- Retention of valued employees who might otherwise quit
- Reduced "carbon footprints" through minimizing daily commuting
- Increased productivity (e.g., reduced wasted office time)
- Lower overhead costs and reduced office space

Although telecommuting offers significant benefits to employers, it also presents potential drawbacks. These include the loss of creativity as employees are not interacting with one another on a regular basis, the difficulty of developing appropriate performance standards and evaluation systems for telecommuters, and the need to formulate an appropriate technology strategy for allocating the necessary equipment.[40] Traditional line managers accustomed to managing by observation may find supervising distributed employees stressful. Additionally, managers may believe that telecommuting negatively affects employee–supervisor relationships through loss of knowledge or information, training or development, and a sense of connectedness.[41]

Employers wishing to have their employees telecommute must comply with wage and hour laws, liability and workers' compensation regulations, equipment purchase or rental agreements with employees, and all employment equity regulations (see Chapter 3). Employees who are denied the opportunity to work from home may feel discriminated against and resent home telecommuters. Figure 4.8 presents suggestions for establishing a successful telecommuting program. Highlights in HRM 4.4 featues work–life balance expert Nora Spinks.

### FIGURE 4.8

KEYS FOR SUCCESSFUL TELECOMMUTING

- *Identify jobs best suited to distance work.* Those involving sales, customer service, and auditing are logical choices.
- *Select responsible employees.* Employees who are self-starters, motivated, and trustworthy and who can work independently are ideal candidates. Establish employee feedback procedures and performance review methods for employee evaluation.
- *Establish formalized telecommuting procedures.* Telecommuting guidelines could cover hours of availability, office reporting periods, performance expectations, and weekly progress reports or email updates.
- *Begin a formal training program.* Training for both telecommuters and managers should include the technical aspects of equipment use and relationship factors such as how and when to contact the office or availability and location of support facilities.
- *Keep telecommuters informed.* Physical separation can make telecommuters feel isolated and invisible. Department and staff updates, inclusion of telecommuters on project teams, required attendance at meetings, and "chat room" discussions all keep telecommuters "in the loop."
- *Recognize when telecommuting is not working.* State in telecommunicating policies that the arrangement may be terminated when it no longer serves company needs or if the employee's performance declines.

**Source:** Adapted from Barbara Hemphill, "Telecommuting Productivity," *Occupational Health and Safety* 73, no. 3 (March 2004): 16.

# HIGHLIGHTS IN HRM 4.4

## Flextime and Work–Life Balance

Nora Spinks, president and CEO of Work–Life Harmony Enterprises, works with employers to create organizational cultures that enable employees to achieve work–life balance. The firm's goal is to develop successful work environments where individuals and organizations have the ability to reach their full potential and where employees have full and satisfying lives outside their work.

Spinks asserts that employers benefit from these family-friendly policies: "The most effective and productive employees are those who do work they enjoy; are challenged; have access to the necessary resources to meet that challenge; have control over how they work; receive recognition, rewards, and compensation based on the effort they put forth; and feel their life outside work is respected and valued. These employees are highly resilient. In today's world of work, individual and organizational resiliency is critical for success. People in resilient, adaptable, responsive environments have the ability to change, the capacity to adapt to change, the energy to drive change and the flexibility to react positively to change, regardless of the intensity or the factors outside of their immediate control such as market forces, economic pressures, and social or political circumstances."

Today's most popular employee-support initiative is workplace flexibility: flextime with core hours and flexible start and end times, compressed workweeks (full workload completed in less than five days per week), and/or permanent part-time hours with equal status, prorated benefits, and the same development opportunities as full-time employees. Gaining in popularity are creative alternatives such as extended workweeks (full workload completed in six days) and self-funded or radical sabbaticals (setting aside a portion of pay for a period of time and taking an extended leave while collecting the banked salary—e.g., 2.5 years working at 85 percent pay and 6 months away from the workplace on a self-funded sabbatical).

Employees are using the time gained from workplace flexibility to fulfill family responsibilities, create a balanced lifestyle, continue their education, make a contribution to their community, or volunteer in developing countries.

Spinks argues strongly for these policies: "Establishing control over hours of work has very specific, well-documented results: reduction in illness, injury, absenteeism, presenteeism (physically present, but mentally and emotionally absent), turnover, conflict, and unhealthy lifestyles and behaviours such as smoking, drinking, and drugs.

"When you work too hard or too long, you tend to rely on substances such as nicotine, caffeine, or sugar boosters to get you through the day. When you are tired all the time, your ability to solve problems and resolve conflicts is decreased significantly. When you are rundown, you become uninterested and disengaged. Employees who have control over their working hours have more energy, more time, and are more engaged at home, at work, and in the community. Employers, customers, and coworkers benefit during the day, and employees, their family, friends, and community benefit at the end of the day."

# SMALL BUSINESS APPLICATION

As we have seen, to effectively provide performance feedback, train, or recruit new employees, developing and optimizing job requirements act as the cornerstone. Although this is not different in small companies, what is different is that in small enterprises, (1) these job requirements may be less structured than in large companies, (2) requirements may be more individualized to factor in the individual talents of team members, and (3) these requirements are less likely to be written down.

Take, for example, a small Internet development company with 25 employees. These 25 employees are involved in either sales, website development, or website maintenance for a variety of clients. Although there may be general classifications of roles, in that some people will be involved in sales, some in development, and some in maintenance, it will likely be the case that every employee in the company, rather than having specific duties, will be drawn on based on his or her skills

*continued*

and how busy that person is. For example, a client may have identified that it would like to have a new feature added to its website. The employee responsible for the support of this site may not be the best person on the team to develop this new feature. The entire team will be consulted to determine not just who has developed or could develop the skill to do this. The end result is that the determination of what is to be done and who is to do it is based on situational requirements and the allocation of talent at that point in time.

This highlights a primary challenge in all organizations: that organizations hire individuals but then manage teams to deliver on changing requirements. In small enterprises, especially, although the core job requirements will consist of a collection of tasks generally associated with the performance of the role, employees will be required to support requirements outside a prescribed job requirement. Small enterprises often neglect actions such as written job requirements or written performance reviews. These acts may be deemed to be unnecessary formalities that are counter to the informal culture in small companies. The advantages to both the company and employees are twofold. First, documenting job requirements increases operational efficiency in recruiting and training future employees. Second, performance evaluations result in improving the effectiveness and morale of existing staff. What is different in small enterprises is that each of these will be carried out by a manager without the support of an HR professional.

# SUMMARY

## SUMMARY

**OUTCOME 1** Job requirements reflect the different duties, tasks, and responsibilities contained in jobs. Job requirements, in turn, influence HR functions performed by managers, including recruitment, selection, training and development, performance appraisal, compensation, and various labour relations activities.

**OUTCOME 2** Job analysis data may be gathered using several collection methods—interviews, questionnaires, observations, and diaries. Other, more quantitative approaches include the PAQ system, critical incident method, task inventory analysis, and competency-based analysis. It is the prevailing opinion of the courts that HRM decisions on employment, performance appraisal, and promotions must be based on specific criteria that are job related. These criteria can be determined objectively only by analyzing the requirements of each job.

**OUTCOME 3** The format of job descriptions varies widely, often reflecting the needs of the organization and the expertise of the writer. At a minimum, job descriptions should contain a job title, a job identification section, and a job duties, or essential functions, section. A job specification section also may be included. Job descriptions should be written in clear and specific terms with consideration given to their legal implications.

**OUTCOME 4** Job design is a combination of four basic considerations: organizational objectives; industrial engineering concerns of analyzing work methods and establishing time standards; ergonomic considerations, which accommodate human capabilities and limitations to job tasks; and employee contributions.

**OUTCOME 5** In the job characteristics model, five job factors contribute to increased job performance and satisfaction: skill variety, task identity, task significance, autonomy, and feedback. All factors should be built into jobs because each factor influences different employee psychological states. When jobs are enriched through the job characteristics model, employees experience more meaningfulness in their jobs, acquire more job responsibility, and receive direct feedback from the tasks they perform.

**OUTCOME 6** To improve the internal process of organizations and increase productivity, greater efforts are being made by organizations to involve groups of employees in work operations. Employee involvement groups are composed of employees in work units charged with offering suggestions for improving product or service quality or fostering workplace effectiveness. Employee teams stress employee collaboration over individual accomplishment. Teams rely on the expertise and different abilities of members to achieve a specific goal or objective. Self-directed teams are characterized by their willingness to perform traditional managerial tasks.

**OUTCOME 7**  Changes in work schedules—which include the compressed workweek, flextime, job sharing, and telecommuting—permit employees to adjust their work periods to accommodate their particular lifestyles. Employees can select from among these HR techniques to accommodate diverse employee needs while fostering organizational effectiveness.

## KEY TERMS

critical incident method, 127
employee empowerment, 135
employee involvement groups
  (EIs), 138
employee teams 139
ergonomics 136
flextime, 143
industrial engineering, 136

job, 122
job analysis, 124
job characteristics model 134
job description, 122
job design, 133
job enrichment 134
job family, 122
job sharing, 143

job specification, 122
position, 122
position analysis questionnaire
  (PAQ), 127
task inventory analysis 129
telecommuting, 144
virtual team, 141

## DISCUSSION QUESTIONS

1. Why is job analysis often described as the "bedrock" of HRM practices? In your answer, explain how job analysis helps with HRM practices such as recruitment, selection, compensation, and performance appraisals.
2. Discuss the various methods by which job analysis can be completed. Compare these methods, noting the pros or cons of each.
3. The description of the "administrative assistant" position often varies across organizations. Search the Internet for a few of these job descriptions and compare them. How can this "problem" be solved?
4. Explain how industrial engineering and behavioural considerations can both clash with and complement each other in the design of jobs.

5. The job characteristics model has five components that enhance employee jobs: skill variety, task identity, task significance, autonomy, and feedback. Give an example illustrating how each component can be used to improve the organization and the job of the employee. (Suggestion: Consider your present or a recent job to answer this question.)
6. Figure 4.7 shows the different forms of employee teams. Provide an example of where each type of team can be used. How do teams create synergy?
7. An argument could be advanced that some job design methods, including those involving industrial engineering, have led to employees being "deskilled" and "alienated from their work." Debate this issue.

# HRM EXPERIENCE

## Establishing Ground Rules for Team Success

Professional trainers understand that setting ground rules for teams is a cornerstone for continued team success. Ground rules—or team norms—are agreed-on formal rules that guide group member behaviour. Norms established prior to the team's task regulate the behaviour of group members. Ground rules simply state how members want to be treated and how members agree to treat others. When team members follow the established norms, the norms help maintain order and promote positive behaviour and can be used to correct undesirable actions. Remember, because teams operate in different settings, different norms may be appropriate in different arrangements.

*continued*

## Assignment

1. Working within your team, select what you believe are the 10 most important norms for team behaviour.

2. From the following Behaviour List, have each team member *silently* select 2 lists of 10 items each of the behaviours they believe most critical for team success. The first list of 10 items (your A list) is considered the most important for group conduct. The second list (the B list) is desired items but those not of major importance.

3. In a group discussion, have all team members select a final list of 10 items from both lists. These become your team's final norms. Select no more than 10 items. During your discussion, items can be modified or combined to meet your team's specific needs.

4. Prepare a written document of chosen behaviours and have all team members sign the form. You have now established a written contract for positive team conduct.

## Behaviour List

While working in our team, individuals should . . .

1. Do their fair share of the work.

2. Check to ensure that everyone clearly understands what is to be done.

3. Encourage planning, including short-range agendas and long-range goals.

4. Encourage open and candid opinions about issues.

5. Listen willingly and carefully to other people's ideas, even if those people have a different viewpoint.

6. Prepare thoroughly before meetings.

7. Make team members feel at ease in discussion.

8. Ask questions when they do not clearly understand tasks or procedures.

9. Propose specific analyses of the pros and cons of decisions faced by the team.

10. Follow through on task assignments.

11. Help other members when assistance is requested.

12. Treat all team members as equals.

13. Paraphrase or restate what someone else says to check meaning.

14. Openly voice opinions and share ideas.

15. Be flexible in arranging meeting schedules.

16. Compliment others for things they have said or done.

17. Be willing to meet whenever it is necessary to discuss a problem.

18. Deal with conflict directly, bringing it to the attention of the team.

19. Express enthusiasm about what the team is doing.

20. Encourage budgeting of the team's time.

21. At the end of a meeting, restate their own responsibilities to check for agreement.

22. Be serious about the team's work.

23. Arrive on time for regularly scheduled meetings.

24. Be willing to listen to other team members' ideas.

25. Get the team's approval on important matters before proceeding.

 **CourseMate**

Visit the *Managing Human Resources* CourseMate website at http://www.belcourt7e.nelson.com for quizzes, flashcards, videos, games, and more!

# CASE STUDY 1

## FAIRMONT HOTELS AND RESORTS

Corporate social responsibility through environmental sensitivity, among others, has recently surfaced as a pressing organizational issue. However, Fairmont Hotels and Resorts has been one of the firms in the forefront with its Green Partnership program. The Toronto-based company initiated a chain-wide environmental program in 1990; it has now spread to more than 40 locations globally,

winning several international awards along the way. Fairmont became particularly interested in the initiatives because of its locations in sensitive environments such as national parks, biosphere reserves, and wetlands. The environmental program now includes eco-innovation projects at its hotels, such as turtle conservation in Mexico, coral reef protection in Hawaii, and whale adoption in Quebec. Empowered employees are vital to the success of the programs. Employees were first encouraged to buy in before implementation through involvement in the development of the programs and effective communication; new employees are given an orientation on the green programs; volunteer teams meet monthly and discuss how to improve on the green programs; and there is an incentive program for the green teams with the best results. Fairmont management claims that employees feel empowered because they have an ownership in the programs.

## Questions

1. What arguments could be advanced both for and against the use of employee empowerment?
2. Assume you are a manager at Fairmont. What would you do differently to further empower employees?
3. Let us say that employees begin to resist the changes and prefer to perform their traditional duties. How would you manage such resistance and at the same time sustain empowerment?

**Source:** Adapted from Sarah Dobson, "Fairmont finds it's easy being green," *Canadian HR Reporter*, 20, no. 6, (Mar 26, 2007): 14–16.

---

## CASE STUDY 2

### BUT MY JOB HAS CHANGED

Job descriptions are a critical tool used for job orientation and training and, importantly, in annual employee performance evaluations. When the duties and responsibilities listed in the job description do not reflect current job content, employee/management disagreements can arise, as this case illustrates.

Both employees and managers agree that Brenda Batten has been an exceptional employee. As a senior technical representative (STR) for Blackhawk Aironics, she is valued for her knowledge in airplane instrumentation. One manager described her as "simply an expert in the complex technology of satellite weather systems."

In May 2007, Blackhawk Aironics implemented a new work reorganization plan. STRs such as Brenda now work largely by telecommuting with managers and engineers at company headquarters and with customers scattered throughout North America. Additionally, under the new work plan, STRs were given more freedom to deal directly with customers and engineers without supervisory intervention. This freedom greatly facilitated customer service needs and demands in an aviation market everyone considers highly dynamic.

Brenda's current job description reflects the technical dimensions of her position but not the telecommuting requirements now performed. Personal competencies such as decision making, self-motivation, problem solving, and communication skills are not covered.

In May 2008, Brenda met with her manager, Martin Eaton, for her annual performance review. Unfortunately, unlike past meetings, which were highly satisfactory, this meeting quickly developed into a disagreement. At the centre of the controversy were the factors to be used to measure Brenda's new job demands. Martin wanted to place major emphasis on the tasks and duties listed in her current job description. As he explained to Brenda, "I hardly see you anymore, and I have no objective criteria or performance data by which to measure those behaviours you now use." Brenda, in response, acknowledged that some things in the current job description were still important aspects of her job, but, overall, the current job description did not capture the full scope of her new duties and responsibilities. Brenda concluded that she was satisfied with Martin's evaluation of the technical aspects of her job, but she was clearly not pleased with the overall evaluation of her performance. As she told Martin, "It's simply not fair; you just don't know what I do now."

### Questions

1. Given the facts of this case, is it possible for Brenda and Martin to reach a satisfactory result? Explain.
2. How can an organization identify and measure the personal competencies of employees?
3. How can the company prevent this problem from occurring in the future? Explain.

**Source:** Based on an actual case known to the authors. All names and locations are fictitious.

# SUMMARY

## NOTES AND REFERENCES

1. Michael Hammer and J. Champy, *Reengineering the Corporation* (New York: Harper Collins, 2003); Narasimhaiah Gorla, Ravi Chinta, and Tam Wai Chu, "An Enhanced Business Process Re-engineering Model for Supply Chain Management and a Case Study," *Journal of Information Technology Case and Application Research* 9, no. 2 (2007): 5.

2. Michael Hammer, "The Process Audit," *Harvard Business Review* 85, no. 4 (April 2007): 111.

3. Peter Coy, "COG or Co-worker?; The Organization Man Isn't Extinct or Even Endangered—But the Role Has Been Refined Over the Past 100 Years," *Business Week*, August 2007, 58.

4. Arnold B. Bakker, Evangelia Demeroob, and Willem Verbeke, "Using the Job Demands Resources Model to Predict Burnout and Performance," *Human Resources Management* 43, no. 1 (Spring 2004): 83; Rehman Safdar, Ajmal Waheed, and Khattak Hamid Rafiq, "Impact of Job Analysis on Job Performance: Analysis of A Hypothesized Model," *Journal of Diversity Management* 5, no. 2 (Summer 2010): 17–36.

5. Parbudyal Singh, "Job Analysis for a Changing Workplace," *Human Resource Management Review* 18, no. 2 (2008): 87–99.

6. George T. Milkovich and Jerry M. Newman, *Compensation*, 10th ed. (Boston: McGraw-Hill Companies, 2010).

7. Fredenick P. Morgeson, Kelly Delaney Klinger, Melinda S. Mayfield, Philip Ferrara, and Michael A. Campion, "Self-Presentation Processes in Job Analysis: A Field Experiment Investigating Inflation in Abilities, Tasks, and Competencies," *Journal of Applied Psychology* 89, no. 4 (August 2004): 674.

8. Interview with job analyst Carol Tucker, Mesa, Arizona, May 10, 2006.

9. Human Resources and Skills Development Canada, "The National Occupational Classification," http://www5.hrsdc.gc.ca/NOC/English/NOC/2006/Welcome.aspx, retrieved July 2012.

10. A detailed description of different job analysis techniques is beyond the scope of this text. For those interested in more comprehensive information or job analysis tools, see Michael T. Bannick, Edward L. Levine, and Frederick P. Morgeson, *Job and Work Analysis: Methods, Research, and Applications for Human Resource Management*, 2nd ed. (Thousand Oaks, CA: Sage, 2007).

11. Michael Campion, Alexis Fink, Brian Ruggeberg, Linda Carr, et al. "Doing Competencies Well: Best Practices in Competency Modeling," *Personnel Psychology* 64, no. 1 (2011): 225–262.

12. Marqie Mader-Clark, *Job Description Handbook* (Berkeley, CA: Nolo Press, 2006).

13. Gensheng Liu, Rachna Shah, and Roger G. Schroeder, "Linking Work Design to Mass Customization: A Socio-technical Systems Perspective," *Decision Sciences* 37, no. 4 (November 2006): 519.

14. Pooja Garg and Renu Rastogi, "New Models of Job Design: Motivating Employees' Performance," *The Journal of Management Development* 25, no. 6 (2006): 572.

15. For Herzberg's important article on job enrichment, see Frederick Herzberg, "One More Time: How Do You Motivate Employees?" *Harvard Business Review* 46, no. 2 (January–February 1968): 53–62.

16. For the original article on the job characteristics model, see J. Richard Hackman and Greg R. Oldham, "Motivation through the Design of Work: Test of a Theory," *Organizational Behavior and Human Performance* 16, no. 2 (August 1976): 250–279.

17. Jed DeVaro, Robert Li, and Dana Brookshire, "Analyzing the Job Characteristics Model: New Support from a Cross-Section of Establishments," *The International Journal of Human Resource Management* 18, no. 6 (June 2007): 986.

18. Richard E. Wilmot and Robert Galford, "A Commitment to Trust," *Communication World* 24, no. 2 (March/April 2007): 34.

19. Denise Robitaille, "Invaluable Contributions," *Industrial Engineering* 39, no. 1 (January 2007): 32.

20. Laura Baron, James Vander Spek, and Wendy Young, "The Economics of Ergonomics," *Journal of Accountancy* 222, no. 6 (December 2006): 34.

21. Julian Faraway and Matthew P. Reed, "Statistics for Digital Human Motion Modeling in Ergonomics," *Technometrics* 49, no. 3 (August 2007): 277.

22. Andrew J. DuBrin, *Fundamentals of Organizational Behavior*, 4th ed. (Cincinnati, OH: South-Western, 2007), Chapter 10.

23. Keith Ayers, "Get Employees to Help You Increase Productivity and Profitability," *Rural Telecommunications* 26, no. 5 (September/October 2007): 26.

24. Brian Hindo, "The Empire Strikes at Silos," *Business Week*, August 20, 2007, 63.

25. Roy C. Herrenkohl, *Becoming a Team: Achieving a Goal* (Mason, OH: South-Western, 2004).

26. Vojko Potocan and Bostjan Kuralt, "Synergy in Business: Some New Suggestions," *Journal of American Academy of Business* 12, no. 1 (September 2007): 199.

27. Leigh Thompson, "Improving the Creativity of Organizational Work Groups," *The Academy of Management Executive* 17, no. 1 (February 2003): 96.

28. Michael Mandel, "Which Way to the Future," *BusinessWeek*, August 20, 2007, 45.

29. Laura A. Hambley, Thomas A. O'Neil, and Theresa J. B. Klien, "Virtual Team Leadership: The Effects of Leadership Style and Communication Medium on Team Interaction Styles and Outcomes," *Organizational Behavior and Human Decision Processes* 103, no. 1 (May 2007): 1.

30. Interview with Paulette Tichenor, Arizona State University, Tempe, Arizona, January 18, 2007.

31. For a discussion of the stages of team development, see Don Hellriegel and John W. Slocum, Jr., *Organizational Behavior*, 11th ed. (Cincinnati, OH: South-Western, 2007).

32. Michelle Conlin, "Smashing the Clock," *BusinessWeek*, December 11, 2006, 60. See also Susan Meisinger, "Flexible Schedules Make Powerful Perks," *HR Magazine* 52, no. 4 (April 2007): 12.

33. Kathy Gurchiek, "Good News for Moms Reconsidering Work," *HR Magazine* 51, no. 7 (August 2006): 39.

34. James A. Breaugh and N. Kathleen Frye, "An Examination of the Antecedents and Consequences of the Use of Family-Friendly Benefits," *Journal of Management Issues* 19, no. 1 (Spring 2007): 35.

35. Rita Zeidner, "Bending with the Times," *HR Magazine* 53, no. 7 (July 2008): 10.

36. Nancy Sutton Bell and Marvin Narz, "Meeting the Challenges of Age Diversity in the Workplace," *The CPA Journal* 77, no. 2 (February 2007): 56.

37. "Have You Considered Job Sharing as a Retention Tool?" *HRfocus* 83, no. 9 (September 2006): 10.

38. Susan Berfield, "Two for the Cubicle," *BusinessWeek*, July 24, 2006, 88.

39. Tammy Dewar, "Virtual Teams—Virtually Impossible," *Performance Improvement* 45, no. 5 (May/June 2006): 22.

40. Wendell Joice, "Implementing Telework: The Technology Issue," *Public Manager* 36, no. 2 (Summer 2007): 64.

41. Marjorie Deruen, "The Remote Connection," *HR Magazine* 52, no. 3 (March 2007): 111.

# Branding the Talent Pool: Recruitment and Careers

# After studying this chapter, you should be able to

**OUTCOME 1**    Describe how a firm's strategy affects its recruiting efforts.

**OUTCOME 2**    Outline the methods by which firms recruit internally.

**OUTCOME 3**    Outline the methods by which firms recruit externally.

**OUTCOME 4**    Explain the techniques organizations can use to improve their recruiting efforts.

**OUTCOME 5**    Explain how career management programs integrate the needs of individual employees and their organizations.

In the past, recruiting was often a reactive process firms engaged in periodically when a position needed to be filled. Today, however, more companies see the recruiting function as a strategic imperative and, therefore, an ongoing process. Instead of waiting for a job opening, HR managers are studying their firms' strategies in conjunction with their organizational charts, job analysis information, and external factors such as the labour market and the competition and then recruiting proactively and continually. The greater competition for talent means that recruiting has become more important for managers. Recruiting involves not only looking for talented pools of employees but also making an effort to figure out what they want and establishing the firm as an employer of choice so people will want to work for it.

The Container Store, which regularly tops *Fortune*'s "100 Best Companies to Work For," is a good example of a company that makes recruiting an ongoing process. Individual managers spend two to three hours a week on recruiting activities to locate good candidates, regardless of whether there are job openings at their stores. Employees are also encouraged to focus their efforts on recruiting. "Basically we have mini human resources departments in each of our stores. We challenge each of our 4,000 employees to be recruiters and refer us to great people," says The Container Store's director of recruiting.[1]

In this chapter, we will discuss the many strategies and techniques organizations use both internally and externally to recruit the talent they need. For example, to find ways to reach out to and recruit the right kinds of candidates, some companies develop **employee profiles** by surveying their top performers about what they like to do, what events they attend, and how they like to be contacted and recruited. They then pursue candidates using this information. We will also discuss the approaches that organizations take toward career management over time. This is important because, unlike physical assets, human assets (employees) can decide to leave the firm of their own accord. The Internet has helped make workers better informed about opportunities and allowed them to telecommute or work off-site. As a result, rival firms are in a better position to lure good employees away.

AVAVA/Shutterstock

# STRATEGIC ASPECTS OF RECRUITING

OUTCOME 1

**employee profile**
A profile of a worker developed by studying an organization's top performers to recruit similar types of people

**recruiting process outsourcing (RPO)**
The practice of outsourcing an organization's recruiting function to an outside firm

Decisions about talent—regardless of whether they pertain to recruiting, transferring, promoting, developing, or deploying people—need to be considered within the context of a business's strategies and priorities. Consider the decision to outsource and offshore work: most North American clothing makers have outsourced or offshored work because labour costs are cheaper outside North America. (Nearly all of the clothing purchased in Canada today is imported. Just check your clothing labels.)

The broad factors that can affect a firm's recruiting strategy include a firm's recruiting abilities, whether to recruit externally versus internally, the labour market for the types of positions it is recruiting for, including global labour markets, and the strength of a firm's employment "brand." We will talk about each of these factors next. Note that at any given time, a firm might need to use multiple recruiting strategies. Moreover, a strategy that works for one firm or one job might not work for another firm (or job). For example, an engineering firm might place a premium on finding highly qualified applicants, whereas an amusement park ramping up for a new season might place a premium on hiring quickly. Recruiting strategies and their effectiveness can change over time as well. As a result, firms need to continuously examine their recruiting efforts and refine them. So, for example, if the engineering firm landed a huge construction contract, being able to hire engineers quickly could become a priority.

## WHO SHOULD DO THE RECRUITING?

The size of an organization often affects who performs the recruitment function. Most large firms have full-time, in-house HR recruiters. In smaller organizations, the recruiting might be done by an HR generalist. If the organization has no HR function, managers and/or supervisors recruit their own employees. At companies such as Williams-Sonoma, the members of work teams help select new employees for their groups.

Organizations that want to focus on their core functions, including small businesses that lack time or HR personnel, sometimes outsource their recruiting functions to outside firms. This practice is known as **recruiting process outsourcing (RPO)**. Organizations also sometimes use RPO providers when they need to hire a lot of employees or hire employees quickly. RPO providers can also be useful when a firm has had trouble finding suitable candidates in the past or needs a different way to tap different talent pools, perhaps to find more diverse candidates.

Regardless of who does the recruiting, it is imperative that these individuals have a good understanding of the knowledge, skills, abilities, experiences,

Many companies use their own internal intranet websites as well as the public-facing website and other job posting websites to recruit candidates.

Rido/Shutterstock

and other characteristics required for the job and be personable, enthusiastic, and competent. Recruiters can often enhance the perceived attractiveness of a job and an organization—or detract from it. They are often a main reason why applicants select one organization over another.

internal labour market
Labour market in which workers are hired into entry-level jobs and higher levels are filled from within

## SHOULD A FIRM RECRUIT INTERNALLY OR EXTERNALLY?

Most managers try to follow a policy of filling job vacancies above the entry-level position through promotions and transfers. By filling vacancies in this way, an organization can capitalize on the investment it has made in recruiting, selecting, training, and developing its current employees, who might look for jobs elsewhere if they lack promotion opportunities.

Promoting employees rewards them for past performance and encourages them to continue their efforts. It also gives other employees a reason to believe that if they perform similarly, they will be promoted too. This can improve morale within the organization and support a culture of employee engagement. Furthermore, the employee's familiarity with the organization and its operations can eliminate the orientation and training costs that recruitment from the outside would entail. Most important, the transferee's performance record is likely to be a more accurate predictor of the candidate's success than the data gained about outside applicants. Promotion-from-within policies at Marriott and Whole Foods have contributed to the companies' overall growth and success.[2]

Managers need to be aware of the potential limitations of recruiting internally as well, however. For example, jobs that require specialized training and experience cannot always be easily filled from within the organization and may need to be filled from the outside. This is especially common in small organizations, where the existing talent pool is limited. Potential candidates from the outside should also be considered to prevent the "inbreeding" of ideas and attitudes. Chief executive officers (CEOs) are often hired externally. Applicants hired from the outside, particularly for certain technical and managerial positions, can be a source of creativity and innovation and may bring with them the latest knowledge acquired from their previous employers. It is not uncommon for firms to attempt to gain secrets from their competitors by hiring away their employees. Procter & Gamble (P&G) sued a rival papermaker when it hired former employees who had a great deal of knowledge about the making of Charmin toilet paper and Bounty paper towels—both P&G products. Amazon.com was sued by Walmart, which accused Amazon of hiring away employees who had in-depth knowledge about Walmart's sophisticated inventory systems.[3]

Some applicants bring more than knowledge to their new employers. They bring revenue. Talented salespeople, doctors, accountants, lawyers, and hairdressers are examples. When these people leave their organizations, their clients often go with them. Recruiting externally in this case makes sense. Reaching an employer's diversity goals is another factor that can lead a firm to recruit externally.

## LABOUR MARKETS

The condition of the labour can have a big effect on a firm's recruiting plans. During periods of high unemployment in the economy, organizations might be able to maintain an adequate supply of qualified applicants from unsolicited résumés and from their **internal labour markets**. Internal labour markets are those where workers are hired into entry-level jobs and higher levels are filled from within.[4] A tight labour market, one with low unemployment, might force the employer to advertise heavily and/or seek assistance from local employment agencies. Keep in mind that the actual labour market a company faces depends on the industry in which the firm operates and the types of positions it is seeking to fill. In one industry, the supply of qualified individuals might be plentiful for a particular position. Other jobs are chronically hard to fill, such as the jobs for machinists, engineers, and IT professionals.

**global sourcing**
The business practice of searching for and utilizing goods and services from around the world

**branding**
A company's efforts to help existing and prospective workers understand why it is a desirable place to work

## Using the Internet

Learn how to hire a temporary foreign worker by visiting this website and clicking on the "Temporary Foreign Worker Program" link:

**http://www.hrsdc.gc.ca**

## Regional and Global Labour Markets

Have you ever noticed that competing firms are often located in the same areas? Oil and gas companies are plentiful in the Calgary area. Film and television companies are clustered around Toronto and Vancouver. This is not a coincidence. The clustering occurs because the resources these firms need—both human and natural—are located in some areas and not others. Likewise, because the University of Waterloo is one of the top computer science schools in the country, high-tech companies have flocked to the city of Waterloo in Ontario. You could open a high-tech firm in Churchill, Manitoba, but you might have a hard time getting talent to relocate there.

In addition to locating near their talent, to stay apace of their competitors and expand their operations around the world, companies are also looking globally for goods and services, including labour. This practice is referred to as **global sourcing**. As we explained earlier in the book, companies are no longer simply offshoring work to save labour costs. They are also looking abroad to develop better products around the clock via a global workforce and to attract the best talent wherever it may be. For example, after the fall of the Soviet Union in the 1990s, firms abroad began recruiting talented Soviet scientists who had worked for the government and no longer had jobs. Emerging countries such as China and India are also heating up the competition for talent as firms there attempt to staff the burgeoning high-tech industries in these nations.

Firms are trying to fill not just technical positions firms but also lower skilled positions. Resorts and vacation areas are among the businesses having trouble finding employees to staff their operations. Recruiting abroad can be very complicated, however. In addition to having to deal with a myriad of local, national, and international laws, employers also have to take into account the different labour costs, preemployment and compensation practices, and cultural differences associated with the countries in which they are recruiting. In volatile areas of the world, security is a concern.

To help them navigate challenges such as these, many companies utilize firms such as Genpact and Robert Half International, which specialize in global recruiting. These firms help companies address the numerous legal complications associated with obtaining various types of visas and work permits for the foreign workers they are trying to hire. Foreign workers can be hired through Human Resources and Skills Development Canada and Service Canada, which will provide foreign workers with temporary work permits.

## BRANDING

Whomever and wherever a firm is recruiting, it wants to be *the* employer of choice to attract and hire top candidates before its competitors do. Branding can help organizations do this. **Branding** refers to a company's efforts to help existing and prospective workers understand why it is a desirable place to work.

So how does a company "burnish" its employment brand? One way is to think of applicants as consumers and focus on what they want in terms of jobs and careers as opposed to what an organization has to "sell" them. Companies have to listen to and reach out to applicants just like they do consumers. In fact, some firms make their customers their employers. A high percentage of the people Ikea recruits are customers who like doing business with the company.

Some of the newer ways firms are building their employer brands is by reaching out to people via social networks. Instead of just posting jobs on the Internet, firms are creating Facebook pages to promote the careers they have to offer, striking up conversations with potential applicants on those pages, and giving them a preview of what it is like to work for their firms. Writing blogs and articles for industry publications is another way. (We will talk more about social networks as a recruiting tool later in the chapter.)

Philanthropic activities are another avenue for reaching out to prospective employees, especially Generation Y applicants, who are looking for more than just a paycheque and promotions in their careers. For example, to establish relationships with promising young employees, the accounting and consulting firm Deloitte has teamed up with United Way Worldwide to sponsor alternative spring-break programs for undergraduate students who work alongside employees to help communities in need.

In the global arena, branding can be enormously helpful because locals are often unfamiliar with foreign firms. In India, the firms people work for are very important to applicants and their families. Genpact has set up "storefronts" in major Indian cities to promote the employment brands of its corporate clients. Candidates can walk in and chat with company representatives about what these firms do and the kinds of opportunities they offer.

Firms need to be sure that the brand they promote to prospective employees truly reflects their internal cultures, however. Painting a rosier picture of your organization can backfire because it can leave applicants disillusioned after they have been hired. (To help prevent this from occurring, some firms use realistic job previews, which are discussed later in this chapter.) Highlights in HRM 5.1 shows

# HIGHLIGHTS IN HRM 5.1

## Marriott's Recruitment Princples: Living Up to the Employment Brand

1. **Build the employment brand.** Marriott attracts employees the same way it attracts customers. Just as consumers buy experiences, not just products, potential employees are looking for a great work experience when they shop for jobs. Communicating the promise of a great work experience is what employment branding is all about. It is basically a value proposition. According to CEO J. W. Marriott, "For more than 70 years, we've lived by a simple motto: If we take care of our associates, they'll take care of our guests. That isn't just a sentiment. It is a strategy—one all businesses must adopt to remain competitive in an environment where our most valuable resource, human capital, drives economic value for our company."

2. **Get it right the first time.** Marriott "hires friendly" and "trains technical." It is better to hire people with "the spirit to serve" and train them to work than hire people who know business and try to teach them to enjoy serving guests. Marriott hires cooks who love to cook and housekeepers who love to clean. They have learned that this approach works for both delivering excellent service and retaining their employees.

3. **Money is a big thing, but** . . . The top concern of Marriott associates is total compensation. But intangible factors taken together, such as work–life balance, leadership quality, opportunity for advancement, work environment, and training, far outweigh money in their

decisions to stay or leave. Pay matters less, and the other factors matter more the longer someone works for Marriott. From flexible schedules to tailored benefit packages and development opportunities, Marriott has built systems to address these nonmonetary factors.

4. **A caring workplace is a bottom-line issue.** When employees come to work, they feel safe, secure, and welcome. Committed associates are less likely to leave, and associate work commitment is one of the key drivers of guest satisfaction. Managers are accountable for associate satisfaction ratings and for turnover rates. Every day, associates in each of Marriott's full-service hotels participate in a 15-minute meeting to review basic values, such as respect. Managers also encourage associates to raise their personal concerns. They take the time to celebrate birthdays and anniversaries. Marriott calls this the loyalty program because it builds loyalty among associates and repeat business from customers. The result is that everyone has a stake in making the hotel a success.

5. **Promote from within.** More than 50 percent of Marriott's current managers have been promoted from within. All associates are given the opportunity to advance as far as their abilities will carry them. Elevating veterans to positions of leadership helps Marriott pass on the soul of its business—its corporate culture—from one generation to the next. In addition, promoting from within is a powerful tool for recruitment and retention. Associates cite "opportunity for advancement" as a key factor in their decisions to stay with Marriott. (Accompanying that is a $100-million-a-year commitment to training.)

Sources: J. W. Marriott, "Competitive Strength," *Executive Excellence* 18, no. 4 (April 2001): 3–4; J. W. Marriott, "Our Competitive Strength: Human Capital," *Executive Speeches* 15, no. 5 (April/May 2001): 18–21.

**9-box grid**
A comparative diagram that includes appraisal and assessment data to allow managers to easily see an employee's actual and potential performance

how the hotel chain Marriott has been able to establish its brand as an employer of choice by engaging in good recruiting practices. The brand reflects Marriott's culture.

# RECRUITMENT CHANNELS

## RECRUITING INTERNALLY

**OUTCOME 2**

It is only natural for a firm to look internally first when it needs talent. Internal candidates are readily available and get up to speed faster, and there is less uncertainty about how they will perform. You also do not have to run advertisements to find them, which can be costly.

### Internal Job Postings

Internal job postings are a quick way to find qualified employees interested in a position. A small business might simply post a notice on a bulletin board in its break room. Larger companies generally post their openings on their intranet sites. The intranets of some companies alert employees about jobs in which they may be interested. As a position becomes available, a list of employees interested in that position is retrieved, and the records of these employees are reviewed to select possible candidates for interviews. The employees can be electronically notified about interview schedules and track their progress electronically through the various hiring stages.[5]

### Identifying Talent through Performance Appraisals

Successful performers are often good candidates for a promotion. Identifying and developing all employees is a role that all managers should take seriously. A tool called a **9-box grid** is helping firms such as General Electric (GE), Novartis, and others do this. The grid helps managers assess appraisal and assessment data to be compiled into a single visual reference so they can see both an employee's actual performance and potential performance. This can then help managers determine what the developmental needs of the employee are and what the person's next steps within the organization might be. Figure 5.1 is an example of a 9-box grid.

## FIGURE 5.1

### AN EXAMPLE OF A 9-BOX GRID

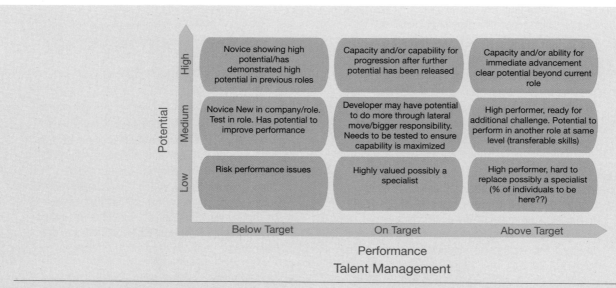

**Source:** Mike Morrison RapidBI.com

## Skill Inventories and Replacement Charts

As we discussed in Chapter 2, firms use skill inventories to help track an employee's education, past work experience, vocational interests, specific abilities and skills, compensation history, and job tenure to see how they can best be used. P&G and HSBC are among the firms that track their employees this way to locate capable employees who can be recruited to fill open positions. Along with skill inventories, replacement charts are an important tool for succession planning. At GE, for every position at or above a director level, two or three people are usually identified who can easily step in when the current job holder moves on.[6]

As we also discussed in Chapter 2, more firms are electronically capturing the qualifications of each of their employees. Companies such as PeopleSoft and SAP have developing automated staffing and skills management software. These information systems allow an organization to rapidly screen its entire workforce to locate suitable candidates to fill an internal opening. The data can also be used to predict the career paths of employees and to anticipate when and where promotion opportunities might arise.[7]

At least one research study has found that managers often hire external candidates rather than promote their current employees because they have a tendency to overvalue unfamiliar candidates and undervalue known ones.[8] This tendency can leave a firm's current employees disillusioned to the point where they begin looking elsewhere for jobs, even when the external candidates hired end up being very qualified for their positions. When experienced employees leave an organization, they take with them years of corporate know-how that is hard to replace. Some signs that the firm needs to work harder at grooming internal talent are shown in Figure 5.2. To lessen the chances of losing top performers, some managers actively identify high-potential "at-risk" employees and take steps to retain these people.

## RECRUITING EXTERNALLY

The sources from which employers recruit externally will vary with the type of position to be filled. A computer programmer, for example, is not likely to be recruited from the same source as a machine operator. Trade schools can be a good source of applicants for entry-level positions, although these recruitment sources are not as useful when highly skilled employees are needed. Some firms keep detailed statistics by job type on the sources from which their employees are hired. This helps HR managers make better decisions about the places to begin recruiting when different job openings arise. We will talk more about recruiting statistics later in the chapter.

**OUTCOME 3**

## Advertisements

Advertising job openings on websites and in newspapers and trade journals is a common way to attract candidates. But Help Wanted signs, billboards, and even Craigslist are sometimes used. In countries in which literacy rates are low, radio

## FIGURE 5.2

### WARNING SIGNS OF A WEAK TALENT BENCH

1. It takes a long time to fill key positions.
2. Key positions can be filled only by hiring from the outside.
3. Vacancies in key positions cannot be filled with confidence in the abilities of those chosen for them.
4. Replacements for positions often are unsuccessful in performing their new duties.
5. Promotions are made on the basis of whim, favouritism, or nepotism.

**Source:** Adapted from William Rothwell, *Effective Succession Planning* (New York: AMACOM, 2000).

and television ads can be more effective. Ads and pages on social networking sites, email campaigns, Twitter, and text messages are new ways recruiters are getting the word out about job openings.

Advertising has the advantage of reaching a large audience of possible applicants. However, some degree of selectivity can be achieved by using newspapers and journals directed toward a particular group of readers. Professional and trade journals, blogs, the professional social networking groups on LinkedIn, and the publications of unions and various fraternal or nonprofit organizations will attract different types of candidates than help wanted signs, for example.

Preparing recruiting advertisements not only is time-consuming, it also requires creativity in terms of developing their design and message content. Well-written advertisements highlight the major assets of the position while showing the responsiveness of the organization to the job, career, and lifestyle needs of applicants. Also, there appears to be a correlation between the accuracy and completeness of information provided in job advertisements and an organization's recruitment success. The more information disclosed, the better. Among the information typically included in advertisements is that the recruiting organization is an equal opportunity employer.

However, even when a job opening is described thoroughly in an advertisement, many unqualified applicants will still apply. HR personnel often have to sift through stacks of inquiries and résumés to locate qualified candidates. In fact, for each vacant position, HR staff and managers typically review 20 to 100 résumés. Fortunately, software developers are designing new tools companies can use to prescreen applicants online, digitize their résumés, distribute the data into company databases, and automate the process of candidate referrals from in-house personnel.[9]

## Walk-ins and Unsolicited Applications and Résumés

Walk-in job seekers seeking jobs that pay hourly wages are common in smaller organizations. Employers also receive unsolicited applications and résumés. Walk-in applicants and individuals who send unsolicited résumés to firms may or may not be good prospects for employment. However, they are a source that cannot be ignored. In fact, it is often believed that individuals who contact employers on their own initiative will be better employees than those recruited through college placement services or newspaper advertisements.

In some segments, such as retail stores and restaurants, it is quite common to find excellent prospective employees through walk-in applications.

© Melanie Stetson Freeman/Christian Science Monitor/The Image Works

Good public relations dictate that any person contacting an organization for a job be treated with courtesy and respect. Not treating applicants with respect will harm a company's employer brand. If there is no present or future possibility of employment in the organization, the applicant should be tactfully and frankly informed. Research has shown that a candidate who has been treated well by a potential employer will, on average, tell one other person. On the other hand, a candidate who has been treated poorly—perhaps receiving a tardy rejection letter or no letter at all—will, on average, tell 11 other people.[10]

**passive job seekers**
People who are not looking for jobs but could be persuaded to take new ones given the right opportunity

## The Internet, Social Networking, and Mobile Recruiting

Looking on the Internet is the most commonly used search tactic by job seekers and recruiters to get the word out about new positions. Both companies and applicants find the approach cheaper, faster, and potentially more effective. Monster has a premium service that narrows down applicants, ranks candidates, and compares them side by side. Staffing experts say it is also a good idea to post your firm's jobs at free association and trade group sites, where your specific talent pool is most likely to congregate.[11] Of course, most large companies post job openings on their own corporate websites, usually under a link titled "Careers." Some companies are now posting podcasts that profile the working lives of their different employees.

As we indicated earlier in the chapter, to help establish their employer brands and recruit talent, many companies are making use of social networking tools to recruit employees. Recruiters are joining groups on LinkedIn that target certain types of professionals. And, of course, companies are flocking to Facebook, for example, to create free recruiting sites where recruiters post job information, showcase their company's attractive features, offer job advice, and post company news. The organizations then buy advertisements on Facebook directing potential candidates to their sites.

Software developers have created talent search software, which can be customized to search the Web for valuable but passive job candidates, based on information they post on industry blogs, social networking sites, and so forth. **Passive job seekers** are people who are not looking for jobs but could be persuaded to take new ones given the right opportunity.

Mobile recruiting has given creative recruiters another new tool to use in the war for talent. Mobile recruiting is the process of recruiting candidates via their mobile devices. It is no secret that people are glued to their mobile phones these days. For this reason, recruiting experts advise that whatever social networking or Internet platform an organization uses, it should have a mobile application tied to it. On the three-block walk between his office and parking spot, Owen Williams, Macy's executive recruiting director, uses a mobile application of LinkedIn and Twitter to post job openings and extend invitations to connect to potential candidates and to keep up with what is happening in his industry. Williams says that mobile recruiting has the advantage of speed, which is important in competitive labour markets and when a firm needs to recruit talent fast. "You never know how long a great candidate will be on the market, so you have to capitalize on the moment," says Williams.[12]

Text messages are also being used to send prospective employees information about jobs. Some surveys show that it is the most popular type of e-recruiting, perhaps because people know how to use it the best. Text messages work well because they are inexpensive, easy to send, fast, and work with any cell phone. Moreover, because most people have their mobile devices on all the time, they get the messages immediately instead of having to launch applications on their phones to get to a site such as Facebook or LinkedIn.

Using social networks is an inexpensive way to recruit people compared to print ads, which can cost hundreds of dollars to run. But there can still be costs a recruiter might not necessarily think about. Patrice Rice, the president of Patrice and Associates Inc., a hospitality industry recruiter, figures that in one year alone she spent $60,000 on branding, a Facebook campaign, and employing a part-time social media manager to maintain the company's online presence, partly so recruiters do not have to, but also to be quicker to respond to queries from potential candidates.[13]

Another potential drawback of using social media, such as Facebook, Twitter, and the Internet in general, is that some groups of people are less likely to be "wired." The disabled are an example. A 2010 study found that whereas 85 percent of adults without disabilities access the Internet, only 54 percent of adults with disabilities do. As a result, relying too heavily on electronic recruiting could hurt a company's diversity efforts. And despite the fact that social media is a burgeoning way to recruit employees, some surveys show that the number of employees actually hired via social media recruiting is still relatively small compared to other methods.

## Job Fairs

Job fairs can be a good way to cast a wide net for diverse applicants in a certain region. At a job fair, companies and their recruiters set up booths, meet with prospective applicants, and exchange employment information. Often the fairs are industry specific.

One drawback of job fairs is that although they attract a lot of applicants, many of them might not be qualified. Another problem is that they only attract applicants in the regional area in which they are held. One way to get around the latter problem is to hold a "virtual job fair" that anyone, anywhere can attend. During a virtual job fair, recruiters staff "virtual booths" online, where they provide links to their career resources, collect résumés, and talk with candidates via online chat functions. Companies can also administer screening questionnaires and, if a webcam feature is incorporated, see the candidates. Holding a virtual job fair can also be cost effective for both recruiters and attendees because they do not have to pay travel costs.

## Employee Referrals

The recruitment efforts of an organization can be greatly aided by employee referrals or recommendations from the firm's current employees about potential candidates. In fact, word-of-mouth recommendations are the way most job positions are filled. (Apparently, there is truth to the phrase, "It is not what you know, but who you know.") Managers have found that the quality of employee-referred applicants is normally quite high because employees are generally hesitant to recommend individuals who might not perform well. In general, applicants who are referred by a current employee, if hired, tend to remain with the organization longer as well.[14]

Some firms have created referral pages on their intranets to make it easier for employees to refer candidates and track their progress through the hiring process.[15] Accenture is a company that has such a site. Highlights in HRM 5.2 shows some additional ways firms can encourage employee referrals.

There are some negative factors associated with employee referrals and profiles, however, including the possibility of corporate "inbreeding." Since employees and their referrals tend to have similar backgrounds, employers who rely heavily on employee referrals to fill job openings may intentionally or unintentionally screen out, and thereby discriminate against, protected classes. Some researchers have found that inbreeding occurs gradually as part of a three-stage trend. According to the Attraction-Selection-Attrition model, in the first stage (Attraction), people with values similar to those of an organization are attracted to it and become employees. In the second stage (Selection), these employees then choose applicants similar to themselves. In the final

# HIGHLIGHTS IN HRM 5.2

## Employee Referral Programs That Work

A company's current employees may be its greatest source of future employees thanks to a well-designed and well-promoted employee referral program (ERP). Here are several suggestions for creating an effective program:

- Make the ERP part of the company culture. Companies typically need more of certain types of skills than others and often have a general profile of background, education, values, and ethics in mind for their candidates. So a big part of building an effective referral program is educating employees about the kinds of people the organization wants to hire—and continuing to keep that profile in the forefront. Helping employees see how finding the right types of candidates will enhance the overall team also adds to their enthusiasm for the program.

- *Be responsive.* Failing to acknowledge referrals promptly makes employees feel as if their efforts have disappeared into a black hole, which is demotivating. Instead, let the candidate and the referring employee know right away when a referral has entered the system. Then give the referred candidate priority processing in terms of screening and interviewing to demonstrate how much good referrals are valued.

- *Up the ante.* Consider creating two tiers of financial incentives for referrals: small rewards for candidates who meet the company's requirements but are not selected and larger rewards for successful matches.

- *Provide rewards that employees value.* Some companies offer healthy bonuses, all-expenses-paid weekend trips, donations to the referring employee's favourite charity, or free insurance as incentives for successful referrals, but plenty of other options are available. Many experts agree that public recognition, perhaps at a company meeting or department luncheon, can be equally rewarding.

- *Give employees the right tools.* Consider supplying employees with special "we're recruiting" business cards to hand out when meeting people face to face. And make it easy for employees to post or tweet information about job openings to their online network of associates.

- *Measure results.* It should go without saying that after the program is implemented, managers need to study the results in terms of the volume of referrals, qualifications of candidates, and success of new hires on the job. These results can then be used to fine-tune the program.

Sources: "How a Talent Management Plan Can Anchor Your Company's Future," *HR Focus 81*, no. 10 (October 2004): 7–10; Susan M. Heathfield, "You Can Inspire Great Employee Referrals," http://humanresources.about.com; John Sullivan, "Advanced Employee Referral Programs—Best Practices You Need to Copy," www.drjohnsullivan.com.

---

stage (Attrition), employees who do not fit in leave. The result is an ultra-homogenized organization.[16]

The practice of hiring relatives, referred to as **nepotism**, can invite charges of favouritism, especially in appointments to desirable positions. HR personnel hiring globally, however, need to realize that in other cultures, including Asia and the Middle East, nepotism is the norm. Even in the United States, nepotism gets mixed reviews, in part because family members are in an ideal position to pass job knowledge and skills on to one another. Many corporate dynasties (Ford Motor Company and McCain Foods among them) have been built on nepotism. Labour unions would not have flourished without it. In the United States, a number of law firms and universities have dropped restrictions against hiring spouses on the basis that they are prejudicial.[17]

**nepotism**
A preference for hiring relatives of current employees

**rerecruiting**
The process of keeping track of and maintaining relationships with former employees to see if they would be willing to return to the firm

## Rerecruiting

**Rerecruiting** is the process of keeping track of and maintaining relationships with former employees to see if they would be willing to return to the firm. Rerecruiting is not uncommon. At the accounting and consulting firm Deloitte, over 75,000 former employees are kept track of via an "alumni network." Other organizations that have alumni networks include Microsoft, Oshkosh, and Ernst & Young.[18]

## Executive Search Firms

In contrast to public and private employment agencies, which help job seekers find the right job, executive search firms (often called "headhunters") help employers find the right person for a job. Firms such as Korn/Ferry International and Mercer & Associates are top recruiting firms for executives. Executive search firms do not advertise in the media for job candidates, nor do they accept a fee from the individual being placed.

The fees charged by search firms can range anywhere from 25 to 40 percent of the annual salary for the position to be filled. For the recruitment of senior executives, this fee is paid by the client firm, whether or not the recruiting effort results in a hire. Search firms receive the greatest criticism for this practice.

Nevertheless, as we noted earlier, hiring new CEOs from outside the organization has become commonplace. A large number of these new CEOs are placed in those positions through the services of an executive search firm. However, newer data suggest that CEOs who are promoted from within their organizations actually outperform those hired from the outside. Moreover, due to high-profile CEO-related scandals and bankruptcies that have occurred in recent times, HR personnel are increasingly being called on to demand more from executive search firms and to assist boards of directors in the careful selection of top executives. In some instances, executive search firms have been criticized for selling the "Superman" qualities of outside CEOs—for which firms pay a premium.

## Educational Institutions

Educational institutions typically are a source of young applicants with formal training but relatively little full-time work experience. High schools are usually a source of employees for clerical and blue-collar jobs. Community colleges, with their various types of specialized training, can provide candidates for technical jobs. These institutions can also be a source of applicants for a variety of white-collar jobs, including those in the sales and retail fields. Some management trainee jobs are also staffed from this source.

For technical and managerial positions, colleges and universities are generally the primary source. Given these numbers and the strong demand for highly skilled employees, colleges are likely to remain a good recruiting source. In addition, some Canadian universities are setting up campuses overseas. As a result, HR professionals in the coming years will have a new source from which to recruit employees abroad.[19]

Not using campus placement offices effectively and trying to visit too many campuses instead of concentrating on select institutions are common mistakes firms make when recruiting on campus. Rather than recruiting students from dozens of schools, as they have done in the past, companies such as Nestlé are targeting fewer schools and forming closer partnerships with them. Employees guest lecture at the schools and develop relationships with instructors, who then recommend students for jobs. (Yes, it pays to be nice to your teacher.) Another mistake recruiting firms make is not continuing the recruiting effort on a long-term basis once it is begun.

Furthermore, some recruiters sent to campuses are not sufficiently trained or prepared to talk to interested candidates about career opportunities or the requirements of specific openings or do not follow up with them. This is a grave mistake because research shows that students' perceptions of recruiters have a big impact on which jobs and companies they choose to pursue. "It is all about how [students] are treated in the campus recruiting process and the feeling that they get from the people they interact with," says the founder of a college

## FIGURE 5.3

### STEPS FOR STRENGTHENING A FIRM'S ON-CAMPUS RECRUITING RELATIONSHIPS

- Invite professors and advisors to visit your office and take them to lunch.

- Invite them to bring a student group to the office.

- Send press releases and newsletters by mail or email to bring them up to date on the firm's latest news and innovations.

- Provide guest speakers for classes.

- Conduct mock interviews, especially in years when not interviewing for full-time or internship positions.

- Provide scholarships to students.

- Attend the campus career fair, even when the firm is not going to be hiring, so that its name becomes known by the faculty and students.

- Offer job-shadowing programs for students.

**Sources:** Bruce Busta, D'Arcy Becker, and Jane P. Saly, "Effective Campus Recruiting: The Faculty Perspective," *CPA Journal* 77, no. 7 (July 2007): 62–65; Deborah J. Sessions, "Recruiting Made Easy," *Journal of Accountancy* 201, no. 5 (May 2006): 31–34.

recruitment consulting firm. Figure 5.3 shows some of the steps firms can take to strengthen their on-campus recruiting relationships.

To attract high-demand graduates, in addition to offering higher pay, firms sometimes employ innovative recruitment techniques such as work–study programs, low-interest loans for promising recruits, scholarships, and internships. Internships can be a great way for firms to "try out" college students who want to work in their fields and for students to decide if they want to work for an organization long term. However, many internships are not as successful as they should be because the sponsoring firms have not thought through how to effectively utilize their interns. This can lead to bored interns, who can, in turn, become disillusioned about their fields. Highlights in HRM 5.3 shows steps companies can take to ensure that their internships are truly successful.

## HIGHLIGHTS IN HRM 5.3

### Making Your Internship Program a Success

Let's assume your company's management has realized that internships benefit both your firm and the students they employ. And let's assume management understands that, statistically, interns usually make the best future full-fledged employees. So now let's look at how to make your internship program a success. Experts agree that you should do the following:

- Reach out to colleges and universities to begin building relationships with them. Let the career advisors at these schools know what you are looking for and what you have to offer the interns and continue to promote your program on an ongoing basis.

- Clearly define what you are looking for in a candidate in terms of current enrollment, GPA, preferred or required major, specific skills, attributes, and other experience.

- Devise a budget for intern recruiting, selection, compensation, relocation, housing, and travel.

- For each intern position, develop a work plan—a list of responsibilities and tasks that will be performed by this person. Since the intern will probably be assigned to a supervisor who will serve as the intern's mentor, it might be useful to get input from the supervisor regarding the position.

- Write an internship handbook that includes information on intern orientation, mentoring, executive engagement, project work, and cross-functional activity opportunities. Provide this to all of the supervisor/mentors in the program and the interns.

- Set up a system for providing interns with feedback on their performance, preferably at the midpoint of their internship and again at the conclusion. Make the experience a teachable moment.

Sources: Getting the Most from Internship Programs," *Supply Chain Management Review* 13, no. 8 (2009): 34; Audrey Watters, "5 Tips for Creating an Internship Program for Your Startup," www.readwriteweb.com; Jean Scheid, "Designing Internship Programs," www.brighthub.com; Penny Loretto, "Developing an Internship Program," http://internships.about.com.

## Professional Associations

Many professional associations and societies offer a placement service to members as one of their benefits. Lists of members seeking employment may be advertised in their journals or publicized at their national meetings. For the mutual benefit of employers and job seekers, placement centres are usually included at the national meetings of professional associations. The Human Resource Professionals Association (HRPA), for example, helps employers and prospective HR employees come together.

## Labour Unions

Labour unions have been a principal source of applicants for blue-collar and some professional jobs. Some unions, such as those in the maritime, printing, and construction industries, maintain hiring halls that can provide a supply of applicants, particularly for short-term needs. Employers wishing to use this recruitment source should contact the local union under consideration for employer eligibility requirements and applicant availability.

## Public Employment Agencies

Each province maintains an employment agency that administers its employment insurance program. Many of these agencies bear such titles as Human Resources Development and have local public employment offices in most communities of any size. Individuals who become unemployed must register at one of these offices and be available for "suitable employment" to receive their weekly employment insurance cheques. As a result, the agencies are able to refer to employers with job openings those applicants with the required skills who are available for employment. In addition to matching unemployed applicants with job openings, public employment agencies sometimes assist employers with apprenticeship programs, employment testing, job analysis, evaluation programs, and community wage surveys.

## Private Employment and Temporary Agencies

Charging a fee enables private employment agencies to tailor their services to the specific needs of their clients. However, it is common for agencies to specialize in serving a specific occupational area or geographic area. When recruiting abroad, companies frequently use local employment agencies because they understand a country's culture, labour markets and methods of recruiting workers there.

Depending on who is receiving the most service, the fee may be paid by the employer, the job seeker, or both. It is not uncommon for private employment agencies to charge an employer a 25 to 30 percent fee, based on the position's annual salary, if the employer hires an applicant found by the agency.

Private employment agencies differ in the services they offer, their professionalism, and the calibre of their counsellors. If counsellors are paid on a commission basis, their desire to do a professional job may be offset by their desire to earn a commission. Thus, they may encourage job seekers to accept jobs for which they are not suited. Because of this, job seekers would be wise to take the time to find a recruiter who is knowledgeable, experienced, and professional. When talking with potential recruiters, individuals should discuss openly their philosophies and practices with regard to recruiting strategies, including advertising, in-house recruiting, screening procedures, and costs for these efforts. They should try to find a recruiter who is flexible and who will consider their needs and wants.

In addition to placing permanent workers, many private agencies hire and place workers in temporary positions. "Temps" are typically used for short-term assignments or to help when managers cannot justify hiring a full-time employee, such as for vacation fill-ins, for peak work periods, or during an employee's pregnancy leave or sick leave. Increasingly, temps have been employed to fill positions once staffed by permanent employees.

Temps give organizations added flexibility because they can be hired and laid off as needed. Also, the employment costs of temporaries are often lower than those of permanent employees because temps are not provided with benefits. To keep their costs down and gain flexibility, some companies use a just-in-time staffing approach, in which a core staff of employees is augmented by a trained and highly skilled supplementary workforce.

Many temporary employees are eventually hired full-time. Temping allows them and the firms they contract with to try one another out before a permanent commitment is made. One concern related to using temps is that they have less of an incentive to be loyal to an employer and its clients or to go the extra mile to help a company achieve success.

For reasons such as these, some organizations are scaling back their use of temporary help. Instead of hiring temps, the Hilton hotel chain sends full-time employees from one hotel to another to address temporary spikes in demand. This strategy not only makes efficient use of the hotel chain's staff but also helps develop an agile workforce.[20]

## Employee Leasing

**Employee leasing** by professional employer organizations (PEOs) has grown rapidly in the United States but is not as common in Canada. We discuss it here because trends in the United States often migrate here a few years later. Basically, a PEO—typically a larger company—takes over the management of a smaller company's HR tasks and becomes a coemployer to its employees. The PEO performs all the HR duties of an employer—recruiting, background checks, hiring, payroll, performance appraisal, benefits administration, and other day-to-day HR activities—and in return is paid a placement fee of normally 4 to 8 percent of payroll cost plus 9 to 20 percent of gross wages. Because PEOs can coemploy a large number of people working at many different companies, they can provide employees with benefits and health plans that small companies cannot afford. Unlike temporary agencies, which supply workers only for limited periods, employee leasing companies place their employees with subscribers on a permanent basis. The Society for Human Resource Management reports that companies with fewer than 50 employees can save anywhere from $5,000 to $50,000 in time and labour costs annually by hiring a PEO.[21]

# IMPROVING THE EFFECTIVENESS OF RECRUITING

OUTCOME 4

How well is a company doing when it comes to recruiting talent from all sources? Have the firm's recruiters been able to hire enough employees to meet the company's needs, including key personnel? Are the recruiters slow or fast when it comes to filling positions? Are line managers happy with the process and the quality of the people hired? Are the people who have been hired happy with their jobs and likely to remain with the firm and advance in the organization? HR managers have many tools available to them to gauge their efforts and improve their recruiting. Let's look at a few of them.

## USING REALISTIC JOB PREVIEWS

One way organizations may be able to increase the effectiveness of their recruitment efforts is to provide job applicants with a **realistic job preview (RJP)**. An RJP informs applicants about all aspects of the job, including both its desirable and undesirable facets. In contrast, a typical job preview presents the job only in positive terms. The RJP might also include a tour of the working area, combined with a discussion of any negative health or safety considerations. Proponents of RJPs believe that applicants who are given realistic information regarding a position are more likely to remain on the job and be successful because there will be fewer unpleasant surprises. In fact, a number of research studies on RJPs report that they can yield results such as realistic job expectations on the part of employees, better job satisfaction, and lower turnover.

Some companies are taking their RJPs online. For example, the North Shore Health Region, in British Columbia, realized that it had unique attributes that could give a competitive advantage in recruiting nurses. Recruitment materials were prepared that captured the main appeal of this employer: a small, friendly, full-service hospital. This message was reinforced in all recruitment efforts and was credible (realistic) because it was based on research with existing employees.[22]

## SURVEYS

Another way to improve a company's recruiting is to survey managers about how satisfied they are with the process. Are managers happy with the time it takes to hire new employees, the degree to which they need to be involved in the process, and, ultimately, the overall quality of the people recruited? Why or why not? New hires can also be surveyed to see how satisfied they are. Lastly, candidates who turned down jobs often can provide valuable information about why they did not accept the firm's offer.

## RECRUITING METRICS

As we explained earlier in the chapter, recruiters should keep statistics on the sources from which candidates are recruited and hired as well as the costs of each source. The time it takes to recruit various employees from various sources and the quality of employees are other statistics recruiters collect and study. Doing so helps them understand which recruiting sources work best for different employees, which allows them to find better employees faster and at a lower cost.

### Quality-of-Fill Statistics

As we indicated in the Appendix to Chapter 2, hiring quality employees is a primary concern of recruiters. Firms have attempted to develop a quality-of-fill statistic they can use to improve their recruiting processes. The following is one suggested way of calculating an annual quality-of-fill metric for an organization:

$$\text{Quality of Hire} = (PR + HP + HR)/N$$

$PR$ = average job performance rating of new hires

$HP$ = percentage of new hires reaching acceptable productivity within an acceptable time frame

$HR$ = percentage of new hires retained after one year

$N$ = number of indicators

Example:

$PR$ = average 3.5 on a 5.0 scale = 70 percent

$HP$ = of 100 hires made one year ago, 75 are meeting acceptable productivity levels = 75 percent

$HR$ = 20 percent turnover = 80 percent HR

$N$ = 3

$$\text{Quality of Hire} = (70 + 75 + 80)/3 = 75$$

The result is a quality level of 75 percent for new employees hired during the year.

FIGURE 5.4

## TIME-TO-FILL CALCULATIONS

| Position | Date Position Approved | Date Offer Accepted | Date Started Work | Selection Time | Time to Start |
|---|---|---|---|---|---|
| Engineer | 10/10/12 | 11/30/12 | 12/15/12 | 51 | 15 |
| Marketing manager | 10/11/12 | 11/24/12 | 12/16/12 | 44 | 22 |
| Salesperson | 10/12/12 | 11/13/12 | 11/20/12 | 32 | 7 |
| Administrative assistant | 10/13/12 | 11/7/12 | 11/14/12 | 25 | 7 |
| Clerk | 10/13/12 | 10/30/12 | 11/14/12 | 17 | 15 |
| **Averages** | | | | **33.8** | **13.2** |

## Time to Fill

The **time-to-fill** metric refers to the number of days from when a job opening is approved to the date the person ultimately chosen for the job is selected. Figure 5.4 shows an example of how the time-to-fill metric is calculated. Generally speaking, lower time-to-fill statistics are better. However, a tradeoff has to be made between the time to fill a position and the quality of the candidates needed for the position.

**time-to-fill metric**
The number of days from when a job opening is approved to the date the candidate is selected

**yield ratio**
The percentage of applicants from a recruitment source that make it to the next stage of the selection process

## Yield Ratios

Yield ratios help indicate which recruitment sources are most effective at producing qualified job candidates. Quite simply, a **yield ratio** is the percentage of applicants from a particular source who make it to the next stage in the selection process. For example, if 100 résumés were obtained from an employment agency and 17 of the applicants submitting those résumés were invited for an on-site interview, the yield ratio for that agency would be 17 percent (17/100). This yield ratio could then be recalculated for each subsequent stage in the selection process (e.g., after the interview and again after the final offer), which would result in a cumulative yield ratio. By calculating and comparing yield ratios for each recruitment source, it is possible to find out which sources produce qualified applicants.

## Costs of Recruitment

The costs of various recruiting procedures can be computed using a fairly simple set of calculations. For example, the average source cost per hire (SC/H) can be determined by the following formula:

$$SC/H = AC + AF\_ + RB + NC/H$$

where AC = advertising costs, total monthly expenditure (e.g., $32,000);

    AF = agency fees, total for the month (e.g., $21,000);

    RB = referral bonuses, total paid ($2,600);

    NC = no-cost hires, walk-ins, nonprofit agencies (e.g., $0);

    H = total hires (e.g., 119).

Substituting the example numbers into the formula gives

$$\frac{SC}{H} = \frac{\$32,000 + \$21,000 + \$2,600 + \$0}{119}$$

$$= \frac{\$55,600}{119}$$

$$= \$467.23 \text{ (source cost of recruits per hire)}$$

**applicant tracking system (ATS)**
A software application recruiters use to post job openings, screen résumés, contact potential candidates for interviews via email, and track the time and costs related to hiring people

When combined with information about yield ratios, these calculations can provide invaluable information to managers about the utility of different approaches to and sources of recruitment. In that way, they can make more informed decisions about both controlling the costs of recruitment and increasing its effectiveness. For example, although advertisements and employee referrals may both yield qualified applicants, managers may find that referral bonuses are a more economical alternative.

An **applicant tracking system (ATS)** can help a firm automatically track and calculate the statistics we have discussed. An ATS is a software application recruiters use to post job openings, screen résumés, contact potential candidates for interviews via email, and track the time and costs related to hiring people. About 50 percent of all midsized companies and almost all large corporations use some type of ATS.[23]

# CAREER MANAGEMENT: DEVELOPING TALENT OVER TIME

**OUTCOME 5**

Regardless of the source from which employees are recruited—internally or externally—managers play a key role in expanding the talent pools of firms. Good managers listen to their employees' aspirations, act as coaches, identify their strengths and areas for improvement, and offer them continual feedback about their performance. They also ensure that employees receive training and are provided with self-assessment tools and information about the organization and possible career paths within it. Compared to recruiting, helping employees grow and working to develop their skills is a more proactive—and strategic—approach to systematically expanding the talent pool relative to bringing people in from the outside and banking on them being right for the job.

Integrating career development with other HR programs creates synergies in which all aspects of HR reinforce one another. Figure 5.5 illustrates how

## FIGURE 5.5

### HR'S ROLE IN CAREER MANAGEMENT

**1 THE GOAL: MATCH INDIVIDUAL AND ORGANIZATION NEEDS**

**The Goal: Matching**

- Create a supportive environment.
- Communicate the direction of the company.
- Establish mutual goal setting and planning

**2 IDENTIFY CAREER OPPORTUNITIES & REQUIREMENTS**

**Opportunities & Requirements**

- Identify future competency needs.
- Establish job progressions/career paths.
- Balance promotions, transfers, exits, etc.
- Establish dual career paths.

**4 INSTITUTE CAREER DEVELOPMENT INITIATIVES**

**Career Development Initiatives**

- Provide workbooks and workshops.
- Provide career counseling.
- Provide career self-management training.
- Give developmental feedback.

**3 GAUGE EMPLOYEE POTENTIAL**

**Gauge Employee Potential**

- Measure competencies (appraisals).
- Establish talent inventories.
- Establish succession plans.
- Use assessment centers.

HR structures relate to some of the essential aspects of the career management process. For example, to plan their careers, employees need organizational information—information that strategic planning, forecasting, succession planning, and skill inventories can provide. Similarly, as they obtain information themselves and use it to plan their careers, employees need to know what the career paths within their organizations are and how management views their performance.

## THE GOAL: MATCHING INDIVIDUAL AND ORGANIZATIONAL NEEDS

A career development program should be viewed as a dynamic process that matches the needs of the organization with the needs of employees. Each party has a distinctive role to play.

### The Employee's Role

Changes in the workplace are occurring so rapidly that employees need to take an active role in planning their careers. What new technological skills will they need to be successful in the workforce in the future? What careers utilize those skills? What career options would a person be able to pursue if he or she were downsized? At some point in their careers, most employees will face this situation.

Because having a successful career involves creating your own career path—not just following a path that has been established by the organization—employees need to identify their knowledge, skills, abilities, interests, and values and to seek out information about career options in conjunction with their managers. Managers can help with the process by offering their subordinates continual feedback about their performance and providing them with self-assessment tools, training, and information about the organization and possible career paths within it. General Motors, for example, has prepared a career development guide that groups jobs by fields of work such as engineering, manufacturing, communications, data processing, financial services, HR, and scientific fields. These categories give employees an understanding of the career possibilities in various fields.

### The Organization's Role: Establishing a Favourable Career Development Climate

If career development is to succeed, it must receive the complete support of top management. Ideally, senior line managers and HR department managers should work together to design and implement a career development system. The system should reflect the goals and culture of the organization, and the HR philosophy should be woven throughout. An HR philosophy can provide employees with a clear set of expectations and directions for their own career development. Says the director of recruitment with The Container Store: "There is constant, consistent communication with management on growth opportunities. Rather than follow one career path, the company works to leverage employees' talents for new and different roles, as well as giving them as much exposure as possible to other positions and responsibilities in the company to ensure they're challenged."[24]

### Blending the Goals of Individual Employees with the Goals of the Organization

Of course, a career development program should be based on the organization's goals and needs as well. As Figure 5.6 shows, the organization's goals and needs should be linked with the individual career needs of its employees in a way that

**FIGURE 5.6**

BLENDING THE NEEDS OF INDIVIDUAL EMPLOYEES WITH THE NEEDS OF THEIR ORGANIZATIONS

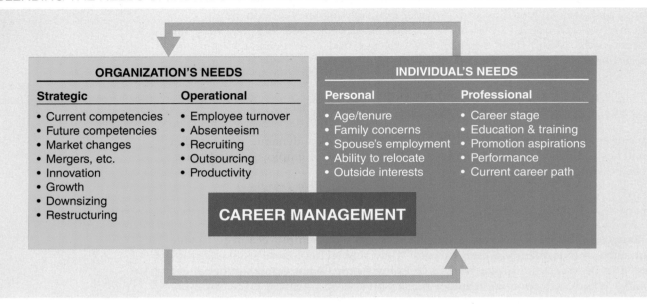

| ORGANIZATION'S NEEDS | | INDIVIDUAL'S NEEDS | |
| --- | --- | --- | --- |
| **Strategic** | **Operational** | **Personal** | **Professional** |
| • Current competencies | • Employee turnover | • Age/tenure | • Career stage |
| • Future competencies | • Absenteeism | • Family concerns | • Education & training |
| • Market changes | • Recruiting | • Spouse's employment | • Promotion aspirations |
| • Mergers, etc. | • Outsourcing | • Ability to relocate | • Performance |
| • Innovation | • Productivity | • Outside interests | • Current career path |
| • Growth | | | |
| • Downsizing | | | |
| • Restructuring | | | |

**CAREER MANAGEMENT**

improves the effectiveness of workers and their satisfaction as well as achieving the firm's strategic objectives. Before a firm's employees can engage in meaningful career planning, however, not only must they have an awareness of the organization's philosophy, they must also have a good understanding of the organization's more immediate goals. Otherwise, they might plan for personal change and growth without knowing whether or how their own goals match those of the organization. For example, if the technology of a business is changing and new skills are needed, will the organization retrain its employees to meet this need or hire new talent? Is there growth, stability, or decline in the number of employees needed? How will turnover affect this need?

## IDENTIFYING CAREER OPPORTUNITIES AND REQUIREMENTS

Although talent management integrates a number of related HR activities, those who direct the process have to keep a steady watch on the needs and requirements of the organization. This involves an analysis of the competencies required for jobs, progression among related jobs, and the supply of ready (and potential) talent available to fill those jobs. A variety of approaches can be used to do this, including surveys, informal group discussions, and interviews. The process should involve personnel from different groups, such as new employees, managers, long-time employees, minority employees, and technical and professional employees. Identifying the needs and problems of these groups provides the starting point for the organization's career development efforts.

### Begin with a Competency Analysis

It is important for an organization to study its jobs carefully to identify and assign weights to the knowledge and skills that each one requires. This can be achieved with job analysis and evaluation systems such as those used in compensation programs. The system used at Sears measures three basic competencies for each job: know-how, problem solving, and accountability. Know-how is broken down into three types of job knowledge: technical, managerial, and human relations. Problem solving and accountability also have several dimensions. Scores for each of these three major competencies are assigned to each job, and a total value is computed for each job. For any planned job transfer, the amount of increase (or decrease) the next job represents in each of the skill areas, as well as in the total point values, can be computed. This information is then used to make certain that a transfer to a different job is a move that requires growth on the part of the employee.

Sears designs career development paths to provide the following experiences: (1) an increase in at least one skill area on each new assignment, (2) an increase of at least 10 percent in total points on each new assignment, and (3) assignments in several different functional areas.[25]

## Identify Job Progressions and Career Paths

Once the skill demands of jobs are identified and weighted according to their importance, it is then possible to plan **job progressions**. A new employee with no experience is typically assigned to a "starting job." After a period of time in that job, the employee can be promoted to one that requires more knowledge and/or skill. Although most organizations concentrate on developing job progressions for managerial, professional, and technical jobs, progressions can be developed for all categories of jobs. Job progressions can then serve as a basis for developing **career paths**—the lines of advancement within an organization—for individuals. Figure 5.7 illustrates a typical line of advancement in the HR area of a large multinational corporation. As you can see from the figure, in this firm, a person has to be prepared to move geographically to advance very far in the HR department. This might also be true of other career fields within the organization.

Although these analyses can be quite helpful to employees—and are perhaps essential for organizations—a word of caution is appropriate here. Even with the best career planning, it is almost impossible for people to have perfect certainty about where their careers are going. People change over time, and because of that, their needs and interests change. Moreover, successful career paths often do not proceed in a lockstep manner. Many successful individuals readily admit that their career paths are idiosyncratic to their circumstances. These people often note that they were either "in the right place at the right time" or carved out entirely new career paths for themselves. Other people's careers progress quite predictably and linearly.

## Track Career Stages

A person's knowledge, skills, abilities, and attitudes as well as career aspirations change with age and maturity. The challenges and frustrations people face at the

**job progressions**
The hierarchy of jobs a new employee might experience, ranging from a starting job to jobs that successively require more knowledge and/or skill

**career paths**
Lines of advancement in an occupational field within an organization

PART 3

**FIGURE 5.7**

TYPICAL LINE OF ADVANCEMENT IN HR MANAGEMENT

| | | | | Vice president, HR |
|---|---|---|---|---|
| | | | Corporate HR director | |
| | | Corporate HR manager | Division HR director | |
| | | Asst. division HR director | | |
| | Regional HR manager | Plant HR manager | | |
| | Asst. plant HR manager | | | |
| Regional HR associate | HR supervisor | | | |
| HR associate | | | | |

same stages in their careers are remarkably similar. A model describing these stages is shown in Figure 5.7. The stages are (1) preparation for work, (2) organizational entry, (3) early career, (4) midcareer, and (5) late career. The typical age range and the major tasks of each stage are also presented in the figure.

The first stage—preparation for work—encompasses the period prior to entering an organization, often extending until age 25. It is a period in which individuals must acquire the knowledge, abilities, and skills they will need to compete in the marketplace. It is a time when careful planning, based on sound information, should be the focus. Reality Check outlines how Career Edge helps people in this stage find their first job. The second stage, typically from ages 18 to 25, is devoted to soliciting job offers and selecting an appropriate job. During this period, a person might also be involved in preparing for work. The next three stages entail fitting into a chosen occupation and organization(s), modifying one's goals, remaining productive, and, finally, preparing for retirement. In the remainder of the chapter, we will look at the challenges faced by students, many of whom are likely to be in the early stages of their careers. Retirement planning will be discussed in Chapter 11.

## Recognize Different Career Paths

Career development and planning systems were once primarily focused on promotions. However, in today's flatter organizations and more dynamic work environment, an individual's career advancement can move along several different

# REALITY CHECK

## Career Edge Making a Difference

Career Edge is Canada's youth internship program that helps university, college, and high school graduates launch their careers as full-time paid interns. For recent graduates with no work experience, obtaining that first job can be difficult. They are caught in the cycle of "no experience, no job; no job, no experience." Career Edge helps graduates obtain that first job, which then leads, in most cases, to a permanent job. Career Edge also operates Ability Edge, a national internship program for graduates with disabilities. Career Edge contacts host organizations, which agree to provide an internship combining four elements: employment experience, learning, coaching, and networking. Because the interns are employed by Career Edge, employers do not have to fight for additional positions (a very difficult task in any organization) but can employ the interns from contract budgets. The interns are paid a stipend of $1,500 per month.

All job posting is done electronically. Employers post internships on the Career Edge website (http://www.careeredge.org). Underemployed or unemployed graduates can sign on and search for internships by sector, company, educational discipline, date of posting, city, and length of internship desired. When a fit is found, the full job description is made available. The site also offers information on job search skills such as résumé and interview preparation.

Frances Randle, former president and CEO of Career Edge, says:

> The contact is made directly between the candidate and the host organization because these students have to learn how to market themselves, and companies have to commit to the intern directly. Interns are looking for practical experience, increased confidence in their abilities, learning about their fields, getting experience in that field, having challenging work, developing a network, and getting feedback on performance, in that order. Companies want recent university graduates who are enthusiastic, flexible, interested in learning, yet with some technical skills and the ability to communicate.

Since opening for business in October 1996, when the youth unemployment rate was nearly 18 percent, Career Edge has placed thousands of interns at over 1,000 companies. About 50 percent of the interns find full-time work with their host organizations.

Source: Interview with Francis Randle, 2006.

paths via promotions, transfers, demotions, and even exits. A **promotion** is a change of assignment to a job at a higher level in the organization. The new job normally provides an increase in pay and status and demands more skill or carries more responsibility. The three principal criteria for determining promotions are merit, seniority, and potential. Often the problem is to determine how much consideration to give each factor. A common problem in organizations that promote primarily on past performance and seniority is called the Peter Principle. This refers to the situation in which individuals are promoted as long as they have done a good job in their previous jobs. The situation continues until someone does poorly in his or her new job. Then he or she is no longer promoted. This results in people being promoted to their level of incompetence. There are other intrafirm challenges related to promotions. Sometimes extremely good employees are prevented from being promoted to other departments because their current managers are reluctant to lose them. And as we pointed out earlier in the chapter, some managers favour external candidates versus internal candidates because they are not familiar with the external candidates' flaws. This helps explain why companies so often look outside their firms in an effort to hire "saviour" CEOs.[26] In flatter organizations, there are fewer promotional opportunities, so many individuals find career advancement through lateral moves. A **transfer** is the placement of an employee in another job for which the duties, responsibilities, status, and pay and benefits are approximately equal to those of the previous job he or she held (although as an incentive to make a transfer, organizations sometimes offer transferred employees small pay increases). Individuals who look forward to change or want a chance to learn more about their organizations and obtain different skills often seek transfers. Frequently, these employees do so with an effort to augment their skills so that they will be more promotable in the future.

A transfer sometimes requires the employee to change his or her work group, workplace, work shift, or organizational unit; it may even necessitate moving to another geographic area. Thus, transfers make it possible for an organization to place its employees in jobs where there is a greater need for their services and where they can acquire new knowledge and skills.

A downward transfer, or *demotion*, moves an individual into a lower level job that can provide developmental opportunities. Although such a move is ordinarily considered unfavourable, some individuals may request it to return to their "technical roots." It is not uncommon, for example, for organizations to appoint temporary leaders (especially in team environments) to positions with the understanding that they will eventually return to their former jobs.

Transfers, promotions, and demotions require individuals to adjust to new job demands and usually to a different work environment. A transfer that involves moving to a new location within Canada or abroad places greater demands on an employee because it requires the person to adapt to a new work environment and new living conditions. The employee with a family has the added responsibility of helping family members adjust to the new living arrangements. Even though some employers provide all types of **relocation services**—including covering moving expenses, helping to sell a home, and providing cultural orientation and language training—there is always some loss in the employee's productivity during the relocation process. Pretransfer training, whether related to job skills or to lifestyle, has been suggested as one of the most effective ways to reduce lost productivity.

Of course, many employees choose to exit their organizations as part of their career development. When a person's career opportunities within a firm are limited and his or her skills are in demand externally, the best career options could be for the individual to switch companies or to work as freelancers, consultants, or entrepreneurs. Although some employees leave voluntarily, other employees are forced to leave. Larger organizations often provide **outplacement services** to help terminated employees find jobs elsewhere. Jack Welch, the former chairman of GE, was one of the first executives to make a commitment to employees to try to ensure *employability* when the company could no longer guarantee lifetime employment. That is, GE has committed to providing employees with the skills and support they would need to find a job in another organization.[27]

**promotion**
A change of assignment to a job at a higher level in the organization

**transfer**
Placement of an individual in another job for which the duties, responsibilities, status, and remuneration are approximately equal to those of the previous job

**relocation services**
Services provided to an employee who is transferred to a new location, which might include help in moving, selling a home, orienting to a new culture, and/or learning a new language

**outplacement services**
Services provided by organizations to help terminated employees find a new job

**career plateau**
A situation in which, for either organizational or personal reasons, the probability of moving up the career ladder is low

Human Resources and Skills Development Canada offers several programs to support the unemployed, the underemployed, and those facing barriers in employment. Every provincial and territorial government also offers employment assistance.[28]

## Consider Dual Career Paths for Employees

One of the most obvious places where career paths have been changing is in technical and professional areas. One of the ironies of organizations in the past has been that the most successful engineers, scientists, and professionals were often promoted right out of their area of specialization into management. Instead of doing what they were good at, they were promoted into a job they often did not understand or enjoy.

It has become apparent that there must be another way to compensate these types of professionals without putting them in management positions. The solution has been to develop dual career paths, or tracks, that provide for progression in special areas such as information technology, finance, marketing, and engineering, with compensation that is comparable to that received by managers at different levels. As we explained in Chapter 2, Microsoft offers software engineers both a management-focused and a technical specialist career track and allows them to move back and forth between the two.

## Consider the Boundaryless Career

A generation ago, career success was synonymous with ascending a corporate hierarchy over the course of a lifetime spent in a single firm. Today, however, individuals pursuing *boundaryless careers* prefer to see themselves as self-directed "free agents" who develop a portfolio of employment opportunities by proactively moving from employer to employer, simultaneously developing and utilizing their marketable skills.

Under the boundaryless career model, success depends on continually learning new skills, developing new relationships, and capitalizing on existing skills and relationships. These individuals place a premium on flexibility and the capacity to do several different types of tasks, learn new jobs, adjust quickly to different group settings and organizational cultures, and move from one firm, occupation, or industry to another. Their employment security depends on their marketable skills rather than their dedication to one organization over time. A number of studies have shown that people with boundaryless careers find them very satisfying. Organizations can also benefit from boundaryless careers because it allows them to attract top talent from all over the world on a project-by-project basis.[29]

## Help Employees Progress beyond Career Plateaus

Career plateaus are common obstacles in the career development of employees. A **career plateau** is a situation in which, for either organizational or personal reasons, the probability of moving up the career ladder is low. There are three types of plateaus: structural, content, and life. A *structural plateau* marks the end of promotions. A *content plateau* occurs when a person has learned a job too well and is bored with day-to-day activities. A *life plateau* is more profound and may feel like a midlife crisis. People who experience life plateaus often have allowed work or some other major factor to become the most significant aspect of their lives, and they experience a loss of identity and self-esteem when they are no longer advancing in their careers.

Organizations can help individuals cope with plateaus by providing them with opportunities for lateral growth or allowing them to choose their own assignments when opportunities for advancement do not exist. Companies with international divisions can encourage employees to take assignments abroad to expand their horizons, lead philanthropic and volunteer activities for their firms, or take sabbaticals. A **sabbatical** is an extended period of time during which an employee leaves an organization to pursue other activities before returning to the firm. Career enrichment programs can help people learn more about what gives them satisfaction within a company, as well as what kinds of opportunities will make them happiest if they go elsewhere.

**sabbatical**
An extended period of time in which an employee leaves an organization to pursue other activities and later returns to his or her job

## CAREER DEVELOPMENT INITIATIVES

In a study undertaken by the HR consulting firm Drake Beam Morin (DBM), the six most successful career management practices used within organizations are as follows:

- Placing clear expectations on employees so they know what is expected of them throughout their careers with the organization
- Giving employees the opportunity to transfer to other office locations, both domestically and internationally
- Providing a clear and thorough succession plan to employees
- Encouraging performance through rewards and recognition
- Giving employees the time and resources they need to consider short- and long-term career goals
- Encouraging employees to continually assess their skills and career direction

In contrast, organizations also need to be mindful of the internal barriers that inhibit employees' career advancement. Generally, these barriers can include such things as the following:

- Lack of time, budgets, and resources for employees to plan their careers and to undertake training and development
- Rigid job specifications, lack of leadership support for career management, and a short-term focus
- Lack of career opportunities and pathways within the organization for employees[30]

A variety of tools are available to help employees further their careers within an organization. Informal counselling by HR staff and supervisors is used widely. Career planning workbooks and workshops are also popular tools for helping employees identify their potential and the strength of their interests. Supporting career development activities can help the organization achieve retention and productivity goals as outlined in the Business Case.

---

# THE BUSINESS CASE

## The Value of Career Development Programs

Career development programs may not appear to offer the obvious return on investments that absenteeism or safety management programs offer. However, employers should start to measure the following to make the business case for career development:

- *Attraction.* Do organizations establish reputations as "academies" that develop talent through solid career development and mentoring programs?

- *Retention.* Do units with strong career development programs have higher retention rates of top talent than those without?

- *Employability.* If organizations cannot guarantee lifetime employment, do they have a moral responsibility to provide career development programs that ensure that employees are employable?

- *Commitment.* In those organizations with career development programs, is there a correlation between employee commitment and productivity?

*continued*

---

One company did measure retention and commitment changes that occurred as a result of a career development program, and the return on investment was 190 percent. A manufacturer of technical equipment was experiencing a 37 percent turnover among highly valuable engineers. As part of the solution, the company created a high-potential development program. The participants attended workshops, identified learning projects, and were paired with an executive sponsor and an external mentor. Eighteen months later, turnover was down from 37 percent to 1 percent, and participants were more productive, as measured by their superiors.

Sources: Jack Ito and Celeste Brotheridge, "Does Supporting Employees Career Adaptability Lead to Commitment, Turnover, or Both?" *Human Resource Management*, Spring 2005, 44, 1, 05–19; Catherine Mossop, "Mentoring Can Drive Business Goals," *Canadian HR Reporter*, July 12, 2004, 6.

**career counselling**
The process of discussing with employees their current job activities and performance, personal and career interests and goals, personal skills, and suitable career development objectives

**fast-track program**
A program that encourages new managers with high potential to remain with an organization by enabling them to advance more rapidly than those with less potential

## Career Planning Workbooks and Workshops

Several organizations have prepared workbooks to guide their employees individually through systematic self-assessment of values, interests, abilities, goals, and personal development plans. General Motors' *Career Development Guide* contains a section called "What Do You Want Your Future to Be?" in which the employee makes a personal evaluation. GE has developed an extensive set of career development programs, including workbooks to help employees explore life issues that affect career decisions.

Some organizations prefer to use workbooks written for the general public. Popular ones include Richard N. Bolles's *What Color Is Your Parachute?* and Dan Zadra and Kristel Wills's *Where Will You Be Five Years from Today?* These same books are recommended to students for help in planning their careers.

Like workbooks, career planning workshops help employees seek career planning information, make career decisions, set goals, and, at the same time, build confidence and self-esteem.[31] However, workshops give employees the opportunity to compare and discuss their concerns and plans with other people in similar situations and the professionals who conduct the workshops. Some workshops focus on current job performance and development plans. Others deal with broader life and career plans and values.

## Career Counselling

**Career counselling** is the process of talking with employees about their current job activities and performance, personal and career interests and goals, personal skills, and suitable career development objectives. Career counselling can be provided by HR staff members, managers and supervisors, specialized staff counselors, or outside consultants. To truly expand an organization's talent pool, managers should make career counselling part of the performance appraisals. They can do so by simply asking employees what their career aspirations are. Once the conversation has begun, how those goals can be achieved and fit in with the organization's goals can be discussed and a career "action" plan for the employees established. Several techniques for career counselling are outlined at the end of this chapter (see the Appendix). The obligations of employees to return the organizational investments in their development are outlined in Ethics in HRM. As employees approach retirement, they may be encouraged to participate in preretirement programs, which often include counselling. Preretirement programs will be discussed in Chapter 11.

In helping individuals plan their careers, it is important for organizations to recognize that younger employees today seek meaningful training assignments that are interesting and involve challenge, responsibility, and a sense of empowerment. They also have a greater concern for the contribution that their work in the organization will make to society. Unfortunately, they are frequently given responsibilities they view as rudimentary, boring, and composed of too many "busy-work" activities. Some organizations are attempting to retain young managers with high potential by offering a **fast-track program** that enables them to advance more

# ETHICS IN HRM

## Individual Investment or Organizational Investment?

Organizations such as P&G and IBM invest a great deal of time and money in developing their professional sales staff and management personnel. Similarly, the federal government offers new university recruits up to six months of language training and tuition-paid university courses, as well as several weeks of skills training, within the first two years on the job.

Other organizations refuse to invest in the long-term development of their employees. They cite statistics suggesting that over one-third of university recruits will quit within the first year. In addition, they argue that other corporations will raid these highly trained personnel.

Do employees who have received the benefit of extensive development programs at the employer's expense have an obligation to remain with the organization so that it can realize a return on its investment?

rapidly than those with less potential. A fast-track program can provide for a relatively rapid progression—lateral transfers or promotions—through a number of managerial positions designed to expose the employee to different functions within the organization.

**mentors**
Individuals who coach, advise, and encourage individuals of lesser rank

## Mentoring

It is common to hear people mention individuals at work who influenced them. They frequently refer to their immediate managers, who were especially helpful as career developers. But they also mention others at higher levels in the organization who provided them with guidance and support in the development of their careers. Executives and managers who coach, advise, and encourage employees are called **mentors**.

A mentoring relationship need not be formal. In reality, informal mentoring goes on daily within every type of organization. Generally, the mentor initiates the relationship, but sometimes an employee will approach a potential mentor

### Using the Internet

This site provides links to mentoring resources:

**http://www.mentors.ca**

Managers may act as mentors to those in early career stages.

CHAPTER 5: BRANDING THE TALENT POOL: RECRUITMENT AND CAREERS

## FIGURE 5.8

### TOP 10 MYTHS ABOUT MENTORS

**Myth 1:** *Mentors exist only for career development.* Sometimes the mentor focuses on formal career development. Sometimes the mentor is teacher, counsellor, and friend. Some mentors assume all of these roles. This enhances both personal and professional development.

**Myth 2:** *You need only one mentor.* We can have multiple mentors in our lives. Different mentors provide different things to help protégés with their careers.

**Myth 3:** *Mentoring is a one-way process.* Learning flows both ways. The mentor often learns from the protégé, so the growth is reciprocal.

**Myth 4:** *A mentor has to be older than the protégé.* Age does not matter. Experience and wisdom matter. Do not deprive yourself of learning opportunities from others who have rich experiences.

**Myth 5:** *A mentor has to be the same gender and race as the protégé.* The purpose of mentoring is to learn. Do not deprive yourself. Seek mentors who are different from you.

**Myth 6:** *Mentor relationships just happen.* Being in the right place at the right time can help, but the key to selecting a good mentor is what (not whom) you need. Do not be afraid to actively seek a mentor.

**Myth 7:** *Highly profiled people make the best mentors.* Prestige and success can be good, but good advice, leadership styles, and work ethics vary by individuals. Good mentors are people who challenge you according to your needs, readiness, and aspirations.

**Myth 8:** *Once a mentor, always a mentor.* Over time, the mentor should pull back and let the protégé go his or her own way. Although the two may maintain contact, the relationship changes over time.

**Myth 9:** *Mentoring is a complicated process.* The most complicated part is getting out of a bad mentor relationship. If the relationship is not productive, find a tactful way to disengage.

**Myth 10:** *Mentor–protégé expectations are the same for everyone.* Individuals seek mentors for the same reasons: resources, visibility, enhanced skills, and counsel. But each individual brings different expectations. The key is understanding where the protégé is now, not where he or she should be.

for advice. Most mentoring relationships develop over time on an informal basis. They frequently end that way too. However, proactive organizations emphasize formal mentoring plans that assign a mentor to employees considered for upward movement in the organization. GE, for example, selects the top 20 percent of its performers and allows these people to choose their own mentors from a list of top executives. Under a good mentor, learning focuses on goals, opportunities, expectations, standards, and assistance in fulfilling one's potential.[32]

The top 10 myths about mentors are shown in Figure 5.8. Figure 5.9 shows a list of the most effective features of mentors as well as partners. To form an

## FIGURE 5.9

### MENTORING FUNCTIONS

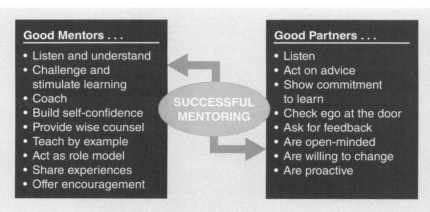

**Source:** Matt Starcevich, PhD and Fred Friend, "Effective Mentoring Relationships from the Mentee's Perspective," *Workforce*, supplement (July 1999): 2–3. Used with permission of the Center for Coaching and Mentoring, Inc., http://coachingandmentoring.com.

effective mentoring relationship, an employee seeking a mentor should follow a few general guidelines:

career networking
The process of establishing mutually beneficial relationships with other businesspeople, including potential clients and customers

1. *Research the person's background.* Do your homework. The more you know about your potential mentor, the easier it will be to approach him or her and establish a relationship that will work for both of you.
2. *Make contact with the person.* Have a mutual friend or acquaintance introduce you or get involved with your potential mentor in business settings. That will help the mentor see your skills in action.
3. *Request help on a particular matter.* Let the mentor know that you admire him or her and ask for help in that arena. For example, you might say, "You're good at dealing with customers. Would it be okay if I came to you for advice on my customers?" Keep your request simple and specific.
4. *Consider what you can offer in exchange.* Mentoring is a two-way street. If you can do something for your potential mentor, then, by all means, tell him or her.
5. *Arrange a meeting.* Once your specific request has been accepted, you are ready to meet with your potential mentor. Never go into this meeting cold. Set goals, identify your desired outcomes, and prepare a list of questions. Listen attentively. Then ask your prepared questions and request specific suggestions.
6. *Follow up.* After the meeting, try some of your potential mentor's suggestions and share the results. Express appreciation by identifying something in particular that was significant to you.
7. *Ask to meet on an ongoing basis.* After your potential mentor has had a chance not only to meet and interact with you but also to see the value of what he or she can provide, you are in a good position to request an ongoing relationship. Suggest that you meet with him or her regularly or ask permission to get help on an ad hoc basis.[33]

When done well, the mentoring process is beneficial for both the pupil and the mentor. One survey found, for example, that 77 percent of companies with successful mentoring programs reported that they effectively increased employee retention.[34] Firms can help facilitate mentoring by rewarding mentors in their performance appraisals.

Not surprisingly, mentoring is also being done via email or using software or online programs, a type of mentoring that has become known as *e-mentoring*. E-mentoring is commonplace at IBM. "A lot of our people work virtually, and mentoring can erase geographic and business-unit borders," explained one IBM manager.[35] At Rockwell Collins, a communication and aviation electronics company, nearly 6,000 employees utilize an e-mentoring software solution developed by Triple Creek. The software can connect to a firm's existing talent management software, gauge competency gaps, and match mentors and mentees based on their knowledge and learning needs.[36]

## Networking

As the number of contacts grows, mentoring broadens into a process of **career networking**. As a complement to mentoring, in which relationships are more selective, networking relationships tend to be more varied and temporary. The networks can be internal to a particular organization or connected across many different organizations.

According to the Monster career advice centre, there are many ways to identify networking contacts. Some of the best places to consider are the following:

- Your educational alumni association or career office networking lists
- Your own extended family
- Your friends' parents and other family members
- Your professors, advisors, coaches, tutors, and clergy
- Your former bosses and your friends' and family members' bosses

- Members of clubs, religious groups, and other organizations to which you belong
- All of the organizations near where you live or go to school

Monster also has a networking feature that allows job seekers to meet with other people who have similar career interests. Social networking sites such as LinkedIn.com and Tribe.net have begun connecting professionals in formal and informal ways as well. Through networking, individuals often find out about new jobs, professional trends, and other opportunities. In a survey of executives by the HR firm DBM, 61 percent said that they had found new positions in the previous year through networking. Another study of 15 high-ranking executive women found that although many of them lacked formal mentors, they had successfully engaged in a kind of "360-degree" networking: the women made it a point to form and maintain relationships with people above, below, and at the same level as themselves, which helped advance their careers.[37]

## Career Self-Management Training

Many organizations are establishing programs for employees on how they can engage in *career self-management*. The training focuses on two major objectives: (1) helping employees learn to continuously gather feedback and information about their careers and (2) encouraging them to prepare for mobility. The training is not geared to skills and behaviours associated with a specific job but rather toward long-term personal effectiveness. Essentially, career self-management is not a process but an event. Employees typically undertake self-assessments to increase their awareness of their own career attitudes and values. In addition, they are encouraged to widen their viewpoint beyond the next company promotion to broader opportunities in the marketplace, attend conferences, and develop good long-term relationships with their bosses or other mentors. Participants might be encouraged to engage in career networking or to identify other means to prepare for job mobility, such as hearing reports from employees who made transitions to new job opportunities both within and outside the organization.[38]

# SMALL BUSINESS APPLICATION

Recruiting generally applies to small business in much the same way as to large business, with the exception of one significant factor: scale. Whereas large companies will have a continuous ongoing need to recruit people into roles and may require large numbers of employees, small businesses may require only one or two persons every now and then. This difference is significant as small companies may not justify the time and expense associated with developing recruiting strategies to hire a few people. Also, because small business hiring needs are lower, the determination of recruitment channels will be based on ensuring a small number of suitable candidates rather than a large number of general candidates.

For example, if a large company needs to hire 20 customer service people because of growth and turnover, the hiring volume would support hiring a designated recruiter, developing and posting an effective job advertisement screening large numbers of candidates, and developing a set of behavioural competencies for the role to be used in selections. If a small company had the need for one customer service person, it certainly would not follow the same approach.

So how do small companies recruit successful staff? Because (1) the hiring needs of small companies are lower, (2) small companies are generally more closely allied with friends and family, and (3) small companies are typically more closely involved with the local community, small companies usually avoid the cost and administration of major promotion of jobs on large job boards or newspapers and rely on networking through employee referrals or small targeted industry groups. That does not mean that small companies cannot benefit from recruiting tools such as Web job boards. When small companies need to create a job posting, they can go to these sites to review the jobs posted and then tailor an existing posting to reflect their specific requirements. What will be different is that the small company will post that job at its place of business, or circulate it to those in its network, rather than post it on a large-scale job board.

# SUMMARY

**OUTCOME 1** To expand the talent pool of organizations—the number and kind of people available for employment—organizations must focus on multiple approaches to recruitment and career management. Which internal and outside sources and methods are used in recruiting will depend on the strategy and goals of the organization, conditions of the labour market, and specifications of the jobs to be filled.

**OUTCOME 2** Employers usually find it advantageous to use internal promotions and transfers to fill as many openings as possible above the entry level. By recruiting from within, an organization can capitalize on the previous investments they have made in recruiting, selecting, training, and developing its current employees and rewarding them. Internal job postings, performance appraisals, skill inventories, replacement charts, and assessment centres are ways in which firms identify internal talent.

**OUTCOME 3** Outside candidates are recruited when internal talent is lacking or a firm wants to hire employees with expertise from other organizations for competitive reasons and to prevent the inbreeding of ideas within their organization.

To diversify its talent pools, firms also look externally for candidates. Advertisements, the Internet, social networks, mobile recruiting, employment agencies, tapping educational institutions and professional associations, and rerecruiting are among the many ways firms recruit external candidates.

**OUTCOME 4** HR managers have many tools available to them to gauge their efforts and improve their recruiting. Using realistic job previews, surveying managers and applicants about the process, and examining metrics such as the cost per hire, time to fill a position, and yield ratios are some of the ways in which firms evaluate their recruiting efforts. An ATS can help a firm automatically track and calculate many of these statistics.

**OUTCOME 5** Identifying and developing talent are the responsibility of all managers. A career development program is a dynamic process that should integrate the career goals of employees with the goals of the organization. Job opportunities can be identified by studying jobs and determining the knowledge and skills each one requires. Once that is accomplished, key jobs can be identified, and job progressions can be planned. These progressions can then serve as a basis for developing the career paths of employees. Employees need to be made aware of the organization's philosophy and its goals; otherwise, they will not know how their goals match those of the organization. Mentoring has been found to be valuable for providing guidance and support to employees and potential managers.

## KEY TERMS

9-box grid, 158
applicant tracking system (ATS), 170
branding, 156
career counselling, 178
career networking, 181
career paths, 173
career plateau, 176
employee leasing, 167

employee profile, 153
fast-track program, 178
global sourcing, 156
internal labour market, 155
job progressions, 173
mentors, 179
nepotism, 163
outplacement services, 175
passive job seekers, 161
promotion, 175

realistic job preview (RJP), 167
recruiting process outsourcing, (RPO) 154
relocation services, 175
rerecruiting, 163
sabbatical, 177
time-to-fill metric, 169
transfer, 175
yield ratio, 169

## DISCUSSION QUESTIONS

1. Name some companies with which you have done business. Then discuss how you view their employer brands. Would you want to work for them or not? How might these firms improve their employer brands?
2. More than 50 percent of all MBAs leave their first employer within five years. Although the change may mean career growth for these individuals,

it represents a loss to the employers. What are some of the probable reasons a MBA would leave his or her first employer?
3. Companies are finding candidates through searches of LinkedIn profiles. They also use LinkedIn and other social media to screen candidates. Discuss the advantages and disadvantages of using social media as a recruitment channel.

4. Explain how RJPs operate. Why do they appear to be an effective recruitment technique?

5. The Ottawa Police Services recognized that traditional recruiting practices may not work in a multicultural society. New immigrants may not view policing as an honourable profession, based on their previous experiences. Sitting in large groups hearing about opportunities in the police force is not effective as many are reluctant to ask questions. Newcomers also do not know about the "ride along" program that most forces operate as a way to introduce potential recruits to the daily work of a police officer. Design a recruitment campaign for the police force that would be sensitive to the perceptions and needs of a multicultural candidate base.

# HRM EXPERIENCE

## Career Management

We often think that successful people plan their careers in advance and then work toward their goals in a very logical, sequential manner. Although some successes are designed and implemented this way, others are created through insight, preparedness, and taking advantages of opportunities as they arise.

## Assignment

1. Form teams of four to six members. Identify three people to interview about their careers. One person should be in the early stages of his or her career, one should be in midcareer, and one should be in the final stages of his or her career.

2. Ask each person to identify his or her career goals and how they have changed or are expected to change over time.

3. Ask each person to describe the sequence of events that led to where he or she is. How well does that story align with the traditional model of careers?

4. Ask each person what (if anything) he or she would do differently. Ask what advice he or she has for you about how to approach your career.

Visit the *Managing Human Resources* CourseMate website at http://www.belcourt7e.nelson.com for quizzes, flashcards, videos, games, and more!

## CASE STUDY 1

### IMPRIMAX

Imprimax is a family business, specializing in commercial printing, that has been operating for more than 45 years. The founder's son, who now heads the company, has maintained the authoritative management style introduced by his predecessor. Imprimax has experienced strong growth thanks to the acquisition of major contracts and the introduction of new technologies. In addition, its workforce has increased from 300 to 500 employees. The company's management team is composed of managers who came up through the ranks of the organization and are experienced in printing techniques.

Like all the businesses in its region, Imprimax is facing both internal and external challenges. Over the past year, its staff turnover doubled and many employees retired. The problem was exacerbated by the current lack of experienced workers available on the labour market. As part of its succession plan, the company launched a massive recruitment campaign among students from trade and technical schools and universities. The generation clash between the two groups of employees is already being felt. Although the young recruits are more technologically advanced, the older employees are the ones with the specific know-how and experience. Networking between the different generations seems to be problematic, and the retention rate among the younger generation is low. In fact, a number of them quit after only several months with the company. Knowledge transfer and employee retention are key success factors for Imprimax's survival.

## Questions

As a trainee hired by the plant's HR manager, you are asked to analyze the situation and make recommendations to reduce the turnover by retaining young new hires and promoting an intergenerational synergy. With this in mind,

1. Identify five probable causes as to why young new hires are leaving the company.
2. What could be developed as this employer's brand to make it realistic and attractive to candidates?
3. Develop solutions to the recruitment issues facing this firm.

## CASE STUDY 2

### RECRUITMENT CHANNELS

LoyaltyOne is one of the world's leading loyalty marketing organizations and the creator and operator of Canada's premier coalition loyalty program, the AIR MILES® Reward Program. As of early 2012, with more than 10 million Collector accounts, approximately two-thirds of all Canadian households actively participate in the AIR MILES Reward Program. Working with many of North America's leading brands in the retail, financial services, grocery, petroleum retail, travel, and hospitality industries, LoyaltyOne designs, implements, and manages coalition loyalty programs and customer analytics and loyalty management solutions, which include loyalty consulting and creative, insight-driven marketing services. LoyaltyOne's research group *COLLOQUY* provides a worldwide audience of more than 30,000 marketers with news, insights, and best practices from the loyalty marketing industry. LoyaltyOne's website is http://www.loyalty.com.

LoyaltyOne is a unit of Alliance Data Systems Corporation (NYSE:ADS). Alliance Data is a leading provider of loyalty marketing solutions derived from transaction-rich data for some of the most recognizable brands in North America. Already influencing over 120 million consumer relationships, Alliance Data is also expanding its reach into Europe, South America, and Asia.

With over 1,500 associates across a multitude of functions such as consumer intelligence analysts, marketing specialists, customer care representative, IT, and business developers, LoyaltyOne is continuously looking for top-calibre talent. It is one of many organizations to utilize the World Wide Web, job boards such as Workopolis.ca, and niche boards such as the HRPA and also maintains a strong staffing division.

LoyaltyOne is looking to proactively source candidates to fill a variety of roles within multiple business units and suspects its current practices may not be sufficiently proactive or effective in targeting both passive and active candidates across the organization.

Currently, LoyaltyOne

- employs a well-developed recruitment team using talent acquisition methods to source candidates;
- is looking for very specialized segments of the workforce, and these individuals are in limited supply;
- is determined and must work hard to find and hire candidates that meet both job requirements and fit the corporate culture;
- considers its approach somewhat traditional and is looking to become more "leading edge";
- wishes to hire qualified individuals across all age groups; and
- would welcome the creative use of mobile and social networking tools but currently already uses LinkedIn and Facebook.

LoyaltyOne faces challenges:
1. The organization's brand image may not be clearly recognized by candidates as AIR MILES has historically been the company's most predominant brand.
2. Its businesses are diverse, as are the knowledge and skills that it would be seeking in its prospective associates.

### Question

1. Provide recommendations for proactive best practices and leading-edge sourcing approaches.

# GET PAID FOR AN EMPLOYEE REFERRAL

At Accenture, Inc. based in Toronto, an employee was given a $6000 bonus for referring a candidate for a senior-level job. The candidate was his long-time friend, and the employee felt that the real rewards were having his recommendation validated through the selection process and having a friend at work. According to the director of HR at Accenture, 24 percent of experienced hires come from staff referrals.

At Ernst and Young LLP, employee referrals are used because it is more economical than a search firm, and employees understand the culture of the firm. Another advantage of employee referral programs is the increased engagement with the firm's goals. At Mars Canada Inc., employees care about the business results and success of the organization, so they are cautious in their recommendations, and act as a first screening. Companies are also cautious about keeping the referring employee in the loop, and submitting all referred candidates to the same rigorous selection process.

Employee referrals and social recruiting, which already began melding through Jobvite, and other tools are growing even closer as new vendors enter the field and corporations test how well their jobs spread on Facebook and other sites. A New York startup called Referrio is quietly entering this niche. On the Referrio site, Cisco, for example, lists eleven jobs and is offering about $2,500 per job for people who fill the openings by spreading the word through social media sites or email.

Experienced nurses and occupational/speech/physical therapists are among the highest in demand and so many hospitals are using employee referrals to generate leads. At one hospital, there was "unreal" interest when the 36,000-employee organization moved to an electronic employee referral system two months ago. About 1,500 people referred candidates in about a month. This was not a social media campaign per se, but that is likely coming soon.

This smart marriage of referrals and social sites is where we are headed.

## Questions

1. How does automating the employee referral process encourage referrals?
2. What do you think some of the drawbacks of getting referrals from social network sites might be?

**Source:** Excerpted from Todd Raphael, "Employee Referral Programs Using More Social Media" (June 22, 2010), http://www.ere.net; A. Dwyer, "When the Best Talent Is Close to Home," *The Globe and Mail*, November 16, 2011,E1, E6.

## NOTES AND REFERENCES

1. Blake Landau, "The Uncontained Culture of the Container Store," *Human Resources IQ* (March 6, 2008), http://www.humanresourcesiq.com.

2. J. W. Marriott, "Our Competitive Strength: Human Capital," *Executive Speeches* 15, no. 5 (April–May 2001): 18–21.

3. Debbie Mack, "P&G Fights to Protect Its Bounty," *Corporate Legal Times* 13, no. 135 (February 2003): 64.

4. Edward P. Lazear and Paul Oyer, *Internal and External Labor Markets: A Personnel Economics Approach*, NBER (working paper, 2003), http://www.nber.org/papers /w10192.

5. "The Pros and Cons of Online Recruiting," *HRfocus* 81 (April 2004 supplement): S2.

6. Robert Rodriguez, "Filling the HR Pipeline," *HR Magazine* 49, no. 9 (September 2004): 78–84; James W. Walker, "Perspectives," *Human Resource Planning* 25, no. 1 (2002): 12–14; Stanley Ragalevsky, "CEO Succession: Five Best Practices for Internal Candidates," *Community Banker* 17, no. 2 (February 2008): 24–25.

7. "How to Implement an Effective Process for a New HR Management System," *HRfocus* 82, no. 1 (January 2005): 3–4.

8. "Heading for the Fast Track: New Studies Examine Who Gets Promoted and Why" (August 10, 2005), http:// knowledge.wharton.upenn.edu.

9. Rob Yeung, "Finders Keepers," *Accountancy Magazine* 134, no. 1335 (November 2004): 42–44; Joe Dysart, "New Directions in Internet Recruiting," *Contractor Magazine* 53, no. 7 (July 2006): 33–36.

10. Ibid.

11. Jennifer Taylor Arnold, "Employee Referrals at a Keystroke," *HR Magazine* 51, no. 10 (October 2006):

82–88; Victoria Furnes, "The New Frontier," *Personnel Today* (January 22, 2008): 13–16.

12. Michelle V. Rafter, "Goin' Mobile," *Workforce Management* (February 2011): 26.

13. Ibid.

14. Douglas P. Shuit, "Monster Board Games," *Workforce Management* 82, no. 2 (November 2003): 37–42; Joe Dysart, "New Directions in Internet Recruiting," *Contractor Magazine* 53, no. 7 (July 2006): 33–36.

15. Jennifer Salopek, "Employee Referrals Remain a Recruiter's Best Friend," *Workforce Management* (December 2010), http://www.workforce.com.

16. Greg Patrick Haudek, "A Longitudinal Test of the Attraction-Selection-Attrition Model," *ETD Collection for Wayne State University* (January 1, 2001), Paper AAI3010091, http://digitalcommons.wayne.edu.

17. "In Praise of Nepotism?" *Business Ethics Quarterly* 15, no. 1 (January 2005): 153–161; Richard Reeve and Gavin Sheridan, "Nepotism: Is It Back?" *New Statesman* 135 (September 29, 2003): 22–25.

18. Madeline Laurano, "Best Practices in Re-Recruiting Top Talent," Bersin & Associates (blog) (August 6, 2009), http://www.bersin.com.

19. Leslie Stevens-Huffman, "Commitment, Consistency Are Key to College Recruiting," *Workforce Management* 85, no. 6 (March 27, 2006): 42–43.

20. Ed Frauenheim, "Companies Focus Their Attention on Flexibility," *Workforce Management* (February 2011): 3–4.

21. Chris Pentilla, "Got It Covered: If You Can't Afford to Offer Employee Benefits on Your Own, Why Not Join Forces with a PEO?" *Entrepreneur* 32, no. 2 (February 2004): 66–68; Bill Leonard, "Small Firms Prepare for Aging Workforce," *HR Magazine* 53, no. 5 (May 2008): 32.

22. Connie Winkler, "Job Tryouts Go Virtual," *HR Magazine* 51, no. 9 (September 2006): 131–134; J. O'Krafka, "Vancouver Health Region Brands Its Advantages," *Canadian HR Reporter* (April 25, 2005): 8.

23. "Applicant Tracking System," *SearchCIO.com*, http://searchcio.techtarget.com, retrieved March 18, 2011.

24. Blake Landau, "The Uncontained Culture of the Container Store," *Human Resources IQ* (March 6, 2008), http://www.humanresourcesiq.com.

25. Peg O'Herron and Peggy Simonsen, "Career Development Gets a Charge at Sears Credit," *Personnel Journal* 74, no. 5 (May 1995): 103–106. See also Jules Abend, "Behind the Scenes at: Sears," *Bobbin* 39, no. 11 (June 1998): 22–26; Shari Caudron, "The De-Jobbing of America," *Industry Week* 243, no. 16 (September 5, 1994): 30–36; Edward E. Lawler III, "From Job-Based to Competency-Based Organizations," *Journal of Organizational Behavior* 15, no. 1 (January 1994): 3–15; Douglas T. Hall, "Accelerate Executive

Development—At Your Peril!" *Career Development International* 4, no. 4 (1999): 237–239.

26. "How a Talent Management Plan Can Anchor Your Company's Future," *HRfocus* 81, no. 10 (October 2004): 7–10; "Heading for the Fast Track? New Studies Examine Who Gets Promoted and Why," *Knowledge@Wharton* (August 10, 2005), http://knowledge.wharton. upenn.edu.

27. Elizabeth Craig, John Kimberly, and Hamid Bouchikhhi, "Can Loyalty Be Leased?" *Harvard Business Review* 80, no. 9 (September 2002): 24–34; Edward Potter, "Improving Skills and Employability in the 21st Century," *Industrial and Labor Relations Review* 55, no. 4 (July 2002): 739–745.

28. Service Canada, "Training and Employment Initiatives," http://www.servicecanada.gc.ca/eng/epb/ebsm/index. shtml, retrieved March 30, 2012.

29. Suzanne C. de Janasz, Shery E. Sullivan, and Vicki Whiting, "Mentor Networks and Career Success: Lessons for Turbulent Times," *Academy of Management Executive* 17, no. 4 (November 2003): 78–92; Kate Walsh and Judith Gordon, "Creating an Individual Work Identity," *Human Resource Management Review* 18, no. 1 (March 2008): 46–61.

30. Larry Cambron, "Career Development Pays," *Far Eastern Economic Review* 164, no. 42 (October 25, 2001): 83.

31. Susan Wells, "Smoothing the Way," *HR Magazine* 46, no. 6 (June 2001): 52–58; Heath Row, "Market Yourself," *Fast Company* 58 (May 2002): 24.

32. de Janasz, Sullivan, and Whiting, "Mentor Networks and Career Success," 78–92; Carole Gaskell, "Reward Coaching Behavior to Encourage Its Use," *People Management* 14, no. 4 (February 21, 2008): 70.

33. Jeff Barbian, "The Road Best Traveled," *Training* 39, no. 5 (May 2002): 38–42; Kathleen Barton, "Will You Mentor Me?" *Training and Development* 56, no. 5 (May 2002): 90–92.

34. Elaine Biech, "Executive Commentary," *Academy of Management Executive* 17, no. 4 (November 2003): 92–94.

35. Jennifer Alsever, "How to Start a Mentorship Program," *BNET* (June 24, 2008), http://www.bnet.com.

36. Laura M. Francis, "The Shifting Shape of Mentoring," *Training & Development* (September 2009), http://www. astd.org/.

37. de Janasz, Sullivan, and Whiting, "Mentor Networks and Career Success," 78–92; Jill Rachline Marabix, "Job Search 2. Oh!" *U.S. News & World Report* 136, no. 8 (March 8, 2004): 60–63.

38. Thomas A. Stewart, "What's in It for Me?" *Harvard Business Review* 83, no. 1 (January 2005): 8; Marilyn Clarke and Margaret Patrickson, "The New Covenant of Employability," *Employee Relations* 30, no. 2 (2008): 121–141.

# APPENDIX

# Personal Career Development

Because you are likely to spend more time working during your life than doing anything else, it makes sense to plan your career. There are numerous ways for an employer to contribute to an individual employee's career development and at the same time meet the organization's HR needs. Although organizations can certainly be a positive force in the development process, the primary responsibility for personal career growth still rests with the individual. After all, your career is likely to begin before and often continue after a period of employment with a particular organization. To help you, as students and prospective employees, achieve your career objectives, this appendix is included to provide some background for your personal development and decisions.

## DEVELOPING PERSONAL SKILLS AND COMPETENCIES

Planning for a career involves more than simply acquiring specific job knowledge and skills. Job know-how is clearly essential, but you must also develop other skills to be successful as an employee. To succeed as a manager, you must achieve still higher level skills in the areas of communication, time management, self-motivation, interpersonal relationships, and leadership.

Hundreds of self-help books, professional journals, and magazines have been written on these topics or contain articles about them, and myriad opportunities to participate in workshops are available, often sponsored by employers.[1] For example, the pointers on the basic skills of successful career management listed in Highlights in HRM 5.A1 shows the competencies candidates "must have" to embark on a career in any field.

## CHOOSING A CAREER

Many years ago, when the management expert Peter Drucker was asked about career choices, he said, "The probability that the first job choice you make is the right one for you is roughly one in a million. If you decide your first choice is the right one, chances are that you are just plain lazy."[2] The implications of this statement are just as true today. You often have to do a lot of searching and changing to find a career path that is psychologically and financially satisfying.

# HIGHLIGHTS IN HRM 5.A1

## Preparing a Career Development Plan

The following are "must haves" according to a broad range of employers surveyed:

1. Basic Skills

   - Comprehend, explain, and analyze information
   - Interpret the meaning of written material
   - Perform all basic math functions with whole numbers, decimals, and fractions
   - Interpret and solve algebraic equations, use math in business, i.e., calculating discounts and percentages
   - Create and use tables and graphs and integrate information from multiple sources
   - Employ basic and business writing skills, including accuracy in spelling, punctuation, and grammar and the ability to create business letters, emails, and other written communications
   - Have effective oral communication skills, including the ability to speak professionally and speak so others can understand

2. Computer Literacy

   - Keyboarding skills
   - General data entry skills
   - Ability to navigate in Microsoft Windows
   - Understand and use computer terminology appropriately
   - Connect to the Internet or an online service
   - Use email (compose, retrieve, read, respond in a professional manner)

3. Customer Service

   - Appropriately address customers, either in person or by telephone, email, or other means
   - Identify customer needs by gathering information, assessing customer's knowledge of products/ services
   - Provide accurate, courteous, and timely information, including responding to customer comments and questions
   - Work calmly with "difficult" or upset customers
   - Work in a team environment
   - Solve customer problems and know when to escalate a problem to a manager

4. Problem-Solving and Decision-Making Skills

   - Read and follow multistep directions
   - Learn, reason, and think creatively
   - Make appropriate and reasonable decisions
   - Prioritize workload
   - Ask pertinent questions

5. Interpersonal Skills

   Individuals meeting this competency can

   - Work without supervision
   - Work well with people from culturally diverse backgrounds
   - Develop and maintain productive group relations
   - Cooperate with others and accept supervision

6. Personal Qualities

   - Has a positive, "can do" attitude
   - Is a self-starter
   - Habitually arrives on time and does not leave early
   - Understands and can adapt to workplace culture
   - Can control emotional outbursts
   - Shows flexibility and adaptability
   - Demonstrates self-management and dependability
   - Comes to work appropriately dressed
   - Demonstrates honesty and integrity
   - Has addressed barriers to employment, such as substance abuse, the need for childcare or related services, transportation, or criminal justice involvement

7. Job-Seeking Skills

   - An up-to-date, accurate résumé customized for each job using key words from advertisement and listing accomplishments; résumé should include accurate spelling and grammar, action words, appropriate white space, bullets, not paragraphs, and appropriate email name and phone voice message
   - Cover letter
   - List of up-to-date professional references
   - "Dress for Success" interview clothing
   - Proof of education attainment (e.g., diploma) and any certificates earned
   - At least one work-based learning experience obtained through internship (paid or unpaid); a job; work experience provided by the program with a skill rating from the supervisor in addition to letters of reference

Source: Capital Workforce Partners

A variety of resources are available to aid in the process of choosing a satisfying career path. Counsellors at colleges and universities, as well as those in private practice, are equipped to assist individuals in evaluating their aptitudes, abilities, interests, and values as they relate to career selection. Placement offices and continuing education centres offer some type of career planning assistance. In addition to career exploration, most of them offer résumé writing help, interview preparation, and job placement assistance. Looking on the Internet is also a great way to jump-start your career planning. For example, About.com's career planning website contains a wealth of information that will help get you started. Most job-posting websites, including Monster and CareerBuilder, contain free career information as well.

## ACCURACY OF SELF-EVALUATION

Successful career development depends in part on an individual's ability to conduct an accurate self-evaluation. When you are doing a self-evaluation, you need to consider factors that are personally significant to you. The most important internal factors are your interests, academic aptitude and achievement, occupational aptitudes and skills, social skills, communication skills, and leadership abilities. What activities do you like to do? Do you like working alone or with other people? Do you like technical work or creative work? Do you think you would like working in an office, or would you prefer another setting? What have you always dreamed of doing?

You also need to consider the salary level, status, opportunities for advancement, and growth for the job you seek. External factors that should be assessed include your family values and expectations, economic conditions, employment trends, and job market information.

### INTEREST INVENTORIES

Psychologists who specialize in career counselling typically administer a battery of tests. The *Strong Vocational Interest Bank* (SVIB), developed by E. K. Strong, Jr., was among the first of the interest tests.[3] Strong found substantial differences in interests that vary from occupation to occupation and that a person's interest pattern, especially after age 21, tends to become quite stable. By taking his test, now known as the *Strong Interest Inventory*, you can learn the degree to which your interests correspond to those of successful people in a wide range of occupations. Your personality type can also be obtained by using a special scoring key on the *Strong Interest Inventory* answer sheet. This key, developed by John Holland, provides scores on six personality types: (1) realistic, (2) investigative, (3) artistic, (4) social, (5) enterprising, and (6) conventional. These categories characterize not only a type of personality but also the type of working environment that a person would find most satisfying. The *Strong Interest Inventory* must be administered by someone certified by the product's distributor, CPP.[4]

Another inventory that measures both interests and skills is the *Campbell Interest and Skill Survey (CISS)*, which can be taken online at a number of sites for a fee, as can the *Strong Interest Inventory*.[5] People report their levels of interest and skill using a 6-point response scale on 200 interest items and 120 skill items. This information is then translated into 7 orientations—influencing, organizing, helping, creating, analyzing, producing, and adventuring—and further categorized into 29 basic scales such as leadership and supervision to identify occupations with advice about whether each of the occupations should be "pursued," "explored," or "avoided" by the person who took the test.

Profiles such as these help individuals see how their interests and skills compare to those of a sample of people happily employed in a wide range of occupations. The About.com website includes a number of free self-assessments, as do other sites, such as MyPlan.com, CareerPath, LiveCareer, and JobDiagnosis. Note, however, that people have taken interest and skill inventories that dissuaded them from their chosen careers, pursued them anyway, and become extremely successful. If you find yourself in such a situation, do not be discouraged about your career choice. Consider exploring the career further via internships, informational interviews, and job shadowing (discussed next). Also, keep in mind that most people change careers multiple times during the lives. If your first choice of a career is not what you hoped it would be, you are always free to pursue another.

**informational interview**
An informal meeting with someone in an occupation that interests you

**job shadowing**
The process of observing an employee in his or her work environment to obtain a better understanding of what the employee does

## INFORMATIONAL INTERVIEWS, JOB SHADOWING, AND INTERNSHIPS

An **informational interview** is a conversation you have with someone in an occupation in which you are interested. You invite the person to lunch or for coffee and ask him or her what the job is really like—the good and the bad, qualifications needed, the outlook for the career, and so forth. Most people are flattered to be asked to provide career information and like to talk about what they do. However, make it clear that you are not soliciting the person for a job—just seeking information.

**Job shadowing** is the process of observing someone in his or her own work environment to better understand what he or she does. Generally, this is done for a few hours to half a day.

The Internet is giving people a virtual way to shadow professionals. Virtualjobshadow.com, for example, is a website where you can watch professionals in about 100 different careers explain their jobs. The site also contains information about the earnings and outlook of the profession, its educational requirements, and a search function that shows the colleges that offer degrees appropriate for the profession. People who sign up for the site can also ask professional questions they might have. As we explained earlier in this chapter, internships can be a great way to "try out" a particular field of work, as is volunteering. Check with your college advisor and career placement centre to find opportunities such as these.

## EVALUATING LONG-TERM EMPLOYMENT OPPORTUNITIES

When choosing a career, you should attempt to determine the probable long-term opportunities in the occupational fields you are considering. The federal government's National Occupational Classification, which we discussed in Chapter 4, contains comprehensive information about hundreds of jobs, the education they require, the types of people who enjoy doing them, the types of working conditions job holders experience, the wages they earn, and the employment outlook associated with jobs. The information is free and should be a first research step for anyone considering a particular career. Many libraries also have publications that provide details about jobs and career fields.

## CHOOSING AN EMPLOYER

Once an individual has made a career choice, even if only tentatively, the next major step is deciding where to work. The choice of employer may be based primarily on location, the immediate availability of a position, starting salary, or other basic considerations. Douglas Hall proposes that people frequently choose an organization on the basis of its climate and how it appears to fit their needs. According to Hall, people with high needs for achievement are more likely to choose aggressive, achievement-oriented organizations. Power-oriented people are more likely to choose influential, prestigious, power-oriented organizations.

# HIGHLIGHTS IN HRM 5.A2

## Questions to Ask Yourself before You Accept a Job Offer

- Have I been offered a fair salary? Is it comparable to what other people in the same position are making?
- Have I met my potential boss? Does he or she seem like someone with whom I can have a good working relationship?

- What do I know about my potential coworkers?
- Will I be comfortable in this office environment?
- Is the corporate culture in line with my own values, attitudes, and goals?
- Can I handle the commute to this job?

---

**entrepreneur**
Someone who starts, organizes, manages, and assumes responsibility for a business or other enterprise

Affiliative people are more likely to choose warm, friendly, supportive organizations. We know that people whose needs fit with the climate of an organization are rewarded more and are more satisfied than those who fit in less well, so it is natural to reason that fit would also be a factor in a person's choice of an organization.[6]

Knowing something about an employer and industry can give you a competitive edge in terms of getting an interview, landing a job, and negotiating a good salary. Numerous company directories containing information about privately and publicly held companies are available. Corporate websites are another source. Often under the "Investors" or "Media" tabs you can find press releases issued by the companies in which you are interested. The releases often highlight the initiatives companies are pursuing and the directions in which they are taking their businesses. Business, industry, and professional publications are a good source too. Simply "googling" a company can turn up a great deal of information.

Once you have landed an interview, you have the opportunity to learn more about an employer, including the type of people who work there, its corporate culture, benefits, and so forth. If you are offered a job with the firm, a website such as Salary.com can help you determine whether the firm's offer is appropriate. Highlights in HRM 5.A2 shows the questions you should ask yourself before you accept a job offer with a particular company.

## BECOMING AN ENTREPRENEUR

No discussion of careers would be complete if entrepreneurship opportunities were not mentioned. Being an **entrepreneur**—someone who starts, organizes, manages, and assumes responsibility for a business or other enterprise—offers a personal challenge that many individuals prefer over being an employee. Small businesses are typically run by entrepreneurs who accept the personal financial risks that go with owning a business but who also benefit directly from the success of the business.[7]

Many government departments and financial institutions offer advice on how to start a business.[8] Since the details of organizing a business are beyond the scope of this book, Figure 5.A1 is presented to provide an overview of the basic steps in starting a new business.[9]

FIGURE 5.A1

TWELVE STEPS FOR STARTING A NEW BUSINESS

Source: From Cunningham/Aldag/Block. Business in a Changing World, 3E. © 1993 South-Western, a part of Cengage Learning, Inc. Reproduced by permission. www.cengage.com/permissions

## KEEPING A CAREER IN PERSPECTIVE

For most people, work is a primary factor in the overall quality of their lives. It provides a setting for satisfying practically the whole range of human needs and is thus of considerable value to the individual. Nevertheless, it is advisable to keep one's career in perspective so that other important areas of life are not neglected.

### DEVELOPING OFF-THE-JOB INTERESTS

Satisfaction with one's life is a product of many forces. Unfortunately, when people complain about not having a good work–life balance, often the problem is not too much work but too little "life," according to Randall Craig of Pinetree Advisors, an HR strategy consulting firm.[10] Some of the more important ingredients of "life" are physical health, emotional well-being, financial security, harmonious inter-personal relationships, freedom from too much stress, and achievement of one's goals. Although a career can provide some of the satisfaction a person needs, most people find it necessary to turn to interests and activities outside their career. Off-the-job activities not only provide a respite from daily work responsibilities but also offer satisfaction in areas unrelated to work. With that said, it is up to you to decide what is important to you and how to spend your work and off-the-job time. Your life is yours to live, and it is shorter than you think.

### BALANCING MARITAL AND/OR FAMILY LIFE

As we have said, the one event that often poses the greatest threat to family needs is relocation. Families often experience conflicts between the desire to advance the careers of different parents and the desire to stay in one place and put down family roots. Many employers now provide assistance in this area, including relocation counselling, in an effort to reduce the severity of the pain that can accompany relocations.

Although relocation is a serious threat to employees with families, there are also other sources of conflict. Some work-related sources of conflict include the number of hours a person must work per week, the frequency of the overtime they work, and the frequency and irregularity of shift work. If an employee is experiencing ambiguity and/or conflict with his or her work role, a low level of supervisory support, or disappointment due to unfulfilled work expectations, this can affect his or her family life as well. Other sources of conflict include the need to spend an unusually large amount of time with a person's family members, to care for children, aging elders, or a spouse. The different employment patterns in a family and dissimilarity in a couple's career orientations are also commonplace and can take a toll on employees.

A number of employers are doing more today to help their employees cope with these problems via alternative work options. Many employees are also actively looking for companies that have family-friendly policies. Understand that "to be a success in the business world takes hard work, long hours, persistent effort, and constant attention. To be a success in marriage takes hard work, long hours, persistent effort, and constant attention.... The problem is giving each its due and not shortchanging the other."[11]

## PLANNING FOR RETIREMENT

Although you might be many years from retirement, it is never too early to plan for it. In your twenties, you will want to begin a savings plan and perhaps pay off your student loans. As you get older, your goals will probably change. Perhaps you will want to buy a home, and you will need money for a downpayment. Regardless of what stage of your life you are in, you should never neglect saving for your retirement throughout your working years. This is because a small sum of money saved early, compounded with interest over years, can amount to millions of dollars. But if you wait until later, you will have to save a lot of money for it to amount to as much.

Your employer can help you with some aspects of retirement planning by providing you with information about tax-advantaged employer and individual savings plans. But although employer-sponsored preretirement programs can be helpful (as we will see in Chapter 11), planning for your retirement is up to you. Do you want to travel or live in another province or country? What kind of retirement does your spouse envision? How much money will all of this require? Your employer will not be able to answer these questions. However, by reading about the subject of retirement and taking it seriously while you are young, you will be able to answer these questions yourself. Planning early will help you set the stage for a healthy and satisfying retirement as free from worries as possible—especially worries that could have been avoided or minimized had you taken a few easy steps earlier in life.

## KEY TERMS

entrepreneur, 192
informational interview, 191
job shadowing, 191

## NOTES AND REFERENCES

1. A selection of self-help publications on a variety of topics may be found in any bookstore. College and university bookstores typically have a wide selection in their trade or general books department. One such book is Paul D. Tieger and Barbara Barron's *Do What You Are: Discover the Perfect Career for You through the Secrets of Personality Type*, 4th ed. (New York: Little Brown and Company, 2007).

2. Mary Harrington Hall, "A Conversation with Peter Drucker," *Psychology Today* (March 1968): 22.

3. E. K. Strong, Jr., of Stanford University, was active in the measurement of interests from the early 1920s until his death in 1963. Since then, his work has been carried on by the staff of the Measurement Research Center, University of Minnesota. The *Strong Interest Inventory* is distributed by Consulting

Psychologists Press, Inc., to qualified people under an exclusive licence from the publisher, Stanford University Press.

4. Gary D. Gottfredson and John L. Holland, *Dictionary of Holland Occupational Codes* (Lutz, FL: Psychological Assessment Resources, December 1996); Derek Parker, "The Skills Shortage: Making Headway, but No Easy Answers," *Manufacturers' Monthly* (September 2007), http://www.manmonthly.com.au/news/the-skills-shortage-making-headway-but-no-easy-ans, retrieved July 10, 2012.

5. David Lubinski, Camilla P. Benbow, and Jennifer Ryan, "Stability of Vocational Interests among the Intellectually Gifted from Adolescence to Adulthood: A 15-Year Longitudinal Study," *Journal of Applied Psychology* 80, no. 1 (February 1995): 196–200; Hope Samborn, "Left Click, Left Law," *ABA Journal* 92, no. 7 (July 2006): 58.

6. Douglas T. Hall and Jonathan E. Moss, "The New Protean Career Contract: Helping Organizations and Employees Adapt," *Organizational Dynamics* 26, no. 3 (Winter 1998): 22–37. See also Douglas T. Hall, *The Career Is Dead, Long Live the Career: A Relational Approach to Careers* (San Francisco: Jossey-Bass, 1996); Douglas T. Hall, "Protean Careers of the 21st Century," *Academy of Management Executive* 10, no. 4 (1996): 8–16; Douglas T. Hall and Associates, *Career Development in Organizations* (San Francisco: Jossey-Bass, 1986); Yue-Wah Chay and Samuel Aryee, "The Moderating Influence of Career Growth Opportunities on Careerist Orientation and Work Attitudes: Evidence of the Protean Career Era in Singapore," *Journal of Organizational Behavior* 20, no. 5 (September 1999): 613–623.

7. Julie Rose, "The New Risk Takers," *Fortune Small Business* 12, no. 2 (March 2002): 28–34; Jack Howard, "Balancing Conflicts of Interest When Employing Spouses," *Employee Responsibilities & Rights* 20, no. 1 (March 2008): 29–43.

8. Business Development Bank of Canada, http://www.bdc.ca/EN/Pages/home.aspx; RBC Advice Centre, "Starting a Business," https://www.rbcadvicecentre.com/business_advice/starting_a_business, retrieved March 30, 2012.

9. For information on starting a business, the interested reader might look into Bob Adams, *Adams Streetwise Small Business Startup* (Holbrook, MA: Adams Media Corporation, 1996); Linda Pinson and Jerry Jinnett, *Anatomy of a Business Plan: Starting Smart, Building a Business and Securing Your Company's Future* (Chicago: Upstart, 1996); Kenneth Cook, *AMA Complete Guide to Strategic Planning for Small Business* (Lincolnwood, IL: NTC Business Books, 1995); Priscilla Y. Huff, *101 Best Small Businesses for Women* (Rocklin, CA: Prima, 1996); Constance Jones, *The 220 Best Franchises to Buy: The Sourcebook for Evaluating the Best Franchise Opportunities* (New York: Bantam Doubleday Dell, 1993).

10. Jamie Eckle, "Randall Craig," *Computerworld* 42, no. 26 (June 23, 2008): 36.

11. Christopher Caggiano, "Married ... with Companies," *Inc.* 17, no. 6 (May 1995): 68–76; Sue Shellenbarger, "Sustaining a Marriage When Job Demands Seem to Be Endless," *The Wall Street Journal*, December 8, 1999, B1; Johan A. Turner, "Work Options for Older Americans: Employee Benefits for the Era of Living Longer," *Benefits Quarterly* 24, no. 3, (2008): 20–25.

# 6

# Employee Selection

## After studying this chapter, you should be able to

**OUTCOME 1**    Explain the objectives of the personnel selection process.

**OUTCOME 2**    Explain what is required for an employee selection tool to be reliable and valid.

**OUTCOME 3**    Illustrate the different approaches to conducting an employment interview.

**OUTCOME 4**    Compare the value of different types of employment tests.

**OUTCOME 5**    Describe the various decision strategies for selection.

Regardless of whether the company is large or small, hiring the best and the brightest employees lays a strong foundation for excellence. But how should this be done? And what happens if it is not done right? A study by the Society for Human Resource Management (SHRM) found that the cost of hiring someone for an intermediate position that has not been carefully planned is approximately $20,000, and the cost of hiring the wrong person for a senior manager's position is $100,000. The bottom line is that good selection decisions make a difference. So do bad ones.

# OVERVIEW OF THE SELECTION PROCESS

**selection**
The process of choosing individuals who have relevant qualifications to fill existing or projected job openings

**Selection** is the process of choosing individuals who have the relevant qualifications to fill existing or projected job openings.

Figure 6.1 shows in broad terms that the overall goal of selection is to maximize "hits" and avoid "misses." Hits are accurate predictions, and misses are inaccurate ones. The cost of one type of miss would be the direct and indirect expense of hiring an employee who turns out to be unsuccessful. The cost of the other type of miss is an opportunity cost—someone who could have been successful did not get a chance. Although the overall selection program is often the formal responsibility of the HR department, line managers typically make the final decision about hiring people in their unit. It is important, therefore, that managers understand the objectives, policies, and practices used for selection.

## BEGIN WITH A JOB ANALYSIS

In Chapter 4, we discussed the process of analyzing jobs to develop job descriptions and specifications. Job specifications, in particular, help identify the *individual competencies* employees need for success—the knowledge, skills, abilities, and other factors (KSAOs) that lead to superior performance. Managers then use selection methods such as interviews, references, and preemployment tests to measure applicant KSAOs against the competencies required for the job. Complete and clear specification of required competencies helps interviewers differentiate between qualified and unqualified applicants and reduces the effect of an interviewer's biases and prejudices. Research also shows that applicants whose KSAOs are well matched to the jobs they are hired for perform better and are more satisfied.[1]

Ordinarily, line managers are well acquainted with the requirements pertaining to the skills, physical demands, and other characteristics of the jobs in their organizations. In addition to the requirements of the job, many organizations, such as Edward Jones, a Toronto-based brokerage firm, and Intuit, an Edmonton-based financial software company, place a high priority on selecting individuals who match the values and culture of their organizations. Recall from Chapter 2 that this process is referred to as values-based hiring. The drawback of

**FIGURE 6.1**

THE GOAL OF SELECTION: MAXIMIZE "HITS"

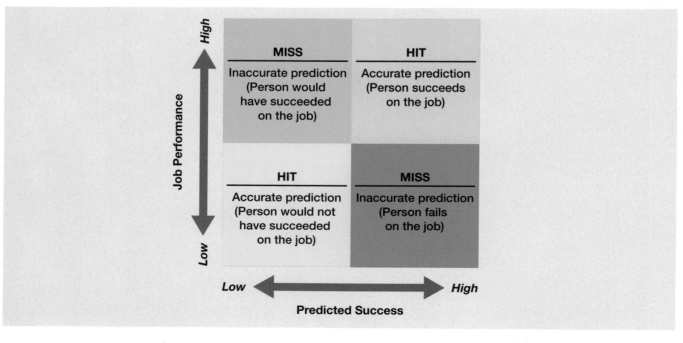

values-based hiring is that it can result in a lack of diversity, so firms need to be cautious about hiring too many of the same types of people.

## THE SELECTION PROCESS

The number of steps in the selection process and their sequence will vary not only with the organization but also with the type and level of jobs to be filled. Each step should be evaluated in terms of its contribution to the process. The steps that typically make up the selection process are shown in Figure 6.2. Not all applicants will go through all of these steps. Some may be rejected after the preliminary interview, others after taking tests, and so on.

As Figure 6.2 shows, organizations use several different means to obtain information about applicants. These include gathering résumés and applications and conducting interviews, tests, and investigations.

## OBTAINING RELIABLE AND VALID INFORMATION

Regardless of whether a position is filled internally or externally, it is essential that the information obtained be reliable and valid and gathered legally and that the privacy of the applicants be safeguarded. The degree to which interviews, tests, and other selection procedures yield comparable data over a period of time is known as **reliability**. For example, unless interviewers judge the capabilities of a group of applicants to be the same today as they did yesterday, their judgments are unreliable (i.e., unstable). Likewise, a test that gives widely different scores when it is administered to the same individual a few days apart is unreliable.

Reliability also refers to the extent to which two or more methods (e.g., interviews and tests) yield similar results or are consistent. Interrater reliability—agreement among two or more raters—is one measure of a method's consistency.

In addition to having reliable information pertaining to a person's suitability for a job, the information must be as valid as possible. **Validity** refers to what a test

OUTCOME 2

## FIGURE 6.2

### STEPS IN THE SELECTION PROCESS

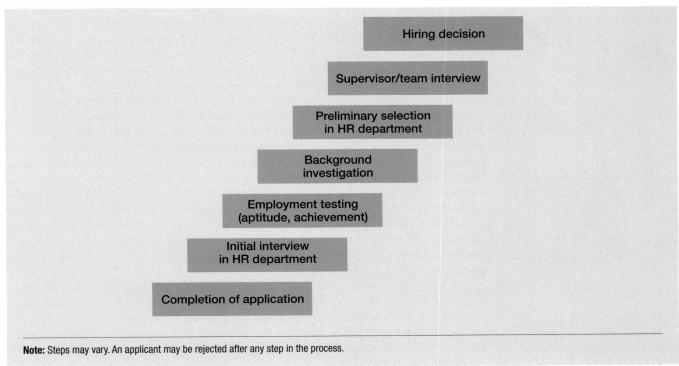

Hiring decision

Supervisor/team interview

Preliminary selection in HR department

Background investigation

Employment testing (aptitude, achievement)

Initial interview in HR department

Completion of application

**Note:** Steps may vary. An applicant may be rejected after any step in the process.

or other selection procedure measures and how well it measures it. In other words, the selection process should be able to predict how well a person performs on the job. Like a new medical procedure, a selection procedure must be validated before it is used. There are two reasons for validating a procedure. First, validity is directly related to increases in employee productivity, as we will demonstrate. Second, employment equity regulations require valid selection procedures.[2]

## INITIAL SCREENING

Employers use many different pieces of information to try to determine whether an applicant will be successful on the job. The initial pieces of information for screening candidates include cover letters, résumés, and applications and often the Internet.

Résumés and cover letters have been used for decades to assess the suitability of applicants, especially for salaried positions. Generally, these documents are reviewed first with an eye toward who can be eliminated because they do not have the skills, abilities, education, or experience outlined in the job description for the application. Did the applicant submit a thoughtful cover letter? Or is he or she simply "spamming" companies with résumés? A lack of a cover letter could be one way of eliminating applicants. Was the cover letter well written? Well-written cover letters are important if a requirement of the job is having good written communication skills, which is the case for many jobs. So, for example, if a person who applied for an online customer service job that includes writing chat messages to customers submitted a cover letter with numerous typos, this could be grounds for passing over the person. Good writing skills might be less important for a person who works as a Walmart greeter. Good verbal or interpersonal skills might suffice for this position.

Evaluating résumés can be a subjective process. Evaluators often have a difficult time applying a set of consistent standards across multiple candidates or consistently apply standards that are irrelevant to success on the job. The fact that there is no "set" format for writing résumés—that they vary from person to person—can make them difficult for people to screen. Bias can also enter the process. A University of British Columbia study found that job applicants with English names have a greater chance of getting interviews than those with Chinese, Indian, or Pakistani names.[3]

Developing explicit evaluation criteria and a structured way to review résumés can help make the process less subjective. Once applicants who clearly are not qualified are eliminated, a company might use an assessment grid such as the one shown in Figure 6.3 to take some of the guesswork out of the process. Job description criteria are placed in the left-hand column of the grid, and candidates are then ranked based on a scale as to whether the skills outlined in their résumés and cover letters match the job. The totals for the candidates are then compared.

The downside of manually screening and assessing cover letters is that it is not uncommon for a firm to receive hundreds of résumés for a single position. To speed up the evaluation process, many firms are now using software to scan résumés to find qualified applications. For example, a hiring manager or HR representative will specify the educational and experience levels a job requires and key words indicative of that experience. The software then scans the résumés collected for that position, pulls a list of qualified candidates, and ranks them according to how closely they match the job criteria. Applicant tracking systems generally include a résumé screening feature. Some of the systems also prescreen people who submit résumés by first asking them to take a short questionnaire to determine how qualified they are.

Not all HR professionals are fans of résumé-screening software, however. There is concern that capable people are routinely being rejected by machines, even before a human lays eyes on their credentials. Also, applicants have learned to "pepper" their résumés with a job's key words to get past résumé-screening software. Considering the volume of résumés firms can receive, however, the practice is probably here to stay.

Many HR professionals use computer software to make the process of screening résumés faster and easier.

EDHAR/Shutterstock

FIGURE 6.3

## APPLICATION/RESUME ASSESSMENT GRID

Rate each candidate on a scale of 1–5, with 5 being the highest rating.

| | Applicant A | Applicant B | Applicant C | Applicant D |
|---|---|---|---|---|
| **Quantitative requirements** | | | | |
| Business degree and/or MBA | 5 | | | |
| Two years' managerial experience | 5 | | | |
| Ability to develop strategies | 2 | | | |
| Ability to manage budgets | 2 | | | |
| **Qualitative requirements** | | | | |
| Demonstrated interpersonal skills | 4 | | | |
| Demonstrated coaching and development skills | 4 | | | |
| Ability to manage diverse teams and work with other departments | 4 | | | |
| Flexibility | 3 | | | |
| Writing and verbal skills | 4 | | | |
| Presentation skills | 4 | | | |
| Level of integrity | 4 | | | |
| **Total** | **41** | | | |

## INTERNET CHECKS AND PHONE SCREENING

HR professionals and hiring managers will often "google" applicants' names and check online social networking sites before deciding whether or not to invite them for a face-to-face interview. The downside of conducting Internet searches relates to the privacy of applicants. In Finland, the practice is illegal. It is also difficult to verify the authenticity of information posted online (did the candidate really post the information, or did someone else?) and easy to confuse an applicant with someone else who has the same name.

Short phone interviews, or screening interviews, are also often conducted, many times by HR personnel, to narrow down the field and save managers time by eliminating candidates who are not likely to be hired. Video is being used to prescreen applicants as well.

iCandidateScreener is a product that allows candidates to interview themselves with their webcams. Managers can quickly screen through the candidates when they have time before bringing applicants in for a face-to-face interview. To give employers a "preview" of themselves, candidates are also posting **video résumés** on YouTube and other sites. Video résumés are short video clips that highlight applicants' qualifications beyond what they can communicate via their résumés and cover letters. The videos allow employers to see how well they present themselves and decide whether they should be called in for an interview. However, there is some concern that video résumés will cause employers to screen people based on their looks rather than their qualifications.

**video résumés**
Short video clips that highlight applicants' qualifications beyond what they can communicate on their résumé

## APPLICATION FORMS

Most organizations require application forms to be completed because they provide a fairly quick and systematic means of obtaining a variety of information about the applicant. Application forms serve several purposes. They provide information for deciding whether an applicant meets the minimum requirements for experience, education, and so on. They provide a basis for questions the interviewer will ask about the applicant's background. They also offer sources for reference checks. For certain jobs, a short application form is appropriate. For example, McDonald's uses a form that is quite brief but asks for information that is highly relevant to job performance. The form also provides information regarding the employer's conformity with various laws and regulations. For scientific, professional, and managerial jobs, a more extended form is likely to be used. Even when applicants come armed with elaborate résumés, it is important that they complete an application form early in the process. People, even those in high positions, frequently exaggerate their qualifications on their résumés and omit unflattering information.

Asking applicants to transcribe specific résumé material onto a standardized application form can help alleviate this problem. Far fewer people lie on application forms relative to their résumés, a 2006 survey by CareerBuilder.com found. The applicant is then asked to sign a statement that the information contained on the form is true and that he or she accepts the employer's right to terminate the candidate's employment if any of the information is subsequently found to be false.[4] The consequences of falsifying information on applications and résumés are frequently high, as described in Ethics in HRM.

# ETHICS IN HRM

## Writing It Wrong

Most candidates for white-collar jobs prepare a résumé and submit it to prospective employers. They also complete the application form, answering questions required by employers for comparison purposes. Some recruitment agencies noticed during the last recession that résumé padding increased. Applicants were "stretching" the dates of their employment, misleading employers about the nature of their duties, and misrepresenting their salaries. While you are writing a résumé, adding three months to your previous employment, saying you were a night auditor instead of a clerk, and adding $950 to your last salary seem like relatively harmless lies.

What are the facts? Studies of "creative" résumé writing indicate that about 25 percent of résumés contain inaccuracies; one-third report incorrect dates, one-tenth misrepresent reasons for leaving, and the rest exaggerate education attainments or omit criminal records. The probability is that about two-thirds of employers check references. Some former employers give only dates of employment and previous salary ranges.

Most organizations require applicants to sign a statement saying that the information they supply is true and that if it is not, they will be dismissed. Some cases of résumé padding have been heavily publicized. A Toronto Stock Exchange manager was dismissed for lying about having a master's degree. A member of Parliament listed an ILB on his résumé, which normally stands for International Baccalaureate of Law but that he claimed stood for Incomplete Baccalaureate of Law. In one heart-wrenching case, a person who was ready to retire was found to have lied about his age decades earlier to get a job. On discovery, he was dismissed and lost his pension. In another case, a Canadian businessman was sentenced to eight months in jail in New Zealand for lying on his résumé by listing false qualifications, such as an MBA. Academic fraud happens 5 percent of the time. The president of Selection Protection Services, a background check firm, offers this advice to job seekers: "Don't lie." She describes one candidate who wrote "Honours Degree" on her résumé when she did not have one. She did not get the job because dishonesty is a deal breaker.

In a labour market where there are too many people chasing too few jobs, candidates will also lie on their résumés by dropping experience and educational qualifications. This practice, called "stripping," is used because job seekers are ready to take any job to survive or to hold them over until the jobs they want are available. Knowing that graduate degrees will act as barriers to jobs as labourers or administrative assistants, applicants simply do not list the degrees or previous professional jobs. Understandably, employers do not want to hire those who are overqualified and who would soon quit for better jobs.

Sources: Jason Chow, "Job Shadow," *Financial Post Business*, May 2006, 29; Rick Spence, "Should Executives Do Their Own Reference Checks?" *The Toronto Star*, May 13, 2004; E. Urquhart, "Should We Edit Our Job Skills?" *The Globe and Mail*, June 20, 2003, C1; P. Waldie, "Davy Sentenced to Eight Months in N.Z. Court," *The Globe and Mail*, May 30, 2002, B6; J. Schilder, "Trial by Hire," *Human Resource Professional* 11, no. 2 (March 1994): 21–23.

Many managers remain unclear about the questions they can ask on an application form. Although most know they should steer clear of issues such as age, race, marital status, and sexual orientation, other issues are less clear. In addition to consulting the province's employment laws, some of which are more restrictive than others, managers should use the following suggestions for putting together an application form:

- *Application date.* The applicant should date the application. This helps managers know when the form was completed and gives them an idea of the time limit (e.g., one year) for keeping the form on file.

- *Educational background.* The form should contain information about grade school, high school, college, and university attendance but not the dates attended because that can be connected with age.

- *Experience.* Virtually any questions that focus on work experience related to the job are permissible.

- *Arrests and criminal convictions.* Questions about arrests, convictions, and criminal records are to be avoided. If bonding is a requirement, the candidate can be asked whether she or he is eligible.

- *Country of citizenship.* Such questions are not permitted. It is allowable to ask whether the person is legally entitled to work in Canada.

- *References.* It is both permissible and advisable that the names, addresses, and phone numbers of references be provided. (We will cover this in more detail later.)

- *Disabilities.* Employers should avoid asking about disabilities or hospitalization or whether candidates have received workers' compensation.

Some organizations use what is referred to as a *weighted application blank* (*WAB*). The WAB involves the use of a common standardized employment application that is designed to distinguish between successful and unsuccessful employees. If managers can identify application items that have predicted employee success in the past, they may use that information to screen other applicants. Some evidence suggests that use of the WAB has been especially helpful for reducing turnover costs in the hospitality industry.

## ONLINE APPLICATIONS

Most large companies accept applications online, and some conduct screening tests online. One of the key advantages of accepting applications online is that companies can recruit candidates and fill their job openings much faster.

Companies report that the downside of posting jobs and accepting online applications is that it can lead to a large volume of them being submitted—many of which fail to meet minimum qualifications. The upside, however, is that generating a larger number of applicants tends to promote greater employee diversity. Home Depot, for example, successfully implemented an online application system called the Job Preference Program to obtain a broader pool of applicants than it had previously been getting. It ultimately enabled the company to hire more women.[5]

## EMPLOYMENT INTERVIEWS

OUTCOME 3

The next step after screening résumés, cover letters, and applications for qualified candidates is often interviewing them. Traditionally, the employment interview has a central role in the selection process—so much so that it is rare to find an instance in which an employee is hired without some sort of interview. Depending on the type of job, applicants may be interviewed by one person, members of a work team, or other individuals in the organization. Although researchers have raised some doubts about its validity, the interview remains a mainstay of selection because (1) it is especially practical when there are only a small number of applicants; (2) it serves other purposes, such as public relations; and (3) interviewers

**nondirective interview**
An interview in which the applicant is allowed the maximum amount of freedom in determining the course of the discussion, while the interviewer carefully refrains from influencing the applicant's remarks

**structured interview**
An interview in which a set of standardized questions with an established set of answers is used

**situational interview**
An interview in which an applicant is given a hypothetical incident and asked how he or she would respond to it

maintain great faith and confidence in their judgments. In this section, we review the characteristics, advantages, and disadvantages of various types of employment interviews. We highlight the fact that the structure of the interview and the training of interviewers strongly influence the success of the hiring process.[6]

Interview methods differ in several ways, most significantly in terms of the amount of structure, or control, exercised by the interviewer. In highly structured interviews, the interviewer determines the course that the interview will follow as each question is asked. In the less structured interview, the applicant plays a larger role in determining the course the discussion will take. Let's look at how the different types of interviews, from the least structured to the most structured, reveal these differences.

## THE NONDIRECTIVE INTERVIEW

In the **nondirective interview**, the interviewer carefully refrains from influencing the applicant's remarks. The applicant is allowed the maximum amount of freedom in determining the course of the discussion. The interviewer asks broad, open-ended questions—such as "Tell me more about your experiences on your last job"—and permits the applicant to talk freely with a minimum of interruption. Generally, the nondirective interviewer listens carefully and does not argue, interrupt, or change the subject abruptly. The interviewer also uses follow-up questions to allow the applicant to elaborate, makes only brief responses, and allows pauses in the conversation; the pausing technique is the most difficult for the novice interviewer.

The greater freedom afforded to the applicant in the nondirective interview helps bring to the interviewer's attention any information, attitudes, or feelings a candidate might not disclose during more structured questioning. However, because the applicant determines the course of the interview and no set procedure is followed, little information that comes from these interviews enables interviewers to cross-check agreement with other interviewers. Thus, the reliability and validity of these interviews are not likely to be as great. This method is most likely to be used in interviewing candidates for high-level positions and in counselling, which we will discuss in Chapter 13.

## THE STRUCTURED INTERVIEW

Because a **structured interview** has a set of standardized questions (based on job analysis) and an established set of answers against which applicant responses can be rated, it provides a more consistent basis for evaluating job candidates. For example, staff members of Weyerhaeuser Company's HR department have developed a structured interviewing process with the following characteristics:

1. The interview process is based exclusively on job duties and requirements critical to job performance.
2. There are sample (benchmark) answers, determined in advance, to each question.
3. Candidates are interviewed by multiple people, who rate the responses.
4. The interviewers take notes for future reference and in case of a legal challenge.

A structured interview is more likely to provide the type of information needed for making sound decisions. According to one report, structured interviews are twice as likely as nondirective interviews to predict on-the-job performance. Structured interviews are also less likely than nondirective interviews to be attacked in court.[7]

## THE SITUATIONAL INTERVIEW

One variation of the structured interview is called the **situational interview**. With this approach, an applicant is given a hypothetical incident and asked how he or she would respond to it. The applicant's response is then evaluated relative to preestablished benchmark standards. Highlights in HRM 6.1 shows a sample question from a situational interview used to select systems analysts at a chemical plant. Highlights in HRM 6.2 lists some of the oddest statements made by job applicants.

# HIGHLIGHTS IN HRM 6.1

## Sample Situational Interview Question

**QUESTION:**

It is the night before your scheduled vacation. You are packed and ready to go. Just before you get into bed, you receive a phone call from the plant. A problem has arisen that only you can handle. You are asked to come in to take care of things. What would you do in this situation?

**RECORD ANSWER:**

_____

_____

_____

**SCORING GUIDE:**

Good: "I would go in to work and make certain that everything is okay. Then I would go on vacation."
Good: "There are no problems that only I can handle. I would make certain that someone qualified was there to handle things."
Fair: "I would try to find someone else to deal with the problem."
Fair: "I would go on vacation."

## THE BEHAVIOURAL DESCRIPTION INTERVIEW

In contrast to a situational interview, which focuses on hypothetical situations, a **behavioural description interview (BDI)** focuses on *actual* work incidents in the interviewee's past. The BDI format asks the job applicant what he or she actually did in a given situation. For example, to assess a potential manager's

> **behavioural description interview (BDI)**
> An interview in which an applicant is asked questions about what he or she did in a given situation

# HIGHLIGHTS IN HRM 6.2

## Hiring Managers Reveal Mistakes Candidates Make during Job Interviews

Hiring managers often share the most memorable blunders that caused them to pass on a particular candidate. Below is a sample of some of them.

- "The candidate spoke no English, so he brought his mother to translate for him during the interview. It was for a customer-service position."

- "She kept telling me about her marital problems."

- "The candidate knew nothing about the job being offered or our organization."

- "One guy ate a sandwich."

- "The candidate asked me to hurry up because she left her child in the car."

- "He told me the only reason he was here was because his mother wanted him to get a job. He was 37."

- "One candidate did not wear shoes to the interview."

- "Body odor so bad I had to excuse myself midinterview and put lip gloss in my nose in order to get through the rest."

- "One guy mentioned his arrest during the interview after stating on his application that he had never been arrested."

- "One guy asked if we drug-tested and if we gave advance notice (we are a drug treatment facility)."

Sources: CareerBuilder.com; *Reader's Digest*.

# HIGHLIGHTS IN HRM 6.3

## Behavioural Interviews at BMO

The BMO Financial Group has been using behavioural interviewing for almost every position it fills and after several revisions feels that it is a solid predictive tool in the hiring process. Below is a list of competencies and the questions BMO uses to evaluate them:

### Business acumen behaviours

- Tell me about a time when you had to accomplish something that had a tight deadline and when you had to accomplish many things at once.
- Tell me about a challenging assignment that you had in the past year and how you handled this challenge.
- Describe a time when you had to decide what to do about a business situation where no guidelines existed or no precedents had been set.

### Analytical and systems thinking behaviours

- Tell me how you approached the most difficult or challenging project that you had to solve.
- Give me an example of a situation where you had to handle a project unlike anything you ever had to do.
- Tell me about a time when your team had to complete a challenging project.

### Customer and client service behaviours

- Describe to me a time when you turned around a very angry client and how you did it.
- Give me an example of a particularly difficult situation involving an external client and how you handled it.
- Tell me about a time when you felt particularly effective in establishing or maintaining a business relationship with a client.

Source: Adapted from Todd Humber, "How BMO Financial Selects Employees," *Canadian HR Reporter*, December 6, 2004, G2.

---

ability to handle a problem employee, an interviewer might ask, "Tell me about the last time that you disciplined an employee." Such an approach to interviewing, based on a critical incidents job analysis, assumes that past performance is the best predictor of future performance. It also may be somewhat less susceptible to faking. Recent research indicates that the BDI is more effective than the situational interview for hiring higher level postions such as general managers and executives.[8]

See Highlights in HRM 6.3 for behavioural questions posed by BMO Financial. The Business Case outlines the advantages of the behavioural interview.

## PANEL AND SEQUENTIAL INTERVIEWS

Another type of interview involves a panel of interviewers who question and observe a single candidate. In a typical **panel interview**, the candidate meets with three to five interviewers, who take turns asking questions. After the interview, the interviewers pool their observations and their rating scores if the interview is structured to reach a consensus about the suitability of the candidate. HRM specialists report that panel interviews provide several significant advantages over traditional one-to-one interviews, including higher reliability because they involve multiple inputs. They can also result in a shorter decision-making period, and applicants are more likely to accept the decisions made. Studies also suggest that if the panels are composed of a diverse group of interviewers, hiring discrimination is minimized.[9]

A **sequential interview** is one in which a candidate is interviewed by multiple people, one right after another. Sequential interviews are very common. They allow different interviewers who have a vested interest in the candidate's success to meet and evaluate the person one on one. The interviewers later get together and compare their assessments of the candidates.

# THE BUSINESS CASE

## Behavioural Interviews Bring Big Returns

Fairmont Hotels and Resorts Inc., formerly Canadian Pacific Hotels, with nearly 31,000 employees at 81 hotels in 6 countries, measures the effectiveness of selection tools. Using a Gallup selection tool, Fairmont has tracked the performance of sales personnel by selecting those who matched the characteristics of the best performers. Those superior employees produce two to three times more revenue than others.

A financial organization decided to assess the return on investment (ROI) of competency-based behavioural interviewing. It focused first on the sales and marketing function, which employed about 100 people, with average annual salaries of $135,000 ($90,000 plus a variable bonus of 50 percent for on-target performance). Turnover was about 20 percent a year. Elementary statistics suggest that the output of a group of workers forms a bell-shaped distribution, resulting in a small portion (about 10 percent) of staff working above or below acceptable performance, whereas the majority worked in the acceptable range. The recruiters decided to delineate the competencies that differentiated superior performers from average performers and to use these to improve the selection procedure.

Here is how the ROI was calculated:

Assume 20 new recruits a year.

Two recruits, on average, would be superior performers under the current recruiting system.

Under the new system, all 20 would be superior, for a net increase of 18 new superior employees.

Performing above average is worth about 48 percent of the average annual salary to the company.

Therefore, $18 \times (\$135,000 \times 0.48) = \$1,166,000$

But the recruitment process is not perfect and so must be discounted by 0.545 (the consultants' estimate of how good they were at selecting superior candidates and rejecting inferior candidates).

Therefore, $545 \times \$1,166,000 = \$635,000$

The cost of the competency project for sales and marketing was $130,000.

The benefit was $635,000, for an ROI of 488 percent.

The long-term ROI may be higher as superior recruits may have lower turnover, shorter learning curves, and increasingly effective performance.

Interviews must be as valid as tests because they are so expensive. The average cost per hire of an executive is $43,000, a manager or professional $17,000, a technical person $13,000, and clerical and administrative support around $3,000.

Sources: Adapted from A. Davis, "What Is the Cost of Hiring?" *Canadian HR Reporter* 16, no. 11 (June 2, 2003): 12; T. Tritch, "Fairmont's Talent Strategy Delivers Results," *Gallup Management Journal*, http://www.gmj.gallup.com, May 13, 2003; Lionel LaRoche and Stephen Martin, "Demonstrating the Bottom-Line Impact of HR: A Competencies Case Study," *Canadian HR Reporter* 13, no. 22 (December 18, 2000): 29–31.

In this panel interview, one of the participants is connecting by videoconference.

© Tom Merton/Alamy

## THE COMPUTER AND VIRTUAL INTERVIEWS

With advances in information technology, more and more organizations are using computers and the Internet to help with the interviewing process. Nike and Pinkerton Security have developed expert systems to gather preliminary information and compare candidates.

Typically, a computer interview requires candidates to answer a series (75 to 125) of multiple-choice questions tailored to the job. These answers are compared to either an ideal profile or profiles developed on the basis of other candidates' responses. The computer interview can also be used as a screening device to help filter out unqualified applicants applying online who do not merit a personal interview. Depending on the vendor and the software used, a computer interview conducted in conjunction with online tests can measure everything from contradictory responses and latent responses (time delays related to answering a question) to the applicant's typing speed and ability to use different kinds of software. CareerBuilder.com, for example, offers a service called IntelligentHire that screens out the 10 most qualified and interested applicants posting for a job on CareerBuilder's site. IntelligentHire then generates a report for the employer that includes the applicants' résumés, answers to questions, background check results, and their overall rankings against one another.[10]

A few years ago, Pic N Pay Shoe Stores created a computerized interview that could be conducted over the phone using a toll-free number. The interview focused on honesty, work attitude, drug use, candour, dependability, and self-motivation. After implementing the system, the company cut turnover by 50 percent and reduced employee theft by almost 40 percent. In addition to the benefits of objectivity, some research evidence suggests that applicants may be less likely to engage in "impression management" in computerized interviews than in face-to-face interviews. So far, organizations have used the computer mainly as a complement to, rather than as a replacement for, conventional interviews.[11]

## VIDEO AND DIGITALLY RECORDED INTERVIEWS

Companies such as AT&T, Dell Computer, and Nike are using videoconference technologies to evaluate job candidates. Whereas some use their own in-house systems, others use outside service partners. FedEx Kinko's, for example, rents videoconferencing rooms at a quarter of its 900 stores for about $225 per hour.

Video and digitally recorded interviews have several potential advantages related to flexibility, speed, and cost. Employers can make preliminary assessments about candidates' technical abilities, energy level, and appearance before incurring the costs of a face-to-face meeting. The goal is to enable faster, higher quality decisions at lower cost.

In addition to offering a broad range of candidate assessment services, a number of recruiting companies digitally record job applicants and post their interviews to their websites. Corporations log on to the sites and check out candidates free of charge or for a small fee depending on the vendor. By recording and playing back the interviews to several companies' executives, firms can eliminate complications involved in setting up many more interviews.[12]

## GUIDELINES FOR EMPLOYMENT INTERVIEWERS

Apart from the characteristics of the interviews themselves, there are several important tips for interviewers. Organizations should be cautious in selecting employment interviewers. Qualities that are desirable include humility, the ability to think objectively, maturity, and poise. Given the importance of diversity in the workforce, experience in associating with people from a variety of backgrounds is also desirable. Qualities to avoid in interviewers include overtalkativeness, extreme opinions, and biases.

# Interviewer Training

Training has been shown to dramatically improve the competence of interviewers. If not done on a continuing basis, training should at least be done periodically for managers, supervisors, and HR representatives who conduct interviews. Interviewer training programs should include practice interviews conducted under guidance. Practice interviews may be recorded and evaluated later in a group training session. The following list presents 10 ground rules for employment interviews that are commonly accepted and supported by research findings. Their apparent simplicity should not lead one to underestimate their importance.

1. *Understand the job.* Perhaps the most critical step to ensuring interviewers do a good job is to be sure that they understand the job and its requirements. Research studies have shown that interviewers who understand the parameters of a job are better at interviewing people and evaluating their responses.

2. *Establish an interview plan.* Examine the purposes of the interview and determine the areas and specific questions to be covered. Review the job requirements, application form data, test scores, and other available information before seeing the applicant.

3. *Establish and maintain rapport and listen actively.* This is accomplished by greeting the applicant pleasantly, explaining the purpose of the interview, displaying sincere interest in the applicant, and listening carefully. Try to understand not only what the candidate is saying but also what he or she is implying.

4. *Pay attention to nonverbal cues.* An applicant's facial expressions, gestures, body position, and movements often provide clues to that person's attitudes and feelings. Be aware of what you are communicating nonverbally.

5. *Provide information as freely and honestly as possible.* Answer fully and frankly the applicant's questions. Present a realistic picture of the job.

6. *Use questions effectively.* Ask open-ended questions rather than questions that can be answered with a simple "yes" or "no." Do not ask questions that "lead" candidates to the "right" answer. Phrase the questions in a neutral way.

7. *Separate facts from inferences.* During the interview, record factual information. Later, record your inferences or interpretations of the facts. Compare your inferences with those of other interviewers.

8. *Recognize biases and stereotypes.* Stereotyping involves forming generalized opinions of how people of a given gender, race, or ethnic background appear, think, feel, and act. As we have mentioned, one typical bias is for interviewers to consider candidates who have interests, experiences, and backgrounds similar to their own to be more acceptable. Another bias occurs when interviewers "fall into like" with applicants, especially if a candidate is extroverted and charming. If extroversion is an important characteristic of the job (such as a sales job), choosing an extroverted candidate might be appropriate. However, a less extroverted candidate who is more conscientious might be better for a job that is detail oriented or requires a person to work alone. In other words, evaluate candidates based on the characteristics of the job and not, for example, the fact that they went to the same college you did.

9. *Avoid the "halo error," or judging an individual favourably or unfavourably overall on the basis of only one strong point (or weak point) on which you place high value.* Also avoid the influence of "beautyism." Discrimination against unattractive but talented people is a persistent and pervasive form of employment discrimination. (If you are a candidate, remember that it can be difficult for interviewers to control their biases, so first impressions count. The degrees to which employers are influenced by a candidate's appearance are shown in Figure 6.4.)

## FIGURE 6.4

### HOW CANDIDATES' PHYSICAL ATTRIBUTES INFLUENCE EMPLOYERS

|  | No Influence | Slight Influence | Strong Influence |
|---|---|---|---|
| Grooming | 6% | 21% | 73% |
| Nontraditional interview attire | 13 | 38 | 49 |
| Handshake | 22 | 45 | 33 |
| Body piercing | 26 | 43 | 31 |
| Obvious tattoos | 25 | 46 | 29 |
| Nontraditional hair colour | 26 | 46 | 28 |
| Unusual hairstyle | 30 | 49 | 21 |
| Earring (male) | 54 | 34 | 12 |
| Beard | 73 | 22 | 5 |
| Mustache | 83 | 16 | 1 |

**Source:** Occupational Outlook Quarterly.

10. *Control the course of the interview*. Establish an interview plan and stick to it. Provide the applicant with ample opportunity to talk but maintain control of the situation to reach the interview objectives.
11. *Standardize the questions asked*. To increase the reliability of the interview and avoid discrimination, ask the same questions of all applicants for a particular job. Keep careful notes; record facts, impressions, and any relevant information, including what the applicant was told.

## EMPLOYMENT EQUITY: ARE YOUR QUESTIONS LEGAL?

The entire subject of preemployment questioning is complex. Federal and provincial requirements sometimes vary in the types of questions that may be asked during the interview. However, all jurisdictions forbid direct questions about race, sex, colour, age, religion, and national origin, and most look with disapproval on indirect questions dealing with the same topics. Some of the questions that interviewers once felt free to ask can be potentially hazardous. Human rights commissions have severely limited the areas of questioning. In general, if the question is job related, is asked of everyone, and does not discriminate against a certain class of applicants, it is likely to be acceptable to government authorities. Readers who are interested in a more comprehensive discussion should consult Catano et al., *Recruitment and Selection in Canada*, 5th Edition (Toronto: Nelson Canada, 2013).

Particular care must be given to questions asked of female applicants about their family responsibilities. It is inappropriate, for example, to ask, "Who will take care of your children while you are at work?" or "Do you plan to have children?" or "What is your husband's occupation?" or "Are you engaged?" It is, in fact, inappropriate to ask applicants of either gender questions about matters that have no relevance to job performance.

Employers have found it advisable to provide interviewers with instructions on how to avoid potentially discriminatory questions in their interviews. The examples of appropriate and inappropriate questions shown in Highlights in HRM 6.4 may serve as guidelines for application forms and preemployment interviews. Complete guidelines may be developed from current information

# HIGHLIGHTS IN HRM 6.4

## Appropriate and Inappropriate Interview Questions

| Subject | Avoid Asking | Preferred |
|---|---|---|
| *Name* | about name change; whether it was changed by court order, marriage, or other reason<br>maiden name | |
| *Address* | for addresses outside Canada | ask place and duration of current or recent address |
| *Age* | for birth certificates, baptismal records, or about age in general | ask applicants if they are eligible to work under Canadian laws regarding age restrictions |
| *Sex* | males or females to fill in different applications<br>about pregnancy, child-bearing plans, or childcare arrangements | can ask applicant if the attendance requirements can be met |
| *Marital Status* | whether applicant is single, married, divorced, engaged, separated, widowed, or living common-law<br>whether the applicant's spouse will be transferred<br>about the spouse's employment | if transfer or travel is part of the job, the applicant can be asked if he or she can meet these requirements; ask whether there are any circumstances that might prevent completion of a minimum service commitment |
| *Family Status* | number of children or dependants<br>about childcare arrangements | can ask if the applicant would be able to work the required hours and, where applicable, overtime |
| *National or Ethnic Origin* | about birthplace, nationality of ancestors, spouse, or other relatives<br>whether born in Canada<br>for proof of citizenship | since those who are entitled to work in Canada must be citizens, permanent residents, or holders of valid work permits, applicants can be asked if they are legally entitled to work in Canada |
| *Military Service* | about military service in other countries | inquiry about Canadian military service where employment preference is given to veterans by law |
| *Language* | mother tongue<br>where language skills obtained | ask if applicant understands, reads, writes, or speaks languages required for the job |
| *Race or Colour* | any question about race or colour, including colour of eyes, skin, or hair | |
| *Photographs* | for photo to be attached to applications or sent to interviewer before interview | |
| *Religion* | about religious affiliation, church membership, frequency of church attendance, if applicant will work a specific religious holiday, or for references from clergy or religious leader | explain the required work shift, asking if such a schedule poses problems for the applicant |
| *Height and Weight* | no inquiry unless there is evidence they are genuine occupational requirements | |

*continued*

| Subject | Avoid Asking | Preferred |
|---------|--------------|-----------|
| *Disability* | for listing of all disabilities, limitations, or health problems<br><br>whether applicant drinks or uses drugs<br><br>whether applicant has ever received psychiatric care or been hospitalized for emotional problems<br><br>whether applicant has received workers' compensation | The employer should:<br>disclose any information on medically related requirements or standards early in the application process<br>then ask whether the applicant has any condition that could affect his or her ability to do the job, preferably during a pre-employment medical examination |
| *Medical Information* | if currently under physician's care, name of family doctor<br><br>if receiving counselling or therapy | |
| *Pardoned Conviction* | whether an applicant has ever been convicted<br><br>if an applicant has ever been arrested<br><br>whether an applicant has a criminal record | if bonding is a job requirement ask if applicant is eligible |
| *Sexual Orientation* | about the applicant's sexual orientation | |
| *References* | The same restrictions that apply to questions asked of applicants also apply to questions asked of the applicant's references. | |

Source: A Guide to Screening and Selection in Employment. www.chrc-ccdp.ca/publications/screen-preselection.asp. Canadian Human Rights Commission. Reproduced with the permission of the Minister of Public Works and Government Services Canada, 2012.

available from provincial human rights commissions. Once an individual is hired, the information needed but not asked in the interview may be obtained if there is a valid need for it and if it does not lead to discrimination.

## POST-INTERVIEW SCREENING

When the interviewer is satisfied that the applicant is potentially qualified, information about previous employment and other information provided by the applicant are investigated.

### REFERENCE CHECKS

The most reliable information usually comes from supervisors, who are in the best position to report on an applicant's work habits and performance. Written verification of information relating to job titles, duties, and pay levels from the former employer's HR office is also very helpful. Highlights in HRM 6.5 includes a list of helpful questions to ask about applicants when checking their references.[13]

As a legal protection for all concerned, it is important to ask the applicant to fill out forms permitting information to be solicited from former employers and other reference sources. Even with these safeguards, many organizations are reluctant to put into writing an evaluation of a former employee for fear of being sued by the person. Many employers will verify only former employees' employment dates and positions. Note that there is no legal obligation to provide a reference letter for an employee unless you have promised in writing to do so. A survey by the SHRM found that although 75 percent of companies do provide references, many reported that the information consists only of employment dates and position. This results in problems for the next employers. A survey of Canadian companies found that the majority had to terminate an employee for reasons that

# HIGHLIGHTS IN HRM 6.5

## Sample Reference Checking Questions

- What is your relationship to the applicant? Are you the person's supervisor, peer, or subordinate?
- What were the start and end dates of the applicant's employment?
- What were the applicant's title and responsibilities?
- In what areas did the applicant excel?
- In what areas did the applicant need improvement?
- What was the applicant's biggest accomplishment at your organization?
- How well does the applicant communicate with and get along with others?

- How does the applicant deal with conflicts and stress?
- To what extent is the applicant driven to succeed?
- Did the applicant miss a lot of work?
- Was the applicant punctual?
- For what reason did the applicant leave your organization?
- Would you rehire the applicant?
- Are there any serious problems with the applicant we should know about?
- Is there any additional information about the applicant you would like to share with me?

Sources: Alison Doyle, "Reference Check Questions," About.com, accessed March 24, 2011, http://www.about.com; Carolyn Hirschman, "The Whole Truth," *HRMagazine* 45, no. 6 (June 2000): 86–72.

could have been discovered through a reference check. For example, the City of Waterloo fired its chief administrative officer after it uncovered an employment history in which the candidate broke rules and misled his previous employer, all well publicized but not checked by either the recruiting firm or the city.[14]

## BACKGROUND CHECKS

Following the terrorist attacks in the United States on September 11, 2001 (i.e., 9/11), and a rash of corporate scandals at companies such as Enron, Tyco, and WorldCom, background investigations have become standard procedure for many companies to prevent a variety of problems ranging from embezzlement and theft of merchandise to workplace violence. The vast majority (over 90 percent) of Canadian companies surveyed by the Canadian HR Reporter indicated that they conduct background checks for previous employment history (92 percent), academic qualifications (53 percent), criminal record (50 percent), and credit rating (11 percent).[15]

Like the application process, many checks that were once done manually are now being done online using existing computer databases. However, this frequently requires checking many different databases. Information on international applicants is even harder to obtain. Some companies outsource some or all of the checks to third-party screeners.

Some job boards now have online screening tools allowing an applicant to conduct his or her own self-background check and post it online prior to any sort of interview. The idea is to demonstrate upfront to prospective employers that the applicant has a clean criminal record and a good job history and would make a good employee.[16]

Finally, an increasing number of companies are simply using Internet searches to uncover background information on a potential candidate through social networking sites such as Facebook. Information found on these sites can positively or adversely influence the employer's perspective of a candidate. If the candidate is not hired for the job and learns that the employer has checked his social media sites, and perhaps learned that he is a member of a visible minority, he could potentially file a human rights claim.

**preemployment test**
An objective and standardized measure of a sample of behaviour that is used to gauge a person's knowledge, skills, abilities, and other characteristics (KSAOs) relative to other individuals

Organizations check the references of employees in a number of ways. Generally, telephone checks are preferable because they save time and provide for greater candour. Prescient InfoTech, a computer systems managing company, first calls references to establish contact and then emails them a two-page questionnaire asking them to numerically rank the applicant's various job-related attributes. There is room at the end of the questionnaire for comments and recommendations.

The most reliable information usually comes from supervisors, who are in the best position to report on an applicant's work habits and performance. Written verification of information relating to job titles, duties, and pay levels from the former employer's HR office is also very helpful.

## CREDIT CHECKS

The use of consumer credit reports by employers as a basis for establishing an applicant's eligibility for employment has become more restricted. For positions of trust, such as those involving financial instruments in banks, credit reports must be used. Applicants must agree in writing to a credit report and have the right to review its contents. More importantly, the reason for the credit report must be job related.

## PREEMPLOYMENT TESTS

OUTCOME 4

A **preemployment test** is an objective and standardized measure of a sample of behaviour that is used to gauge a person's KSAOs relative to other individuals.

One of the drawbacks of preemployment testing is that it creates the potential for legal challenges, particularly in the United States. There, a small but growing number of companies are being taken to court by candidates claiming that the tests they took were discriminatory. There is also some evidence that the more tests that are required, the higher the likelihood of a lawsuit. The relative frequency of discrimination suits also appears to vary by industry and job type. Police, firefighting, and teaching areas—which generally require applicants to pass more tests—appear to be more prone to discrimination litigation.[17] Because Canadian HR practices often lag behind U.S. practices, we can expect to see more legal challenges in Canada. Nonetheless, tests have played a more important part in government HR programs in which hiring on the basis of merit is required by law. Although government agencies experienced the same types of problems with their testing programs as did organizations in the private sector, their staff were forced to improve their testing programs rather than abandon them.

Although it is often advisable to use consultants, especially if an organization is considering the use of personality tests, managers should have a basic understanding of the technical aspects of testing and the contributions that tests can make to the HR program. Managers should also do a thorough job analysis to determine the crucial job requirements and related skills that need to be tested for and eliminate any unnecessary or duplicate tests.

## TYPES OF EMPLOYMENT TESTS

### Job Knowledge Tests

Government agencies and licensing boards usually develop job knowledge tests, a type of achievement test designed to measure a person's level of understanding about a particular job. The Uniform CPA Examination used to license certified public accountants is one such test. Most civil service examinations, for example, are used to determine whether an applicant possesses the information and understanding that will permit placement in the job without further training.[18]

## Work Sample Tests

Work sample tests, or job sample tests, require the applicant to perform tasks that are actually part of the work required on the job. Like job knowledge tests, work sample tests are constructed from a carefully developed outline that experts agree includes the major job functions; the tests are thus considered content valid. Organizations that are interested in moving toward *competency-based selection*—that is, hiring based on observation of behaviours previously shown to distinguish successful employees—increasingly use work samples to see potential employees "in action."[19]

Work samples have been devised for many diverse jobs: a map-reading test for traffic control officers, a lathe test for machine operators, a complex coordination test for pilots, an in-basket test for managers, a group discussion test for supervisors, and a judgment and decision-making test for administrators, to name a few. The reports are that this type of test is cost effective, reliable, valid, fair, and acceptable to applicants.[20]

Related to the job sample test is the job simulation, used by nearly one-third of those surveyed in 2005. Prudential Grand Valley Realty, a real estate firm in Kitchener, Ontario, uses an online video-based assessment that simulates the job of a real estate agent. The candidate plays the role of an agent and interacts with virtual clients who are interested in buying or selling a property. The recruit is taken thorough the entire sales cycle, from building rapport to closing the deal, and must demonstrate the ability to handle objections, negotiate price, understand client needs, and handle periodic rejection.[21]

## Assessment Centre Tests

An **assessment centre** is a process (not a place) used to evaluate candidates as they participate in a series of situations that resemble what they might be called on to handle on the job. Candidates engage in the following types of activities at assessment centres:

- *In-basket exercises.* This method is used to simulate a problem situation. The participants are given several documents, each describing a problem or situation requiring an immediate response. They are thus forced to make decisions under the pressure of time and to determine what priority to give each problem.

- *Leaderless group discussions.* With this activity, trainees are gathered in a conference setting to discuss an assigned topic, either with or without designated group roles. The participants are given little or no instruction in how to approach the topic, nor are they told what decision to reach. Leaderless group trainees are evaluated on their initiative, leadership skills, and ability to work effectively in a group setting.

- *Role-playing.* The exercise might involve preparing for and engaging in a customer meeting or a team leader meeting with one's subordinates. A trained assessor then assesses the participant using a structured rating scale.

- *Behavioural interviews.* The interviewer asks the participant a series of questions about what he or she would do in particular work circumstances. Sometimes behavioural interviews are combined with videos showing work simulations, and participants are asked at intervals to make choices about what they would do in the situations shown.

At the end of the assessment centre period, the assessors' observations are combined to develop an overall picture of the strengths and needs of the participants. A report is normally submitted to the organization that commissioned the tests, and feedback is given to the participants. Because of the costs involved, assessment centres are usually used to select managers.

With jobs such as this one that require specific skills, it is quite common for employers to ask candidates to demonstrate their abilities through work sample tests.

## Cognitive Ability Tests

Cognitive ability tests measure mental capabilities such as general intelligence, verbal fluency, numerical ability, and reasoning ability. A host of paper-and-pencil tests measure cognitive abilities, including the General Aptitude Test Battery (GATB), Scholastic Aptitude Test (SAT), Graduate Management Aptitude Test (GMAT), and Bennett Mechanical Comprehension Test (BMCT). Figure 6.5 provides examples of questions from the General Competency Test (GCT) administered by the Public Service Commission of Canada.

Although cognitive ability tests can be developed to measure very specialized areas, such as reading comprehension and spatial relations, many experts believe that the validity of cognitive ability tests simply reflects their connection to general intelligence. However, measures of general intelligence (such as IQ) have been shown to be good predictors of performance across a wide variety of jobs.[22]

### FIGURE 6.5

GENERAL COMPETENCY TEST LEVEL 1

The GCT was developed by the Personnel Psychology Centre, Assessment, Testing and Counselling Directorate, the Public Service Commission of Canada. The GCT 1 has 50 multiple-choice questions, and the test takes 85 minutes. There are three types of questions, and an example from each is found below:

Understanding Written Material Example:

Government of Canada

Memorandum

To: All employees

From: Manager

We are pleased to announce that our Ministry's budget has been increased and consequently we will experience an increase in staff size. Because new positions will become available, we will be holding interviews within the next few weeks.

The main focus of this interview is a change concerning:

1. Better ministerial policy
2. Better budget publicity
3. More human resources
4. More office space

Solving Numerical Questions:

You are in charge of financial services and must calculate overtime pay for employees in your division. Due to a heavy workload, an employee had to do 35 hours of overtime in two weeks. Seven of these hours are at "double time" (i.e., twice usual pay), the rest are at "time and a half." The employee's usual pay is $375 a week at $10 an hour. How much overtime money should the employee be paid for the two-week period?

1. $340
2. $420
3. $560
4. $760

Drawing Logical Conclusions:

One of your duties is the selection and disposal of boxes of obsolete files. According to regulations, ordinary files become obsolete after 24 months, confidential files after 36 months, and classified files after 48 months. Which of the following boxes of files can be disposed of?

A) A box containing ordinary files dated 26 months ago and classified files dated 34 months ago.

B) A box containing ordinary files dated 38 months ago and confidential files dated 28 months ago.

1. A only
2. B only
3. Both A and B
4. Neither A nor B

Answers can be found on page 233.

**Source:** Reproduced with the permission of the Public Service Commission of Canada, 2012.

## Biodata Tests

Biodata tests collect biographical information about candidates that has been shown to correlate with on-the-job success. Candidates are questioned about events and behaviours that reflect attitudes, experiences, interests, skills, and abilities. Typically, the questions relate to events that have occurred in a person's life and ask what the person typically did in those situations. The idea is that past behaviour is the best predictor of future behaviour. For example, a question on a biodata test might ask, "How many books have you read in the last 6 months?" or "How often have you put aside tasks to complete another, more difficult assignment?" Test takers choose one of several predetermined alternatives to best match their past behaviour and experiences.

A response to a single biodata question is of little value. Rather, the pattern of responses across several different situations gives biographical data the power to predict future behaviour on the job. Although biodata tests have been found to be good predictors of on-the job success, they are sophisticated and must be professionally developed and validated. Another drawback is that the questions might not appear to be clearly related to the job being tested for, so applicants might question the test's validity and believe that the test invades their privacy.

## Personality and Interest Inventories

Whereas cognitive ability tests measure a person's mental capacity, personality tests measure disposition and temperament. During the 1990s, for example, testing by the U.S. Army found that cognitive ability tests were the best predictors of how well soldiers were able to acquire job knowledge and, ultimately, of their technical proficiencies. But personality tests were the better predictors of their motivation, such as their leadership efforts and propensity to adhere to rules. Years of research show that five dimensions can summarize personality traits. The "Big Five" factors are the following:

1. *Extroversion*—the degree to which someone is talkative, sociable, active, aggressive, and excitable
2. *Agreeableness*—the degree to which someone is trusting, amiable, generous, tolerant, honest, cooperative, and flexible
3. *Conscientiousness*—the degree to which someone is dependable and organized and perseveres in tasks
4. *Neuroticism*—the degree to which someone is secure, calm, independent, and autonomous
5. *Openness to experience*—the degree to which someone is intellectual, philosophical, insightful, creative, artistic, and curious[23]

Personality tests include the California Psychological Inventory, the Myers-Briggs Type Indicator (MBTI), and the 180-question Caliper test. Although there is some evidence to show that when used in combination with cognitive ability tests, measures of personality traits (such as conscientiousness) can help predict how well a person will perform on the job, historically, the connection between the two has been quite low.[24]

Personality tests can also be problematic if they inadvertently discriminate against individuals who would otherwise perform effectively.[25] Rather than being used to make hiring decisions, personality and interest inventories may be most useful for helping people with their occupational selection and career planning.

## Polygraph Tests

The polygraph, or lie detector, is a device that measures the changes in breathing, blood pressure, and pulse of a person who is being questioned. It consists of a rubber tube around the chest, a cuff around the arm, and sensors attached to the fingers that record the physiological changes in the examinee as the examiner asks questions that call for an answer of yes or no. Questions typically cover such items as whether a person uses drugs, has stolen from an employer, or has committed a serious undetected crime.

The RCMP uses a polygraph test to identify candidates who meet its standards of honesty and suitability. However, the use of lie detector tests for employment purposes is prohibited under the *Employment Standards Acts* in both Ontario and New Brunswick. Check provincial legislation before considering the use of a polygraph.

## Honesty and Integrity Tests

Many employers have dramatically increased their use of pencil-and-paper honesty and integrity tests. These tests have commonly been used in settings such as retail stores, where employees have access to cash or merchandise. Common areas of inquiry include beliefs about the frequency and extent of theft in our society, punishment for theft, and perceived ease of theft. For example, Payless ShoeSource has used a paper-and-pencil honesty test to reduce employee theft. When the company began its program, losses totalled nearly $21 million per year among its 4,700 stores. Within only one year of implementing its screening program, inventory shrinkage fell by 20 percent to less than 1 percent of sales.[26]

Potential items that might be used on an integrity test are shown in Figure 6.4. Although some studies have shown that honesty tests are valid for predicting job performance and a wide range of disruptive behaviours, such as theft, disciplinary problems, and absenteeism, other studies have questioned their validity.[27] It is possible that the tests "work" not because they predict behaviour but because they deter less-than-honest applicants from joining a company. However, applicants sometimes view the tests as an invasion of their privacy. Some candidates find questions such as "I like to take chances" offensive. The British Columbia Civil Liberties Union has called for legislation banning integrity tests as an invasion of privacy. Sobeys, a chain food store based in Stellarton, Nova Scotia, used an integrity test and failed an applicant even though she had worked for them previously for six years without any incident. The applicant filed a complaint with the Nova Scotia Human Rights Commission.

Given these issues, HRM specialists should consider the use of honesty tests very cautiously and most certainly in conjunction with other sources of information.[28]

## Physical Ability Tests

In addition to learning about a job candidate's mental capabilities, employers frequently need to assess a person's physical abilities. Particularly for demanding and potentially dangerous jobs, such as those held by firefighters and police officers, physical abilities such as strength and endurance tend to be good predictors not only of performance but also of accidents and injuries.[29]

Physical ability tests must be used cautiously. In the past, requirements for physical characteristics such as strength, agility, height, and weight were often determined by an employer's unvalidated notion of what should be required. This often put women and disabled job applicants at a disadvantage, a situation that can lead to lawsuits. Evidence suggests that the average man is stronger, faster, and more powerful than the average woman, but women tend to have better balance, manual dexterity, flexibility, and coordination than men. For example, applicants who take the RCMP's Physical Fitness Abilities Requirement Evaluation (PARE) are required to run 350 metres, complete a standing broad jump of about 2 metres, and pick up and carry a heavy bag for 15 metres. According to one RCMP officer, "If you're a bigger person, the PARE test is easier, no doubt." The fact that women fail the test in greater numbers than men has resulted in a complaint before the Canadian Human Rights Commission. The RCMP defended the PARE test on the grounds that it simulates common police activities, such as chasing a suspect on foot, carrying an injured person, and forcing open a door. However, the court struck down as illegal a similar test used for firefighters in

British Columbia because it discriminated against women, who were less likely to meet the standard, which itself was based on a male standard.[30]

On the basis of these differences, it is clear that (as with other methods for screening potential employees) the use of physical ability tests should be carefully validated on the basis of the essential functions of the job.[31]

## Medical Examinations

A medical examination is generally given to ensure that the health and fitness of applicants are adequate to meet the job requirements. It also provides a baseline against which subsequent medical examinations can be compared and interpreted. The last objective is especially important for determining work-caused disabilities under workers' compensation law.

Any requirements that tend to discriminate against women have been questioned and modified to represent typical job demands.

Medical examinations and inquiries about a candidate directed to medical professionals can be conducted only after an offer (preferably written) of employment has been made. The offer can be made conditional on the applicant's ability to perform the essential duties of the job as determined by a job-related medical examination. Any medical inquiries must be directly related to assessing the candidate's abilities to perform the essential duties of the job. This allows the applicant with a disability the opportunity to be considered exclusively on merit during the selection process.

An employer may ask a candidate if she or he has any disability-related needs that would require accommodation to enable performance of the essential duties of the job. The interviewer should be cautioned about probing as to the nature of the disability. Later employment-related decisions may be perceived to be based on this information and thereby characterized as discriminatory. To ensure neutrality, and to avoid the possibility of a complaint to the Canadian Human Rights Commission, such information should remain exclusively with the examining physician, not in the personnel file.

If the employee has a disability, the employer has a duty to accommodate his or her needs. The accommodation can be accomplished either by changing some of the essential duties of the position or by providing the appropriate equipment. To determine whether an individual can do the essential duties of a particular position, the employer should conduct a physical demands analysis, checklists for which are available through most provincial ministries of labour.

## Drug Testing

The Canadian Human Rights Commission and some of its provincial counterparts have issued policies on employment-related drug testing. Addiction to drugs or alcohol is considered a disability, and the employer is to be guided by legislation and by practices such as workplace accommodation. The medical examination cannot be conducted until a conditional offer of employment is made in writing, and the examination can determine only the individual's ability to perform the essential duties. Since drug tests measure neither actual impairment nor the likelihood of a person reporting to work under the influence of drugs, the extent to which they assess the ability to perform essential duties is extremely limited. Therefore, human rights tribunals and courts have imposed very strict limitations on the right of employers to require drug tests.

If the job is a safety-sensitive one, then an employer may be permitted to offer the position conditional on the successful passing of a drug test. The employer then has the right to demand a medical examination of the employee. If an employee refuses, he or she can be dismissed. However, if an employee who fails a drug test is a drug addict, and therefore disabled under human rights statutes, then the employer will be required to accommodate the employee's disability to the point of undue hardship before it can dismiss the employee.

 **Using the Internet**

The Treasury Board Secretariat of the federal government publishes its policies on the accommodation of persons with disabilities at

**http://www.tbs-sct.gc.ca /pubs_pol/hrpubs/TB_852 /ppaed_e.asp**

**criterion-related validity**
The extent to which a selection tool predicts, or significantly correlates with, important elements of work behaviour

**concurrent validity**
The extent to which test scores (or other predictor information) match criterion data obtained at about the same time from current employees

**predictive validity**
The extent to which applicants' test scores match criterion data obtained from those applicants/employees after they have been on the job for an indefinite period

**cross-validation**
Verifying the results obtained from a validation study by administering a test or test battery to a different sample (drawn from the same population)

**content validity**
The extent to which a selection instrument, such as a test, adequately samples the knowledge and skills needed to perform a particular job

The following types of testing are not allowed:

- Preemployment drug testing
- Preemployment alcohol testing
- Random drug testing
- Random alcohol testing of employees in non–safety-sensitive positions

There is widespread opposition to drug testing in the workplace, which is why only about 2 percent of companies in Canada do it compared to about 80 percent of American companies. Canadian companies that operate in both countries, such as those in cross-border trucking, may argue that testing is a bona fide occupational qualification for drivers; otherwise, they would be banned from driving in the United States. Syncor Canada, a world leader in mining and extracting crude oil, believes that drug testing of heavy equipment operators could be justified on safety grounds but not for those in an office environment.

The Canadian Civil Liberties Association takes the position that "no person should be required to share urine with a stranger" as a condition of employment. Employee assistance programs (EAPs) play an important role in helping employees with drug and alcohol problems. EAPs will be discussed in Chapter 12.

## DETERMINING THE VALIDITY OF TESTS

There are three recognized approaches to validation: criterion-related validity, content validity, and construct validity.

### Criterion-Related Validity

The extent to which a selection tool predicts, or significantly correlates with, important elements of work behaviour is known as **criterion-related validity**. How well a person performs on a test, for example, is compared to his or her actual production records, supervisory ratings, training outcomes, and other measures of success that are appropriate to each type of job. In a sales job, for example, it is common to use sales figures as a basis for comparison. In production jobs, the quantity and quality of output are likely to be the best indicators of job success.

There are two types of criterion-related validity: concurrent and predictive. **Concurrent validity** involves obtaining criterion data from *current employees* at about the same time that test scores (or other predictor information) are obtained. For example, a supervisor will be asked to rate a group of clerical employees on the quantity and quality of their performance. These employees are then given a clerical aptitude test, and the test scores are compared to the supervisor's ratings to determine the degree of relationship between them. **Predictive validity**, on the other hand, involves testing *applicants* and obtaining criterion data *after* those applicants have been hired and have been on the job for a certain period of time. For example, applicants are given clerical aptitude tests, which are then filed for later study.

After the individuals have been on the job for several months, supervisors, who should not know the employees' test scores, are asked to rate them on the quality and quantity of their performance. The test scores are then compared to the supervisors' ratings.

Regardless of the method used, cross-validation is essential. **Cross-validation** is a process in which a test or battery of tests is administered to a different sample of people (drawn from the same population) for the purpose of verifying the results obtained from the original validation study. One way to measure a test's validity is to administer it to an organization's current employees and create a benchmark score to which applicants' scores can be compared.

### Content Validity

When it is not feasible to use the criterion-related approach, often because of limited samples of individuals, the content method is used. **Content validity** is assumed to exist when a selection instrument, such as a test, adequately samples the knowledge and skills a person needs to do a particular job.

construct validity
The extent to which a selection tool measures a theoretical construct or trait

The closer the content of the selection instrument is to actual work samples or behaviours, the greater its content validity. For example, a civil service examination for accountants has high content validity when it requires applicants to solve accounting problems representative of those found on the job. Asking an accountant to lift a 25-kilogram box, however, is a selection procedure that has content validity only if the job description indicates that accountants must be able to meet this requirement. Content validity is the most direct and least complicated type of validity to assess. It is generally used to evaluate job knowledge and skill tests. Unlike the criterion-related method, content validity is not expressed in correlational terms. Instead, an index is computed (from evaluations of an expert panel) that indicates the relationship between the content of the test items and a person's performance on the job.[32] Although content validity does have its limitations, it has made a positive contribution to job analysis procedures and to the role of expert judgment in sampling and scoring procedures.

## Construct Validity

The extent to which a selection tool measures a theoretical construct, or trait, is known as **construct validity**. Typical constructs are intelligence, mechanical comprehension, and anxiety. They are broad, general categories of human functions that are based on the measurement of many discrete behaviours. For example, the BMCT consists of a wide variety of tasks that measure the construct of mechanical comprehension.

Measuring construct validity requires showing that the psychological trait is related to satisfactory job performance and that the test accurately measures the psychological trait. There is a lack of literature covering this concept as it relates to employment practices, probably because it is difficult and expensive to validate a construct and to show how it is job related.[33]

# REACHING A SELECTION DECISION

The most critical step is the decision to accept or reject applicants. Thus, it requires systematic consideration of all the relevant information about applicants. It is common to use summary forms and checklists such as the one shown in Figure 6.6 to ensure that all of the pertinent information has been included in the evaluation of applicants. In the Reality Check, read about how The Bay recruits and reaches selection decisions for its candidates.

**OUTCOME 5**

## SUMMARIZING INFORMATION ABOUT APPLICANTS

Fundamentally, an employer is interested in what an applicant can do and will do. Evaluating candidates on the basis of information you have assembled should focus on these two factors. The "can do" factors include a candidate's knowledge and skills, as well as the aptitude (the potential) for acquiring new knowledge and skills. The "will do" factors include the candidate's motivation, interests, and other personality characteristics. Both factors are essential to successful performance on the job. The employee who has the ability (can do) but is not motivated to use it (will not do) is little better than the employee who lacks the necessary ability.

It is much easier to measure what individuals can do than what they will do. The can do factors are readily evident from test scores and verified information. What the individual will do can only be inferred. Employers can use the responses to interview and application form questions and references to obtain information for making inferences about what an individual will do.

# REALITY CHECK

## Selection at The Bay

Canada's oldest corporation and largest department store retailer is the Hudson's Bay Company (HBC), which was established in 1670 and operates as The Bay and Zellers. Tina Peacock, HR manager for Merchandise Services and Corporate Offices, has been with HBC for more than 20 years. She helps the company achieve its goals by carefully applying selection methods to identify key potential candidates for many different positions, such as merchandise buyer, financial manager, and systems manager.

"In addition to succession planning," states Peacock, "we follow established trends, such as growth in our business units, turnover, and performance results, to identify those positions that may become vacant during the year. Through a number of training programs provided in-house, we are able to fill our positions internally. In fact, 80 percent are staffed from internal promotions. For the other 20 percent, we hire externally. As a proactive measure in anticipation of those openings, we run recruiting ads so that we always have a 'stable' of competent candidates.

"It is important that we work closely with the managers because they know what is needed to run their business. My role is to provide them with qualified candidates who possess the basic job knowledge with the right competencies to work in our fast-paced, changing environment. For instance, a number of managers are tapped into the marketplace, so they are able to get the ball rolling by identifying candidates in the industry before an ad is placed. Our role is to prescreen those candidates to ensure they have the attributes needed to successfully perform in our environment.

"We work very closely with an ad agency to assist us in preparing the ad and to provide advice on the marketing strategies of where and when to place the ad. They save you a lot of time, especially when they understand your business. Running our ads for a particular position yields us other qualified candidates for other positions we had not counted on.

"Many of our ads yield as many as 250 résumés. Based on the competencies required for a position, we prescreen the résumés. It is not uncommon for me to receive over 50 phone calls per day when an ad is running. If I can delegate some of those calls, I do; however, if they have asked me for something specific, I make an effort to call them back because they are our customers and they are important to us. Once I have determined a short list, I then conduct a pretty thorough telephone interview before bringing in any candidates. Questions regarding salary expectations, any information that may be missing on the résumé, and some very job-specific questions are reviewed. We are always looking to improve our systems. Our next ad will incorporate a voice response system that has been developed internally by our Information Services Department. Candidates who wish to apply to an ad will be asked to call our system and respond to some basic job-related questions. At the end of the session, the candidate will be advised whether they possess the basic requirements of the job and whether they should apply to this position.

"The questions we ask during the face-to-face interview are open-ended questions that look for behavioural attributes specific to the competencies and key job requirements. For example, we want the candidates to demonstrate how they have gone about performing their job duties in the past. For those candidates who proceed to a final interview, we ask each of them to complete a communications survey. Using an outside consultant, we have developed a prediction performance program profile that has identified benchmark attributes for our buyers, merchandising trainees, and store managers. The results are graphed and compared against the benchmark. This profile is not used as a basis for determining whether we should hire a candidate or not. It provides us with another opportunity to fully assess the individual's capabilities by asking more focused questions. In this way, it ensures that we have fully investigated the individual's background and credentials. We provide each of our candidates with a written assessment of the report, whether they are hired or not, and ask them to comment on the accuracy of the results. Based on these responses, the report has been assessed at an accuracy of over 90 percent."

Peacock says in closing: "Systems in the workplace will continue to change, but the bottom line is that we need the best people to technically do the job and, most importantly, they must be customer focused."

Source: Interview with Tina Peacock.

## DECISION-MAKING STRATEGY

The strategy used for making personnel decisions for one category of jobs might differ from that used for another category. The strategy used to select managerial and executive personnel, for example, will be different from the strategy used to select clerical and technical personnel. Although many factors have to be

**FIGURE 6.6**

PART 3

## CANDIDATE EVALUATION FORM

**Position:**
**Candidate Name:**
**Interviewer Name:**
**Interview Date:**

Complete the comments section as you interview the candidate. After the interview, circle your ratings for each section and then add them together for a final score. The ratings scale is as follows:

**RATINGS SCALE**
1. Negligible or doesn't meet requirements
2. More needed
3. Adequate
4. Exceeds requirements

**Education**
Comments:
Rating: _____

**Experience**
Comments:
Rating: _____

**Job Knowledge**
Comments:
Rating: _____

**Job Skills**
Comments:
Rating: _____

**Interest in Position**
Comments:
Rating: _____

**Problem-Solving Ability**
Comments:
Rating: _____

**Communication Skills**
Comments:
Rating: _____

**Leadership Skills**
Comments:
Rating: _____

_____ TOTAL POINTS

Rater's Recommendation:

considered in terms of making hiring decisions, the following are some of the questions that managers must consider:

1. Should the individuals be hired according to their highest potential or according to the needs of the organization?
2. At what grade or wage level should the individual be started?
3. Should the selection be concerned primarily with finding an ideal employee to match the job currently open, or should a candidate's potential for advancement in the organization be considered?

**compensatory model**
A selection decision model in which a high score in one area can make up for a low score in another area

**multiple cutoff model**
A selection decision model that requires an applicant to achieve a minimum level of proficiency on all selection dimensions

**multiple hurdle model**
A sequential strategy in which only the applicants with the highest scores at an initial test stage go on to subsequent stages

4. To what extent should those who are not qualified but are qualifiable (have potential) be considered?
5. Should overqualified individuals be considered?
6. What effect will a decision have on the organization's meeting its employment equity plans and diversity considerations?

In addition to these types of factors, managers must also consider which approach they will use in making hiring decisions. There are two basic approaches to selection: clinical (personal judgment) and statistical.

## Clinical Approach

In the clinical approach to decision making, those making the selection decision review all the data on the applicants. Then, on the basis of their understanding of the job and the individuals who have been successful in that job, they make a decision. Different individuals often arrive at different decisions about an applicant when they use this approach because each evaluator assigns different weights to the applicant's strengths and weaknesses. Unfortunately, personal biases and stereotypes are frequently covered up by what appear to be rational reasons for either accepting or rejecting a candidate.

## Statistical Approach

In contrast to the clinical approach, the statistical approach to decision making is more objective. It involves identifying the most valid predictors and weighting them using statistical methods, such as multiple regression.[34] Quantified data, such as scores or ratings from interviews, tests, and other procedures, are then combined according to their weighted value. Individuals with the highest combined scores are selected. A comparison of the clinical approach with the statistical approach in a wide variety of situations has shown that the statistical approach is superior. Although this superiority has been recognized for many decades, the clinical approach continues to be the one most commonly used.

With a strictly statistical approach, a candidate's high score on one predictor (such as a cognitive ability test) will make up for a low score on another predictor (such as the interview). For this reason, this model is a **compensatory model**. However, it is frequently important that applicants achieve some minimum level of proficiency on all selection dimensions. When this is the case, a **multiple cutoff model** can be used in which only those candidates who score above the minimum cutoff on all dimensions are considered. The selection decision is made from that subset of candidates.[35]

A variation of the multiple cutoff is referred to as the **multiple hurdle model**. This decision strategy is sequential in that after candidates go through an initial evaluation stage, the ones who score well are provisionally accepted and are assessed further at each successive stage. The process continues through several stages (hurdles) before a final decision is made regarding the candidates. This approach is especially useful when either the testing or training procedures are lengthy and expensive.

Each statistical approach requires that a decision be made about where the cutoff lies—that point in the distribution of scores above which a person should be considered and below which the person should be rejected. The score that the applicant must achieve is the cutoff score. Depending on the labour supply and diversity considerations, it may be necessary to lower or raise the cutoff score.

Of course, the most valid predictors should be used with any selection strategy. Nonetheless, a related factor contributes to selecting the best qualified people: having an adequate number of applicants or candidates from which to make a selection. This formula is typically expressed in terms of a

**selection ratio**, which is the ratio of the number of applicants to be selected to the total number of applicants. A ratio of 0.10, for example, means that 10 percent of the applicants will be selected. A ratio of 0.90 means that 90 percent will be selected. If the selection ratio is low, only the most promising applicants will be hired. When the ratio is high, very little selectivity will be possible because even applicants with mediocre abilities will have to be hired if the firm's vacancies are to be filled. When this is the situation, a firm's managers can fall prey to what some experts call the "desperation bias"—choosing someone because they are in a pinch. It is a common problem among managers because of the many time and operating constraints they face.

**selection ratio**
The number of applicants compared to the number of people to be hired

## FINAL DECISION

After a preliminary selection/screening by a firm's HR department has been conducted, the applicants who appear most promising are then referred to the departments with vacancies. These people are then interviewed by the managers or supervisors, who usually make the final decision and communicate it to the HR department. Because of the weight that is usually given to their choices, managers and supervisors should be trained so that their role in the selection process does not negate the more rigorous efforts of the firm's HR staff.

In large organizations, notifying applicants of the decision that has been made and making job offers is often the responsibility of HR departments. The HR department should confirm the details of the job, such as working arrangements and wages, and specify a deadline by which the applicant must reach a decision.

# SMALL BUSINESS APPLICATION

What is different for small business is twofold. First, in all likelihood, the person conducting the interview will be the business owner or hiring manager rather than an HR generalist. This will not be true in all cases as there may be times when small businesses work through temporary staffing companies or recruitment agencies, in which case, candidates would likely go through an interview with a recruitment specialist prior to being referred for consideration. Second, as we outlined in Chapter 3, the nature of working for a small company is that people must fit in with the team and assist in many different capacities. As a result, where selection for positions in large companies balances the importance of person–job fit and person–organization fit, in small companies, a greater focus is placed on person–organization fit combined with capability and motivation to do the job candidates are being hired for as well as providing assistance to others when needed.

So how do small companies ensure that their selection process effectively assesses a candidate's fit? With the twin goals of selection being to assess a candidate's skills to perform in the role and his or her ability to fit into the organization, many small companies conduct multiple interviews. One interview is conducted by the functional manager, which focuses on assessing the required job skill and fit with the operational leader. A second interview is conducted by the business owner or another manager, with the aim of assessing the candidate's capacity and demonstrated willingness to support other activities, as well as assessing organizational fit. References are then checked, with a cautionary recognition that references are seldom negative, even if past performance was unsatisfactory, as past employers do not wish to get involved in any controversy as a result of providing negative feedback.

As a final note, in Chapter 5, we identified that employee referrals and hiring family members is a common practice in small companies. Small companies need to be very cautious in the selection process when considering referrals, friends, and family. Such selection creates bias, which must be factored into the selection process. This does not mean that small companies should not consider referrals, friends, and family. It just means that all steps should be taken to confirm that the candidate is the best candidate for the job based on job fit and organizational fit and so minimize hiring mistakes that come from incorrectly assuming the skills and fit of referrals, friends, or family.

# SUMMARY

**SUMMARY**

**OUTCOME 1** Selection is the process of choosing individuals who have relevant qualifications to fill existing or projected job openings. The selection process should start with a job analysis. Research shows that complete and clear job specifications help interviewers differentiate between qualified and unqualified applicants and reduces the effect of an interviewer's biases and prejudices. The number of steps in the selection process and their sequence will vary, not only with the organization but also with the type and level of jobs to be filled.

**OUTCOME 2** The employee selection process should provide as much reliable and valid information as possible about applicants so that their qualifications can be carefully matched with the job's specifications. The information that is obtained should be clearly job related or predict success on the job and be free from potential discrimination. Reliability refers to the consistency of test scores over time and across measures. Validity refers to the accuracy of the measurements taken. Validity can be assessed in terms of whether the measurement is based on a job specification (content validity), whether test scores correlate with performance criteria (predictive validity), and whether the test accurately measures what it purports to measure (construct validity).

**OUTCOME 3** Interviews are customarily used in conjunction with résumés, application forms, biographical information blanks, references, background investigations, and various types of preemployment tests. Despite problems with its validity, the employment interview remains central to the selection process. Depending on the type of job, applicants could be interviewed by one person, members of a work team, or other individuals in the organization. Structured interviews have been found to be better predictors of the performance of job applicants than nonstructured interviews. Some interviews are situational and can focus on hypothetical situations or actual behavioural descriptions of a candidate's previous work experiences.

Regardless of the technique chosen, those who conduct interviews should receive special training to acquaint them with interviewing methods and employment equity considerations. The training should also make them more aware of the nature of the job and its requirements.

**OUTCOME 4** Preemployment tests are more objective than interviews and can give managers a fuller sense of the capabilities of different candidates. A wide range of tests exists. Cognitive ability tests are especially valuable for assessing verbal, quantitative, and reasoning abilities. Personality and interest tests are perhaps best used for placement or career development. Job knowledge and work sample tests are achievement tests that are useful for determining whether a candidate can perform the duties of the job without further training. Physical ability tests can be used to prevent accidents and injuries, particularly for physically demanding work. However, they must not be used if they have a disparate impact on candidates in designated groups. Medical examinations and drug tests can be legally administered only after a conditional offer of employment has been made.

**OUTCOME 5** In the process of making decisions, all "can do" and "will do" factors should be assembled and weighted systematically so that the final decision can be based on a composite of the most reliable and valid information. Although the clinical approach to decision making is used more than the statistical approach, the former lacks the accuracy of the latter. Compensatory models allow a candidate's high score on one predictor to make up for a low score on another. When the multiple cutoff model is used, only those candidates who score above a minimum cutoff level remain in the running. A variation of the multiple cutoff is the multiple hurdle model, which involves several stages and cutoff levels. Whichever approach is used, the goal is to select a greater proportion of individuals who will be successful on the job.

# KEY TERMS

## DISCUSSION QUESTIONS

1. In groups, describe to each other the steps in the selection process that you experienced in a recent job search. Compare these experiences and discuss the reasons why there would be differences.

2. What is meant by the term *criterion* as it is used in personnel selection? Give some examples of criteria used for jobs with which you are familiar.

3. Compare briefly the major types of employment interviews described in this chapter. Which type would you prefer to conduct? Why?

4. What characteristics do job knowledge and job sample tests have that often make them more acceptable to the examinees than other types of tests?

5. In what ways does the clinical approach to selection differ from the statistical approach? How do you account for the fact that one approach is superior to the other?

# HRM EXPERIENCE

## Designing Selection Criteria and Methods

Making hiring decisions is one of the most important—and difficult—decisions a manager makes. Without good information, managers have almost no chance of making the right choice. The process begins with a sound understanding of the job: the tasks, duties, and responsibilities associated with it and the knowledge, skills, and abilities needed to do it. A job analysis should be done to make certain that all managers have assembled all of the information they need to ensure a good person–job fit. However, this information may not be enough. Other information about the company's values and philosophy is likely to be required to ensure that a good person–organization fit results.

### Assignment

1. Working in teams of four to six, choose a job with which you are familiar and identify the most important KSAOs needed for someone doing the job to perform well.

2. Next, identify which methods you would use to find candidates with these qualities. Would you use applications, interviews, cognitive or ability tests, work samples, or something else? Explain why you would use these methods you identified and justify the cost and time required to conduct each.

3. After you have identified your selection criteria and methods, do a "reality check" in a real organization. Interview a manager who employs someone in that job. For example, if the job you selected is salesperson, go to a local business to learn how it selects individuals for sales jobs. Compare what you thought would be a good selection approach to what you learned from the company you visited.

4. Identify the reasons for any discrepancies between your approach and theirs. Are the reasons justified and sound?

Visit the *Managing Human Resources* CourseMate website at www.belcourt7e.nelson.com for quizzes, flashcards, videos, games, and more!

## JOB CANDIDATE ASSESSMENT TESTS GO VIRTUAL

When it comes to preemployment tests, companies are not necessarily just handing candidates a pen and a pencil or having them answer multiple-choice questions via a computer or phone anymore. A small but growing number of assessments have gone virtual. The assessments, which are often conducted via the computer or the Web, simulate a job's functions. You can liken them to video games but within a work setting. Toyota, Starbucks, and the paint maker Sherwin-Williams have successfully used virtual job simulations to assess applicants. The national real estate firm Royal LePage placed a banner on its careers section inviting candidates to try a real estate simulation to determine whether real estate was the right career. Recruitment leads jumped 300 percent. CIBC's call centre also uses a simulation of the work of a call centre employee, allowing candidates to experience the work of a call centre employee while simultaneously having their skills assessed by CIBC recruiters.

At Toyota, applicants participating in simulations read dials and gauges, spot safety problems, and use their ability to solve problems; at the same time, their general ability to learn is assessed. The candidates can see and hear about the job they are applying for from current Toyota employees. National City Bank has used virtual assessments to test call centre candidates and branch manager candidates. Call centre candidates are given customer service problems to solve, and branch manager candidates go through a simulation that assesses their ability to foster relationships with clients and make personnel decisions.

Virtual assessment tools, which are produced by companies such as Shaker Group Consulting and Profiles International, do not come cheap. Although they can cost tens of thousands of dollars, larger companies that can afford them are saying they are worth it. The benefits are better-qualified candidates, faster recruiting, and lower turnover among employees hired. KeyBank says that by using virtual testing tools, it realized savings of more than $1.75 million per year due to lower turnover. Toyota began using computer-based assessments in the early 2000s, which have been so successful that the company has since introduced them to its other plants around the world.

Candidates also seem to like the assessments because they provide a more realistic job preview and make them feel as if they are being chosen for jobs based on more than just their personalities or how they performed during an interview. "It was a very insightful experience that made you think about what exactly you like and dislike in the workplace and if you really enjoy helping customers and have patience to do so," says one candidate tested for a customer service job.

HR experts warn that companies need to be sure they are not simply buying glitzy simulations that do not translate well to the jobs for which they are hiring. Also, the screening tools could potentially eliminate candidates who have trouble with simulations or computers but might make good employees. You should ask the vendor to provide evidence that these methods are reliable and valid.

### Questions

1. What do you think are the primary advantages and disadvantages of "virtual tryouts"?
2. Do you think there would be any employment equity concerns regarding this system?
3. Do you think virtual job tryouts might be better suited for some jobs than others? If so, which ones?

**Sources:** Karen Vilardo, "KeyBank's Success With the 'Virtual_Job_Tryout,'" *Journal of Corporate Recruiting Leadership* 5, no. 4 (May 2010): 24; Ira S. Wolfe, "Success Performance Solutions," *The Total View Newsletter* (May 12, 2010); Connie Winkle, "HR Technology: Job Tryouts Go Virtual," *HR Magazine* (September 1, 2006), http://www.shrm.org/; Gina Ruiz, "Job Candidate Assessment Tests Go Virtual," *Workforce Management Online* (January 2008), http://www.workforce.com; Shaker Consulting Group, "Clients and Case Studies," http://www.shakercg.com, retrieved March 27, 2011; Igor Kotlyar and Ravit Abelman, *Canadian HR Reporter* 16, no. 21 (December 1, 2003): G6.

## TESTS AT AN ELECTRONICS CORPORATION

An electronics plant in Midland, Ontario, has begun using tests as part of its selection process. Before new candidates will be considered for new job openings and for promotions, they must pass eight different tests. One test for manual dexterity requires applicants to move small metal pegs from holes on one side of a board to holes on the other side as fast as they can. In another test, employees are shown pictures of two cows—one white and the other spotted—and asked, "Which cow would be easier to see from an airplane?"

The company's employees see no relationship between their jobs and the cow test; they also find it humiliating to have to move pegs on a board in order to qualify for jobs they have been doing for years. In one testing session, 80 percent of employees failed. The price of failure is exclusion from higher paying and more desirable jobs. Even more shameful is the fact that people with less seniority and little plant experience are passing these tests.

The dispute is deeply rooted. The union feels that the tests are allowing management to replace experienced workers with new hires who work for less pay. The fact that test results are almost always confidential has led to suspicions that the results are being manipulated in some way. After seeing their colleagues fail the tests, some workers are so discouraged that they don't even try for new jobs or promotions. Other changes that have been introduced along with the tests include 12-hour rotating shifts, the "flexible" replacement of workers, and new computerized inspection systems.

Management defends the testing, claiming that new plants and new work methods require aptitudes such as problem solving and flexible thinking. These skills are not usually associated with the stereotype of the senior blue-collar worker. In the past, young people had no need to even graduate from high school if there was a plant in town offering big paycheques for manual labour. The tests that have been introduced discriminate against older workers with less formal education. In demand today are employees who can do many jobs, solve problems, make decisions, provide creative solutions, and function effectively as part of an empowered work team.

### Questions

1. Do you see any problems with the way the company's testing program is being managed? Discuss.
2. Suggest how the program might be modified.
3. The union is fighting to eliminate the testing. On what grounds could the union base its arguments?
4. If an employee files a complaint with the Ontario Human Rights Commission on the grounds that the test discriminated against him as an older worker, what kinds of information will have to be gathered to determine the validity of his claim?

**Source:** Reprinted by permission of the author, Megan Terepocki.

## SEARCHING FOR SPIES

The Canadian Security Intelligence Service (CSIS) is a civilian-run agency, formerly the Security Services of the RCMP. Its role is defensive: to protect Canada from terrorists and foreign spies. It does not send armed spies overseas. Curiously, for an extremely private organization, CSIS has been named a top employer three years in a row by Mediacorp Canada, a specialty publisher of employment-related periodicals.

Since the 9/11 attacks, CSIS has added about 500 new staff, and now new hires represent about 15 percent of its workforce. Selecting spies used to be a secret process. There was no public knowledge about how spies were recruited, what the job description was, and what the selection criteria and methods were.

Each year, CSIS receives 3,000 unsolicited applicants for about 100 openings. However, most of these applications are from unqualified James Bond "wannabes". CSIS wants highly qualified, well-educated, multilingual, multiskilled employees. It recruits openly, and its selection criteria and processes are public.

In 2008, CSIS recruited at 53 career fairs, 142 information sessions, and 18 special career events. However, in an effort to recruit more visible minorities, it also uses the Internet, business breakfasts, professional associations, and academic connections. If you want to apply, CSIS looks for Canadian citizens who are university graduates, preferably with advanced degrees. You must have a valid driver's licence and be able to relocate anywhere in Canada at any time. You will have lived or studied abroad, be proficient in English and French, and have a third or fourth language. CSIS looks for generalists: people who are knowledgeable about international and political issues and who have investigative and analytical skills. As a CSIS employee, you will not be able to discuss your work with outsiders at any time.

As an applicant, you must go through the following selection process:

- Submit a résumé
- Complete a 12-page application, which also involves writing a 500-word essay explaining why you want to become an intelligence officer
- Attend a group information session, where recruiters and intelligence officers answer questions
- Attend a suitability interview, where your motivation and verbal and people skills are judged
- Take a battery of psychological and aptitude tests
- Have your language skills tested
- Attend a national assessment panel—veterans will assess your motivation, knowledge of CSIS, and general awareness of public affairs
- Be submitted to security clearance procedures (including a polygraph test, fingerprints, lie detector test, credit check, criminal record check, and references back to teen years), which take three months and cost thousands of dollars
- Go to a final interview

This is a multiple-hurdle model of selection. As a candidate, you will have to pass each hurdle before being allowed to continue to the next. If successful, you will be on probation for five years, undergo 12 weeks of classroom training and language training, and spend two or three years at an operations desk at headquarters before being transferred to the field under the guidance of a mentor.

## Questions

1. Do you think the selection system used by CSIS is valid? Using your knowledge of validity, rate each step in this process.
2. One reason CSIS went public was to increase the representation of women from 10 percent to a target of 50 percent. Are there any possible problems with discrimination in this selection system? Discuss.

**Sources:** Adapted from J. Sallot, "The Spy Masters' Talent Hunt Goes Public," *The Globe and Mail*, June 22, 1999, A1, A10; "Wanna Be a Spy? Your Country Needs You," *The Province*, March 14, 2008, A.24; "Spies Like Us," *Canadian HR Reporter* 16, no. 10 (May 19, 2003): G2.

## NOTES AND REFERENCES

1. Misty L. Loughry, Matthew W. Ohland, and D. Dewayne Moore, "Development of a Theory-Based Assessment of Team Member Effectiveness," *Educational & Psychological Measurement* 67, no. 3 (June 2007): 505–524; Patrick D. Converse, Fredrick L. Oswald, Michael A. Gillespie, Kevin A. Field, and Elizabeth B. Bizot, "Matching Individual to Occupations Using Abilities and the O*NET," *Personnel Psychology* 57, no. 2 (Summer 2004): 451–488.

2. Mary-Kathryn Zachary, "Discrimination without Intent," *Supervision* 64, no. 5 (May 2003): 23–29; Neal Schmitt, William Rogers, David Chan, Lori Sheppard, and Danielle Jennings, "Adverse Impact and Predictive Efficiency of Various Predictor Combinations," *Journal of Applied Psychology* 82, no. 5 (October 1997): 719–730.

3. "Employers Discriminate against Applicants with Non-English Names," http://www.publicaffairs.ubc.ca/media/releases/2009/mr-09-056.html, retrieved March 26, 2012.

4. "Busted," *Training Development* 60, no. 12 (December 2006): 19; Pamela Babock, "Spotting Lies," *HR Magazine* 48, no. 10 (October 2003): 46–51; Tammy Prater and Sara Bliss Kiser, "Lies, Lies, and More Lies," *A.A.M. Advance Management Journal* 67, no. 2 (Spring 2002): 9–14.

5. Connie Walker, "Job Tryouts Go Virtual," *HR Magazine* 51, no. 9 (September 2006): 131–134; "The Pros and Cons of Online Recruiting," *HRfocus* 81 (April 2004): S1; Rob Drew, "Career Portals Boost Online Recruiting," *HR Magazine* 49, no. 4 (April 2004):

111–114; Samuel Greengard, "Smarter Screening Takes Technology and HR Savvy," *Workforce* 81, no. 6 (June 2002): 56–62.

6. Amy Maingault, John Sweeney, and Naomi Cossack, "Interviewing, Management Training, Strikes," *HR Magazine* 52, no. 6 (June 2007): 43; James Bassett, "Stop, Thief!" *Gifts & Decorative Accessories* 104, no. 1 (January 2003): 130–134; Richard A. Posthuma, Frederick Morgeson, and Michael Campion, "Beyond Employment Interview Validity: A Comprehensive Narrative Review of Recent Research and Trends over Time," *Personnel Psychology* 55, no. 1 (Spring 2002): 1–8.

7. Yen-Chun Chen, Wei-Chi Tsai, and Changya Hu, "The Influences of Interviewer-Related and Situational Factors on Interviewer Reactions to High Structured Job Interviews," *International Journal of Human Resource Management* 19, no. 6 (June 2008): 1056–1071. For an excellent review of research on the structured interview, see Michael A. Campion, David K. Palmer, and James E. Campion, "A Review of Structure in the Selection Interview," *Personnel Psychology* 50, no. 3 (Autumn 1997): 655–702. See also Karen vanderZee, Arnold Bakker, and Paulien Bakker, "Why Are Structured Interviews So Rarely Used in Personnel Selection?" *Journal of Applied Psychology* 87, no. 1 (February 2002): 176–184.

8. Jesus F. Salgado and Silvia Moscoso, "Comprehensive Meta-Analysis of the Construct Validity of the Employment Interview," *European Journal of Work and Organizational Psychology* 11, no. 3 (September 2002): 299–325.

9. Peter Herriot, "Assessment by Groups: Can Value Be Added?" *European Journal of Work & Organizational Psychology* 12, no. 2 (June 2003): 131–146; Jesus F. Salgado and Silvia Moscoso, "Comprehensive Meta-Analysis of the Construct Validity of the Employment Interview"; Amelia J. Prewett-Livingston, John G. Veres III, Hubert S. Field, and Philip M. Lewis, "Effects of Race on Interview Ratings in a Situational Panel Interview," *Journal of Applied Psychology* 81, no. 2 (April 1996): 178–186. See also Damodar Y. Golhar and Satish P. Deshpande, "HRM Practices of Large and Small Canadian Manufacturing Firms," *Journal of Small Business Management* 35, no. 3 (July 1997): 30–38.

10. Jack Welch and Suzy Welch, "Hiring Is Hard Work," *BusinessWeek Online*, no. 4091 (July 7, 2008); Michele V. Rafter, "Candidates for Jobs in High Places Sit for Tests That Size Up Their Mettle," *Workforce Management* 83, no. 5 (May 2004): 70–73; Patricia Buhler, "Computer Interview: Managing in the New Millennium," *Supervision* 63, no. 10 (October 2002): 20–23.

11. Victoria Reitz, "Interview without Leaving Home," *Machine Design* 76, no. 7 (April 1, 2004): 66; Jessica Clark Newman, Don Des Jarlais, Charles Turner, Jay Gribble, Phillip Cooley, and Denise Paone, "The Differential Effects of Face-to-Face and Computer Interview Modes," *American Journal of Public Health* 92, no. 2 (February 2002): 294; David Mitchell, "ijob.com Recruiting Online," *Strategic Finance* 80, no. 11 (May 1999): 48–51.

12. Dan Hanover, "Hiring Gets Cheaper and Faster," *Sales and Marketing Management* 152, no. 3 (March 2000): 87.

13. Kira Vermond, "References Done Right," *Profit* 26, no. 2 (May 2007): 101; Kathleen Samey, "A Not-So-Perfect Fit," *Adweek* 44, no. 47 (December 1, 2003): 34; Ann Fisher, "How Can We Be Sure We're Not Hiring a Bunch of Shady Liars?" *Fortune* 147, no. 10 (May 26, 2003).

14. Victor Catano, Willi Wiesner, Rick Hackett, and Laura Methot, *Recruitment and Selection in Canada*, 3rd ed. (Toronto: Thomson Nelson, 2005).

15. Todd Humber, "Recruitment Isn't Getting Any Easier," *Canadian HR Reporter*, May 23, 2005, R2, R3.

16. Doug Eisenschenk and Elaine Davis, "Background Checks in Hiring and Compensation: The Next Generation," *Benefits & Compensation Digest* 41, no. 10 (October 2004): 1–4; "What's New," *HR Magazine* 49, no. 4 (April 2004): 153–156; "Why You Should Update Your Background Checks," *HRfocus* (February 1, 2004): 12–13; Merry Mayer, "Background Checks in Focus," *HR Magazine* 47, no. 1 (January 2002): 59–62. In addition, organizations use other resources, such as the following: *The Guide to Background Investigations: A Comprehensive Source Directory for Employee Screening and Background Investigations*, 8th ed. (TISI, 2000).

17. Ely A. Leightling and Pamela M. Ploor, "When Applicants Apply through the Internet," *Employee Relations Law Journal* 30, no. 2 (Autumn 2004): 3–13; "EEOC Clarifies the Definition of Who Is an 'Applicant' in the Context of Internet Recruiting and Hiring," *Fair Employment Practices Guidelines*, no. 587 (April 1, 2004): 3–13; Kathryn Tyler, "Put Applicants' Skills to the Test," *HR Magazine* 45, no. 1 (January 2000): 74–80.

18. John Bret Becton, Hubert S. Feild, William F. Giles, and Allison Jones-Farmer, "Racial Differences in Promotion Candidate Performance and Reactions to Selection Procedures: A Field Study in a Diverse Top-Management Context," *Journal of Organizational Behavior* 29, no. 3 (April 2008): 265–285.

19. Rachel Suff, "Testing the Water: Using Work Sampling for Selection," *IRS Employment Review*, no. 802 (June 18, 2004): 44–49; Leonard D. Goodstein and Alan D. Davidson, "Hiring the Right Stuff: Using Competency-Based Selection," *Compensation & Benefits Management* 14, no. 3 (Summer 1998): 1–10.

20. Noelle Murphy, "Testing the Waters: Employers' Use of Selection Assessments," *IRS Employment Review* 852 (August 4, 2006): 42–48; Florence Berger and Ajay Ghei, "Employment Tests: A Facet of Hospitality Hiring," *Cornell Hotel and Restaurant Administration Quarterly* 36, no. 6 (December 1995): 28–31; Malcolm James Ree, Thomas R. Carretta, and Mark S. Teachout, "Role of Ability and Prior Job Knowledge in Complex Training Performance," *Journal of Applied Psychology* 80, no. 6 (December 1995): 721–730.

21. Igor Kotlyar and Ravit Ableman, "Simulation Turns Recruitment into a Two-Way Street," *Canadian HR Reporter* (December 1, 2003): G6.

22. Justin Menkes, "Interviewing for Executive Intelligence," *HR Professional* 25, no. 3 (April–May 2008): 54; Chris Piotrowski and Terry Armstrong," Current Recruitment and Selection Practices: A National Survey of Fortune 1000 Firms," *North American Journal of Psychology* 8, no. 3 (2006): 489–496; Sara Rynes, Amy Colbert, and Kenneth Brown, "HR Professionals' Beliefs about Effective Human Resource Practices: Correspondence between Research and Practice," *Human Resource Management* 41, no. 2 (Summer 2002): 149–174.

23. Kris Frieswick, "Casting to Type," *CFO* 20, no. 9 (July 2004): 71–73; Timothy Judge and Joyce Bono, "Five-Factor Model of Personality and Transformational Leadership," *Journal of Applied Psychology* 85, no. 5 (October 2000): 751–765; J. Michael Crant and Thomas S. Bateman, "Charismatic Leadership Viewed from Above: The Impact of Proactive Personality," *Journal of Organizational Behavior* 21, no. 1 (February 2000): 63–75.

24. Frederick P. Morgeson, Michael A. Campion, Robert L. Dipboye, John R. Hollenbeck, Kevin Murphy, and Neal Schmitt, "Reconsidering the Use of Personality Tests in Personnel Selection Contexts," *Personnel Psychology* 60, no. 3 (Autumn 2007): 683–729; Arielle Emmett, "Snake Oil or Science? The Raging Debate on Personality Testing," *Workforce Management* 83, no. 10 (October 2004): 90–93; Gregory Hurtz and John Donovan, "Personality and Job Performance: The Big Five Revisited," *Journal of Applied Psychology* 85, no. 6 (December 2000): 869–879.

25. George B. Yancey, "The Predictive Power of Hiring Tools," *Credit Union Executive Journal* 40, no. 4 (July–August 2000): 12–18; Jeffrey A. Mello, "Personality Tests and Privacy Rights," *HRfocus* 73, no. 3 (March 1996): 22–23.

26. Constance L. Hays, "Tests Are Becoming Common in Hiring," *The New York Times,* November 28, 1997, D1. See also Gregory M. Lousig-Nont, "Avoid Common Hiring Mistakes with Honesty Tests," *Nation's Restaurant News* 31, no. 11 (March 17, 1997): 30; "If the Shoe Fits," *Security Management* 40, no. 2 (February 1996): 11; Michelle Cottle, "Job Testing: Multiple Choices," *The New York Times*, September 5, 1999, 10.

27. Thomas J. Ryan, "Nerves of Steal," *SGB* 37, no. 6 (June 2004): 8–10; D. S. Ones, C. Viswesvaran, and F. L. Schmidt, "Comprehensive Meta-Analysis of Integrity Test Validities: Findings and Implications for Personnel Selection and Theories of Job Performance," *Journal of Applied Psychology* 78 (August 1993): 679–703. See also Deniz S. Ones and Chockalingam Viswesvaran, "Gender, Age and Race Differences on Overt Integrity Tests: Results across Four Large-Scale Job Applicant Data Sets," *Journal of Applied Psychology* 83, no. 1 (February 1998): 35–42.

28. James Krohe, Jr., "Are Workplace Tests Worth Taking?" *Across the Board* 43, no. 4 (July–August 2006): 16–23; "Honesty Tests Flawed," *People Management* 3, no. 2 (January 23, 1997): 15; Hays, "Tests Are Becoming Common in Hiring"; Stephen A. Dwight and George M. Alliger, "Reactions to Overt Integrity Test Items," *Educational and Psychological Measurement* 57, no. 6 (December 1997): 937–948.

29. Walter C. Borman, Mary Ann Hanson, and Jerry W. Hedge, "Personnel Selection," *Annual Review of Psychology* 48 (1997): 299–337; Charles Sproule and Stephen Berkley, "The Selection of Entry-Level Corrections Officers: Pennsylvania Research," *Public Personnel Management* 30, no. 3 (Fall 2001): 377–418.

30. British Columbia (Public Service Employee Relations Commission) v. BCGSEU, [1999] 3 S.C.R. 3; "Using the Global to Support the Local," http://csc.lexum .umontreal.ca/en/1999/1999rcs3-3/1999rcs3-3.html, retrieved July 30, 2009.

31. M. Brewster, "RCMP Ease Fitness Rules for Women," *The Globe and Mail*, July 14, 1997, A4.

32. Philip Bobko, Philip L. Roth, and Maury A. Buster, "The Usefulness of Unit Weights in Creating Composite Scores: A Literature Review, Application to Content Validity, and Meta-Analysis," *Organizational Research Methods* 10, no. 4 (October 2007): 689–709; Kobi Dayan, Ronen Kasten, and Shaul Fox, "Entry-Level Police Candidate Assessment Center: An Efficient Tool or a Hammer to Kill a Fly?" *Personnel Psychology* 55, no. 4 (Winter 2002): 827–849.

33. Deniz S. Ones, Chockalingam Viswesvaran, and Frank L Schmidt, "No New Terrain: Reliability and Construct Validity of Job Performance Ratings," *Industrial & Organizational Psychology* 1, no. 2 (June 2008): 174–179; D. Brent Smith and Lill Ellingson, "Substance versus Style: A New Look at Social Desirability in Motivating Contexts," *Journal of Applied Psychology* 87, no. 2 (April 2002): 211–219; Ken Craik, Aaron Ware, John Kamp, Charles O'Reilly III, Barry Staw, and Sheldon Zedeck, "Explorations of Construct Validity in a Combined Managerial and Personality

Assessment Programme," *Journal of Occupational and Organizational Psychology* 75, no. 2 (June 2002): 171–193.

34. Multiple regression is a statistical method for evaluating the magnitude of effects of more than one independent variable (e.g., selection predictors) on a dependent variable (e.g., job performance) using principles of correlation and regression.

35. Patricia M. Buhler, "Managing in the New Millennium," *Supervision* 68, no. 11 (November 2007): 17–20; David E. Bowen and Cheri Ostroff, "Understanding HRM—Firm Performance Linkages: The Role of the Strengths of the HRM System," *Academy of Management Review* 29, no. 2 (April 2004): 203–222; Ann Marie Ryan, Joshua Sacco, Lynn McFarland, and David Kriska, "Applicant Self-Selection: Correlates of Withdrawal from a Multiple Hurdle Process," *Journal of Applied Psychology* 85, no. 2 (April 2000): 163–179.

Answers to Figure 6.5: 3, 3, 4

PART 3

CHAPTER

# 7

# Training and Development

# After studying this chapter, you should be able to

| OUTCOME 1 | Discuss the strategic approach to training and development. |
| OUTCOME 2 | Describe the components of training needs assessment. |
| OUTCOME 3 | Identify the principles of learning and describe how they facilitate training. |
| OUTCOME 4 | Identify the types of training methods used for managers and nonmanagers. |
| OUTCOME 5 | Discuss the advantages and disadvantages of various evaluation criteria. |
| OUTCOME 6 | Describe additional training programs. |

Workplace training used to be rather boxlike. It focused on teaching employees to do particular activities, such as operate machines and process work. However, as the workplace has shifted from "touch labour" to "knowledge workers" (see Chapter 1), the focus of training has shifted as well. Companies are realizing that workers need not only operational know-how but also superior job expertise; knowledge about competitive, industry, and technological trends; and the ability to continually learn and utilize new information. These characteristics help an organization adapt and innovate to compete far more effectively in today's fast-paced global business world. Because training plays a central role in nurturing, strengthening, and expanding the capabilities of a firm in this way, it has become part of the backbone of strategic management.

**Using the Internet**

The Canadian Society for Training and Development is the professional association for those working in training and development in Canada:

**http://www.cstd.ca**

## THE SCOPE OF TRAINING

Many new employees come equipped with most of the knowledge, skills, abilities, and other factors (KSAOs) needed to start work. Others require extensive training before they are ready to make much of a contribution to the organization.

The term *training* is often used casually to describe almost any effort initiated by an organization to foster learning among its members. However, many experts distinguish between training, which tends to be more narrowly focused and oriented toward short-term performance concerns, and *development*, which, as you learned in Chapter 5, tends to be oriented more toward broadening an individual's skills for future responsibilities. The two terms tend to be combined into a single phrase, *training and development*, to recognize the combination of activities organizations use to increase the skill base of employees.

### INVESTMENTS IN TRAINING

Research shows that an organization's revenues and overall profitability are positively correlated to the amount of training it gives its employees. Here are some interesting training statistics from the Conference Board of Canada's *Learning and Development Outlook 2011*:

- Canadian businesses spend about $688 per employee on training.
- The average number of hours per employee in training is 25.
- Training of managers is done by 90 percent of organizations surveyed.[1]

Each employee of the Ritz–Carlton hotel chain, for example, receives nearly 200 hours of training each year. The types of training being offered by Canadian organizations are outlined in Figure 7.1. In addition to the billions of dollars

### FIGURE 7.1

COURSE CONTENT BEING OFFERED BY ORGANIZATIONS, 2010

| Content Area | Percentage of Overall Content | Percentage of Organizations Offering |
| --- | --- | --- |
| Management/supervisory skills training | 15 | 91 |
| Professional and technical training | 13 | 67 |
| Occupational health and safety/compliance | 11 | 80 |
| New employee orientation | 10 | 85 |
| Interpersonal skills | 9 | 77 |
| Product knowledge | 8 | 51 |
| Executive development | 7 | 69 |
| Information technology skills | 7 | 68 |
| Customer relations and/or service | 7 | 65 |
| Sales (excluding product knowledge) | 5 | 41 |
| Quality competition and business practices | 5 | 59 |
| Other | 2 | 6 |
| Basic skills training (literacy/numeracy) | 1 | 20 |

**Source**: C. Lavas, Learning and Development Outlook 2011, The Conference Board of Canada.

# ETHICS IN HRM

## Mandatory or Voluntary?

There is only one payroll training tax in North America. The Quebec government program that forces employers to spend 1 percent of payroll on training may not have the intended consequences of increasing training investments in employees. Using data from a Statistics Canada survey, Alan Saks of the University of Toronto and Robert Haccoun of the Université de Montréal matched Quebec employers with Ontario employers and found that there were no differences in amounts spent on training. The paperwork is so cumbersome that many employers prefer to pay the 1 percent tax rather than go through the thick guidebooks necessary to report the training.

If little effect is gained by forcing employers to provide training, are there benefits by forcing employees to attend training? The answer is not clear: some studies report some slight benefits in outcomes (such as improved job performance) when employees voluntarily attend courses; other studies see no differences.

There may be more serious problems than performance results created by forcing employees to attend courses. Half of the 24 employees of SaskTel who participated in a training program on process reengineering required psychological counselling, stress leave, or both in its aftermath. Trainees said they were subjected to a greenhouse environment: windows were papered over, employees were not allowed to communicate with one another, and all were subjected to verbal abuse from the training consultants. As the president of the Ontario Society for Training and Development commented, "That's not training, that's assault."

Seagulls Pewter and Silversmiths of Pugwash, Nova Scotia, sent its employees to seminars based on the controversial EST (Erhard Seminars Training) therapy. Employees complained to their union that the seminars, in which participants were encouraged to delve into painful emotions, often drove participants to breakdowns. In another example, a large insurance company hired a consultant to conduct management training for hundreds of supervisors and managers. The company did not realize that the consultant was a member of L. Ron Hubbard's Church of Scientology and was teaching management principles developed by scientologists. Critics contend that scientology is a cult, not a religion. Employees resented being subjected to psychological concepts based on "tones" that catalogue emotions, to the ruthless devotion to ferreting out and firing problem employees, and to "religious scriptures."

The employees in these organizations were required to participate in programs that caused them undue stress and sometimes violated their moral or religious beliefs. Those who organized the programs believed that employees with the "right" attitudes would be more effective.

Sources: K. Harding, "A Taxing Way to Train Staff," *The Globe and Mail*, June 4, 2003, C1; D. Brown, "Legislated Training, Questionable Results," *Canadian HR Reporter* 15, no. 9 (May 6, 2002): 1; A. Thomlinson, "Mandatory or Voluntary?" *Canadian HR Reporter* 15, no. 6 (March 25, 2002): 1; Edward Kay, "Trauma in Real Life," *The Globe and Mail Report on Business Magazine*, November 1996, 82–92; J. Saunders, "How Scientology's Message Came to Allstate," *The Globe and Mail*, April 24, 1995, B1; R. Sharpe, "Agents of Intimidation," *The Globe and Mail*, March 28, 1995, B8.

spent by businesses each year on formal training, nearly four times that amount is spent on informal instruction. The types of training given employees range from simple, on-the-job instruction to sophisticated skills training conducted on multimillion-dollar simulators.[2]

Ethics in HRM presents the debate about the effectiveness of mandatory training for employees.

## A STRATEGIC APPROACH TO TRAINING

From the broadest perspective, the goal of training is to contribute to the organization's overall goals. Training programs should be developed with this in mind. Managers should keep a close eye on their firms' goals and strategies and orient

**OUTCOME 1**

## FIGURE 7.2

### TOP THREE STRATEGIC LEARNING GOALS

(percent, n = 102*)

| Strategic Goal | 1st | 2nd | 3rd | Total |
|---|---|---|---|---|
| Improve organizational performance | 31% | 16% | 8% | 54% |
| Develop organizational leaders | 18 | 18 | 16 | 51 |
| Align learning and business objectives | 22 | 13 | 14 | 49 |
| Improve individual (employee) performance | 7 | 17 | 18 | 41 |
| Enable employees to obtain/maintain competencies and certifications | 2 | 10 | 13 | 24 |
| Comply with industry and other regulatory training environments | 12 | 6 | 5 | 22 |
| Knowledge management/transfer | 2 | 9 | 8 | 18 |
| Increase the use of information technologies for learning | 1 | 6 | 9 | 16 |
| Keep pace with rapid organizational and technological change | 3 | 1 | 7 | 11 |
| Increase in-house content development | 2 | 2 | 2 | 6 |
| Reduce learning and development costs | 1 | 2 | 2 | 5 |
| Maximize reuse of internal learning content | 0 | 2 | 1 | 3 |

*Organizations reporting strategic goals for learning.

**Note:** Respondents were provided with a list of 12 possible choices and asked to select their top three goals in order.

**Source:** C. Lavis, Training and Development Outlook, 2011, The Conference Board of Canada.

their training accordingly. For example, is it the firm's goal to develop new product lines? If so, how should this goal affect its training initiatives? Is the firm trying to lower its costs of production so it can utilize a low-cost strategy to capture new business? If so, are there training initiatives that can be undertaken to deliver on this strategy? Figure 7.2 outlines the top strategic learning goals. The most important goal is to improve organizational performance, followed by the development of leaders and aligning business and learning objectives.

Unfortunately, many organizations never make the connection between the two. Instead, fads, fashions, or "whatever the competition is doing" can sometimes be the main drivers of an organization's training agenda. As a result, training programs are often misdirected, poorly designed, and inadequately evaluated—not to mention a waste of money. First, not all of a firm's strategic initiatives can be accomplished with training. Second, not all training programs—no matter how widely they are adopted by other organizations—will be a strategic imperative for a firm.

To ensure that a firm's training and development investment has the maximum impact possible, a strategic approach should be used that involves four phases: (1) needs assessment, (2) program design, (3) implementation, and (4) evaluation. A model that is useful to designers of training programs is presented in Figure 7.3. We will use this model as a framework for organizing the material throughout this chapter.

FIGURE 7.3

STRATEGIC MODEL OF TRAINING

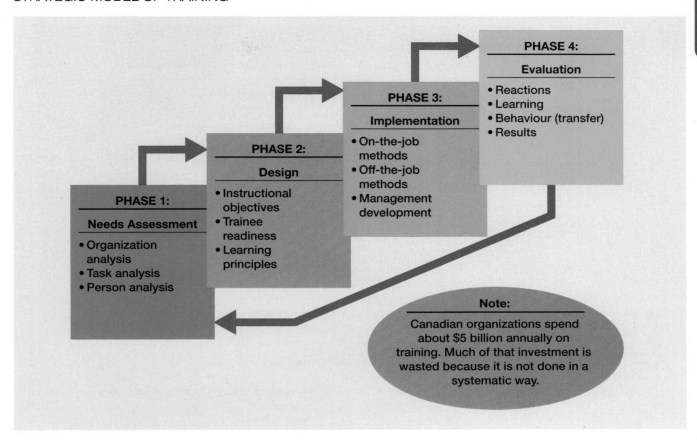

# PHASE 1: CONDUCTING THE NEEDS ASSESSMENT

Because business conditions change rapidly, as does technology, keeping abreast of the types of training a firm's employees need to remain competitive can be a challenge. If employees consistently fail to achieve their productivity objectives, this might be a signal that training is needed. Likewise, if organizations receive an excessive number of customer complaints, this, too, might suggest that a firm's training is inadequate. About 30 percent of larger firms, including GE, Walmart, and IBM, have what are called **chief learning officers**. These people are top executives within their firms who are responsible for making certain that a company's training is timely and focused on the firm's top strategic issues. However, regardless of who does the needs assessment within an organization, it should be conducted systematically by utilizing the three different types of analysis shown in Figure 7.4: organization analysis, task analysis, and person analysis. Each of these will be discussed.

Unfortunately, because of the costs, expertise, and time required, a study by the American Society for Training and Development found that organizations conduct needs assessment less than 50 percent of the time. Ironically, as the speed of change increases and time and resources are at a premium, the need for good needs assessment increases. In these cases, the process need not be so daunting and laborious. Highlights in HRM 7.1 provides some tips for rapidly assessing training needs.[3]

## ORGANIZATION ANALYSIS

The first step in a needs assessment is identifying the broad forces that can influence a firm's training needs. An **organization analysis** is an examination of the

---

**OUTCOME 2**

**chief learning officer**
A high-ranking manager directly responsible for fostering employee learning and development within the organization

**organization analysis**
Examination of the environment, strategies, and resources of the organization to determine where training emphasis should be placed

---

## FIGURE 7.4

NEEDS ASSESSMENT FOR TRAINING

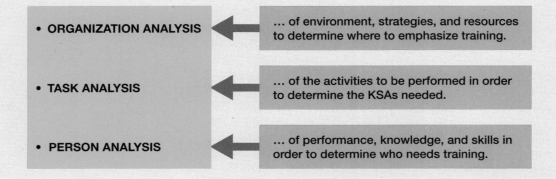

- **ORGANIZATION ANALYSIS** ← ... of environment, strategies, and resources to determine where to emphasize training.

- **TASK ANALYSIS** ← ... of the activities to be performed in order to determine the KSAs needed.

- **PERSON ANALYSIS** ← ... of performance, knowledge, and skills in order to determine who needs training.

# HIGHLIGHTS IN HRM 7.1

## Notes on Rapid Needs Assessment

**NOTE 1: Look at the problem scope.** Common sense suggests that small, local matters may require less information gathering than big problems with a major impact on the organization. Ask managers a series of questions about the nature of the problem and its impact on the organization and gear your analysis accordingly.

**NOTE 2: Do organizational scanning.** Stay connected with what is going on in the organization in order to anticipate upcoming training needs. If a new technology is about to be launched, the need for training should take no one by surprise. In short, needs assessment isn't an event with a start-and-stop switch. It is the process of being engaged in your business.

**NOTE 3: Play "give and take."** Get the information you need, but don't drag your feet with excessive analysis before reporting back to managers. Show them that you are sensitive to their need for action by giving them updates on the information you have collected. If necessary, explain that better value may be gained by further analysis.

**NOTE 4: Check "lost and found."** Often, information gathered for a different purpose may bear on your training issue. Performance data (such as errors, sales, and customer complaints) and staffing data (such as proficiency

testing, turnover, and absenteeism) can be very helpful as a starting point.

**NOTE 5: Use plain talk.** Instead of using clinical terms such as analysis or assessment, use straight talk with managers that tells them what you are doing: (1) identify the problem, (2) identify alternative ways to get there, (3) implement a solution based on cost/benefit concerns, and (4) determine the effectiveness and efficiency of the solution.

**NOTE 6: Use the Web.** Information technology allows you to communicate with others, perhaps by setting up an electronic mailing list to post questions, synthesize responses, share resources, get feedback, gather information on trends, and the like.

**NOTE 7: Use rapid prototyping.** Often the most effective and efficient training is that which is "just-in-time, just enough, and just for me." Create a rapid prototype of a training program, evaluating and revising as you implement, and learn more about the problems.

**NOTE 8: Seek out exemplars.** Find those in the organization that currently demonstrate the performance the organization wants. Bring others together with them to talk about the performance issues, and let the exemplars share their experiences and insights. This avoids the risk of packaging the wrong information, and people learn just what they need to know from each other.

Source: Condensed from Ron Zemke, "How to Do a Needs Assessment When You Think You Don't Have Time," *Training* 35, no. 3 (March 1998): 38–44. Reprinted with permission from the March 1998 issue of *Training Magazine*. Copyright 1998. Bill Communications, Inc., Minneapolis, MN. All Rights Reserved. Not for resale.

environment, strategies, and resources the firm faces so as to determine what training it should emphasize. As we have explained, a firm's training should revolve around the strategic initiatives of the organization. Mergers and acquisitions, for example, frequently require that employees take on new roles and responsibilities and adjust to new cultures and ways of conducting business. Nowhere is this more prevalent than in grooming new leaders within organizations. Other issues, such as technological change, globalization, and quality improvements, influence the way work is done and the types of skills needed to do it. Still other concerns may be more tactical but no less important in terms of their impact on training. If an organization is restructuring, downsizing, or undertaking new employee empowerment or teamwork initiatives, these efforts will impact the firm's training requirements.

Economic and public policy issues influence corporate training needs as well. For example, since the September 11, 2001, terrorist attacks, the training of airport security personnel has increased substantially. It has also increased for flight crews of airlines, employees in the transportation industry, workers in nuclear power plants, and even security staff at theme parks.[4]

Conducting an organization analysis also involves closely examining a firm's resources—technological, financial, and human—available to meet the company's training objectives. HR personnel typically collect data such as information on their companies' direct and indirect labour costs, quality of goods or services, absenteeism, turnover, and number of accidents. The availability of potential replacements and the time required to train them are other important factors in organization analysis.

To cope with budget constraints yet continue to meet their strategic imperatives, firms have become more focused on efficiently using their training budgets. Companies such as Motorola and Merck have found that by using information technology wisely, they cut their training budget by as much as 30 to 50 percent. To "do more with less," managers have to plan carefully where they will spend their training dollars, and this means doing a rigorous organization analysis. Other companies outsource their training programs, or at least part of it, to external partners to cut costs. Other companies purchase "off-the-shelf" course materials developed by training companies rather than develop their own. A new trend is for companies to partner with other firms in their supply chains to jointly train their employees more cost-effectively.[5]

## TASK ANALYSIS

The second step in training needs assessment is task analysis. **Task analysis** involves reviewing the job description and specifications to identify the activities performed in a particular job and the KSAOs needed to perform them. The first step in task analysis is to list all the tasks or duties included in the job. The second step is to list the steps performed by the employee to complete each task. Once the job is understood thoroughly, the type of performance required (such as speech, recall, discrimination, and manipulation), along with the skills and knowledge necessary to do it, can be defined. For example, in the task of taking a chest x-ray, a radiologist correctly positions the patient (manipulation), gives special instructions (speech), and checks the proper distance of the x-ray tube from the patient (discrimination). The types of skills and knowledge that trainees need can be determined by observing and questioning skilled jobholders and/or by reviewing job descriptions. This information helps trainers select program content and choose the most effective training methods.

Instead of focusing on a fixed sequence of tasks, firms are finding that their employees need more flexible sets of competencies to perform in a superior way. Companies have found that as jobs begin to involve more teamwork, employees need to be flexible and adjust their behaviour as needed. **Competency assessment** focuses on the sets of skills and knowledge employees need to be

**task analysis**
The process of determining what the content of a training program should be on the basis of a study of the tasks and duties involved in the job

**competency assessment**
Analysis of the sets of skills and knowledge needed for decision-oriented and knowledge-intensive jobs

PART 3

As older workers near retirement, younger workers must be trained in the skills and knowledge needed to take their place. The availability of potential replacements and the time required to train them are two factors that must be considered in organization analysis.

successful, particularly for decision-oriented and knowledge-intensive jobs. But competency assessment goes beyond simply describing the traits an employee must have to successfully perform the work. It also captures elements of how those traits, which might include an employee's motivation levels, personality traits, and interpersonal skills, should be used within an organization's context and culture. GE, for example, uses a formal competency assessment program based on 45 different employee behaviours. Although training programs based on a work-oriented task analysis can become dated as jobs change, training programs based on competency assessment are more flexible and perhaps have more durability. The practice has been adopted extensively in the health care industry.[6] Highlights in HRM 7.2 shows an example of a partial competency assessment tool used for evaluating a manager.

# HIGHLIGHTS IN HRM 7.2

## A Competency Assessment for a Managerial Position

For each item, circle the number that best describes the manager's characteristics. For items that do not apply, circle **NA** (not applicable). For other items for which you lack sufficient observations or documentary evidence, circle **DK** (don't know).

4—Exemplary

3—Proficient

2—Progressing

1—Needs Assistance

NA—Not Applicable

DK—Don't Know

Competency 1: Behaves professionally and encourages other staff members to do likewise

4   3   2   1   NA   DK

Evidence _____

_____

_____

_____

_____

Competency 2: Behaves ethically and encourages staff members to do likewise

4   3   2   1   NA   DK

Evidence _____

_____

_____

_____

_____

Competency 3: Uses a variety of modes of communication and conveys information fully and clearly

4   3   2   1   NA   DK

Evidence _____

_____

_____

_____

_____

Competency 4: Seeks input from all levels and demonstrates fairness and consistency

4   3   2   1   NA   DK

Evidence _____

_____

_____

_____

_____

Competency 5: Engages in an open style of management and is open to criticism from supervisors and subordinates

4   3   2   1   NA   DK

Evidence _____

_____

_____

_____

_____

Competency 6: Searches for and embraces innovative solutions to improve department's programs and products

4   3   2   1   NA   DK

Evidence _____

_____

_____

_____

_____

## PERSON ANALYSIS

Along with organization and task analyses, it is necessary to perform a person analysis. A **person analysis** involves determining which employees require training and, equally important, which do not. In this regard, conducting a person analysis is important for several reasons. First, a thorough analysis helps organizations avoid the mistake of sending all employees into training when some do not need it. In addition, a person analysis helps managers determine what prospective trainees are able to do when they enter training so that the programs can be designed to emphasize the areas in which they are deficient.

**person analysis**
Determination of the specific individuals who need training

**CHAPTER 7:** TRAINING AND DEVELOPMENT

**instructional objectives**
Desired outcomes of a training program

Companies such as Hewlett-Packard (HP) have used performance appraisal information as an input for person analysis. Although performance appraisals might reveal which employees are not meeting the firm's expectations, they typically do not reveal why. If the performance deficiencies are due to ability problems, training is likely to be a good solution. However, if the performance deficiencies are due to poor motivation or factors outside an employee's control, training might not be the answer. Ultimately, managers have to sit down with employees to talk about areas for improvement so that they can jointly determine the developmental approaches that will have maximum benefit.[7]

# PHASE 2: DESIGNING THE TRAINING PROGRAM

Once the training needs have been determined, the next step is to design the type of learning environment necessary to enhance learning. Experts believe that the design of training programs should focus on at least four related issues: (1) the training's instructional objectives, (2) the "readiness" of trainees and their motivation, (3) principles of learning, and (4) the characteristics of instructors. Next, we discuss each.

## INSTRUCTIONAL OBJECTIVES

After conducting organization, task, and person analyses, managers should have a more complete picture of their firms' training needs. On the basis of this information, they can more formally state the desired outcomes of training through written instructional objectives. Generally, **instructional objectives** describe the skills or knowledge to be acquired and/or the attitudes to be changed. One type of instructional objective, the performance-centred objective, is widely used because it lends itself to an unbiased evaluation of the results. For example, the stated objective for one training program might be that "employees trained in team methods will be able to perform the different jobs of their team members within six months." Performance-centred objectives typically include precise terms, such as "to calculate," "to repair," "to adjust," "to construct," "to assemble," and "to classify."[8]

## TRAINEE READINESS AND MOTIVATION

Two preconditions for learning affect the success of those who are to receive training: readiness and motivation. *Trainee readiness* refers to whether or not the experience of trainees has made them receptive to the training that they will receive. Prospective trainees should be screened to ensure that they have the background knowledge and the skills necessary to absorb what will be presented to them. Recognizing the individual differences of trainees in terms of their readiness is as important in organizational training as it is in any other teaching situation. Consequently, it is often desirable to group individuals according to their capacity to learn, as determined by test scores or other assessment information, and to provide alternative types of instruction for those who need it.

The receptiveness and readiness of participants in training programs can be increased by having them complete questionnaires about why they are attending training and what they hope to accomplish as a result. Participants can also be asked to give copies of their completed questionnaires to their managers.

The other precondition for learning is *trainee motivation*. The organization needs to help employees understand the link between the effort they put into training and the payoff. Why is the training important? What will happen if it does not occur? Moreover, what is in it for the individual employee? By focusing on the trainees themselves, managers can create a training environment that is conducive to learning. Although most employees are motivated by certain common needs, they differ from one another in the relative importance of these needs at any given time. For example, new college or university graduates often have a high desire for advancement and have established specific goals for career progression. The training objectives should therefore be clearly related to trainees' individual needs to succeed.[9] Allowing employees to undergo training in areas that they want to pursue rather than merely assigning them certain training activities can also be very motivating—so can enlisting employees to train other employees with the information they learn. Who in an organization does not want to be called on for their expertise?

## PRINCIPLES OF LEARNING

OUTCOME 3

As we move from assessing an organization's needs and instructional objectives to employee readiness and motivation, we obviously shift our focus from the organization to employees. Ultimately, however, training has to build a bridge between employees and the organization. One important step in this transition involves giving full consideration to the psychological principles of learning— that is, the characteristics of training programs that help employees grasp new material, make sense of it in their own lives, and transfer it back to their jobs. All things considered, training programs are likely to be more effective if they incorporate the principles of learning shown in Figure 7.5.

### Goal Setting

The value of goal setting for focusing and motivating behaviour extends into training. When trainers take the time to explain the training's goals and objectives to trainees—or when trainees are encouraged to set goals on their own—the level of interest, understanding, and effort directed toward the training is likely to increase. In some cases, goal setting can simply take the form of a "road map" of the course/program, its objectives, and its learning points.[10]

## FIGURE 7.5

PRINCIPLES OF LEARNING

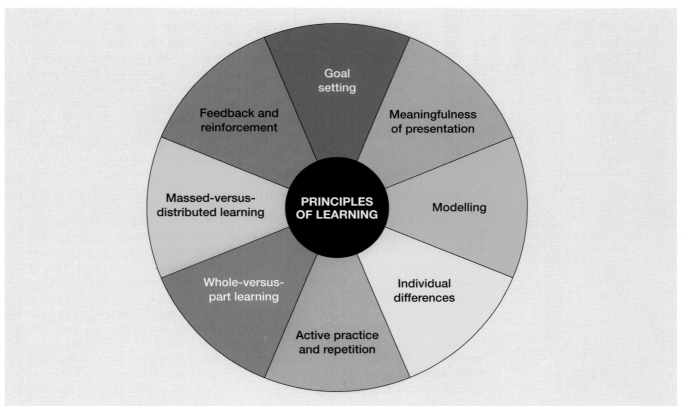

**CHAPTER 7:** TRAINING AND DEVELOPMENT

## Meaningfulness of Presentation

One principle of learning is that the material to be learned should be presented in as meaningful a manner as possible. Quite simply, trainees will be better able to learn new information if they can connect it with things that are already familiar to them. This is the reason why trainers frequently use colourful examples to which trainees can relate. The examples make the material meaningful. In addition, material should be arranged so that each experience builds on preceding ones. In this way, trainees are able to integrate the experiences into a usable pattern of knowledge and skills.

## Modelling

The old saying "a picture is worth a thousand words" applies to training. Just as examples increase the meaningfulness of factual material or new knowledge in a training environment, modelling increases the salience of behavioural training. Quite simply, we learn by watching. For example, if you were learning to ride a horse, it would be much easier to watch someone do it—and then try it yourself—than to read a book or listen to a lecture and hope you can do it right.[11]

Modelling can take many forms. Real-life demonstrations and demonstrations on DVDs are often helpful; even pictures and drawings can get the visual message across. The point is that modelling demonstrates the desired behaviour or method to be learned. In some cases, modelling the wrong behaviour can be helpful even if it shows trainees what not to do and then clarifies the appropriate behaviour.

## Individual Differences

People learn at different rates and in different ways. Visual learners absorb information best through pictures, diagrams, and demonstrations. Verbal learners absorb information best through spoken or written words. Similarly, some students who do horribly in large lecture settings will excel in small discussion classes. Trainers can help accommodate different learning styles in a variety of ways. The key is to avoid delivering the material in only one way. So, for example, instead of delivering a monologue, trainers should incorporate variety into their presentations. They should use visualize aids, encourage the participation of learners by including them in demonstrations, and ask them questions about their own experiences. Hands-on activities and breaking large groups into smaller groups for specific activities can also help trainers accommodate different learning styles. To the extent possible, training programs should try to account for and accommodate these individual differences to facilitate each person's style and rate of learning.[12]

## Active Practice and Repetition

Those things we do daily become part of our repertoire of skills. Trainees should be given frequent opportunities to practise their job tasks in the way that they will ultimately be expected to perform them. The individual who is being taught how to operate a machine should have an opportunity to practise on it. The manager who is being taught how to train should be given supervised practice in training.

In some cases, the value of practice is that it causes behaviours to become second nature. For example, when you first learned to drive a car, you focused a great deal on the mechanics: "Where are my hands, where are my feet, and how fast am I going?" As you practised driving, you began to think less about the mechanics and more about the road, the weather, and the traffic. Other forms of learning are no different—by practising, a trainee can forget about distinct behaviours and concentrate on the subtleties of how they are used.

## Whole-versus-Part Learning

Most jobs and tasks can be broken down into parts that lend themselves to further analysis. Determining the most effective manner for completing each part then provides a basis for giving specific instruction. Learning to sell a product, for example, is made up of several skills that are part of the total process. Although the process sounds daunting, it can essentially be broken down into a few discrete steps: finding customer opportunities; eliciting a prospective customer's needs by learning the proper questions to ask him or her; presenting the firm's product in a way that meets those needs; and, finally, learning how and when to ask the customer to buy the product (closing the deal). In evaluating whole-versus-part learning, it is necessary to consider the nature of the task to be learned. If the task can be broken down successfully, it probably should be broken down to facilitate learning; otherwise, it should probably be taught as a unit.

## Massed-versus-Distributed Learning

Another factor that determines the effectiveness of training is the amount of time devoted to practice in one session. Should trainees be given training in 5 two-hour periods or in 10 one-hour periods? It has been found in most cases that spacing out the training will result in faster learning and longer retention. This is the principle of distributed learning.

## Feedback and Reinforcement

Can any learning occur without feedback? Some feedback comes from trainees themselves via self-monitoring, whereas other feedback comes from trainers and fellow trainees. Feedback can help individuals focus on what they are doing right and what they are doing wrong. Think about when you first learned how to throw a baseball, ride a bicycle, or swim. Someone, perhaps a parent, told you what you were doing right and what things to correct. As you corrected those things, you likely got better.

In addition to providing participants with information about their performance, feedback also plays an important motivational role. For example, a person's training progress, measured in terms of either mistakes or successes, can be plotted on a chart commonly referred to as a "learning curve." Figure 7.6

**FIGURE 7.6**

A TYPICAL LEARNING CURVE

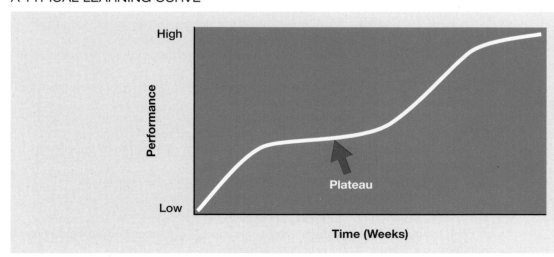

presents an example of a learning curve common in the acquisition of many job skills. In many learning situations, there are times when progress does not occur. Such periods show up on the curve as a fairly straight horizontal line called a *plateau*. A plateau can occur because of reduced motivation or because a person gets discouraged when he or she does not always perform a new task as well as hoped. It is a natural phenomenon, and learners usually experience a spontaneous recovery later, as Figure 7.6 shows.

Over the years, organizations have used **behaviour modification**, a technique that operates on the principle that behaviour that is rewarded—positively reinforced—will be exhibited more frequently in the future, whereas behaviour that is penalized or unrewarded will decrease in frequency. For example, in safety training, it is possible to identify "safe" behavioural profiles—that is, actions that ensure fewer accidents—as well as unsafe profiles. As a follow-up to training or as part of the training itself, managers can use relatively simple rewards to encourage and maintain desired behaviour. Companies such as Monsanto have found that nothing more than words of encouragement and feedback are needed to strengthen employee behaviours. However, the idea behind behaviour modification is that a person's behaviour can be motivated and gradually shaped toward what managers desire when he or she exhibits positive behaviours and is rewarded for them.[13]

Verbal encouragement or more tangible rewards, such as prizes, awards, and ceremonies, can help reinforce the behaviour firms desire of trainees over time as well as help them get over plateaus they might experience. Encouragement is most effective when it is given immediately after a trainee successfully accomplishes a certain task. This is why some employers have instituted spot rewards programs. **Spot rewards** programs award employees "on the spot" when they do something particularly well during training or on the job. The awards can consist of cash, gift cards, time off, or anything else employees value.

## CHARACTERISTICS OF INSTRUCTORS

The success of any training effort will largely depend on the teaching skills and personal characteristics of those responsible for conducting the training. What separates good trainers from mediocre ones? Often a good trainer is one who shows a little more effort or demonstrates more instructional preparation. However, training is also influenced by the trainer's personal manner and characteristics. Here is a short list of desirable traits:

1. *Knowledge of subject*. Employees expect trainers to know their job or subject thoroughly. Furthermore, they are expected to demonstrate that knowledge.
2. *Adaptability*. Because some individuals learn faster or slower than others, the instruction should be matched to the trainee's learning ability.
3. *Sincerity*. Trainees appreciate sincerity in trainers. Along with this, trainers need to be patient with trainees and demonstrate tact in addressing their concerns.
4. *Sense of humour*. Learning can be fun; very often a point can be made with a story or anecdote.
5. *Interest*. Good trainers have a keen interest in the subject they are teaching; this interest is readily conveyed to trainees.
6. *Clear instructions*. Naturally, training is accomplished more quickly and retained longer when trainers give clear instructions.
7. *Individual assistance*. When training more than one employee, successful trainers always provide individual assistance.
8. *Enthusiasm*. A dynamic presentation and a vibrant personality show trainees that the trainer enjoys training; employees tend to respond positively to an enthusiastic climate.[14]

For training programs to be most successful, organizations should reward managers who prove to be excellent trainers.

# PHASE 3: IMPLEMENTING THE TRAINING PROGRAM

A major consideration in choosing among various training methods is determining which ones are appropriate for the KSAOs to be learned. For example, if the material is mostly factual, methods such as lecture, classroom, or programmed instruction may be fine. However, if the training involves a large behavioural component, other methods, such as on-the-job training, simulation, or computer-based training, might work better.[15]

To organize our discussion of various training methods, we will break them down into two primary groups: those used for nonmanagerial employees and those used for managers. Keep in mind that many of the methods are used to train both types of employees.

## TRAINING METHODS FOR NONMANAGERIAL EMPLOYEES

A wide variety of methods are available for training employees at all levels. Some methods have a long history of being used. Newer methods have emerged over the years out of a greater understanding of human behaviour, particularly in the areas of learning, motivation, and interpersonal relationships. More recently, technological advances, especially in computer hardware and software, have resulted in training devices that in many instances are more effective and economical than traditional training methods.

### On-the-Job Training

By far, the most common method used for training nonmanagerial employees is **on-the-job training (OJT)**. By some estimates, 80 to 90 percent of employee learning occurs via OJT. OJT has the advantage of providing hands-on experience under normal working conditions and an opportunity for the trainer—a manager or senior employee—to build good relationships with new employees. OJT is viewed by some to be potentially the most effective means of facilitating learning in the workplace.[16]

Although it is used by all types of organizations, OJT is often one of the most poorly implemented training methods. Three common drawbacks are (1) the lack of a well-structured training environment, (2) poor training skills on the part of managers, and (3) the absence of well-defined job performance criteria. To overcome these problems, training experts suggest the following:

1. Develop realistic goals and/or measures for each OJT area.
2. Plan a specific training schedule for each trainee, including set periods for evaluation and feedback.
3. Help managers establish a nonthreatening atmosphere conducive to learning.
4. Conduct periodic evaluations after training is completed to prevent regression.[17]

Figure 7.7 shows the basic steps of an OJT program. The method is used frequently in organizations to ensure that new employees have adequate guidance before taking on work responsibilities on their own. For example, KLM Royal Dutch Airlines uses OJT to train its cabin attendants. The airline started a program that places cabin attendant trainees in the classroom for a certain period and then gives them additional training during an evaluation flight. On these flights, experienced cabin attendants provide the trainees with OJT, based on a list of identified job tasks. Some tasks, such as serving meals, are demonstrated during the actual delivery of services to passengers. Other tasks are presented to trainees away from passengers between meal service.[18]

### Apprenticeship Training

An extension of OJT is **apprenticeship training**. With this method, individuals entering an industry, particularly in skilled trades such as machinist, laboratory

**on-the-job training (OJT)**
A method by which employees are given hands-on experience with instructions from their supervisor or other trainer

**apprenticeship training**
A system of training in which a worker entering the skilled trades is given thorough instruction and experience, both on and off the job, in the practical and theoretical aspects of the work

| OUTCOME 4

## FIGURE 7.7

### THE PROPER WAY TO DO ON-THE-JOB TRAINING

**P**    **Prepare.** Decide what employees need to be taught. Identify the best sequence or steps of the training. Decide how best to demonstrate these steps. Have materials, resources, and equipment ready.

**R**    **Reassure.** Put each employee at ease. Learn about his or her prior experience, and adjust accordingly. Try to get the employee interested, relaxed, and motivated to learn.

**O**    **Orient.** Show the employee the correct way to do the job. Explain why it is done this way. Discuss how it relates to other jobs. Let him or her ask lots of questions.

**P**    **Perform.** When employees are ready, let them try the job themselves. Give them an opportunity to practise the job and guide them through rough spots. Provide help and assistance at first, then less as they continue.

**E**    **Evaluate.** Check the employees' performance, and question them on how, why, when, and where they should do something. Correct errors; repeat instructions.

**R**    **Reinforce and Review.** Provide praise and encouragement, and give feedback about how the employee is doing. Continue the conversation and express confidence in his or her doing the job.

**Source:** Scott Snell, University of Virginia.

---

**cooperative training**
Training program that combines practical on-the-job experience with formal educational classes

technician, and electrician, are given thorough instruction and experience, both on and off the job. For example, Bonneville Power Administration and General Physics Corporation developed an apprenticeship program for substation operators to give employees both a strong technical foundation in the fundamentals of electricity and a hands-on ability to operate equipment within the power substation. Ultimately, the program was also designed to help future electrical operators respond to emergencies. In Europe, organizations such as BAE Systems and Ford Motor Company use apprenticeship programs extensively for their engineers.[19]

Although apprenticeship programs originated in Europe as part of its guild system, they have been adapted for use in Canada. Typically, the programs involve cooperation between organizations and their labour unions, between industry and government, or between organizations and local school systems. For example, Red River College in Winnipeg offers 31 apprenticeship programs, all with long waiting lists because its graduates find work immediately.

However, apprenticeships are available in a wide range of other industries, including the telecommunications, arts, and health fields. Generally, an apprentice is paid 50 percent of a skilled journey worker's wage to start with, but the wage increases at regular intervals as the apprentice's job skills increase. When the apprentice successfully completes the apprenticeship, he or she becomes a certified journey-level worker earning full pay. According to the Bureau of Apprenticeship and Training, many journey workers earn as much as post-secondary graduates, and some earn more.[20]

## Cooperative Training, Internships, and Governmental Training

Similar to apprenticeships, **cooperative training** programs combine practical on-the-job experience with formal classes. However, the term *cooperative training* is typically used in connection with high school and college programs that incorporate part- or full-time experiences. In recent years, there has been an increased effort to expand opportunities that combine on-the-job skill training with regular classroom training so that students can pursue either technical work or a college degree program. EnCana, an oil and gas company based in Calgary, has developed the Oil and Gas Production Field Operator Career Pathway program,

# HIGHLIGHTS IN HRM 7.3

## Internship Program at Durham College

The work–study program in HR at Durham College, Ontario, is designed to transition an HR student into an HR practitioner. According to the coordinator of the HR program, Dr. Carolin Rekar Munro, each project must allow for the transfer of theories learned in class to a project management format at the field placement location. Students are required to write objectives in a draft proposal, similar to management by objectives, in which the criteria used to measure the success of the placement must be both qualitative and quantitative in content.

For the three-year diploma program, students in their final year will work two days per week from October to April and gain 344 hours of field placement experience. For the one-year post-diploma certificate program, students will attain 200 hours of field placement experience over a five-week block following final exams. Cohorts

are also put into teams during the experience and attend weekly seminars in which the students can share their experiences and get advice on issues they are facing at their respective placements. According to Dr. Rekar Munro, this peer group process helps establish a network of HR professionals.

By focusing on application-based projects, students will be in a position to decide if they wish to pursue careers in HR and will have acquired valuable experience in project management. Employers also benefit as they receive both a quality HR project and the chance to preview a potential new staff member. This work–study program gives employers a unique probationary period, and 30 to 40 percent of students are hired at their field placements to continue their projects. For example, Dr. Rekar Munro points to a student who created a health and safety manual for people with English as a second language (ESL), who was then hired by her field placement employer to complete the work.

Source: Interview with Dr. Carolin Rekar Munro.

---

which offers high school students an opportunity to earn credits while learning about field production work, in alliance with the Southern Alberta Institute of Technology (SAIT). The courses are offered as an option, and students graduate with a field operator certificate from SAIT and have a chance to obtain a paid internship in the summer.[21] The internship program of a community college is described in Highlights in HRM 7.3.

The federal government and various provincial governments have begun working with private employers to sponsor a multitude of training programs. For example, the federal government has invested money in the Information Technology program at the Nova Scotia Community College, Marconi Campus, which installed a high-tech infrastructure to support customized training for the petroleum industry.[22]

**Internship programs**, jointly sponsored by colleges, universities, and a variety of organizations, offer students the chance to get real-world experience while finding out how they will perform in work organizations. Organizations benefit by getting student–employees with new ideas, energy, and eagerness to accomplish their assignments. Many universities and community colleges allow students to earn credits on the basis of successful job performance and fulfillment of established program requirements. The following are steps firms can take to increase the effectiveness of their internships:

1. Assign the intern to projects that are accomplishable and provide training as required.
2. Appoint a mentor or supervisor to guide the intern.
3. Solicit project suggestions from other staff members.
4. Rotate interns throughout the organization.
5. Treat interns as part of the organizational staff and invite them to staff meetings.
6. Establish a process for considering interns for permanent hire.[23]

> **internship programs**
> Programs jointly sponsored by colleges, universities, and other organizations that offer students the opportunity to gain real-life experience while allowing them to find out how they will perform in work organizations

**blended learning**
The use of multiple training methods to achieve optimal learning on the part of trainees

## Classroom Instruction

When most people think about training, they think about classrooms. According to the Conference Board of Canada's *Learning and Development Outlook 2007*, 75 percent of training still takes place in the classroom.[24] Classroom training enables the maximum number of trainees to be handled by the minimum number of instructors. This method lends itself particularly well to what is called **blended learning**, in which lectures and demonstrations are combined with films, DVDs, videotapes, or computer instruction. Despite the rise of many other types of learning—electronic and otherwise—classroom instruction is still the number one training method, as Figure 7.8 shows.[25]

## Programmed Instruction

One method of instruction that is particularly good for allowing individuals to work at their own pace is programmed instruction. Programmed instruction—increasingly referred to as self-directed learning—involves the use of books, manuals, or computers to break down subject matter content into highly organized, logical sequences that demand a continual response on the part of the trainee. After being presented with a small segment of information, the trainee is required to answer a question. If the response is correct, the trainee is told so and is presented with the next step (screen) in the material. If the response is incorrect, further explanatory information is given, and the trainee is told to try again.

A major advantage of programmed instruction is that it incorporates a number of the established learning principles discussed earlier in the chapter. With programmed instruction, training is individualized, trainees are actively involved in the instructional process, and the feedback and reinforcement provided are immediate.

## Audiovisual Methods

To teach skills and procedures for many production jobs, audiovisual devices can be used. For example, video recordings are often used to illustrate the

Apprenticeships are a good way to train employees, especially in skilled trade industries.

**FIGURE 7.8**

DELIVERY METHOD OF TRAINING

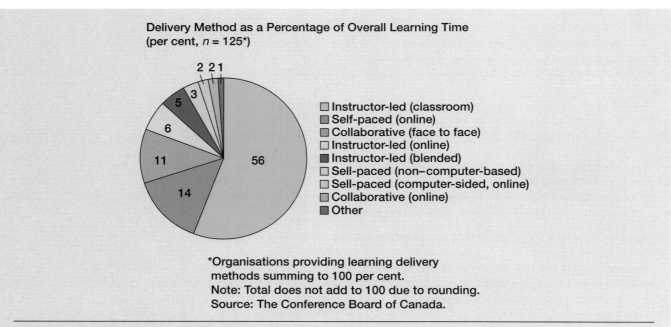

Delivery Method as a Percentage of Overall Learning Time
(per cent, *n* = 125*)

- Instructor-led (classroom) — 56
- Self-paced (online) — 14
- Collaborative (face to face) — 11
- Instructor-led (online) — 6
- Instructor-led (blended) — 5
- Sell-paced (non–computer-based) — 3
- Sell-paced (computer-sided, online) — 2
- Collaborative (online) — 2
- Other — 1

*Organisations providing learning delivery methods summing to 100 per cent.
Note: Total does not add to 100 due to rounding.
Source: The Conference Board of Canada.

**Source:** The Conference Board of Canada, Learning and Development Outlook 2011. Used by permission.

steps in a procedure such as assembling electronic equipment or working with a problem employee. Trainers and trainees can view an on-the-spot recording to receive immediate feedback. Golf and tennis coaches frequently record their students to let them see their mistakes. CDs and DVDs allow trainees to access any segment of the instructional program, which is especially useful for individualized instruction when employees have different levels of knowledge and ability.

Teleconferencing and videoconferencing allow an instructional program to be transmitted to many locations simultaneously and trainees to interact with one another. Electronic Data Systems has used teleconferencing to train its employees wherever they are in the world rather than having them travel to one location. The company recently conducted a "coaching skills for leaders" program that was disseminated to 1,500 managers in 41 countries via teleconferencing.[26]

Web conferencing is used to conduct live meetings or presentations over the Internet. During a web conference, trainees sit at their own computers and are connected to other participants via the Web. To attend the conference, they simply enter a website address and dial in to a 1-800 number to talk to one another and the trainer via the telephone. A webinar is a one-way conference, from the speaker to the audience, with limited audience interaction. A number of organizations are also using podcasts to provide their employees, such as sales representatives, with information on the go. Podcasts allow them to learn about new products while they are in the field rather than having to take time off to travel to corporate headquarters to get the information.

## Simulation Method

Sometimes it is either impractical or unwise to train employees on the equipment used on the job. One obvious example is training nurses and doctors. At St. Michael's Hospital in Toronto, high-tech mannequins can simulate, for example, heart ailments, trauma, and neonatal problems, allowing trainees to practise without endangering the patient. Another obvious example is training employees to operate aircraft, spacecraft, and other highly technical and expensive equipment. The simulation method emphasizes realism in equipment and its operation at minimum cost and maximum safety.

Southwest Airlines boasts perhaps the most technologically advanced flight simulator in the airline industry: a $10.8 million full-motion Boeing 737–700 unit housed in an 110,000-square-foot flight operations training centre. The facility can house up to six 737 simulators and can train up to 300 (of Southwest's 4,100) pilots at one time. The centre has a staff of 110 employees. In addition to the simulators and their associated briefing and computer programming rooms, the training centre houses eight classrooms, each fully equipped with closed-circuit television, computers, conventional audiovisual equipment, and telephone and Internet hookups. The Canadian Forces uses simulation software to train new recruits about aviation technology. Using the software enables students to disassemble and reassemble a propeller system many times, compared to the traditional training style of observing an instructor do it and perhaps having one opportunity to practise.[27] Trainees who do poorly in certain situations are then targeted for additional training in those areas. Simulators that represent human patients are being integrated into medical training as well.[28]

The distinction between simulation and computer-based training has blurred. For example, a simulation developed by the Wireless Internet Center for Advanced Technology (WICAT) in partnership with Airbus and Singapore Airlines runs on a PC and replicates a cockpit with control displays and throttle/flap controls. Even though the PC-based simulation is relatively inexpensive, it is powerful. Pilots are taken through a self-paced program that simulates "taxi, takeoff, climb, cruise, descent, approach, landing, and go-around." These types of technologies are making it easier to offer training in new and different ways. Given advances in telecommunications, the possibilities seem limitless.[29]

**e-learning**
Learning that takes place via electronic media

**just-in-time training**
Training delivered to trainees when and where they need it to do their jobs, usually via computer or the Internet

**learning management system (LMS)**
On-line system that provides a variety of assessment, communication, teaching, and learning opportunities

## E-Learning

The training methods we just discussed are evolving into what trainers today refer to as e-learning. **E-learning** covers a wide variety of applications, such as Web- and computer-based training and social networks. It includes delivery of content via the Internet, intranets and extranets, mobile devices, DVDs, CD-ROMs, MP3 players, and virtual classrooms found in the gaming platform Second Life. Today one of every three hours of training is delivered via some form of technology, and companies are reporting that they are saving anywhere from 30 to 70 percent on their training costs by doing so. E-learning makes it possible to provide drills and practice, problem solving, simulation, and gaming forms of instruction and certain very sophisticated forms of individualized tutorial instruction in a way that is more engaging for learners than traditional classroom instruction. E-learning is also cheaper for employers to administer because, in many instances, it can be delivered directly to the PCs of multiple employees. Today, one of every three hours of training is delivered via some form of technology, and companies are reporting that they are saving anywhere from 30 to 70 percent on their training costs by doing so.[30]

E-learning transforms the learning process in several ways. First, as we have said, it allows the firm to bring the training to employees rather than vice versa, which is generally more efficient and cost effective. The nuclear power plant industry is a case in point. Nuclear power plant training is frequent and time consuming. Just for workers to remove their protective gear and commute to a separate training venue can take anywhere from an hour or more. One nuclear power company that switched to e-learning reported that it saved nearly $1 million and 10,000 employee hours in one year by doing so.

E-learning also allows employees to search online training libraries to customize their learning in their own time and space. This type of training, which is referred to as **just-in-time training**, helps alleviate the boredom trainees experience during full-blown training courses, and employees are more likely to retain the information when they can immediately put it to use. Cisco has thousands of training videos that employees can download off the company's intranet as needed.[31] Microsoft's product experts have created hundreds of short audio and video podcasts that the company's sales professionals can download on their mobile devices as they need them. The company realized that full-blown training courses pulled people away from making sales and that with so many products continually being launched, it was difficult for them to keep up to date if they had to take frequent training sessions. Also, employees did not remember the training if they could not put it to use immediately.[32]

E-learning systems need not be overly expensive. Many e-learning training programs use existing applications employees are familiar with, such as PowerPoint, Word, and Adobe Acrobat, that can easily be uploaded.

## Learning Management Systems

Organizations are combining their e-learning, employee assessment tools, and other training functions into electronic **learning management systems (LMSs)** built for them by software vendors. Using the software, managers can assess the skills of employees, register them for courses, deliver interactive learning modules to them directly to their desktops when they need or want them, evaluate and track their progress, and determine when they are ready to be promoted. Purchasing an LMS does not alleviate HR personnel and a firm's managers from conducting a thorough needs assessment, however, especially because the systems are costly. After conducting a thorough needs analysis, managers then have to address the types of systems that will work best.

## METHODS FOR MANAGEMENT DEVELOPMENT

Many of the methods used to train front-line employees are also used to train supervisors and first-level managers. But other methods are used primarily to improve the preparation and development of mid- to senior-level managers. Over the past decade, the importance of management development has grown because so many experienced baby boomer managers have begun retiring and firms are having a hard time replacing the expertise they provided. Most companies reported moderate to major leadership shortages, and many expected the problem to get worse.[33]

## On-the-Job Experiences

Some skills and knowledge can be acquired just by listening and observing or by reading. But others must be acquired through practice and experience. By presenting managers with the opportunities to perform under pressure and to learn from their mistakes, on-the-job development experiences are some of the most powerful and commonly used techniques. Methods of providing on-the-job experiences include the following:

1. *Coaching* involves a continuing flow of instructions, comments, and suggestions from the manager to the subordinate. (*Mentoring*, discussed in Chapter 5, is a similar approach to personal and informal management development.)
2. *Understudy assignments* groom an individual to take over a manager's job by providing experience in handling important functions of the job.
3. *Job rotation* and *lateral transfers* provide, through a variety of work experiences, the broadened knowledge and understanding required to manage more effectively.
4. *Special projects* and *junior boards* provide an opportunity for individuals to study current organizational problems, make decisions, and work on new initiatives.
5. *Action learning* is a training method whereby trainees work full-time on projects with others in the organization and then discuss with them the aspects that went right and wrong. In some cases, action learning is combined with classroom instruction, conferences, and other types of blended learning opportunities.
6. *Managerial staff meetings* enable participants to become more familiar with problems and events occurring outside their immediate areas by exposing them to the ideas and thinking of other managers.
7. *Planned career progressions* (discussed in Chapter 5) utilize all of these different methods to provide employees with the training and development necessary to progress through a series of jobs requiring higher and higher levels of knowledge and/or skills.[34]

Figure 7.9 provides an analysis of the methods used to develop managers in Canada and globally, based on data provided by HR professionals, and Figure 7.10 rates the effectiveness of these methods, as assessed by the managers.

Although these methods are used most often to develop managers for higher level positions, they also provide valuable experiences for those who are being groomed for other types of positions in the organization. Although on-the-job experiences constitute the core of management training and development, other off-the-job methods of development can be used to supplement these experiences.

## Seminars and Conferences

Seminars and conferences, like classroom instruction, are useful for bringing groups of people together for training and development. In terms of developing managers, seminars and conferences can be used to communicate ideas, policies, or procedures, but they are also good for raising points of debate or discussing issues (usually with the help of a qualified leader) that have no set answers or resolutions. For this reason, seminars and conferences are often used when attitude change is a goal.

## FIGURE 7.9

### FREQUENCY OF USE OF DEVELOPMENT METHODS

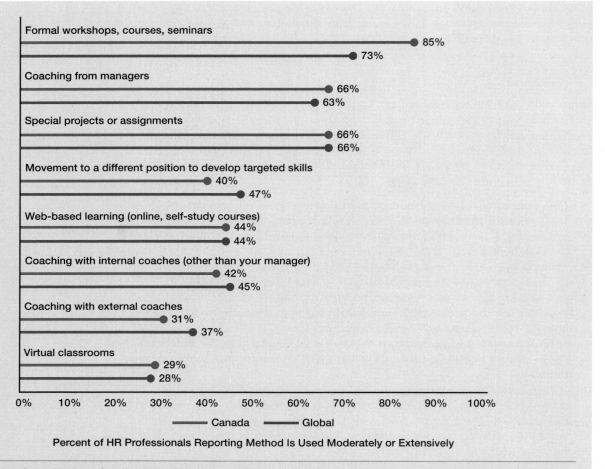

Formal workshops, courses, seminars — 85% / 73%

Coaching from managers — 66% / 63%

Special projects or assignments — 66% / 66%

Movement to a different position to develop targeted skills — 40% / 47%

Web-based learning (online, self-study courses) — 44% / 44%

Coaching with internal coaches (other than your manager) — 42% / 45%

Coaching with external coaches — 31% / 37%

Virtual classrooms — 29% / 28%

0% 10% 20% 30% 40% 50% 60% 70% 80% 90% 100%

— Canada  — Global

**Percent of HR Professionals Reporting Method Is Used Moderately or Extensively**

**Source:** Figures from Canada Highlights: *Global Leadership Forecasts* 2011, DDI. By Jazmine Boatman PhD, Richard Wellins PhD and Vykinta Kligyte-Culver PhD. ©Development Dimensions International, Inc. MMXI. All rights reserved. Reprinted with permission from Development Dimensions International.

Outside seminars and conferences are often conducted jointly with universities and consulting firms. Caterpillar, the construction and mining equipment manufacturer, is one company that, in conjunction with an outside consulting firm, has developed a training program to groom new managers. The challenge for the company is to get enough leaders and managers in place to effectively run the company by 2020. To meet this challenge, Caterpillar launched a leadership development initiative through its Caterpillar University of Leadership. The effort began with a series of high-level meetings and strategy sessions. In those meetings, 11 characteristics were identified that the company seeks in its managers and leaders. So far, some 5,000 managers and executives have gone through the program, which is designed to help them become more self-aware as managers and develop their financial management skills and ability to better formulate strategies to increase Caterpillar's global competitiveness.[35]

### Case Studies

A particularly useful method used in classroom learning situations is the case study. Using documented examples, participants learn how to analyze (take apart) and synthesize (put together) facts, become conscious of the many variables on which management decisions are based, and, in general, improve their decision-making skills. Experienced educators and trainers generally point out that the case study is most appropriate when

## FIGURE 7.10

### EFFECTIVENESS OF DEVELOPMENT METHODS

**PART 3**

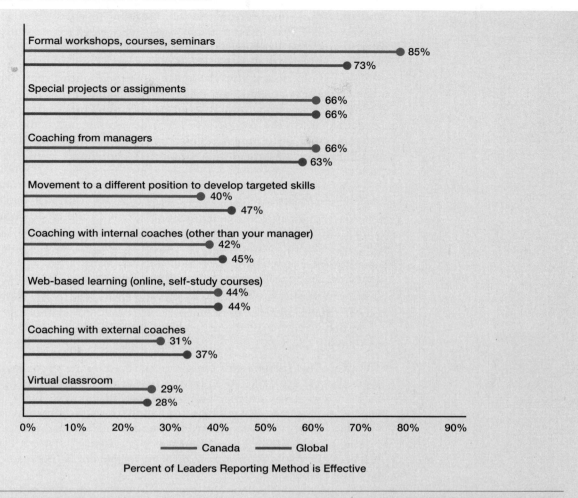

Formal workshops, courses, seminars — 85% / 73%

Special projects or assignments — 66% / 66%

Coaching from managers — 66% / 63%

Movement to a different position to develop targeted skills — 40% / 47%

Coaching with internal coaches (other than your manager) — 42% / 45%

Web-based learning (online, self-study courses) — 44% / 44%

Coaching with external coaches — 31% / 37%

Virtual classroom — 29% / 28%

Canada — Global

**Percent of Leaders Reporting Method is Effective**

1. Analytical, problem-solving, and critical thinking skills are most important
2. The KSAOs are complex, and participants need time to master them
3. Active participation is desired
4. The process of learning (e.g., questioning, interpreting) is as important as the content
5. Team problem solving and interaction are possible[36]

Even when case studies may be appropriate, they are often mismanaged. As with any other development technique, implementation is crucial for effectiveness.

## Management Games and Simulations

Games are now being widely used as a management development method. Generally, players–managers are faced with the task of making a series of management decisions affecting a hypothetical organization. The effects that every decision has on each area within the organization can be simulated with a computer programmed for the game. Bell Canada has its managers play TeleSim, a computer simulation for the telecommunications industry developed by Thinking Tools and Coopers & Lybrand to teach executives how to act in an increasingly open, competitive market.[37] At Marriott International, a computer program called Business Acumen has been used to train its non-U.S. property-level managers on the finer points of hotel operation. The program simulates hotel operations scenarios, such as budgetary decisions.[38]

Project managers at L'Oreal Canada are given a "virtual" company to manage after only three months on the job. Working in pairs for four hours a week, employees are introduced to a new topic every week for six weeks. Based on this new content, the pairs make decisions and learn the next day what impact their decisions have on the market share of the imaginary product.[39]

Simulations do not always require a computer, however. Motorola developed a non–computer-based game called "Equal Employment Opportunity: It's Your Job" to teach the basic principles of equal employment opportunity. The players get caught up in the competitive spirit of a game and at the same time absorb and remember government regulations. They also become aware of how their own daily decisions affect their employer's compliance with these regulations.[40]

## Role-Playing

Role-playing consists of playing the role of others, often a supervisor and a subordinate who are facing a particular problem, such as a performance problem. By acting out another's position, participants in the role-playing can improve their ability to understand and cope with others. Role-playing is used widely in training health care professionals to be empathic and sensitive to the concerns of patients. It is also used widely in training managers to handle employee issues relating to absenteeism, performance appraisal, and conflicts.

At times, participants may be hesitant to try role-playing; therefore, successful role-playing takes planning. Instructors should do the following:

1. Ensure that members of the group have gotten to know each other. In other words, do not make role-play the first activity in a training program.
2. Realize that volunteers make better role-players.
3. Prepare the role-players by introducing a specific situation.
4. Prepare the observers by giving them specific tasks (such as evaluating the role-play and offering feedback once it is over).
5. Guide the role-play enactment through its little errors (because it is not scripted).
6. Keep it short.
7. Discuss the enactment and prepare bulleted points of what was learned.[41]

Role-playing is a versatile teaching model, applicable to a variety of training experiences. Planned and implemented correctly, role-playing can bring realism and insight into dilemmas and experiences that otherwise might not be shared. Computer programs that simulate role-playing have also been developed. Virtual Leader, a product by SimuLearn, is one such program: management trainees interact with animated "employees," some of whom are more cooperative than others. The trainees are then given feedback as to how well they applied their managerial skills to each situation.

## Behaviour Modelling

One technique that combines several different training methods, and therefore multiple principles of learning, is the **behaviour modelling** technique. Behaviour modelling involves four basic components:

1. *Learning points.* At the beginning of instruction, the essential goals and objectives of the program are enumerated. In some cases, the learning points are a sequence of behaviours that are to be taught. For example, the learning points might describe the recommended steps for giving employees feedback.
2. *Modelling.* Participants view videos in which a model manager is portrayed dealing with an employee in an effort to improve his or her performance. The model shows specifically how to deal with the situation and demonstrates the learning points.

3. *Practice and role-play.* Trainees participate in extensive rehearsal of the behaviours demonstrated by the models. The greatest percentage of training time is spent in these skill practice sessions.
4. *Feedback and reinforcement.* As the trainee's behaviour increasingly resembles that of the model, the trainer and other trainees reinforce the behaviour with praise, approval, encouragement, and attention. Digitally recording the sessions can also be very instructive.

Behaviour modelling seems to work, according to various studies. The training can help managers better interact with employees, administer discipline, introduce changes, and increase productivity. Military training is a classic example of how behaviour modelling can work. Drill sergeants model the behaviour expected of new recruits, who, in turn, by emulating them, develop discipline and confidence.[42]

In the final analysis, the most successful training courses for either regular employees or managers do not rely on a single type of training. Instead, utilizing a variety of methods better helps keep the interest of trainees high and accommodates different kinds of learning styles.

## PHASE 4: EVALUATING THE TRAINING PROGRAM

OUTCOME 5

Training, like any other HRM function, has to be evaluated to determine its effectiveness. A variety of methods are available to assess the extent to which a firm's training programs improve learning, affect behaviour on the job, and impact the bottom-line performance of an organization. Unfortunately, over 50 percent of Canadian organizations do not adequately evaluate their training programs. But this is changing. Today, HR departments are under pressure to calculate the return on their firms' training investment dollars. We will explain how this is done later in this section.

Figure 7.11 shows that four basic criteria are available to evaluate training: (1) reactions, (2) learning, (3) behaviour, and (4) results, including return on investment (ROI). Some of these criteria are easier to measure than others, but each is important in that it provides different information about the success of the programs. The combination of these criteria can give a total picture of the training program to help managers decide where problem areas lie, what to change about the program, and whether to continue with a program.[43] The Reality Check shows how these four levels have been applied at Conexus, the largest credit union in Saskatchewan.

### CRITERION 1: REACTIONS

One of the simplest and most common approaches to evaluating a training program is assessing participants' reactions. Happy trainees will be more likely to want to focus on training principles and to utilize the information on the job. Trainees can do

## FIGURE 7.11

CRITERIA FOR EVALUATING TRAINING

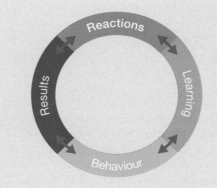

# REALITY CHECK

## A Classic Four-Level Evaluation

Conexus is the largest credit union in Saskatchewan, with assets of $1.1 billion. According to Gayle Johnson, CHRP, executive vice president HR and corporate secretary, its training and development budget for its 465 employees is 6 percent of payroll. Three percent is spent on university education, and the other 3 percent is spent on training. Its largest training program is one that develops financial service representatives. The training consists of several steps, and each is measured.

In-house and classroom-based modules teach content, such as computer literacy, cash duties, and introduction to Conexus's products and services, and progress through to more advanced training, such as consumer lending practices, estates, and minimal mortgage lending. Each three- to five-day module is followed by a work period of 3 to 12 months so that employees can apply their knowledge. The four levels of measurement of the effectiveness of training are the following:

1. *Reaction.* "Smile sheets" are completed by each participant at the end of the classroom training, asking questions such as "What did you get from this session?"

2. *Comprehensive review.* Exams are given after each module, and the results are fed back to the employees and managers.

3. *Employee performance competencies.* Every job family has a number of job-specific competencies, and managers are asked to rate the participants on these performance competencies. The changes in ratings are tracked.

4. *Results.* These vary by module. For example, after the cash-lending module, the performance tracked would be the number of callouts to customers and the number of sales.

Source: Interview with Gayle Johnson.

more than tell you whether they liked a training program. They can give insights into the content and techniques they found most useful. They can critique the instructors or make suggestions about participant interactions, and feedback. Potential questions might include the following:

- What were your learning goals for this program?
- Did you achieve them?
- Did you like this program?
- Would you recommend it to others who have similar learning goals?
- What suggestions do you have for improving the program?
- Should the organization continue to offer it?

Although evaluation methods based on reactions are improving, too many conclusions about training effectiveness are still based on broad satisfaction measures that lack specific feedback. Furthermore, it should be noted that positive reactions are no guarantee that the training has been successful. It may be easy to collect glowing comments from trainees, but as gratifying as this information is, it may not be useful to the organization unless it somehow translates into improved behaviour and job performance that is measurable. In the final analysis, reaction measures should not stop with assessing the training's entertainment value.[44]

## CRITERION 2: LEARNING

Beyond what participants *think* about the training, it might be a good idea to see whether they learned anything. Testing the knowledge and skills of trainees before and after a training program will help determine their improvement. The skill and knowledge levels of employees who have undergone a training program can also be compared to those of employees who have not. FedEx took this approach by studying 20 van drivers who attended a weeklong new-hire training program. The company then compared the performance of these drivers to that of a control group of 20 drivers who had received only OJT. FedEx found that the drivers who had been formally trained made fewer package processing errors, saving the company about $500 per trained driver.[45]

**transfer of training**
Effective application of principles learned to what is required on the job

## CRITERION 3: BEHAVIOUR

You might be surprised to learn that much of what is learned in a training program never gets used back on the job. It is not that the training was necessarily ineffective. But for several reasons, trainees do not demonstrate behaviour change back on the job. The **transfer of training** refers to how well employees apply what they have learned to their jobs. To maximize the transfer of training, managers and trainers can take several approaches:

1. *Feature identical elements*. Transferring the training to the job can be facilitated by having conditions in the training program come as close as possible to those on the job. For example, instead of verbally explaining a manufacturing process, it is better to demonstrate it on a factory floor.

2. *Focus on general principles*, if necessary. When jobs change or the work environment cannot be matched exactly, trainers often stress the general principles behind the training rather than focus on rote behaviour. This approach helps trainees learn how to apply the main learning points to varying conditions on the job.

3. *Establish a climate for transfer*. In some cases, trained behaviour is not implemented because old approaches and routines are still reinforced by other managers, peers, and employees. To prevent this kind of problem, managers need to support, reinforce, and reward trainees for applying the new skills or knowledge. Often this requires firms to train their managers to actively embrace the strategic changes their organizations are seeking to implement.

4. *Give employees transfer strategies*. Particularly in settings that are not conducive to transfer, managers should also provide trainees with strategies and tactics for dealing with their transfer environment. One approach, called relapse prevention, teaches individuals how to anticipate and cope with the inevitable setbacks they will encounter back on the job—that is, a relapse into former behaviours. By identifying high-risk situations that jeopardize transfer and developing coping strategies, relapse prevention can help employees gain better control over maintaining learned behaviours.[46]

There are several methods for assessing transfer of learned skills back to the job. At Xerox, for example, trainers observe trainees once they return to their regular positions, interview the trainees' managers about their progress later on, and examine their post-training performance appraisals.

## CRITERION 4: RESULTS, OR RETURN ON INVESTMENT (ROI)

As we have indicated, HR managers are under pressure to show that their training programs produce "bottom-line" results.[47] Most organizations understand that they should measure their training in terms of its ROI, but less than half do this. ROI is also sometimes referred to as the *utility* the firm gets for its training dollars. A company's ROI refers to the benefits it derives from training its employees relative to the costs it incurs. HR managers are responsible for calculating and presenting these benefits to the company's top managers. The benefits can include higher revenues generated, increased productivity, improved quality, lower costs, more satisfied customers, higher job satisfaction, and lower employee turnover.

The following are the types of questions HR managers should try to answer as they calculate a training program's benefits:

• How much did quality improve because of the training program?

• How much has it contributed to profits?

- What reduction in turnover and wasted materials did the company get after training?
- How much has productivity increased, and by how much have costs been reduced?

To answer these questions, HR managers use various types of data, such as sales data, HR and financial data, and employee survey and control group data gathered from various sources within the organization. Of course, the costs of the training program need to be measured too. The ROI formula can then be calculated fairly simply:

$$ROI = Results/Training\ Costs$$

A firm's training costs include the various expenses it incurs related to the training, including the direct costs of the programs (e.g., materials, employee travel and meals, meeting site costs, equipment, trainers' salaries or fees) and the indirect costs of the programs (participants' salaries and the productivity they lose while they are attending the training). So, for example, if the ROI ratio of the training is >1, its benefits exceed its cost; if the ROI ratio is <1, the costs of the training exceed the benefits. Highlights in HRM 7.4 shows some simple examples of ROI calculations. A firm's training ROI can also be measured in terms of how long it takes before the benefits of the training pay off. This analysis is done by adding the costs and dividing the benefits realized in a single month. The result will indicate the overall time required for the training to pay for itself.[48] The Business Case discusses the return on training investment.

Despite the emphasis on ROI today, some HR experts think managers can become overly preoccupied with ROI calculations because often the benefits of training can be intangible or take a long time to appear. Measuring participants' reactions can be done immediately, of course. However, measuring improved employee skills, and customer satisfaction can take somewhat longer, and factors other than training can also affect these measures. Finally, the development of ground-breaking new products or processes can also be sparked by training but

# HIGHLIGHTS IN HRM 7.4

## Calculating Training ROI: Examples

If the ROI ratio is >1 the benefits of the training program are greater than its costs. By contrast, the training program's costs outweigh the benefits if the ratio is <1

Example 1: A program to train dental hygienists on a new process costs $15,000 to develop and implement. If the average number of patients processed each year increased by 350 following the training, and the profit earned from each patient is $30, this results in an extra $10,500 as a result of the training.

$$ROI = \$10,500/\$5,250 = 2$$

Since the ROI is greater than 1, the training's benefits outweigh its costs.

Example 2: A program to train call centre representatives to better help customers troubleshoot their Internet connectivity problem costs a cable company $225,000. One year later, the number of customers who dropped their service due to connectivity problems fell by 1,250. The average profit earned from each customer per year is $150. This results in an additional $187,500 for the firm.

$$ROI = \$187,500/\$225,000 = 0.83$$

Since the ROI of the training was only 0.83, the costs of the program are greater than the benefits.

Sources: Adapted from Richard J. Wagner and Robert J. Weigand, "Can the Value of Training Be Measured? A Simplified Approach to Evaluating Training," *The Health Care Manager* 23, no. 1 (January–March 2004): 71–78; Ron Drew Stone, "ROI Is Like a Box of Chocolates," *Chief Learning Officer* (January 2011): 36; Howard Prager and Susan Vece, "Simplified ROI: Measuring What Matters Most," *Chief Learning Officer* (November 2009): 28.

# THE BUSINESS CASE

## Return on Training Investment

Organizations spend about 2 percent of payroll on training, an estimated $750 billion around the globe. Most organizations (four out of five) do not measure the ROI on their training dollars, citing barriers such as the difficulty of doing so, the cost, lack of training, and lack of experience. However, at TD Bank, which has 1,500 branches, 45,000 employees, and 30 different businesses, a focus on measuring the ROI of training captures results such as revenues and profitability. TD has a front-end process: the

business units determine the business results expected, the job performance that will generate these results, and the role that training plays.

According to the Conference Board of Canada, a positive relationship exists between formal training expenditures and performance indicators, such as employee productivity and company profitability. H. J. Heinz Company Canada provided training for its staff in response to increased competition and the need for new technologies. The training costs of $869,000 were repaid within 20 months due to increased productivity, reduced absenteeism, and fewer damaged containers.

Sources: S. Carrigan, "Training: Investment in the Future," *Canadian HR Reporter* 14, no. 11 (June 4, 2001): G1; "What Should You Expect from Your Training?" *Strategis*, Industry Canada, "Canadian Training Solutions," www.strategis.gc.ca

---

take years to develop, making them hard to attribute to training. Nonetheless, developments such as these can transform organizations.

## Benchmarking

Closely related to calculating the firm's training ROI is the process of **benchmarking** developmental services and practices against those of recognized leaders in industry.

Although no single model for exact benchmarking exists, the simplest models are based on the late W. Edwards Deming's classic four-step process.[49] The four-step process advocates that managers

1. *Plan.* Conduct a self-audit to define internal processes and measurements; decide on areas to be benchmarked and choose the comparison organization.
2. *Do.* Collect data through surveys, interviews, site visits, and/or historical records.
3. *Check.* Analyze data to discover performance gaps and communicate findings and suggested improvements to management.
4. *Act.* Establish goals, implement specific changes, monitor progress, and redefine benchmarks as a continuous improvement process.

The American Society of Training has developed training benchmarks from hundreds of different companies to which other firms can compare the data on their training costs, staffing, administration, design, development, and delivery of training programs. Benchmarks such as these can help organizations evaluate their current and future training programs.[50] Highlights in HRM 7.5 shows several aspects of training that can be benchmarked against organizations considered superior in the training function and how those aspects are calculated.

The reader might also note that these evaluation criteria can be used as inputs to (further) needs analysis, thereby completing the cycle inherent in the system's approach to training discussed at the beginning of this chapter. By starting the cycle over again, a system's approach to training and development helps establish an ongoing cycle of continuous assessment and improvement over time.

> **benchmarking**
> The process of measuring one's own services and practices against those of recognized leaders to identify areas for improvement

# HIGHLIGHTS IN HRM 7.5

## Benchmarking HR Training

| Measurement | How to Calculate |
|---|---|
| Percentage of payroll spent on training | Total training expenditures ÷ total payroll |
| Training dollars spent per employee | Total training expenditures ÷ total employees served |
| Average training hours per employee | Total number of training hours (hours × participants) ÷ total employees served |
| Percentage of employees trained per year | Total number of employees receiving training ÷ total employee population |
| HR development staff per 1,000 employees | Number of HR development staff ÷ total employee population × 1,000 |
| Cost savings as a ratio of training expenses | Total savings in scrap or waste ÷ dollars invested in training |
| Training costs per student hour | Total costs of training ÷ total number of hours of training |

## ADDITIONAL TOPICS IN TRAINING AND DEVELOPMENT

**OUTCOME 6**

In addition to training that addresses KSAOs reflecting the demands of a particular job, many employers develop training programs to meet the special needs of employees.

In this final section, we summarize some of these programs, including orientation training, basic skills training, team training and cross-training, ethics training, and diversity training. International training will be covered in Chapter 15.

**orientation**

The formal process of familiarizing new employees with the organization, their jobs, and their work units

### ORIENTATION TRAINING

To get new employees off to a good start, organizations generally offer a formal orientation program. **Orientation** is the formal process of familiarizing new employees with the organization, their jobs, and their work units. Training emphasizes the *what* and the *how*, whereas orientation often stresses the *why*. It is designed to influence employee attitudes about the work they will be doing and their role in the organization. It defines the philosophy behind the organization's rules and provides a framework for job-related tasks. Reported benefits include the following:

1. Lower turnover
2. Increased productivity
3. Improved employee morale
4. Lower recruiting and training costs
5. Facilitation of learning
5. Reduction of the new employee's anxiety[51]

Intuit Canada does an excellent job at employee orientation (see Highlights in HRM 7.6).

The HR department ordinarily is responsible for coordinating orientation activities and for providing new employees with information about conditions of employment, pay, benefits, and other areas not directly under a supervisor's

# HIGHLIGHTS IN HRM 7.6

## Wowing the Candidate

Intuit Canada, headquartered in Edmonton, Alberta, is a leading developer of financial software, including personal finance management, small business accounting, and tax preparation, with products such as Quicken. Intuit, like other organizations profiled in this report, is a top employer; it was ranked number two in Canada by *The Globe and Mail* survey and 45th of the 100 Best Companies to Work for in America by *Fortune* magazine. What makes Intuit special is its success in a highly competitive industry. There are many factors, but evidence of its success is its low attrition rate of 3 percent, which is remarkable in a sector where the average turnover is 20 percent. Ninety-four percent of its employees report that Intuit is a "great place to work," according to their annual surveys.

Intuit is very careful about the first few days of a new employee's work life. There are too many stories about employees in other organizations showing up very excited about their new job, only to discover that no one remembers that they are arriving that day, supplies and offices are not ready, and the reporting manager is absent. Intuit is committed to wowing the candidate—now employee—on the first day. On arriving at work, a new employee is greeted by name by the receptionist, who gives him or her a stainless steel coffee mug engraved with the employee's name. The hiring manager is called and arrives promptly. He knows the new employee and takes him or her to the workstation, showing the computer, telephone, and office supplies. The next step is to introduce the new employee to colleagues and other team members and a "buddy" who has volunteered to guide the new employee and answer all questions for the next three weeks. New employees often struggle with simple questions, such as "How does the photocopier work?" "Do most people bring their lunches to work?" The IT person arrives next and helps set up voice mail, email, and Internet access. Intuit considers it vital that when a new employee goes home that night, he or she should be able to answer the universal question, "How was your first day on the job?" with "Wow, am I ever glad that I took this job!"

This informal orientation is completed by a formal orientation, in which information about the strategy, vision, plans, history—including war stories and all the successes—is shared. A key part of this orientation is a discussion of Intuit values. At the end of the first week, and again at the end of the first month, feedback about the new employee's experiences is solicited, such as what worked, what was frustrating, and how the orientation can be improved.

Source: M. Belcourt and S. Taggar, "Making Government the Best Place to Work: Building Commitment," *IPAC, New Directions Series*, no. 8, 2002.

direction. However, the supervisor has the most important role in the orientation program. New employees are interested primarily in what the supervisor says and does and what their new coworkers are like.

Before the arrival of a new employee, the supervisor should inform the work group that a new worker is joining the unit. It is also common practice for supervisors or other managerial personnel to recruit coworkers to serve as volunteer "sponsors," or mentors, for incoming employees. In addition to providing practical help to newcomers, experienced colleagues represent an important source of information about the norms and nuances of the work group, the culture of the organization, and what it expects from its employees. These relationships are vital to the socialization of new employees and contribute significantly to their long-term success within the organization.

Given the immediate and lasting impact of orientation programs, careful planning—with emphasis on program goals, topics to be covered, and methods of organizing and presenting them—is essential. In many cases, organizations devise checklists for use by those responsible for conducting the orientation so that no item of importance to employees is overlooked. The checklist would include such things as (1) an introduction to other employees; (2) an outline of training; (3) expectations for attendance, conduct, and appearance; (4) the conditions of employment, such as hours and pay periods; (5) an explanation of job duties, standards, and appraisal criteria; (6) safety regulations; (7) a list of the chain of command; and (8) an explanation of the organization's purpose and strategic goals. Highlights in HRM 7.7 shows the types of materials new hires can be given and the various steps that can ease their transition into the workplace.[52]

# HIGHLIGHTS IN HRM 7.7

## Checklist for Orienting New Employees

### Items in Orientation Packet

- Welcome letter with company background
- Map of facility, including parking information
- IDs, keys, and parking decals
- Current organization chart
- Telephone numbers, email addresses, and locations of key personnel
- Copy of employee's specific job goals and descriptions
- List of unique terms in the industry, company, and job
- Training class schedules
- Safety and emergency procedures
- Copy of policy handbook, including office hours and telephone and email rules
- List of employee benefits, including insurance plans
- Holiday schedule

### Follow-up Activities

- Ensure that employee has completed required paperwork, including benefit enrollment forms
- Revisit performance standards
- Schedule first performance appraisal meeting

---

**onboarding**
The process of systematically socializing new employees to help them go "on board" with an organization

Some organizations combine orientation programs with computer-based training. New hires at SumTotal Systems go online for virtual tours of the company's various departments, with introductions to company leaders sprinkled throughout. Of course, these types of programs supplement—but do not replace—the value of face-to-face orientation.[53]

## ONBOARDING

**Onboarding** is the process of systematically socializing new employees to help them get "on board" with an organization. Onboarding goes beyond just orienting new employees to their new environments. It brings them into the organization's fold so that they truly feel as if they are a part of it. This is important because new hires are at high risk for quitting.

Many new hires quit their jobs not because they cannot handle the tasks related to them but because they are going through culture shock within their new organizations. When new hires quickly quit, companies often have to begin recruiting, interviewing, and screening candidates all over again. The best recruiting and selection processes are therefore of little value if a firm is not able to retain the people it hires. The more time and effort spent in helping new employees feel welcome, the more likely they are to identify with the organization and become valuable members of it.

To help new hires avoid culture shock, some companies make video and podcasts available to new hires before they even begin work. The mission and goals of an organization, a mini-tour of its facilities, and interviews with current employees talking about what they like about the organization are featured. Executives are often featured as well, which helps new hires develop an early understanding of who's who in the organization.

It is also common practice for supervisors or other managerial personnel to recruit coworkers to serve as volunteer "sponsors," or mentors, for incoming employees. In addition to providing practical help to newcomers, experienced colleagues represent an important source of information about the norms and nuances of the work group, the culture of the organization, and what it expects from its employees. These relationships are vital to the socialization of new employees and contribute significantly to their long-term success within the organization.

Southwest Airlines approaches onboarding as a welcoming party. "It was so much fun and so informative. [The company] stresses that we are a family, so when I speak of Southwest Airlines, I will only speak in terms of *we* and not *they*," remarked one eager new employee after Southwest's onboarding process. New employees always start on Fridays at CityMax.com, a build-your-own-website service in Vancouver, British Columbia. On Fridays, the work is less hectic, people are in a better mood and more relaxed, and everyone has time to introduce themselves.[54]

## BASIC SKILLS TRAINING

Businesses report that they are having a harder time finding workers with the basic skills they seek. Almost half of all Canadians have low literacy skills—meaning that they can cope with everyday tasks but lack the capacity to learn new job skills.[55] Many businesses say it is their top problem. A list of typical basic skills employees need includes the following:

- Reading
- Writing
- Computing
- Speaking
- Listening
- Problem solving
- Managing oneself/self-discipline
- Knowing how to learn
- Working as part of a team
- Leading others

Avon Foods in Nova Scotia and Palliser's Furniture in Manitoba are among the many companies that now offer remedial courses to their employees, many of which are conducted in-house.[56] Recognizing that the skills gap is increasing, colleges and companies have begun teaming up to bridge the gap. To implement a successful program in basic and remedial skills, managers should do the following:

1. Explain to employees why and how the training will help them in their jobs.
2. Relate the training to the employees' goals.
3. Respect and consider participants' experiences and use these as a resource.
4. Use a task-centred or problem-centred approach so that participants "learn by doing."
5. Give employees feedback on their progress toward meeting their learning objectives.

A workplace education program in the City of Charlottetown won an award of excellence for Municipal Workplace Literacy Achievements by following these principles. The key to developing a successful basic skills program is *flexibility*, reinforcing the principle of individual differences while acknowledging the reality of work and family constraints.

Job-specific and general skills are both essential for career success.

## TEAM TRAINING AND CROSS-TRAINING

As we discussed earlier in the book, organizations rely on teams to attain strategic and operational goals. Whether the team is an aircrew, a research team, or a manufacturing or service unit, the contributions of the individual members of the team are a function not only of the KSAOs of each individual but also of the interaction of the team members. Teamwork behaviours that differentiate effective teams are shown in Figure 7.12. They include both process dynamics and behavioural dynamics. The fact that these behaviours are observable and measurable provides a basis for training team members to function more effectively in the pursuit of their goals.[57]

Coca-Cola's Fountain Manufacturing Operation (which makes the syrup for Coke and Diet Coke) developed team training for its manufacturing employees. The program focused on three skill categories: (1) technical, (2) interpersonal,

**CHAPTER 7:** TRAINING AND DEVELOPMENT

## FIGURE 7.12

TEAM TRAINING SKILLS

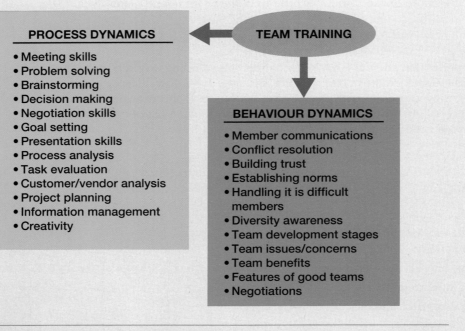

**PROCESS DYNAMICS**

- Meeting skills
- Problem solving
- Brainstorming
- Decision making
- Negotiation skills
- Goal setting
- Presentation skills
- Process analysis
- Task evaluation
- Customer/vendor analysis
- Project planning
- Information management
- Creativity

**TEAM TRAINING**

**BEHAVIOUR DYNAMICS**

- Member communications
- Conflict resolution
- Building trust
- Establishing norms
- Handling it is difficult members
- Diversity awareness
- Team development stages
- Team issues/concerns
- Team benefits
- Features of good teams
- Negotiations

**Source:** George Bohlander and Kathy McCarthy, "How to Get the Most from Team Training," *National Productivity Review* (Autumn 1996): 25–35.

**cross-training**
The process of training employees to do multiple jobs within an organization

and (3) team action. The technical component, called Four-Deep Training, meant that each individual should learn four different jobs to allow for team flexibility. The interpersonal skills component, called Adventures in Attitudes, focused on listening, conflict resolution, influence, and negotiation. Team action training focused on team leadership, management of meetings, team roles, group dynamics, and problem solving—all skills needed to function effectively as a team. The training not only increased quality and customer satisfaction but also helped decrease costs and set up a model for preparing employees for the future.[58]

Closely related to team training is **cross-training**. Cross-trained employees learn how to do different jobs within an organization as well as their own. Part of the motivation for cross-training is that it gives firms flexibility. Workers can be dynamically shifted when and where they are needed, unlike specialized workers and equipment, which cannot. Moreover, by keeping workers interested and motivated, cross-training can cut turnover, increase productivity, pare down labour costs, and lay the foundation for careers rather than dead-end jobs.

In a sense, cross-training represents a shift from Henry Ford's assembly line production to flexible production. Some companies are using cross-training to keep their workers and plants in Canada versus offshoring them. Pace Worldwide, a company that sells soldering equipment, watched all of its competitors move offshore. To keep up with the productivity of its low-cost rivals abroad, Pace grouped workers into teams and trained each team to build an entire product as well as different products. "Some of the people could only do certain things, and if they had no work, they would just sit and wait," said one Pace manager. "Now they have ownership of it all." Employees have an incentive to learn because their hourly wages get bumped up as they master more skills. Now Pace builds products to meet customer demand rather than storing inventory, which is more costly, and has been able to shorten its production times and move its operations into one building versus two. In addition to making them more productive, research shows that cross-training gives employees the "big picture," making them more creative and better problem solvers.[59]

## ETHICS TRAINING

**chief ethics officer**
A high-ranking manager directly responsible for fostering the ethical climate within the firm

Ethics training became more prevalent in companies following the high-profile corporate scandals such as those that occurred at Enron in 2001. As the Enron case showed, ethics training is not just for rank-and-file employees. Top managers also need to attend ethics training and take it seriously or risk jail time. For reasons such as these and because the reputational and financial repercussions of ethical lapses can be devastating, many firms have since created ethics codes and developed ethics training programs for their employees.

Top managers play a key role in terms of ethics training because employees take their cues from them and mirror their behaviour. Thus, a firm's top executives and managers should behave in accordance with their companies' values. If this does not happen, no ethics training program within a company can be effective. Senior managers should also broach the topic of ethics often in their speeches and presentations, and a company's ethics training should be part of the new employee orientation. In addition, a firm's current employees need to undergo ethics training at regular intervals.

Workers who are responsible for areas that expose them to ethical lapses are likely to require special training. Employees who do the purchasing for their firms are one example. Likewise, some firms offer special training to their overseas personnel who work in countries in which corruption and bribery are prevalent. (We will talk more about bribery in Chapter 15, which covers international topics.)

Bringing in an outside expert trained in ethics or values-based management can be helpful, as can surveying employees, managers, and sometimes even customers about what they believe the ethical state of the company is and where improvements could be made. Some firms go so far as to appoint **chief ethics officers**—high-ranking managers directly responsible for fostering the ethical climate within their firms.

HP is one company that has an exemplary ethics program. All employees—from entry-level employees to senior executives—are responsible for holding one another accountable with respect to ethical behaviour. The following are elements of HP's ethics program and training:

- A publicly available ethics code written in 12 languages
- Mandatory ethics training for all employees
- A toll-free ethics hotline complemented by a dedicated electronic mailbox where messages are treated with the highest degree of confidentiality
- An ethics officer with vice president–level leadership and authority
- Conflict resolution procedures
- Communications systems that facilitate and encourage employee feedback without fear of retaliation[60]

# SMALL BUSINESS APPLICATION

Training is very important to small businesses because, typically, employee turnover is high, and as a result, the development of new employees quickly and effectively is one of the key success factors for smaller businesses.

To illustrate the role of training for small business, let's draw on the example of a clothing retailer we will call Style Zone. Style Zone has one store, located in a popular shopping mall. It is open seven days per week from 10 a.m. to 9 p.m. It is located close to two high schools, which provide regular customers, as well as staff. Style Zone has 35 staff in addition to the owner and the assistant manager. Generally speaking, turnover is 50 percent per year, meaning that over the course of the

*continued*

year, half of the staff leave, equating to one or two new hires per month. Style Zone supports the regular integration of staff by the standardization of roles and processes for two positions: cashier and stock associate. Within these two roles, the company has clearly defined and documented the responsibilities for the role, from how the employees should groom and dress, to what they do when they arrive, to how they greet customers, to what procedures to follow, to what they do before they leave for the day.

Why is role specialization important for Style Zone or any other small company managing the integration of staff? There are three primary reasons. First, standardization of roles allows many people to be able to train new workers. In Style Zone, with one owner and one assistant manager, it is imperative that existing staff are able to train new staff so that Style Zone is ready on any

given day to integrate new staff. Second, role standardization allows new workers to be coached and supported by other staff as they learn their roles. Orientation is typically a small part of on-the-job learning as employees will spend days and weeks becoming proficient in their new roles. Lastly, role specialization is important because it allows new employees to have clear visibility into the expectations of the role and quickly become proficient.

So how did Style Zone get there? The owner and assistant manager worked together to document the knowledge and skills required for each job. With this written documentation, the manager then started training, which consisted of a systematic review of the required behaviours with the employee, demonstration of these behaviours, and practice of these behaviours with reinforcement—all done on the job.

# SUMMARY

## SUMMARY

**OUTCOME 1** Training programs cover a broad range of subjects, from simple on-the-job instruction to sophisticated skills training conducted on million dollar simulators. The goal of training is to contribute to an organization's strategic goals. To be effective, training programs need to be developed systematically. This approach consists of four phases: (1) needs assessment, (2) program design, (3) implementation, and (4) evaluation.

**OUTCOME 2** Needs assessment begins with organization analysis. Managers must establish a context for training by deciding where training is needed, how it connects with their firms' strategic goals, and how their companies' resources can best be used in terms of training. A task analysis is used to identify the knowledge, skills, and abilities employees need. A person analysis is used to identify which people need training.

**OUTCOME 3** When designing a training program, managers must consider the two fundamental preconditions for learning: readiness and motivation of trainees. In addition, the principles of learning should be considered to create an environment that is conducive to learning. These principles include goal setting, the meaningfulness of presentation, modelling, individual differences, active practice and repetition, whole-versus-part learning, massed-versus-distributed learning, and feedback and reinforcement.

**OUTCOME 4** A wide variety of methods are available to train nonmanagerial personnel. OJT is one of the most commonly used methods because it provides trainees with hands-on experience and an opportunity to build a relationship with their supervisor and coworkers. Apprenticeship training and internships are especially effective because they provide both on- and off-the-job experiences. Other off-the-job methods include classroom training, programmed instruction, computer-based training, simulations, and interactive e-learning utilizing teleconferencing, videoconferencing, webinars, and the communities of practice method of learning. Using multiple methods, or what is called blended learning, has been found to be the most effective.

The training and development of managers are becoming increasingly critical for firms because they are facing increasing competition from across the globe and the baby boomer generation is retiring.

As with nonmanagerial personnel, a wide variety of training methods are used for developing managers. On-the-job experiences include coaching, understudy assignment, job rotation, lateral transfers, project and committee assignments, and staff meetings. Off-the-job experiences include analysis of case studies, management games and simulations, role-playing, and behaviour modelling.

**OUTCOME 5** Evaluation of a training program should focus on several criteria: participant reactions, learning, behaviour change on the job, and bottom-line results such as ROI. Transfer of training is measured via examination of the degree to which trained skills are demonstrated back on the job. Benchmarking and utility analysis help evaluate the impact of training and provide the information for further needs assessment.

**OUTCOME 6** In addition to training that addresses the KSAOs of a particular job, many employers develop additional training programs for various purposes. Orientation training allows new hires to more quickly acquire the knowledge, skills, and attitudes that increase the probabilities of their success within the organization. Onboarding programs go beyond orientation by bringing new hires into an organization's fold so that they truly feel as if they are part of it. This is important because new hires are at high risk for quitting. Basic skills training, team and cross-training, and ethics training are other programs commonly conducted by organizations.

## KEY TERMS

apprenticeship training, 249
behaviour modelling, 258
behaviour modification, 248
benchmarking, 263
blended learning, 252
chief ethics officer, 269
chief learning officer, 239
competency assessment, 241

cooperative training, 250
cross-training, 268
e-learning, 254
instructional objectives, 244
internship programs, 251
just-in-time training, 254
learning management system (LMS), 254

on-the-job training (OJT), 249
onboarding, 266
organization analysis, 239
orientation, 264
person analysis, 243
spot rewards, 248
task analysis, 241
transfer of training, 261

## DISCUSSION QUESTIONS

1. You have been asked by a colleague to teach her how to use Excel. How would you conduct a needs analysis to determine her current knowledge and skill level?

2. Think about the best teacher whom you have ever experienced and the worst teacher. Go to the list of characteristics of effective instructors on page 248 and assess each teacher against this list.

3. Indicate what training methods you would use for each of the following jobs. Explain your choices.
   a. File clerk
   b. Computer operator
   c. Automobile service station attendant
   d. Pizza maker
   e. Nurse's aide

4. Compare computer-based instruction and e-learning to the lecture method with regard to the way the two methods involve the different psychological principles of learning.

5. Suppose that you are the manager of an accounts receivable unit in a large company. You are switching to a new system of billing and record keeping and need to train your 3 supervisors and 28 employees in the new procedures. What training method(s) would you use? Why?

6. Think of all the training methods that you have experienced. Prepare a grid, with the methods on one column and the four levels of evaluation on another. Rate each method as to its effectiveness in your reaction, learning, behaviour, and results, citing specific examples where possible.

7. Team up with a classmate and design an orientation program for a new student to your school.

# HRM EXPERIENCE

## Training and Learning Principles

Even though it is not difficult to do so, a surprising number of training programs do not explicitly incorporate the principles of learning (goal setting, modelling, individual differences, and feedback) discussed in the chapter. To prove that incorporating them is not difficult, complete the following assignment for building a paper airplane.

## Assignment

1. Form teams of four to six members. Identify someone on the team who knows how to make a paper airplane. That person will be the *trainer*.

2. Identify someone who will be the *observer/recorder*. That person will not participate in the training but will write down how many (and how effectively) principles of learning are used in the instruction:

    a. Goal setting
    b. Modelling
    c. Meaningfulness
    d. Individual differences
    e. Whole-versus-part learning
    f. Mass-versus-distributed learning
    g. Active practice
    h. Feedback

3. Give the trainer 10 to 15 minutes to train the group in making a paper airplane. The observer/recorder will keep notes of effective and ineffective training techniques (demonstrated learning principles).

4. Have someone from each team—not the trainer—volunteer to come before the class for a friendly competition. The instructor will give each team member two minutes to make a paper airplane. Then, just for fun, they can compete by seeing which one flies the farthest. As always, no wagering, please.

5. To finish the exercise, the observers/recorders will lead a discussion of the learning principles that were demonstrated. If they were done in this setting, discuss also why they might not be done in other training settings.

Visit the *Managing Human Resources* CourseMate website at http://www.belcourt7e.nelson.com for quizzes, flashcards, videos, games, and more!

# CASE STUDY 1

## SERVICE AT THE CHATEAU WHISTLER

The Chateau Whistler in Whistler, British Columbia, is one of the world's leading hotels and has been named the number one ski resort in North America for the past eight years. The 557-room hotel opened in 1989 and currently has 650 full-time employees.

The orientation program for new employees at the Chateau Whistler reflects the same standards that guests enjoy at the hotel. New recruits have raw talents such as energy and enthusiasm but have to be trained quickly in the art of excellent service.

On day 1 of the orientation program, an "orientation game" is played; then the employees are introduced to the hotel (e.g., the types of rooms, the amenities). Then the following are discussed:

- Salary and benefits, including health care, pension plan, discounted ski passes, staff meals, food discounts, discounted rates at other properties, and health club access
- Employment standards, human rights, and labour relations (although the hotel is not unionized)
- Health and safety, including the Workplace Hazardous Materials Information System (WHMIS) and Material Safety Data Sheets (MSDSs) and the environmental program
- Harassment policy
- The wellness program
- The incentive program

New employees also receive a tour of the town of Whistler so that they can talk to guests about the key attractions and establish a network of friends.

Day 2 is devoted to the Service Plus Program. The Service Plus Code is spelled out this way:

S support
E empathy
R responsiveness
V valuing differences
I interdependence
C caring
E expectations

The day 2 program focuses on the guest–employee interaction and strives to teach employees how to provide excellent service, deal empathetically and effectively with problems reported by guests, and solve problems creatively. Training consists of role-plays such as "handling the difficult guest." Specifically, the new recruits gain an understanding of the hotel's mission statement and commitment to service, the changing service culture, and the high service expectations of the guests.

The third component of the orientation program is "Guest for a Night," during which employees who have been working at the hotel for three months eat at the restaurants, enjoy the facilities, and spend one night in the hotel as a guest. According to David Roberts, the hotel's general manager, the goal of the Guest for a Night program is to ensure that employees can talk knowledgeably about guest rooms, restaurants, and other facilities and understand the level of quality that the hotel provides.

As part of this program, employees are asked to fill out a feedback survey, just like a guest. Also at this time, employees are invited to be part of a focus group to express concerns and provide feedback about their work experiences.

Through these orientation and training programs, employees develop knowledge and skills in service excellence. More importantly, they develop a commitment to the company. At a 10-year reunion party given for 600 people, 599 said that it was the best working experience of their lives.

## Questions

1. Compare the Chateau Whistler's orientation program to the list of activities presented in Highlights in HRM 7.7. Would you add anything?
2. The hospitality sector has high turnover rates among employees. Why does the Chateau Whistler invest so much time, money, and energy into its orientation program?
3. Describe the activities in the orientation and training programs that would ensure a high degree of transfer of training to the job.
4. How would you measure the success of this program? What results criteria would you try to measure?

## CASE STUDY 2

# PEOPLE DEVELOPMENT STRATEGIES AT CREDIT UNION CENTRAL OF SASKATCHEWAN

There are 128 credit unions in Saskatchewan, with assets ranging from less than $1 million to more than $1 billion. All of these are affiliated with Credit Union Central of Saskatchewan, which facilitates cooperation among credit unions and provides consulting services, trade association functions, and liquidity management.

Credit Union Central, together with the four largest Saskatchewan credit unions, developed a plan to implement a comprehensive HRM system to produce, first, a better alignment of employee performance to organizational objectives and, second, more focused training to produce desired business results and an enhanced ability to retain employees through opportunities for professional development. Working with Hay Management Consultants, the first step was to develop a competency glossary, followed by performance management processes and tools, selection and staffing tools, and then succession planning.

Competencies can be defined as attitudes, skills, knowledge, or behaviours that are essential to perform at work and that differentiate superior performers. The competency glossary defines core competencies, which apply to all roles within the organization, and role-specific competencies. Competency target levels indicating superior performance are set for each role.

An example of a core competency, based on the key values and strategies of the organization, is "results orientation":

When your employee tried to improve his or her own performance, he or she

1. Identified areas of waste or inefficiency but did not take any action
2. Made some changes to work methods to reach particular goals that had been set for him or her
3. Made specific changes in the system and his or her work methods to improve performance beyond goals set
4. Set challenging goals that were accomplished with a significant amount of planning, analysis, and effort
5. Set individual goals by thinking through the costs and benefits and explicitly considered potential profits, risks, and ROI to make decisions that ended up having a positive organizational impact
6. Took a calculated entrepreneurial risk and committed significant organizational resources to act on an idea that ended up significantly improving performance

A role-specific competency might be "concern for order, quality, and compliance," defined as follows:

When your employee demonstrated attention to detail in his or her work, he or she

1. Checked on the work to ensure that it was accurate, complied with all relevant regulations, and followed all standard practices and procedures
2. Monitored the accuracy and quality of his or her work and others' work consistently and systematically and kept a detailed record of work when it was necessary

3. During the project, monitored the progress of the project against milestones and deliverables, took action to ensure that the procedures put in place were effective, and quickly corrected any weaknesses or deficiencies
4. Established and utilized a procedure and/or system to facilitate work efficiency and ensure high-quality output and modified and improved the procedure and/or system when a weakness was identified to ensure that high-quality work was being produced

Managers work with employees to assess competency levels. The competency glossary and a competency assessment questionnaire enable managers and employees to discuss skills, abilities, and behaviours using a common framework. Training and development plans are based on gaps between target performance and actual performance. A developmental resource kit, which includes training courses, seminars, books, and work opportunities, all classified by competency, assists with building development plans.

This approach has resulted in clear direction on performance and development plans to move employees toward optimum performance levels.

## Questions

1. Describe the advantages of the approach used to identify performance gaps.
2. Why would managers resist or support this approach?
3. Describe methods that you would use to evaluate the effectiveness of this approach by levels of learning, behaviour, and results.

## CASE STUDY 3

### ONBOARDING AT CAPITAL POWER

Capital Power is an independent power producer, based in Edmonton, Alberta, but with operations across North America. It has an aggressive growth strategy with the goal of tripling its generating capacity by 2020. With this strategy, Capital Power needs to increase its workforce of 950 employees and retain the talent that it plans to hire. Feeling that traditional orientation programs were not effective, the senior vice president of HR, environment, and health and safety designed and implemented an onboarding program called Strong Start. The features of the program include

- A new hire portal, which directs the new employee to content relevant to the position
- An e-learning module, Capital Power 101: The Basics, which outlines the organization's design, vision, values, leadership team, major policies, and how the company makes money, as well as the growth strategy
- An e-learning module, Capital Power 102: Powering Up and Plugging In, provides the template for a 100-day developmental plan that the new hire must create with the manager
- A day-and-a-half classroom session with other new hires, which includes a personality inventory (to increase self-insight); a

presentation by an executive about the mission, vision, and values; and a plant tour

An assessment of the Strong Start program revealed that over 90 percent felt that the program leads to the engagement of employees, aligns employees with the culture of the company, and enables new hires to be more successful. A majority also felt that it will assist in reducing turnover. There has been a 30 percent increase in organizational knowledge among participants.

According to a study by Alan Saks (University of Toronto) and Jamie Gruman (University of Guelph), structured onboarding tactics result in more engaged employees who believe that they fit both the job and the organization. Onboarding programs, unlike orientation programs, create opportunities for employees to develop a social network and establish where and how to get information.

## Questions

1. Using the checklist in Highlights in HRM 7.7, compare the requirements for an orientation program to Capital Power's Strong Start program. What are the differences?
2. Capital Power has evaluated its program. Using the four levels of evaluation, determine which levels were used. Prepare an evaluation program that will assess the goals of the program and the goals of onboarding outlined by Saks and Gruman.

Sources: "Capital Power: About Us," http://www.capitalpower.com; B. Mitchell, "Power to the People," *Canadian HR Reporter*, January 30, 2012, 23, 25; A. M. Saks and J. A. Gruman, "Getting Newcomers Engaged: The Role of Socialization Tactics," *Journal of Managerial Psychology* 26, no. 5 (January 2011): 383–402.

# NOTES AND REFERENCES

1. Carrie Lavis, *Learning and Development Outlook 2011: Are Organizations Ready for Learning 2.0?* (The Conference Board of Canada, October 2011).

2. Lori Freifeld, "Best of the Best," *Training* 45, no. 2 (February 2008): 8.

3. David Dubois and William Rothwell, "Competency-Based or a Traditional Approach to Training?" *T+D Magazine* 58, no. 4 (April 2004): 46–59; See also Irwin L. Goldstein and J. Kevin Ford, *Training in Organizations: Needs Assessment, Development and Evaluation,* 4th ed. (Belmont, CA: Wadsworth, 2002). For the classic citation on needs assessment, see William McGehee and Paul W. Thayer, *Training in Business and Industry* (New York: John Wiley and Sons, 1961).

4. Laurie Bassi and Daniel McMurrer, "How's Your Return on People?" *Harvard Business Review* 8, no. 3 (March 2004): 18; Tracy Mauro, "Helping Organizations Build Community," *T+D Magazine* 56, no. 2 (February 2002): 25–29; Liam Lahey, "RFIDs Touted as Standard for Airport Security," *Computing Canada* 28, no. 13 (June 21, 2002): 21; Caroline Wilson, "Ensuring a Smooth Ride," *Security Management* 46, no. 8 (August 2002): 92.

5. Brad Long, "Strategic Human Resource Management and the Worker's Experience," *Journal of Individual Employment Rights* 12, no. 3 (2007): 265–282; "E-Learning and Teleconferencing Join Needs Assessment to Control Training Costs," *Managing Training & Development, no.* 3 (December 2003): 1; Thomas Gainey, Brian Klaas, and Darla Moore, "Outsourcing the Training Function: Results from the Field," *Human Resource Planning* 25, no. 1 (2002): 16; Sarah Fister Gale, "Creative Training: Doing More with Less," *Workforce* 80, no. 10 (October 2001): 82–88.

6. Scott A. Yorkovich, Gregory S. Waddell, and Robert K. Gerwig, "Competency-based Assessment Systems: Encouragement Toward a More Holistic Approach," *Proceedings of the Northeast Business & Economics Association* (2007): 77–81; Patty Davis, Jennifer Naughton, and William Rothwell, "New Roles and New Competencies for the Profession: Are You Ready for the Next Generation," *T+D Magazine* 58, no. 4 (April 2004): 26–38; David Dubois and William Rothwell, "Competency-Based or a Traditional Approach to Training?" T+D *Magazine* 58, no. 4 (April 2004): 46–59.

7. Thomas Hoffman, "Motivation: These IT Leaders Keep Staffers Upbeat during Lean Times by Targeting What Drives Them: Technology and Training," *Computerworld 38,* no. 1 (January 5, 2004): 39; Elwood Holton, Reid Bates, and Sharon Naquin, "Large-Scale Performance-Driven Training Needs Assessment: A Case Study," *Public Personnel Management* 29, no. 2 (Summer 2000): 249–267.

8. Gail Johnson, "The Development Framework: Booz Allen Hamilton's Holistic Method of Employee Development Gives Its Employee a Roadmap to Success—Both Professionally and Personally," *Training* 40, no. 2 (February 2003): 32–34; Robert Mager, "Contract Training Tips," *Security Management* 45, no. 6 (June 2001): 30.

9. Debbie Schachter, "How to Set Performance Goals: Employee Reviews Are More Than Annual Critiques," *Information Outlook* 8, no. 9 (September 2004): 26–30; "Burger Olympics," *Training 41*, no. 7 (July 2004): 20; Jason A. Colquitt and Marcia J. Simmering, "Conscientiousness, Goal Orientation, and Motivation to Learn during the Learning Process: A Longitudinal Study," *Journal of Applied Psychology* 83, no. 4 (August 1998): 654–665.

10. Annette Towler and Robert Dipboye, "Effects of Trainer Expressiveness, Organization, and Trainee Goal Orientation on Training Outcomes," *Journal of Applied Psychology* 86, no. 4 (August 2001): 664–673; Steve Kozlowski, Stanley Gully, Kenneth Brown, and Eduardo Salas, "Effects of Training Goals and Goal Orientation Traits on Multidimensional Training Outcomes and Performance Adaptability," *Organizational Behavior and Human Decision Processes* 85, no. 1 (May 2001): 1–31.

11. The classics by Albert Bandura include *Social Foundations of Thought and Action: A Social Cognitive Theory* (Englewood Cliffs, NJ: Prentice Hall, 1986) and *A Social Learning Theory* (Englewood Cliffs, NJ: Prentice Hall, 1977). See also Melesa Altizer Bolt, Larry Killough, and Hian Chye Koh, "Testing the Interaction Effects of Task Complexity in Computer Training Using the Social Cognitive Model," *Decision Sciences 32*, no. 1 (Winter 2001): 1–20; Susan Pedersen and Min Liu, "The Transfer of Problem-Solving Skills from a Problem-Based Learning Environment: The Effect of Modeling an Expert's Cognitive Processes," *Journal of Research on Technology in Education* 35, no. 2 (Winter 2002): 303–321.

12. Stanley Gully, Stephanie Payn, K. Lee Kiechel Koles, and John-Andrew Whiteman, "The Impact of Error Training and Individual Differences on Training Outcomes: An Attribute-Treatment Interaction Perspective," *Journal of Applied Psychology* 87, no. 1 (February 2002): 143–155; Steven John Simon, "The Relationship of Learning Style and Training Method to End-User Computer Satisfaction and Computer Use: A Structural Equation Model," *Information Technology, Learning, and Performance Journal* 18, no. 1 (Spring 2000): 41–59.

13. Maya Dollarhide, "Hits the Spot," *Incentive* 181, no. 10 (October 2007): 102–103; "Can Technology Actually Boost Behavior Change?" *Managing Training & Development,* no. 3 (November 2003): 3; Don Hartshorn, "Reinforcing the Unsafe Worker," *Occupational Hazards* 62, no. 10 (October 2000): 125–128.

14. Joe M. Ricks, Jacqueline A. Williams, and William A. Weeks, "Sales Trainer Roles, Competencies, Skills, and Behaviors: A Case Study," *Industrial Marketing Management* 37, no. 5 (July 2008): 593–609; John L. Bennett, "Trainers as Leaders of Learning," T+D Magazine 55, no. 3 (March 2001): 42–45; Ruth Palombo Weiss, "Deconstructing Trainers' Self-Image," T+D Magazine 55, no. 12 (December 2001): 34–39.

15. Eduardo Salas and Janis Cannon-Bowers, "The Science of Training: A Decade of Progress," *Annual Review of Psychology* 52 (2001): 471–499.

16. Cohn Terry, "Enabling Staff to Access the Knowledge They Need, When They Need It," *Industrial & Commercial Training* 39, no. 7 (2007): 368–371; Diane Walter, *Training on the Job* (Alexandria, VA: American Society for Training and Development, 2001); Toni Hodges, *Linking Learning and Performance: A Practical Guide to Measuring Learning and On-the-Job Application* (Burlington, MA: Butterworth-Heinemann, 2001); Gary Sisson, *Hands-On Training: A Simple and Effective Method for On-the-Job Training* (San Francisco: Barrett-Koehler, 2001).

17. Teresa M. McAleavy, "U.S. Schools Fail to Provide Job Training," *Knight-Ridder/Tribune Business News* (June 9, 2004); "Eight Steps to Better On-the-Job Training," *HRfocus* 80, no. 7 (July 2003): 11; Alison Booth, Yu-Fu Chen, and Gylfi Zoega, "Hiring and Firing: A Tale of Two Thresholds," *Journal of Labor Economics* 20, no. 2 (April 2002): 217–248.

18. Ronald L. Jacobs and Michael J. Jones, "Teaching Tools: When to Use On-the-Job Training," *Security Management* 41, no. 9 (September 1997): 35–39.

19. Information found on the Apprenticeship page, Spokane Community College website, February 9, 2005, http://www.scc.spokane.edu/?apprent, retrieved July 30, 2009.

20. For more information about the Bureau of Apprenticeship and Training, see the Bureau's website at http://oa.doleta.gov.

21. Uyen Vu, "EnCana Builds Talent Pipeline into High School Classrooms," *Canadian HR Reporter*, April 11, 2005, 3.

22. "Major Investment in Training Programs at Nova Scotia Community College, Marconi Campus," News Release, Enterprise Cape Breton Corporation, May 17, 2002.

23. John Byrd and Rob Poole, "Highly Motivated Employees at No Cost? It's Not an Impossible Dream," *Nonprofit World* 19, no. 6 (November/December 2001): 312–332.

24. Michael Grant and P. Derek Hughes, *Learning and Development Outlook 2007: Are We Learning Enough?* (Conference Board of Canada, April 2007).

25. Phil Britt, "E-Learning on the Rise in the Classroom: Companies Move Content Online: Cisco Systems' Employees and Partners Routinely Watch Videos on the Internet," *EContent* 27, no. 11 (November 2004): 36–41; Heather Johnson, "The Whole Picture: When

It Comes to Finding Out How Employees Feel about Training, Many Companies Fail to Get a Clear Picture," *Training* 47, no. 7 (July 2004): 30–35.

26. Laura Chubb, "EDS Uses Teleconferencing to Train Leaders in Coaching Skills," *People Management* 13, no. 23 (November 15, 2007): 13; "What Does Teleconferencing Cost?" *T+D Magazine* 1, no. 10 (October 2007): 96.

27. Matthew Trevisan, "A Smart Lesson from the Airforce, in 3D," *The Globe and Mail*, May 8, 2008, B11.

28. Ericka Johnson, "Surgical Simulators and Simulated Surgeons: Reconstituting Medical Practice and Practitioners in Simulations," *Social Studies of Science* 37, no. 4 (August 2007): 585–608; "Soup to Nuts: Simulator Manufacturing Is a Lucrative but Risky Business, Which Is Why Market Leader CAE Has Tapped into the More Stable World of Flight Training," *Air Transport World* 40, no. 5 (May 2003): 69–71; "SimsSir: Modeling and Simulation Are Leading the Assault on New Learning Technologies That Are Winning Favor with the U.S. Military," *T+D Magazine* 57, no. 10 (October 2003): 46–52.

29. Marc J. Rosenberg, "Technology Euphoria?" *T+D Magazine* 62, no. 6 (June 2008): 24–27. For applications of simulation training used in the U.S. Navy, see John Flink, "This Is Really Neat Stuff," *United States Naval Institute Proceedings* 128, no. 7 (July 2002): 68–69. For applications of simulation training used in medical schools, see David Noonan, "Is the Cadaver Dead?" *Newsweek* 139, no. 25 (June 24, 2002): 62. For applications of simulation training used in the police force, see Jim Weiss and Mickey Davis, "Deadly Force Decision-Making," *Law and Order* 50, no. 6 (June 2002): 58–62.

30. Sarah Fister Gale. "Virtual Training with Real Results," *Workforce Management* (December 2008), http://www.workforce.com.

31. Scott A. Snell, Donna Stueber, and David P. Lepak, "Virtual HR Departments: Getting Out of the Middle," in R. L. Heneman and D. B. Greenberger (eds.), *Human Resource Management in Virtual Organizations* (Greenwich, CT: Information Age Publishing, 2002).

32. Scott A. Snell, Donna Stueber, and David P. Lepak, "Virtual HR Departments: Getting Out of the Middle," in R. L. Heneman and D. B. Greenberger (eds.), *Human Resource Management in Virtual Organizations* (Greenwich, CT: Information Age Publishing, 2002).

33. Garry Kranz, "E-learning Hits Its Stride," *Workforce Management Online* (February 2008); Martin Delahoussaye, Kristine Ellis, and Matt Bolch, "Measuring Corporate Smarts," *Training* 39, no. 8 (August 2002): 20–35; Daniel Crepin, "From Design to Action: Developing a Corporate Strategy," *Quality Progress 35*, no. 2 (February 2002): 49–56; Brad Miller, "Making Managers More Effective Agents of Change," *Quality Progress* 34, no. 5 (May 2001): 53–57.

34. Yabome Gilpin-Jackson and Gervase R. Bushe, "Leadership Development Training Transfer: A Case Study of Post-Training Determinants," *Journal of Management Development* 26, no. 10 (2007): 980–1004; Joseph Alutto, "Just-in-Time Management Education in the 21st Century," *HR Magazine* 44, no. 11 (1999): 56–57; Gordon Dehler, M. Ann Welsh, and Marianne W. Lewis, "Critical Pedagogy in the 'New Paradigm,'" *Management Learning* 493, no. 4 (December 2001): 493–511.

35. Yabome Gilpin-Jackson and Gervase R. Bushe, "Leadership Development Training: A Case Study of Post-Training Determinants," *Journal of Management Development* 26, no. 10 (2007): 980–1004.

36. Chris Whitcomb, "Scenario-Based Training to the F.B.I.," *T+D Magazine* 53, no. 6 (June 1999): 42–46; Anne Hoag, Dale Brickley, and Joanne Cawley, "Media Management Education and the Case Method," *Journalism and Mass Communication Educator* 55, no. 4 (Winter 2001): 49–59.

37. Jason B. Moats, Thomas J. Chermack, and Larry M. Dooley, "Using Scenarios to Develop Crisis Managers: Applications of Scenario Planning and Scenario-Based Training," *Advances in Developing Human Resources* 10, no. 3 (June 2008): 397–424; A. J. Faria, "The Changing Nature of Business Simulation/Gaming Research: A Brief History," *Simulation and Gaming* 32, no. 1 (March 2001): 97–110.

38. Alli McConnon, "The Games Managers Play," *BusinessWeek* (June 25, 2007), 12; Matt Bolch, "Games Employees Play: Delta Air Lines Uses a Blended e-Learning Program to Teach Employees the Economic Realities of the Airline Industry," *Training* 40, no. 4 (April 2003): 44–48.

39. Shannon Klie, "L'Oreal Plays Games with Training," *Canadian HR Reporter*, October 6, 2008, 26.

40. Adam Kirby, "Guest Service Is Fun and Games," *Hotels* 42, no. 5 (May 2008): 71–72; Dan Heilman, "Putting Games to Work: Game-Based Training Is Shaping Up to Be One of This Generation's Primary Teaching Tools, in Business and Elsewhere," *Computer User* 22, no. 2 (February 2004): 14–16.

41. Patricia Robinson, "In Practice: Western Companies Show Asian Counterparts That It Pays to Play," *Chief Learning Officer* 6, no. 12 (December 2007): 30; Christopher Hosford, "Serious Fun: Computer Training Finds a Niche," *Meeting News* 28, no. 7 (December 2004): 16; Rick Sullivan, "Lessons in Smallness," *T+D Magazine* 56, no. 3 (March 2002): 21–23; James W. Walker, "Perspectives," *Human Resource Planning* 23, no. 3 (2000): 5–7.

42. T. L. Stanley, "Be a Good Role Model for Your Employees," *Supervision* 65, no. 5 (January 2004): 5–8; Gary May and William Kahnweiler, "The Effect of a Mastery Practice Design on Learning and Transfer in Behavior Modeling Training," *Personnel Psychology* 53, no. 2 (Summer 2000): 353–373.

43. Wendy Larlee, "Training Programs: Key to Collections: Companies in the Collections Business Face Significant Challenges: Putting Solid Training Program in Place Can Help," *Collections & Credit Risk* 9, no. 2 (December 2004): 42–44; Heather Johnson, "The Whole Picture: When It Comes to Finding Out How Employees Feel about Training, Many Companies Fail to Get a Clear Picture," *Training* 47, no. 7 (July 2004): 30–35; Martin Delahoussaye, "Show Me the Results," *Training* 39, no. 3 (March 2002): 28–29; Reinout van Brakel, "Why ROI Isn't Enough," *T+D Magazine* 56, no. 6 (June 2002): 72–74.

44. "Dissatisfaction with Job Training Contributes to Low Job Satisfaction," *Managing Training & Development* (November 2003): 8; James Pershing and Jana Pershing, "Ineffective Reaction Evaluation," *Human Resource Development Quarterly* 12, no. 1 (Spring 2001): 73–90.

45. Andreas Putra, "Evaluating Training Programs: An Exploratory Study of Transfer of Learning onto the Job at Hotel A and Hotel B, Sydney, Australia," *Journal of Hospitality and Tourism Management* 11, no. 1 (April 2004): 77–78; Thomas Hoffman, "Simulations Revitalize e-Learning," *Computerworld* 37, no. 31 (August 4, 2003): 26–28.

46. Jathan Janove, "Use It or Lose It," *HR Magazine* 47, no. 4 (April 2002): 99–104; Max Montesino, "Strategic Alignment of Training, Transfer-Enhancing Behaviors, and Training Usage: A Posttraining Study," *Human Resource Development Quarterly* 13, no. 1 (Spring 2002): 89–108; Siriporn Yamnill and Gary McLean, "Theories Supporting Transfer of Training," *Human Resource Development Quarterly* 12, no. 2 (Summer 2001): 195–208.

47. Delahoussaye, "Show Me the Results," 28–29; van Brakel, "Why ROI Isn't Enough," 72–74.

48. Richard J. Wagner and Robert J. Weigand, "Can the Value of Training Be Measured? A Simplified Approach to Evaluating Training," *The Health Care Manager* 23, no. 1 (January–March 2004): 71–79; van Brakel, "Why ROI Isn't Enough," 72–74; Sarah Fister Gale, "Measuring the ROI of E-Learning," *Workforce* 81, no. 8 (August 2002): 74–77; Earl Honeycutt, Kiran Karande, Ashraf Attia, and Steven Maurer, "A Utility-Based Framework for Evaluating the Financial Impact of Sales Force Training Programs," *Journal of Personal Selling and Sales Management* 21, no. 3 (Summer 2001): 229–238.

49. Mary Walton, *The Deming Management Method* (New York: The Putnam Publishing Group, 1986).

50. "Three Quick and Easy Ways to Gauge Your Training Outcomes," *IOMA's Report on Managing Training & Development* (January 2005): 4–5; "Use This Eight-Step Process to Predict the ROI of Your Training Programs," *IOMA's Human Resource Department Management Report* (December 2004): 4–5; Ellen Drost, Colette Frayne, Keven Lowe, and J. Michael Geringer, "Benchmarking Training and Development Practices: A Multi-Country Comparative Analysis," *Human Resource Management* 41, no. 1 (Spring 2002): 67–86; Daniel McMurrer, Mark Van Buren, and William Woodwell, "Making the Commitment," *T+D Magazine* 54, no. 1 (January 2000): 41–48.

51. Lisa Bertagnoli, "Basic Training: Orientation Is Proving to Be an Important First Step in Establishing Employee Bonds That Last," *WWD* (September 30, 2004): 40S; Jonathan Thom, "Creating Effective Orientation Programs," *San Diego Business Journal* 25, no. 33 (August 16, 2004): A6; Howard Klein and Natasha Weaver, "The Effectiveness of an Organizational-Level Orientation Training Program in the Socialization of New Hires," *Personnel Psychology* 53, no. 1 (Spring 2000): 47–66.

52. Mike Frost, "Creative New Employee Orientation Programs," *HR Magazine* 47, no. 8 (August 2002): 120–121; Marilyn Moats Kennedy, "Setting the Right Tone, Right Away," *Across the Board* 36, no. 4 (April 1999): 51–52.

53. Emmanuella Plakoyiannaki, Nikolaos Tzokas, Pavlos Dimitratos, and Michael Saren, "How Critical Is Employee Orientation for Customer Relationship Management? Insights from a Case Study," *Journal of Management Studies* 45, no. 2 (March 2008): 268–293.

54. Kathryn Tyler, "Take New Employee Orienation off the Back Burner," *HR Magazine* 43, no. 6 (May 1998); Noel Tichy, "No Ordinary Boot Camp," *Harvard Business Review* 79, no. 4 (April 2001): 63–70.

55. Canadian Council on Learning, "Projection: 15 Million Canadian Adults with Low Literacy by 2031," June 12, 2008, http://www.ccl-cca.ca/CCL/Newsroom/Releases /20080612ReadingtheFuture.htm, retrieved July 30, 2009.

56. "Corporate America Can't Write," *Work & Family* Newsbrief (January 2005): 4; Matt Bolch, "School at Work," *Training* 39, no. 2 (February 2002); Slav Kanyba, "Community Colleges React to Job-Training Request," *San Fernando Valley Business Journal* 9, no. 2 (June 7, 2004): 1–2.

57. Eduardo Salas, Diana R. Nichols, and James E. Driskell, "Testing Three Team Training Strategies in Intact Teams: A Meta-Analysis," *Small Group Research* (August 2007); "What Makes Teams Work?" *HRfocus* 79, no. 4 (April 2002): S1–S3; John Annett, David Cunningham, and Peter Mathias-Jones, "A Method for Measuring Team Skills," *Ergonomics* 43, no. 8 (August 2000): 1076–1094.

58. "Behavior-Based Sales Team Training Produces a 56% Increase in Revenues," *Managing Training & Development* (April 2004): 1.

59. Lorraine Mirabella, "Productivity Gains in Maryland Mean Less Hiring But More Job Cross-Training," *The Baltimore Sun* (via Knight-Ridder/Tribune Business News), April 17, 2004.

60. "Ethics Codes and Ethics Training Issue Brief," *Business for Social Responsibility* (March 2005), http://www.bsr.org/research/issue-brief-details. cfm?DocumentID=50967; Nan Demars, "Office Ethics: News from the Front Lines," *Office Pro* 68, no. 3 (April 2008): 28–31.

# 8

# Performance Management and the Employee Appraisal Process

MANAGINGHU
HUMANRESOU
RESOURCESM

## After studying this chapter, you should be able to

**OUTCOME 1** Explain what performance management is and how the establishment of goals, ongoing performance feedback, and the appraisal process are part of it.

**OUTCOME 2** Explain the purposes of performance appraisals and the reasons they can sometimes fail.

**OUTCOME 3** Describe the different sources of appraisal information.

**OUTCOME 4** Explain the various methods used for performance evaluation.

**OUTCOME 5** Outline the characteristics of an effective performance appraisal interview.

We have discussed some of the ways managers can acquire and develop top-notch employees and train and develop them. But how do managers know if their efforts are really paying off in terms of what their employees are contributing once they are on the job?

# PERFORMANCE MANAGEMENT SYSTEMS

**performance management**
The process of creating a work environment in which people can perform to the best of their abilities

**performance appraisals**
The result of an annual or biannual process in which a manager evaluates an employee's performance relative to the requirements of his or her job and uses the information to show the person where improvements are needed and why

**Performance management** is the process of creating a work environment in which people can perform to the best of their abilities to meet a company's goals. It is an entire work system that emanates from a company's goals. Figure 8.1 shows the elements of a performance management process.

**Performance appraisals,** which are an important part of performance management systems, are the result of an annual or biannual process in which a manager evaluates an employee's performance relative to the requirements of his or her job and uses the information to show the person where improvements are needed and why. Appraisals are therefore a tool organizations can use to maintain and enhance their productivity and facilitate progress toward their strategic goals. But as you can see from Figure 8.1, appraisals are just part of the performance management process. Aligning the goals of employees with that of the firm, providing workers with continual on-the-job feedback, and rewarding them are critical as well.

You might compare a performance appraisal to taking a test in college. Do tests motivate you? Do they make you want to excel, or do you just want to get through them? Now compare your test-taking experience to an experience in which your instructor talked to you about your career plans, complimented you on your performance, and offered you suggestions for improving it. That probably had a greater motivating effect on you.

We hope you can see the analogy we are making. Employers have to appraise you, just as your university has to test you to be sure you graduate with the qualifications people in society expect. But your performance in either scenario consists of so much more than that. That is why organizations need to look at

## FIGURE 8.1

STEPS IN THE PERFORMANCE MANAGEMENT PROCESS

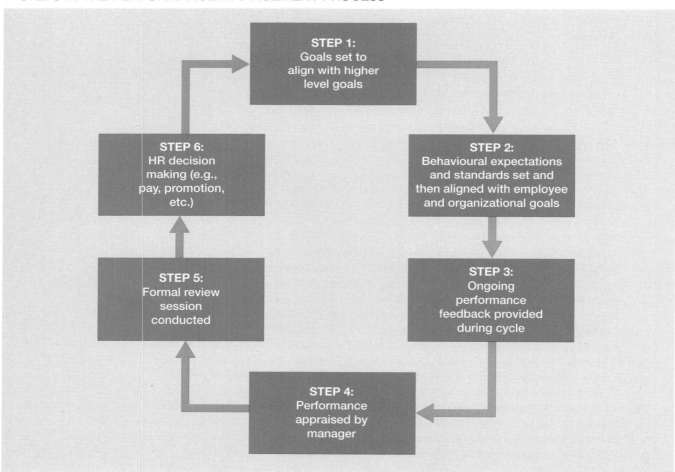

**STEP 1:** Goals set to align with higher level goals

**STEP 2:** Behavioural expectations and standards set and then aligned with employee and organizational goals

**STEP 3:** Ongoing performance feedback provided during cycle

**STEP 4:** Performance appraised by manager

**STEP 5:** Formal review session conducted

**STEP 6:** HR decision making (e.g., pay, promotion, etc.)

the performance management system as a whole rather than just appraisals. Appraisals are simply a logical extension of the day-to-day performance management process.[1]

## ONGOING PERFORMANCE FEEDBACK

Because feedback is most useful when it is immediate and specific to a particular situation, it should be a regularly occurring activity. For example, if you are a sales manager, should you wait to appraise your employees once or twice a year? Probably not. Most likely you would want to monitor their sales on a weekly and monthly basis. Has a particular salesperson met his or her customer contact numbers this week? Why or why not? Is the salesperson closing deals with the people he or she does contact? If, at the six-month mark, the salesperson is not making his or her goals, how can you help the person if you have not provided ongoing feedback? The lack of sales will be hard to make up at this point.

It is not just salespeople who need continual feedback. All types of employees can benefit from ongoing performance conversations with their managers. Managers need to constantly engage in a dialogue with their subordinates. Once the manager and employees have a series of discussions, there is an ebb and flow of ideas, some with the potential to serve as catalysts for improvement within the company.[2] The ultimate purpose is to better both parties.

The HR function at one university provides training and development in the area of employee feedback for its managers and leaders. In that training, the university identifies seven key points to address during feedback sessions:

- *Give specific examples of desirable and undesirable behaviours.* Without specific examples of real-life situations, the employee will only be confused by the vagueness of the feedback.

- *Focus feedback on behaviour, not the person.* This will help the employee "hear" the message and will defuse what could be a confrontational conversation.

- *Frame the feedback in turns of helping the employee be successful.* Let the employee know that you are trying to help him or her be a successful employee within the organization.

- *Direct the feedback toward behaviour the employee can control.* Employees cannot do much about things over which they have no control.

- *The feedback should be timely.* When an event takes place, it is important to provide feedback within a reasonable amount of time.

- *Limit feedback to the amount the employee can process.* Most employees are able to handle feedback on one or two issues at a time.

- *Use active communication skills and confirm that the employee is engaged in the conversation.*

Providing employees with feedback on a continual basis also helps them know where they stand when they receive their formal appraisals. As a result, the anxiety they experience during formal appraisals is often alleviated, and a more meaningful conversation with them and their supervisors can take place. If employees are surprised by their reviews, it is probably safe to say that their supervisors have not been providing them with much ongoing feedback.

## PERFORMANCE APPRAISAL PROGRAMS

A **focal performance appraisal** is one in which all employees of a company are reviewed at the same time of year rather than on the anniversary dates they were hired. This appraisal strategy can be very helpful if a company is experiencing change and must quickly alter its strategy. After the new strategic goals of the firm are established, they can then be translated into individual goals that employees receive all at the same time. That way, all employees can begin working toward those goals immediately. A focal performance appraisal also enables managers to compare the performance of different employees simultaneously, which can result in appraisals that are more accurate and fair. The review of an employee is also less likely to be overlooked if all of an organization's managers review employees at the same time.

## THE PURPOSES OF PERFORMANCE APPRAISAL

It has been said that "what gets measured gets done." Performance appraisals are part of an organization's measurement process. Good appraisal systems have the capability to influence employee behaviour and improve an organization's performance. One study showed that organizations with strong performance management systems are 40 to 50 percent more likely to outperform their competitors in the areas of revenue growth, productivity, profitability, and market value.[3] This is why experts advise companies to continue to appraise their employees during an economic downturn even if they cannot afford to give them raises.

Formal appraisal processes also ensure that employees receive at least *some* feedback from their supervisors. A recent poll by the research company Gallup found that employees who receive no feedback from their supervisors exhibit the least amount of engagement. Jim Harter, a Gallup research scientist and coauthor of the report, says that even negative feedback is better than none. Negative feedback, he says, "at least lets people know that they matter."[4]

In addition to improving a firm's overall performance and profitability, Figure 8.2 shows the other two most common purposes of performance appraisals: *administrative* and *developmental*.

### Administrative Purposes

Appraisal programs provide input that can be used for the entire range of HRM activities, such as promotions, transfers, layoffs, and pay decisions. The practice of "pay for performance," basing employees' pay on their achievements, is found in all types of organizations. Studies have shown that employees who earn performance-based pay are more satisfied.[5] Performance appraisal data may also be used in HR planning, in determining the relative worth of jobs under a job evaluation program, and as criteria for recruiting particular types of employees and validating selection tests. Performance appraisals also provide a "paper trail" for documenting HRM actions that can result in legal action. Employers must

## FIGURE 8.2

PURPOSES OF PERFORMANCE APPRAISAL

| DEVELOPMENTAL | ADMINISTRATIVE |
| --- | --- |
| • Provide performance feedback<br>• Identify individual strengths and weaknesses<br>• Recognize individual performance achievements<br>• Help employees identify goals<br>• Evaluate goal achievement of employees<br>• Identify individual training needs<br>• Determine organizational training needs<br>• Reinforce authority structure<br>• Allow employees to discuss concerns<br>• Improve communication<br>• Provide a forum for leaders to help employees | • Document personnel decisions<br>• Promote employees<br>• Determine transfers and assignments<br>• Identify performance problems and develop ways to correct them<br>• Make retention, termination, and layoff decisions<br>• Validate selection criteria<br>• Meet legal requirements<br>• Evaluate training programs/progress<br>• Assist with human resources planning<br>• Make reward and compensation decisions |

maintain accurate, objective employee performance records to defend themselves against possible charges of discrimination when it comes to promotions, salaries, and terminations. Finally, it is important to recognize that the success of the entire HR program depends on knowing how the performance of employees compares to the goals established for them. This knowledge is best derived from a carefully planned and administered HR appraisal program.

## Developmental Purposes

From the standpoint of individual development, appraisal provides the feedback essential for discussing an employee's goals and how they align with the organization's goals. As with ongoing feedback, the appraisal process provides managers and employees with the opportunity to discuss ways to build on their strengths, eliminate potential weaknesses, identify problems, and set new goals for achieving high performance. Performance appraisals are also used to develop training and development plans for employees. By taking a developmental approach to appraisals, managers help employees understand that the appraisals are being conducted to improve their future competencies and further their careers and are not being conducted simply to judge them based on their past performance.

Companies such as Best Buy and EDS have redesigned their performance appraisal systems to focus more on employee development and learning. EDS, for example, integrated its performance appraisal system to work in concert with the company's learning and career management objectives. The new system, called the Career Resource System, includes a detailed job description, performance review, and career planner to track employees' long-term goals, as well as access to the company's automated career library. The system is ultimately linked to the company's succession policies. By creating this overall system, EDS hopes to shift the role of manager from that of "judge" to one of "coach."[6]

## WHY APPRAISAL PROGRAMS SOMETIMES FAIL

Performance appraisals often fall short of their potential. In an ongoing survey of employee attitudes by the HR consulting firm Watson Wyatt, only 30 percent of employees said they thought their company's performance management process actually improved employee performance; only one in five thought it helped poorly performing employees do better. Some people believe performance appraisals discourage teamwork because they frequently focus on the individual achievements of workers versus what their teams or firms accomplish. (Who gets the best rating and the biggest raise? Who does not?) Others contend that appraisals are useful only at the extremes—for highly effective or highly ineffective employees—and are not as useful for the majority of employees in the middle. Still others point out that appraisals often focus on short-term achievements rather than long-term improvement and learning.

Figure 8.3 shows that the primary culprits include a lack of top-management information and support, unclear performance standards, biased ratings because managers lack training, too many time-consuming forms to complete, and use of the program for conflicting purposes. For example, if an appraisal program is used to determine an employee's future pay and at the same time to motivate the person to perform better, the two purposes can end up conflicting with one another. Often when salary decisions are discussed during a performance appraisal, they tend to become the dominant topic of conversation, and managers spend a lot of time justifying their pay decisions. As a result, ways to improve the employee's future job performance get less discussion.

As with all HR practices, if the support of a firm's top managers is lacking, the appraisal program will not be successful. Even the best-conceived program will not work in an environment where appraisers are not encouraged by their superiors to take the program seriously. To underscore the importance of this

## FIGURE 8.3

### LET ME COUNT THE WAYS

There are many reasons why performance appraisal systems might not be effective. Some of the most common problems include the following:

- Inadequate preparation on the part of the manager
- Employee is not given clear objectives at the beginning of the performance period
- Manager may not be able to observe performance or have all the information
- Performance standards may not be clear
- Inconsistency in ratings among supervisors or other raters
- Manager rating personality rather than performance
- The halo effect, contrast effect, or some other perceptual bias

- Inappropriate time span (either too short or too long)
- Overemphasis on uncharacteristic performance
- Inflated ratings because managers do not want to deal with "bad news"
- Subjective or vague language in written appraisals
- Organizational politics or personal relationships cloud judgments
- No thorough discussion of causes of performance problems
- Manager may not be trained at evaluation or giving feedback
- No follow-up and coaching after the evaluation

**Source:** Patricia Evres, "Problems to Avoid during Performance Evaluations," *Air Conditioning, Heating & Refrigeration News* 216, no. 16 (August 19, 2002): 24–26; Clinton Longnecker and Dennis Gioia, "The Politics of Executive Appraisals," *Journal of Compensation and Benefits* 10, no. 2 (1994): 5–11; "Seven Deadly Sins of Performance Appraisals," *Supervisory Management* 39, no. 1 (1994): 7–8.

responsibility, top management should announce that effectiveness in appraising subordinates is a standard by which the appraisers themselves will be evaluated.

Other reasons performance appraisal programs can fail to yield the desired results include the following:

1. There is little face-to-face discussion between the manager and the employee being appraised.
2. The relationship between the employee's job description and the criteria on the appraisal form is not clear.
3. Managers feel that little or no benefit will be derived from the time and energy they spend on the process or are concerned only with bad performances.
4. Managers dislike the face-to-face confrontation of appraisal interviews.
5. Managers are not sufficiently adept at rating employees or providing them with appraisal feedback.
6. The judgmental role of appraisal conflicts with the helping role of developing employees.
7. The appraisal is just a once-a-year event, and there is little follow-up afterward.

In many organizations, performance appraisals are conducted only once a year. Although this is appropriate in many circumstances, an increasing number of organizations are finding value in conducting them on a semiannual and even quarterly basis. An important principle of performance appraisal is that continual feedback and employee coaching must be a regularly occurring activity. The annual or semiannual performance review should simply be a logical extension of the day-to-day managerial process. It has been found that providing employees with feedback on a continual basis not only improves their performance but also helps them know where they stand in terms of their performance. As a result, the anxiety they experience during formal appraisals is often alleviated. Some organizations do not perform formal evaluations and use coaching, individual development plans, or other feedback systems instead.

One of the main concerns employees have relates to the fairness of the performance appraisal systems of their firms. Organizational politics, a firm's culture, the orientation of its managers, as well as its history and current competitive conditions can all affect how managers conduct and rate their employees.[7] For example, managers sometimes inflate evaluations because they want to obtain higher salaries for their employees or because higher ratings for their subordinates make them look good as supervisors. Alternatively, managers might want to get rid of troublesome employees by inflating their ratings and passing them off to another department. Even when appraisals are supposed to be confidential, employees often have a keen sense about whether or not the process is fair, or at least they think they do. Employees who believe the system is unfair are likely to consider the appraisal interview a waste of time and leave the interview feeling frustrated and cynical. Also, they may view compliance with the appraisal system as perfunctory and thus play only a passive role during the interview process. By addressing these employee concerns during the planning stage of the appraisal process and reassuring them that they can meet the requirements and will be rewarded accordingly, an appraisal program is more likely to be successful.[8]

Figure 8.3 shows the primary reasons why the performance appraisal process often ends up being less effective than it could be. Many managers are as nervous about administering appraisals as employees are about receiving them. Often they just want them to be over. When this happens, managers do not engage employees in much of a conversation during the appraisals, which is a major drawback. Even when appraising an outstanding employee, managers often are reluctant to evaluate an employee's performance. Sometimes it is as simple as the manager lacking the skills to execute an effective performance review session; sometimes there is never enough money to recognize even the top performer. So reviews are postponed or handled poorly, and the result is that the organization's best performers are left frustrated, angry, disillusioned, and demotivated. In addition, these top performers are looking at the organization's competitor.

Employee performance avoidance often starts on the first day of a new job. Rather than clearly outlining the expectations, many managers show the new employees to their workstations and dump them off, leaving the new hires to their own means. Job assignments may be delivered and retrieved on a routine basis with little or no feedback or comments from the manager.

Unclear performance standards, biased ratings because managers lack training, too many time-consuming forms to complete, and use of the program for conflicting purposes can also hamper the effectiveness of performance appraisals.

# DEVELOPING AN EFFECTIVE APPRAISAL PROGRAM

The HR department ordinarily has the primary responsibility for overseeing and coordinating a firm's appraisal program. However, managers from the company's operating departments must also be actively involved, particularly when it comes to helping establish the objectives for the program. Furthermore, employees are more likely to accept and be satisfied with the performance appraisal program when they have the chance to participate in its development. Their concerns about the fairness and accuracy of the program insofar as it determines their raises, promotions, and the like tend to be alleviated somewhat when they have been involved at the planning stage and have helped develop the performance standards themselves. It also helps ensure that the appraisal takes into account all of the tasks that need to be done in an organization, especially when major changes in the firm and its jobs are taking place.[9]

## WHAT ARE THE PERFORMANCE STANDARDS?

Before any appraisal is conducted, the standards by which performance is to be evaluated should be clearly defined and communicated to the employee. As discussed in Chapter 4, these standards should be based on job-related requirements

## FIGURE 8.4

ESTABLISHING PERFORMANCE STANDARDS

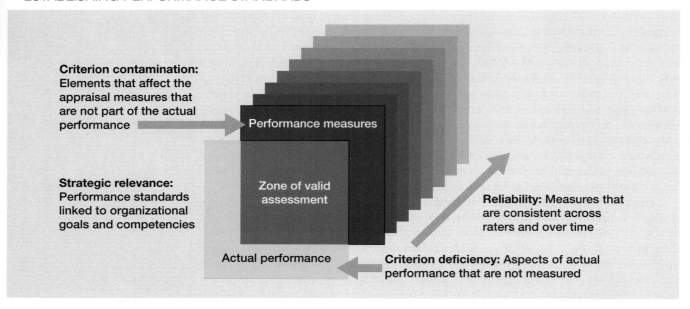

**Criterion contamination:** Elements that affect the appraisal measures that are not part of the actual performance

Performance measures

**Strategic relevance:** Performance standards linked to organizational goals and competencies

Zone of valid assessment

**Reliability:** Measures that are consistent across raters and over time

Actual performance

**Criterion deficiency:** Aspects of actual performance that are not measured

derived from job analysis and reflected in an employee's job description and job specifications. When performance standards are properly established, they help translate an organization's goals and objectives into job requirements that communicate to employees the definitions of acceptable and unacceptable performance levels.

As shown in Figure 8.4, there are four basic considerations in establishing performance standards: strategic relevance, criterion deficiency, criterion contamination, and reliability.

## Strategic Relevance

Strategic relevance refers to the extent to which the standards of an appraisal relate to the strategic objectives of the organization in which they are applied. For example, if an organization has established a standard that "95 percent of all customer complaints are to be resolved in one day," then it is relevant for the customer service representatives to be held to this standard when they are evaluated. Companies such as 3M have strategic objectives to the effect that 25 to 30 percent of their sales are to be generated from products developed within the past five years. These objectives are then translated into performance standards for their employees. General Motors' and Whirlpool's strategic objectives include cost, quality, and speed, and the two companies have developed metrics to identify and compare their performance around the world on these measures. A strategy-driven performance appraisal process also provides the documentation HR managers need to justify various training expenses to close any gaps between employees' current skills and those they will need in the future to execute the firm's strategy.[10]

## Criterion Deficiency

A second consideration in establishing performance standards is the extent to which the standards capture the entire range of an employee's responsibilities. When performance standards focus on a single criterion (such as sales revenues) to the exclusion of other important but less quantifiable performance dimensions (such as customer service), then the appraisal system is said to suffer from criterion deficiency.[11]

## Criterion Contamination

Just as performance criteria can be deficient, they can also be contaminated. There are factors outside an employee's control that can influence his or her performance. A comparison of performance of production workers, for example, should not be contaminated by the fact that some work with newer machines than others do. A comparison of the performance of travelling salespeople should not be contaminated by the fact that territories differ in sales potential.[12]

## Reliability

As we discussed in Chapter 6, reliability refers to the stability or consistency of a standard, or the extent to which individuals tend to maintain a certain level of performance over time. In terms of appraisal ratings, reliability can be measured by correlating two sets of ratings made by a single rater or by two different raters. For example, two managers would rate the same individual and estimate his or her suitability for a promotion. Their ratings would then be compared to determine interrater reliability.

Some companies are now using a process called **calibration** to make sure managers are rating employees consistently. During calibration meetings, a group of supervisors, led by their managers and facilitated by a HR professional, discuss the performance of individual employees to ensure that all managers apply similar standards to all of the firm's employees. The supervisors begin the process by rating employees whose performances are especially good or especially poor. They then attempt to rate employees who lie more in the middle and try to achieve a consensus on their performance. Initially, the ratings are likely to vary considerably simply because some managers are hard raters and others are not. Over subsequent evaluation periods and calibration meetings, however, the ratings should begin to converge, or become more similar. Calibration meetings can be particularly helpful after a merger or acquisition, especially one that is global. Why? Because differences in the corporate cultures and the appraisal standards of the formerly separate companies can cause the same employees to be rated quite differently. For example, when Lawson Software grew from 1,400 employees in 3 countries to 4,000 employees in 30 countries, it successfully used calibration to be sure its managers across the globe were assessing employees accurately.[13]

Performance standards also permit managers to specify and communicate precise information to employees regarding quality and quantity of output. This is why the standards should be defined in quantifiable and measurable terms and written down. For example, "the ability and willingness to handle customer orders" is not as good a performance standard as "all customer orders will be filled in 4 hours with a 98 percent accuracy rate." When the standard is expressed in specific, measurable terms, comparing an employee's performance against the standard results in a more accurate and justifiable appraisal.

## LEGAL ISSUES

Since some performance appraisals are used for HRM actions, they must meet certain legal requirements. Employers might face legal challenges to their appraisal systems when appraisals indicate that an employee's performance is acceptable or above average, but then the person is later passed over for promotion, disciplined for poor performance, discharged, or laid off from the organization. In these cases, the performance appraisals can undermine the legitimacy of the subsequent personnel decision. Intel, for example, was taken to court by a group of former employees on the grounds that the performance appraisal system (used for layoff decisions) was unreliable and invalid. Other companies, such as Goodyear and Ford, have also faced legal battles in the United States because their performance appraisals were viewed as discriminatory against

**CHAPTER 8:** PERFORMANCE MANAGEMENT AND THE EMPLOYEE APPRAISAL PROCESS

Specific, measurable job standards help remove vagueness and subjectivity from performance appraisals.

older workers.[14] In light of cases such as these, performance appraisals should meet the following legal guidelines:

- Performance ratings must be job related, with performance standards developed through a job analysis.

- Employees must be given a written copy of their job standards in advance of their appraisals.

- Managers who conduct the appraisals must be able to observe the behaviour they are rating. This implies having measurable standards with which to compare employee behaviour.

- Do not allow performance problems to continue unchecked. Document problems when they occur and refer to them in performance appraisals.

- Supervisors should be trained to use the appraisal form correctly. They should be instructed as to how to apply the appraisal standards when making judgments.

- The appraisals should be discussed openly with employees and counselling or corrective guidance offered to help poor performers improve their performance.

- An appeals procedure should be established to enable employees to express their disagreement with the appraisals.[15]

Employers must ensure that managers and supervisors document appraisals and reasons for subsequent HRM actions. This information may prove decisive should an employee take legal action. An employer's credibility is strengthened when it can support performance appraisal ratings by documenting instances of poor performance.

## WHO SHOULD APPRAISE PERFORMANCE?

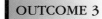

OUTCOME 3

Just as there are multiple standards by which to evaluate performance, there are also multiple candidates for appraising performance. Given the complexity of today's jobs, it is often unrealistic to presume that one person can fully observe and evaluate an employee's performance. At IBM, employees with high potential are regularly reviewed by a broad cross section of the company's leaders, not just their immediate bosses. As shown in Figure 8.5, raters may include

## FIGURE 8.5

ALTERNATIVE SOURCES OF APPRAISAL

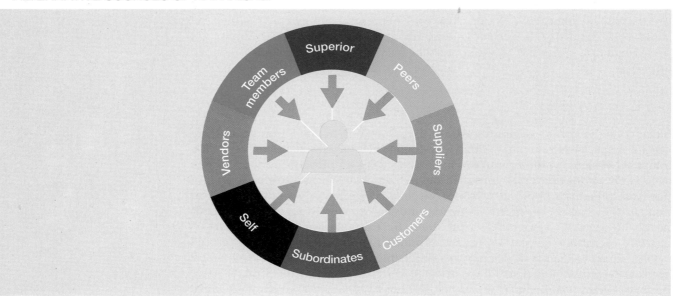

supervisors, peers, team members, self, subordinates, customers, vendors, and suppliers. Each may be more or less useful for the administrative and developmental purposes we discussed earlier. Companies such as Cigna, Black & Decker, and Disney have used a multiple rater approach—or 360-degree appraisal—to evaluate employee performance.[16] We will talk more about 360-degree appraisal at the end of this section.

**manager and/or supervisor appraisal**
A performance appraisal done by an employee's manager and often reviewed by a manager one level higher

**self-appraisal**
A performance appraisal done by the employee being evaluated, generally on an appraisal form completed by the employee prior to the performance interview

**subordinate appraisal**
A performance appraisal of a superior by an employee, which is more appropriate for developmental than for administrative purposes

## Manager/Supervisor Appraisal

**Manager and/or supervisor appraisal** has been the traditional approach to evaluating an employee's performance. In most instances, supervisors are in the best position to perform this function, although it may not always be possible for them to do so. Managers often complain that they do not have the time to fully observe the performance of employees. These managers must then rely on performance records to evaluate an employee's performance. If reliable and valid measures are unavailable, the appraisal may be less than accurate. (Recall our earlier discussion of criterion deficiency and criterion contamination.) In addition, research has shown that the ratings managers give employees they have known for less than one year are less reliable.[17]

When a supervisor appraises employees independently, provision is often made for a review of the appraisals by the supervisor's superior. This reduces the chance of superficial or biased evaluations.

## Self-Appraisal

Sometimes employees are asked to evaluate themselves on a self-appraisal form. The **self-appraisal** is beneficial when managers seek to increase an employee's involvement in the review process. A self-appraisal system requires an employee to complete the appraisal form prior to the performance interview. At a minimum, this gets the employee thinking about his or her strengths and weaknesses and may lead to discussions about barriers to effective performance. During the performance interview, the manager and the employee discuss job performance and agree on a final appraisal. This approach also works well when the manager and the employee jointly establish future performance goals or employee development plans. Critics of self-appraisal argue that self-raters are more lenient than managers in their assessments and tend to present themselves in a highly favourable light. There is also evidence that self-appraisals can lead employees to believe that they will have more influence over the appraisal's outcome. If that expectation is not met, the employee can become frustrated. For this reason, self-appraisals may be best for developmental purposes rather than for administrative decisions. Used in conjunction with other methods, self-appraisals can be a valuable source of appraisal information. They at least serve as a catalyst for discussion during the appraisal.[18]

## Subordinate Appraisal

**Subordinate appraisals** have been used by both large and small organizations to give managers feedback on how their subordinates view them.[19] Subordinates are in a good position to evaluate their managers because they are in frequent contact with their superiors and occupy a unique position from which to observe many performance-related behaviours. Subordinate appraisals have also been shown to improve the performance of managers. The performance dimensions judged most appropriate for subordinates to appraise include a manager's leadership, oral communication, delegation of authority, coordination of team efforts, and interest in his or her subordinates. However, dimensions related to managers' specific job tasks, such as planning and organizing, budgeting, creativity, and analytical ability, are not usually considered

**peer appraisal**
A performance appraisal done by fellow employees, generally on forms that are compiled into a single profile for use in the performance interview conducted by the employee's manager

**team appraisal**
A performance appraisal, based on total quality management concepts, that recognizes team accomplishment rather than individual performance

appropriate dimensions for subordinates to appraise. Because subordinate appraisals give employees power over their bosses, managers may be hesitant to endorse such a system, particularly when it might be used as a basis for compensation decisions. However, when the information is used for developmental purposes, managers tend to be more open to the idea. Available evidence suggests that when managers heed the advice of their subordinates, their own performance can improve substantially. Nevertheless, to avoid potential problems, subordinate appraisals should be submitted anonymously and combined across several individual raters.[20]

## Peer Appraisal

Individuals of equal rank who work together are increasingly asked to evaluate each other. A **peer appraisal** provides information that differs to some degree from ratings by a superior because an employee's peers often see different dimensions of his or her performance. Peers can readily identify leadership and interpersonal skills along with other strengths and weaknesses of their coworkers. For example, a superior asked to rate a patrol officer on a dimension such as "dealing with the public" might not have had much opportunity to observe it. Fellow officers, on the other hand, have the opportunity to observe this behaviour regularly.

One advantage of peer appraisals is the belief that they furnish more accurate and valid information than appraisals by superiors. The supervisor often sees employees on their best behaviour, whereas those who work with their fellow employees on a regular basis may see a more realistic picture. With peer appraisals, coworkers complete an evaluation on the employee. The forms are then usually compiled into a single profile, which is given to the supervisor for use in the final appraisal. For employees who have trouble confronting their coworkers about problems, the reviews provide a forum in which to address issues and resolve conflicts. They also provide an opportunity to hand out praise.[21]

Despite the evidence that peer appraisals are possibly the most accurate method of judging employee behaviour, there are reasons why they have not been used more frequently.[22] The reasons commonly cited include the following:

1. Peer ratings are simply a popularity contest.
2. Managers are reluctant to give up control over the appraisal process.
3. Those receiving low ratings might retaliate against their peers.
4. Peers rely on stereotypes in ratings.

When peers, such as sales associates, for example, are in competition with one another, peer appraisals should not be used to make administrative decisions such as those involving salary or bonuses. Employers using peer appraisals must also be sure to safeguard confidentiality in handling the review forms. Any breach of confidentiality can create interpersonal rivalries or hurt feelings and foster hostility among fellow employees.

### Using the Internet

Review the advantages and limitations of the peer appraisal used by nurses at

**http://nursing.advanceweb. com/editorial/content/editorial. aspx?cc=191092**

## Team Appraisal

An extension of the peer appraisal is the **team appraisal**. In a team setting, it may be nearly impossible to separate an individual's contribution. Advocates of team appraisals argue that, in such cases, individual appraisals can be dysfunctional because they detract from the critical issues of the team. To address this issue, organizations have begun developing team appraisals to evaluate the performance of their teams as a whole. These companies believe that team appraisals can help break down barriers between individual employees and encourage a joint effort on their part.

Much of the interest in team appraisals grew out of company commitments to total quality management (TQM) in the 1980s. But the principles and practices are no less relevant today. At its root, TQM is a control system that involves setting standards (based on customer requirements), measuring a firm's performance against those standards, and identifying opportunities for continuous improvement. In this regard, TQM and performance appraisals complement one another. However, a basic tenet of TQM is that a firm's performance is best understood at the level of the system as a whole, whereas performance appraisals traditionally focus on individual performance.[23] Frequently, the system is complemented by the use of team incentives or group variable pay (see Chapter 10).

## Customer Appraisal

**customer appraisal**
Performance appraisal that, like team appraisals, is based on total quality management concepts and seeks evaluation from both external and internal customers

Also driven by TQM concerns, an increasing number of organizations use internal and external **customer appraisals** as a source of performance appraisal information. External customers' evaluations, of course, have been used for some time to appraise restaurant personnel. However, companies such as FedEx and BMW Canada are among the companies that have utilized external customers as well. Poor customer appraisals undoubtedly explain why some firms, including Dell and others, have reconsidered offshoring their customer service functions. Other companies survey their vendors and suppliers as part of the appraisal process. By including the firm's business partners in the performance reviews, managers hope to produce more objective evaluations, more effective employees, more satisfied customers, and better business performance.[24]

In contrast to external customers, internal customers include anyone inside the organization who depends on an employee's work output. For example, managers who rely on the HR department for selection and training services would be candidates for conducting internal customer evaluations of that department. For both developmental and administrative purposes, internal customers can provide extremely useful feedback about the value added by an employee or team of employees.

Some managers give their teams autonomy but hold them accountable for results.

iStockphoto

As mentioned previously, companies combine various sources of performance appraisal information to create multirater—or 360-degree—appraisal and feedback systems. Jobs are multifaceted, and different people see different things. As the name implies, 360-degree feedback is intended to provide employees with as accurate a view of their performance as possible by getting input from all angles, such as from supervisors, peers, subordinates, and customers. Although in the beginning, 360-degree systems were purely developmental and were restricted mainly to management and career development, they have migrated to performance appraisal and other administrative applications.

Because the system combines more information than a typical performance appraisal, it can become administratively complex. For that reason, organizations have recently begun using performance management software to compile and aggregate the information.[25] For example, Workstream 7.0 developed by Workstream, Inc. gives managers a single view of all their talent management information: performance reviews, 360-degree assessments, compensation planning, development data, and succession planning, all unified in one application.[26] Figure 8.6 shows a list of pros and cons of 360-degree appraisal. When Intel established a 360-degree system, the company observed the following safeguards to ensure its maximum quality and acceptance:

- *Ensure anonymity.* Make certain that no employee ever knows how any evaluation team member responded. (The supervisor's rating is an exception to this rule.)

- *Make respondents accountable.* Supervisors should discuss each evaluation team member's input, letting each member know whether he or she used the rating scales appropriately, whether his or her responses were reliable, and how other participants rated the employee.

- *Prevent "gaming" of the system.* Some individuals may try to help or hurt an employee by giving either too high or too low an evaluation. Team members may try to collude with one another by agreeing to give each other uniformly high ratings. Supervisors should check for obviously invalid responses.

## FIGURE 8.6

PROS AND CONS OF 360-DEGREE APPRAISAL

**PROS**

- The system is more comprehensive in that responses are gathered from multiple perspectives.
- The quality of information is better. (The quality of respondents is more important than the quantity.)
- It complements TQM initiatives by emphasizing internal/external customers and teams.
- It may lessen bias or prejudice because feedback comes from more people, not one individual.
- Feedback from peers and others may increase employee self-development.

**CONS**

- The system is complex in combining all the responses.
- Feedback can be intimidating and cause resentment if an employee feels the respondents have "ganged up."
- There may be conflicting opinions, although they may all be accurate from the respective standpoints.
- The system requires training to work effectively.
- Employees may collude or "game" the system by giving invalid evaluations to one another.
- Appraisers may not be accountable if their evaluations are anonymous.

**Sources:** Compiled from David A. Waldman, Leanne E. Atwater, and David Antonioni, "Has 360-Degree Feedback Gone Amok?" *Academy of Management Executive* 12, no. 2 (May 1998): 86–94; Bruce Pfau, Ira Kay, Kenneth Nowak, and Jai Ghorpade, "Does 360-Degree Feedback Negatively Affect Company Performance?" *HRMagazine* 47, no. 6 (June 2002): 54–59; Maury Peiperl, "Getting 360-Degree Feedback Right," *Harvard Business Review* 79, no. 1 (January 2001): 142–147; Joyce E. Bono and Amy E. Colbert, "Understanding Responses to Multi-Source Feedback: The Role of Core Self-Evaluations," *Personnel Psychology* 58, no. 1 (Spring 2005): 171–205.

- *Use statistical procedures.* Use weighted averages or other quantitative approaches to combining evaluations. Supervisors should be careful about using subjective combinations of data, which could undermine the system.

- *Identify and quantify biases.* Check for prejudices or preferences related to age, gender, ethnicity, or other group factors.[27]

Based on the experiences of companies such as Canadian Tire, described in the Reality Check, it appears that 360-degree feedback can provide a valuable approach to performance appraisal. Its success, as with any appraisal technique, depends on how managers use the information and how fairly employees are treated.

# REALITY CHECK

## Canadian Tire 360-Degree Matrix

"Accentuate the positive; build on leadership strengths" is the principal theme of leadership performance evaluation and development conducted by the Canadian Tire Corporation as described by Janice Wismer, vice president of HR. Canadian Tire is a network of interrelated businesses with retail, financial, and petroleum interests. About 45,000 employees work in 1,000 retail stores across Canada.

The customized 360-degree feedback process used at Canadian Tire is research based and designed to build a cadre of great leaders. The first step in the design of the 360-degree feedback instrument was to benchmark other organizations that had effective 360-degree feedback processes. Twenty-seven key employees at Canadian Tire were interviewed to identify the attributes of their great leaders as measured by the standards of the organization. These key leadership attributes were then discussed and evaluated in workshops with important stakeholders. A total of 16 competencies were identified. Seven related to "who one is"—characteristics such as *trustworthy, passionate, and curious.* Nine others focused on "what one can do for the team, business, and enterprise," such as make *strategic choices, motivate* and *celebrate,* and *communicate authentically.*

To date, about 170 managers have been assessed by an average of nine colleagues, including peers, subordinates, and bosses. Colleagues complete a self-survey, and all feedback assessment is analyzed relative to their own organization and to industry standards, which are maintained in a database. A confidential feedback report is given to each individual.

In addition to the generation of individual reports, an aggregate one-page executive summary is produced. The report, presented as a matrix, provides a visual summary colour-coded under each competency comparing aggregate feedback data for all individuals in a defined business unit. The sample 360-degree matrix shown below lists key attributes across the horizontal axis and the employee's feedback along the vertical axis. To maintain confidentiality, identifiers are assigned to the supervisors and managers so that they can see their relative standing but without knowing the identity of the other employees. In the colour coding, red signifies a weak performance, yellow is an average performance, and green indicates exceptional strengths. By using this 360-degree matrix, HR can identify areas where groups of employees need professional development, thus investing training dollars where it matters most. In the example, Executives A, B, and C are perceived as generally excellent across most of the eight areas of interest, whereas Executives M, N, and O are experiencing considerable difficulty. In addition, most of the executive team performed well in areas 1, 2, and 3, having the most difficulty in area 8. In this case, individual development plans may work well for executives having problems in areas 1, 2, and 3, whereas a group development solution may be best designed for area 8.

According to Ed Haltrecht, Ph.D., CHRP, who specializes in measurement and organizational leadership development, in most organizations when performance feedback is presented, both the employee and the manager focus on the reds—the weaknesses—and try to work out methods of development to improve this area. What is unique about Canadian Tire is that the focus is on the positive. It has found that improvements in weak areas (provided that they are not fundamental flaws) do not affect overall performance, whereas improvements in areas of strength bring managers from good to extraordinary. The goal is to identify and strengthen attributes so employees will distinguish and present themselves as extraordinary. Individuals first address any "fundamental flaws," either a very weak attribute of the individual or, more importantly, elements regarded as critical to the organization. In the sample 360-degree matrix,

*continued*

Executives I, L, N, and O have potential fundamental flaws in areas 1 and 2. If there are no fundamental flaws, then development focuses on building strengths. This combination has resulted in measurable gains in performance.

This approach is research based. One book, *The Extraordinary Leader: Turning Good Managers into Great Leaders* by John Zenger and Joseph Folkman (New York: McGraw-Hill, 2002), presents several significant findings based on 225,000 evaluations of 20,000 people. Poor leaders were identified as those scoring in the bottom 10 percent; extraordinary leaders scored in the top 10 percent. Employee turnover in a call centre was 19 percent for the units managed by the poor managers, 14 percent for the middle group, and 9 percent for the extraordinary leaders. In another case that looked at a bank, net incomes for the bank generated by those groups whose managers were extraordinary, average, and poor were $7 million, $3.7 million, and $1.9 million, respectively. Employee satisfaction indices were at the 80th percentile for top managers compared to the 18th percentile for the bottom-scoring managers. Likewise, union vulnerability indices, which measure how attractive the organization is to a union's membership drive, reflected the 91st percentile for the top-scoring managers compared to the 10th percentile for the poor managers—that is, poorer managers are more likely to attract union interest. Although the pay structure was the same across different departments, those led by the top-scoring managers had employees who were at the 65th percentile in satisfaction with company pay and job security; the employees of average managers were in the 50th percentile; and poor managers' employees scored at the 37th percentile for satisfaction with company pay and job security.

Canadian Tire's leadership development system also recognizes two other significant research findings: first, extraordinary leaders have about three competencies at which they excel, and developing a few strengths to very high performance levels has a greater impact than improving several competencies from poor to average. Second, competencies travel together, and improvement

| Executive | 1. Treats others with respect. | 2. Gives credit to others who have contributed or performed well. | 3. Shows consistency between words and action. | 4. Models the core values of the corporation; leads by example. | 5. Treats team members as individuals based on knowledge of their strengths and development needs. | 6. Takes actions that build a high level of commitment to work group goals and objectives. | 7. Obtains resources so that the team has the knowledge, skills, and experience required to deliver results. | 8. Where there is underlying conflict, helps parties involved bring up their issues and get to the heart of the problem. | Mean |
|---|---|---|---|---|---|---|---|---|---|
| A | 5.0 | 4.9 | 4.9 | 4.6 | 4.8 | 4.6 | 4.6 | 4.5 | 4.7 |
| B | 5.0 | 4.8 | 4.9 | 4.9 | 4.9 | 4.8 | 4.3 | 3.7 | 4.7 |
| C | 5.0 | 4.7 | 4.5 | 4.7 | 4.7 | 4.7 | 4.5 | 4.2 | 4.6 |
| D | 4.8 | 4.6 | 4.2 | 4.7 | 4.3 | 4.3 | 4.6 | 4.1 | 4.4 |
| E | 4.7 | 5.0 | 4.7 | 4.0 | 3.7 | 4.0 | 4.3 | 4.3 | 4.4 |
| F | 4.8 | 4.3 | 4.3 | 4.5 | 4.4 | 4.3 | 4.1 | 3.2 | 4.2 |
| G | 4.6 | 4.2 | 4.2 | 4.2 | 4.2 | 4.1 | 4.2 | 3.9 | 4.2 |
| H | 4.5 | 4.4 | 4.1 | 4.2 | 4.3 | 3.9 | 3.9 | 4.1 | 4.2 |
| I | 4.4 | 3.8 | 4.0 | 4.3 | 4.0 | 4.3 | 4.5 | 3.7 | 4.2 |
| J | 4.4 | 4.3 | 4.5 | 4.2 | 4.1 | 4.2 | 3.9 | 4.0 | 4.2 |
| K | 4.6 | 4.2 | 4.5 | 4.0 | 4.5 | 4.2 | 3.6 | 4.3 | 4.1 |
| L | 3.8 | 4.4 | 4.3 | 4.3 | 3.7 | 4.1 | 4.5 | 3.9 | 4.1 |
| M | 4.4 | 4.2 | 4.4 | 4.1 | 4.2 | 4.0 | 4.0 | 4.2 | 4.1 |
| N | 4.3 | 3.8 | 4.1 | 3.9 | 4.0 | 4.0 | 3.5 | 2.9 | 3.9 |
| O | 3.3 | 4.1 | 4.0 | 3.6 | 3.8 | 3.8 | 3.9 | 3.3 | 3.6 |
| Mean | 4.5 | 4.3 | 4.4 | 4.2 | 4.2 | 4.2 | 4.1 | 3.9 | 4.2 |

in one leads to significant progress in others. Identifying these companion competencies has proven to be extremely worthwhile. In a nutshell, these are the findings: start with the right set of competencies or attributes, focus on strengths, eliminate any fundamental flaws, and pay attention to companion attributes.

The assessment feedback process at Canadian Tire is seen as a tool for dialogue and for focusing on what makes a great company and what matters in leadership. Those employees who try to improve are given a developmental opportunities guidebook. Canadian Tire has discovered that the best development methods are challenging stretch assignments, coaching and mentoring, personal feedback, talks with consultants, and training programs.

Source: Interview with Janice Wismer and Ed Haltrecht.

## TRAINING APPRAISERS

A weakness of many performance appraisal programs is that managers and supervisors are not adequately trained for the appraisal task, so the feedback they provide to their subordinates is not as useful as it might be and can often be meaningless, if not destructive. This is perhaps one reason that some experts believe firms should no longer conduct performance appraisals of their employees. However, training appraisers can vastly improve the performance appraisal process. According to one HR manager: "What's not important is the (appraisal) form or the (measuring) scale. What's important is that managers can objectively observe people's performance and objectively give feedback on that performance." Notwithstanding, in a survey of 55 HR managers from medium and large companies, more than half said their companies did either little or no evaluation of how well their managers do appraisals.[28]

### Establishing an Appraisal Plan

A training program for raters is most effective when it follows a systematic process that begins with an explanation of the objectives of the firm's performance appraisal system. It is also important for the rater to know the purpose for which the appraisal is to be used. For example, using the appraisal for compensation decisions rather than development purposes can affect how the rater evaluates the employee and may change the rater's opinion of how the appraisal form should be completed. The mechanics of the rating system should also be explained, including how frequently the appraisals are to be conducted, who will conduct them, and what the standards of performance are. In addition, appraisal training should alert raters to the weaknesses and problems of appraisal systems so that they can be avoided.

### Eliminating Rater Error

Appraisal training should focus on eliminating the subjective errors made by managers in the rating process. Gary Latham of the University of Toronto and Kenneth Wexley, an American industrial psychologist, stress the importance of performance appraisal training by noting that

> [R]egardless of whether evaluations are obtained from multiple appraisers or from only the employee's immediate superior, all appraisers should be trained to reduce errors of judgment that occur when one person evaluates another. This training is necessary because to the degree to which a performance appraisal is biased, distorted, or inaccurate, the probability of increasing the productivity of the employee is greatly decreased. Moreover, wrong decisions could be made regarding whom to promote, retain, or replace, which in turn will penalize the organization's bottom line. In addition, when a performance appraisal is affected by rating errors, the employee may be justified in filing a discrimination charge.[29]

With any rating method, certain types of errors can arise that should be considered. The "halo error" is common with respect to rating scales, especially those

**error of central tendency**
A performance rating error in which all employees are rated about average

**leniency or strictness error**
A performance rating error in which the appraiser tends to give employees either unusually high or unusually low ratings

**recency error**
A performance rating error in which the appraisal is based largely on the employee's most recent behaviour rather than on behaviour throughout the appraisal period

**contrast error**
A performance rating error in which an employee's evaluation is biased either upward or downward because of comparison with another employee just previously evaluated

that do not include carefully developed descriptions of the employee behaviours being rated. Provision for comments on the rating form tends to reduce halo error. The "horn error" is the opposite of the halo effect. It occurs when a manager focuses on one negative aspect about an employee and generalizes it into an overall poor appraisal rating. A personality conflict between a manager and his or her employees increases the probability of the horn effect, which can lead to a high level of frustration on the employee's part if it is not corrected.[30] Some types of rating errors are *distributional errors* in that they involve a group of ratings given across various employees. For example, raters who are reluctant to assign either extremely high or extremely low ratings commit the **error of central tendency**. In this case, all employees are rated about average. To such raters, it is a good idea to explain that, among large numbers of employees, one should expect to find significant differences in their behaviour, productivity, and other characteristics. In contrast to central tendency errors, it is also common for some raters to give unusually high or low ratings. For example, a manager may erroneously assert, "All my employees are excellent" or "None of my people are good enough." These beliefs give rise to what is called **leniency or strictness error**.[31] One way to reduce this error is to clearly define the characteristics or dimensions of performance and to provide meaningful descriptions of behaviour, known as "anchors," on the scale. Another approach is to require ratings to conform to a *forced distribution,* a type of system initially developed by GE, purportedly with good results. Managers appraising employees under a *forced distribution* system are required to place a certain percentage of employees into various performance categories. For example, it may be required that 10 percent of ratings be poor (or excellent). This is similar to the requirement in some schools that instructors grade on a curve. A variation of this is *peer ranking*, a system whereby employees in a work group are ranked against one another from best to worst.

Although forced distribution and peer ranking may solve leniency and strictness errors, they can create other rating errors—particularly if most employees are performing above standard. Even so, more organizations are using forced ranking systems. However, other companies, including Ford and Goodyear, described in the Business Case, abandoned their forced ranking systems after lawsuits, lower morale, decreased teamwork, and destructive employee competition ensued following their use. In addition, not all corporate cultures are conducive to forced ranking systems. For example, at Starbucks, which fosters a corporate climate based on teamwork, using a forced ranking system would probably be counterproductive. Because of the legal issues related to forced ranking, companies that use these methods obviously need to carefully train their appraisers.[32]

Some rating errors are *temporal* in that the performance review is biased either favourably or unfavourably, depending on the way performance information is selected, evaluated, and organized by the rater over time. For example, when the appraisal is based largely on the employee's recent behaviour, good or bad, the rater has committed the **recency error**. Managers who give higher ratings because they believe an employee is "showing improvement" may unwittingly be committing recency error. Without work record documentation for the entire appraisal period, the rater is forced to recall recent employee behaviour to establish the rating. Having the rater routinely document employee accomplishments and failures throughout the whole appraisal period can minimize the recency error. One way for managers to do this is by keeping a diary or a log. Rater training also will help reduce this error.

**Contrast error** occurs when an employee's evaluation is biased either upward or downward because of another employee's performance, evaluated just previously. For example, an average employee may appear especially productive when compared to a poor performer. However, that same employee may appear unproductive when compared to a star performer. Contrast errors are most likely when raters are required to rank employees in order from the best to the poorest. Employees are evaluated against one another, usually on the basis of some organizational standard or guideline. For example, they may be compared on the basis of their ability to meet production standards or their "overall" ability

# THE BUSINESS CASE

## Rank and Yank

Research shows that performance appraisals can have a positive financial impact, but there is the potential to lose money if the wrong system is chosen. Goodyear Tire & Rubber Co. abandoned a performance-rating system for salaried employees just as discrimination attorneys were planning to file a class-action lawsuit over it. Goodyear said it was dropping major parts of its program, including its so-called 10-80-10 feature, which essentially graded all salaried employees on a curve. The top 10 percent were rated A, the middle 80 percent were rated B, and the bottom 10 percent were rated C. Those falling in the bottom 10 percent weren't eligible for raises or bonuses and were warned that they might lose their jobs.

The lawsuit alleged that the workers who got C ratings were humiliated and stigmatized among their peers and managers. The legal arm of the AARP, formerly known as the American Association of Retired Persons, joined the lawsuit as co-counsel. Most of the plaintiffs who got C rankings in the case were Goodyear employees who were over 50 years old. "This case will send a clear message that performance rating schemes that target older workers for unfair treatment are illegal and will not be tolerated," said Laurie McCann of AARP.

Jack McGilvrey, a 59-year-old salaried employee, was one of those named in the suit. He claimed that he always received ratings of at least "good/effective performer" in his formal performance reviews up through the late 1990s. In 2000, he was ranked "highly effective." But in February 2001, he was transferred to a new department and shortly thereafter was given a C rating in his performance review. The suit asserted that Mr. McGilvrey didn't deserve the rating and received it as part of Goodyear's plan to discriminate against older employees. He was later dismissed.

The lawsuit against Goodyear has many parallels to one filed in 2001 against Ford Motor Co. In that case, also joined by AARP, the company modified its plans in the face of a legal challenge. The Ford case was eventually settled.

In modifying its white-collar ranking system, Goodyear said it would replace those A, B, and C rankings with the terms *exceeds expectations, meets expectations,* and *unsatisfactory.* There will be no requirement to assign those ratings to set percentages of employees. The company also said it was stepping up training for managers so they learn to do a better job of conducting performance reviews. Goodyear has about 28,000 salaried employees around the world.

Source: Timothy Aeppel, "Goodyear Ends Ratings System Ahead of Discrimination Suit," *The Wall Street Journal Online*, September 12, 2002: B8. Copyright © 2002 Dow Jones & Company, Inc. Reprinted with permission of Dow Jones & Company, Inc. in the format Textbook, via Copyright Clearance Center.

---

to perform their job. As with other types of rating errors, contrast error can be reduced through training that focuses on using objective standards and behavioural anchors to appraise performance.[33]

The **similar-to-me error** occurs when appraisers inflate the evaluations of people with whom they have something in common. For example, if both the manager and the employee are from small towns, the manager may unwittingly have a more favourable impression of the employee. The effects of a similar-to-me error can be powerful, and when the similarity is based on race, religion, or gender, it can result in discrimination.

Furthermore, raters should be aware of any stereotypes they may hold toward particular groups—such as male/female or white/black—because the observation and interpretation of performance can be clouded by these stereotypes. For example, one study found that men who experience conflicts between family and work received lower overall performance ratings and lower reward recommendations than men who did not experience such conflicts. Women, on the other hand, were judged no differently, whether they experienced family–work conflicts or not. A host of organizations such as Avenor, a Montreal-based pulp-and-paper company, have developed formal training programs to reduce the subjective errors commonly made during the rating process. This training can pay off, particularly when participants have the opportunity to (1) observe other managers making errors, (2) actively participate in discovering their own errors, and (3) practise job-related tasks to reduce the errors they tend to make.[34]

**similar-to-me error**
A performance rating error in which an appraiser inflates the evaluation of an employee because of a mutual personal connection

# HIGHLIGHTS IN HRM 8.1

## Supervisor's Checklist for the Performance Appraisal

### Scheduling

1. Schedule the review and notify the employee 10 days to 2 weeks in advance.

2. Ask the employee to prepare for the session by reviewing his or her performance, job objectives, and development goals.

3. Clearly state that this will be the formal annual performance appraisal.

### Preparing for the Review

1. Review the performance documentation collected throughout the year. Concentrate on work patterns that have developed.

2. Be prepared to give specific examples of above- or below-average performance.

3. When performance falls short of expectations, determine what changes need to be made. If performance meets or exceeds expectations, plan to discuss this and how to reinforce it.

4. After the appraisal is written, set it aside for a few days and then review it again.

5. Follow whatever steps are required by your organization's performance appraisal system.

### Conducting the Review

1. Select a location that is comfortable and free of distractions. The location should encourage a frank and candid conversation.

2. Discuss each topic in the appraisal one at a time, considering both strengths and shortcomings.

3. Be specific and descriptive, not general and judgmental. Report occurrences rather than evaluating them.

4. Discuss your differences and resolve them. Solicit agreement with the evaluation.

5. Jointly discuss and design plans for taking corrective action for growth and development.

6. Maintain a professional and supportive approach to the appraisal discussion.

## Feedback Training

Finally, a training program for raters should provide some general points to consider for planning and providing feedback during the appraisal interview. Managers need to understand that employees want feedback—that is, they want to know how they are doing and how they can improve. They are less eager to be appraised or judged. This is why it is important for their managers to provide them with ongoing feedback and not just "dump on them" during a formal appraisal. Feedback training should cover at least three basic areas: (1) communicating effectively, (2) diagnosing the root causes of performance problems, and (3) setting goals and objectives. A checklist such as the one in Highlights in HRM 8.1 can be used to assist supervisors in preparing for the appraisal interview.[35]

## PERFORMANCE APPRAISAL METHODS

OUTCOME 4

Since the early years of their use by the federal government, methods of evaluating personnel have evolved considerably. Old systems have been replaced by new methods that reflect technical improvements and legal requirements and are more consistent with the purposes of appraisal. Likewise, paper appraisals are being replaced by electronic appraisals built into firms' performance management systems. In the discussion that follows, we will examine in some detail the methods that have found widespread use, and we will briefly touch on other methods that are used less frequently.

Performance appraisal methods can be broadly classified as measuring traits, behaviours, or results. Trait approaches continue to be more popular despite their inherent subjectivity. Behavioural approaches provide more action-oriented information to employees and therefore may be best for development. The results-oriented approach is gaining popularity because it focuses on the measurable contributions that employees make to the organization.

## TRAIT METHODS

Trait approaches to performance appraisal are designed to measure the extent to which an employee possesses certain characteristics—such as dependability, creativity, initiative, and leadership—that are viewed as important for the job and the organization in general. The fact that trait methods are the most popular is due in large part to the ease with which they are developed. However, if not designed carefully on the basis of job analysis, trait appraisals can be notoriously biased and subjective.

**graphic rating scale method**
A trait approach to performance appraisal whereby each employee is rated according to a scale of characteristics

### Graphic Rating Scales

In the **graphic rating scale method**, each trait or characteristic to be rated is represented by a scale on which a rater indicates the degree to which an employee possesses that trait or characteristic. An example of this type of scale is shown in Highlights in HRM 8.2. There are many variations of the graphic

# HIGHLIGHTS IN HRM 8.2

## Graphic Rating Scale with Provision for Comments

Appraise employee's performance in PRESENT ASSIGNMENT. Check (✔) most appropriate square. Appraisers are *urged to freely use* the "Remarks" sections for significant comments descriptive of the individual.

| | Needs instruction or guidance | Has required knowledge of own and related work | Has exceptional knowledge of own and related work |
|---|---|---|---|
| **1. KNOWLEDGE OF WORK:** Understanding of all phases of his/her work and related matters | ☐ ☐ | ☐ ☐ | ✔☐ |
| | Remarks: *Is particularly good on gas engines.* | | |

| | Lacks imagination | Meets necessary requirements | Unusually resourceful |
|---|---|---|---|
| **2. INITIATIVE:** Ability to originate or develop ideas and to get things started | ☐ ✔ | ☐ ☐ | ☐ ☐ |
| | Remarks: *Has good ideas when asked for an opinion, but otherwise will not offer them. Somewhat lacking in self-confidence.* | | |

| | Wastes time Needs close supervision | Steady and willing worker | Exceptionally industrious |
|---|---|---|---|
| **3. APPLICATION:** Attention and application to his/her work | ☐ ☐ ✔ | ☐ ☐ | ☐ |
| | Remarks: *Accepts new jobs when assigned.* | | |

| | Needs improvement | Regularly meets recognized standards | Consistently maintains highest quality |
|---|---|---|---|
| **4. QUALITY OF WORK:** Thoroughness, neatness, and accuracy of work | ☐ ☐ | ☐ ☐ | ✔ |
| | Remarks: *The work he turns out is always of the highest possible quality.* | | |

| | Should be increased | Regularly meets recognized standards | Unusually high output |
|---|---|---|---|
| **5. VOLUME OF WORK:** Quantity of acceptable work | ☐ ☐ | ✔ ☐ | ☐ |
| | Remarks: *Would be higher if he did not spend so much time checking and rechecking his work.* | | |

**mixed-standard scale method**
A trait approach to performance appraisal similar to other scale methods but based on comparison with (better than, equal to, or worse than) a standard

**forced-choice method**
A trait approach to performance appraisal that requires the rater to choose from statements designed to distinguish between successful and unsuccessful performance

rating scale. The differences are to be found in (1) the characteristics or dimensions on which individuals are rated, (2) the degree to which the performance dimension is defined for the rater, and (3) how clearly the points on the scale are defined. In Highlights in HRM 8.2, the dimensions are defined briefly, and an attempt is made to define the points on the scale. Subjectivity bias is reduced somewhat when the dimensions on the scale and the scale points are defined as precisely as possible. This can be achieved by training raters and by including descriptive appraisal guidelines in a performance appraisal reference packet.[36]

Also, the rating form should provide sufficient space for comments on the behaviour associated with each scale. These comments improve the accuracy of the appraisal because they require the rater to think in terms of observable employee behaviours while providing specific examples to discuss with the employee during the appraisal interview.

## Mixed-Standard Scales

The **mixed-standard scale method** is a modification of the basic rating scale method. Rather than evaluating traits according to a single scale, the rater is given three specific descriptions of each trait. These descriptions reflect three levels of performance: superior, average, and inferior. After the three descriptions for each trait are written, they are randomly sequenced to form the mixed-standard scale. As shown in Highlights in HRM 8.3, supervisors evaluate employees by indicating whether their performance is better than, equal to, or worse than the standard for each behaviour.

## Forced-Choice Method

The **forced-choice method** requires the rater to choose from statements, often in pairs, that appear equally favourable or equally unfavourable. The statements,

# HIGHLIGHTS IN HRM 8.3

## Example of a Mixed-Standard Scale

DIRECTIONS: Please indicate whether the individual's performance is above (+), equal to (0), or lower than (−) each of the following standards.

1. ___ Employee uses good judgment when addressing problems and provides workable alternatives; however, at times does not take actions to prevent problems. *(medium PROBLEM SOLVING)*

2. ___ Employee lacks supervisory skills; frequently handles employees poorly and is at times argumentative. *(low LEADERSHIP)*

3. ___ Employee is extremely cooperative; can be expected to take the lead in developing cooperation among employees; completes job tasks with a positive attitude. *(high COOPERATION)*

4. ___ Employee has effective supervision skills; encourages productivity, quality, and employee development. *(medium LEADERSHIP)*

5. ___ Employee normally displays an argumentative or defensive attitude toward fellow employees and job assignments. *(low COOPERATION)*

6. ___ Employee is generally agreeable but becomes argumentative at times when given job assignments; cooperates with other employees as expected. *(medium COOPERATION)*

7. ___ Employee is not good at solving problems; uses poor judgment and does not anticipate potential difficulties. *(low PROBLEM SOLVING)*

8. ___ Employee anticipates potential problems and provides creative, proactive alternative solutions; has good attention to follow-up. *(high PROBLEM SOLVING)*

9. ___ Employee displays skilled direction; effectively coordinates unit activities; is generally a dynamic leader and motivates employees to high performance. *(high LEADERSHIP)*

however, are designed to distinguish between successful and unsuccessful performance. The rater selects one statement from the pair without knowing which statement correctly describes successful job behaviour. For example, forced-choice pairs might include the following:

1. ____ a) Works hard      ____ b) Works quickly
2. ____ a) Shows initiative      ____ b) Is responsive to customers
3. ____ a) Produces poor quality      ____ b) Lacks good work habits

The forced-choice method is not without limitations, the primary one being the cost of establishing and maintaining its validity. The fact that it has been a source of frustration to many raters has sometimes caused the method to be eliminated from appraisal programs. In addition, it cannot be used as effectively as some of the other methods as a tool for developing employees.

## Essay Method

Unlike rating scales, which provide a structured form of appraisal, the **essay method** requires the appraiser to compose a statement that best describes the employee being appraised. The appraiser is usually instructed to describe the employee's strengths and weaknesses and to make recommendations for his or her development. Often the essay method is combined with other rating methods. Essays may provide additional descriptive information on an employee's performance that cannot be generated with a structured rating scale, for example.

The essay method provides an excellent opportunity to point out the unique characteristics of the employee being appraised. This aspect of the method is heightened when a supervisor is instructed to describe specific points about the employee's promotability, special talents, skills, strengths, and weaknesses. A major limitation of the essay method is that composing an essay that attempts to cover all of an employee's essential characteristics is a very time-consuming task (although when combined with other methods, this method does not require a lengthy statement). Another disadvantage of the essay method is that the quality of the performance appraisal may be influenced by the supervisor's writing skills and composition style. Good writers may simply be able to produce more favourable appraisals. A final drawback of this appraisal method is that it tends to be subjective and may not focus on the relevant aspects of a person's job performance.

## BEHAVIOURAL METHODS

As we mentioned, one of the potential drawbacks of a trait-oriented performance appraisal is that traits tend to be vague and subjective. We discussed earlier that one way to improve a rating scale is to have descriptions of behaviour along a scale, or continuum. These descriptions permit the rater to readily identify the point where a particular employee falls on the scale. Behavioural methods have been developed to specifically describe which actions should (or should not) be exhibited on the job. They are often used to provide employees with developmental feedback.

## Critical Incident Method

The critical incident method, described in Chapter 4 in connection with job analysis, is also used as a method of appraisal. Recall that a **critical incident** occurs when employee behaviour results in unusual success or unusual failure in some part of the job. An example of a favourable critical incident occurs when a janitor observes that a file cabinet containing classified documents has been left unlocked at the close of business and calls the firm's security officer to correct the problem. An example of an unfavourable incident occurs when a mail clerk fails to deliver an express mail package immediately, instead putting it in with regular mail to be routed two hours later. The manager keeps a log or diary for

**essay method**
A trait approach to performance appraisal that requires the rater to compose a statement describing employee behaviour

**critical incident**
An unusual event that denotes superior or inferior employee performance in some part of the job

<br>

**behaviourally anchored rating scale (BARS)**
A behavioural approach to performance appraisal that consists of a series of vertical scales, one for each important dimension of job performance

each employee throughout the appraisal period and notes specific critical incidents related to how well they perform. When completing the appraisal form, the manager refers to the critical incident log and uses this information to substantiate an employee's rating of outstanding, satisfactory, or unsatisfactory in specific performance areas and overall. This method can also help a manager counsel employees when they are having performance problems while the problem is still minor. It also increases the objectivity of the appraisal by requiring the rater to use job performance criteria to justify the ratings.[37]

## Behavioural Checklist Method

One of the oldest appraisal techniques is the behavioural checklist method. It consists of having the rater check the statements on a list that the rater believes are characteristic of the employee's performance or behaviour. A checklist developed for computer salespeople might include a number of statements such as the following:

___ Is able to explain equipment clearly
___ Keeps abreast of new developments in technology
___ Tends to be a steady worker
___ Reacts quickly to customers' needs
___ Processes orders correctly

## Behaviourally Anchored Rating Scale (BARS)

A **behaviourally anchored rating scale (BARS)** consists of a series of 5 to 10 vertical scales, one for each important dimension of performance identified through job analysis. These dimensions are anchored by behaviours identified through a critical incident job analysis. The critical incidents are placed along the scale and are assigned point values according to the opinions of experts. A BARS for the job of firefighter is shown in the upper portion of Highlights in HRM 8.4. Note that this particular scale is for the dimension described as "Firefighting Strategy: Knowledge of Fire Characteristics."

A BARS is typically developed by a committee that includes both subordinates and managers. The committee's task is to identify all the relevant characteristics or dimensions of the job. Behavioural anchors in the form of statements are then established for each job dimension. Several participants are asked to review

# HIGHLIGHTS IN HRM 8.4

## BARS and BOS Examples

**Example of a BARS for Municipal Fire Companies**
*FIREFIGHTING STRATEGY: Knowledge of Fire Characteristics.* This area of performance concerns the ability of a firefighter to understand fire characteristics to develop the best strategy for fighting a fire.

HIGH   7 — Finds the fire when no one else can
       6 — Correctly assesses best point of entry for fighting fire

          5 — Uses type of smoke as indicator of type of fire
AVERAGE   4 — Understands basic hydraulics
          3 — Cannot tell the type of fire by observing the color of flame
          2 — Cannot identify location of the fire
LOW       1 — Will not change firefighting strategy in spite of flashbacks and other signs that accelerants are present

Source: Adapted from Landy, Jacobs, and Associates. Reprinted with permission.

the anchor statements and indicate which job dimension each anchor illustrates. The only anchors retained are those that at least 70 percent of the group agrees belong with a particular dimension. Finally, anchors are attached to their job dimensions and are placed on the appropriate scales according to values that the group assigns to them.

At present, there is no strong evidence that a BARS reduces all of the rating errors mentioned previously. However, some studies have shown that scales of this type can yield more accurate ratings. One major advantage of a BARS is that personnel outside the HR department participate with HR staff in its development. Employee participation can lead to greater acceptance of the performance appraisal process and of the performance measures that it uses.

The procedures followed in developing a BARS also result in scales that have a high degree of content validity. The main disadvantage of a BARS is that it requires considerable time and effort to develop. In addition, because the scales are specific to particular jobs, a scale designed for one job might not apply to another.

**behaviour observation scale (BOS)**
A behavioural approach to performance appraisal that measures the frequency of observed behaviour

PART 3

## Behaviour Observation Scale (BOS)

A **behaviour observation scale (BOS)** is similar to a BARS in that they are both based on critical incidents. However, Highlights in HRM 8.5 shows that rather than asking the evaluator to choose the most representative behavioural anchor, a BOS is designed to measure how frequently each behaviour has been observed.

The value of a BOS is that this approach allows the appraiser to play the role of observer rather than of judge. In this way, he or she can more easily provide constructive feedback to the employee, who will be more willing to accept it. Research shows that users of the system frequently prefer it over the BARS or trait scales for (1) maintaining objectivity, (2) distinguishing good performers from poor performers, (3) providing feedback, and (4) identifying training needs.[38]

# HIGHLIGHTS IN HRM 8.5

## Sample Items from Behaviour Observation Scales

For each behaviour observed, use the following scale:

| 5 represents *almost always* | 95–100% of the time |
|---|---|
| 4 represents *frequently* | 85–94% of the time |
| 3 represents *sometimes* | 75–84% of the time |
| 2 represents *seldom* | 65–74% of the time |
| 1 represents *almost never* | 0–64% of the time |

| Sales Productivity | Never | | | | Always |
|---|---|---|---|---|---|
| Reviews individual productivity results with manager | 1 | 2 | 3 | 4 | 5 |
| Suggests to peers ways of building sales | 1 | 2 | 3 | 4 | 5 |
| Formulates specific objectives for each contact | 1 | 2 | 3 | 4 | 5 |
| Focuses on product rather than customer problem | 1 | 2 | 3 | 4 | 5 |
| Keeps account plans updated | 1 | 2 | 3 | 4 | 5 |
| Follows up on customer leads | 1 | 2 | 3 | 4 | 5 |

Rather than looking at the traits of employees or the behaviours they exhibit on the job, many organizations evaluate employee accomplishments—the results they achieve through their work. Advocates of results appraisals argue that they are more objective and empowering for employees. Looking at results such as sales figures and production output involves less subjectivity and therefore may be less open to bias. Furthermore, results appraisals often give employees responsibility for their outcomes while giving them discretion over the methods they use to accomplish them (within limits). This is empowerment in action.

## Productivity Measures

A number of results measures are available to evaluate performance. Salespeople are evaluated on the basis of their sales volume (both the number of units sold and the dollar amount in revenues). Production workers are evaluated on the basis of the number of units they produce and perhaps the scrap rate or number of defects that are detected. Executives are frequently evaluated on the basis of company profits or growth rate. Each measure directly links what employees accomplish and the results that benefit the organization. In this way, results appraisals can directly align employee and organizational goals.

But there are some problems with results appraisals. First, recall our earlier discussion of criteria contamination. Results appraisals can be contaminated by external factors that employees cannot influence. Sales representatives who have extremely bad markets or production employees who cannot get materials will not be able to perform up to their abilities. In this case, it is unfair to hold these employees accountable for results that are contaminated by circumstances beyond their control. Furthermore, results appraisals can inadvertently encourage employees to "look good" on a short-term basis while ignoring the long-term ramifications. Line supervisors, for example, might let their equipment suffer to reduce maintenance costs. If the appraisal focuses on a narrow set of results criteria to the exclusion of other important process issues, the system may suffer from criterion deficiency and unintentionally foster the attitude that "what gets measured gets done." In fact, in any job involving interaction with others, it is not enough to simply look at production or sales figures. Factors such as cooperation, adaptability, initiative, and concern for human relations are important to the job success of employees too. If these factors are important job standards, they should be added to the appraisal review. Thus, to be realistic, both the results and the methods or processes used to achieve them should be considered.[39]

## Management by Objectives

One method that attempts to overcome some of the limitations of results appraisals is **management by objectives (MBO)**. MBO is a philosophy of management that has employees establish objectives (such as production costs, sales per product, quality standards, and profits) through consultation with their superiors and then uses these objectives as a basis for evaluation.[40] MBO is a system involving a cycle (Figure 8.7) that begins with setting the organization's common goals and objectives and ultimately returns to that step. The system acts as a goal-setting process whereby objectives are established for the organization (Step 1), departments (Step 2), and individual managers and employees (Step 3).

As Figure 8.7 illustrates, a significant feature of the cycle is the establishment of specific goals by the employee, but those goals are based on a broad statement of the employee's responsibilities prepared by the person's supervisor. Employee-established goals are discussed with the supervisor and jointly reviewed and modified until both parties are satisfied with them (Step 4). The goal statements are accompanied by a detailed account of the actions the employee proposes to take to reach the goals. During periodic reviews, as objective data are made available, the progress that the employee is making toward the goals is then

# FIGURE 8.7

## PERFORMANCE APPRAISAL UNDER AN MBO PROGRAM

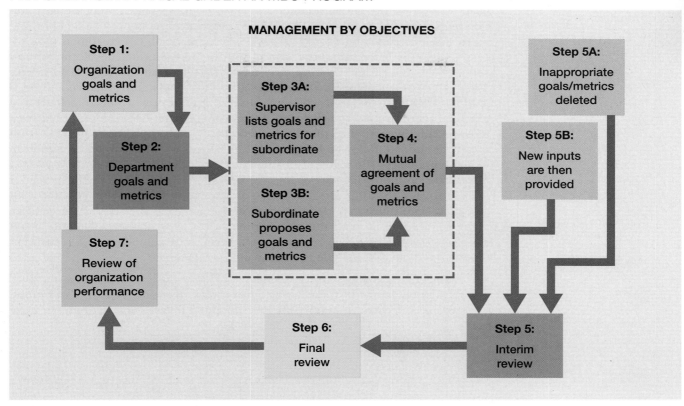

assessed (Step 5). Goals may be changed at this time as new or additional data are received. At the conclusion of a period of time (usually six months or one year), the employee makes a self-appraisal of what he or she has accomplished, substantiating the self-appraisal with factual data wherever possible. The "interview" is an examination of the employee's self-appraisal by the supervisor and the employee together (Step 6). The final step (Step 7) is reviewing the connection between individual and organizational performance. To ensure success, MBO programs should be viewed as part of a total system for managing, not as merely an addition to the manager's job. Managers must be willing to empower employees to accomplish their objectives on their own, giving them discretion over the methods they use (but holding them accountable for outcomes). The following guidelines may be especially helpful:

1. Managers and employees must be willing to establish goals and objectives together. Goal setting has been shown to improve employee performance, typically ranging from 10 to 25 percent. Goal setting works because it helps employees focus on important tasks and makes them accountable for completing these tasks. It also establishes an automatic feedback system that aids learning because employees can regularly evaluate their performance against their goals.[41]
2. The objectives should be quantifiable and measurable for the long and short terms. However, goal statements should be accompanied by a description of how that goal will be accomplished.
3. The results that are expected must be under the employee's control. Recall our early discussion of criterion contamination.
4. The goals and objectives must be consistent for each employee level (top executive, manager, and employee).
5. Managers and employees must establish specific times when the goals are to be reviewed and evaluated.

## The Balanced Scorecard

The balanced scorecard (BSC), which we first discussed in Chapter 2, can be used to appraise individual employees, teams, business units, and the corporation itself. The idea behind the BSC model was shown in Chapter 2. The appraisal takes into account four related categories: (1) financial, (2) customer, (3) processes, and (4) learning. These internal processes—product development and service—are critical for creating customer satisfaction and loyalty. In turn, creating value for customers is what drives a firm's financial performance and profitability. Highlights in HRM 8.6 shows an example of how a BSC translates to a personal scorecard for an employee. As you can see, the corporation's objectives have already been spelled out on the scorecard. Then the various business unit targets are added, followed by the target objectives of the firm's teams and individual employees. The value of this is that each individual can see more clearly how his or her performance ties into the overall performance of the firm. Similar in some ways to MBO, the BSC enables managers to translate broad corporate goals into divisional, departmental, and team goals in a cascading fashion. Many firms have adopted the BSC approach, but it is neither a flawless nor a simple performance management system. Some recommendations for ensuring the method's success include the following:

- *Translate the strategy into a scorecard of clear objectives.* Because the BSC process begins with strategic objectives, unless these are clear, the rest of the system is doomed to ambiguity and potential failure. Translating a strategy

# HIGHLIGHTS IN HRM 8.6

## Personal Scorecard

| CORPORATE OBJECTIVES |
| --- |

- Double our corporate value in seven years.
- Increase our earnings by an average of 20% per year.
- Achieve an internal rate of return 2% above the cost of capital.
- Increase both production and reserves by 20% in the next decade.

☑ Corporate
☐ Business Unit
☐ Team/Individual

| CorporateTargets | | | | Scorecard Measures | Bus. Unit Targets | | | | Team/Individual Objectives |
| --- | --- | --- | --- | --- | --- | --- | --- | --- | --- |
| 2013 | 2014 | 2015 | 2016 | | 2013 | 2014 | 2015 | 2016 | 1. |
| | | | | **Financial** | | | | | |
| 100 | 120 | 160 | 180 | Earnings (millions of dollars) | | | | | |
| 100 | 450 | 200 | 210 | Net cash flow | | | | | |
| 100 | 85 | 75 | 70 | Overhead and operating costs | | | | | 2. |
| | | | | **Operating** | | | | | |
| 100 | 75 | 73 | 70 | Production costs/barrel | | | | | |
| 100 | 97 | 93 | 90 | Development costs/barrel | | | | | |
| 100 | 105 | 108 | 110 | Total annual production | | | | | 3. |
| **Team/Individual Measures** | | | | | **Targets** | | | | |
| 1. | | | | | | | | | |
| 2. | | | | | | | | | 4. |
| 3. | | | | | | | | | |
| 4. | | | | | | | | | |

into objectives provides managers and front-line employees with goals that are more understandable and attainable. Typically, having fewer goals adds clarity and focus.

- *Attach measures to each objective.* For managers and employees to know if and when the objectives are achieved, clear measures must be attached to each goal. Each objective should be given at least one metric that can be measured either by a preexisting system or manually within an organization.

- *Cascade scorecards to the front line.* It is often said that the real strategic work happens at the front line. For all employees to understand how their roles and job duties are aligned with the firm's higher level goals, the scorecards should be cascaded to the individual level. Cascading scorecards ensures that strategy then becomes "everyone's" job.

- *Provide performance feedback based on measures.* As with other performance management systems, unless managers provide employees with solid feedback on how they are doing, the system is likely to be ineffective. As part of this process, employees must know that they are accountable for achieving their objectives and providing an explanation when they do not hit their targets.

- *Empower employees to make performance improvements.* Individuals, on their own or working in teams, may understand ways of achieving higher performance. One of the benefits of a results-based system such as the BSC is that it gives employees the latitude to continuously improve best practice methods.

- *Reassess strategy.* One of the key benefits of the BSC is that it is a continuous loop process. Managers should monitor performance and use this information to reassess the strategy and make continuous adjustments. Those who have had the best success with the BSC argue that the system helps improve communication and learning rather than fixing in place a mechanical set of controls.[42]

## WHICH PERFORMANCE APPRAISAL METHOD TO USE?

The method chosen should be based largely on the purpose of the appraisal. Figure 8.8 lists some of the strengths and weaknesses of trait, behaviour, and results approaches to appraisal. Note that the simplest and least expensive techniques often yield the least accurate information. However, research has not always supported a clear choice among appraisal methods. Although researchers and HR managers generally believe that the more sophisticated and more time-consuming methods offer more useful information, this may not always be the case. Ronald Gross, an industrial psychologist and HR consultant, states: "I can't judge a performance appraisal system just by looking at the paperwork. The back of an envelope can work just fine. I've seen many systems fail miserably because they're too complex, too time consuming, and too burdensome. I've never seen a system fail because it was too simple."[43] One way to assess whether an organization's appraisal system is effective is by doing an annual, or at least periodic, audit of the process using a survey instrument that both managers and employees complete on a periodic basis. This should give HR a better sense of whether the appraisal processes is improving.

Of course, having a first-rate appraisal method does no good if the manager simply "shoves it in a drawer." Even a rudimentary system, when used properly, can initiate a discussion between managers and employees that genuinely leads to superior performance. These issues are discussed next under the topic of performance appraisal interviews. In addition, as we have explained, performance appraisals should not be just for middle managers and rank-and-file employees. If the organization's goals are to cascade downward, the firm's top executives need to be involved in the appraisal process as well.

**FIGURE 8.8**

SUMMARY OF VARIOUS APPRAISAL METHODS

| | **Advantages** | **Disadvantages** |
|---|---|---|
| *Trait methods* | 1. Are inexpensive to develop | 1. Have high potential for rating errors |
| | 2. Use meaningful dimensions | 2. Are not useful for employee counselling |
| | 3. Are easy to use | 3. Are not useful for allocating rewards |
| | | 4. Are not useful for promotion decisions |
| *Behavioural methods* | 1. Use specific performance dimensions | 1. Can be time consuming to develop /use |
| | 2. Are acceptable to employees and superiors | 2. Can be costly to develop |
| | 3. Are useful for providing feedback | 3. Have some potential for rating error |
| | 4. Are fair for reward and promotion decisions | |
| *Results methods* | 1. Have less subjectivity bias | 1. Are time consuming to develop/use |
| | 2. Are acceptable to employees and superiors | 2. May encourage a short-term perspective |
| | 3. Link individual performance to organizational performance | 3. May use contaminated criteria |
| | 4. Encourage mutual goal setting | 4. May use deficient criteria |
| | 5. Are good for reward and promotion decisions | |

## APPRAISAL INTERVIEWS

**OUTCOME 5**

The appraisal interview is perhaps the most important part of the entire performance appraisal process. The appraisal interview gives a manager the opportunity to discuss a subordinate's performance record and to explore areas of possible improvement and growth. Unfortunately, the interviewer can become overburdened by attempting to discuss too much, such as the employee's past performance and future development goals. Dividing the appraisal interview into two sessions, one for the performance review and the other for the employee's growth plans, can be helpful. Moreover, by separating the interview into two sessions, the interviewer can give each session the proper attention it deserves. It can be difficult for a supervisor to perform the role of both evaluator and counsellor in the same review period. Dividing the sessions can also improve the communication and cooperation between the parties, thereby reducing any stress and defensiveness that might arise. Interviews should be scheduled far enough in advance to allow the interviewee, as well as the interviewer, to prepare for the discussion. Usually, 10 days to 2 weeks is a sufficient amount of lead time.

### THREE TYPES OF APPRAISAL INTERVIEWS

The individual who has probably studied different approaches to performance appraisal interviews most thoroughly is Norman R. F. Maier. In his classic book, *The Appraisal Interview*, he analyzes the cause-and-effect relationships in three types of appraisal interviews: tell-and-sell, tell-and-listen, and problem solving.[44]

## Tell-and-Sell Interview

The skills required in the tell-and-sell interview include the ability to persuade an employee to change in a prescribed manner. This may require the development of new behaviours on the part of the employee and skillful use of motivational incentives on the part of the appraiser or supervisor.

## Tell-and-Listen Interview

In the tell-and-listen interview, the skills required include the ability to communicate the strong and weak points of an employee's job performance during the first part of the interview. During the second part of the interview, the employee's feelings about the appraisal are thoroughly explored. The tell-and-listen method gives both managers and employees the opportunity to release any feelings of frustration they might have. Today, most experts advise supervisors to encourage their employees to speak freely and to listen closely to what they have to say, emphasizing the fact that the communication during performance appraisals should be a two-way street.

## Problem-Solving Interview

Listening, accepting, and responding to feelings are essential elements of the problem-solving interview. However, this method goes beyond an interest in the employee's feelings. It seeks to stimulate growth and development in the employee by discussing the problems, needs, and on-the-job satisfactions and dissatisfactions. Managers should not assume that only one type of appraisal interview is appropriate for every review session. Rather, they should be able to use one or more of the interview types, depending on the topic being discussed or on the behaviour of the employee being appraised. The interview should be seen as requiring a flexible approach.

## CONDUCTING THE APPRAISAL INTERVIEW

Although there are probably no hard-and-fast rules for how to conduct an appraisal interview, some guidelines can increase an employee's willingness to discuss his or her performance and improve it, accept feedback from his or her supervisors, and increase the person's overall satisfaction with the interview. Many of the principles

The purpose of a performance appraisal interview is to initiate a dialogue that will help an employee improve his or her performance, making the employee an active participant in the discussion. Such participation is strongly related to an employee's satisfaction with appraisal feedback.

of effective interviewing discussed in Chapter 6 apply to performance appraisal interviews as well. Here are some other guidelines that should also be considered.

## Ask for a Self-Assessment

As we noted earlier in the chapter, it is useful to have employees evaluate their own performance prior to the appraisal interview. Even if this information is not used to determine the final rating on the review, the self-appraisal starts the employee thinking about his or her accomplishments. Self-appraisal also ensures that the employee knows against what criteria he or she is being evaluated, thus eliminating any potential surprises.

Recent research evidence suggests that employees are more satisfied and view the appraisal system as providing more *procedural justice* when they have input into the process.

When the employee has evaluated his or her own performance, the interview can be used to discuss areas in which the manager and the employee have reached different conclusions—not so much to resolve the "truth" but to work toward a resolution of problems.

## Invite Participation

The core purpose of a performance appraisal interview is to initiate a dialogue that will help an employee improve his or her performance. To the extent that an employee is an active participant in that discussion, the more likely it is that the root causes and obstacles to performance will be uncovered and the more likely it is that constructive ideas for improvement will be raised. In addition, research evidence suggests that participation is strongly related to an employee's satisfaction with the appraisal feedback, the extent to which the employee believes it is fair and useful, and his or her intention to improve performance. As a rule of thumb, supervisors should spend only about 30 to 35 percent of the time talking during the interview. They should spend the rest of the time listening to the information their employees volunteer and their responses to questions.

## Express Appreciation

Praise is a powerful motivator, and in an appraisal interview, particularly, employees are seeking positive feedback. It is frequently beneficial to start the appraisal interview by expressing appreciation for what the employee has done well. In this way, he or she may be less defensive and more likely to talk about aspects of the job that are not going so well. However, supervisors should try to avoid the obvious use of the "sandwich technique" in which positive statements are followed by negative ones, which are then followed by positive statements. This approach may not work for several reasons. Praise often alerts the employee that criticism will be coming. If managers follow an appraisal form, the problem of the sandwich technique will often be avoided. Furthermore, if employees are kept informed of their behaviour on a regular basis, there will be no need to use this appraisal technique.

## Minimize Criticism

Even the most stoic employees can absorb only so much criticism before they start to get defensive. If an employee has many areas in need of improvement, managers should focus on those few objective issues that are most problematic or most important to the job. In other words, criticism should be given in small doses.

Some tips for using criticism constructively include the following:

- Consider *whether it is necessary*. Frustration with performance problems sometimes leads to criticism that is little more than a manager "letting off steam." Make certain that the criticism focuses on a recurrent problem or a consistent pattern of behaviour over which the employee has control.

- *Consider the person.* Everyone handles criticism differently. Some people are able to handle it well. Others react very negatively to even the slightest criticism.
- *Be specific and do not exaggerate.* Even managers who dislike criticizing may find that, once they get started, they tend to overdo it. Sometimes we over-state problems to be convincing or to demonstrate our concern. Try to keep criticism simple, factual, and to the point. Avoid using terms such as *always*, *completely*, and *never*.
- *Watch your timing.* Properly timed criticism can often mean the difference between success and failure. Even good criticism given late in the day, for example, can touch a raw nerve if the employee is tired. If the employee gets emotional, take a break, even if it means finishing the appraisal the fol-lowing day.
- *Make improvement your goal.* Frankly, it is hard to change a person's behav-iour with a single conversation, so "laying it on the line" is probably not a good idea. Moreover, any criticism needs to be complemented with manage-rial support. This point is elaborated on next.[45]

## Change the Behaviour, Not the Person

Managers frequently try to play psychologist, to "figure out" why an employee has acted a certain way. Empathy is a good thing, and attempts to understand the employee's point of view can be very helpful. However, when dealing with a problem area, in particular, remember that it is not the person who is bad but the actions exhibited on the job. Avoid making suggestions to employees about per-sonal traits to change; instead, suggest more acceptable ways of performing. For example, instead of focusing on a person's "unreliability," a manager might focus on the fact that the employee "has been late to work seven times this month." It is difficult for employees to change who they are; it is usually much easier for them to change how they act.

## Focus on Solving Problems

When addressing performance issues, it is also frequently tempting to get into the "blame game" in which both manager and employee enter into a potentially endless discussion of why a situation has arisen. Frequently, solving problems requires an analysis of the causes, but, ultimately, the appraisal interview should be directed at devising a solution to the problem.

## Be Supportive

One of the better techniques for engaging an employee in the problem-solving process is for the manager to ask, "What can I do to help?" Employees frequently attribute performance problems to either real or perceived obstacles (such as bureaucratic procedures or inadequate resources). By being open and sup-portive, the manager conveys to the employee that he or she will try to elimi-nate roadblocks and will work with the employee to achieve a higher standard of performance.

## Establish Goals

Since a major purpose of the appraisal interview is to make plans for improve-ment, it is important to focus the interviewee's attention on the future rather than the past. Toward that goal, managers should

- Emphasize strengths on which the employee can build rather than weak-nesses to overcome and how the employee's efforts will contribute to the organization during the coming year

- Concentrate on opportunities for growth that exist within the framework of the employee's present position and drop unproductive tasks
- Limit plans for growth to a few important items that can be accomplished within a reasonable period of time
- Establish specific action plans that spell out how each goal will be achieved. The plans may also include a list of contacts, resources, and timetables for follow-up.
- End the review on a positive note by highlighting how both the employee and the firm will excel if the goals are achieved

Many managers are as nervous about administering appraisals as employees are about receiving them. Some supervisors may be tempted to establish difficult goals with their subordinates. The ethical issues surrounding unreasonable goals are discussed in Ethics in HRM.

# ETHICS IN HRM

## Stretch Goals

Employees are being asked to set performance goals, labelled "stretch goals," that ask them to do such things as double their sales or increase response time to customers threefold. Research has shown that the establishment of goals results in higher productivity. So if goals are good, are supergoals better?

"Not necessarily," says Steve Kerr, General Electric's chief learning officer. In his opinion, most managers do not know how to manage stretch targets. Companies set ambitious goals for their employees but fail to provide them with the resources they need to achieve them. They are saying, in effect, "We aren't going to give you any more people or money, so your solution is to work smarter and be creative." The only resource left to employees is their personal time, and so North Americans are working harder than employees in any other developed country. They are working evenings and weekends, with fewer vacations. "That's immoral," says Kerr. "Companies have a moral obligation to provide the tools to meet tough goals." The other risk is that stretch goals may lead to risk-taking behaviour on the part of employees. For instance, U.S. banks set numerical goals for mortgages that resulted in selling mortgages to high-risk customers, who subsequently defaulted, causing a massive meltdown in the home real estate market.

How should stretch goals be managed? The goal must be seen as achievable and not provoke a reaction of "You've got to be kidding." People must also realize that creative energy can be increased. For example, in one innovation training program, teams are given an orange and told that each person must handle the orange, but the orange must end up in the hands of the person who started with it. All teams start by throwing the orange to team members; this takes nine seconds. They try to reduce the time to seven seconds by throwing faster or in tighter circles. When told that it is possible to do this task in one second, they get creative: they stack their hands, and the first person drops the orange through the stacked but open hands and catches it at the bottom.

If the stretch goals are not achieved, then punishment should not be used. Be careful with high achievers who are already stretching or these winners will feel like losers if they cannot meet impossible goals. Provide the tools; asking people to double their quota without ensuring backup is demoralizing. Finally, share the wealth. If the achievement results in additional funds flowing to the organization, split the incremental savings or gains.

Some employees, masters at the politics of organizations, play games with stretch goals. They negotiate hard for modest, achievable goals while arguing that these are stretch targets. Others, with high needs for achievement, accept the stretch targets. At bonus time, the modest goal setters have met or surpassed their goals and receive merit increases. Having failed to achieve impossible targets, the less Machiavellian employees receive nothing.

Sources: Adapted from S. Sherman, "Stretch Goals: The Dark Side of Asking for Miracles," *Fortune*, November 13, 1995, 231; W. Immen, "The Goal: To Set Goals That Really Can Be Met," *The Globe and Mail*, March 20, 2009, B12.

# HIGHLIGHTS IN HRM 8.7

## Feedback for Generation Y

- *Focus on growth.* This generation was raised hearing a lot of praise, and this may be one of their first experiences with negative feedback. So the negative feedback must be discussed in terms of developmental opportunities.

- *Give specific feedback frequently and informally and use technology.* For a generation accustomed to real-time interaction, the once-a-year appraisal does not work. Yes, use a text message to compliment a successful presentation or report.

- *Encourage peers and colleagues to provide feedback.* It is powerful to receive feedback from peers that they trust and colleagues that they respect. At Facebook, the social network's 2,000 employees are encouraged to give small nuggets of feedback after meetings, presentations, and projects. Soliciting comments may be as simple as asking "How did that go? What could be done better?"

Sources: Adapted from K. Gordon, "Feedback that Gets Results with Gen Y," *HR Professional* (February 2010): 40; R. E. Silverman, "Every Year Is Not Enough; Try Weekly Performance Reviews," *The Globe and Mail*, September 12, 2011, B8.

## Follow Up Day to Day

As you have learned, feedback is most useful when it is immediate and specific to a particular situation. Unfortunately, both managers and employees are frequently happy to finish the interview and file away the appraisal form. A better approach is to have informal talks periodically, perhaps quarterly, to follow up on the issues raised in the appraisal interview. Levi Strauss, for example, offers employees informal feedback and coaching sessions on an ongoing basis. This puts managers in more of a coaching role versus that of a judge. Some managers believe that Generation Ys do not like feedback. But if it is done in the right way, they love feedback, as discussed in Highlights in HRM 8.7.

## IMPROVING PERFORMANCE

In many instances, the appraisal interview will provide the basis for noting deficiencies in employee performance and for making plans for improvement. Unless these deficiencies are brought to the employee's attention, they are likely to continue until they become quite serious. Sometimes underperformers do not understand exactly what is expected of them. However, once their responsibilities are clarified, they are in a position to take the corrective action needed to improve their performance.

## Identifying Sources of Ineffective Performance

A person's performance is a function of several factors, but perhaps it can be boiled down to three primary concerns: ability, motivation, and environment. Each individual has a unique pattern of strengths and weaknesses that play a part. But talented employees with low motivation are not likely to succeed. In addition, other factors in the work environment—or even in the external environment, which includes personal, family, and community concerns—can affect a person's performance either positively or negatively. Figure 8.9 provides a better picture of how these three factors (ability, motivation, and environment) can influence people's performance.

## FIGURE 8.9

**FACTORS THAT INFLUENCE PERFORMANCE**

| ABILITY | MOTIVATION | ENVIRONMENT |
|---|---|---|
| • Technical skills | • Career ambition | • Equipment/materials |
| • Interpersonal skills | • Employee conflict | • Job design |
| • Problem-solving skills | • Frustration | • Economic conditions |
| • Analytical skills | • Fairness/satisfaction | • Unions |
| • Communication skills | • Goals/expectations | • Rules and policies |
| • Physical limitations | | • Management support |
| | | • Laws and regulations |

It is recommended that a diagnosis of poor employee performance focus on these three interactive elements. As Figure 8.9 shows, if an employee's performance is not up to standard, the cause could be an ability problem (knowledge, skills, technical competencies), a motivation problem (effort to get the job done), and/or some problem in the work environment (poor economic conditions, worker shortages due to downsizing, difficult sales territories).[46] Any one of these problem areas could cause performance to suffer.

### Performance Diagnosis

Although performance appraisal systems can often tell us who is not performing well, they typically cannot reveal why. Unfortunately, managers often assume that poor performance is first due to lack of ability, second to poor motivation, and third to external conditions an employee faces. Ironically, research also suggests that we tend to make just the opposite attributions about our own performance. We first attribute poor performance to external constraints such as bad luck or factors out of our control. If the problem is internal, then we typically attribute it to temporary factors such as motivation or energy ("I had a bad day") and only as a last resort admit that it might be due to ability.

So what can be done to diagnose the real reasons for poor performance? More specifically, how can managers identify the root causes and get to work on a solution that improves performance? By comparing different performance measures, managers can begin to get an idea of the underlying causes of performance problems. For example, as shown in Figure 8.10, results measures cannot distinguish between ability, motivation, and environmental determinants of performance. So if someone is not achieving desired results, it could be due to ability, motivation, or external constraints. On the other hand, behavioural measures are less affected by external constraints. So if someone is demonstrating all the desired behaviours but is not achieving the desired results, logic suggests that it might be due to factors beyond his or her control.

Other kinds of diagnoses are possible by comparing different measures of performance. Only by correctly diagnosing the causes of performance problems can managers—and employees—hope to improve them.

### Managing Ineffective Performance

Once the sources of performance problems are known, a course of action can be planned. This action may lie in providing training in areas that would increase the knowledge and/or skills needed for effective performance. A transfer to another

## FIGURE 8.10

### PERFORMANCE DIAGNOSIS

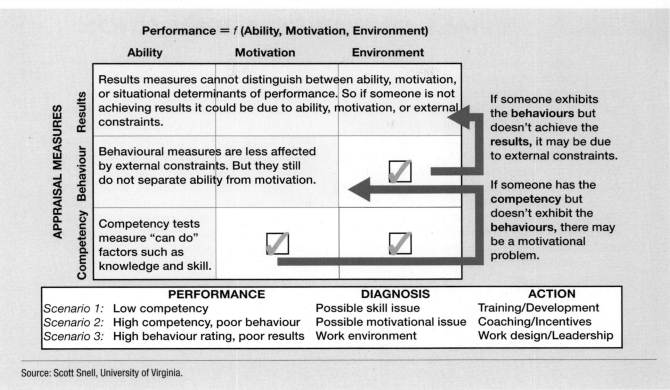

**Performance = $f$ (Ability, Motivation, Environment)**

|  | Ability | Motivation | Environment |
|---|---|---|---|
| **Results** | Results measures cannot distinguish between ability, motivation, or situational determinants of performance. So if someone is not achieving results it could be due to ability, motivation, or external constraints. | | |
| **Behaviour** | Behavioural measures are less affected by external constraints. But they still do not separate ability from motivation. | | |
| **Competency** | Competency tests measure "can do" factors such as knowledge and skill. | | |

If someone exhibits the **behaviours** but doesn't achieve the **results**, it may be due to external constraints.

If someone has the **competency** but doesn't exhibit the **behaviours**, there may be a motivational problem.

| | PERFORMANCE | DIAGNOSIS | ACTION |
|---|---|---|---|
| *Scenario 1:* | Low competency | Possible skill issue | Training/Development |
| *Scenario 2:* | High competency, poor behaviour | Possible motivational issue | Coaching/Incentives |
| *Scenario 3:* | High behaviour rating, poor results | Work environment | Work design/Leadership |

Source: Scott Snell, University of Virginia.

job or department might give an employee a chance to become a more effective member of the organization. In other instances, greater attention may have to be focused on ways to motivate the individual.

If the ineffective performance persists, it may be necessary to transfer the employee, take disciplinary action, or discharge the person from the organization. The ineffective behaviour is likely affecting not only the manager and the organization as a whole but also the person's coworkers. Whatever action is taken, however, should be done objectively, fairly, and with an understanding of the feelings of the individual involved. A new manager is likely to need training in this area because it is one of the most difficult aspects of being a manager.

A final word of caution when it comes to managing performance problems: because research consistently shows that managers often attribute poor performance to characteristics of the individuals (ability or motivation), although employees themselves typically blame external factors for their miscues, this can establish a negative cycle if not handled properly. Managers who assume that employees are not motivated or not capable may begin to treat them differently (perhaps supervising them too closely or watching for their next mistake). This can actually decrease an employee's motivation and cause him or her to withdraw. Seeing this, the manager may confirm his or her initial beliefs that the employee does not "measure up." As you can probably tell, this "set-up-to-fail" syndrome can be self-fulfilling and self-reinforcing. We hope the ideas and suggestions in this chapter will help managers accurately identify who is performing well (and why) and give them some focus for improving the productivity of their employees.[47]

# SMALL BUSINESS APPLICATION

In this chapter, we have covered many appraisal methods under the broad categories of trait, behavioural, and results models. Depending on the context, any of these may be suitable for a small business. However, in a small business, where one's role is unique, a results-based model is likely going to be the most suitable model. For clarity, a results-based model considers the employee's objective outcomes against preestablished objectives. Let's use the example of a carpenter named John working for a small contracting company. Although there are periods when there is enough carpentry work for him to be occupied for the full day, the company regularly also turns to John for assistance on client calls, as well as other miscellaneous work, such as painting. So how does one evaluate John's performance? In essence, John's core responsibility is carpentry, so John will be evaluated based on the effectiveness of his carpentry in terms of quantity, quality, and the manner in which it was

delivered. This is a results-based assessment. The other components of John's role fall into the category of "other duties as required." Recognizing that these, even though they are unstructured, form a regular part of John's role, John's manager will likely speak to John regarding his performance in these areas, drawing on the behavioural methods we have reviewed, likely the critical incident method.

Finally, although small business typically employs a less formal and less structured approach to performance appraisal programs, the legal considerations outlined in this chapter apply equally to small business as to large companies. Small companies looking for assistance in training in or development of effective performance appraisal may consider working with outside training companies or HR consultants to effectively establish performance appraisal processes.

# SUMMARY

## SUMMARY

**OUTCOME 1** Performance management is the process of creating a work environment in which people can perform to the best of their abilities to meet a company's goals. Performance appraisals are the result of an annual, biannual, or quarterly process in which a manager evaluates an employee's performance relative to the requirements of his or her job and uses the information to show the person where improvements are needed and why. Appraisals are just part of the performance management process, however. Aligning the goals of employees with that of the firm, providing employees with continual on-the-job feedback, and rewarding them are critical as well.

**OUTCOME 2** Performance appraisal programs serve many purposes, but, in general, those purposes can be clustered into two categories: administrative and developmental. The administrative purposes include decisions about who

will be promoted, transferred, or laid off. Appraisals are also conducted to make compensation decisions. Developmental decisions include those related to improving and enhancing an individual's capabilities. These include identifying a person's strengths and weaknesses, eliminating external performance obstacles, and establishing training needs.

Some HR experts and firms believe that performance appraisals are ineffective. In other organizations, performance appraisals are seen as a necessary evil. Managers frequently avoid conducting appraisals because they dislike passing judgment on people. Furthermore, if managers are not adequately trained, subjectivity and organizational politics can distort employee reviews. Managers do not develop good feedback skills and are often not prepared to conduct an appraisal. As a consequence, the appraisal is done begrudgingly once a year and then forgotten. The ultimate success or failure of a performance appraisal program depends on the philosophy underlying it, its connection with the firm's business goals, and the attitudes and skills of those responsible for its administration.

**OUTCOME 3** To determine the contributions of each individual, it is necessary to have a formal appraisal program with clearly stated objectives. Carefully defined performance standards that are reliable, strategically relevant, and free from either criterion deficiency or criterion contamination are essential foundations for evaluation. Appraisal systems must also comply with the law and, like selection tests, be valid and reliable. For example, ratings must be job related, employees must understand their performance standards in advance, appraisers must be able to observe job performance, appraisers must be trained, feedback must be given, and an appeals procedure must be established. Some companies now hold calibration meetings to ensure that their managers are accurately rating employees. Using multiple raters is frequently a good idea because different individuals see different facets of an employee's performance. The supervisor, for example, has legitimate authority over an employee and is in a good position to discern whether he or she is contributing to the goals of the organization. Peers and team members, on the other hand, often have an unfiltered view of an employee's work activity, particularly related to issues such as cooperation and dependability. Subordinates often provide good information about whether an employee is facilitating their work, and customers (both internal and external) can convey the extent to which an employee adds value and meets their requirements. Self-appraisal is useful, if for no other reason than it encourages employees to think about their strengths, weaknesses, and future goals. An increasing number of organizations are using multiple raters—or 360-degree appraisal—to get a more comprehensive picture of employee performance. Regardless of the source of appraisal information, appraisers should be thoroughly trained in the particular methods they will use in evaluating their subordinates.

**OUTCOME 4** Several methods can be used for performance appraisals. These include trait approaches (such as graphic rating scales, mixed-standard scales, forced-choice forms, and essays), behavioural methods (such as critical incident ratings, checklists, BARS, and BOS), and results methods (MBO). The choice of method depends on the purpose of the appraisal. Trait appraisals are simple to develop and complete, but they have problems in subjectivity and are not useful for feedback. Behavioural methods provide more specific information for giving feedback but can be time consuming and costly to develop. Results appraisals are more objective and can link individual performance to the organization as a whole, but they may encourage a short-term perspective (such as annual goals) and may not include subtle yet important aspects of performance.

**OUTCOME 5** The degree to which a performance appraisal program benefits an organization and its members is directly related to the quality of the appraisal interviews that are conducted. Interviewing skills are best developed through instruction and supervised practice. Although there are various approaches to the interview, research suggests that employee participation and goal setting lead to higher satisfaction and improved performance. Discussing problems, showing support, minimizing criticism, and rewarding effective performance are also beneficial practices. During the interview, performance deficiencies can be discussed and plans for improvement can be made.

## KEY TERMS

behaviour observation scale
   (BOS), 305
behaviourally anchored rating
   scale (BARS), 304
calibration, 289
contrast error, 298
critical incident, 303
customer appraisal, 293
error of central tendency, 298

essay method, 303
focal performance appraisal, 283
forced-choice method, 302
graphic rating scale method, 301
leniency or strictness error, 298
management by objectives
   (MBO), 306
manager and/or supervisor
   appraisal, 291

mixed-standard scale method, 302
peer appraisal, 292
performance appraisal, 282
performance management, 282
recency error, 298
self-appraisal, 291
similar-to-me error, 299
subordinate appraisal, 291
team appraisal, 292

# SUMMARY

## DISCUSSION QUESTIONS

1. Eighty percent of Canadian organizations have performance appraisal systems. List some reasons why 20 percent would not choose to implement one.

2. Develop a list of the characteristics of effective service for fast-food servers at places such as Tim Hortons. Over your next five visits, rate the servers against the criteria that you have developed. Did your criteria meet the performance standards of relevant and reliable, or were they subject to criterion deficiency or contamination?

3. Develop a 10-item checklist to be used to rate student behaviour (e.g., *Always submits assignments on time*). Rate your own behaviour against this list. Then ask friends and family members to rate your behaviour. Are there differences? If so, how would you explain them?

4. Take two of the items from question 3 and develop a BARS for each of these items. Then rate yourself and ask others to rate you using the BARS. Did the ratings change? If so, why?

5. Think of a friend or a family member whose behaviour you wish to change (e.g., your friend is usually late for events that you have organized). Using the problem-solving interview and the suggestions for conducting an effective appraisal interview, provide appraisal feedback to your friend.

6. What sources could be used to evaluate the performance of people working in the following jobs?

   a. Sales representative
   b. TV repairer
   c. Director of nursing in a hospital
   d. HR manager
   e. Air traffic controller

7. In many organizations, evaluators submit ratings to their immediate superiors for review before discussing them with the individual employees they have rated. What advantages are there to this procedure?

8. Three types of appraisal interviews are described in this chapter.

   a. What different skills are required for each type of appraisal interview? What reactions can one expect from using these different skills?
   b. How can one develop the skills needed for the problem-solving type of interview?
   c. Which method do you feel is the least desirable? Why?

9. A member of your study team usually misses the deadline for submitting his part of the assignment. Using Figure 8.10, conduct a performance diagnosis.

# HRM EXPERIENCE

## Performance Diagnosis

Managing performance is an important—yet delicate—process for managers to undertake. They need to make tough calls at times regarding who is performing well or not. Also, they need to play the role of coach to help each employee improve his or her performance. One of the toughest aspects of performance management is assessing why someone is not performing well. Although it may be easy to spot who is not performing well, it is not always easy to diagnose the underlying causes of poor performance (such as ability, motivation, and environment). But without a correct diagnosis, it is nearly impossible to cure the problem.

### Assignment

The following are descriptions of three different employees. Describe the potential causes of poor performance in each case. For each potential cause, identify appropriate solutions to enhance performance.

1. Carl Spackler is the assistant greenskeeper at Bushwood Country Club. Over the past few months, members have been complaining that gophers

are destroying the course and digging holes in the greens. Although Carl has been working evenings and weekends to address the situation, the problem persists. Unfortunately, his boss is interested only in results, and because the gophers are still there, he contends that Carl is not doing his job. He has accused Carl of "slacking off" and threatened his job.

2. Susan Griswold works in research and development for a chemical company that makes nonnutritive food additives. Her most recent assignment has been the development of a nonstick aerosol cooking spray, but the project is way behind schedule and seems to be going nowhere. CEO Frank Shirley is decidedly upset and has threatened that if things do not improve,

he will suspend bonuses again this year, as he did last year. Susan feels dejected because without the bonus she will not be able to take her family on vacation.

3. Bonnie Molloy is the host of a local television talk show called *Morning Metro*. Although she is a talented performer and comedian, Bonnie has an unacceptable record of tardiness. The show's producer, David Bellows, is frustrated because the problem has affected the quality of the show. On several occasions, Bonnie was unprepared when the show went on the air. Bellows has concluded that Bonnie is not a morning person and has thought about replacing her with a different host.

Visit the *Managing Human Resources* CourseMate website at http://www.belcourt7e.nelson.com for quizzes, flashcards, videos, games, and more!

## CASE STUDY 1

### JUST-IN-TIME FEEDBACK

Critics of formal performance evaluation programs cite "timeliness" as the major disadvantage of the annual formal performance appraisal interview. This criticism is gaining force as more people become accustomed to instant dialogue on BlackBerries, Facebook, and Twitter. The second criticism of the traditional performance appraisal interview is the one-way nature of the communication. The Net generation wants dialogue, not lectures. They want instant feedback and information about everything. The traditional process does not deliver what employees want: constant, timely, and interactive feedback. Daily feedback is more important and effective than annual feedback.

Technology may be the answer. A Canadian company, Rypple, has created a Web-based service to replace the performance review. Instead of waiting one year to sit down with a boss, employees choose some advisors who could be mentors, coworkers, managers, or clients. These employees can then contact the advisors with direct questions (How do I prepare for the report to the board?) or career queries (How can I be more effective on my job?). The advisors can respond quickly and anonymously to provide real-time, just-in-time performance feedback.

### Questions

1. What are the advantages and limitations of this kind of performance feedback?
2. Who would you choose as mentors in your current job and why?
3. What questions would you ask them?

---

**Sources:** Adapted from Dan Tapscott, "The Just-in-Time Performance Review," *The Globe and Mail*, February 13, 2009, B15; Malcolm Gabriel and Pierre Robitaille, "Sustaining High Performance with Generation-Y Employees," *Canadian HR Reporter* 21, no. 1 (January 14, 2008): 13.

# PERFORMANCE APPRAISAL AT A NOT-FOR-PROFIT ORGANIZATION

More than 3,000 people work for the Zoological Society of San Diego, a nonprofit organization that operates the San Diego Zoo, the San Diego Zoo's Wild Animal Park, and San Diego Zoo's Institute for Conservation Research. The people who work for the society are not quite as varied as the 800 species of animals the society deals with, but they do represent a wide cross section of all sorts of employees. They include everyone from veterinarians and scientists to food service personnel and security staff.

For years, the society had used a paper-and-pen system to evaluate employees. However, there were no consequences if a supervisor did not bother to complete his or her reviews and submit them to HR. Enter Tim Mulligan, the society's new HR director. "The old review process was spotty at best," says Mulligan. "There were managers within the organization who had not received reviews in ten years," says Mulligan. There was simply no way to monitor whether the reviews were getting done, and, more importantly, there was no understanding by employees or managers of the need for them, says Mulligan.

Mulligan wanted to change the situation. He wanted the society and its managers to set some goals for themselves and their workers and for people to be paid based on those goals. "It's hard to insist on accountability if there are no goals to hold anyone to," he says.

Consequently, Mulligan put together a team to explore the possibility of adopting a performance management system. After some research, the team determined that the zoo needed a system that would

- Be easy to use, even for those with limited computer skills; many people in the company were leery of having to learn how to operate a piece of software, so this was a top priority
- Effectively link employee goals with the Zoological Society's objectives
- Objectively measure employee performance so that it could be linked with compensation

- Better manage the process of tracking the review process
- Contain a journal feature so employees could record their achievements on a year-round basis

Eventually, the society decided to adopt Halogen Software's eAppraisal system. The software has built-in prompts that guide managers through the review process and frees HR professionals from the task of reminding managers that appraisals are due. The appraisal process can also be tailored to include multiple raters.

There was just one problem: the society had no goals. So, a second team of more than 200 managers was formed to establish goals and determine the key competencies that lead to a manager's success in the organization. At the beginning of the year, each manager chooses five goals, at least three of which must be linked to the organization's overall objectives. Those goals are based on everything from guest satisfaction to revenue. "The solution was not shoved down their throats by HR," said Mulligan. "No matter what department you worked in, you had a vote on the competencies that were going to be included."

Since implementing the eAppraisal system, the appraisal completion rate has gone from about 50 percent to a full 100 percent. "At first, I think our employees found it hard to believe this was all really happening," says Mulligan. "Seeing managers being held accountable for customer satisfaction, employee satisfaction, budgets, and training and development is helping to strengthen our organization's employee accountability and to boost overall morale." Nor is the human touch lost when it comes to appraisals. Performance appraisals must be delivered in person, and supervisors and their employees discuss the results as they review the appraisals together. An employee cannot just pull up his appraisal on the Web and read it.

"People come to work at the Zoo and the Wild Animal Park because they believe in our efforts to conserve endangered species," said Douglas Myers, executive director and CEO for the Zoological Society. "Tim has worked to ensure that this dedication is recognized and rewarded."

## Questions

1. Why do nonprofit organizations such as the San Diego Zoological Society need an appraisal system if their goal is not to maximize their profits?

2. What do you think are the pros and cons of using a Web-based appraisal system?
3. How will the new appraisal system affect employees and the types of employees who work at the zoo?

**Sources:** "The Zoological Society of San Diego Redefined Its Corporate Culture with Its New Employee Performance Management System," Halogen Software [case study], accessed April 23, 2011; Todd Henneman, "Employee Performance Management: What's Gnu at the Zoo," *Workforce Management*, September 11, 2006; "San Diego Zoo Human Resources Director Honored," *Imperial Valley News* (July 16, 2008), http://www.ivpressonline.com.

# CASE STUDY 3

## WOW PRODUCTIONS

Wow Productions is a Canadian company specializing in the production of films, documentaries, dramas and animation programs for television. The quality of its productions has earned the company an excellent reputation on the market. Over the last three years, the organization has grown substantially, doubling its workforce. With over 800 employees working in four studios across the country, it has become a major industry player. Furthermore, since it was founded in 1990, Wow Productions has won a number of international awards. A cloud has however appeared on the horizon: in the last 18 months reactions to its productions have been cool and profits have fallen.

The company's president believes that what sets Wow Productions apart in its market segment is its strong talent. Since its inception, it has been able to depend on reliable directors. At their strategic meeting each year, the company reminds the directors of their responsibility to maintain tight control over the management of their studio's productivity and performance.

During a team meeting, some Studio 2 employees learned that, unlike them, Studio 3 employees weren't evaluated each year by their director. The company's president heard about these discussions and wants to understand exactly what's happening. She therefore asks the HR manager to analyze the situation.

The HR manager first meets each of the four studio directors individually before summing up the situation as follows:

| Studio 1 | Studio 2 | Studio 3 | Studio 4 |
|---|---|---|---|
| The director: | The director: | The director: | The director: |
| • sets performance goals for poor performers only; | • sets performance goals for all the employees; | • does not set any employee performance goals; | • meets with top performers once a year to congratulate them and recognize their efforts and good performance. |
| • meets these employees as often as necessary during the year. In some cases, they are let go or dismissed. | • holds one-on-one meetings with all the employees twice a year (in mid-year and at year-end). | • holds several one-on-one meetings as needed during the year. | |

The names and characters in this case study are fictitious, and any resemblance to actual persons living or dead is purely coincidental.

## Questions

You are the HR manager and you decide to prepare a report for the president, setting out an overview of the situation and proposing recommendations.

1. Identify four probable causes for the lack of uniformity in the application of performance management practices.

2. What are your top three recommendations to ensure effective management of performance within the organization? Justify your answers.

## NOTES AND REFERENCES

1. Susan Scherreik, "Your Performance Review: Make It Perform," *Business Week*, no. 3762 (December 17, 2001): 139; Dick Grote, "Performance Evaluations: Is It Time for a Makeover?" *HRfocus* 77, no. 11 (November 2000): 6–7; "Employers Need to Do a Better Job of Performance Management," *Managing Training & Development* (April 2003): 8; Christopher D. Lee, "Feedback, Not Appraisal," *HR Magazine* 51, no. 11 (November 2006): 111–114. R. Cardy and B. Leonard, *Performance Management: Concepts, Skills, and Exercises* (Armonk, NY: M. E. Sharpe, Inc., 2011).

2. Dana Jarvis, "Why Should We Continue Performance Appraisals if We Can't Give Raises, *Workforce Management* (September 26 2010), http://www.workforce.com.

3. David Allen and Rodger Griffeth, "Test of a Mediated Performance-Turnover Relationship Highlighting the Moderating Roles of Visibility and Reward Contingency," *Journal of Applied Psychology* 86, no. 5 (October 2001): 1014–1021; Charles Pettijohn, Linda Pettijohn, and Michael D'Amico, "Characteristics of Performance Appraisals and Their Impact on Sales Force Satisfaction," *Human Resource Development Quarterly* 12, no. 2 (Summer 2001): 127–146; Scott and Einstein, "Strategic Performance Appraisal in Team-Based Organizations," *The Academy of Management Executive* 15, no. 2, 107–116; "Organizations Seek Stronger Performance Management—and PFP," *Pay for Performance Report* 4, no. 6 (June 2004): 2–4.

4. Garry Kranz, "Employees Want Feedback Even If It's Negative," *Workforce Management* (February 17, 2010), http://www.workforce.com.

5. Janet Wiscombe, "Can Pay for Performance Really Work?" *Workforce* 80, no. 8 (August 2001): 28–34; Charlotte Garvey, "Meaningful Tokens of Appreciation: Cash Awards Aren't the Only Way to Motivate Your Workforce," *HR Magazine* 49, no. 8 (August 2004): 101–106; Lisa D. Sprenkle, "Forced Ranking: A Good Thing for Business?" *Workforce.com,* http://homepages.uwp.edu/crooker/790-iep-pm/Articles/meth-fd-workforce.pdf.

6. Donna Doldwasser, "Me a Trainer?" *Training* 38, no. 4 (April 2001): 60–66; Rebecca Ganzel, "Mike Carter," *Training* 38, no. 7 (July 2001): 28–30; Carla Joinson, "Making Sure Employees Measure Up," *HR Magazine* 46, no. 3 (March 2001): 36–41; Morton D. Rosenbaum, "Gratitude Adjustment: When a Pat on the Back Isn't Enough," *Meetings & Conventions* 39, no. 7 (June 2004): 20; James W. Smither, Manuel London, and Richard R. Reilly, "Does Performance Improve Following Multisource Feedback?" *Personnel Psychology* 58, no. 1 (Spring 2005): 33–67.

7. Deanna M. Merritt "Appraising the Performance Appraisal" *Supervison* 68,. n0. 4 (April 2007): 3–5. Rebecca M. Chory-Asaad, "Room for Improvement" *Training*, 40. no. 11, (December 2003); 18–20.

8. John Newman, J. Mack Robinson, Larry Tyler, David Dunbar, and Joseph Zager, "CEO Performance Appraisal: Review and Recommendations/Practitioner Application," *Journal* of *Healthcare Management* 46, no. 1 (January/February 2001): 21–38; Bob Losyk, "How to Conduct a Performance Appraisal," *Public Management* 84, no. 3 (April 2002): 8–12; Arup Varma and Shaun Pichler, "Interpersonal Affect: Does It Really Bias Performance Appraisals?" *Journal of Labor Research* 28, no. 2 (Spring 2007): 397–412.

9. David Javitch, "How to Survive Employee Appraisals," http://www.entrepreneur.com, retrieved April 23, 2011.

10. Doug Cederblom, "From Performance Appraisal to Performance Management: One Agency's Experience," *Public Personnel Management* 31, no. 2 (Summer 2002): 131–140; "Anonymous 360-Feedback Drives Vauxhall Strategy," *Personnel Today* (August 19, 2003): 16; Cindy Romaine, "Staying Relevant: Competencies and Employee Reviews," *Information Outlook* 8, no. 7 (April 2004): 21–25; Jerry K. Palmer and James M. Loveland, "The Influence of Group Discussion on Performance Judgments: Rating Accuracy, Contrast Effects, and Halo," *Journal of Psychology* 142, no. 2 (March 2008): 117–130.

11. Jason D. Shaw and Nina Gupta, "Job Complexity, Performance, and Well-Being: When Does Supplies-Values Fit Matter?" *Personnel Psychology* 57, no. 4 (Winter 2004): 847–880.

12. Joel Lefkowitz, "The Role of Interpersonal Affective Regard in Supervisory Performance Ratings: A Literature Review and Proposed Causal Model," *Journal of Occupational and Organizational Psychology* 73, no. 1 (March 2000): 67–85; Scott Highhouse, "Assessing the Candidate As a Whole: A Historical and Critical Analysis of Individual Psychological Assessment for Personnel Decision Making," *Personnel Psychology* 55, no. 2 (Summer 2002): 363–397.

13. Joanne Sammer, "Calibrating Consistency," *HR Magazine* 53, no. 1 (January 2008): 73–75.

14. Timothy Aeppel, "Goodyear Ends Ratings System Ahead of Lawsuit," *The Wall Street Journal,* September 12, 2002, B8; "How to Stay 'Legal' with Performance Evaluation and Testing," *Managing Training & Development,* no. 4 (February 2004): 9.

15. Gillian Flynn, "Getting Performance Reviews Right," *Workforce* 80, no. 5 (May 2001): 76–78; David C. Martin, Kathryn M. Bartol, and Patrick E. Kehoe, "The Legal Ramifications of Performance Appraisal: The Growing Significance," *Public Personnel Management* 29, no. 3 (Fall 2000): 381; Deanna M. Merritt, "Appraising the Performance Appraisal," *Supervision* 68, no. 4 (April 2007): 3–5; Kevin R. Murphy, "Perspectives on the Relationship Between Job Performance and Ratings of Job Performance," *Industrial & Organizational Psychology* 1, no. 2 (June 2008): 197–205.

16. Joan Brett and Leanne Atwater, "360-Degree Feedback: Accuracy, Reactions, and Perceptions of Usefulness," *Journal of Applied Psychology* 86, no. 5 (October 2001): 930–942; Bruce Pfau, Ira Kay, Kenneth Nowak, and Jai Ghorpade, "Does 360-Degree Feedback Negatively Affect Company Performance?" *HR Magazine* 47, no. 6 (June 2002): 54–59; Maury Peiperl, "Getting 360-Degree Feedback Right," *Harvard Business Review* 79, no. 1 (January 2001): 142–147; Robert Gandossy and Tina Kao, "Talent Wars: Out of Mind, Out of Practice," *Human Resource Planning* 27, no. 4 (December 2004): 15–20.

17. Corey E. Miller and Carl L. Thornton, "How Accurate Are Your Performance Appraisals?" *Public Personnel Management* (Summer 2006): 153–162; Edward J. Inderrieden, Robert E. Allen, and Timothy J. Keaveny, "Managerial Discretion in the Use of Self-Ratings in an Appraisal System: The Antecedents and Consequences," *Journal of Managerial Issues* 16, no. 4 (Winter 2004): 460–484.

18. Bob Rosner, "Squeezing More Respect Out of Your Team," *Workforce* 79, no. 7 (July 2000): 78–79; Dick Grote "The Secrets of Performance Appraisal: Best Practices from the Masters," *Across the Board* 37, no. 5 (May 2000): 14–20; Edward J. Inderrieden, Robert E. Allen, and Timothy J. Keaveny, "Managerial Discretion in the Use of Self-Ratings in an Appraisal System: The Use of Antecedents and Consequences," *Journal of Managerial Issues,* 16. no. 4 (Winter 2004): 460–484.

19. Jeffrey Seglin, "Reviewing Your Boss," *Fortune* 143, no. 12 (June 11, 2001): 248; Ann Harrington, "Workers of the World, Rate Your Boss!" *Fortune* 142, no. 6 (September 18, 2000): 340–342; Robert Thompson, "Management Lite: Less Control, More Innovation," *HR Magazine* 44, no. 8 (August 1999): 10.

20. Brett and Atwater, "360-Degree Feedback," 930–942; Paula Silva and Henry L. Tosi, "Determinants of the Anonymity of the CEO Evaluation Process," *Journal of Managerial Issues* 16, no. 1 (Spring 2004): 87–103.

21. Ann Pomeroy, "Great Places, Inspired Employees: The Nation's Best Employers Show That Inspiring Employee Involvement through Good HR Practices Makes Good Business Sense," *HR Magazine* 49, no. 7 (July 2004): 44–64; Sue Browness, "Full-Circle Feedback," *Profit* 25, no. 2 (May 2006): 77.

22. John Drexler, Jr., Terry Beehr, and Thomas Stetz, "Peer Appraisals: Differentiation of Individual Performance on Group Tasks," *Human Resource Management* 40, no. 4 (Winter 2001): 333–345.

23. Scott and Einstein, "Strategic Performance Appraisal in Team-Based Organizations," 107–116; Debbie Kibbe and Jill Casner-Lotto, "Ralston Foods: From Greenfield to Maturity in a Team-Based Plant," *Journal of Organizational Excellence* 21, no. 3 (Summer 2002): 57–67; Simon Taggar and Mitchell Neubert, "The Impact of Poor Performers on Team Outcomes: An Empirical Examination of Attribution Theory," *Personnel Psychology* 57, no. 4 (Winter 2004): 935–969; Bradley Kirkman and Benson Rosen, "Powering Up Teams," *Organizational Dynamics* 28, no. 3 (Winter 2000): 48–66; Matthew Valle and Kirk Davis, "Teams and Performance Appraisal: Using Metrics to Increase Reliability and Validity," *Team Performance Management* 5, no. 8 (1999): 238–243; Ebrahim Soltani, Robert Van der Meer, Terry M. Williams, and Pei-chun Lai, "The Compatibility of Performance Appraisal Systems with TQM Principles: Evidence from Current Practice," *International Journal of Operations & Production Management* 26, no. 1 (2006): 92–112.

24. Michael Cohn, "Best Buy Beefs Up Customer Value at the Call Center," *Internet World* 8, no. 6 (June 2002): 42–43; Joe Kohn, "Isuzu Has IDEA for Boosting Sales," *Automotive News* 76, no. 5973 (March 4, 2002): 41; D. L. Radcliff, "A New Paradigm of Feedback," *Executive Excellence* 19, no. 4 (April 2002): 20; Neeraj Bharadwaj and Anne Roggeveen, "The Impact of Offshored and Outsourced Call Service Centers on Customer Appraisals," *Marketing Letters* 19, no. 1 (January 2008): 13–23.

25. Pfau, Kay, Nowak, and Ghorpade, "Does 360-Degree Feedback Negatively Affect Company Performance?" 54–59; Peiperl, "Getting 360-Degree Feedback Right," 142–147; Jack Kondrasuk, and Matt Graybill, "From Paper to Computer," *The Human Resource Professional* 13, no. 6 (November/December 2000): 18–19.

26. Gary Meyer, "Performance Reviews Made Easy, Paperless," *HR Magazine* 45, no. 10 (October 2000): 181–184; Douglas P. Shuit, "Huddling with the Coach—Part 2," *Workforce Management* 84, no. 2 (February 1, 2005): 5; "Ceridian and Softscape Announce an Agreement to Deliver Employee Performance and Development Solutions," *Payroll Manager's Report* (May 2004): 13; K. Sanwong, "The Development of a 360-Degree Performance Appraisal System: A University Case Study," *International Journal of Management* 25, no. 1 (March 2008): 16–22.

27. "Performance Appraisal," *HR Magazine* 47, no. 10 (October 2002): 146; Frank E. Kuzmits, Arthur J. Adams, Lyle Sussman, and Louis E. Raho, "360-Feedback in Health Care Management: A Field Study," *The Health Care Manager* 23, no. 321 (October–December 2004): 321–329; Jerry K. Palmer and James M. Loveland, "The Influence of Group Discussion on Performance Judgments: Rating Accuracy, Contrast Effects, and Halo. Preview," *Journal of Psychology* 142, no 2 (March 2008): 117–130; S. Bartholomew Craig and Kelly Hannum, "Research Update: 360-Degree Performance Assessment," *Consulting Psychology Journal: Practice & Research* 58, no. 2 (Spring 2006): 117–124.

28. Gary E. Roberts, "Perspectives on Enduring and Emerging Issues in Performance Appraisal," *Public Personnel Management* 27, no. 3 (Fall 1998): 301–320; William Hubbartt, "Bring Performance Appraisal Training to Life," *HR Magazine* 40, no. 5 (May 1995): 166, 168; Filip Lievens, "Assessor Training Strategies and Their Effects on Accuracy, Interrater Reliability, and Discriminant Validity," *Journal of Applied Psychology* 86, no. 2 (April 2001): 255–264; Dick Grote, "Performance Appraisals: Solving Tough Challenges," *HR Magazine* 45, no. 7 (July 2000): 145–150; Leslie A. Weatherly, "Performance Management: Getting It Right from the Start," *HR Magazine* 49, no. 3 (March 2004): S1–S12.

29. Gary P. Latham and Kenneth N. Wexley, *Increasing Productivity through Performance Appraisal,* 2nd ed. (Reading, MA: Addison-Wesley, 1994), 137.

30. Lefkowitz, "The Role of Interpersonal Affective Regard in Supervisory Performance Ratings," 67–85; Edwin Arnold and Marcia Pulich, "Personality Conflicts and Objectivity in Appraising Performance," *The Health Care Manager* 22, no. 3 (July–September 2003): 227; Krista Uggersly and Lorne M. Suksy, "Using Frame-of-Reference Training to Understand the Implications of Rater Idiosyncrasy for Rating Accuracy," *Journal of Applied Psychology* 93, no. 3 (May 2008): 711–719.

31. Deidra J. Schleicher and David V. Day, "A Cognitive Evaluation of Frame-of-Reference Rater Training: Content and Process Issues," *Organizational Behaviour and Human Decision Processes* 73, no. 1 (January 1998): 76–101; Wanda Smith, K. Vernard Harrington, and Jeffery Houghton, "Predictors of Performance Appraisal Discomfort: A Preliminary Examination," *Public Personnel Management* 29, no. 1 (Spring 2000): 21–32; Krista L. Uggerslev and Lorne M. Sulsky, "Using Frame-of-Reference Training to Understand the Implications of Rater Idiosyncrasy for Rating Accuracy," *Journal of Applied Psychology* 93, no. 3 (May 2008): 711–719.

32. Gail Johnson, "Forced Ranking: The Good, the Bad, and the Alternative," *Training* 41, no. 5 (May 2004): 24–31; Christine A. Amalfe and Eileen Quinn Steiner, "Forced Ranking Systems: Yesterday's Legal Target?" *New Jersey Law Journal* CLXXIX, no. 13 (March 28, 2005), Index 1289; Jessica Marquez, "Is GE's Ranking System Broken?" *Workforce Management* 86, no. 12 (June 25, 2007): 1–3.

33. Lisa Keeping and Paul Levy, "Performance Appraisal Reaction: Measurement, Modeling, and Method Bias," *Journal of Applied Psychology* 85, no. 5 (October 2000): 708–723.

34. Adam B. Butler and Amie Skattebo, "What Is Acceptable for Women May Not Be for Men: The Effect of Family Conflicts with Work on Job-Performance Ratings," *Journal of Occupational and Organizational Psychology* 77, no. 4 (December 2004): 553–564; Cheri Ostroff, Leanne E. Atwater, and Barbara J. Feinberg, "Understanding Self-Other Agreement: A Look at Rater and Ratee Characteristics, Context, and Outcomes," *Personnel Psychology* 57, no. 1 (Summer 2004): 333–337; Mike Schraeder and Jim Simpson, "How Similarity and Liking Affect Performance Appraisals," *Journal for Quality & Participation* 29, no. 1 (Spring 2006): 34–40.

35. Kristina E. Chirico, M. Ronald Buckley, Anthony R. Wheeler, Jeffrey D. Facteau, H. John Bernardin, and Danielle S. Beu, "A Note on the Need for True Scores in Frame-of-Reference (FOR) Training Research," *Journal of Managerial Issues* 16, no. 3 (Fall 2004): 382–398; Christopher D. Lee, "Feedback, Not Appraisal," *HR Magazine* 51, no. 11 (November 2006): 111–114.

36. Stephen C. Behrenbrinker, "Conducting Productive Performance Evaluations in the Assessor's Office," *Assessment Journal* 2, no. 5 (September/October 1995): 48–54; Aharon Tziner, Christine Joanis, and Kevin Murphy, "A Comparison of Three Methods of Performance Appraisal with Regard to Goal Properties, Goal Perception, and Ratee Satisfaction," *Group & Organization Management* 25, no. 2 (June 2000): 175–190.

37. Elaine Pulakos, Sharon Arad, Michelle Donovan, and Kevin Plamondon, "Adaptability in the Workplace: Development of a Taxonomy of Adaptive Performance," *Journal of Applied Psychology* 85, no. 4 (August 2000): 612–624; Weatherly, "Performance Management: Getting It Right from the Start," S1–S12; Edwin Arnold and Marcia Pulich, "Personality Conflicts and Objectivity in Appraising Performance," *The Health Care Manager* 22, no. 3 (July–September 2003): 227.

38. Latham and Wexley, *Increasing Productivity*; Tziner, Joanis, and Murphy, "A Comparison of Three Methods of Performance Appraisal," 175–190; Simon Taggar and Travor Brown, "Problem-Solving Team Behaviours: Development and Validation of BOS and a Hierarchical Factor Structure," *Small Group Research* 32, no. 6 (December 2001): 698–726; Paul Falcone, "Big-Picture Performance Appraisal," *HRfocus* 84, no. 9 (September 2007): 1–15.

39. Daniel Bachrach, Elliot Bendoly, and Philip Podsakoff, "Attributions of the 'Causes' of Group Performance as an Alternative Explanation of the Relationship between Organizational Citizenship Behavior and Organizational Performance," *Journal of Applied Psychology* 86, no. 6 (December 2001): 1285–1293; Susan Leandri, "Measures That Matter: How to Fine-Tune Your Performance Measures," *Journal for Quality and Participation* 24, no. 1 (Spring 2001): 39–41.

40. Peter F. Drucker, *The Practice of Management* (New York: Harper & Brothers, 1954; reissued by HarperCollins in 1993); Janice S. Miller, "High Tech and High Performance: Managing Appraisal in the Information Age," *Journal of Labor Research* 24, no. 3 (Summer 2003): 409–425.

41. E. Locke and G. Latham, *A Theory of Goal Setting and Task Performance* (Englewood Cliffs, NJ: Prentice Hall, 1990). See also John J. Donovan and David J. Radosevich, "The Moderating Role of Goal Commitment on the Goal Difficulty-Performance Relationship: A Meta-Analytic Review and Critical Reanalysis," *Journal of Applied Psychology* 83, no. 2 (April 1998): 308–315; Cindy Romaine, "Staying Relevant: Competencies and Employee Reviews," *Information Outlook* 8, no. 4 (April 2004): 21–25; Gail Johnson, "Room for Improvement," *Training* 40, no. 11 (December 2003): 18–20.

42. Jack Steele, "Transforming the Balanced Scorecard into Your Strategy Execution System," *Manage* 53, no. 1 (September/October 2001): 22–23. See also Robert Kaplan and David Norton, "Strategic Learning and the Balanced Scorecard," *Strategy & Leadership* 24, no. 5 (September/October 1996): 18–24; Robert Kaplan and David Norton, "Using the Balanced Scorecard as a Strategic Management System," *Harvard Business Review* (January–February 1996): 75–85; Joe Mullich, "Get in Line: People Talk about Aligning Corporate, Departmental and Employee Goals, But Not Many Actually Do It," *Workforce Management* 82, no. 13 (December 2003); "Good Appraisal Is Simple, Happens Often, Experts Say," *The Orlando Sentinel* (Knight-Ridder/Tribune News Service), December 3, 2003; Li-cheng Chang, "The NHS Performance Assessment Framework as a Balanced Scorecard Approach," *International Journal of Public Sector Management* 20, no 2 (2007): 101–117.

43. Deloris McGee Wanguri, "A Review, an Integration, and a Critique of Cross-Disciplinary Research on Performance Appraisals, Evaluations, and Feedback," *Journal of Business Communications* 32, no. 3 (July 1995): 267–293; Tziner, Joanis, and Murphy, "A Comparison of Three Methods of Performance Appraisal," 175–190; "Good Appraisal Is Simple, Happens Often, Experts Say"; Joanna Haworth, "Measuring Performance," *Nursing Management*—UK 15, no. 3 (June 2008): 22–28.

44. Norman R. F. Maier, *The Appraisal Interview* (Tucson, AZ: University Associates, 1976).

45. Kwok Leung, Steven Su, and Michael Morris, "When Is Criticism Not Constructive? The Roles of Fairness Perceptions and Dispositional Attributions in Employee Acceptance of Critical Supervisory Feedback," *Human Relations* 54, no. 9 (September 2001): 1155–1187; Ted Pollock, "Make Your Criticism Pay Off," *Electric Light & Power* 81, no. 1 (January 2003): 31; "Five Ways to Tackle Poor Performers," *Law Office Management & Administration Report* 6, no. 12 (December 2006): 9.

46. "Focus on Success," *Aftermarket Business* 115, no. 2 (February 2005): 1.

47. Helen Wilkie, "The Tricky Art of Criticism," *HR Magazine* 49, no. 12 (December 2004): 77–83.

# Managing Compensation

MANAGINGHU
HUMANRESOU
RESOURCESM

## After studying this chapter, you should be able to

| | |
|---|---|
| **OUTCOME 1** | Explain how to develop a strategic compensation system. |
| **OUTCOME 2** | Indicate the various factors that influence the setting of wages. |
| **OUTCOME 3** | Describe the mechanics of each of the major job evaluation systems. |
| **OUTCOME 4** | Discuss how and why wage surveys are done. |
| **OUTCOME 5** | Define the wage curve, pay grades, and rate ranges as parts of the compensation structure. |
| **OUTCOME 6** | Identify the major provisions of the laws and regulations affecting compensation. |
| **OUTCOME 7** | Discuss the current issues of equal pay for work of equal value and pay compression. |

People enjoy their work for many reasons, including the challenge of the work, good leadership, interesting job assignments, equitable rewards, and rewarding careers. It is doubtful, however, whether many employees would continue working were it not for the money they earn. Employees desire compensation systems that they perceive as being fair and commensurate with their skills and expectations.

In 2011, Google gave all its employees a 10 percent raise. The company-wide pay boost, spread across 20,300 employees, probably cost the company $1 billion a year. In an email to employees, former Google CEO Eric Schmidt explained that the company had received feedback that salary is more important than other sources of pay (i.e., bonuses and stock in the company).[1] Schmidt explained that even in a slowed-down economy, they are in a "war for talent," and employees had expressed concerns "dealing with sky-high property prices, mortgages, and those kinds of things." But, ultimately, Schmidt stated that the primary reason for the raise was that "we just thought it was good for the whole company!"[2]

Compensation is a way to increase employee loyalty. In Google's case, it was seen as a way to decrease the likelihood that its employees will be hired away by competitors such as Facebook.[3] It reflects a strategic move on the part of the company to show that its employees are the most important component for Google's success. So why focus on compensation? Why not better select employees who will be more loyal? Why not improve the training programs or evaluation systems? The answer is simple. Compensation is directly linked to an employee's livelihood. Employees can receive stellar training

Masterfile

and copious growth opportunities and be completely satisfied with their work and the environment, but they will not show up to work if there is no paycheque in return.

So what is compensation? Compensation consists of three main components. *Direct compensation* encompasses employee wages and salaries, incentives, bonuses, and commissions. *Indirect compensation* comprises the many benefits supplied by employers. *Nonfinancial compensation* includes employee recognition programs, rewarding jobs, organizational support, work environment, and flexible work hours to accommodate personal needs. In this chapter, we will explain one aspect of direct compensation (base pay through wages and salaries) and discuss how pay is determined. Included will be a discussion of laws and regulations that affect wage and salary rates. Chapter 10 reviews pay-for-performance and incentive plans for employees. Employee benefits that are part of the total compensation package are discussed in Chapter 11.

# STRATEGIC COMPENSATION

| OUTCOME 1 |

What is strategic compensation? Simply stated, it is the compensation of employees in ways that enhance motivation and growth while at the same time aligning their efforts with the objectives, philosophies, and culture of the organization. Strategic compensation planning goes beyond determining what market rates to pay employees—although market rates are one element of compensation planning— to purposefully linking compensation to the organization's mission and general business objectives. For example, although Google's decision to increase base pay for all its employees was a strategic move to be more competitive with market rates, Google also recognizes that base pay is not everything. Google offers flexible work schedules, innovative benefits, and an opportunity to work on exciting new products. In this regard, Google has not only aligned its compensation strategy with the external market, it has also aligned it with its desire to be a flexible and innovative company whose core competency is found in the creativity of its people.

Additionally, strategic compensation planning serves to mesh the monetary payments made to employees with specific functions of the HR program. For example, in the recruitment of new employees, the rate of pay for jobs can increase or limit the supply of applicants. A compensation specialist speaking to one of the authors noted, "The linkage of pay levels to labour markets is a strategic policy issue because it serves to attract or retain valued employees while affecting the organization's relative payroll budget." For example, community colleges and universities know that they cannot attract or retain qualified professors unless their pay strategy is linked to competitive market rates.

Many fast-food restaurants, such as Burger King and Taco Bell—traditionally low-wage employers—have had to raise their starting wages to attract a sufficient number of job applicants to meet staffing requirements. If pay rates are high, creating a large applicant pool, then organizations may choose to raise their selection standards and hire better qualified employees. This in turn can reduce employer training costs. When employees perform at exceptional levels, their performance appraisals may justify an increased pay rate. For these reasons and others, an organization should develop a formal HR program to manage employee compensation. We will discuss three important aspects of strategic compensation planning: linking compensation to organizational objectives, the pay-for-performance standard, and motivating employees through compensation.

## LINKING COMPENSATION TO ORGANIZATIONAL OBJECTIVES

The financial crisis of 2007–2010 changed the landscape for compensation. Now companies are more heavily scrutinized by shareholders, government, and the public for how much they pay their people. For example, due to complaints of bloated federal government salaries, exorbitant Wall Street banker bonuses, and generous autoworker benefits, managers are trying to ensure that their compensation plans are in strict alignment with the organization's objectives. In Canada, where the crisis was not as severe as in the United States, the impact on compensation systems has been broadly similar. There is pressure on both private- and public-sector organizations to make their pay systems more performance based. For instance, restrictions were placed on public-sector organizations, such as hospitals in Ontario, on bonuses and salary increases.

Additionally, compensation has been revolutionized by heightened domestic competition, globalization, increased employee skill requirements, and new technology. Therefore, an outcome of today's dynamic business environment is that managers have had to change their pay philosophies from paying for a specific position or job title to also rewarding employees on the basis of their individual competencies or work contributions to organizational success. One study showed that 91 percent of responding organizations had a company compensation philosophy linking their pay strategy with organizational performance. As the authors of this study noted, "A written compensation philosophy indicates senior management understands and is committed to aligning their business strategy with pay, suggesting that alignment can have a positive impact on organizational effectiveness."[4]

Increasingly, compensation specialists are asking which components of the compensation package (benefits, base pay, incentives, and so on), both separately and in combination, create value for the organization and its employees. Managers are asking questions such as, "How will this pay program help retain and motivate valued employees?" and "Does the benefit or pay practice affect the administrative cost?" Payments that fail to advance either the employee or the organization tend to be removed from the compensation program.[5]

It is not uncommon for organizations to establish very specific goals for linking their organizational objectives to their compensation program.[6] Formalized compensation goals serve as guidelines for managers to ensure that wage and benefit policies achieve their intended purpose. The more common goals of a strategic compensation policy include the following:

1. To reward employees' past performance[7]
2. To remain competitive in the labour market
3. To maintain salary equity among employees
4. To mesh employees' future performance with organizational goals
5. To control the compensation budget
6. To attract new employees
7. To reduce unnecessary turnover[8]

One of the key purposes of the compensation system, as suggested by many compensation analysts, is to motivate employees.[9] We will examine this issue in more detail below.

## MOTIVATING EMPLOYEES THROUGH COMPENSATION: THEORETICAL EXPLANATIONS

Although scholars use several theories to explain the potential motivating effects of an organization's compensation systems, we will focus on two of the more popular theories: equity theory and expectancy theory.

### Equity Theory

Pay constitutes a quantitative measure of an employee's relative worth. For most employees, pay has a direct bearing not only on their standard of living

## FIGURE 9.1

### RELATIONSHIP BETWEEN EQUITY AND MOTIVATION

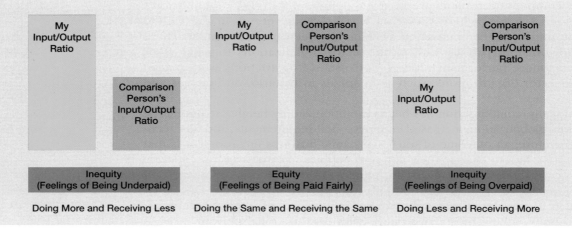

but also on the status and recognition they may be able to achieve both on and off the job. Because pay represents a reward received in exchange for an employee's contributions, it is essential, according to the equity theory, that the pay be equitable in terms of those contributions. It is also essential that an employee's pay be equitable in terms of what other employees are receiving for their contributions. Simply defined, equity embraces the concept of fairness. Equity theory is a motivation theory that explains how people respond to situations in which they feel they have received less (or more) than they deserve.[10]

Central to the theory is the role of perception in motivation and the fact that individuals make comparisons.[11] It states that individuals form a ratio of their inputs (abilities, skills, experiences) in a situation to their outcomes (salary, benefits) in that situation. They then compare the value of that ratio to the value of the input/output ratio for other individuals in a similar class of jobs either internal or external to the organization. If the value of their ratio equals the value of another's, they perceive the situation as equitable, and no tension exists. However, if they perceive their input/output ratio as inequitable relative to others', this creates tension and motivates them to eliminate or reduce the inequity. The strength of their motivation is proportional to the magnitude of the perceived inequity. Figure 9.1 illustrates pay equity and feelings of being fairly paid.

For employees, equity is achieved when their perceived input/output ratio equals the input/output ratio of *referent others* (or those to whom they compare themselves). Research clearly demonstrates that employees' perceptions of equity, or inequity, can have dramatic effects on their motivation for both work behaviour and productivity.[12] Managers must therefore develop strategic pay practices that are both internally and externally equitable. Compensation policies are *internally* equitable when employees believe that the wage rates for their jobs approximate the job's worth to the organization. Perceptions of external pay equity exist when the organization is paying wages that are relatively equal to what other employers are paying for similar types of work.

General Motors' failure to align compensation with the company's objectives is partly to blame for its massive layoffs in recent years.

## Expectancy Theory

The expectancy theory of motivation predicts that one's level of motivation depends on the attractiveness of the rewards sought and the probability of obtaining those rewards.[13] The theory has developed from the work of psychologists who consider humans as thinking, reasoning people who have beliefs and anticipations concerning future life events. Expectancy theory therefore holds that employees should exert greater work effort if they have reason to expect that it will result in a reward that is valued.[14] To motivate this effort, the value of any monetary reward should be attractive. Employees also must believe that good performance is valued by their employer and will result in their receiving the expected reward.

Expectancy theory suggests that three conditions must be met for a reward to be motivational. First, it must have high valence; that is, it must be valued by employees. Second, compensation packages must have high *instrumentality*; that is, employees must believe that the attainment of goals and objectives set by the organization must result in the promised rewards. Third, employees must have an *expectancy* that they can do the required tasks; that is, although goals can be challenging, they must be attainable.

In summary, how employees view compensation can be an important factor in determining the motivational value of compensation. Furthermore, the effective communication of pay information together with an organizational environment that elicits employee trust in management can contribute to employees having more accurate perceptions of their pay. The perceptions employees develop concerning their pay are influenced by the accuracy of their knowledge and understanding of the compensation program's strategic objectives.

## THE BASES FOR COMPENSATION

Work performed in most private, public, and not-for-profit organizations has traditionally been compensated on an hourly basis. It is referred to as **hourly work**, in contrast to **piecework**, in which employees are paid according to the number of units they produce. Hourly work is far more prevalent than piecework as a basis for compensating employees.

Employees compensated on an hourly basis are classified as *hourly employees*, or wage earners. Those whose compensation is computed on the basis of weekly, biweekly, or monthly pay periods are classified as *salaried employees*. Hourly employees are normally paid only for the time they work. Salaried employees, by contrast, are generally paid the same for each pay period, even though they occasionally may work more hours or fewer than the regular number of hours in a period. They also usually receive certain benefits not provided to hourly employees.

Employment practices are a provincial jurisdiction, and each province has its own employment standards act. Each act contains a provision that requires the employer to reimburse the employee at a specified rate after he or she has worked the minimum required hours. This rate is usually 1.5 times the employee's base hourly rate of pay. Some employers offer overtime pay that is more generous than what the act specifies. Some acts provide for time in lieu of overtime; thus, 4 hours of overtime paid at 1.5 would be the equivalent of 6 hours in either pay or time off in lieu of payment. Supervisory and management personnel are not usually paid overtime; still other personnel work overtime for free (see Ethics in HRM). Each employment standards act includes a list of people who are exempt from the overtime provision.

Because so many American companies are operating in Canada, the terms exempt (to describe employees not covered in the overtime provisions of the *U.S. Fair Labor Standards Act*) and *nonexempt* (to describe employees covered by the overtime provisions of the *U.S. Fair Labor Standards Act*) are often heard, although neither has any relevance in Canadian legislation. These terms are used specifically to denote *supervisory* and *nonsupervisory* roles. U.S. legislation stipulates that only nonexempt (i.e., nonsupervisory) workers are entitled to overtime pay.

 **Using the Internet**

You can determine the salary of almost any job by using sites such as

**http://www.workopolis.ca**

# ETHICS IN HRM

## Unpaid Interns: Working for Free?

Many college and university students, without much work experience, are usually encouraged by their professors, counsellors, parents, and others to "get their foot in the door" through internships. In general, this seems to be good advice, especially when these are paid internships and the assigned roles are in the career trajectories of students. There is, however, a potential concern when employers do not pay interns for their time. This issue was recently highlighted in a *Globe and Mail* article. Interns are often lured into believing that they will get valuable work experience with organizations, only to realize that the tasks they are given are not challenging; in fact, they may include mostly custodial work such as cleaning the kitchen and taking out the trash. In

other cases, the work mostly involves filing and making coffee. On top of this, the interns have to pay for transportation and other expenses. There is some debate as to when unpaid internships can be illegal. According to Professor David Doorey of the School of Human Resource Management at York University, in keeping with Ontario's *Employment Standards Act*, unless the internship is part of a degree or diploma requirement, it is likely that the "intern" is an employee and should be paid. Others feel that although the practice may appear to be "exploitative," it does give students an opportunity to get on-the-job-training. But is this practice ethical? Is it fair to students?

Source: Dakshana Baskaramurthy, "Unpaid interns: working for free," *The Globe and Mail,* July, 11, 2011, B2.

## DETERMINING COMPENSATION— THE WAGE MIX

OUTCOME 2

Employees may inquire of their managers, "How are the wages for my job determined?" In practice, a combination of *internal* and *external* factors can influence, directly or indirectly, the rates at which employees are paid. Through their interaction, these factors constitute the wage mix, as shown in Figure 9.2. For example, the area wage rate for administrative assistants might be $11.50 per hour. However, one employer may elect to pay its administrative assistants $14.25 per hour because of their excellent performance. The influence of government legislation on the wage mix will be discussed later in the chapter.

**FIGURE 9.2**

FACTORS AFFECTING THE PAY MIX

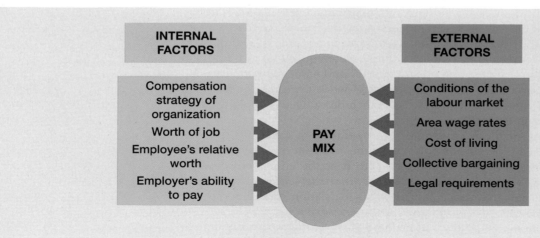

# HIGHLIGHTS IN HRM 9.1

## Comparison of Compensation Strategies

Compensation strategies and objectives can differ widely across large and small employers as well as across employers in the private and public sectors. Here are the compensation strategies at Tri Star Performance and Preventive Health Care.

| Tri Star Performance | Preventive Health Care |
| --- | --- |
| • Promote pay-for-performance practices | • Be a pay leader in the health care industry |
| • Pay market-competitive compensation | • Promote open and understandable pay practices |
| • Achieve internal and external pay equity | • Ensure fair employee treatment |
| • Achieve simplicity in compensation programs | • Offer benefits promoting individual employee needs |
| • Strive for employee commitment and a collaborative work environment | • Offer compensation rewarding employee creativity and achievements |
| • Promote gender fairness in pay and benefits | • Offer compensation to foster the strategic mission of the organization |
| • Comply with all governmental compensation regulations | • Obtain employee input when developing compensation practices |
| • Minimize increased fixed costs | • Emphasize performance through variable pay and stock options |

## INTERNAL FACTORS

The internal factors that influence wage rates are the employer's compensation strategy, the worth of a job, an employee's relative worth in meeting job requirements, and an employer's ability to pay.

### Employer's Compensation Strategy

Highlights in HRM 9.1 illustrates the compensation strategies of two organizations, Tri Star Performance and Preventive Health Care. The pay strategy of Preventive Health Care is to be an industry pay leader, whereas Tri Star Performance seeks to be wage competitive. Both employers strive to promote a compensation policy that is internally fair.

Tri Star Performance and Preventive Health Care, like other employers, will establish numerous compensation objectives that affect the pay employees receive. As a minimum, both large and small employers should set pay policies reflecting (1) the internal wage relationship among jobs and skill levels, (2) the external competition or an employer's pay position relative to what competitors are paying, (3) a policy of rewarding employee performance, and (4) administrative decisions concerning elements of the pay system such as overtime premiums, payment periods, and short-term or long-term incentives.

### Worth of a Job

Organizations without a formal compensation program generally base the worth of jobs on the subjective opinions of people familiar with the jobs. In such

Several factors should be taken into consideration when determining how much workers such as these should be paid.

instances, pay rates may be influenced heavily by the labour market or, in the case of unionized employers, by collective bargaining. Organizations with formal compensation programs, however, are more likely to rely on a system of *job evaluation* to aid in rate determination. Even when rates are subject to collective bargaining, job evaluation can assist the organization in maintaining some degree of control over its wage structure.

The use of job evaluation is widespread in both the public and the private sector. The City of Mississauga and Star Data Systems use job evaluation in establishing wage structures. The jobs covered most frequently by job evaluation are clerical, technical, and various blue-collar groups. Other jobs covered are managerial and top executive positions.

In today's competitive environment, compensation professionals believe that the worth of a job should be based on more than market prices or using only an internally driven job evaluation program. Rather, a job's value should be based on the total value delivered to the organization. That is, some jobs may simply be more important to organizational success than others regardless of how they are internally evaluated. Valuing work properly not only enables organizations to price "important" jobs effectively but also provides insight into how a job relates to overall organizational success. Additionally, valuing work properly serves to attract and retain the right talent to drive organizational performance.[15]

## Employee's Relative Worth

In both hourly and salary jobs, employee performance can be recognized and rewarded through promotion and with various incentive systems. (The incentive systems used most often are discussed in Chapter 10.) Superior performance can also be rewarded by granting merit raises on the basis of steps within a rate range established for a job class. If merit raises are to have their intended value, however, they must be determined by an effective performance appraisal system that differentiates between employees who deserve the raises and those who do not. This system, moreover, must provide a visible and credible relationship between performance and any raises received. Unfortunately, too many so-called merit systems provide for raises to be granted automatically. As a result, employees tend to be rewarded more for merely being present than for being productive on the job. Also, as previously noted, most increases may lack motivational value to employees when organizational salary budgets are low.[16]

## Employer's Ability to Pay

Pay levels are limited by earned profits and other financial resources available to employers. This is clearly illustrated by financially burdened companies that ask their employees for pay cuts. Furthermore, an organization's ability to pay is determined in part by the productivity of its employees. This productivity is a result not only of their performance but also of the amount of capital the organization has invested in labour-saving equipment. Generally, increases in capital investment reduce the number of employees required to perform the work and increase an employer's ability to provide higher pay for those it employs.

Economic conditions and competition faced by employers can also significantly affect the rates they are able to pay. Competition and recessions can force prices down and reduce the income from which compensation payments are derived. In such situations, employers have little choice but to reduce wages and/or lay off employees or, even worse, to go out of business.

General Motors and Chrysler have had to both reduce wages and lay off employees.

## EXTERNAL FACTORS

The major external factors that influence wage rates include labour market conditions, area wage rates, cost of living, collective bargaining if the employer is unionized, and legal requirements. The legal requirements of compensation will be discussed later in the chapter.

**consumer price index (CPI)**
A measure of the average change in prices over time in a fixed "market basket" of goods and services

### Labour Market Conditions

The labour market reflects the forces of supply and demand for qualified labour within an area. These forces help influence the wage rates required to recruit or retain competent employees. It must be recognized, however, that counterforces can reduce the full impact of supply and demand on the labour market. The economic power of unions, for example, may prevent employers from lowering wage rates even when unemployment is high among union members. Government regulations also may prevent an employer from paying at a market rate less than an established minimum set by each province.

### Area Wage Rates

A formal wage structure should provide rates that are in line with those being paid by other employers for comparable jobs within the area. Data pertaining to area wage rates may be obtained from local wage surveys. Wage survey data also may be obtained from a variety of sources, including compensation consulting firms such as Mercer Management Consulting, at a cost, and from some companies such as Monster.ca for free. The Conference Board of Canada also conducts an annual compensation survey. Smaller employers use government or local board of trade surveys to establish rates of pay for new and senior employees. Others engage in a cooperative exchange of wage information or rely on various professional associations for these data.

Wage surveys (discussed fully later in the chapter) serve the important function of providing external wage equity between the surveying organization and other organizations competing for labour in the surrounding labour market. Importantly, data from area wage surveys can be used to prevent the rates for jobs from drifting too far above or below those of other employers in the region. When rates rise above existing area levels, an employer's labour costs may become excessive. Conversely, if they drop too far below area levels, it may be difficult to recruit and retain competent personnel. Wage survey data must also take into account indirect wages paid in the form of benefits.

### Cost of Living

Because of inflation, compensation rates have had to be adjusted upward periodically to help employees maintain their purchasing power. Employers make these changes with the help of the **consumer price index (CPI)**. The CPI is a measure of the average change in prices over time in a fixed "market basket" of goods and services. The CPI is based on prices of food, clothing, shelter, and fuels; transportation fares; and prices of other goods and services that people buy for day-to-day living. Statistics Canada collects price information on a monthly basis and calculates the CPI for the nation as a whole and various Canadian cities. Employers in a number of communities monitor changes in the CPI as a basis for compensation decisions.

CPI figures can have important consequences for organizational morale and productivity. Granting wages based largely on "cost-of-living" figures will not inspire higher employee performance and may cause valued employees to leave the organization. Cost-of-living payments, when traditionally given, may be seen by employees as "entitlements" unrelated to individual performance. Furthermore, should cost-of-living increases be discontinued, managers can expect disgruntled employees, particularly those not likely to receive merit raises.

Employees who work under a union contract may receive wage increases through **escalator clauses** found in their collective agreement. These clauses provide for cost-of-living adjustments (COLAs) in wages based on changes in the CPI. The most common adjustments are 1 cent per hour for each 0.3- or 0.4-point change in the CPI. COLAs are favoured by unions during particularly high periods of inflation.

## Collective Bargaining

One of the primary functions of a labour union, as emphasized in Chapter 14, is to bargain collectively over conditions of employment, the most important of which is compensation.[17] The union's goal in each new agreement is to achieve increases in **real wages**—wage increases larger than the increase in the CPI—thereby improving the purchasing power and standard of living of its members. This goal includes gaining wage settlements that equal or exceed the pattern established by other unions within the area.

The agreements negotiated by unions tend to establish rate patterns within the labour market. As a result, wages are generally higher in areas where organized labour is strong. To recruit and retain competent personnel and avoid unionization, nonunion employers must either meet or exceed these rates. The "union scale" also becomes the prevailing rate that all employers must pay for work performed under government contract. The impact of collective bargaining therefore extends beyond the segment of the labour force that is unionized.

# JOB EVALUATION SYSTEMS

**OUTCOME 3**

As we discussed earlier, one important component of the wage mix is the worth of the job. Organizations formally determine the value of jobs through the process of job evaluation. **Job evaluation** is the systematic process of determining the *relative* worth of jobs to establish which jobs should be paid more than others within the organization. Job evaluation helps establish internal equity between various jobs. The relative worth of a job may be determined by comparing it to others within the organization or by comparing it to a scale that has been constructed for this purpose. Each method of comparison, furthermore, may be made on the basis of the jobs as a whole or on the basis of the parts that constitute the jobs.[18]

Three traditional methods of comparison provide the basis for the principal systems of job evaluation. We will begin by discussing the simpler non-quantitative approaches and conclude by reviewing the more popular quantitative system. Also discussed is a newer method of job evaluation: work evaluation. Regardless of the methodology used, it is important to remember that all job evaluation methods require varying degrees of managerial judgment.

## JOB RANKING SYSTEM

The simplest and oldest system of job evaluation is the **job ranking system**, which arrays jobs on the basis of their relative worth. One technique used to rank jobs consists of having the raters arrange cards listing the duties and responsibilities of each job in order of the importance of the jobs. Job ranking can be done by a single individual knowledgeable about all jobs or by a committee composed of management and employee representatives.

The basic disadvantage of the job ranking system is that it does not provide a very precise measure of each job's worth. Another weakness is that the final ranking of jobs indicates the relative importance of the job, not the differences in the degree of importance that may exist between jobs. A final limitation of the job ranking method is that it can be used only with a small number of jobs, probably no more than 15. Its simplicity, however, makes it ideal for use by smaller employers.

# JOB CLASSIFICATION SYSTEM

In the **job classification system**, jobs are classified and grouped according to a series of predetermined grades. Successive grades require increasing amounts of job responsibility, skill, knowledge, ability, or other factors selected to compare jobs. For example, Grade GS-1 from the federal government (U.S.) grade descriptions reads as follows:

> GS-1 includes those classes of positions the duties of which are to perform, under immediate supervision, with little or no latitude for the exercise of independent judgment (A) the simplest routine work in office, business, or fiscal operations; or (B) elementary work of a subordinate technical character in a professional, scientific, or technical field.[19]

The descriptions of each of the job classes constitute the scale against which the specifications for the various jobs are compared. Managers then evaluate jobs by comparing job descriptions with the different wage grades to "slot" the job into the appropriate grade. Although this system has the advantage of simplicity, it is less precise than the point system because the job is evaluated as a whole.

# POINT SYSTEM

The **point system** is a quantitative job evaluation procedure that determines a job's relative value by calculating the total points assigned to it.[20] It has been successfully used by high-visibility organizations such as the Province of Alberta.

Although point systems are rather complicated to establish, once in place, they are relatively simple to understand and use. The principal advantage of the point system is that it provides a more refined basis for making judgments than either the ranking or classification systems and thereby can produce results that are more valid and less easy to manipulate.

The point system permits jobs to be evaluated quantitatively on the basis of factors or elements—commonly called *compensable factors*—that constitute the job.[21] The skills, efforts, responsibilities, and working conditions that a job usually entails are the more common major compensable factors that serve to rank one job as more or less important than another. More contemporary factors might include fiscal accountability, leadership, teamwork, and project accountability. The number of compensable factors an organization uses depends on the nature of the organization and the jobs to be evaluated. Once selected, compensable factors will be assigned weights according to their relative importance to the organization. For example, if responsibility is considered extremely important to the organization, it could be assigned a weight of 40 percent. Next, each factor will be divided into a number of degrees. Degrees represent different levels of difficulty associated with each factor.

## The Point Manual

The point system requires the use of a *point manual*. The point manual is, in effect, a handbook that contains a description of the compensable factors and the degrees to which these factors may exist within the jobs. A manual also will indicate—usually by means of a table—the number of points allocated to each factor and to each of the degrees into which these factors are divided. The point value assigned to a job represents the sum of the numerical degree values of each compensable factor that the job possesses.

For example, the job factors illustrated in Highlights in HRM 9.2 represent those covered by the American Association of Industrial Management point manual. Each factor listed in this manual has been divided into five degrees. The number of degrees into which the factors in a manual are to be divided, however, can be greater or smaller than this number, depending on the relative weight assigned to each factor and the ease with which the individual degrees can be defined or distinguished. A statement is provided defining each degree, as well as each factor as a whole. The definitions should be concise and yet distinguish the factors and each of their

# HIGHLIGHTS IN HRM 9.2

## Sample Rating Chart for Point Method Job Evaluation

Job Title: _____ Degree Rating

| Factors | 1 | 2 | 3 | 4 | 5 |
|---|---|---|---|---|---|
| **Skill** | | | | | |
| Education | 10 | 20 | 30 | 40 | 50 |
| Experience | 15 | 30 | 45 | 60 | 75 |
| Knowledge | 10 | 20 | 30 | 40 | 50 |
| **Effort** | | | | | |
| Physical effort | 10 | 20 | 30 | 40 | 50 |
| Mental effort | 10 | 20 | 30 | 40 | 50 |
| **Responsibility** | | | | | |
| Equipment and materials | 10 | 20 | 30 | 40 | 50 |
| Supervisory responsibility | 10 | 20 | 30 | 40 | 50 |
| **Job Conditions** | | | | | |
| Working conditions | 10 | 20 | 30 | 40 | 50 |
| Job hazards | 5 | 10 | 15 | 20 | 25 |
| **Customer/Client Service** | 10 | 20 | 30 | 40 | 50 |

degrees. Highlights in HRM 9.3 represents another portion of the point manual used by the American Association of Industrial Management to describe each degree for the education factor. These descriptions enable those conducting a job evaluation to determine the degree to which the factors exist in each job being evaluated.

# HIGHLIGHTS IN HRM 9.3

## Sample of Compensable Factor Showing Degrees

### 1. EDUCATION

This factor deals with the level of formal education required to perform a job.

**Degree 1:** Completion of high school ................................................ **10 points**

**Degree 2:** College diploma ........................................................... **20 points**

**Degree 3:** University undergraduate degree or major professional designation ... **30 points**

**Degree 4:** University master's degree .............................................. **40 points**

**Degree 5:** University doctoral degree .............................................. **50 points**

## Using the Point Manual

Job evaluation under the point system is accomplished by comparing the job descriptions and job specifications, factor by factor, against the various factor-degree descriptions contained in the manual. Each factor within the job being evaluated is then assigned the number of points specified in the manual. When the points for each factor have been determined from the manual, the total point value for the job as a whole can be calculated. The relative worth of the job is then determined from the total points that have been assigned to that job.

## WORK VALUATION

Work valuation is a relatively new job evaluation system championed to meet the demands of a dynamic business environment. The cornerstone for **work valuation** is that work should be valued relative to the business goals of the organization rather than by an internally applied point-factor job evaluation system.[22] As noted by one compensation specialist, "Valuing work properly enables organizations to not only price individual jobs effectively, but provides insight into how jobs relate to overall organizational goals and objectives and how roles ultimately contribute to organizational success."[23] Additionally, work valuation serves to direct compensation dollars to the type of work pivotal to organizational goals.

With work valuations, work is measured through standards that come directly from business goals. For example, jobs might be valued relative to financial, operational, or customer service objectives. All forms of work, employee roles, and ways of organizing work (such as teams) are valued. The work evaluation process ends with a work hierarchy that is an array of work by value to the organization. The work hierarchy is eventually priced through wage surveys to determine individual pay rates.

## JOB EVALUATION FOR MANAGEMENT POSITIONS

Because management positions are more difficult to evaluate and involve certain demands not found in jobs at the lower levels, some organizations do not attempt to include them in their job evaluation programs for hourly employees. Rather, they either employ a standardized (purchased) program or customize a point method to fit their particular jobs. However, regardless of the approach adopted, point plans for executive and managerial employees operate similarly to those for other groups of employees.

One of the better known standardized job evaluation programs for evaluating executive, managerial, and professional positions is the **Hay profile method**, developed by Edward N. Hay. The three broad factors that constitute the evaluation in the "profile" are knowledge (or know-how), mental activity (or problem solving), and accountability. The Hay method uses only three factors because it is assumed that these factors represent the most important aspects of all executive and managerial positions. The profile for each position is developed by determining the percentage value to be assigned to each factor. Jobs are then ranked on the basis of each factor, and point values that make up the profile are assigned to each job on the basis of the percentage-value level at which the job is ranked.

## THE COMPENSATION STRUCTURE

Job evaluation systems provide for internal equity and serve as the basis for wage rate determination. They do not in themselves determine the wage rate. The evaluated worth of each job in terms of its rank, class, points, or monetary worth must be converted into an hourly, daily, weekly, or monthly wage rate. The compensation tool used to help set wages is the wage and salary survey.

**OUTCOME 4**

# WAGE AND SALARY SURVEYS

The **wage and salary survey** is a survey of the wages paid by employers in an organization's relevant labour market—local, regional, or national, depending on the job. The labour market is frequently defined as the area from which employers obtain certain types of workers. The labour market for office personnel would be local, whereas the labour market for engineers would be national. The wage and salary survey permits an organization to maintain external equity—that is, to pay its employees wages equivalent to the wages similar employees earn in other establishments.

When job evaluation and wage survey data are used jointly, they link the likelihood of both internal and external equity. Although surveys are conducted primarily to gather competitive wage data, they can also collect information on employee benefits or organizational pay practices (such as overtime rates or shift differentials).

## Collecting Survey Data

Although many organizations conduct their own wage and salary surveys, a variety of "preconducted" pay surveys are available to satisfy the requirements of most public and not-for-profit or private employers. Companies such as Watson Wyatt (http://www.watson.wyatt.com), Hewitt Associates (http://www.hewitt.com), Mercer Human Resources Consulting (http://www.mercerHR.com), Hay Management Associates (http://www.haygroup.com), and the Conference Board of Canada (http://www.conferenceboard.ca) conduct annual surveys.

Highlights in HRM 9.4 describes the results of compensation surveys for those working in HRM and accounting.

# HIGHLIGHTS IN HRM 9.4

## Compensation Surveys for HR and Accounting Professionals in Canada

Salaries for HR professionals and managers and accounting positions are as follows:

| Title | Low ($) | Median ($) | High ($) |
|---|---|---|---|
| Accounting clerk | 31,773 | 35,640 | 40,170 |
| HR assistant | 34,384 | 39,125 | 44,739 |
| Accounts receivable clerk | 32,790 | 36,679 | 40,773 |
| Recruiter | 35,586 | 42,404 | 51,100 |
| Accountant | 40,317 | 45,933 | 52,552 |
| Accounting manager | 54,633 | 65,348 | 78,005 |
| Manager, compensation | 65,329 | 75,126 | 86,940 |
| Director | 86,554 | 104,024 | 122,379 |
| VP HR | 115,687 | 137,924 | 162,574 |

A study done by the Human Resources Professionals Association of Ontario showed the value of professional certification. Those people working in HR who had achieved the CHRP (Certified Human Resources Professional) tend to earn about 3 to 4 percent more than their counterparts without a CHRP. Clearly, the CHRP has an economic value in employers' minds.

Sources: http://workopolis.ca, retrieved February 22, 2012; Shannon Klie, "It Pays to Have HR Designation," *Canadian HR Reporter* 23, no. 7 (April 5, 2010), p. 1, 12.

Many provinces and cities conduct surveys and make them available to employers. Besides these government surveys, boards of trade and professional associations conduct special surveys tailored to their members' needs.

Employers with global operations can purchase international surveys through large consulting firms. The overseas compensation survey offered by *TPF&C* reports on payment practices in 20 countries. Although all of these third-party surveys provide certain benefits to their users, they also have various limitations. Two problems with all published surveys are that (1) they are not always compatible with the user's jobs and (2) the user cannot specify what specific data to collect. To overcome these problems, organizations may collect their own compensation data.

## HRIS and Salary Surveys

Wage and benefits survey data can be found on numerous websites. Also readily available are commercial products such as those offered at http://www.salary.com: the Salary Wizard, Comp Analyst, and Survey Finder surveys. Survey Finder has a database of hundreds of compensation surveys offered by more than 50 independent vendors. Managers and compensation specialists can search for applicable surveys for either purchase or participation.[24]

## Employer-Initiated Surveys

Employers wishing to conduct their own wage and salary survey must first select the jobs to be used in the survey and identify the organizations with which they compete for employees. Since it is not feasible to survey all the jobs in an organization, normally, only key jobs, also called benchmark jobs, are used. The characteristics of key jobs include the following:

1. They are important to employees and the organization.
2. They contain a large number of positions.
3. They have relatively stable job content.
4. They have the same job content across many organizations.
5. They are acceptable to employees, management, and unions as appropriate for pay comparisons.

The survey of key jobs will usually be sent to 10 or 15 organizations that represent a valid sample of other employers likely to compete for the employees of the surveying organization. A diversity of organizations should be selected—large and small, public and private, new and established, and union and nonunion—because each classification of employer is likely to pay different wage rates for surveyed jobs.

After the key jobs and the employers to be surveyed have been identified, the surveying organization must decide what information to gather on wages, benefit types, and pay policies. For example, when requesting pay data, it is important to specify whether hourly, daily, or weekly pay figures are needed. In addition, those conducting surveys must state whether the wage data are needed for new hires or for senior employees. Precisely defining the compensation data needed will greatly increase the accuracy of the information received and the number of purposes for which it can be used.[25] Once the survey data are tabulated, the compensation structure can be completed.

## THE WAGE CURVE

The relationship between the relative worth of jobs and their wage rates can be represented by means of a **wage curve**. This curve may indicate the rates currently paid for jobs within an organization, new rates resulting from job evaluation, or rates for similar jobs currently being paid by other organizations within the labour market. A curve may be constructed graphically by preparing a

**wage curve**
A curve in a scattergram representing the relationship between the relative worth of jobs and wage rates

**OUTCOME 5**

**CHAPTER 9:** MANAGING COMPENSATION

## FIGURE 9.3

FREEHAND WAGE CURVE

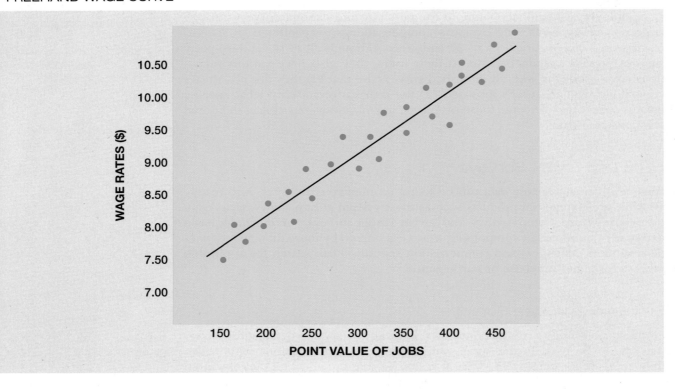

scattergram consisting of a series of dots that represent the current wage rates. As shown in Figure 9.3, a freehand curve is then drawn through the cluster of dots in such a manner so as to leave an approximately equal number of dots above and below the curve. The wage curve can be relatively straight or curved. This curve can then be used to determine the relationship between the value of a job and its wage rate at any given point on the line.

## PAY GRADES

From an administrative standpoint, it is generally preferable to group jobs into **pay grades** and to pay all jobs within a particular grade the same rate or rate range. When the classification system of job evaluation is used, jobs are grouped into grades as part of the evaluation process. When the point system is used, however, pay grades must be established at selected intervals that represent either the point or the evaluated monetary value of these jobs. The graph in Figure 9.4 illustrates a series of pay grades designated along the horizontal axis at 50-point intervals.

The grades within a wage structure may vary in number.[26] The number is determined by factors such as the slope of the wage curve, the number and distribution of the jobs within the structure, and the organization's wage administration and promotion policies. The number utilized should be sufficient to permit difficulty levels to be distinguished but not so great as to make the distinction between two adjoining grades insignificant.

## RATE RANGES

Generally, organizations provide a range of rates for each pay grade. The rate ranges may be the same for each grade or proportionately greater for each successive grade, as shown in Figure 9.4. Rate ranges constructed on the latter basis

FIGURE 9.4

## WAGE STRUCTURE WITH INCREASING RATE RANGES

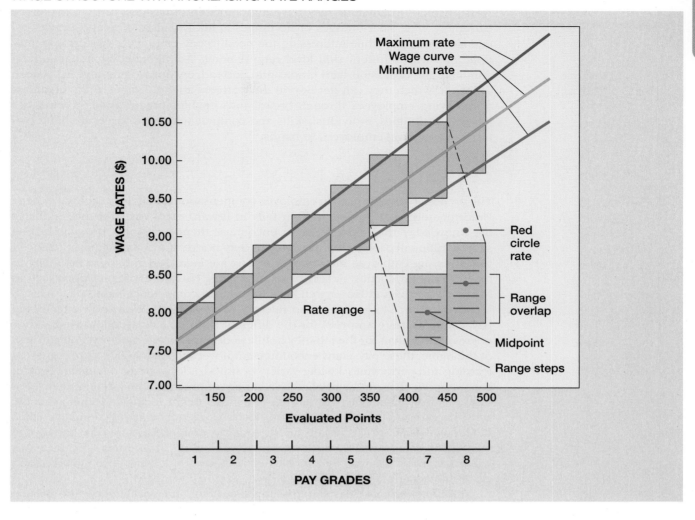

provide a greater incentive for employees to accept a promotion to a job in a higher grade.

Rate ranges are generally divided into a series of steps that permit employees to receive increases up to the maximum rate for the range on the basis of merit or seniority or a combination of the two. Most salary structures provide for the ranges of adjoining pay grades to overlap. The purpose of the overlap is to permit an employee with experience to earn as much as or more than a person with less experience in the next higher job classification.

The final step in setting up a wage structure is to determine the appropriate pay grade into which each job should be placed on the basis of its evaluated worth. Traditionally, this worth is determined on the basis of job requirements without regard to the performance of the person in that job. Under this system, the performance of those who exceed the requirements of a job may be acknowledged by merit increases within the grade range or by promotion to a job in the next higher pay grade.[27]

Organizations may pay individuals above the maximum of the pay range when employees have high seniority or promotional opportunities are scarce. Wages paid above the range maximum are called **red circle rates**. Because these rates are exceptions to the pay structure, employers often "freeze" these rates until all ranges are shifted upward through market wage adjustments.

**red circle rates**
Payment rates above the maximum of the pay range

## Broadbanding

*Broadbanding* simply collapses many traditional salary grades into a few wide salary bands. Broadbands may have midpoints and quartiles, or they may have extremely wide salary ranges or no ranges at all. Broadbanding encourages lateral skill building while addressing the need to pay employees performing multiple jobs with different skill level requirements. Additionally, broadbands help eliminate the obsession with grades and, instead, encourage employees to move to jobs in which they can develop in their careers and add value to the organization. Paying employees through broadbands enables organizations to consider job responsibilities, individual skills and competencies, and career mobility patterns in assigning employees to bands.[28]

## COMPETENCE-BASED PAY

The predominant approach to employee compensation is still the job-based system. Unfortunately, such a system often fails to reward employees for their skills or the knowledge they possess or to encourage them to learn a new job-related skill. Additionally, job-based pay systems may not reinforce an organizational culture stressing employee involvement or provide increased employee flexibility to meet overall production or service requirements. Therefore, organizations such as Nortel Networks and Honeywell have introduced competence-based pay plans.

**Competence-based pay**, also referred to as skill-based or knowledge-based pay, compensates employees for the different skills or increased knowledge they possess rather than for the job they hold in a designated job category.[29] Regardless of the name, these pay plans encourage employees to earn higher base wages by learning and performing a wider variety of skills (or jobs) or displaying an array of competencies that can be applied to a variety of organizational requirements. For example, in a manufacturing setting, new tasks might include various assembly activities carried out in a particular production system or a variety of maintenance functions. Within service organizations, employees might acquire new knowledge related to advanced computer systems or accounting procedures. Organizations will grant an increase in pay after each skill or knowledge has been mastered and can be demonstrated according to a predetermined standard.

Competence-based pay systems represent a fundamental change in the attitude of management regarding how work should be organized and how employees should be paid for their work efforts. The most frequently cited benefits of competence-based pay include greater productivity, increased employee learning

Employee wages may be based in part on how much money people in that area need for day-to-day living

lightpoet/Shutterstock

and commitment to work, improved staffing flexibility to meet production or service demands, and reduced effects of absenteeism and turnover because managers can assign employees where and when needed. Competence-based pay also encourages employees to acquire training when new or updated skills are needed by an organization.

Unfortunately, competence-based plans bring some long-term difficulties. Some plans limit the amount of compensation employees can earn, regardless of the new skills or competencies they acquire. Thus, after achieving the top wage, employees may be reluctant to continue their educational training. Perhaps the greatest challenge in paying individuals for their skills, knowledge, and competencies is developing appropriate measures. It is difficult to write specific knowledge and skill descriptions for jobs that employees perform and then establish accurate measures of acquired skills or knowledge.

# GOVERNMENT REGULATION OF COMPENSATION

Compensation management, like the other areas of HRM, is subject to provincial and federal regulations. Each province has an employment standards act that establishes minimum requirements with respect to wages, hours of work, and overtime. Provincial and federal minimum requirements can be obtained by contacting the appropriate federal or provincial office.

**OUTCOME 6**

> **Using the Internet**
>
> The *Canada Labour Code* can be found at
>
> **http://laws.justice.gc.ca**

## THE *CANADA LABOUR CODE*

Part III of the *Canada Labour Code* and the *Canada Labour Standards Regulations* set minimum labour standards for all employees and employers in works or undertakings that fall within federal jurisdiction, including interprovincial highway and rail transportation, pipelines, telecommunications, air transport, fishing, and banking. Federal Crown corporations are covered by the *Canada Labour Code*, but federal public service employees are not. Employees working under these classifications are subject to a 40-hour workweek. Managerial and professional employees are not covered by the hours-of-work provisions and may be required to exceed those hours. Revisions are constantly being made to these standards; HR managers must keep abreast of these changes to ensure compliance in the workplace.

## EMPLOYMENT STANDARDS ACTS

The employment standards acts of each province and territory establish minimum standards with a view to protecting both employees and employers in certain employment situations. Collective agreements are permitted to override the provisions of these acts as long as employees are not being provided with less than what the acts have stipulated and as long as these overrides benefit the employee. Employers who operate in more than one province must become fully informed of the different requirements that exist in each province. This information is generally available on the Internet.

Each province's act contains a provision that stipulates that an overtime rate, usually about 1.5 times the base rate, must be paid for all hours worked in excess of the set minimum prescribed in the province. For example, if an employee works 45 hours in a province that legislates the minimum workweek as 40 hours, he or she is entitled to overtime for the extra 5 hours at 1.5 times his or her base rate. Particular groups, including lawyers, doctors, engineers, and managers, are exempt from overtime requirements.

## OTHER LEGISLATION

Employment equity is under federal jurisdiction for all federally regulated companies, as well as for provincially regulated companies that are suppliers to the federal government. Pay equity is covered provincially where applicable. As we

discussed in Chapter 3, legislation relating to employment equity and pay equity is designed to ensure that fair employment practices are applied to all members of designated groups.

# SIGNIFICANT COMPENSATION ISSUES

**OUTCOME 7**

As with other HR activities, compensation management operates in a dynamic environment. We will discuss two of these issues here: (1) equal pay for work of equal value and (2) wage-rate compression.

## PAY EQUITY: EQUAL PAY FOR WORK OF EQUAL VALUE

One of the most important gender issues in compensation is **pay equity**, or equal pay for work of equal value. In Ontario, the definition is "equal pay for work of equal or comparable value." The issue stems from the fact that jobs performed predominantly by women are paid less than those performed by men.

This practice results in what critics term *institutionalized sex discrimination*, causing women to receive lower pay for jobs that may be different from but comparable in worth to those performed by men. The issue of equal pay for work of equal value goes beyond providing equal pay for jobs that involve the same duties for women as for men. It is not concerned with whether a female secretary should receive the same pay as a male secretary. Rather, the argument for comparable worth is that jobs held by women are not compensated the same as those held by men, even though both job types may contribute equally to organizational success.

## MEASURING COMPARABILITY

Advocates of comparable worth argue that the difference in wage rates for predominantly male and female occupations rests in the undervaluing of traditional female occupations. To remedy this situation, they propose that wages should be equal for jobs that are "somehow" equivalent in total worth or compensation to the organization. Unfortunately, there is no consensus on a comparable worth standard by which to evaluate jobs, nor is there agreement on the ability of current job evaluation techniques to remedy the problem. Indeed, organizations may dodge the comparable worth issue by using one job evaluation system for clerical and secretarial jobs and another system for other jobs. Reality Check outlines some of the issues that face pay equity specialists. Furthermore, the advocates of comparable worth argue that current job evaluation techniques simply serve to continue the differences in pay between the sexes. However, others believe that job evaluation systems can be designed to measure different types of jobs, in the same way that apples and oranges can be compared (see Figure 9.5). The Business Case describes two large settlements that have resulted from pay equity issues.

## FIGURE 9.5

### HOW CAN YOU COMPARE APPLES AND ORANGES?

| 150.0 grams | Weight | 150.0 grams |
|---|---|---|
| 87 | Calories | 73 |
| 21.7 grams | Carbohydrates | 18.3 grams |
| 0.3 grams | Protein | 1.5 grams |
| 1.5 grams | Fibre | 1.8 grams |
| 140 IU | Vitamin A | 300 IU |

**Source:** M. Belcourt, "Human Resource Management" in *Introduction to Canadian Business,* edited by J. Plinuissen (Toronto: McGraw-Hill Ryerson and Captus Press, 1994): 410.

# REALITY CHECK

## Pay Equity

Linda Sullivan, a former program specialist of the Ontario Pay Equity Commission and currently a learning specialist in the Ministry of Labour in Ontario, talks about current issues in pay equity:

"Most private-sector employers should have implemented pay equity by now, and our role is to monitor them for compliance. However, organizations with 10 to 99 employees have the highest rate of noncompliance because they do not have resources, including a dedicated HR professional, and some positions are held by family members. One year, we monitored the food services sector. A family-owned bakery, for example, would need to identify female and male jobs, compare them, and make the required pay adjustments. In these family-owned enterprises, one can find the traditional breakdown where, for example, the bakers are male, and the customer service positions (i.e., the [people] working at the counter) are female. The bakers are paid more than positions in customer service. The multitude of tasks needed in customer service, such as communication skills, organizational skills, dealing with people who are upset, and dealing with customers quickly, are typically overlooked in female-dominated jobs and are not credited. These tasks within each job must be carefully identified and compensated.

"Smaller organizations in the public sector have different types of problems. In the public sector, it is difficult to do pay equity in a lot of organizations because these organizations only have jobs held by women. For example, women usually hold all jobs in a daycare centre. These organizations cannot compare male and female jobs because there are no male jobs. So, in 1993, when the pay equity act was amended, another method of comparing jobs for these types of organizations was added: a proxy comparison method. The proxy comparison method allowed organizations to take key jobs, such as a daycare supervisor or an early childhood educator, and compare these to similar jobs in a larger public-sector employer, such as a large municipal daycare centre. The municipal sector had already done pay equity, comparing male and female jobs in the daycare centre to male jobs in the municipality. The small daycare centre could compare the early childhood educator job and borrow the pay equity results, i.e., through a proxy comparison method.

"A third issue is, without a doubt, the degree of emotion felt by those who believe that they are being paid unfairly. For example, I had an email from a woman about her work situation, where she had been hired and was doing what she felt was an equivalent job to a male colleague but was being paid less. So she went to her manager and raised the issue with her, and a change was made to her wage, which she felt was justified. Then she realized once again, while they had raised her wage, she was still being paid considerably less than her male colleague doing work of equal or less value. The employer has not done pay equity. To me, what was striking about this situation was how emotional and betrayed the woman felt. The employers don't realize that employees feel so strongly about this unfair treatment. In a lot of these situations, women end up looking for other work, leaving the organization and costing the employer thousands of dollars required to recruit and train new employees."

Source: Interview with Linda Sullivan.

# THE BUSINESS CASE

## Cashing Out

Bell Canada had to pay $100 million in cash and added pension benefits to over 4,000 mostly female employees to settle a pay equity dispute started in the early 1990s. The union argued that thousands of Bell employees, who were mostly women, were underpaid compared to those in male-dominated positions. Those working in female-dominated jobs were making, on average, $2 to $5 less an hour than men in comparable jobs. The request for salary adjustments was based on a study of the work performed by telephone operators, clerical staff, sales associates, and others. Most of those employees were women. Their salaries were compared to other job functions that were dominated by men.

*continued*

In November 2011, the Supreme Court of Canada settled a 28-year epic battle when it ruled in favour of a Canadian Human Rights Tribunal decision in 2005 that there was a wage gap between clerical workers, who were mostly women, and male-dominated employees in an operations group who did work of comparable value to the organization. As a result, Canada Post would have to pay about 6,000 current and former clerical workers $150 million in back pay. The tribunal previously determined that the federal government had underpaid those mainly female workers in administrative support occupational categories. Each employee was entitled to about $30,000 in retroactive pay. The Public Service Alliance of Canada, the union representing the workers affected by the tribunal ruling, calculates that the average annual pension of workers from these groups is only $10,000 per year. The pay equity settlement would make an important difference in the standard of living for these workers and their families now and in the future.

Sources: Colin Freeze, "Bell Settles Pay Equity Dispute," *The Globe and Mail*, May 16, 2006, A5; Neco Cockburn, "Tribunal Rules Systemic Sex Discrimination at Canada Post," *CanWest News*, October 8, 2005, 1; Kathryn May, "After 28-year pay equity fight, female postal workers awarded $150-million," *National Post*, November 17, 2011.

## THE ISSUE OF WAGE-RATE COMPRESSION

**wage-rate compression**
Compression of differentials between job classes, particularly the differential between hourly workers and their managers

Pay compression is a compensation problem that has its roots in low salary budgets. **Wage-rate compression** occurs when less experienced, often junior, employees earn as much or more than experienced employees due to high starting salaries for new employees. For example, the scarcity of qualified applicants in IT, engineering, and other professional and technical fields has forced starting salaries for these occupations to be at or near the salaries paid employees with considerable experience and seniority. Pay compression can also occur when hourly employees, at the top of their pay grades, earn only slightly less than managers at the low end of their pay grades.

Identifying wage-rate compression and its causes is far simpler than implementing organizational policies to alleviate its effect. Organizations wishing to minimize the problem may incorporate the following ideas into their pay policies:

- Reward high-performing and merit-worthy employees with large pay increases.
- Design the pay structure to allow a wide spread between hourly and supervisory employees.
- Prepare high-performing employees for promotions to jobs with higher salary levels.
- Provide equity adjustments for selected employees hardest hit by pay compression.[30]

Since wage-rate compression is largely an internal equity concern, if not addressed fairly, it can cause low employee morale, leading to issues of reduced employee performance, hard feelings between employees, higher absenteeism and turnover, and even delinquent behaviour, such as employee theft.

# SMALL BUSINESS APPLICATION

As compensation is one of the biggest costs for small businesses, employees are often the first to be short-changed. At the same time, the old adage holds true: "You get what you pay for." The ability to attract and retain talented employees depends largely on a company's ability to offer suitable compensation. For small businesses, what is considered suitable differs from that of larger businesses.

Big business can woo job candidates by offering comprehensive compensation packages that include stock options, consistent pay raises, security, and sometimes even a Starbucks in the lobby. Although small businesses cannot offer these things, they can offer more customized pay packages to deal with employees' individual needs. For example, not having a complex and bureaucratic compensation system means that a small company can more readily adjust its employees' wages to match those of the external market. Furthermore, small companies offer more opportunity for upward growth and the chance to more rapidly increase one's pay.

If the small business is private, there are many opportunities to attract and retain top talent by padding lower salaries with stock in the company. By offering shares of a private company as a form of compensation, small private companies can offer the possibility for their employees to make larger sums of money in the future. Offering shares or options to buy shares as a form of compensation can be extremely attractive as employees can make a lot of money when their young company finally goes public and is sold on the stock market. In fact, this form of compensation is enough to make employees leave secure, hefty salaries in a big company for lower salaries and shares of a private company. For example, when Google became a public company on August 18, 2004, it sold shares of its company for $85 per share. Some of the employees who were with the company early on had been awarded shares that were worth as little as $0.30 per share. As you can imagine, someone who had just 10,000 Google shares at this rate was quickly made a millionaire. In fact, hundreds of employees became millionaires at this time.

As a result, a smart manager in a small business can enhance compensation packages that consist of lower salaries through greater opportunities to increase wealth in the future by issuing stock and stock options as part of the pay mix.

Below is a list of specific things small businesses can do to compete with the compensation packages of big business:

1. **Tailor the pay mix to individual employee needs and wants.** For example, one employee may value greater bonus opportunities than base pay, whereas another may want the money the company would spend on health insurance to be paid in salary.

2. **Provide stock options in high-growth environments.** Potential employees will find the opportunity to be part of a high-growth company an exciting and potentially lucrative risk.

3. **Provide faster promotions.** Express how the smallness of your company allows people to move into new and exciting positions quickly, without the bureaucratic red tape found in big business.

4. **Provide frequent contact with top management.** Not being able to interact with and receive mentoring from top management is a major concern for young talent. Smaller companies are able to offer more of these types of growth opportunities than larger competitors.

5. **Provide a greater sense of personal involvement.** One of the advantages of a small company is that they can treat their employees like family. In an age of depersonalized billion-dollar companies, a sense of belongingness, where you know the company cares about you, can go a long way in compensating for lower pay.

Sources: How to attract talent to a small company," *The Wall Street Journal* (November 18, 2010), http://guides.wsj.com/small-business/hiring-and-managing-employees/how-to-attract-talent-to-a-small-company/print/; Miguel Helft, "Mark Zuckerberg's most valuable friend," *New York Times* (October 2, 2010); SME Toolkit. Build Your Business. "Compensation Management from Buzgate.org," http://us.smetoolkit.org/us/en/content/en/2188/Compensation-Management.

## SUMMARY

| OUTCOME 1    Establishing compensation programs requires both large and small organizations to consider specific goals: for example, employee retention, compensation distribution, and adherence to a budget. Compensation must reward employees for past efforts (pay for performance) while motivating employees' future performance. Internal and external equity of the pay program affect employees' concepts of fairness. Organizations must balance each of these concerns while still remaining competitive. The ability to attract qualified employees while controlling labour costs is a major factor in allowing organizations to remain viable in domestic or international markets.

| OUTCOME 2    The basis on which compensation payments are determined and the way they are administered can significantly affect employee productivity and the achievement of organizational goals. Internal influences include the employer's compensation policy, worth of the job, performance of the employee, and the employer's ability to pay. External factors influencing wage rates include labour market conditions, area wage rates, cost of living, outcomes of collective bargaining, and legal requirements.

| OUTCOME 3 | Organizations use one of four basic job evaluation techniques to determine the relative worth of jobs. The job ranking system arranges jobs in numerical order on the basis of the importance of the job's duties and responsibilities to the organization. The job classification system slots jobs into preestablished grades. Higher rated grades will require more responsibilities and more important job duties. The point system of job evaluation uses a point scheme based on the compensable job factors of skill, effort, responsibility, and working conditions. The more compensable factors a job possesses, the more points are assigned to it. Jobs with higher accumulated points are considered more valuable to the organization. The work valuation system evaluates jobs based on their value relative to organizational goals—financial, customer service, and so on—and the job's contribution to organization success. |

| OUTCOME 4 | Wage surveys determine the external equity of jobs. Data obtained from surveys will facilitate establishing the organization's wage policy while ensuring that the employer does not pay more, or less, than needed for jobs in the relevant labour market. |

| OUTCOME 5 | The wage structure is composed of the wage curve, pay grades, and rate ranges. The wage curve depicts graphically the pay rates assigned to jobs within each pay grade. Pay grades represent the grouping of similar jobs on the basis of their relative worth. Each pay grade will include a rate range. Rate ranges will have a midpoint and minimum and maximum pay rates for all jobs in the pay grade. |

| OUTCOME 6 | The federal and provincial governments regulate compensation through the *Canada Labour Code*, employment standards acts, and employment equity/pay equity legislation. |

| OUTCOME 7 | The concept of equal pay for work of equal value seeks to overcome the fact that jobs held by women are compensated at a lower rate than those performed by men. This happens even though both types of jobs may contribute equally to organizational productivity. Wage-rate compression largely affects managerial and senior employees as the pay given to new employees or the wage increases gained through collective agreements erode the pay differences between these groups. |

## KEY TERMS

competence-based pay, 346

consumer price index (CPI), 337

escalator clauses, 338

Hay profile method, 341

hourly work, 333

job classification system, 339

job evaluation, 338

job ranking system, 338

pay equity, 348

pay grades, 344

piecework, 333

point system, 339

real wages, 338

red circle rates, 345

wage and salary survey, 342

wage curve, 343

wage-rate compression, 350

work valuation, 341

## DISCUSSION QUESTIONS

1. Nurses at Adelphi Hospital, located in British Columbia, have been quitting their jobs for more lucrative deals in the United States. The hospital's administration would like to pursue a coherent strategy that would address not only its compensation issues but also patient care and overall client satisfaction. Suggest different compensation objectives to match Adelphi's goals.

2. Discuss how factors internal to the organization may affect compensation levels and the wage mix.

3. What is job evaluation? Explain the differences between the major job evaluation systems, noting the advantages and disadvantages of each.

4. What are pay grades and pay ranges? In a step-by-step manner, discuss how an organization's wage structure is determined.

5. Laws governing compensation raise important issues for both employers and employees. Discuss the following:
   a.  The effect of mandatory overtime
   b.  The effects of raising the minimum wage
   c.  Pay equity: is it needed?

6. The Pay Equity Commission proposes three methods to make pay equity comparisons:

   • The job-to-job comparison method
   • The proportional value comparison method
   • The proxy comparison method

   Read about these methods at http://www.payequity.gov.on.ca/peo/english/pubs/proxycomp.html. What are some of the problems of developing a pay system based on each method?

# HRM EXPERIENCE

## Why This Salary?

A question frequently asked is, "Why is that person paid more than I am when we both perform the same job?" The answer to this question lies in understanding the components of the wage mix, as discussed in this chapter. Although we may disapprove of the idea that someone is paid more or less than we are for similar work, nevertheless, factors both internal and external to the organization influence the final salary paid to a job or a specific person. Often we have little control over the wage mix factors. However, at other times, we can improve our wage by gaining additional job experience or seniority or by obtaining increases in job knowledge or skills. This project is designed to give you experience in understanding why jobs are paid different salaries.

## Assignment

The website http://www.workopolis.ca provides a salary calculator for the Canadian market, giving salary ranges for jobs and a comparison tool for the national average. For example, an HR assistant working in Brandon, Manitoba, earned a median salary of $35,117. Using this site, determine the salaries paid to these occupations, nationally (do not enter city and province in the relevant boxes on this site), and then answer the questions that follow as to why the differences in salaries exist. Relate these reasons to the internal and external factors of the wage mix that are discussed in the text.

| Occupation | National Median Annual Salary ($) | Low ($) | High ($) |
|---|---|---|---|
| HR assistant | 35,640 | 34,384 | 40,170 |
| Librarian | | | |
| Construction labourer | | | |
| Computer systems administrator | | | |
| Police officer | | | |
| Motor coach operator | | | |
| Lawyer | | | |

1. What factors may account for the wide differences among salaries for different occupations?

2. Now check on compensation rates in your city and compare these to those in Toronto or Vancouver and Lethbridge, Alberta. What factors account for the differences among salaries for identical occupations in different cities?

3. What factors may account for the differences among salaries for the identical occupation in different organizations?

You may work individually or in teams to complete this skill-building exercise.

Visit the *Managing Human Resources* CourseMate website at http://www. belcourt7e.nelson.com for quizzes, flashcards, videos, games, and more!

## PAY DECISIONS AT UNIVERSITY HEALTH FOODS ON WHEELS

During her first year at university, Amelia Gomez became quickly aware that there were not many healthy food and drinks on her campus. After taking a few business courses, she learned how to start a business and manage employees. In February 2010, after extensive development of a strategic business plan and a loan in the amount of $75,000 from the Business Development Bank, she started Health Foods on Wheels. Based on a marketing plan that stressed fast delivery on campus, excellent customer service, and healthy foods, the firm grew rapidly. In short, students would call a telephone number and order their food from a menu. Health Foods would deliver it for them. At present, the company employs 16 people: 8 cooks earning between $14.75 and $16.25 per hour; 8 delivery persons paid between $12.50 and $14.50 per hour; two phone order clerks, each earning $11.75 per hour; an assistant manager earning $17.10 per hour; and a general manager with a wage of $20.00 per hour.

Amelia intends to create a new managerial position, purchasing agent, to handle the complex duties of providing healthy food items for the company's numerous suppliers. Since the position of purchasing agent is new, Amelia is not sure how much to pay this person. She wants to employ an individual with five to eight years of experience in food-related purchasing.

### Questions

1. What factors should Amelia consider when setting the wage for the purchasing agent position? What resources are available for them to consult when establishing this wage?
2. Are there any incentive pay systems Amelia should consider? Discuss a few options.

## CANADA POST

Canada Post Corporation employs 67,000 workers, which makes it one of Canada's largest employers. In 1997, it revised its job evaluation system for postmasters and assistants. The old system, which had been in place since 1976, did not take into account changes that had arisen since 1981, when Canada Post became a Crown corporation.

An HR consulting firm, Watson Wyatt Worldwide, was hired to assist with the entire process. According to Linda Tremblay of Organization Planning and Development, Canada Post, the job evaluation system was revised to incorporate employee input, to be responsive to federal pay equity legislation, and, most importantly, to reflect corporate culture and values.

The new job evaluation system measured the content and relative value of jobs. The system evaluated jobs according to their "typical" or "normal" components—that is, tasks that were done on a regular basis. These compensable factors were a function of the job itself, not of the performance of the person doing the job.

The four factors considered and their relative weights were as follows:

A: Responsibilities—What type of responsibilities does the job entail? 60 percent

B: Skills—What particular skills are needed to accomplish the job? 25 percent

C: Working conditions—What working conditions apply to the job? 11 percent

D: Effort—What amount of effort does the job require? 4 percent

Total: 100 percent

### An Example of An Item Under C: Working Conditions

This factor measures the surroundings or physical conditions under which work must be done and the extent to which they make the job disagreeable. Consider whether elements such as those listed are present and the relative amount and continuity of exposure:

Place a checkmark beside all those that apply:

- Adverse weather conditions
- Confined work space
- Dirt/dust
- Fumes

- Inadequate lighting
- Lack of privacy
- Noisy conditions

- Temperature extremes
- Verbal abuse/public harassment
- Other

Job evaluation criteria, such as in the above example, were used in each of the four areas and are summarized below:

## JOB EVALUATION CRITERIA

| Compensable Factors | Components |
|---|---|
| Responsibilities | Internal and external contacts |
| | Decision making |
| | Supervision of employees |
| | Responsibility for property maintenance |
| | Responsibility for rural routes, suburban services, and/or stage services |
| | Points of call |
| | Responsibility for contractor invoices |
| | Responsibility for a till and/or authorized allowance |
| Skills | Knowledge areas (such as budget process, collective agreement, contacted services in mail operations or property management, financial practices, procedures knowledge, product knowledge, primary sortation, final sortation, sales and customer service techniques, personnel management techniques) |
| | Job-related experience |
| Working conditions | Physical work environment |
| | Travel |
| Effort | Physical effort |
| | Multiple demands |

Employees completed the job evaluation questionnaire for their own jobs. The completed questionnaires were reviewed by supervisors, managers, and HR staff.

Total points were then allocated to each job, which corresponded to one of six job bands. Collective agreement negotiations were used to set the rates of pay for each job band.

## Questions

1. What type of job evaluation did Canada Post use?
2. What are the advantages and limitations of this system?
3. If you were asked to review both the questionnaire and the process used to obtain the job information, what recommendations for changes would you make?

**Source:** Interview and correspondence with Linda Tremblay, Canada Post Corporation, April 2006.

## NOTES AND REFERENCES

1. Henry Blodget, "Google Gives All Employees Surprise $1000 Cash Bonus and 10% Raise," *Business Insider SAI* (November 9, 2010), http://articles. businessinsider.com/2010-11-09/tech/30024423_1_ google-ceo-googlers-eric-schmidt, retrieved July 2012.

2. O'Reilly Media. Web 2.0 Summit 2010: Eric Schmidt, "A Conversation with Eric Schmidt," http://www. youtube.com/watch?feature=player_embedded&v =AKOWK2dR4Dg#!.

3. John Dorian, "Google's 10% Salary Increase, $1000 Cash Bonus Part of Company's Competitive Compensation Plan," *International Business Times* (November 10, 2010), http://au.ibtimes. com/articles/80714/20101111/google-s-10-salary-increase-1000-cash-bonus-part-of-company-s-competitive-compensation-plan.htm, retrieved July 2012.

4. Fay Hansen, "Control and Customization," *Workforce Management* 86, no. 19 (November 2007): 42.

5. Hai-Ming Chen and Yi-Hua Hsien, "Key Trends in the Total Reward System of the 21st Century," *Compensation and Benefits Review* 38, no. 6 (November/December 2006): 64.

6. George T. Milkovich and Jerry M. Newman, *Compensation*, 10th ed. (Boston: McGraw-Hill Irwin, 2010).

7. Patricia K. Zingheim and Jay R. Schuster, "What Are Key Issues Right Now?" *Compensation and Benefits Review* 39, no. 3 (June 2007): 51. See also "Reward 'Stars' and Pay for Performance Lead in Pay Control Strategies," *HRfocus* 84, no. 11 (November 2007): 3.

8. Valerie L. Myers and Janice L. Dreachslin, "Recruitment and Retention of a Diverse Workforce: Challenges and Opportunities," *Journal of Healthcare Management* 52, no. 5 (September/October 2007): 290.

9. Parbudyal Singh, "Strategic Compensation and Firm Performance, *International Journal of Human Resource Development and Management* 6, no. 1 (2006): 1–5.

10. For one of the classic articles on equity theory, see J. Stacey Adams, "Integrity in Social Exchange," in L. Berkowitz (ed.), *Advances in Experimental Social Psychology* (New York: Academic Press, 1965): 276–299.

11. Andrew J. DuBrin, *Fundamentals of Organization Behavior*, 4th ed. (Mason, OH: South-Western, 2007), Chapter 6.

12. Parbudyal Singh and Natasha Loncar, "Antecedents of Pay Satisfaction in a Unionized Environment," *Relations Industrielles/Industrial Relations* 65, no. 3 (2010): 470–490.

13. Victor H. Vroom, *Work and Motivation* (San Francisco: Jossey-Bass, 1994). This landmark book, originally published in 1964, integrates the work of hundreds of researchers seeking to explain choice of work, job satisfaction, and job performance.

14. Joseph Champoux, *Organizational Behavior: Integrating Individuals, Groups, and Organizations*, 3rd ed. (Mason, OH: South Western, 2006), Chapter 8.

15. James R. Bowers, "Valuing Work: An Integrated Approach," *WorldatWork* 12, no. 2 (Second Quarter 2003): 28–39. See also Robert L. Heneman, Peter V. LeBlanc, and Tim L. Reynolds, "Using Work Valuation to Identify and Protect the Talent Pool," *WorldatWork* 11, no. 2 (Third Quarter 2002): 31–41.

16. Kathryn Cohen and Alison Avalos, "Salary Budget Increases: Slow but Steady," *Workspan* (September 2007): 29.

17. William H. Holley, Jr., Kenneth H. Jennings, and Rogert W. Wolters, *The Labor Relations Process*, 9th ed. (Mason, OH: South-Western, 2009), Chapter 6.

18. Robert L. Heneman, "Job and Work Evaluation," *Public Personnel Management* 32, no. 1 (Spring 2003): 1–25.

19. http://www.gpo.gov/fdsys/pkg/USCODE-2010-title5/html/USCODE-2010-title5-partIII-subpartD-chap51-sec5104.htm, retrieved July 2012.

20. Emin Kahya, "Revising the Metal Industry Job Evaluation System for Blue-Collar Jobs," *Compensation and Benefits Review* 38, no. 6 (November/December 2006): 49.

21. Lance A. Berger and Dorothy R. Berger, *The Compensation Handbook*, 5th ed. (Boston: McGraw-Hill, 2008).

22. Robert L. Heneman, Peter V. LeBlanc, and Howard Risher, "Work Valuation Addresses Shortcomings of Both Job Evaluation and Market Pricing," *Compensation and Benefits Review* 35, no. 1 (January–February 2003): 7–11.

23. James R. Bowers, "Valuing Work," *WorldatWork* 12, no. 1 (Second Quarter 2003): 28.

24. Nona Tobin, "Can Technology Ease the Pain of Salary Surveys?" *Public Personnel Management* 31, no. 1 (Spring 2002): 65–76.

25. Charles H. Fey and Madhura Tare, "Market Pricing Concerns," *WorldatWork* 16, no. 2 (Second Quarter 2007): 61.

26. Curt Finch, "How to Create an Effective Pay Structure," *Employee Benefit Plan Review* 61, no. 10 (April 2007): 26. See also Gregory A. Stoskopf, "Choosing the Best Salary Structure for Your Organization," *WorldatWork* 11, no. 4 (Fourth Quarter 2004): 28–36.

27. Organizations may have a compensation program that pays a differential based on geographic location. See Thomas J. Atchison, "Branch Office Salary Structure," *Compensation and Benefits Review* 39, no. 3 (June 2007): 35.

28. Howard Risher, "Second-Generation Banded Salary Systems," *WorldatWork* 16, no. 1 (First Quarter 2007): 20.

29. Carri Baca and Gary Starzmann, "Clarifying Competencies: Powerful Tools for Driving Business Success, Part Two," *Workspan* (April 2006): 53.

30. Susan Ladika, "Decompression Pay," *HR Magazine* 50, no. 10 (December 2005): 79.

# 10

# Pay for Performance: Incentive Rewards

# After studying this chapter, you should be able to

**OUTCOME 1** Discuss the basic requirements for successful implementation of incentive programs.

**OUTCOME 2** Identify the types of and reasons for implementing individual incentive plans.

**OUTCOME 3** Explain why merit raises may fail to motivate employees adequately and discuss ways to increase their motivational value.

**OUTCOME 4** Indicate the advantage of each of the principal methods used to compensate salespeople.

**OUTCOME 5** Identify the key aspects of team and group-level pay-for-performance plans.

**OUTCOME 6** Differentiate between profit-sharing plans and explain the advantages and disadvantages of these programs.

**OUTCOME 7** Describe the main types of employee stock ownership plans and discuss their advantages to employers and employees.

Although the recent economic downturn did not affect the Canadian economy as much as the U.S. or European economy, there were several ways in which Canadian organizations were forced to adapt. In addition to pressures on employees to curb their pay and benefits and/or grant concessions, especially in the public sector, organizations were forced to take a second and third look at their pay-for-performance and incentive systems. Compensation analysts and others trace the financial crisis in the housing and banking sectors that spawned the national and international economic troubles to pay-for-performance systems that encouraged aggressive selling on the part of mortgage brokers and real estate agents. Organizations are now likely to tie compensation more closely to performance.[1] Whether you are a heavily scrutinized big bank on Bay Street, Toronto, or a belt-tightening small store in Nova Scotia, you want the biggest bang for your buck; that is, you would want the best efforts from your employees for the rewards you provide. For many, this means aligning the interests of the employees with the interests of the company. One of the best ways to do this is to reward people for their performance. But this is no small task. The process of (1) choosing the right incentive plans based on organizational objectives, (2) setting up performance measures, and (3) administering those incentive plans may seem a bit daunting, especially because so much can go wrong if not done properly.

In this chapter, we will discuss incentive plans in terms of the objectives they hope to achieve and the various factors that may affect their success.

Because many organizations have implemented broad-based incentive programs, for discussion purposes, we have grouped incentive plans into three broad categories: individual incentive plans, group incentive plans, and enterprise incentive plans, as shown in Figure 10.1.[2]

# STRATEGIC REASONS FOR INCENTIVE PLANS

**variable pay**

Tying pay to some measure of individual, group, or organizational performance

A major element of strategic compensation management is the use of incentive plans, also called **variable pay** programs, for employees throughout the organization.

Incentive rewards are based entirely on a pay-for-performance philosophy (see Chapter 9). Incentive pay programs establish a performance "threshold" (a baseline performance level) that an employee or group of employees must reach to qualify for incentive payments. Additionally, incentive plans emphasize a shared focus on organizational objectives by broadening the opportunities for incentives to employees throughout the organization. Incentive plans create an operating environment that champions a philosophy of shared commitment through the belief that every individual contributes to organizational performance and success.

## INCENTIVE PLANS AS LINKS TO ORGANIZATIONAL OBJECTIVES

Contemporary arguments for incentive plans focus on linking compensation rewards, both individual and group, to organizational goals and strategy. Specific company goals or objectives might be to lower labour costs, improve customer satisfaction, expand product markets, or maintain high levels of productivity and quality, which in turn improve the market for the company's goods and services in a global economy. By meshing compensation and organizational objectives, managers believe that employees will assume "ownership" of their jobs, thereby improving their effort and overall job performance. Incentives are designed to encourage employees to put out more effort to complete their job tasks—effort they might not be motivated to expend under hourly and/or seniority-based compensation systems. Also, incentive pay is highly valued as a compensation strategy to attract and retain top-performing employees.[3] Figure 10.2 summarizes the major advantages of incentive pay programs as noted by researchers and HR professionals.

## FIGURE 10.1

TYPES OF INCENTIVE PLANS

| Individual | Group | Enterprise/Organization |
|---|---|---|
| Piecework | Team compensation | Profit sharing |
| Standard hour plan | Scanlon Plan | Stock options |
| Bonuses | Improshare | Employee stock ownership plans (ESOPs) |
| Merit pay | | |
| Lump-sum merit pay | | |
| Incentive awards | | |
| Sales incentives | | |
| Incentives for professional employees | | |
| Executive incentives | | |

## FIGURE 10.2

ADVANTAGES OF INCENTIVE PAY PROGRAMS

- Incentives focus employee efforts on specific performance targets. They provide real motivation that produces important employee and organizational gains.
- Incentive payouts are variable costs linked to the achievement of results. Base salaries are fixed costs largely unrelated to output.
- Incentive compensation is directly related to operating performance. If performance objectives (quantity and/or quality) are met, incentives are paid. If objectives are not achieved, incentives are withheld.
- Incentives foster teamwork and unit cohesiveness when payments to individuals are based on team results.
- Incentives are a way to distribute success among those responsible for producing that success.
- Incentives are a means to reward or attract top performers when salary budgets are low.

Do incentive plans work? The answer is both yes and no. Various studies, along with reports from individual organizations, show a measurable relationship between incentive plans and improved organizational performance.[4] However, the degree of success obtained depends on several factors, including (1) identifying important organizational metrics by which to measure employee performance and (2) a customized incentive plan that effectively measures employee output and rewards exceptional employee performance.[5] For example, at one hospital, health care employees are eligible for up to a 10 percent merit raise depending on whether they meet or exceed important hospital performance expectations. Importantly, in a survey designed to assess the hospital's incentive pay program, employee responses showed a high relationship between hospital goals and the linkage between pay and performance.[6] At an insurance company, salespeople who achieve sales targets receive significant bonuses, merchandise awards, and recognition through the company's website and in-house publications.[7]

Unfortunately, studies also show that variable pay plans may not achieve their proposed objectives or lead to organizational improvements.[8] First, incentive plans sometimes fail to satisfy employee expectations for pay gains. Second, management may have failed to give adequate attention to the design and implementation of the plan, leaving employees confused about how incentive payments are calculated. Third, employees may have little ability to affect performance standards. Furthermore, the success of an incentive plan will depend on the environment that exists within an organization. A plan is more likely to work in an organization where morale is high, employees believe they are being treated fairly, and there is harmony between employees and management.

# REQUIREMENTS FOR A SUCCESSFUL INCENTIVE PLAN

For an incentive plan to succeed, employees must have some desire for the plan. This desire can be influenced in part by how successful management is in introducing the plan and convincing employees of its benefits. Encouraging employees to participate in developing and administering the plan is likely to increase their willingness to accept it.

Employees must be able to see a clear connection between the incentive payments they receive and their job performance. This connection is more visible if there are objective quality or quantity standards by which they can judge their performance. Commitment by employees to meet these standards is also essential for incentive plans to succeed. This requires mutual trust and understanding between employees and their supervisors, which can be achieved only through open, two-way channels of communication. Management should never allow incentive payments to be seen as an *entitlement*. Instead, these payments should be viewed as a reward that must be earned through effort. This perception can be strengthened if the incentive money is distributed to employees in a separate cheque.

| OUTCOME 1

Furthermore, the best managed incentive pay programs are clearly and continuously communicated to employees. This is true during both good and bad economic periods. Proactive organizations find it advisable to continually evaluate the operation and administration of their variable pay programs.

## SETTING PERFORMANCE MEASURES

Measurement is key to the success of incentive plans because it communicates the importance of established organizational goals. What gets measured and rewarded gets attention.[9] For example, if the organization desires to be a leader in quality, then performance indexes may focus on customer satisfaction, timeliness, or being error free. If being a low-priced producer is the goal, then emphasis should be on cost reduction or increased productivity with lower acceptable levels of quality. Although a variety of performance options are available, most focus on quality, cost control, or productivity. Highlights in HRM 10.1 provides six proven guidelines on how to establish and maintain an effective performance measurement program.

For some organizations, linking incentive payments to formalized performance measures has not obtained positive results for either employees or the organization. Failure can often be traced to the choice of performance measures.[10] Therefore, measures that are quantitative, simple, and structured to show a clear relationship to improved performance are best. Overly quantitative, complex measures are to be avoided. Also, when selecting a performance measure, it is necessary to evaluate the extent to which the employees involved can actually influence the measurement. Finally, employers must guard against

# HIGHLIGHTS IN HRM 10.1

## Setting Performance Measures: The Keys

Both large and small organizations have established performance measures to improve operational success while rewarding employees for their performance outcomes. Establishing meaningful performance measures is one of the important and difficult challenges facing management today. Before managers or supervisors develop and implement organizational measures, they should consider the following guidelines:

- *Performance measures—at all organizational levels—must be consistent with the strategic goals of the organization.* Avoid irrelevant measures or metrics that are not closely linked to the business or what employees do in their work.

- *Define the intent of performance measures and champion the cause relentlessly.* Demonstrate that performance measures are good business management and hold managers and employees accountable for their success.

- *Involve employees.* A critical step in any measurement program is the development of an employee

involvement strategy outlining the nature of employee participation, implementation, and ongoing management of the performance management program. Segment the workforce based on the nature of the work and the potential for impact. Consider which metrics require customization. Acceptance of a performance measurement program is heightened when employees "buy into" the process.

- *Consider the organization's culture and workforce demographics when designing performance measures.* For example, organizations with a more traditional hierarchical structure may need more time to introduce performance metrics compared to flatter organizations, which are more fluid and less steeped in control and command characteristics.

- *Set challenging but attainable goals.* Goals that are unattainable demotivate employees.

- *Widely communicate the importance of performance measures.* Performance messages are the principles and guidelines that communicate to employees about required performance levels and why the organization needs to achieve those levels of success.

"ratcheting up" performance goals by continually trying to exceed previous results. This eventually leads to employee frustration and employee perception that the standards are unattainable. The result will be a mistrust of management and a backlash against the entire incentive program.

## ADMINISTERING INCENTIVE PLANS

**straight piecework**
An incentive plan under which employees receive a certain rate for each unit produced

**differential piece rate**
A compensation rate under which employees whose production exceeds the standard amount of output receive a higher rate for all of their work than the rate paid to those who do not exceed the standard amount

Although incentive plans based on productivity can reduce direct labour costs, to achieve their full benefit, they must be carefully thought out, implemented, and maintained. A cardinal rule is that thorough planning must be combined with a "proceed with caution" approach. Compensation managers repeatedly stress a number of points related to the effective administration of incentive plans. Three of the more important points are as follows:

1. Incentive systems are effective only when managers are willing to grant incentives based on differences in individual, team, or organizational performance. Allowing incentive payments to become pay guarantees defeats the motivational intent of the incentive. The primary purpose of an incentive compensation plan is not to pay off under almost all circumstances but rather to motivate performance. Thus, if the plan is to succeed, poor performance must go unrewarded.
2. Annual salary budgets must be large enough to reward and reinforce exceptional performance. When compensation budgets are set to ensure that pay increases do not exceed certain limits (often established as a percentage of payroll or sales), these constraints may prohibit rewarding outstanding individual or group performance.
3. The overhead costs associated with plan implementation and administration must be determined. These may include the cost of establishing performance standards and the added cost of record keeping. The time consumed in communicating the plan to employees, answering questions, and resolving any complaints about it must also be included in these costs.

# INDIVIDUAL INCENTIVE PLANS

In today's competitive world, one word, *flexibility*, describes the design of individual incentive plans.[11] For example, technology, job tasks and duties, and/or organizational goals (such as being a low-cost producer) impact the organization's choice of incentive pay programs. Incentive payments may be determined by the number of units produced, achievement of specific performance goals, or productivity improvements in the organization as a whole. In addition, in highly competitive industries such as food and retailing, low profit margins will affect the availability of monies for incentive payouts. All of these considerations suggest that tradition and philosophy, as well as economics and technology, help govern the design of individual incentive systems.

**OUTCOME 2**

## PIECEWORK

One of the oldest incentive plans is based on piecework. Under **straight piecework**, employees receive a certain rate for each unit produced. Their compensation is determined by the number of units they produce during a pay period. At Steelcase, an office furniture maker, employees can earn more than their base pay, often as much as 35 percent more, through piecework for each slab of metal they cut or chair they upholster. Under a **differential piece rate**, employees whose production exceeds the standard output receive a higher rate for all of their work than the rate paid to those who do not exceed the standard.

Employers include piecework in their compensation strategy for several reasons. The wage payment for each employee is simple to compute, and the plan permits an organization to predict its labour costs with considerable accuracy, because these costs are the same for each unit of output. The piecework system is

**standard hour plan**
An incentive plan that sets rates based on the completion of a job in a predetermined standard time

more likely to succeed when units of output can be measured readily, the quality of the product is less critical, the job is fairly standardized, and a constant flow of work can be maintained.

## Computing the Piece Rate

Although time standards establish the time required to perform a given amount of work, they do not by themselves determine what the incentive rate should be. The incentive rates must be based on hourly wage rates that would otherwise be paid for the type of work being performed. For example, the standard time for producing one unit of work in a job paying $12.75 per hour was set at 12 minutes. The piece rate would be $2.55 per unit, computed as follows:

$$60 \text{ (minutes per hour)}$$
$$12 \text{ (standard time per hour)} = 5 \text{ units per hour}$$
$$\$12.75 \text{ (hourly rate)} = 2.55 \text{ per unit}$$
$$5 \text{ (units per hour)}$$

## Piecework: The Drawbacks

Despite their obvious advantages—including their direct tie to a pay-for-performance philosophy—piecework systems have a number of disadvantages that offset their usefulness. One of the most significant weaknesses of piecework, as well as of other incentive plans based on individual effort, is that it may not always be an effective motivator. If employees believe that an increase in their output will provoke disapproval from fellow workers (often referred to as "rate busting"), they may avoid exerting maximum effort because their desire for peer approval outweighs their desire for more money. Also, jobs in which individual contributions are difficult to distinguish or measure or in which the work is mechanized to the point that the employee exercises very little control over output may be unsuited to piecework. Piecework may also be inappropriate in the following situations:

Employees in manufacturing plants often work under individual incentive plans such as piecework.

- When quality is more important than quantity
- When technology changes are frequent
- When productivity standards on which piecework must be based are difficult to develop

Importantly, piecework incentive systems can work against an organizational culture promoting workforce cooperation, creativity, or problem solving because each of these goals can infringe on an employee's time and productivity and, therefore, total incentive earned.

## STANDARD HOUR PLAN

Another common incentive technique is the **standard hour plan**, which sets incentive rates on the basis of a predetermined "standard time" for completing a job. If employees finish the work in less than the expected time, their pay is still based on the standard time for the job multiplied by their hourly rate. Standard hour plans are popular in service departments in automobile dealerships. For example, if the standard time to install an engine in a truck is five hours and the mechanic completes the job in four and a half hours, the payment would be the mechanic's hourly rate times five hours. Standard hour plans are particularly suited to long-cycle operations or jobs or tasks that are non-repetitive and require a variety of skills. However, although standard hour plans can motivate employees to produce more, employers must ensure that equipment maintenance and product quality do not suffer as employees strive to do their work faster to earn additional income.

# BONUSES

A **bonus** is an incentive payment that is given to an employee beyond his or her normal base wage. It is frequently given at the end of the year and does not become part of base pay. Bonuses have the advantage of providing employees with more pay for exerting greater effort, while at the same time the employees still have the security of a basic wage. Bonus payments are common among managerial and executive employees, but recent trends show that they are increasingly given to employees throughout the organization.[12] The recent economic downturn, however, has resulted in fewer bonuses being awarded to all employee groups.[13]

Depending on who is to receive the bonus, the incentive payment may be determined on the basis of cost reduction, quality improvement, or performance criteria established by the organization. At the executive level, for example, performance criteria might include earnings growth or enterprise-specific agreed-on objectives.

When some special employee contribution is to be rewarded, a **spot bonus** is used. A spot bonus, as the name implies, is given "on the spot," normally for some employee effort not directly tied to an established performance standard. For example, a customer service representative might receive a spot bonus for working long hours to fill a new customer's large order. Spot bonuses are championed as useful retention and motivational tools for overburdened employees, especially during lean financial times. Lauren Sejen, compensation expert with Watson Wyatt Worldwide, notes, "I think spot bonuses are one of the most underutilized forms of rewards, given how well employees respond to them. These plans make perfect sense."[14]

> **bonus**
> An incentive payment that is supplemental to the base wage
>
> **spot bonus**
> An unplanned bonus given for employee effort unrelated to an established performance measure

## MERIT PAY

A merit pay program (merit raise) links an increase in base pay to how successfully an employee performs his or her job. The merit increase is normally given on the basis of an employee having achieved some objective performance standard—although a superior's subjective evaluation of subordinate performance may play a large role in the increase given. Merit raises can serve to motivate if employees perceive the raise to be related to the performance required to earn it.[15]

Theories of motivation, in addition to behavioural science research, provide justification for merit pay plans as well as other pay-for-performance programs.[16] However, research shows that a merit increase in the range of 7 to 9 percent is necessary to serve as a pay motivator.[17] Employees may welcome lower percentage amounts, but low salary increases may not lead to significantly greater effort on the part of employees to drive business results. Consequently, with low salary budgets (see Chapter 9), organizations wishing to reward top performers will be required to distribute a large portion of the compensation budget to these individuals.[18] A meaningful merit increase will catch the attention of top performers while sending a signal to poor-performing employees. A strategic compensation policy *must differentiate* between outstanding and good or average performance. Furthermore, increases granted on the basis of merit should be distinguishable from cost-of-living or other general increases.

## Problems with Merit Raises

Merit raises may not always achieve their intended purpose. Unlike a bonus, a merit raise may be perpetuated year after year even when performance declines. When this happens, employees come to expect the increase and see it as an entitlement, unrelated to their performance. Furthermore, what are referred to as merit raises often turn out to be increases based on seniority or favouritism. A superior's biased evaluation of subordinate performance may play a large role in the increase given. Even when merit raises are determined by performance, the employee's gains may be offset by inflation and higher income taxes. Recent research also suggests a "new" problem: women generally receive less than men

**OUTCOME 3**

**merit guidelines**
Guidelines for awarding merit raises
that are tied to performance objectives

**lump-sum merit program**
Program under which employees
receive a year-end merit payment,
which is not added to their base pay

in merit pay.[19] Compensation specialists also recognize the following problems with merit pay plans:

1. Money available for merit increases may be inadequate to satisfactorily raise all employees' base pay.
2. Managers may have no guidance in how to define and measure performance; there may be vagueness regarding merit award criteria.
3. Employees may not believe that their compensation is tied to effort and performance; they may be unable to differentiate between merit pay and other types of pay increases.
4. Employees and their managers may hold different views of the factors that contribute to job success.
5. Merit pay plans may create feelings of pay inequity.[20]

Although there are no easy solutions to these problems, organizations using a true merit pay plan often base the percentage pay raise on **merit guidelines** tied to performance appraisals. For example, a certain pay increase, "3 percent," will be tied to a certain performance evaluation, "above average." The percentages may change each year, depending on various internal or external concerns such as profit levels or national economic conditions, as indicated by changes in the consumer price index. To prevent all employees from being rated outstanding or above average, managers may be required to distribute the performance rating according to some preestablished formula (such as only 10 percent can be rated outstanding). Additionally, when setting merit percentage guidelines, organizations should consider individual performance along with such factors as training, experience, and current earnings.

## LUMP-SUM MERIT PAY

To make merit increases more flexible and visible, some organizations have implemented a **lump-sum merit program**. Under this type of plan, employees receive a single lump-sum increase at the time of their review, an increase that is not added to their base salary. Lump-sum merit programs offer several advantages. For employees, an advantage is that receiving a single lump-sum merit payment can provide a clear link between pay and performance. For example, a 5 percent merit increase granted to an industrial engineer earning $72,000 a year translates into a weekly increase of $69.23—a figure that looks small compared to a lump-sum payment of $3,600. For employers, lump-sum payments essentially freeze base salaries, thereby maintaining annual salary and benefit costs, because the level of benefits is normally calculated from salary levels. Organizations using a lump-sum merit program will want to adjust base salaries upward after a certain period of time. These adjustments should keep pace with the rising cost of living and increases in the general market wage.

## INCENTIVE AWARDS AND RECOGNITION

Incentive awards and employee recognition are an important part of an employer's pay-for-performance compensation strategy. Awards are used to recognize productivity gains, special contributions or achievements, and service to the organization. Popular noncash incentive awards include merchandise, personalized gifts, theatre or sports tickets, vacations, dining out, gift certificates or gift cards, and personalized clothing. Tangible awards presented with the right message and style can make employees feel appreciated while at the same time underscoring a company value. Research clearly shows that noncash incentive awards are most effective as motivators when the award is combined with a meaningful employee recognition program. Tyler Gentry, employee recognition specialist, notes this about the importance of noncash incentive awards: "Recognition and rewards aren't so much about recognizing someone for going 'above and beyond' and giving gifts as they are about letting employees know that they are *valued* and *appreciated*. Recognition is a conduit that shows employees that the company

Nonmonetary rewards let employees know they are valued, which is why more and more companies are using incentives such as this to recognize high performance.

gosphotodesign/Shutterstock.com

appreciates their efforts, their unique gifts, and their contributions."[21] Employers should take care to tie awards to performance and deliver awards in a timely, sincere, and specific way. Generally, the more public the recognition, the more powerful the effect.[22]

Importantly, noncash incentive awards should support business goals and objectives. Greg Boswell, a director of performance recognition, notes, "Employers are now thinking of awards and employee recognition more strategically with programs closely aligned to their business goals."[23] For example, if quality improvement is a business goal, then recognition needs to be tied to those behaviours that further the achievement of quality. Additionally, incentive awards work best when awards are appreciated and valued by employees. At one advertising agency, the employee-of-the-month is allowed to drive the president's car for one month—the car is a Maserati. Highlights in HRM 10.2 provides suggestions for noncash incentive awards based on the generational grouping of employees.

## SALES INCENTIVES

The enthusiasm and drive required in most types of sales work demand that sales employees be highly motivated. This fact, as well as the competitive nature of selling, explains why financial incentives for salespeople are widely used. These incentive plans must provide a source of motivation that will elicit cooperation and trust. Motivation is particularly important for employees away from the office who cannot be supervised closely and who, as a result, must exercise a high degree of self-discipline.

**OUTCOME 4**

### Unique Needs of Sales Incentive Plans

Incentive systems for salespeople are complicated by wide differences in the types of sales jobs. These range from department store clerks who ring up customer purchases to industrial salespeople who provide consultation and other highly technical services. Salespeople's performance may be measured by the dollar volume of their sales and by their ability to establish new accounts. Other measures are the ability to promote new products or services and to provide various forms of customer service and assistance that do not produce immediate sales revenues.[24]

# HIGHLIGHTS IN HRM 10.2

## Customize Your Noncash Incentive Awards

There is an increased need for compensation specialists to recognize the importance of leveraging noncash incentives to motivate their generationally diverse workforce. The one-size-fits-all approach will not keep their workforce engaged and happy as what appeals to older employees may not be attractive to younger employees.

- *Traditionalists (born before 1945).* These employees are extremely loyal to their organization and see their employment as a duty and an obligation. They are big savers, and as a result, they are a wealthy group. Attractive awards include entertainment venues, vacations, and technology items. They also appreciate health and wellness opportunities.

- *Boomers (born between 1946 and 1964).* They thrive on personal achievement and recognition. They are

very materialistic, placing very high value on working hard and achieving career success. Boomers are an optimistic group that is responsible for several social movements. Boomers favour incentive rewards in the areas of travel, luxury gifts, health and wellness options, and personalized plaques and awards.

- *Generation X (born between 1965 and 1981).* These employees grew up with both parents working outside the home. As a result, they value work–life balance and flexible work arrangements. They are more likely to be satisfied by challenges, learning, and development and value being promoted and being paid equitably.

- *Generation Y (born between 1982 and 1999).* These tech-savvy employees desire easy and quick access to information and immediate performance feedback; they learn quickly and value diversity. Gen Y enjoys freedom at work and places huge emphasis on social networking/media.

Sources: Jo-Ida C. Hansen and Melanie E. Leuty, "Work Values Across Generations," *Journal of Career Assessment* 20, no. 1 (2012): 34–52; Jean Twenge, Stacy M. Campbell, Brian J. Hoffman, and Charles E. Lance, "Generational Differences in Work Values: Leisure and Extrinsic Values Increasing, Social and Intrinsic Values Decreasing," *Journal of Management* 36, no. 5 (2010): 1117–1142; Alison Avalos, "Recognition: A Critical Component of the Total Reward Mix," *Workspan* (July 2007): 33.

---

**straight salary plan**
A compensation plan that permits salespeople to be paid for performing various duties that are not reflected immediately in their sales volume

**straight commission plan**
A compensation plan based on a percentage of sales

Performance standards for sales employees are difficult to develop, however, because their performance is often affected by external factors beyond their control. Economic and seasonal fluctuations, sales competition, changes in demand, and the nature of the sales territory can all affect an individual's sales record.[25] Sales volume alone therefore may not be an accurate indicator of the effort salespeople have expended.

In developing incentive plans for salespeople, managers are also confronted with the problem of how to reward extra sales effort and at the same time compensate for activities that do not contribute directly or immediately to sales. Furthermore, sales employees must be able to enjoy some degree of income stability.[26] Many schemes to reward employees for reaching sales goals are threatened by instances of unethical behaviour where the needs of employees are not aligned with the needs of the customers, as reported in Ethics in HRM.

## Types of Sales Incentive Plans

Compensation plans for sales employees may consist of a straight salary plan, a straight commission plan, a combination salary and commission plan, or a sales plus bonus plan.[27] A **straight salary plan** permits salespeople to be paid for performing various duties not reflected immediately in their sales volume. It enables them to devote more time to providing services and building up the goodwill of customers without jeopardizing their income. The principal limitation of the straight salary plan is that it may not motivate salespeople to exert sufficient effort in maximizing their sales volume.

On the other hand, the **straight commission plan**, based on a percentage of sales, provides maximum incentive and is easy to compute and understand.

# ETHICS IN HRM

## Executive Incentives and Perks: Nortel Networks

In 2010, Canadian executives earned an average of $8.38 million, which is an increase of 27 percent from 2009. In fact, the top executive in Canada earned $62 million in 2010. When one compares these figures to that of the average Canadian worker, who makes $44,366 per year, it is no surprise that there is so much criticism of executive pay and the income inequality gap in Canada.

As seen in the case of Nortel, where executives have been accused of engaging in unethical conduct to cash in on their bonuses, organizations have to be careful in how they take their fiduciary responsibilities. Executives at Nortel allegedly "booked $80 million worth of fraudulent entries in order to transform a loss in the first quarter of 2003 into a profit," which would have stimulated executive bonuses in the amount of $26 million. If this is what

happened, not only would it have breached public disclosure rules, but it also would have been a direct violation of the accounting practices set out by Nortel and further goes against generally accepted accounting practices.

Three of Nortel's executives are currently battling in court over fraudulent and unethical activities that allegedly triggered bonus payments in the amount of $12.2 million for some of the company's top executives. Although executives are still trying to get their bonuses in legal battles, many Nortel employees are unemployed. This brings into question ethical consideration for the nonexecutive employees who are without jobs, pensions and benefits, or disability plans.

Sources: Rachel Mendleson, "CEO Compensation in Canada Jumped 27 Percent in 2010," *Huffington Post*, February 1, 2012, http://www.huffingtonpost.ca/2012/01/02/ceo-compensation-canada-jumps-27-percent_n_1180168.html?ref=canada-business; James Bagnall, "Nortel Bonuses Were Legitimate: Defence," *Financial Post*, February 2, 2012, http://business.financialpost.com/2012/02/02/nortel-bonuses-were-legitimate-defence/; Jamie Sturgeon, "Ex-Nortel CEO Pushed for Fast Turnaround of Restatement, Court Hears," *Financial Post*, February 13, 2012, http://business.financialpost.com/2012/02/13/nearly-a-billion-dollars-in-reserves-incorrectly-booked-nortel-trial-told/.

---

For example, total cash compensation might equal total sales volume times some percentage of total sales, perhaps 2 percent. Straight commission plans encourage aggressive selling, which might be needed in highly competitive industries. Under a straight commission plan, salespeople may be allowed a salary draw. A *draw* is a cash advance that must be paid back as commissions are earned.

However, the straight commission plan is limited by the following disadvantages:

1. Salespeople will stress high-priced products.
2. Customer service after the sale is likely to be neglected.
3. Earnings tend to fluctuate widely between good and poor periods of business, and turnover of trained sales employees tends to increase in poor periods.
4. Salespeople are tempted to grant price concessions.

> **combined salary and commission plan**
> A compensation plan that includes a straight salary and a commission

The **combined salary and commission plan** is the most widely used sales incentive program. For example, the most common pay mix for salespersons responsible for *new* accounts is 50 percent base pay and 50 percent variable pay. For salespersons servicing *existing* accounts, a pay distribution of 70 percent base pay and 30 percent commission is typical.[28] The ratio of base salary to commission can be set to fit organizational objectives. The following advantages indicate why the combination salary and commission plan is so widely used:

1. The right kind of incentive compensation, if linked to salary in the right proportion, has most of the advantages of both the straight salary and the straight commission forms of compensation.
2. A salary-plus-incentive compensation plan offers greater design flexibility and can therefore be more readily set up to help maximize company profits.

**salary plus bonus plan**
A compensation plan that pays a salary plus a bonus achieved by reaching targeted sales goals

3. The plan can develop the most favourable ratio of selling expense to sales.
4. The field sales force can be motivated to achieve specific company marketing objectives in addition to sales volume.

Some companies pay their sales representatives on a salary plus bonus program. Under **salary plus bonus plans**, the payout can be paid on a monthly, quarterly, or yearly schedule contingent upon the salesperson achieving targeted sales goals, such as number of sales calls made, account servicing, or quality of sales.

## INCENTIVES FOR PROFESSIONAL EMPLOYEES

Like other salaried workers, professional employees—engineers, scientists, and attorneys, for example—may be motivated through bonuses and merit increases. In some organizations, unfortunately, professional employees cannot advance beyond a certain point in the salary structure unless they are willing to take an administrative assignment. When they are promoted, their professional talents are no longer utilized fully. In the process, the organization may lose a good professional employee and gain a poor administrator. To avoid this situation, some organizations have extended the salary range for professional positions to equal or nearly equal that for administrative positions. The extension of this range provides a double-track wage system, whereby professionals who do not aspire to become administrators still have an opportunity to earn comparable salaries. Professional employees can receive compensation beyond base pay. For example, scientists and engineers employed by high-tech firms are included in performance-based incentive programs such as profit sharing or stock ownership. These plans encourage greater levels of individual performance. Cash bonuses can be awarded to those who complete projects on or before deadline dates. Payments may also be given to individuals elected to professional societies, granted patents, or meeting professional licensing standards.

### THE EXECUTIVE PAY PACKAGE

Executive compensation plans consist of five basic components: (1) base salary, (2) short-term incentives or bonuses, (3) long-term incentives or stock plans, (4) benefits, and (5) perquisites.[29] Each of these elements may receive different emphasis in the executive's compensation package depending on various organizational goals and executive needs.

Today's HR managers need to be creative in finding ways to motivate and retain their professional employees.

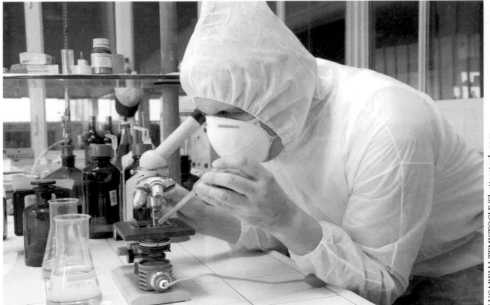

LUCARELLI TEMISTOCLE/Shutterstock.com

## Executive Base Salaries

Executive base salaries represent between 30 and 40 percent of total annual compensation.[30] An analysis of executive salaries shows that the largest portion of executive pay is received in long-term incentive rewards and bonuses. Regardless, executives of Fortune 500 firms routinely earn an annual base salary in excess of $500,000, with executives in very large corporations earning considerably more. The levels of competitive salaries in the job market exert perhaps the greatest influence on executive base salaries. An organization's compensation committee—normally members of the board of directors—will order a salary survey to find out what executives earn in comparable enterprises.[31] For example, by one estimate, 96 percent of companies in Standard & Poor's 500 Stock Index use a technique called *competitive benchmarking* when setting executive pay or to remain competitive for executive talent. CEOs who do not earn as much as their peers are likely to "take a hike." Comparisons may be based on organization size, sales volume, or industry groupings. Thus, by analyzing the data from published studies, along with self-generated salary surveys, the compensation committee can determine the equity of the compensation package outside the organization.

## Executive Short-Term Incentives

Annual bonuses represent the main element of executive short-term incentives.[32] A bonus payment may take the form of cash or stock and may be paid immediately (which is frequently the case), deferred for a short time, or deferred until retirement. Most organizations pay their short-term incentive bonuses in cash (in the form of a supplemental cheque), in keeping with their pay-for-performance strategy. By providing a reward soon after the performance and thus linking it to the effort on which it is based, they can use cash bonuses as a significant motivator. Deferred bonuses are used to provide a source of retirement benefits or to supplement a regular pension plan.

Incentive bonuses for executives should be based on the contribution the individual makes to the organization. A variety of formulas have been developed for this purpose. Incentive bonuses may be based on a percentage of a company's total profits or a percentage of profits in excess of a specific return on stockholders' investments. In other instances, the payments may be tied to an annual profit plan whereby the amount is determined by the extent to which an agreed-on profit level is exceeded. Payments may also be based on performance ratings or the achievement of specific objectives established with the agreement of executives and the board of directors.

In a continuing effort to monitor the pulse of the marketplace, more organizations are tying operational yardsticks to traditional financial gauges when computing executive pay. Called *balanced scorecards*, these yardsticks may measure things such as customer satisfaction, the ability to innovate, or product or service leadership.[33] Notes David Cates, a compensation principal with Towers Perrin: a balanced scorecard "allows companies to focus on building future economic value, rather than be driven solely by short-term financial results." Mobil Oil uses a balanced scorecard that better indicates exactly where the company is successful and where improvement is needed.

## Executive Long-Term Incentives

Stock options are the primary long-term incentive offered to executives.[34] The principal reason driving executive stock ownership is the desire of both the company and outside investors for senior managers to have a significant stake in the success of the business—to have their fortunes rise and fall with the value they create for shareholders. Stock options can also be extremely lavish for executives. In 2010, the average pay for the top 100 CEOs in Canada was $8.38 million, a 27 percent increase from the $6.6 million in 2009. The highest paid executives

**FIGURE 10.3**

PART 4

## TYPES OF LONG-TERM INCENTIVE PLANS

| Stock options | Rights granted to executives to purchase shares of their organization's stock at an established price for a fixed period of time. Stock price is usually set at the market value at the time the option is granted. |
| --- | --- |
| Stock appreciation rights (SARs) | Cash or stock award determined by an increase in stock price during any time chosen by the executive in the option period; does not require executive financing |
| Stock purchase | Opportunities for executives to purchase shares of their organization's stock valued at full market or a discount price, often with the organization providing financial assistance |
| Phantom stock | Grant of units equal in value to the fair market value or book value of a share of stock; on a specified date, the executive will be paid the appreciation in the value of the units up to that time |
| Restricted stock | Grant of stock or stock units at a reduced price with the condition that the stock not be transferred or sold (by risk of forfeiture) before a specified employment date |
| Performance units | Grants analogous to annual bonuses except that the measurement period exceeds one year. The value of the grant can be expressed as a flat dollar amount or converted to a number of "units" of equivalent aggregate value. |
| Performance shares | Grants of actual stock or phantom stock units. Value is contingent on both predetermined performance objectives over a specified period of time and the stock market. |

in 2010 were Frank Stronach of Magna International with $61,811,287 (including stock options of $17 million and a bonus of $41 million), followed by fellow Magna executives Donald Walker at $16.6 million (including stock options of $1.1 million and a bonus of $11,253,530) and Siegfried Wolf at $16.5 million (including stock options of $3.8 million and a bonus of $9.2 million).[35] Not surprisingly, the creativity in designing a stock option program seems almost limitless. Figure 10.3 highlights several common forms of long-term incentives.

Short-term incentive bonuses are criticized for causing top executives to focus on quarterly profit goals to the detriment of long-term survival and growth objectives. Therefore, corporations such as Sears and Manulife have adopted compensation strategies that tie executive pay to long-term performance measures. Each of these organizations recognizes that compensation strategies must also take into account the performance of the organization as a whole. Important to stockholders are such performance results as growth in earnings per share, return on stockholders' equity, and, ultimately, stock price appreciation.

A variety of incentive plans, therefore, have been developed to tie rewards to these performance results, particularly over the long term. Additionally, stock options can serve to retain key executive personnel when exercising the options is linked to a specified vesting period, perhaps two to four years (this type of incentive is called "golden handcuffs").

Stock options are under attack.[36] The Canadian Coalition for Good Governance, which represents Canada's largest institutional shareholders, is having meetings with large organizations to change their compensation packages and tie them more closely to long-term goals. Many object to the sheer magnitude of these incentive rewards. The link between pay and performance that options are championed to provide can also be undermined when compensation committees grant additional options to executives even when company stock prices fall or performance indexes decline. Peter Clapman, chief counsel for TIAA-CREF, the world's largest pension system, notes, "It's sort of heads you win, tails let's flip again." Even worse for shareholders is the dilution problem. Every option granted to executives makes the shares of other stockholders less valuable.

## Executive Benefits

The benefits package offered executives may parallel one offered to other groups of employees. Various programs for extended health insurance, life insurance, retirement plans, and vacations are common. However, unlike other employee groups, the benefits offered executives are likely to be broader in coverage and free of charge. Additionally, executives may be given financial assistance in the form of trusts for estate planning, payment of mortgage interest, and legal help.[37]

## Executive Perquisites

**Perquisites** are nonmonetary rewards given to executives. Perquisites, or *perks*, are a means of demonstrating the executive's importance to the organization. The status that comes with perks—both inside and outside the organization—shows a pecking order and conveys authority. Corporate executives may simply consider perks a "badge of merit."

The dark side of perks is that they are viewed as wasteful spending and overly lavish. A recent study, however, shows that perks can facilitate company productivity by saving executive time (e.g., private planes and chauffeur service) or improve or maintain executive health (e.g., spas, health clubs, and company cabins). Therefore, the cost of perks should be weighed against the added efficiency and managerial effectiveness they generate.[38] Highlights in HRM 10.3 shows the more common perks offered to executives.

# HIGHLIGHTS IN HRM 10.3

## The "Sweetness" of Executive Perks

Compensation consulting firms such as Coopers & Lybrand LLP, WorldatWork, and Hewitt Associates regularly survey companies nationwide to identify the perks they provide for executives and other top managers. The following are popular executive perks:

- Company car
- Company plane
- Executive eating facilities
- Financial consulting
- Company-paid parking
- Personal liability insurance
- Estate planning
- First-class air travel
- Home computers
- Chauffeur service
- Children's education
- Spouse travel
- Physical examinations
- Mobile phones
- Large insurance policies
- Income tax preparation
- Country club membership
- Luncheon club membership
- Personal home repairs
- Loans
- Legal counselling
- Vacation cabins

**team incentive plan**
A compensation plan in which all team members receive an incentive bonus payment when production or service standards are met or exceeded

# EXECUTIVE COMPENSATION: ETHICS AND ACCOUNTABILITY

Top CEO pay packages in Canada were discussed in a previous section. In the United States, the top executive paycheques in 2011 were, as usual, off the chart. Consider the total compensation drawn in 2011 by the following executives[39]:

| | |
|---|---|
| John Hammergren, McKesson | $131,190,000 |
| Ralph Lauren, Ralph Lauren | $ 66,650,000 |
| Michael Fascitelli, Vornado Realty | $ 64,400,000 |
| Richard Kinder, Kinder Morgan | $ 60,940,000 |
| David Cote, Honeywell | $ 55,790,000 |

Interestingly, respected management expert Peter F. Drucker argued in a 1984 essay that CEO pay had rocketed out of control and implored compensation committees to hold CEO compensation to no more than 20 times what rank-and-file employees made. He warned that the growing pay gap between CEOs and employees would threaten the very credibility of leadership, particularly when CEOs fire thousands of their workers and their companies underperform.[40]

Given the large amount of various compensation packages, the question asked by many is, "Are top executives worth the salaries and bonuses they receive?" The answer may depend on whom you ask. Corporate compensation committees justify big bonuses in the following ways:

1. Large financial incentives are a way to reward superior performance.
2. Business competition is pressure filled and demanding.
3. Good executive talent is in great demand.
4. Effective executives create shareholder value.[41]

Others justify high compensation as a fact of business life, reflecting market compensation trends.

Nevertheless, in an era of massive downsizing, low wage increases, and increased workloads for layoff survivors, strong criticism is voiced regarding the high monetary awards given to senior executives. Furthermore, with the large compensation packages awarded to senior managers and top-level executives, cries for performance accountability and openness abound. In 2007, *Forbes* noted that whereas some high-paid executives do improve performance measures, such as return on equity, earnings per share, and return to shareholders, clearly, many others do not, and their pay far exceeds their performance outcomes.[42] Although not all executive pay is exorbitant and not all executive performance is poor, angry employees, union groups, government officials, and stockholders are arguing for change. Recently, shareholders in firms have begun to increasingly voice their anger and criticism of high executive pay.[43]

# GROUP INCENTIVE PLANS

OUTCOME 5

The emphasis on cost reduction and total quality management has led many organizations to implement a variety of group incentive plans. Group plans enable employees to share in the benefits of improved efficiency realized by major organizational units or various individual work teams. These plans encourage a cooperative—rather than individualistic—spirit among all employees and reward them for their total contribution to the organization. Such features are particularly desirable when working conditions make individual performance difficult, if not impossible, to measure.

## TEAM COMPENSATION

**Team incentive plans** reward team members with an incentive reward when agreed-on performance standards are met or exceeded. Team incentives seek to establish a psychological climate that fosters team member cooperation and a collective desire to fulfill organizational goals and objectives. Although team incentive plans promote a pay-for-performance philosophy, unfortunately, establishing an effective organization-specific incentive team plan is not easy.

One catch with setting team compensation is that not all teams are alike (see Chapter 4). For example, cross-functional teams, self-directed teams, and task force teams make it impossible to develop one consistent type of team incentive plan. With a variety of teams, managers find it difficult to adopt uniform measurement standards or payout formulas for team pay.[44] According to Steven Gross, Hay manager, "Each type of team requires a specific pay structure to function at its peak." Highlights in HRM 10.4 lists important considerations when designing a team incentive plan.

PART 4

# HIGHLIGHTS IN HRM 10.4

## Lessons Learned: Designing Effective Team Incentives

Will your team incentive program be successful? Although there is no exact science for ensuring the success of team incentives, several authors suggest some best practices for designing and implementing them:

- The organization at all levels must embrace a team-based structure—not just by word of mouth as the right resources to empower employees must be in place. This should be evidenced by a holistic change in the organization's culture (i.e., team-based compensation), values, leadership, and overall work atmosphere.

- To facilitate this paradigm shift, communication and post-completion evaluation are fundamental. Provide employees with the right amount of information at the right time and in an effective manner. Develop mechanisms to measure goal achievement, project completion, and effectiveness. Ensure that employees understand what the "do this" is in order to "get this." Incentive plans must be customized based on each team's project.

- Enlist managerial support at all levels. Although top management is instrumental in terms of the time and resources required to customize the "performance measures, objectives, deliverables, and rewards for each team project incentive plan," middle- to lower level managers are directly involved with the program's implementation.

- Select representatives from management, labour, and employees to champion the team-based project. This inclusiveness serves to build trust among them.

- Establish the legitimacy of the group incentives; use written contracts as they put the onus on individuals as teams to be accountable for the end results. Each team member's role must be clearly stipulated, along with the major deliverables, completion date, and team composition.

- Ensure that the incentive payout is perceived as fair and equitable. It should be easy for employees to calculate their incentives, which can be further achieved by establishing an internal resource centre that stores various documents to promote knowledge sharing.

- Celebrate the team's accomplishments collectively rather than singling out individuals who have made outstanding contributions. Recognition from the upper echelon goes a long way to motivating teams.

Team incentive programs are not without their problems. The following are some noted problems associated with team compensation:

- Individual team members may perceive that "their" efforts contribute little to team success or to the attainment of the incentive reward.

- Team members may be afraid that one individual may make the others look bad, or that one individual may put in less effort than others but share equally in team rewards—the "free rider" effect.

- The payout formulas may be complex, or there may be insufficient payout rewards.

---

Sources: Harshada Patel, Michael Pettitt, and John R. Wilson, "Factors of Collaborative Working: A Framework for a Collaboration Model," *Applied Ergonomics* 43, no. 1 (2012): 1–26; Tom Taylor, "The Challenge of Project Team Incentives," *Compensation & Benefits Review* 42, no. 5 (2010): 411–419.

**gainsharing plans**
Programs under which both employees and the organization share financial gains according to a predetermined formula that reflects improved productivity and profitability

**profit sharing**
Any procedure by which an employer pays, or makes available to all regular employees, in addition to base pay, special current or deferred sums based on the profits of the enterprise

### Using the Internet

Read about gainsharing plans at **http://www.qualitydigest.com /jul/gainshre.html** and **http://www.hr-guide.com/data /G443.htm**

When team compensation is decided on, organizations typically use the three-step approach to establishing team incentive payments. First, they set performance measures on which incentive payments are based. Improvements in efficiency or product quality and a reduction in materials or labour costs are common benchmark criteria. For example, if labour costs for a team represent 30 percent of the organization's sales dollars and the organization pays a bonus for labour cost savings, then whenever team labour costs are less than 30 percent of sales dollars, a portion of those savings is paid as an incentive bonus to team members. Information on the size of the incentive bonus is reported to employees on a weekly or monthly basis, explaining why incentive pay was or was not earned.

Second, the size of the incentive bonus must be determined. At one insurance company, health insurance underwriters can receive team incentive bonuses of up to 10 percent of base salary; however, the exact level of incentive pay depends on overall team performance and the company's performance over one year. Team incentives are paid annually.

Third, a payout formula is established and fully explained to employees. The team bonus may be distributed to employees equally, in proportion to their base pay, or on the basis of their relative contribution to the team. With discretionary formulas, managers or, in some cases, team members themselves agree on the payouts to individual team members.

## GAINSHARING INCENTIVE PLANS

**Gainsharing plans** are organizational programs designed to increase productivity or decrease labour costs and share monetary gains with employees. These plans are based on a mathematical formula that compares a baseline of performance to actual productivity during a given period. When productivity exceeds the baseline, an agreed-on savings is shared with employees. Inherent in gainsharing is the idea that involved employees will improve productivity through more effective use of organizational resources.

Although productivity can be measured in various ways, it is usually calculated as a ratio of outputs to inputs. Sales, pieces produced, pounds, total standard costs, direct labour dollars earned, and customer orders are common output measures. Inputs frequently measured include materials, labour, energy, inventory, purchased goods or services, and total costs. An increase in productivity is normally gained when

- Greater output is obtained with less or equal input
- Equal production output is obtained with less input

There are many variations of gainsharing plans; however, the Scanlon Plan and Improshare are representative of gainsharing programs. The Scanlon Plan emphasizes participative management and encourages cost reductions by sharing with employees any savings resulting from those reductions. Improshare is based on the number of finished goods that the employee work teams complete in an established period.

## ENTERPRISE INCENTIVE PLANS

Enterprise incentive plans differ from individual and group incentive plans in that all organizational members participate in the plan's compensation payout. Enterprise incentive plans reward employees on the basis of the success of the organization over an extended time period—normally one year, but the period can be longer. Enterprise incentive plans seek to create a "culture of ownership" by fostering a philosophy of cooperation and teamwork among all organizational members. Common enterprise incentive plans include profit sharing, stock options, and employee stock ownership plans (ESOPs).

### PROFIT-SHARING PLANS

**OUTCOME 6**

**Profit sharing** is any procedure by which an employer pays, or makes available to all regular employees, special current or deferred sums based on the organization's profits. As defined here, profit sharing represents cash payments made to eligible employees at designated time periods, as distinct from profit sharing in the form of contributions to employee pension funds.

Profit-sharing plans are intended to give employees the opportunity to increase their earnings by contributing to the growth of their organization's profits. These contributions may be directed toward improving product quality, reducing operating costs, improving work methods, and building goodwill rather than just increasing rates of production. Profit sharing can help stimulate employees to think and feel more like partners in the enterprise and thus concern themselves with the welfare of the organization as a whole. Its purpose therefore is to motivate a total commitment from employees rather than simply to have them contribute in specific areas.

A popular example of a highly successful profit-sharing plan is the one in use at Lincoln Electric Company, a manufacturer of arc welding equipment and supplies. This plan was started in 1934 by J. F. Lincoln, president of the company. Each year, the company distributes a large percentage of its profits to employees in accordance with their salary level and merit ratings. It is not uncommon for employees' annual bonuses to exceed 50 percent of annual wages. The success of Lincoln Electric's incentive system depends on a high level of contribution by each employee. Unquestionably, there is a high degree of respect among employees and management for Lincoln's organizational goals and for the profit-sharing program.

## Variations in Profit-Sharing Plans

Profit-sharing plans differ in the proportion of profits shared with employees and in the distribution and form of payment. The amount shared with employees may range from 5 to 50 percent of the net profit.

In most plans, however, about 20 to 25 percent of the net profit is shared. Profit distributions may be made to all employees on an equal basis, or they may be based on regular salaries or some formula that takes into account seniority and/or merit. The payments may be disbursed in cash, deferred, or made on the basis of combining the two forms of payments.

## Weaknesses of Profit-Sharing Plans

In spite of their potential advantages, profit-sharing plans are also prone to certain weaknesses. The profits shared with employees may be the result of inventory speculation, climatic factors, economic conditions, national emergencies, or other factors over which employees have no control. As one HR manager noted to the authors, "Since there is little linkage between what employees do and their profit bonus, there is an absence of any employee involvement initiatives." Conversely, losses may occur during years when employee contributions have been at a maximum. The fact that profit-sharing payments are made only once a year or deferred until retirement may reduce their motivational value. If a plan fails to pay off for several years in a row, this can have an adverse effect on productivity and employee morale.

## EMPLOYEE STOCK OPTION PLANS

What do the following companies—Apple Computer, Yahoo, Coca-Cola, Starbucks, Nike, Quaker Oats, and Sara Lee—have in common? Each of these diverse organizations offers a stock option program to its employees. According to *WorldatWork*, a compensation association, the use of stock options is a very prevalent method of motivating and compensating hourly employees, as well as salaried and executive personnel. This appears true regardless of the industry surveyed or the organization's size.[45]

Stock option programs are sometimes implemented as part of an employee benefit plan or as part of a corporate culture linking employee effort to stock performance. However, organizations that offer stock option programs to employees do so with the belief that there is some incentive value to the systems.

# HIGHLIGHTS IN HRM 10.5

## Employee Stock Option Plans

Traditionally, stock option plans have been used as a way to reward company executives or "key" employees and to link their interests with those of the company and their shareholders. Today, companies use employee stock option plans to reward, retain, and attract all levels of employees. Stock options are an effective way to share ownership with employees and to gain commitment to organizational goals.

### What Is a Stock Option?

A stock option gives an employee the right to buy a certain number of shares in the company at a fixed price for a certain number of years. The price at which the option is provided is called the "grant" price and is usually the market price at the time the options are granted. Employees who have been granted stock options hope

that the share price will go up and that they will be able to "cash in" by exercising (purchasing) the stock at the lower grant price and then selling the stock at the current market price.

### How Stock Option Plans Work

Here is an example of a typical employee stock option plan. An employee is granted the option to purchase 1,000 shares of the company's stock at the current market price of $5 per share. The employee can exercise the option at $5 per share; typically, the exercise price will be equal to the price when the options are granted. Plans allow employees to exercise their options after a certain number of years or when the company's stock reaches a certain price. If the price of the stock increases to $20 per share, for example, the employee may exercise his or her option to buy 1,000 shares at $5 per share and then sell the stock at the current market price of $20 per share.

Source: Adapted from Employee Stock Options Fact Sheet, National Center for Employee Ownership at http://www.nceo.org/

By allowing employees to purchase stock, the organization hopes they will increase their productivity, assume a partnership role in the organization, and thus cause the stock price to rise.[46] Furthermore, stock option programs have become a popular way to boost the morale of disenfranchised employees caught in budget cuts and downsizing.

Stock option plans grant to employees the right to purchase a specific number of shares of the company's stock at a guaranteed price (the option price). during a designated time period. Although there are many types of options, most options are granted at the stock's fair market value. Not uncommon are plans for purchasing stock through payroll deductions. Highlights in HRM 10.5 explains employee stock option plans in greater detail. Reality Check describes stock option and other pay-for-performance plans at Lombard Canada.

# REALITY CHECK

## Pay for Performance at Lombard Canada

HR Director and former Manager of Compensation & Benefits at Lombard Canada Sandy Bernier is always aware that pay policies are critical to ensuring a stable and productive workforce. Lombard's overall compensation strategy is to lead the marketplace at the 75th percentile for base pay and to have an incentive plan that is based on performance. This mixed approach to compensation

allows Lombard to pay competitively and to reward high performers based on the value they add to the company. For example, an individual's bonus will depend partly on his or her own achievements and partly on corporate performance. According to Bernier, corporate performance has exceeded its target every year for the last four years, which has permitted full bonuses to be awarded to all employees.

To ensure that all systems and processes are up to date, a thorough job analysis for all positions under the senior management team has been conducted using a hybrid point-factor system. All jobs are then graded, and employees are paid within the salary range for the position they are performing. Lombard has 11 salary ranges and regularly participates in external salary surveys to ensure that the company is using the most up-to-date salary information. Furthermore, each time a new hire is recruited, the job description is reviewed to ensure its accuracy and relevance to the position, and any updates needed are made immediately. For all senior-level positions, an individual ad hoc analysis is conducted annually that compares each position to the marketplace. This is an effective approach to executive compensation as it looks at each position and its uniqueness and is not trying to slot a senior position into a restrictive salary range.

According to Bernier, one of the greatest challenges facing today's compensation and benefits teams is the soaring cost of health care—many companies are seeing double-digit premium increases each year. A lot of psychological claims are also being introduced; these are challenging as they are difficult to manage. To add to this challenge, with the new privacy legislation, many companies find it difficult to administer their short-term disability in-house. One way to combat rising health care costs is to educate employees about their benefits plan and ways to contain costs. Bernier has done these types of presentations to employees across Canada.

As a major insurance company, Lombard is fairly traditional in its approach to benefits, but being an employee of this type of company provides its own unique perks. Along with a flexible extended health and dental plan, Lombard offers its employees a stock ownership plan in which 1 to 10 percent of an employee's salary can be voluntarily deducted from payroll; the company matches this amount by 30 percent. If company return on equity targets are met for the year, the company will then put an additional 20 percent into the plan for a total 50 percent match. This plan provides employees with an opportunity to invest in the company's long-term performance, and employees have a vested interest in how the company is doing. To add to this perk, the money in the fund can also be withdrawn once a year at any time, without penalty, and the employee can use it or place it in an individual RRSP for additional tax savings. Finally, employees are offered a perk that is not easily attained in today's marketplace: after four years of service, they are eligible to apply for the mortgage subsidy program and are also given a 40 percent discount on home and auto insurance if they have their insurance coverage with Lombard.

Unfortunately, in the wake of various corporate scandals, employee stock option plans have come under attack from stockholder groups, government officials, and the general public. Criticism largely focuses on the extravagance of executive stock option plans and dubious corporate accounting procedures.[47]

Nevertheless, despite these faults, stock options continue to be a popular and efficient way to pay for the performance of employees and managers. When stock prices rise, employee stock plans can be financially rewarding to employees.

**employee stock ownership plans (ESOPs)**
Stock plans in which an organization contributes shares of its stock to an established trust for the purpose of stock purchases by employees

## EMPLOYEE STOCK OWNERSHIP PLANS (ESOPS)

Canadian Tire and Sears Canada have established **employee stock ownership plans (ESOPs)**—stock plans in which employees can acquire shares in the firm that employs them. There are three main types of employee stock plans. An employee stock bonus plan is the simplest. An employer provides company shares to employees at no cost to the employee by just granting them or by linking the granting to some kind of performance pay plan. An employee stock purchase plan allows employers to purchase shares but not pay full market price for these shares. Under an employee stock option plan, employees are given the option to purchase shares in the company at some future date, at a set price, which they would exercise if the market price rises to exceed this price.

**OUTCOME 7**

**Using the Internet**

The ESOP Association Canada outlines four main motives for implementing stock ownership plans in Canada:

**http://www.esop-canada.com**

## Advantages of ESOPs

ESOPs can increase employees' pride of ownership in the organization, providing an incentive for them to increase productivity and help the organization prosper and grow. Employees may become more interested in how the company is managed and hold managers to higher and different performance standards, such as maximizing share value. Stock plans have the additional advantage of not requiring companies to pay out in cash, so firms can reward employees with shares. For employees, the advantages include a form of saving for retirement, and in some cases, such as at Microsoft, employees could become millionaires.

## Problems with ESOPs

Generally, ESOPs are more likely to serve their intended purposes in publicly held companies than in privately held ones. A major problem with the privately held company is its potential inability to pay back the shares of employees when they retire. These employees do not have the alternative of disposing of their shares on the open market. Thus, when large organizations suffer financial difficulties and the value of the companies' shares falls, so does the value of the employees' retirement plan. Other problems with ESOPs include the following:

- The more retirement income comes from these plans, the more dependent a pensioner becomes on the price of company shares. Future retirees are vulnerable to stock market fluctuations and to management mistakes.

- Employees may become demotivated and frustrated if the share price falls, even though they have worked productively.

- Finally, although studies show that productivity improves when ESOPs are implemented, these gains are not guaranteed. ESOPs help little unless managers are willing to involve employees in organizational decision making. Unfortunately, ESOPs are sometimes set up in ways that restrict employee decision making and expose the ESOP to risk, although providing investors with large potential gains.

Overall, do incentive plans work? The answer can be found in the Business Case.

# THE BUSINESS CASE

## Incentive Plan at WestJet

Incentive pay is a strategic tool used most often to attract and retain employees and to improve organizational outcomes. Organizations spend an average of 9 percent of total payroll dollars on variable compensation programs. Is this money well spent?

- Four out of five organizations report that incentive compensation is an effective tool for attracting and retaining employees.

- About one-third of employers reported that compensation had a positive effect on operating results. Higher-performing companies are more likely to provide stock options and feel strongly that these options influence behaviour among professional ranks.

- The offering of stock options is associated with improved company performance. Bonuses seem to be more tightly linked to increased profits than are long-term incentives.

Executives and senior management at WestJet enjoy long-term incentives: the value of the incentive plan comprises 50 percent stock options and 50 percent restricted share units (RSUs).

This long-term incentive is also extended to pilots, who can choose to receive it as stock options or as RSUs. Along with the long-term incentives, WestJet's president and CEO, executive vice president, and vice president also receive a short-term incentive. WestJet has made incentive pay an instrumental part of its total compensation. This is an excellent idea given the positive link between incentives and overall organization performance.

Sources: Case prepared by Parbudyal Singh, School of Resource Management, York University, "WestJet Airlines–Turbulence or Clear Skies Ahead," May 2012; Business BC, "More Firms Tie Executive Pay to Performance," *The Vancouver Sun*, December 1, 2005; D. Scott, "Survey of Compensation Policies and Practices," *WorldatWork*, March 2003, http://www.worldatwork.org/research, retrieved August 26, 2009; D. J. Gherson, "Getting the Pay Thing Right," *Workspan* 43, no. 6 (June 2000): 47–51; K. H. Van Neek and J. E. Smilko, "Variable Pay Plans," *WorldatWork* 11, no. 4 (Fourth Quarter 2002).

# SMALL BUSINESS APPLICATION

A number of incentives exist that work particularly well with small businesses: for example, annual bonus plans if targets are met, stock options or membership interest options, and restricted ownership rights. Such incentive plans can be both a blessing and a curse. They provide a great way to align the interests of the employees directly with those of the owner, but managing them can also be time consuming and lead to feelings of inequity. Many small businesses do not possess pay-for-performance plans because they think they are too complicated and potentially more harmful than helpful.

Although the potential pitfalls of incentive systems in small businesses are great, the potential benefits are worth the risk. The key is to understand these risks and then to manage them. Below are some things small businesses can do to help administer incentive plans:

1. Keep incentive plans simple. The easier it is for employees to know how they can be rewarded, the more likely it is that they will buy into the incentive system.

2. Treat the plan as a "work in process." Small business owners need to be open with their employees by communicating that they are trying to reward them in a fair and equitable manner. Being open to feedback is key to continually improving the plan.

3. Set a minimum requirement around what constitutes average performance. Employees need to know that

only after the employee exceeds general expectations will the additional rewards begin to kick in. This first ensures that employees will feel less concerned about being able to maintain a baseline wage. Second, it shows that general performance only brings profits needed to sustain the company. Above and beyond this subsistence level, the owner can say, "Now we share in the profits." Finally, this also shows that high performance is highly rewarded and that if you do well for the company, then you do well for yourself.

4. Decide when the rewards will be provided to the employee. The closer you can tie incentives to performance, the more likely it is that you will be able to sustain that behaviour.

5. Separate rewards from employees' regular pay. When employees can see that they are being given something extra based on their performance, they make a clearer distinction between just showing up for work and contributing. It is also important to make sure that these bonuses are known by others in the organization as this helps motivate them.

6. Refine your measures and make sure employees are happy with them. Communicating with your employees is key to making sure incentive plans do not end up being scrapped the month after they are administered.

# SUMMARY

## SUMMARY

**OUTCOME 1** The success of an incentive pay plan depends on the organizational climate in which it must operate, employee confidence in it, and its suitability to employee and organizational needs. Importantly, employees must view their incentive pay as being equitable and related to their performance. Performance measures should be quantifiable, be easily understood, and bear a demonstrated relationship to organizational performance.

**OUTCOME 2** Piecework plans pay employees a given rate for each unit satisfactorily completed. Employers implement these plans

when output is easily measured and when the production process is fairly standardized. Bonuses are incentive payments above base wages paid on either an individual or a team basis. A bonus is offered to encourage employees to exert greater effort. Standard hour plans establish a standard time for job completion. An incentive is paid for finishing the job in less than the preestablished time. These plans are popular for jobs with a fixed time for completion.

**OUTCOME 3** Merit raises will not serve to motivate employees when they are seen as entitlements, which occurs when these raises are given yearly without regard to changes in employee performance. Merit raises are not motivational when they are given because of seniority or favouritism or when merit budgets are inadequate to sufficiently reward employee performance. To be motivational, merit raises must be such that employees see a clear relationship between pay and performance, and the salary increase must be large enough to exceed inflation and higher income taxes.

**OUTCOME 4** Salespeople may be compensated by a straight salary, a combination of salary and commission, salary plus bonus, or a commission only. Paying employees a straight salary allows them to focus on tasks other than sales, such as service and customer goodwill. A straight commission plan causes employees to emphasize sales goals. A combination of salary and commission or bonus provides the advantages of both the straight salary and the straight commission form of payments.

**OUTCOME 5** There are several types of team and group-level incentive plans, including the Scanlon and Improshare gainsharing plans. These plans encourage employees to maximize their performance and cooperation through suggestions offered to improve organizational performance.

**OUTCOME 6** Profit-sharing plans pay to employees sums of money based on the organization's profits. Cash payments are made to eligible employees at specified times, normally yearly. The primary purpose of profit sharing is to provide employees with additional income through their participation in organizational achievement. Employee commitment to improved productivity, quality, and customer service will contribute to organizational success and, in turn, to their compensation. Profit-sharing plans may not achieve their stated gains when employee performance is unrelated to organizational success or failure. This may occur because of economic conditions, other competition, or environmental conditions. Profit-sharing plans can have a negative effect on employee morale when plans fail to consistently reward employees.

**OUTCOME 7** With an ESOP, each year the organization contributes stock or cash to buy stock that is then placed in an ESOP trust. The ESOP holds the stock for organizational improvement. Employees, however, may lose their retirement income should the company fail or stock prices fall.

## KEY TERMS

bonus, 365
combined salary and commission plan, 369
differential piece rate, 363
employee stock ownership plans (ESOPs), 379
gainsharing plans, 376

lump-sum merit program, 366
merit guidelines, 366
perquisites, 373
profit sharing, 376
salary plus bonus plan, 370
spot bonus, 365
standard hour plan, 364

straight commission plan, 368
straight piecework, 363
straight salary plan, 368
team incentive plan, 374
variable pay, 360

## DISCUSSION QUESTIONS

1. Individual-level performance pay systems have been heavily criticized by scholars and other experts. Using merit pay as an example, discuss the pros and cons of individual performance pay systems.
2. Assume you are a consultant for a small fast-food retail outlet. What would be your suggestions for key steps in designing a successful incentive plan? Discuss a few recommendations you would suggest with respect to incentives for exceptional performance. Why?
3. CEO pay has been heavily criticized in North America, especially in the United States. Discuss

both *reasons for* and *reasons against* high executive pay.
4. Many students are attracted to companies that promote themselves as "green" or environmentally friendly. What kinds of incentives could a "green" company offer to its employees?
5. Because of competitive forces within your industry, you have decided to implement a profit-sharing plan for your employees. Discuss the advantages of profit sharing and identify specific characteristics that will ensure success for your plan.
6. What are some of the advantages and disadvantages of ESOPs?

# HRM EXPERIENCE

## Awarding Salary Increases

Because pay for performance is an important factor governing salary increases, managers must be able to defend the compensation recommendations they make for their employees. Merit raises granted under a pay-for-performance policy must be based on objective appraisals if they are to achieve their intended purposes of rewarding outstanding employee performance. As managers know, however, they must deal with other factors that can affect salary recommendations. These may include the opinions of the employee's peers or extenuating circumstances such as illness or family responsibilities. The purpose of this exercise is to provide you with the experience of granting salary increases to employees based on their work performance and other information.

## Assignment

Following are the work records of five employees. As their supervisor, you have just completed their annual appraisal reviews, and it is now time to make recommendations for their future salary. Your department budget has $5,780 allocated for salary increases. Distribute the $5,780 among your employees based on the descriptions for each subordinate.

a. Janet Jenkins currently earns $41,000. Her performance appraisal rating was very high. She is respected by her peers and is felt to be an asset to the work group. She is divorced and has three young children to support.

b. Russell Watts earns a salary of $36,000. His annual performance appraisal was average. Several members of the work group have spoken to you about the difficulty involved in Russell's job. They feel that it is a tough and demanding job and that he is doing his best.

c. Jack Perkins earns $31,250. His performance appraisal was below average, and he seems to have difficulty adjusting to his coworkers. Jack has had a difficult time this past year. His wife passed away early in the year, and his father has recently been diagnosed as terminally ill.

d. Rick Jacobson earns $28,000. His performance appraisal was above average. He is respected by his peers and is generally considered to be a "good guy."

e. Paula Merrill earns $28,850. Her performance appraisal was very high. Her peers are upset because they feel that she is working only to provide a second income to her household. Moreover, her peers see her as trying to "show them up."

Share your results with other class members. Be prepared to explain your allocation of money.

---

Visit the *Managing Human Resources* CourseMate website at http://www. belcourt7e.nelson.com for quizzes, flashcards, videos, games, and more!

---

## CASE STUDY 1

### EXECUTIVE COMPENSATION: THE CASE OF ONTARIO HOSPITAL EXECUTIVES

Ontario hospital executives are being criticized for their relatively high pay and lucrative perks. The perks include car allowances, free parking spots, and up to six weeks of paid vacation; they also receive a hefty annual salary, up to $100,000 per year in pension top-ups, and severance in excess of $1 million. This type of executive compensation is a hot topic being debated nationally, from Queen's Park, to union leaders, to activists, to employees, all of whom have, in general, voiced their disapproval of hospital executive pay. Andrea Horwath, leader of the NDP in Ontario, believes it is time to start being more careful with taxpayers' money, suggesting that hospital CEO salaries should be capped at $418,000, which is twice what Ontario's premier makes.

Case in point: In 2010, president and CEO of St. Michael's Hospital, Dr. Robert Howard, earned $450,000 a year, plus a 17 percent end-of-year supplement and a 5 percent pay-for-performance bonus. He also benefited from a $75,000 travel allowance to pay for a car, and all expenses (such as gas, car insurance, parking, maintenance) are covered by the hospital. In addition, Howard accepted an annual pension top-up of $100,000, which the hospital offered as an incentive for him to stay on as CEO. Mathew Anderson, president and CEO of the William Osler Health System (three hospitals in Etobicoke and Brampton), received a base annual salary of $445,000, with performance-related bonuses of up to $40,000 per year, alongside car and travel allowances.

The Ontario health care sector has been reeling under financial pressure, with nurses being let go, emergency wards being closed, and continuing longer wait times in the province's emergency rooms. Yet executive pay for some

hospital executives remains relatively high; apart from CEOs, other hospital executives make similar amounts. For example, the chief of staff at the William Osler Health System, Dr. Ian Smith, gets $325,000 base salary plus $1,475 per month for his vehicle and a $215,784 clinical guarantee, which is the additional amount he can make over and above his chief of staff duties.

## Questions

1. Are CEOs and key executives worth the large pay packages they receive? Explain.
2. Do you agree with Peter Drucker that corporate executives should receive compensation packages no larger than a percentage of the pay of hourly workers? Explain.
3. Do you think that executives in the broader public sector, such as hospital executives, should receive such large pay packages?

**Sources:** The Hay Group. *Performance-Based Compensation: Guidelines for Implementation*, Ontario Hospital Association, http://www.oha.com/CurrentIssues/Issues/Documents/Moshe_Greengarten_Presentation.pdf, retrieved February 9, 2011; Megan Ogilvie and Laura Stone, "Generous Perks Given to Ontario Hospital Executives, Contracts Reveal," *The Star.com*, January 4, 2012, http://www.thestar.com/news/article/1109999–generous-perks-given-to-ontario-hospital-executives-contracts-reveal.

## CASE STUDY 2

## TEAM-BASED INCENTIVE REWARDS: IT'S NOT ALL ROSES

Network Cable, Inc. is a service provider for cable TV and high-speed Internet connections. Network Cable operates in an area described as a "high-growth market."

In January 2003, Tara Gilbert, vice president of HR for Network Cable, convinced company president and CEO Jeff Lesitner that restructuring the organization workforce into teams would benefit both Network Cable and its employees. Cost savings, improved morale, and team synergy were cited as inherent benefits of teams. Based on these assessments, in June 2003, a select group of three senior managers, plus Tara Gilbert and the company's financial officer, implemented teams within the company's installation department. Here, 40 service installers were formed into eight teams of five installers each. Management set performance goals for the installation teams linked to attractive incentive rewards (cash bonuses above

base salaries) when performance goals were reached. Performance measures included indexes for improved installation time, customer satisfaction scores, additional sales, equipment maintenance, and repair/callback problems. Each team could earn incentive bonuses up to a maximum of $15,000 annually with cash bonuses shared equally by each team member—a possible cash reward of $3,000 for each installer. Team bonuses after the first year were as follows: two teams, $15,000; one team, $12,500; one team, $7,300; one team, $3,150.

During August 2008, Tara Gilbert sent to all installers and their supervisors a survey requesting feedback on the satisfaction with teams and, specifically, the incentive rewards program. Although the survey results were generally positive, not all was rosy. Problems could be grouped into the following categories:

1. Some installers believed that various team members did not "buy into" the team concept and were simply "free riders"—average

employees who benefited from the efforts of superior employees.

2. There was a general feeling that several teams were routinely assigned difficult installations that prevented them from achieving high-performance goals.

3. Teams did not always display the motivation and synergy expected because "bickering" was prevalent between average performers and super performers. Average performers complained that high performers made them look bad.

4. A high percentage of survey respondents (29 percent) felt the incentive rewards program was unfair and asked for a return to fixed across-the-board salary increases.

## Questions

1. Do the results from the survey illustrate typical complaints about teams and specifically about team incentive rewards? Explain.

2. If appropriate, what changes would you recommend to improve the incentive reward program? Be specific.

3. Would management have benefited from employee involvement in the initial design and implementation of the program? Explain.

## NOTES AND REFERENCES

1. Christine Bevilaqua and Parbudyal Singh, "Pay-for-Performance—Panacea or Pandora's Box? Revisiting an Old Debate in a New Economic Environment," *Compensation and Benefits Review* 41, no. 5 (2009): 20–26.

2. Patricia K. Zingheim and Jay R. Schuster, "Designing Pay and Rewards in Professional Service Companies," *Compensation and Benefits Review* 39, no. 1 (January/February 2007): 55.

3. John A. Menefee and Ryan O. Murphy, "Rewarding and Retaining the Best," *Benefits Quarterly* 20, no. 3 (Third Quarter 2004): 13–21.

4. Enno Siemsen, Sridhar Balasubramanian, and Aleda V. Roth, "Incentives That Induce Task-Related Effort, Helping, and Knowledge Sharing in Workgroups," *Management Science* 53, no. 10 (October 2007): 1533; Shahbaz Sheikh, "Do Compensation Incentives Affect Firm Innovation?" *Review of Accounting and Finance* 10, no. 1 (2012): 4–39.

5. Fay Hansen, "Control and Customization," *Workforce Management* 86, no. 19 (November 5, 2007): 42.

6. Corey Helm, Courtney L. Holladay, Frank R. Tortorella, and Christine Candio, "The Performance Management System: Applying and Evaluating a Pay-for-Performance Initiative," *Journal of Healthcare Management* 52, no. 1 (January/February 2007): 49.

7. Leo Jakobson, "All It's Quacked Up To Be," *Incentive* 181, no. 9 (September 2007): 24.

8. Bevilaqua and Singh, "Pay-for-Performance—Panacea or Pandora's Box?"

9. Ann Pomeroy, "Business Strategy, Not Just HR Strategy," *HR Magazine* 52, no. 11 (November 2007): 46.

10. Jim McCoy, "How to Align Employee Performance with Business Strategy," *Workforce Management* 86, no. 12 (June 27, 2007): 55.

11. George T. Milkovich and Jerry M. Newman, *Compensation*, 10th ed. (Boston: McGraw-Hill Irwin, 2010).

12. Patty Kujawa, "Private Firms Recognize Value of Cash Bonuses," *Workforce Management* 86, no. 21 (December 10, 2007): 11.

13. Brett Philbin, "Wall Street Bonuses Shrink," *Wall Street Journal* (March 2012), http://online.wsj.com/article/SB10001424052970203986604577253111846696908.html, retrieved July 2012.

14. Chris Taylor, "On-the-Spot Incentives," *HR Magazine* 49, no. 5 (May 2004): 80–84.

15. Don Hellriegel and John W. Slocum, Jr., *Organizational Behavior*, 12th ed. (Mason, OH: South-Western, 2009), Chapter 6.

16. Debra L. Nelson and James Campbell Quick, *Organizational Behavior: Science, The Real World, and You*, 6th ed. (Mason, OH: South-Western, 2009).

17. Employee perceptions of appropriate pay raises likely depend on the employer's ability to pay and the economics of the period. For example, when it is known that an employer's ability to pay is great and the economics of the industry are strong, then employees will expect larger percentage merit raises.

18. Susan J. Wells, "No Results, No Raise," *HR Magazine* 50, no. 5 (May 2005): 76.

19. Stephen Bernard, "Why His Merit Raise Is Bigger than Hers," *Harvard Business Review* 90, no. 4 (April 2012): 26.

20. David E. Terpstra and Andre L. Honoree, "Employees Responses to Merit Pay Inequity," *Compensation and Benefits Review* 37, no. 1 (January/February 2005): 51.

21. Tyler Gentry, "Re-engineering Recognition," *Workspan* (February 2007): 47; Ray Saunderson, "How to Get Your Recognition Strategy Right," *Workspan* (May 2011): 66–71.

22. Alison Avalos, "Recognition: A Critical Component of the Total Reward Mix," *Workspan* (July 2007): 33. See also Scott Dow, Tom McMullen, Richard S. Sperling, and Bill Bowbin, "Reward Programs: What Works and What Needs to be Improved," *WorldatWork* 16, no. 3 (Third Quarter 2007): 6.

23. Charlotte Garvey, "Meaningful Tokens of Appreciation," *HR Magazine* 49, no. 9 (August 2004): 102.

24. Michele Marchetti, "Rethinking Compensation Plans," *Sales and Marketing Management* 159, no. 7 (September 2007): 14.

25. Paul R. Dorf and Lisette F. Masur, "The Tough Economy Prompts Companies to Shift Their Approach to Sales Compensation," *Journal of Organizational Excellence* 23, no. 2 (Spring 2004): 35–42.

26. Joseph Dimisa, "How to Sell Your Sales Compensation Plan," *Workspan* (December 2007): 25.

27. Jim Stockmann, "Change on the Horizon: An Analysis of Sales Compensation Practices," *Workspan* (April 2007): 41.

28. Donald L. Caruth and Gail D. Handloggten-Caruth, "The Formula for Compensating Sales Personnel," *The American Salesman* 51, no. 4 (April 2006): 6.

29. Mark Reilly and Brian Enright, "A New Approach to Executive Compensation," *Workspan* (August 2007): 45; Parbudyal Singh, "Executive Compensation: Examining an Old Issue from a New Perspective," *Compensation and Benefits Review* (March/April 2003): 48–54.

30. Total annual compensation is the sum of an executive's annual and long-term compensation. Annual compensation consists of salary, bonus, and other yearly pay. Long-term compensation consists of stock awards, the value of any stock options exercised during the year, and any other long-term compensation (such as payouts from long-term incentive plans, director's fees, and special bonuses).

31. Edward E. Lawler III and David Finegold, "CEO Compensation: What Board Members Think," *WorldatWork* 16, no. 3 (Third Quarter 2007): 38.

32. Brandon Cherry, "Executive Bonus Plans: Recent Trends in Equity Compensation," *Workspan* (January 2007): 22.

33. Darrell Rigby and Barbara Bilodeau, "Selecting Management Tools Wisely," *Harvard Business Review* 85, no. 12 (December 2007): 20.

34. Brad Hill and Christine Tande, "What's Next for Executive Incentives Now That Options Are Limited?" *Workspan* (September 2007): 47.

35. "Richest CEOs earn 189 times average Canadian," *CBC News*, January 3, 2012, http://www.cbc.ca/news /canada/story/2012/01/03/business-ceo-pay.html; Dana Flavelle, "Highest-Paid Canadian CEOs Got 27 Per Cent Pay Hike," January 2, 2012, http://www.thestar.com/business/article/1109514 -highest-paid-canadian-ceos-got-27-per-cent -pay-hike.

36. Peter Burrows, "He's Making Hay as CEOs Squirm," *Business Week*, January 15, 2007, 64. See also John Morrisy, "Firms Move Away from Stock Options; Move to Bonuses," *National Post*, September 18, 2009, 4.

37. Pam Delaney, "Filling the Executive Benefits Gap," *Workspan* (November 2007): 69.

38. "An Unfair Rap for CEO Perks?" *BusinessWeek*, June 7, 2004, 32.

39. Scott DeCarlo, "Gravity-Defying CEO Pay," *Forbes*, April 4, 2012, http://www.forbes.com/lists/2012/12 /ceo-compensation-12_land.html.

40. John A. Byrne, "The Man Who Invented Management: Why Peter Drucker's Ideas Still Matter," *BusinessWeek*, November 2004, 97.

41. Steven N. Kaplan, "Are CEOs Overpaid?" *WorldatWork* 16, no. 3 (Third Quarter 2007): 22. See also Ira Kay and Steve Van Putten, *Myths and Realities of Executive Pay* (Cambridge, MA: Cambridge University Press, 2007); Jessica Marquez, "5 Questions: In Defense of CEO Pay," *Workforce Management* 86, no. 16 (September 27, 2007): 8.

42. Lawler and Finegold, "CEO Compensation," 112.

43. "A New Kind of Outrage; Shareholder Activism and the Banks," *The Economist* 403 (May 5, 2012): 70.

44. Milkovich and Newman, *Compensation*.

45. Jason Kovac, "Stock Options," *Workspan* (August 2006): 23. See also Seymour Burchman and Blair

Jones, "The Future of Stock Options: From Starring Role to Ensemble Player," *WorldatWork* 13, no. 1 (First Quarter 2004): 29–38.

46. Ira T. Kay and Steve Seelig, "Revising the Use of a Management Stock Purchase Plan to Increase Management Ownership," *Journal of Deferred Compensation* 11, no. 3 (Spring 2006): 24; Samita Sawardekar, "Stock Options, or Not?" *Wall Street Journal*, May 13, 2011, http://online.wsj.com/article /SB10001424052748703864204576320742618109046. html, retrieved July 2012.

47. Raquel Meyer Alexander, Mark Hirchey, and Susan Scholz, "Backdating Employee Stock Options: Tax Implications," *The CPA Journal* 77, no. 10 (October 2007): 24. See also T. Thomas Cottingham III, "The Stock Options Backdating Scandal: Critical First Response," *Risk Management* 54, no. 6 (June 2007): 12.

# 11

# Employee Benefits

## After studying this chapter, you should be able to

| OUTCOME 1 | Describe key aspects of managing employee benefits and the characteristics of an effective benefits program. |

| OUTCOME 2 | Indicate management concerns about the costs of employee benefits and discuss ways to control those costs. |

| OUTCOME 3 | Identify and explain the employee benefits required by law. |

| OUTCOME 4 | Discuss ways to control the costs of health care programs. |

| OUTCOME 5 | Describe benefits that involve payment for time not worked. |

| OUTCOME 6 | Discuss recent trends in retirement policies and programs. |

| OUTCOME 7 | Indicate the major factors involved in managing pension plans. |

| OUTCOME 8 | Describe the types of work–life benefits employers can provide. |

Canadian firms are becoming increasingly innovative in the types of benefits and work–life balance opportunities they offer to employees. At GlaxoSmithKline Inc., a Mississauga, Ontario–based pharmaceutical company, the benefits include free yoga and cycling classes, access to a nutritionist, and healthy food choices offered by the firm's cafeteria and even in the snack bowls offered during meetings. Cisco Canada uses technology to cut commuting and travel time to improve work–life balance. Its TelePresence technology connects boardrooms across the globe via high-definition screens.[1] Conexus, a small credit union in southern Saskatchewan, offers full medical insurance, a pension plan with matched contributions, and 72 hours per year of flextime (called "your time"), on top of regular vacation time, which employees can use to do whatever they want.[2] Cool stuff by employers—and great results in employee loyalty and productivity.

Employers have several reasons for offering benefits to employees, including attracting and retaining top talent, as well as improving the firm's bottom line. Great benefits are also helping organizations brand themselves as "best employers" and "great places to work."[3] However, compensation surveys indicate that most employees are unable to name accurately the benefits they receive, and about 50 percent of employees underestimate the value of their benefits.[4] Although benefits are largely undervalued and misidentified, they are still an important issue for both employers and employees. It is clear that benefits are not a "fringe" but rather an integral part of the compensation package. Additionally, because most benefits are provided voluntarily by employers, they become a significant cost and an employment advantage

Thinkstock

for employers, while providing needed psychological and physical assistance to employees. The importance of benefits to both sides cannot be overstated.

Virtually all employers provide a variety of benefits to supplement the wages or salaries they pay their workers. These benefits, some of which are required by law, must be considered part of total compensation. Therefore, in this chapter, we look at the characteristics of employee benefits programs. We will study the types of benefits required by law, the major discretionary benefits that employers offer, the employee services they provide, and the retirement programs in use. The chapter concludes with a discussion of popular and highly important work–life benefit programs.

## MANAGING EMPLOYEE BENEFITS PROGRAMS

**OUTCOME 1**

Employee benefits constitute an indirect form of compensation intended to improve the quality of the work lives and personal lives of employees. Benefits constitute a significant percentage of total payroll costs. In Canada, the figures range from 20 to 25 percent of payroll costs; however, they are higher in the United States, about 30 to 35 percent.[5] The difference is largely attributed to the fact that Canadian firms do not have to provide some basic health benefits as these are provided by various governments. In return, employers generally expect employees to be supportive of the organization. Since employees have come to expect an increasing number of benefits, the value of these benefits depends on how the benefits program is designed and communicated. Once viewed as a gift from the employer, benefits are now considered rights to which all employees are entitled.

## REQUIREMENTS FOR AN EFFECTIVE BENEFITS PROGRAM

**Using the Internet**

A broad view of benefits in Canada can be found at
**http://www.benefitscanada.ca**

The effectiveness of a benefits program hinges on two factors: (1) selecting benefits that target important employee needs while promoting strategic organizational objectives and (2) effective administration of benefits programs. Gone are the days of providing a particular benefit because other employers are doing it, because someone in authority believes it is a good idea, or because the benefit is "popular" at the moment. Therefore, benefit specialists recommend paying attention to certain basic considerations.

### Strategic Benefits Planning

Like any other component of the HR program, an employee benefits program should be based on specific objectives. The objectives an organization establishes will depend on many factors, including the size of the firm, its location, its degree of unionization, its profitability, and industry patterns. Most important, these aims must be compatible with the organization's strategy and the strategic compensation plan (see Chapter 9), including its philosophy and policies. The chief objectives of most benefits programs are to

- Improve employee work satisfaction
- Meet employee health and security requirements
- Attract and motivate employees
- Retain top-performing employees
- Maintain a favourable competitive position

In a 2009 survey of employees, about half stated that a good benefits plan would make them stay with their current employer and would prefer their health benefits over increased compensation.[6] Another survey found that 4 out of 10 employers use wellness programs and subsidized fitness programs as a retention strategy.[7] Furthermore, these objectives must be considered within the framework of cost containment—a major issue in today's programs.

Unless the organization plans to develop a flexible benefits plan (to be discussed later), a uniform package of benefits should be developed. This involves carefully considering the various benefits that can be offered, the relative preference shown for each benefit by management and the employees, the estimated cost of each benefit, and the total amount of money available for the entire benefits package.

## Allowing for Employee Involvement

Before a new benefit is introduced, the need for it should first be established. Many organizations create committees composed of managers and employees to administer, interpret, and oversee their benefits policies. Opinion surveys are also used to obtain employee input. Having employees participate in designing benefits programs helps ensure that management is moving in the direction of satisfying employee wants. Monsanto Canada reviews its benefits each year through biannual and quarterly "pulse" surveys of different segments of the workforce; this has helped the firm be ranked as one of Canada's Top Family-Friendly Employers.[8]

## Benefits for a Diverse Workforce

To serve their intended purpose, employee benefits programs must reflect the social changes that Canada is constantly facing. Particularly significant are changes in the diversity and lifestyles of the workforce; the changes make it necessary to develop new types of benefits to meet shifting needs. Therefore, more employers are tailoring their benefits programs to be family friendly. (Specific family-friendly benefits are discussed later in the chapter.) For example, as we have indicated throughout this book, the number of women in the workforce is continuing to grow. Which benefits are most valuable to them (and to men) will be determined largely by whether they have dependent children and whether they have a spouse who has benefits coverage.

Unfortunately, benefits plans sometimes provide little advantage to employees, limiting the organization's ability to attract and retain quality employees. For example, many employers provide unneeded medical benefits to those who are young and single and without dependants in the form of dependants' coverage. Likewise, a well-designed—and costly—defined-benefits pension program may not serve the needs of employees or the employer of a predominantly younger workforce. Similarly, the employer's contribution to the pension plan for a 30-year-old employee is roughly one-quarter the contribution for a 50-year-old employee for the same amount of pension commencing at age 65. This difference in funds spent on older workers in effect discriminates against younger workers, although in legal terms, it is not regarded as discriminatory.

## Providing for Flexibility

To accommodate the individual needs of employees, many organizations are embracing **flexible benefits plans**, also known as cafeteria plans. When Zabeen Hirji, senior vice president of HR for RBC, surveyed 16,000 of the bank's 65,000 employees about their benefits preferences, the number one request was for flexibility.[9] These plans enable individual employees to choose the benefits that are best suited to their particular needs. They also prevent certain benefits from being wasted on employees who have no need for them. Typically, employees are offered a basic or core benefits package of life and health insurance, sick leave, and vacation. Requiring a core set of benefits ensures that employees have a minimum level of coverage to protect against unforeseen financial hardships. Employees are then given a specified number of credits that they may use to "buy" whatever other benefits they need. Other benefits options might include prepaid legal services, financial planning, or long-term care insurance.[10] Compensation specialists often see flexible benefits plans as ideal. Employees select the benefits of greatest value to them, whereas employers manage benefits costs by limiting the dollars employees have to spend.

**flexible benefits plans (cafeteria plans)**
Benefits plans that enable individual employees to choose the benefits that are best suited to their particular needs

**FIGURE 11.1**

FLEXIBLE BENEFITS PLANS: ADVANTAGES AND DISADVANTAGES

**Advantages**

- Employees select benefits to match their individual needs.
- Benefit selections adapt to a constantly changing (diversified) workforce.
- Employees gain greater understanding of the benefits offered to them and the costs incurred.
- Employers maximize the psychological value of their benefits program by paying only for the highly desired benefits.
- Employers limit benefit costs by allowing employees to "buy" benefits only up to a maximum (defined) amount.

- Employers gain competitive advantage in the recruiting and retention of employees.

**Disadvantages**

- Poor employee benefits selection results in unwanted financial costs.
- There are certain added costs to establishing and maintaining the flexible plan.
- Employees may choose benefits of high use to them that might increase employer premium costs.

Honeywell Canada considered three types of flexible benefits programs: cafeteria style, whereby employees could choose any benefits they wanted; a module approach, whereby employees could select among prepackaged sets of benefits; and a core-plus-options plan, whereby employees could choose among options to augment a basic level of protection. Employees were able to select health and dental benefits that suited their life stages and that matched well with the plans their spouses had. Figure 11.1 lists the most commonly cited advantages and disadvantages of flexible benefits programs.

Because cafeteria plans increase the complexity of administering the entire benefits program, organizations may elect to outsource the handling of this function to a professional benefits vendor. About one-third of Canadian firms rely on third parties to perform these types of transactional services for their plans.[11] Paying a service or contract fee to these firms may be particularly cost effective for the smaller employer. Furthermore, benefits programs must be flexible enough to accommodate the constant flow of new laws and regulations that affect them. A number of consulting firms specializing in benefits can help managers track changes in all phases of the programs they oversee.

## COMMUNICATING EMPLOYEE BENEFITS INFORMATION

Many employees do not believe what their employers tell them about soaring benefits' costs, and employees and employers are at loggerheads over how effectively benefits are used. Therefore, it becomes critical that organizations effectively—and frequently—communicate the benefits package to employees. Court cases in Canada have established that it is the employer's responsibility to properly inform and disclose information about benefits. In *Spinks v. Canada*, an employee was not advised of certain pension options when he started with a new employer—specifically, that he was eligible to purchase past service in connection with his previous employment. The Federal Court of Appeal ruled that the employee had been poorly advised. In other cases, such as *Schmidt v. Air Products of Canada*, the courts have ruled that employee brochures, which usually are not considered legal documents, may be legally binding.[12]

Although it is important to communicate information about employee benefits, there is no legislation that mandates how this is to be done. Various provincial pension benefits acts and federal laws regulating pension benefits state that employers operating a pension plan must provide specific information to employees. However, there are differences among provinces about what must be communicated. The sponsor of a registered retirement plan (RPP) has until six months after the end of the plan's fiscal year to provide active plan members with statements of their pension benefits. (Quebec regulations require annual pension statements for retired and deferred vested members.) The employee's name, date of birth, and date of hire must be included in the pension statement, along with the pension plan membership date, vesting date, and normal retirement date. Most provinces also require the name of the employee's spouse and/or pension plan beneficiary.[13]

Employers use a number of methods to communicate benefits to employees, such as the following:

- In-house publications (employee handbooks and organizational newsletters)
- Group meeting and training classes
- Online modules
- Bulletin boards
- Payroll inserts/pay stub messages
- Specialty brochures

Also, the topic is usually covered in new-hire orientation programs. Managers who are conducting orientations should be allowed plenty of time to inform new employees of the benefits program and to answer any questions. The Calgary Health Region solved the problem of communicating benefits to thousands of workers in 115 locations who did not have ready access to computers by providing free-standing interactive information kiosks in more than 100 high-traffic areas. Using a touch-screen display, employees can access email, websites, and personal information.[14] Highlights in HRM 11.1 provides a list of recommendations for communicating benefits.

Employee self-service systems have made it possible for employees to gather information about their benefits plans, enroll in their plans of choice, change their benefits coverage, or simply inquire about the status of their various benefits accounts without ever contacting an HR representative. Coopers & Lybrand uses a benefits information line to provide its employees with instant access to a wide variety of HR and benefits information by telephone. Employees can access

# HIGHLIGHTS IN HRM 11.1

## Crafting an Effective Benefits Communication Program

A well-designed benefits communication program will greatly enhance employees' appreciation of their benefits while ensuring that employers receive the intended value of these offerings. An effective program provides information to employees frequently and in a timely and cost-effective manner. Compensation specialists recommend the following when administering a benefits communication program.

### In Building an Identity:

- Design materials that are eye-catching and of high interest to employees.
- Develop a graphic logo for all material.
- Identify a theme for the benefits program.

### In Writing Benefits Materials:

- Avoid complex language when describing benefits. Clear, concise, and understandable language is a must.

- Provide numerous examples to illustrate benefits specifics.
- Explain all benefits in an open and honest manner. Do not attempt to conceal unpleasant news.
- Explain the purpose behind the benefit and the value of the benefit to employees.

### In Publicizing Benefits Information:

- Use all popular employee communication techniques.
- Maintain employee self-service (ESS) technology to disseminate benefits information and to update employee benefits selections.
- Use voice mail to send benefits information.
- Employ presentation software to present information to groups of employees.
- Maintain a benefits hot line to answer employee questions.

Employees can access their benefit plans online.

© Blue Jean Images/Alamy

their individual account information by entering a personal identification number (PIN). Other organizations use networked PCs or multimedia kiosks for the same purpose. These latter approaches enable employees to click on icons to access different benefits and to type in new information to update their records. Once an update or change has been made, the new information is permanently entered into the organization's human resources information system (HRIS) without the need for paperwork.

It is also important for each employee to have a current statement of the status of her or his benefits. The usual means is a personalized computer-generated statement, as illustrated in Figure 11.2

As the field of benefits becomes increasingly complex, and as employees become more sophisticated about financial planning, the need to hire and train benefits experts also grows. For those interested in specializing in this field, a good career move would be to become a certified employee benefit specialist (CEBS).

## HRIS AND EMPLOYEE BENEFITS

The benefits of an HRIS are reduced costs, increased efficiencies, and accuracy.[15] Online benefits programs create a form of self-service administration. One intent of online programs is to eliminate the annual open enrollment period for various benefits, thereby providing greater flexibility in benefits selection. An important advantage to an interactive benefits program is the significant savings in administration costs. Once an online system is operational, it is easy and inexpensive to adapt to employer and employee demands. However, although the Internet can be used effectively in benefits administration, security must always be a concern when transmitting benefits information.[16]

Perhaps no part of the HR function is more technologically advanced than benefits administration. A wide variety of commercially developed software packages have been developed that serve to facilitate benefits administration in areas such as pensions, variable pay, workers' compensation, health benefits, and time-off programs. Descriptions of and advertisements for a variety of benefits software programs are regularly found in HR journals such as *Canadian HR Reporter and Human Resource Professional*. Software programs represent a cost-effective way to manage employee benefits programs when employers lack the resources or expertise.

## FIGURE 11.2

COMMUNICATING BENEFITS AS PART OF TOTAL REWARDS

This statement summarizes the scope and value of your total rewards package at ABC. It was prepared with data current as of December 31, 2012, and it includes your 2013 benefit elections. We encourage you to review this statement carefully and to share it with your family.

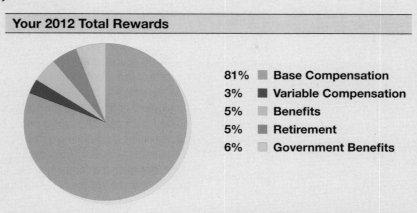

**Your 2012 Total Rewards**

| | | |
|---|---|---|
| 81% | ■ | Base Compensation |
| 3% | ■ | Variable Compensation |
| 5% | ■ | Benefits |
| 5% | ■ | Retirement |
| 6% | ■ | Government Benefits |

| | ABC Pays | You Pay |
|---|---|---|
| Base compensation | $49,000 | — |
| Variable compensation | $ 1,500 | — |
| • Long-term incentive plan | $ 0 | — |
| • Other bonus/incentive plan | $ 1,500 | — |
| Benefits | $ 2,954 | $ 1,412 |
| • Health and dental plans | $ 1,797 | $ 576 |
| • Flexible spending account | — | $ 500 |
| • Long-term disability plan | $ 346 | — |
| • Basic life/AD&D insurance | $ 201 | — |
| • Optional life/AD&D insurance | — | $ 183 |
| • Optional dependant life insurance | — | $ 153 |
| • Other benefits | $ 610 | — |
| Retirement | $ 2,944 | $ 998 |
| • Pension plan | $ 2,495 | — |
| • Savings plan | $ 499 | $ 998 |
| Government benefits | $ 3,808 | $ 2,620 |
| Your 2012 Total Rewards | $60,256 | |

**Source:** Made available with permission from Mercer (Canada) Limited, with adaptations. Copyright 2012. (http://www.mercer.ca)

# CONCERNS OF MANAGEMENT

| OUTCOME 2 |

Managing an employee benefits program requires close attention to the many forces that must be kept in balance if the program is to succeed. Management must consider union demands, the benefits other employers are offering, tax consequences, and rising costs, which are discussed in the Business Case.

The escalating cost of health care benefits is a concern to employers, who must strike an appropriate balance between offering quality benefits and keeping costs under control. The shift in benefit planning from entitlement to self-responsibility is discussed in the Reality Check.

PART 4

# THE BUSINESS CASE

## Managing the Costs of Benefits: Klohn Crippen Berger (KCB)

The rising costs of benefits continue to pose a problem for organizations big and small. These costs reportedly range anywhere from 14 to 50 percent of payroll when voluntary benefits are accounted for. Hewitt Associates reports that flexible benefit plans are gaining momentum in Canada as not only do they help contain the costs of benefits, they are also instrumental in meeting the needs of Canada's diverse employee population and move benefits away from the one-size-fits-all paradigm. Moreover, companies that have used flex plans to date have reported much success in managing benefits costs in their organizations.

A Vancouver-based international engineering and environmental group, Klohn Crippen Berger (KCB), recently revamped its traditional benefits program and will begin offering flexible benefits to its 350-plus employees as of March 1, 2012. Director of HR at KCB, Sharon Batchelor, believes that this flex program will be instrumental not only in capturing talented employees but also in retaining them. KCB has ensured that the plan is as close as possible to traditional benefits, with a massive change in the cost sharing from 60 percent to 35 percent employee paid. KCB educated employees at all levels about the benefits of this program and put in place "flex champions" and "benefits 101" to promote the program and secure employee buy-in. To ease the administrative burden for both HR staff and employees, plan enrollment was conducted online. KCB offered a free pizza lunch to the first division that achieved 100% enrollment and put count-down clocks on the company's intranet. These initiatives helped raise awareness of the new flex plan and led to a full enrollment when the program went live. A recent company survey revealed a 70 percent employee satisfaction rate with the flex plan.

Flex arrangements can benefit rapidly growing organizations as they can be easily adapted to organizational changes. And as the KCB example shows, clear focus and ongoing communication with employees can make the shift to flexible benefit plans nearly seamless.

Sources: Gloria Gonzalez, "Canadian Firms Seek to Stem Rising Costs of Benefits," *Business Insurance*, March 22, 2004, 3; D. Brown, "Runaway Drug Costs Make Benefit Upgrades Impractical," *Canadian HR Reporter* 16, no. 12 (June 16, 2003): 2; S. Felix, "Gimme Gimme," *Benefits Canada* 24, no. 7 (July 2000): 20–21.

# REALITY CHECK

## Benefits Planning: From Entitlement to Self-Responsibility

In recent years, we have witnessed major upheavals in the area of benefits. Never before have there been such large increases in the cost of providing benefits as senior executives in companies throughout Canada try to change the "entitlement mindset" so prevalent in employees. HR professionals and senior executives can no longer make decisions regarding benefits plans without the assistance of benefits consultants. We met with Daphne Woolf, senior vice president of Aon-Hewitt, a global HR consulting and outsourcing firm, to discuss trends in benefit coverage. Among other HR areas, Woolf specializes in the design and implementation of flexible benefits plans, strategic planning as it relates to compensation and benefits, and the design and monitoring of programs for promoting workplace health.

"First of all, we need to look at the drivers of change. We see five things happening: our demographics are changing as people age; we have double-income families; the workplace is becoming increasingly diverse; benefits are being taxed to greater extents; and human rights legislation is changing with respect to who should be covered. Due to the high costs of providing benefit coverage, we are seeing a shift in responsibility from the provinces to third parties and individuals. The provinces are covering less, and this trend will continue to grow. The final, most important, underlying issue is increased sensitivity to the magnitude of these trends and the resulting benefit cost impacts.

"The entitlement mindset stems from the fact that, 15 years ago, benefits were considered fringe. Now they are viewed as part of total compensation, which is a change in mentality. Employers are starting to move away from this entitlement mindset to self-responsibility. Employees are not used to making their own health care decisions, and it is a challenge for employers to educate their employees sufficiently and sway them to a different way of thinking. As the population ages, employees' needs for benefits are increasing; at the same time, the quality of their benefits must decrease in response to the high costs. Based on some of our studies, what we are seeing for the first time is that employees are making employment decisions based on benefits. Employers look at dealing with these benefit trends by revisiting their philosophy and benefits objectives. For example, does an employer pay for smoking cessation, include high deductibles, offer choice, or provide coverage for dependents?

"We are seeing an increase in flexible benefit plans. My belief is that in five years the majority of plans will be flexible, and an employer who waits may be disadvantaged. Employers are better off as flex leaders than flex followers. You want to create your own plan, not have to base your program design on what someone else has done. Now you can 'anti-select' the benefit costs of the spouse's plan, allowing your employee to 'cash out' or allocate flex credits to stock plans or an RRSP [registered retirement savings plan]. In the future, however, employees and their dependents may not opt out of your plan, and this would potentially increase your costs. So going flex sooner than later, if it's in keeping with corporate objectives, makes sense for many employers who have employees with spouses who work elsewhere.

"There is an increase in health promotion. We are talking about wellness programs, which may focus on stress reduction, fitness in the workplace, and smoking-cessation programs. Employers are seeing the value in keeping employees healthy and productive, that is, preventing the claims costs. Employers can yield a favourable return on investment if they ensure the right steps are taken to implement health promotion to secure effective cost containment. We are also diverging from traditional medicine to naturopathy and other paramedic services."

"In the future, flexible benefit plans will be the plan of choice so that educating the employee will be paramount if we are to move from an entitlement mindset to self-responsibility. Your plan should be devised considering an overall philosophy with particular attention to the strategic plan of your organization. Benefits can no longer be taken for granted as the costs of providing this commodity are at a premium. What constitutes benefits must be expanded beyond the basic dental, life insurance, and drug plans. Benefits strategies cannot be short term but rather must be long range, and in this regard, benefit consultants can provide value-added advice. Selecting the right consultant to work with you is just as important as determining your overall benefits philosophy. This philosophy is key to the design of your program as it sets the stage for what your benefit plan will entail."

About 20 percent of employers are choosing at least one of these methods to control costs. Lafarge Canada is one of those employers trying to contain the costs of benefits for its 8,000 employees, which have been rising at 6 to 10 percent per year. The organization's goal is to keep the escalation in costs at the annual rate of inflation. Air Canada is requiring its employees to pay 30 percent of the costs of the benefits.[18] All employers should try to uncover instances of fraudulent claims, as discussed in Ethics in HRM.

# ETHICS IN HRM

## Benefits Fraud

Benefits fraud has been crippling organizations across North America in both the private and public spheres. The National Health Care Anti-Fraud Association (NHCAA) reports that between 2 and 10 percent of annual health care cost, representing between $3.2 and $16 billion, is lost to fraudulent activities each year, and this amount is increasing at an alarming rate. In the same vein, Service Canada reports that "[employment insurance (EI)] fraud threatens the effective operation of one of Canada's most important social programs. Our investigations reveal that fraudulent claims result in approximately $142 million in EI overpayments each year." Although only a few employees submit falsified benefit claims, given the magnitude of health and dental claims ($15 billion) paid out by group providers, even a 1 percent falsification amounts to considerable cost to plan sponsors and can be quite damaging. According to this antifraud association, the most common type of frauds are malingering (exaggerating illnesses or injuries to collect additional disability benefits, doctor shopping), collecting multiple prescriptions, misrepresenting dependents (making claims for children who are no longer dependent or not coordinating spousal plans), and submitting false claims.

## Case in Point

Reports indicate that six ramp workers at Pearson International Airport were arrested

*continued*

for a series of fraudulent benefits claims against Air Canada, which were successfully paid out to employees. Corporate security at Air Canada alerted the police, and investigation into the case revealed $126,000 in counterfeit benefits claims. To combat fraud, organizations should consider implementing whistle-blowing policies, continue to educate their employees about the costs of fraudulent activities, establish a code of ethical conduct for employees and work with providers to ensure that fraud detection mechanisms are in place.

Sources: Peer to Peer: Challenges for Trustees—Identity Theft and Fraud. *Benefits & Compensation Digest*, May 2010, 47(5), 24–25; http://www.servicecanada.gc.ca/eng/ei/fraud/fraud_serious.shtml; Robert M. Nicholas, (2005). Health and Dental Benefits Fraud: The Bottom Line. *Benefits & Compensation Digest*, 42 (12), 18–21; S. Maxwell, "Fraud Squad," *Benefits Canada* vol. 32, Iss. 10 (2008): 25; Bob Mitchell. Air Canada workers charged with benefits fraud; *Thestar.com*, Feb 3, 2011

The Conference Board of Canada has published a list of cost containment strategies, which include the following:

- Contribution changes, such as increasing deductibles
- Dollar limits, such as a dollar cap on specific benefits, such as eyeglasses
- Coverage changes (e.g., limits on hospital upgrades)
- Benefit caps (e.g., on dispensing fees)
- Use of preferred providers and flexible benefits[17]

## EMPLOYEE BENEFITS REQUIRED BY LAW

**OUTCOME 3**

Legally required employee benefits amount to 12 percent of the benefits packages that Canadian employers provide.[19] These benefits include employer contributions to the Canada and Quebec pension plans, employment insurance, workers' compensation insurance, and, in some provinces, provincial medicare.

### CANADA AND QUEBEC PENSION PLANS (CPP/QPP)

The Canada and Quebec pension plans cover almost all Canadian employees between the ages of 18 and 70. (Certain migratory and casual workers who earn less than the specified amount may be excluded.) To receive a retirement benefit, an individual must apply to Human Resources and Social Development Canada at least six months in advance of retirement.

Although similar in concept, CPP and QPP differ in how much they pay out to participants. Both plans require employers to match the contributions made by employees. The revenues generated by these contributions are used to pay three main types of benefits: retirement pensions, disability benefits, and survivors' benefits. Governments do not subsidize these plans; all contributions come from employers and employees. Self-employed individuals can also contribute to the plan. With Canada's population aging, the funds from CPP will not be able to meet the needs of retirees unless those currently working, and their employers, significantly increase their contributions.

Canada has cross-border agreements with several countries to protect the acquired social security rights of people who have worked and lived in both countries and who meet the minimum qualifications for benefits from either country. A contributor's rights to benefits under CPP or QPP are not affected or impaired in any way by a change in employment or residence in Canada. All Canadian workers have "universal portability," that is, the right to claim benefit credits wherever they are employed in Canada.

### EMPLOYMENT INSURANCE (EI)

Employment insurance (EI) benefits are payable to claimants who are unemployed and are actively seeking employment. A person who becomes unemployed is usually entitled to what most Canadians still call "unemployment insurance" (or UI), the former name of this program. The new name reflects a change in focus from basic income support to active employment measures.[20]

The amount of benefit paid is determined by the number of hours of employment in the past year and the regional unemployment rate. Individuals are entitled to unemployment insurance after they have contributed enough for a qualifying period and after a waiting period. The waiting period may vary with the individual's situation. Also, employees who resign from their jobs or who are terminated for cause may be ineligible for benefits unless they can prove there was no reasonable alternative to leaving their jobs. Just causes include sexual harassment, health concerns, and moving to another town or city because of a spouse's reassignment.

Additional benefits may be extended for situations involving illness, injury, or quarantine or for maternity, parental, or adoption leave. If an organization does not offer sick leave benefits, the employee may have to apply to EI for sick benefits. The benefit amount, which is calculated on the same basis as the regular benefit, varies across jurisdictions. Sickness or disability benefits are available for up to 15 weeks. A combination of maternity, parental, or adoptive benefits may be available up to a cumulative maximum of one year in some provinces.

Employees and employers both contribute to the EI fund, and there are numerous types of EI plans. For details on these, see http://www.servicecanada.gc.ca/eng/sc/ei/.

## WORKERS' COMPENSATION INSURANCE

**Workers' compensation insurance** is based on the theory that compensation for work-related accidents and illnesses should be considered one of the costs of doing business and should ultimately be passed on to the consumer. Individual employees should not be required to bear the cost of their treatment or loss of income; nor should they be subjected to complicated, delaying, and expensive legal procedures.

Workers' compensation is a form of insurance. It was created by an act of Parliament to help workers injured on the job return to the workplace. Each provincial and territorial board is empowered by the relevant legislation to amend and collect assessments (i.e., insurance premiums), to determine the right to compensation, and to pay the amount due to the injured worker. This system of collective liability is compulsory. Employers' contributions are assessed as a percentage of their payroll. The percentage varies with the nature of the industry. For example, in a high-risk industry such as mining, the assessment rates are higher than in knowledge-based industries.

Workers' compensation is based on the following principles:

- Employers share collective liability, although contributions may vary among employers in the same industry (e.g., some provinces punish employers who do not maintain a safe and healthy work environment by levying additional fines).

- This compensation is based on loss of earnings.

- The system is no fault and nonadversarial and thus offers no recourse to the courts.

Benefits are paid out of an employer-financed fund and include medical expenses stemming from work-related injuries, survivors' benefits (including burial expenses and pensions), and wage loss payments for temporary, total, or partial disability. Permanent disability benefits may be disbursed as a lump-sum payment or as a permanent disability pension with rehabilitation services. The amount paid depends on the employee's earnings and provincial legislation.

Employees cannot be required either to make contributions toward a workers' compensation fund or to waive their right to receive compensation benefits. Payments made to claimants are effectively nontaxable. Premiums paid for by the employer may be deducted as expenses and are not deemed a taxable benefit for employees.

Figure 11.3 lists the steps that an HR department can take to control workers' compensation costs.

PART 4

ANDA CHU/MCT/Landov

Walk while you work? Companies such as GlaxoSmithKline and Best Buy have been utilizing treadmill desks like the one shown here. The treadmills move at a slow speed so that employees do not get hot, sweaty, and out of breath.

## FIGURE 11.3

### REDUCING WORKERS' COMPENSATION COSTS: KEY AREAS

1. Perform an audit to assess high-risk areas in the workplace.
2. Prevent injuries by proper ergonomic design of the workplace and effective assessment of job candidates.
3. Provide quality medical care to injured employees from physicians with experience and preferably with training in occupational health.
4. Reduce litigation by ensuring effective communication between the employer and the injured worker.
5. Manage the care of the injured worker from the time of the injury until the return to work.
6. Keep a partially recovered employee at the worksite.
7. Provide extensive worker training in all related health and safety areas.

## PROVINCIAL HOSPITAL AND MEDICAL SERVICES

People who have been resident in a Canadian province for three months are eligible to receive health care benefits. Applications must be made and approval given before coverage starts. Benefits include services provided by physicians, surgeons, and other qualified health professionals; hospital services such as standard ward accommodation and laboratory and diagnostic procedures; and hospital-administered drugs. Many employers offer third-party benefit coverage, which entitles their employees to additional benefits such as semiprivate or private accommodation, prescription drugs, private nursing, ambulance services, out-of-country medical expenses that exceed provincial limits, vision and dental care, and paramedic services. Depending on the employer, all or just a portion of the services may be covered.

## DISCRETIONARY MAJOR EMPLOYEE BENEFITS

Besides the mandated benefits, most employers offer other benefits, such as health care, a dental plan, payment for time not worked, life insurance, retirement programs, and pension plans.

## HEALTH CARE BENEFITS

The benefits receiving the most attention from employers today, owing to sharply rising costs and employee concerns, are health care benefits. In the past, health insurance plans covered only medical, surgical, and hospital expenses. Today, employers are under pressure to include prescription drugs as well as dental, optical, and mental health care benefits in the packages they offer their workers. Drugs now represent the second largest health expenditures, second only to hospital costs.

### Cost Containment

**OUTCOME 4**

The growth in health care costs can be attributed to a number of factors, including the greater need for health care by an aging population, the costs associated with technological advances in medicine, the growing costs of health care labour, and the overuse of costly health care services.

With the significant rise in health care costs, it is understandable that employers seek relief from these expenses. The approaches used to contain the costs of health care benefits include reductions in coverage, increased deductibles or copayments, and increased coordination of benefits to ensure that the same expense is not paid by more than one insurance reimbursement. A list of cost containment strategies is provided in Figure 11.4.

Employee assistance programs and wellness programs can help organizations cut the costs of health care benefits. Highlights in HRM 11.2 focuses on a team approach to cost reduction.

**FIGURE 11.4**

## COST CONTAINMENT STRATEGIES

Employers can reduce the cost of benefits in the following ways:

1. Education and Motivation
   - Communicate the costs of benefits.
   - Provide incentives to employees to reduce costs.
   - Teach employees how to live healthy lifestyles and how to plan for retirement.
2. Change Coverage
   - Introduce dollar limits on benefits.
   - Eliminate duplicate coverage for spouses.
   - Remove upgrades.
   - Introduce minimum fees to be paid by employees.
3. Change the System
   - Form partnerships with pharmacies to provide discounts.
   - Move to defined-contribution plans.
   - Move to a claims management approach and audit claims.

## Other Health Benefits

In the past two decades, more and more employees have been receiving dental care insurance as a benefit. Besides their obvious purpose, dental plans encourage employees to receive regular dental attention. Typically, the insurance pays a portion of the charges and the subscriber pays the remainder.

Another fairly new benefit that many employers are offering is optical care. Typically, the coverage includes visual examinations and a percentage of the costs of lenses and frames.

# HIGHLIGHTS IN HRM 11.2

## Team Approach to Cost Containment at The Economical Insurance Group (TEIG)

TEIG is one of Canada's largest casualty and property insurance groups, providing coverage for customers all across the country. TEIG offers its employees a range of rewards and benefits, such as competitive base and incentive pay, flexible benefits, training and development (e.g., Economical Learning Institute for Training—ELITE program, tuition reimbursement, e-learning), and a variety of perks (e.g., rewarding employee performance, on-site fitness or reimbursements for outside programs, concession tickets to various attractions). TEIG also values work–life balance, promoting diversity and a culture of inclusiveness in the workplace.

TEIG realized that with the growing cost of employee benefits, a fixed plan could not offer limited forms of cost containment as the company normally absorbs the increase or recoups it from employees through salary deduction. This was not a good way to attract and retain top candidates or contain the cost of benefits. A flexible approach was brought on board that allowed employees to pick and choose what works for them (e.g., trade-off with their spouse), thus reducing duplication of benefits and lowering the coverage cost to the employee and employer. Employees who opt to maintain a high level of coverage will have to pay the difference through payroll deductions.

With this shared approach, the initial cost is covered by TEIG with flex dollars; once those are exhausted, the second set of funds is deducted from employee payroll. Depending on the level of coverage that the employees opt for, the flex dollars might cover the total cost while enhanced coverage is paid for through payroll deductions. If money is left over from the flex dollars, employees can choose to funnel those funds into their health care expense accounts or group RRSP contributions, take time off work, or receive credit of up to $300 in their wellness accounts. This team-based approach to cost containment not only saves the employer a lot of money, but 86% of employees surveyed also said that they have a good understanding of their benefits.

Source: Jennifer Hubbard and Parbudyal Singh, "The Evolution of Employee Benefits at the Economical Insurance Group; *Compensation and Benefits Review*, 41, no. 6 (2009): 27–35; TEIG Website: http://talentegg.ca/employer/the-economical-insurance-group/highlights

**severance pay**
A lump-sum payment given to terminated employees by an employer at the time of an employer-initiated termination

The "payment for time not worked" category of benefits includes the following: statutory holiday pay and vacation pay; time off for bereavement, jury duty, and military duty; rest periods and coffee breaks; and maternity/paternity benefits (which usually involve some form of salary continuance).

## Vacations with Pay

It is generally agreed that vacation time is essential to the well-being of employees. Eligibility for vacations varies by industry, locale, and size of the organization. To qualify for longer vacations of 3, 4, or 5 weeks, one may expect to work for 5, 10, or 15 years. The average annual number of vacation days in Canada is 19, but about 1 in 4 employees does not take all of his or her vacation allotment, and a surprising 10 percent never take their vacation time allotment. The reasons? They did not schedule in advance, prefer cash in lieu of time, and are too busy at work.[21] However, some companies are now forcing employees to take time off as an internal control to avoid fraud. For example, Deutsche Bank has a global policy to force traders to take 10 consecutive days of work off a year so that any concealed positions (secret trading) become evident in their absence. This was a result of the $79 million that a trader placed in undetected gambling bets, and he only took 4 vacation days a year.[22]

## Paid Holidays

Both hourly and salaried workers can expect to be paid for statutory holidays as designated by each province. The standard statutory holidays are New Year's Day, Good Friday, Canada Day (Memorial Day in Newfoundland), Labour Day, and Christmas Day. Other holidays commonly recognized by the various provinces are Victoria Day and Thanksgiving Day. Some provinces have their own special statutory holidays. Many employers give workers an additional one to three personal days off (i.e., personal use days).

## Sick Leave

Employees who cannot work because of illness or injury are compensated in various ways. Most employers offer short-term disability and long-term disability plans. Short-term disability plans include salary continuance programs, sick leave credits, and weekly indemnity plans. Most public employees, and many in private firms—especially in white-collar jobs—receive a set number of sick leave days each year to cover such absences. Sometimes employees are permitted to accumulate the sick leave they do not use to cover prolonged absences. Accumulated vacation leave is sometimes treated as a source of income when sick leave benefits have been exhausted. Group insurance that provides income protection during a long-term disability is also becoming more common. Long-term disability plans normally provide a disabled employee with 50 to 70 percent of predisability income. Yet another alternative, depending on the situation, is workers' compensation insurance, which was discussed earlier in the chapter.

## Severance Pay

An employee who is being terminated is sometimes given a one-time payment. Known as **severance pay**, it can amount to anywhere from a few days' wages to several months', with the exact payment depending on length of service. There are no strict rules for severance pay, but the following are guidelines based on court decisions:

- Two weeks per year of service for those working as labourers, production workers, and administrative support staff

- Three weeks per year of service for those employed in technical, professional, supervisor, and managerial jobs
- Four weeks per year of service for those employed as senior managers[23]

Employers that are downsizing often use severance pay to soften the impact of unexpected termination on employees. An employee is not entitled to severance pay if a reasonable offer of alternative employment is refused.

## LIFE INSURANCE

Group life insurance is the benefit most commonly provided by an employer. The purpose is to provide financial security to the dependants of the employee in case of his or her death.

## RETIREMENT PROGRAMS

Retirement is an important part of life and requires careful preparation. When convincing job applicants to work for them, employers usually emphasize the retirement benefits that can be expected after a certain number of years of employment. As we noted earlier, it is common for each employee, once a year, to receive a personalized statement of benefits that contains information about projected retirement income from pensions and employee investment plans.

**silver handshake**
An early retirement incentive in the form of increased pension benefits for several years or a cash bonus

**OUTCOME 6**

### Retirement Policies

With the federal government repealing legislation forcing retirement at age 65 for federal employees, mandatory retirement in Canada is being abolished.[24] Statistics Canada reported that 61 is the average age of retirement, with women leaving work at 58 and men at 62. The higher the household income, the lower the age of retirement.[25] Many are retiring because they have lost their jobs and cannot find other work. However, as we have seen, there is a growing trend for individuals in their 60s to take on part-time employment as a means of supplementing their income.

To avoid making layoffs and to reduce salary and benefits costs, employers often encourage early retirement. This encouragement often takes the form of increased pension benefits or cash bonuses, sometimes referred to as the **silver handshake**. Some companies, including IBM Canada, have given generously to encourage the early retirement of workers. Ontario Hydro presented its employees with various options to retire early; these included an early retirement allowance, a voluntary separation allowance, a special retirement program, and a voluntary retirement program. The incentives succeeded; most employees with 25 years of service opted for the special retirement program.[26] An employer can offset the cost of retirement incentives by paying lower compensation to replacements and/or by reducing its workforce.

For employees, the main factors in a decision to retire early are health, personal finances, and job satisfaction. Lesser factors include an attractive pension and the possibility of future layoffs.

### Preretirement Programs

Most people are eager to retire; some are bitterly disappointed once they do. In an attempt to lessen the disappointment, some employers offer programs to help employees prepare for retirement. These programs typically include seminars and workshops, where lectures, videos, and printed materials are offered. Usually, they cover topics such as how to live on a reduced, fixed income and how to cope with lost prestige, family conflict, and idleness. Also discussed are more concrete topics such as pension plans, health insurance coverage, retirement benefits and provincial health care, and personal financial planning.

**contributory plan**
A pension plan in which contributions are made jointly by employees and employers

**noncontributory plan**
A pension plan in which contributions are made solely by the employer

**defined-benefit plan**
A pension plan in which the amount an employee is to receive on retirement is specifically set forth

**defined-contribution plan**
A pension plan that establishes the basis on which an employer will contribute to the pension fund

## PENSION PLANS

Originally, pensions were based on a *reward philosophy*; in other words, employers viewed pensions mainly as a reward to employees who stayed with them until retirement. Employees who quit or were terminated before retirement were not seen as deserving retirement benefits. Since then, most unions have negotiated vesting requirements into their contracts, and vesting has become required by law. Put another way, pensions are now based on an *earnings philosophy*; they are seen as deferred income that employees accumulate during their working lives. In other words, the pension belongs to the employee after a specified number of years of service whether or not she or he remains with the employer until retirement.

Since the CPP/QPP legislation was enacted in 1966, pension plans have been used to supplement the protection provided by government-sponsored programs. Most private pension plans and a significant number of public plans now integrate their benefits with CPP/QPP benefits.

It is up to the employer whether to offer a pension plan. Because these plans are so expensive, companies are always looking for the least expensive ways to provide them to their employees.

### Types of Pension Plans

**OUTCOME 7**

Pensions can be categorized in two basic ways: according to contributions made by the employer and according to the amount of pension benefits to be paid. In a **contributory plan**, contributions to a pension plan are made jointly by employees and employers. In a **noncontributory plan**, the contributions are made solely by the employer. Most plans in privately held organizations are contributory.

When pension plans are classified by the amount of pension benefits to be paid, there are two basic types: the defined-benefit plan and the defined-contribution plan. Under a **defined-benefit plan**, the retirement benefit is determined according to a predefined formula. This amount is usually based on the employee's years of service, average earnings during a specific period of time, and age at the time of retirement. A variety of formulas exist for determining pension benefits; the one used most often is based on the employee's average earnings (usually over a three- to five-year period immediately preceding retirement) multiplied by the number of years of service with the organization. A deduction is then made for each year the retiree is under 65. As noted earlier, pension benefits are usually integrated with CPP/QPP. Very few employers introduce this type of plan because it places them under the legal obligation to pay benefits regardless of the performance of the pension plan.

A **defined-contribution plan** establishes the basis on which an employer will contribute to the pension fund. These plans come in a variety of forms: some involve profit sharing; others involve employers matching employee contributions; still others are employer-sponsored registered retirement saving plans (RRSPs). The size of the pension the employee will get is determined by the funds in his or her account at the time of retirement and what retirement benefits (usually in the form of an annuity) these funds will purchase. These plans are not as predictable (i.e., secure) as defined-benefit plans. However, even under defined-benefit plans, retirees may not receive the benefits promised them if the plan is not adequately funded.

Defined-benefit plans, with their fixed payouts, are falling out of use and have dropped to less than 40 percent of companies.[27] They are less popular with employers nowadays because they cost more and because they require compliance with complicated government rules. Many new pension plans in Canada, such as those introduced by MacMillan Bloedel and Molson Breweries, are defined-contribution plans.

RRSPs have experienced tremendous growth in recent years because the funds in these plans are allowed to accumulate tax free until they are withdrawn.

RRSPs have annual contribution limits; also, if withdrawals are made from them before retirement, tax must be paid on them. Some employers offer group RRSPs, which have some advantages over individual RRSPs: they are deducted from payroll and have mass-purchasing power.

**vesting**
A guarantee of accrued benefits to participants at retirement age, regardless of their employment status at the time

## Federal Regulation of Pension Plans

Registered pension plans (RPPs) are subject to federal and provincial regulations. The federal *Income Tax Act* prescribes limits and standards that affect the amount of contributions that can be deducted from income; it also mandates how pension benefits can be taxed. In the federal jurisdiction and most provincial ones, there are laws that state how pension plans must be operated. For example, the actuarial assumptions on which the funding is based must be certified by an actuary at specified intervals.

An important issue to employees is vesting. **Vesting** is a guarantee of accrued benefits to participants at retirement age, regardless of their employment status at that time. Vested benefits that have been earned by the employee cannot be revoked by the employer. Employees with two years of service in an organization are considered, with regard to their pension plans, fully vested and locked in.

## Pension Portability

For a long time, most pension plans lacked portability; in other words, employees who changed jobs were unable to maintain equity in a single pension. Unions addressed this concern by encouraging multiple-employer plans. These plans cover the employees of two or more unrelated organizations in accordance with a collective agreement. They are governed by boards of trustees on which both the employers and the union are represented. Multiple-employer plans tend to be found in industries in which few companies have enough employees to justify an individual plan. They are also found often in industries in which employment tends to be either seasonal or irregular. These plans are found in the following manufacturing sectors: apparel, printing, furniture, leather, and metalworking. They are also found in nonmanufacturing industries such as mining, construction, transport, entertainment, and private higher education.

Employees who leave an organization can leave their locked-in funds in their current pension plan, or they can transfer those funds into a locked-in RRSP or into their new employer's pension plan (if one exists).

## Pension Funds

A pension fund can be administered through a trusted plan or through an insured one. In a *trusted plan*, the pension contributions are placed in a trust fund. The fund is then invested and administered by trustees. The trustees are appointed by the employer, but if there is a union, the union sometimes appoints them. Contributions to an *insured* pension plan are used to purchase insurance annuities. These funds are administered by the insurance company that is providing the annuities.

Government benefits such as CPP/QPP and Old Age Security will be stretched thin as baby boomers grow older, and some private pensions may be vulnerable to poorly performing investments. It should also be noted that the pension funds of some organizations are not adequate to cover their obligations. Here is another interesting question: "Whose money is it?" When a pension fund has generated a surplus over plan (and many of them have), management tends to see this surplus as part of the organization's portfolio of assets; not surprisingly, employees tend to view it as their own money. Highlights in HRM 11.3 describes this debate.

# HIGHLIGHTS IN HRM 11.3

## Whose Money Is It?

Ray Bekeris worked 12-hour shifts as a steelworker for 30 years for Cold Metal Products, a steel-manufacturing plant based in Hamilton, Ontario. Cold Metal Products went bankrupt, and Ray discovered that his pension plan was gone too. After the banks and other secured creditors got their money, almost none was left for the employees. Canadian bankruptcy laws favour secured creditors, and employees are at the bottom of the list. Actuaries view this as reasonable because creditors would not risk their investment if they were not at the top of the list to be repaid. This is not heartless because banks are investing people's money and want some expectation of a return. But this means that employees become unwitting investors. To illustrate, a company is in trouble, and the employer stops making its contributions to the pension plan. It uses this money to finance the company, perhaps

prolonging the bankruptcy. The employees, who are likely unaware of this, become unintentional investors, but with no rights and no voice.

And it is not just private companies using pension plan funds as if the funds were their own money. There is a case before the courts that is deemed the most important pension court case in history. Legal firms representing 670,000 public service employees and retirees are suing the federal government because it appropriated the pension surplus (of $30 billion in 1999). Employees believed that they were paying into a pension plan where the money would be held safely and then distributed to them, not to the general coffers of the government.

Bankruptcies and appropriation of pension surpluses are not the only threats to pension plans. Most pension plans can cover only 80 percent of their obligations. These facts should stimulate employees to not rely on organizational pension plans but to save wisely for their own retirements.

Source: Diane Swain, "How Safe Is Your Pension?" *CBC News online*. From The National, November 15, 2004. Retrieved March 10, 2006 from www.cbc.ca/news/background/pension and from "Public Service Pension Plan: Pension Grab Court Case Begins," www.pipsc.ca/english/newsletteres/c-dec05/6.html.

## EMPLOYEE SERVICES: CREATING A WORK–LIFE SETTING

| OUTCOME 8

Employee services, like other benefits, represent a cost to the employer. But they are often well worth the cost. More and more different services are being offered by employers to make life at work more rewarding and to enhance the well-being of employees. "Wellness is good for business," says Ann Coll of Husky Injection Molding Systems. The employees at Husky's plant in Bolton, Ontario, enjoy a subsidized cafeteria with organic vegetarian meals, a $500 stipend for vitamins, and a fitness centre that is open around the clock.

**employee assistance programs (EAPs)**
Services provided by employers to help workers cope with a wide variety of problems that interfere with the way they perform their jobs

### CREATING A FAMILY-FRIENDLY SETTING

Eddie Bauer, an outdoor clothing and equipment supplier, offers its employees takeout dinners and one paid "balance day" off a year. AltaGas, based in Calgary, offers many benefits: a share purchase plan, extra vacation days, quarterly corporate events such as cross-country skiing, emergency short-term daycare, and discounts on home computers.[28] These organizations, and many others, are seeking to create a family-friendly organizational environment that allows employees to balance work and personal needs. Programs such as these help employees manage their time; employers benefit by attracting good workers and by reducing the various interruptions that affect workplace productivity.[29] Figure 11.5 lists some of the more popular employer-sponsored work–life benefits.

### EMPLOYEE ASSISTANCE PROGRAMS

To help workers cope with a wide variety of problems that interfere with their work performance, organizations have developed **employee assistance programs (EAPs)**. Typically, an EAP provides diagnosis, counselling, and referral services for alcohol or drug problems, emotional problems, and financial or family

FIGURE 11.5

## FAMILY-FRIENDLY BENEFITS: BALANCING WORK AND HOME NEEDS

- Childcare/eldercare referral services
- Time off for children's school activities
- Employer-paid on-site or near-site childcare facilities
- Flexible work hours scheduling
- Employee-accumulated leave days for dependant care
- Subsidized temporary or emergency dependant care
- Extended leave policies for childcare/eldercare
- Sick child programs (caregiver on call)
- Work-at-home arrangements/telecommuting
- Partial funding of childcare costs
- Customized career paths

crises. (EAPs are discussed in more detail in Chapter 12.) It has been estimated that employees' stress adds as much as 8 percent to payroll costs. The point of EAPs is to help employees solve their personal problems or at least to prevent those problems from turning into crises that affect their ability to work productively. To handle crises, many EAPs offer 24-hour hotlines. Between 7 and 10 percent of employees use EAPs.[30] The Public Service Commission of the Yukon Government provides a summary of employee and employer responsibilities when using the EAP to deal with the personal problems of employees that affect their work performance (see Highlights in HRM 11.4).

# HIGHLIGHTS IN HRM 11.4

## Yukon Government's Public Service Commission

### Employee Assistance Program

To assist employees to deal with personal problems that are affecting or have the potential to affect their work performance.

### Employee Rights and Responsibilities

- To maintain work performance at an acceptable level.
- To voluntarily seek or accept confidential assistance or advice when deteriorating or impaired work performance is being caused by a personal, health, or behavioural problem.
- To cooperate in any treatment program that is established and continue the program to completion.
- An employee who accepts the referral, counseling, and rehabilitation available under EAP does so without prejudice to job security.

### Supervisory Responsibilities

- Recognize that a problem exists.
- Document the facts.
- Confront the employee with the facts.
- Try to find a solution within the work situation without diagnosing the underlying personal/behavioural problem.
- Refer employee to EAP if the problem cannot be resolved in the workplace.
- Follow up with the EAP adviser on the employee's progress.
- Work with the EAP adviser in establishing course of action to reintegrate employee into work environment.
- Monitor the work performance of the employee against clearly established objectives and support the employee in the integration process.

Source: Printed with the permission of the Government of Yukon, Public Service Commission.

**eldercare**
Care provided to an elderly relative by an employee who remains actively at work

## COUNSELLING SERVICES

An important part of an EAP is the counselling services it provides to employees. Although most organizations expect managers to counsel subordinates on work-related issues, some employees will have problems that require professional counselling. Most organizations refer these employees to outside services such as family counselling services, marriage counsellors, and mental health clinics. Some organizations have a clinical psychologist, counsellor, or comparable specialist on staff to whom employees may be referred.

## CHILDCARE AND ELDERCARE

Consider these statistics:

- About 32 percent of Canadians have eldercare responsibilities.
- Employees spend an average of 23 hours each month on eldercare.[31]

Those responsible for caregiving are more likely to miss work because of the emotional and physical fatigue associated with caregiving.[32] Great-West Life Insurance Company, based in Winnipeg, has hired a family services coordinator to help its employees with family issues. The coordinator recommends products, such as personal alarm systems, or services, such as adult daycare in the community.[33] In the past, working parents had to make their own arrangements with sitters or with nursery schools for preschool children. Today, benefits may include financial assistance, alternative work schedules, and family leave. For many employees, on-site or near-site childcare centres are the most visible, prestigious, and desired solutions.

Ontario Hydro has provided the space and is paying the occupancy costs for a program it calls Hydro Kids. This program encompasses three on-site daycare centres, which are open to company employees. These nonprofit centres are operated by the parents themselves, who hire the childcare staff and manage day-to-day operations. Parents pay market rates for the childcare services.[34] Ford Motor Company of Canada offers its employees as much as $2,000 a year in childcare assistance.

A growing benefit offered employees with children experiencing a short illness is called mildly ill child care. Medical supervision is the primary difference between these facilities and traditional daycare arrangements. Mildly ill care facilities serve children recovering from colds, flu, ear infections, chickenpox, or other mild illnesses that temporarily prevent them from attending regular school or day care. See Highlights in HRM 11.5 for examples of childcare benefits at Statistics Canada.

Responsibility for the care of aging parents and other relatives is another fact of life for more and more employees. The term **eldercare**, as used in the context of employment, refers to situations in which an employee provides care to an elderly relative while remaining actively at work. Most caregivers are women.

There is no doubt that eldercare responsibilities detract from work efficiency: from time lost to take a parent to the doctor to loss of concentration due to worry, work time being spent making care arrangements, never knowing when an emergency will occur, and calls from neighbours and relatives disrupting the workday. When combined, these responsibilities lead to a situation where neither the caregiver nor the employee role is filled adequately. Lost productivity due to absenteeism of those caring for elders can cost a 1,000-employee company without an eldercare program as much as $400,000 per year. TransAmerica Corporation, an insurance and financial services organization, reported that 1,600 missed workdays per year were attributed to 22 percent of its employees who were caring for an elderly relative, for an annual loss to the corporation of $250,000. For larger companies, these costs can run into the millions.[35]

To reduce the negative effects of caregiving on productivity, organizations can offer eldercare counselling, educational fairs and seminars, printed resources, support groups, and special flexible schedules and leaves of absence.

# HIGHLIGHTS IN HRM 11.5

## Statistics Canada Makes Childcare a Priority

The Conference Board of Canada reports that employees who have a great deal of stress maintaining work–life balance are more prone to absenteeism (7.2 days per year) as opposed to those who have less stress balancing their work life (3.6 days). It is no wonder that Statistics Canada decided to make work–life balance a key component of its organization. Statistics Canada, employer of some 5,550 employees, ranked among the top 20 of Canada's Top Family-Friendly Employers in 2012. Although Statistics Canada's overall ranking in each component was way above average/excellent, when it comes to health and family-friendly benefits, Statistics Canada not only makes the top 100 best employers in Canada, it also

gets an A+. Among some of the benefits offered are full family health care (fixed/traditional coverage), alternative and traditional medicine coverage, maternity top-up of 93 percent for one year, 93 percent salary top-up for 37 weeks for new fathers and adoptive parents, and 100 percent top-up for 1 week for compassionate leave, to name a few.

The childcare programs available to employees are particularly appealing. They include "subsidized onsite daycare; onsite daycare centre with 49 spaces; 14 childcare workers; a 12-month waiting list for available spaces; and pre-arranged emergency short-term daycare" with flexible work arrangements. This on-site daycare centre is operated by a charitable, nonprofit organization in conjunction with Statistics Canada. The programs are bilingual and are geared toward preschool-age children.

Sources: http://www.hrs.ualberta.ca/HPaWS/CMHA-Employer_Brochure.pdf; http://www.eluta.ca/top-employer-statistics-canada

---

Schering-Plough, a pharmaceuticals manufacturer, uses an 800-line for eldercare referrals. IBM has established a nationwide telephone network of more than 200 community-based referral agencies. Some employers band together to come up with better solutions to the challenge of eldercare.

AT&T has given grants to community organizations to recruit, train, and manage eldercare volunteers where its employees live and work. Travellers Corporation, a financial services company, is part of a consortium of employers that trains family care workers; it also shares with employees the cost of three days' in-home care for family emergencies.[36] Interest in and demand for eldercare programs will increase dramatically as baby boomers age and find themselves managing organizations and experiencing eldercare problems with their own parents.

Caring for one's aging parents and relatives is a growing concern for employees.

Henglein and Steets/Getty Images

# HIGHLIGHTS IN HRM 11.6

## Business Development Bank of Canada (BDC)

BDC, employer of some 1,700 employees across Canada, was ranked number 1 on the list of Canada's best employers for pension and benefits in 2007. Among the various benefits offered by BDC, employees are given the opportunity to buy and sell vacation time as part of their benefits package. This began in 2003 as part of the corporation's total rewards plan. The corporation is charged with delivering financial investment and consulting services to Canadian small businesses, with emphasis on the technology and export sector of the Canadian economy.

Due to comprehensive communication efforts, the company has gained buy-in from all provinces. This flexibility is being touted as improving things "a whole lot" given that employees are empowered to make choices about their vacation days. BDC places in the top 30 employers with the best benefits; however, the term "best benefits" makes Maryse Corbella, Total Rewards Director, uncomfortable. "Saying it that way bothers me. What we have done is maximized flexibility and leveraged people's understanding and ability to make things work

for them, and that's what they really, really appreciate." On an annual basis, between 30 and 35 percent of their employees have the ability to release funds to buy one to five vacation days each year, and "they love it," says Corbella.

Other ways employees can distribute their excess flex dollars include receiving them in cash, allocating them to their HSA, putting them into an employee savings plan where the funds are matched by BDC, or earmarking them to pay a portion of their pension contribution. Corbella says that her biggest challenge with respect to benefits is ensuring that service providers really deliver. Plan members are savvy consumers and expect high-quality service. "You could have the best design and the best enrollment, then if it all falls apart when employees go to use it, you lose credibility," she says. The decision to move to flexible benefits was prompted by demographic pressures and the realization that benefits can be an important attraction and retention tool. "We need this edge to hold on to people and retain people," says Corbella. "I don't think benefits are a 'gimme' anymore. They're not a throwaway. People do pay attention to them a lot more than they used to."

Source: Andrea Davis, (2007). Canada's Best Pension and Benefits Plans: The people's choice. *Benefits Canada*, 31(6), 44–57.

## OTHER SERVICES

The variety of benefits and services that employers offer today could not have been imagined a few years ago. Some are fairly standard, such as legal services, financial planning, housing and moving expenses, transportation pooling, credit unions, and recreational and social services. Others are unique and obviously grew out of specific concerns, needs, and interests. Some of the more creative and unusual benefits are group insurance for employee pets, free baseball tickets for families and friends, on-site barbers and car washers, and drop-offs for dry cleaning. Highlights in HRM 11.6 illustrates examples of various types of flexible benefits.

# SMALL BUSINESS APPLICATION

Small business aims to address three issues with the prevalence of benefit programs in Canada. First, such programs help employees remain healthy, reducing the cost of absenteeism. Second, such programs help keep small businesses competitive with other employers. Third, these programs provide a tax advantage as contributions

to such programs may be tax exempt, whereas compensation is taxable.

So what options are available to small business? From the standpoint of benefits programs, many insurance providers have benefits programs available for as few as one or two employees. Such programs can be employer paid, employee paid, or cost shared. Coverage can be 100 percent, 80 percent, or any other level. Plans may cover full-time employees, part-time employees, or both. It is critical to identify the plan that best meets the objectives and budget of the organization. Regarding retirement plans, assuming that the set-up and management of pension plans is cost-prohibitive and administratively burdensome, small employers may wish to provide an incentive to employees to contribute to a retirement savings plan (RSP) managed by the employee. Simple programs where a company matches employee contributions to an RSP up to a certain maximum can have the same positive effect of a company pension, with much lower cost and program administration challenges.

In conclusion, not all small companies have benefit or retirement programs. However, recognizing the benefit of such programs and that many can be implemented with relative ease and low cost, small companies certainly should consider them.

# SUMMARY

**OUTCOME 1** Benefits are an established and integral part of the total compensation package. To have an effective benefits program, there are certain basic considerations. It is essential that a program be based on specific objectives that are compatible with the organization's philosophy and policies, as well as affordable. Through committees and surveys, a benefits package can be developed to meet employees' needs. Through the use of flexible benefits plans, employees are able to choose those benefits that are best suited to their individual needs. An important factor in how employees view the program is the full communication of benefits information through meetings, printed materials, and annual personalized statements of benefits.

**OUTCOME 2** Since many benefits represent a fixed cost, management must pay close attention in assuming more benefit expense. Increasingly, employers are requiring employees to pay part of the costs of certain benefits. Employers also shop for benefits services that are competitively priced.

**OUTCOME 3** Nearly one-quarter of the benefits packages provided by employers are legally required. These benefits include employer contributions to retirement plans, employment insurance, and workers' compensation insurance.

**OUTCOME 4** The cost of health care programs has become the major concern in the area of employee benefits. Several approaches can be used to contain health care costs, including reduction in coverage, increased coordination of benefits, and increased deductibles. EAPs and wellness programs can also help cut the costs of health care benefits.

**OUTCOME 5** Included in the category of benefits that involve payments for time not worked are vacations with pay, paid holidays, sick leave, and severance pay. Most Canadian workers receive 10 to 15 days' vacation leave plus statutory holidays. In addition to vacation time, most employees—especially in white-collar jobs—receive a set number of sick leave days. A one-time payment of severance pay may be given to employees who are being terminated.

**OUTCOME 6** Many provinces have abolished mandatory retirement, and now employees can choose when to retire. However, many employers provide incentives for early retirement in the form of increased pension benefits or cash bonuses. Some organizations now offer preretirement programs, which typically include seminars, workshops, and informational materials.

**OUTCOME 7** Once a pension plan has been established, it is subject to federal and provincial regulation to ensure that benefits will be available when the employee retires. Although two types of plans are available—defined benefit and defined contribution—most employers now opt for the latter. The amount an employee receives on retirement is based on years of service, average earnings, and age at the time of retirement. Usually, pension benefits are integrated with CPP/QPP. Pension funds are administered through either a trustee or an insurance plan.

**OUTCOME 8** The types of service benefits that employers typically provide include EAPs, counselling services, childcare, and eldercare. Other benefits are prepaid legal services, financial planning, housing and moving, transportation pooling, credit unions, and social and recreational opportunities.

# SUMMARY

## KEY TERMS

contributory plan, 404
defined-benefit plan, 404
defined-contribution
   plan, 404
eldercare, 408

employee assistance programs
   (EAPs), 406
flexible benefits plans (cafeteria
   plans), 391
noncontributory plan, 404

severance pay, 402
silver handshake, 403
vesting, 405
workers' compensation
   insurance, 399

## DISCUSSION QUESTIONS

1. Assume that you have been hired as the HR manager of a small computer software firm with 180 employees. The CEO has asked you to design a strategic benefits plan for the firm. Using the knowledge gained in this chapter and book, discuss the key steps you would suggest in such a plan.

2. Many organizations are concerned about the rising cost of employee benefits and question their value to the organization and to the employees.

   a. In your opinion, what benefits are of greatest value to employees? To the organization? Why?

   b. What can management do to increase the value to the organization of the benefits provided to employees?

3. Benefits account for a significant percentage of payroll costs for organizations. Name three ways in which you, as an employer, would try to reduce the costs of benefits.

4. Do you agree with the argument that the benefits for time not worked are the ones most readily available to reduce employer costs? Explain.

5. As was mentioned in the opening of this chapter, many employees do not know the details of the benefits they receive. Discuss how you would go about designing and implementing a communications plan to address this issue.

6. Many organizations are introducing flexible benefit plans. Why? What are the advantages and disadvantages?

7. Given the costs of employee benefits, should cash-strapped organizations provide discretionary benefits? Why or why not? Support your answer with reference to examples.

8. Assume that your team has been hired as a benefits consultant by a small business with 50 to 60 employees. What benefits do you believe this employer should offer, given its limited resources? Explain why you would offer these benefits.

# HRM EXPERIENCE

## Understanding Employer Benefit Programs

Compensation surveys indicate that a majority of employees are unable to accurately name the benefits they receive, and employees vastly underestimate the cost of benefits paid by their employers.

   This exercise will help you more fully understand the benefits discussed in this chapter. Additionally, you will explore, in detail, the benefits and services offered by your employer and other employers in your area.

## Assignment

Working in teams of four to six, obtain information on the benefits package offered by your employer or other employers in your area. Once the information is gathered, be able to identify (1) each benefit offered, (2) what the benefit provides the employee, (3) employee eligibility (if required), and (4) how the benefit is paid for (employer, employee, or a combination of both). Compare benefit packages. Be prepared to discuss your findings with the class.

Visit the *Managing Human Resources* CourseMate website at http://www.belcourt7e.nelson.com for quizzes, flashcards, videos, games, and more!

# CASE STUDY 1

## EVALUATE THE WORK–LIFE CLIMATE IN YOUR COMPANY

What is the quality of the work–life environment in your company? The following survey provided by the Work and Family Connection will help provide a "case analysis" of the climate in your organization. Answers to the 20 questions will provide clear insights about your company's position in the work–life area.

### Agree or Disagree with the Following Statements:

1. My manager/supervisor treats my work–life needs with sensitivity.
2. It is usually easy for me to manage the demands of both work and home life.
3. My career path at this company is limited because of the pressure of home life demands.
4. My job at this company keeps me from maintaining the quality of life I want.
5. My manager/supervisor is supportive when home life issues interfere with work.
6. My manager/supervisor focuses on results, rather than the time I am at my desk.
7. My manager/supervisor has a good understanding of flexible work hour practices.
8. If I requested a flexible work arrangement my manager/supervisor would support me.
9. My manager/supervisor is often inflexible or insensitive about my personal needs.
10. I believe my manager/supervisor treats me with respect.
11. My manager/supervisor allows me informal flexibility as long as I get the job done.
12. My manager/supervisor tends to treat us like children.
13. My manager/supervisor seldom gives me praise or recognition for the work I do.
14. My manager/supervisor seems to care about me as a person.
15. I would recommend this company to others.
16. The work I do is not all that important to this company's success.
17. If I could find another job with better pay, I would leave this organization.
18. If I could find another job where I would be treated with respect, I would take it.
19. If I could find another job where I could have more flexibility, I would take it.
20. I am totally committed to this company.

For a perfect score, you should answer "Disagree" to questions 3, 4, 9, 12, 13, 16, 17, 18, and 19 and "Agree" to all the rest (questions 1, 2, 5, 6, 7, 8, 10, 11, 14, 15, and 20).

To score, begin by giving yourself 20 points. Then deduct one point for every "wrong" response from the total score.

If your score is 18 to 20: Congratulations! Your organization is leading the nation in flexibility and supportiveness.

If your score is 14 to 17: Your organization is probably more supportive and flexible than most, but you have room to grow.

If your score is 11 to 13: You could be open to other job offers in the race for talent among employees.

If your score is 10 or less: Your managers will need help to manage the 21st century workforce.

**Source:** Used with permission of the Work and Family Connection, 5195 Beachside Drive, Minnetonka, Minnesota 55343; phone 1-800-487-7898 or http://www.workfamily.com

# CASE STUDY 2

## MAPLE LEAFS' FAMILY-FRIENDLY BENEFITS: AN UNEXPECTED BACKLASH

Maple Leafs Computing Services (MLCS), a provider of HR software application systems, prides itself on the variety of benefits it offers employees. In addition to health care, pension, and vacation benefits, the company also offers an attractive family-friendly benefits package including flexible schedules, child- and eldercare assistance, counselling services, adoption assistance, and extended parental leave. Unfortunately, in recent months, the company's progressive work–life policy has experienced a backlash from several employees, as the following case illustrates.

In March 2012, Mala Wifey was hired by MLCS as a software accounts manager. With excellent administrative and technical skills, plus four years of experience at Adaptable Software, MLCS's main competitor, Mala became a valued addition to the company's marketing team. As a mother with two grade-school children, Mala received permission to take Fridays off. She was also allowed to leave work early or come in late to meet the demands of her children. Mala is one of 11 software account managers at MLCS.

The problem for MLCS, and particularly Janis Blancero, HR manager, began in the fall of 2012. On September 15, Lana Bajana, citing "personal reasons"—which she refused to discuss—requested a 4-day workweek for which she was willing to take a 20 percent cut in pay. When Lana asked for the reduced work schedule, she sarcastically quipped, "I hope I don't have to have kids to get this time off." On October 3, Lilman Cutee, a world-class marathon runner, requested a flexible work hours arrangement to accommodate his morning and afternoon training schedule. Lilman is registered to run the London, England, marathon. Just prior to Lilman's request, Amelia Gomez asked for, and was granted, an extended leave for her university examinations in December. If these unexpected requests were not enough, Blancero has heard comments from senior account managers about how some employees seem to get "special privileges," whereas the managers work

long hours that often require them to meet around-the-clock customer demands. Janis has adequate reason to believe that there is hidden tension over the company's flexible work hours program. Currently, MLCS has no formal policy on flexible schedules. Furthermore, with the company's growth in business combined with the increasing workload of software account managers and the constant service demands of some customers, Blancero realizes that she simply cannot grant all the time-off requests of her employees.

## Questions

1. Do managers such as Janis Blancero face a more complicated decision when evaluating the personal requests of employees versus evaluating employees' individual work performance? Explain.

2. a. Should MLCS establish a policy for granting flexible work schedules? Explain.

   b. If you answered yes, what might that policy contain?

3. If you were Janis Blancero, how would you resolve this dilemma? Explain.

**Source:** Adapted from Alden M. Hayashi, "Mommy-Track Backlash," *Harvard Business Review* 79, no. 3 (March 2001): 33–42.

## NOTES AND REFERENCES

1. Erica Alini, "Healthy and Happy," *Macleans Canada*, Thursday, October 18, 2010, http://www2.macleans.ca/tag/best-employers/.

2. Tom Henfeffer, "Fair and Flexible", *Macleans Canada*, Thursday, October 18, 2010, http://www2.macleans.ca/tag/best-employers/.

3. Linda Love and Parbudyal Singh, "Employer Branding through Human Resource Management," *Journal of Business and Psychology* 26, no. 2 (2011): 175–181.

4. J. Taggart, "Putting Flex Benefits through Their Paces," *Canadian HR Reporter* 15, no. 21 (December 2, 2002): G3.

5. Richard Long, *Strategic Compensation in Canada*, 4th ed, (Toronto: Nelson, 2010).

6. http://www.benefitscanada.ca, retrieved June 11, 2009.

7. Jeff Holloway, "Recruiting On Principle: Selling A Company's Values," *Canadian HR Reporter*, November 22, 2004, 7; Jacqueline Taggart and Joy Sloane, "If the Pitch Is Total Rewards, Flex Benefits Are the Home Run," *Canadian HR Reporter* 17, no. 4 (February 23, 2004), G3.

8. Sarah Dobson, "Collection of Family Friendly Perks Boost Monsanto's Image as an Employer," *Canadian HR Reporter* 23, no. 19 (November 1, 2010): 13, 15.

9. Todd Humber, "RBC Organizes Pay, Benefits Training, Work Environment into a Single Package," *Canadian HR Reporter* 17, no. 4 (February 23, 2004), G1.

10. Ronald W. Perry and N. Joseph Cayer, "Cafeteria Style Health Plans in Municipal Govt.," *Public Personnel Management* 28, no. 1 (Spring 1999): 107–117; Jon J. Meyer, "The Future of Flexible Benefit Plans," *Employee Benefits Journal* 25, no. 2 (June 2000): 3–7. See also Rosaline Koo, "The Global Added Value of Flexible Benefits," *Benefits Quarterly*, 27, no. 4 (Fourth Quarter, 2011): 17–20.

11. L. Byron and R. Dawson, "Flex Benefits Are More Popular Than Ever with Employers and Employees," *Benefits Canada*, http://www.benefitscanada.com/magazine/article.jsp?content= 20030624_134506_4312, April 2003.

12. "Communication Break Down: Employers Must Properly Inform Employees of Their Entitlement Benefits or Face Expensive and Time Consuming Court Challenges," *Benefits Canada* 21, no. 1 (January 1997): 27, 29.

13. M. Paterson, "Making a Statement: Are You Ready to Turn an Obligation into an Opportunity?" *Benefits Canada*, February 1995: 19–21.

14. T. Belford, "The 24/7 Personnel Office," *The Globe and Mail*, November 20, 2007, B13.

15. S. Felix, "Techno Benefits," *Benefits Canada* 24, no. 1 (January 2000): 27–34.

16. Jan Everett, "Internet Security," *Employee Benefits Journal* 23, no. 3 (September 1998): 14–18. See also Alan R. Parham, "Developing a Technology Policy," *Employee Benefits Journal 23*, no. 3 (September 1998): 3–5.

17. J. MacBride-King, *Managing Corporate Health Care*, Conference Board of Canada, October 1995, Report 158–195: 10.

18. Neil Mrkvicka, "The Cost Also Rises," *Benefits Canada* 34, no. 11 (November 2010): 71; David Brown, "Employees Willing to Help Defray the Costs of Benefits," *Canadian HR Reporter*, June 14, 2004, 1; Uyen Vu, "HR Responds to Cost Crunch with Workforce Cuts," *Canadian HR Reporter*, May 31, 2004, 1; Greg Keenan, "Stelco Cuts Benefits for Salaried Workers," *The Globe and Mail,* May 15, 2006, B3; Gloria Gonzalez, "Canadian Firms Seek to Stem Rising Costs of Benefits," *Business Insurance*, March 22, 2004, 3; Jacqueline Taggart, "No Easy Answer for Cost Conundrum," *Canadian HR Reporter 17*, no. 8 (April 19, 2004), 11.

19. Taggart, "No Easy Answer for Cost Conundrum," 11.

20. "FTNT Employment Insurance: More Than a New Name," *Work Life Report* 10, no. 2 (1996): 1–4, 5.

21. Wallance Immen, "Working Life Blues: Can't Shake the Job," *The Globe and Mail*, May 17, 2006, C1.

22. "Deutsche Bank Traders Told to Take Time Off," *The Globe and Mail*, March 23, 2008, B1.

23. Richard Long, *Strategic Compensation in Canada.*

24. Mandatory retirement fades in Canada, *CBC News*, October 18, 2010, http://www.cbc.ca/news/canada /story/2009/08/20/mandatory-retirement-explainer523. html; Kathryn Blaze Carlson, "Tories End Forced Retirement, Decades of 'Age Discrimination,'" *National Post*, December 18, 2011, http://news.nationalpost. com/2011/12/18/tories-end-forced-retirement-decades -of-age-discrimination/.

25. Dorothy Lipovenko, "Job Losses Force Early Retirement," *The Globe and Mail*, September 8, 1995, A8.

26. Doug Burn, "Wheel of Fortune: How Much Should an Organization Gamble on Early Retirement Planning?" *Human Resources Professional* 11, no. 4 (May 1994): 13–17.

27. Richard Long, *Strategic Compensation in Canada.*

28. S. Dobson, "Benefits Go Beyond Financials," *Canadian HR Reporter* 21, no. 15 (2008): 15, 20; Sarah Dobson, "Revisiting Total Rewards a Constant Cycle," *Canadian HR Reporter* 24, no. 14 (August 15, 2011): 27.

29. "Employers Help Workers Achieve Balance in Life," *HRfocus* 75, no. 11 (November 1998): S3.

30. T. Humber, "Stress Attack," *Canadian HR Reporter* 16, no. 3 (February 10, 2003): G1, G10.

31. Cindy Goodman, "Work-Life Conflicts Present New Evolution of Challenges," *Saskatoon Star*, 14 (January 2012): F14; A. Tomlinson, "Trickle Down Effect of Retiring Boomers," *Canadian HR Reporter* 15, no. 11 (June 3, 2002): 1, 12.

32. Linda Duxbury, Christopher Higgins, and Rob Smart, "Elder Care and the Impact of Caregiver Strain on the Health of Employed Caregivers," *Work* 40, no. 1 (2011): 29; G. Joseph, "Embracing Elder Care," *Benefits Canada* 2, no. 4, 2008: 57.

33. Betty Healey, "Support for Employees Providing Support," *Canadian HR Reporter*, September 13, 2004: 17; Uyen Vu, "At Great-West There's Elder Care Help on Staff," *Canadian HR Reporter* 17, no. 15 (September 13, 2004): 18.

34. Sonya Felix, "Running on Empty," *Benefits Canada* 21, no. 16 (June 1997): 109–114.

35. Elaine Davis and Mary Kay Krouse, "Elder Care Obligations Challenge the Next Generation," *HR Magazine* 41, no. 7 (July 1996): 98–103; Rodney K. Platt, "The Aging Workforce," *Workspan* 44, no. 1 (January 2001): 26.

36. Sue Shellenbarger, "Firms Try Harder, but Often Fail, to Help Workers Cope with Elder-Care Problems," *Wall Street Journal*, June 23, 1993: B1.

# 12

# Promoting Safety and Health

Photodisc

## After studying this chapter, you should be able to

| OUTCOME 1 | Summarize the common elements of federal and provincial occupational health and safety legislation. |

| OUTCOME 2 | Describe the measures managers and employees can take to create a safe work environment. |

| OUTCOME 3 | Identify ways to control and eliminate various on-the-job health hazards. |

| OUTCOME 4 | Describe the programs organizations utilize to build better health among their workforces. |

| OUTCOME 5 | Indicate the methods for coping with stress. |

Occupational safety and health accidents are both numerous and costly to employers. To prevent losses such as these, employers are concerned with providing working conditions, in all areas of employment, that provide for the safety and health of their employees.

Although the laws safeguarding employees' physical and emotional well-being are certainly an incentive, many employers are motivated to provide desirable working conditions by virtue of their sensitivity to human needs and rights. The more cost-oriented employer recognizes the importance of avoiding accidents and illnesses wherever possible. One in every 21 workers can expect to be injured at work each year.[1] Costs associated with sick leave, disability payments, replacement of employees who are injured or killed, and workers' compensation far exceed the costs of maintaining a safety and health program. One study found that employers saved $1.95 and $3.75 for each $1 invested in workplace safety.[2] Accidents and illnesses attributable to the workplace may also have pronounced effects on employee morale and on the goodwill that the organization enjoys in the community and in the business world.

Employers are motivated by more than costs and their reputations to keep their workers safe and healthy, however. Most organizations provide their employees with good working conditions (1) because it is the right thing to do and (2) because firms realize that people are the most strategic asset they have. But truly proactive companies can go further than this using total quality management (TQM). TQM is a set of principles and practices whose core ideas include understanding customer needs, doing things right the first time, and striving for continuous improvement. Interestingly, a study that looked at companies that had won awards for TQM concluded that these firms not only had maintained above-average earnings, productivity, and growth rates but also had improved worker safety by a remarkable amount. Perhaps part of the reason why this is so is that programs such as TQM result in greater employee engagement. We will talk more about employee engagement and safety later in the chapter.

After discussing the legal requirements for safety and health, the rest of the chapter will focus on the creation of a safe and healthy work environment and on the management of stress.

# SAFETY AND HEALTH: IT'S THE LAW

OUTCOME 1

Consider these facts:

- According to the Association of Workers' Compensation Boards of Canada, in 2009, there were 939 workplace-related deaths, which means that about 4 Canadian workers die every working day.
- There are over 1 million work-related injuries each year.
- There are 260,000 injuries serious enough to cause the worker to miss at least one day of work.
- Over $12 billion is paid out to injured workers and their families annually.[3]

**occupational injury**
Any cut, fracture, sprain, or amputation resulting from a workplace accident or from an exposure involving an accident in the work environment

**occupational illness**
Any abnormal condition or disorder, other than one resulting from an occupational injury, caused by exposure to environmental factors associated with employment

The burden on Canada's commerce as a result of lost productivity and wages, medical expenses, and disability compensation is staggering. And there is no way to calculate the human suffering involved.

Occupational health and safety is regulated by the federal, provincial, and territorial governments. Statutes and standards vary slightly from jurisdiction to jurisdiction, although attempts have been made to harmonize the various acts and regulations. An **occupational injury** is any cut, fracture, sprain, or amputation resulting from a workplace accident. The worker's involvement in the accident can be direct, or the worker can simply be near enough to the accident to be injured as a result of it. An **occupational illness** is any condition or disorder (other than one resulting from an occupational injury) caused by the work environment. An occupational illness can be acute or chronic; it can result from inhaling, absorbing, ingesting, or directly contacting an illness-causing agent. Those working in the field agree that occupational illnesses are underreported because few diseases are caused solely by work-related factors, and cause and effect can be difficult to determine. Consider, for example, the case of a mine worker who has contracted a lung disease but who also smokes heavily.

## ACTS AND REGULATIONS

All HR managers should become familiar with the occupational health and safety laws that apply to their organization. The various acts and government departments that enforce the legislation are listed in Figure 12.1.

## DUTIES AND RESPONSIBILITIES

The fundamental duty of every employer is to take every reasonable precaution to ensure employee safety. The motivating forces behind workplace legislation were effectively articulated in the landmark case *Cory v. Wholesale Travel Group*, in which Judge Cory stated: "From cradle to grave, we are protected by regulations; they apply to the doctors attending our entry into this world and to the morticians present at our departure. Every day, from waking to sleeping, we profit from regulatory measures which we often take for granted."[4]

Regulatory legislation is essential to the operation of our complex industrial society; it plays a legitimate and vital role in protecting those who are most vulnerable and least able to protect themselves. The extent and importance of that role have increased continuously since the onset of the Industrial Revolution. Before effective workplace legislation was enacted, labourers—including children—worked unconscionably long hours in dangerous and unhealthy surroundings that evoke visions of Dante's Inferno. Regulatory legislation, with its enforcement provisions,

**FIGURE 12.1**

OCCUPATIONAL HEALTH AND SAFETY IN CANADA

| Jurisdiction | Legislation | Enforcement | Source |
|---|---|---|---|
| Canada | *Canada Labour Code* | Ministry of Labour | http://www.hrsdc.gc.ca/eng/lp/lo/ohs /publications/overview.shtml |
| Alberta | *Occupational Health and Safety Act* | Occupational Health and Safety Council (OHSC) | http://employment.alberta.ca/documents/WHS /WHS-LEG_ohsc_2009.pdf |
| British Columbia | *Workers Compensation Act* | WorkSafeBC | http://www.worksafebc.com/ |
| Manitoba | *The Workplace Safety and Health Act* | Workplace Safety and Health Division (WSHD) | http://safemanitoba.com/about.aspx |
| New Brunswick | *Occupational Health and Safety Act* | WorkSafeNB | http://www.worksafenb.ca/emp12_e.asp |
| Newfoundland and Labrador | *Occupational Health and Safety Act* | Occupational Health and Safety Branch | http://www.gs.gov.nl.ca/ohs/about.stm |
| Nova Scotia | *Occupational Health and Safety Act* | Department of Labour and Workforce Development | http://www.gov.ns.ca/lwd/ |
| Ontario | *Occupational Health and Safety Act* | Ministry of Labour | http://www.labour.gov.on.ca/english/hs/ |
| Prince Edward Island | *Occupational Health and Safety Act* | Workers Compensation Board of PEI | http://www.wcb.pe.ca/index. php3?number=58768&lang=E |
| Quebec | *An Act Respecting Occupational Health and Safety (AOHS)* | Commission de la santé et de la sécurité du travail (CSST) | http://www.csst.qc.ca/Portail/en /lois_politiques/index_loi.htm |
| Saskatchewan | *Occupational Health and Safety Act* | Saskatchewan Labour | http://www.labour.gov.sk.ca/overview-hs |
| Northwest Territories | *Safety Act* | Workers' Safety and Compensation Commission | http://www.wcb.nt.ca/safety_and_training /occupational_safety_health.html |
| Nunavut | *Safety Act* | For information only; not an official act | http://www.wcb.nt.ca/your_wcb/Legislation /General_Safety.pdf |

brought an end to the shameful situations that existed in mines, factories, and workshops in the 19th century. The differential treatment of regulatory offences is justified by their common goal of protecting the vulnerable.

## Duties of Employers

Besides providing a hazard-free workplace and complying with the applicable statutes and regulations, employers must inform their employees about safety and health requirements. Employers are also required to keep certain records, to compile an annual summary of work-related injuries and illnesses, and to ensure that supervisors are familiar with the work and its associated hazards (the supervisor, in turn, must ensure that workers are aware of those hazards). An organization with many employees may have a full-time health and safety officer.

In all jurisdictions, employers are required to report to the Workers' Compensation Board all accidents that cause injuries and diseases. Accidents resulting in death or critical injuries must be reported immediately; the accident must then be investigated and a written report submitted. In addition, employers must provide safety training

# HIGHLIGHTS IN HRM 12.1

## Health and Safety Checklist for New Employees

### Employee Orientation Checklist

| Areas to be Covered | Description | Completed | |
|---|---|---|---|
| | | Yes | No |
| Company Safety Rules | Explain safety rules that are specific to your company. | | |
| Company Policies | Explain the health, safety and wellness policies of your company. | | |
| Previous Training | Ask the employee if she/he has taken any safety training. | | |
| Training | Provide any necessary safety, environmental, compliance or policy/procedural training. | | |
| Health and Safety | Inform the health and safety specialist that a new employee has joined the company who may need safety training. Arrange for this training and education to occur. | | |
| Potential hazards | Tour your work areas and facility and discuss associated work area hazards and safe work practices. | | |
| Emergency Procedures | Show and explain how to use emergency eyewashes and showers, first aid kits, fire blankets, fire extinguishers, fire exits and fire alarm pull boxes, as applicable. Demonstrate the evacuation procedures. | | |
| Toxic Products | Identify workspaces where hazardous materials are used, stored or disposed. Provide training as necessary. | | |
| Food and Beverages | Explain that food and beverages are only permitted to be stored in refrigerators clearly labelled "FOOD ONLY". | | |
| Emergency Notification Form | Have employee complete the Emergency Notification form. Keep a copy for your files and send a copy to your Emergency Coordinator. | | |
| WHMIS | Identify the location of the Material Safety Data Sheets (MSDSs). Review the MSDSs for all hazardous materials to be used by the employee. Explain hazardous material labelling requirements. Conduct job specific training. | | |
| Emergency Evacuation | Review the company's Emergency Evacuation Plan and explain the evacuation signals and procedures, point out proper exit routes and the designated assembly area for your Branch. | | |
| Personal Protective Equipment (PPE) | Review the PPE program if the employee will be required to wear protective equipment. Issue appropriate personal protective equipment (PPE) that must be worn as required by the work being performed. | | |
| In Case of Injury or Illness | Review the reporting procedures in the event of an injury and/or accident. | | |
| Health and Safety Committee | Supply a copy of the facility telephone list with names of Safety Committee Members highlighted. Identify the location of the safety bulletin board. Explain how the employee can participate in the health and safety process (e.g., report hazards). | | |

Henryk Sadura/Shutterstock

Supervisors are required to advise employees of potential workplace hazards and ensure that workers wear safety equipment.

establish a nonadversarial climate for creating safe and healthy workplaces. In Ontario, at least one management representative and one worker representative must be certified. The certification program provides training in the following subjects: safety laws, sanitation, general safety, rights and duties, and indoor air quality. Read about how a world leader in health and safety structures committees to produce award-winning safety environments in Highlights in HRM 12.2.

**industrial disease**
A disease resulting from exposure to a substance relating to a particular process, trade, or occupation in industry

## PENALTIES FOR EMPLOYER NONCOMPLIANCE

The penalties for violating occupational health and safety regulations vary across provinces and territories. Most health and safety acts provide for fines up to $500,000, and offenders can be sent to jail. A Nova Scotia wind farm was fined $95,000 when two workers died of carbon monoxide poisoning while working in a shed with an improperly installed generator. General Motors Canada was fined $325,000 for a violation that resulted in an employee's death.[5] Bill C-45, also known as the corporate killing law, makes it possible for criminal charges to be brought against coworkers, supervisors, and executives when a worker is killed or injured on the job.

## WORKERS' COMPENSATION

Under workers' compensation, injured workers can receive benefits in the form of a cash payout (if the disability is permanent) or wage loss payments (if the worker can no longer earn the same amount of money). Unlimited medical aid is also provided, along with vocational rehabilitation, which includes physical, social, and psychological services. The goal is to return the employee to his or her job (or some modification thereof) as soon as possible. Sun Life Assurance Company of Canada has a return-to-work awards program that gives premium credits to employers that allow injured workers to change jobs or duties to enable these employees to return to work. A person who has been off work for 6 months has a 50 percent chance of returning; after 12 months, a 20 percent chance; and after 2 years, a 10 percent chance. Weyerhaeuser Co. Ltd of Vancouver's coordinated back-to-work program resulted in a 47 percent reduction in the duration of claims and a 39 percent reduction in the costs of the claims.

Compensation has become a complex issue. The definitions of accidents and injuries have recently been expanded to include industrial diseases and stress. An **industrial disease** is a disease resulting from exposure to a substance relating to a particular process, trade, or occupation in industry.

 **Using the Internet**

The National Institute of Disability Management and Research was established by business, labour, government, insurance, and rehabilitation representatives to promote best practices in disability management:

**http://www.nidmar.ca**

Equally problematic is compensation for stress, which is discussed in more detail later in the chapter. Stress-related disabilities are usually divided into three groups: physical injuries leading to mental disabilities (e.g., clinical depression after a serious accident); mental stress resulting in a physical disability (ulcers or migraines); and mental stress resulting in a mental condition (anxiety over workload or downsizing, leading to depression). Most claims, it should be pointed out, result from accidents or injuries.

The emphasis in workers' compensation has been shifting away from simply making assessments and payments toward creating safety-conscious environments where there will be fewer work-related accidents, disabilities, and diseases. In some industrial sectors, employers are working together to establish rules and training programs to further the cause of accident prevention.

## PROMOTING A SAFE WORK ENVIRONMENT

**OUTCOME 2**

We have seen that employers are required by law to provide safe working conditions for their employees. To achieve this objective, the majority of employers have a formal safety program. Typically, the HR department or the industrial relations department is responsible for the safety program. Although the success of a safety program depends largely on managers and supervisors of operating departments, the HR department typically coordinates the safety communication and training programs, maintains safety records required by legislation, and works closely with managers and supervisors in a cooperative effort to make the program a success. As Dennis Locking, HR manager for Calgary-based Volker Stevin, a growing road building company with more than 1,000 employees, states, "Safety is all about the way that you run your business. Wherever you see poor safety, there is always a poorly run company. If a company has a poor attitude towards safety, then it makes us wonder if that attitude is indicative of other aspects of their business."[6]

Organizations with formal safety programs generally have an employee–management safety committee that includes representatives from management, each department or manufacturing/service unit, and employee representatives. Committees are typically involved in investigating accidents and helping to publicize the importance of safety rules and their enforcement.

### CREATING A CULTURE OF SAFETY

Probably the most important role of a safety awareness program is motivating managers, supervisors, and subordinates to be champions of safety considerations. In one study, "survey results showed a direct correlation between an increase in management's commitment to safety in the workplace and a decrease in accidents."[7]

Firms today try to create a "culture" of safety within their organizations that goes beyond managing operational processes and reducing accidents. A culture of safety exists when everyone within an organization consciously works to improve its safety and health conditions. HR managers play a key role in this effort. Furthermore, experts are advocating for a culture of safety that focuses specifically on *process safety metrics*. For example, instead of counting injuries, managers should set goals on how many unit safety meetings should be held quarterly and measure goal attainment.

### Interviewing for Safety

One of the ways HR managers can help create a culture of safety within in an organization is to encourage supervisors to incorporate safety into their interviews with job candidates. Have you ever known someone who seemed accident prone? What about someone who rarely experienced a scratch? Several researchers have reported finding a correlation between different employees and their propensity for safety. Although asking job candidates about the injuries they have experienced is off-limits, interviewers can ask candidates other behavioural-type questions designed to elicit their propensity for safety. For example, interviewers might ask candidates a question about an unsafe incident they witnessed and how they handled it.

If managers and supervisors fail to demonstrate awareness, their subordinates can hardly be expected to do so. Unfortunately, many managers and supervisors wear their "safety hats" far less often than their "production, quality control, and methods of improvement hats."

Most organizations have a safety awareness program that entails the use of several different media. Safety lectures, commercially produced films, specially developed videocassettes, and other media, such as pamphlets, are useful for teaching and motivating employees to follow safe work procedures.

## The Key Role of the Supervisor

One of a supervisor's major responsibilities is to communicate to an employee the need to work safely. Beginning with new-employee orientation, safety should be emphasized continually. Proper work procedures, the use of protective clothing and devices, and potential hazards should be explained thoroughly. Furthermore, employees' understanding of all of these considerations should be verified during training sessions, and employees should be encouraged to take some initiative in maintaining a concern for safety. Since training by itself does not ensure continual adherence to safe work practices, supervisors must observe employees at work and reinforce safe practices. Where unsafe acts are detected, supervisors should take immediate action to find the cause. Supervisors should also foster a team spirit of safety among the work group.

## Proactive Safety Training Program

Safety training is not only good business; in certain occupational areas, safety and health training is legally required. When training is mandated, employers must keep accurate records of all employee education. Violations can incur criminal penalties.

In companies that voluntarily undertake safety and health training, one study found the most frequent topics to be (1) first aid, (2) defensive driving, (3) accident prevention techniques, (4) hazardous materials, and (5) emergency procedures.[8] Most programs emphasize the use of emergency first-aid equipment and personal safety equipment.

HR professionals, and safety directors in particular, advocate employee involvement when designing and implementing safety programs.[9] Employees can offer valuable ideas regarding specific safety and health topics to cover, instructional methods, and proper teaching techniques.[10] Furthermore, acceptance for safety training is heightened when employees feel a sense of ownership in the instructional program.

Many associations, such as the Canadian Centre for Occupational Health and Safety and the Industrial Accident Prevention Association, promoting occupational health and safety offer services and products to assist employers. Of course, the Web has become a popular way to disseminate safety training materials as well. Several reasons are advanced for the use of the Internet and information technology in safety and health training. First, enhanced delivery modes facilitate the development of both managers and employees.[11] Videos, PowerPoint presentations, and interactive CD-ROM training are ideal methods for standardized safety, environmental, and health instruction. Second, information technology allows organizations to customize their safety and health training needs.[12] At Stanley Works, the company's Internet is the number one tool for reducing health and safety problems. According to Kevin Nelson, employee health and safety director, "The Internet functions as the organization's SWAT team to develop and implement timely and efficient health and safety programs." Third, information technology is ideally suited for regulatory instruction.[13]

Safety begins with proper instruction, as these firefighters demonstrate in this training exercise.

**CHAPTER 12:** PROMOTING SAFETY AND HEALTH

Specific rules and regulations concerning safety are communicated through supervisors, bulletin board notices, employee handbooks, and signs attached to equipment. Safety rules are also emphasized in regular safety meetings, at new-employee orientations, and in manuals of standard operating procedures.[14]

Penalties for violation of safety rules are usually stated in the employee handbook. In a large percentage of organizations, the penalties imposed on violators are the same as those for violations of other rules. They include an oral or written warning for the first violation, suspension for repeated violations, and, as a last resort, dismissal. However, for serious violations—such as smoking around volatile substances—even the first offence may be cause for termination.

Although discipline may force employees to work safely, safety managers understand that the most effective enforcement of safety rules occurs when employees willingly obey and "champion" safety rules and procedures. This can be achieved when management actively encourages employees to participate in all aspects of the organization's safety program. For example, opportunities for employee involvement include (1) jointly setting safety standards with management, (2) participation in safety training, (3) involvement in designing and implementing special safety training programs, (4) involvement in establishing safety incentives and rewards, and (5) inclusion in accident investigations. Other ways to engage employees is to solicit their ideas and opinions when assessing the risk of jobs during the job analysis process. The idea behind this is to help identify potential hazards and develop protective measures before accidents occur. Establishing an employee safety suggestion program and asking employees to formally participate in the process of observing the safety behaviour of their coworkers are two other ways. Soliciting employees' opinions about the safety of the tools a company is considering purchasing is another way. At one railway company, not only do employees offer suggestions on the tools the company is considering buying, it is also not uncommon for the company's mechanical group to create new tools or retrofit them so they are safer for employees to use.

Safety rewards are another popular way to encourage workplace health and safety. There are many workable incentives—for example, gift certificates, cash awards, trips, dinners, and gifts such as clothing or jewellery. Economy Carriers, a transportation company based in Edmonton, offers an employee points program. It audits 18 operational areas for safety; on the basis of that audit, employees accumulate safety points, which they can use for purchases. Two researchers looked at 24 studies in which positive reinforcement and feedback were used to enhance safe behaviour. In all studies, incentives were found to improve safety conditions or reduce accidents.[15]

The Procter & Gamble (P&G) plant in Belleville, Ontario, won an award for its novel approach to incentives. The plant manager calculated that P&G would receive a refund from workers' compensation of about $200,000 a year if injuries were eliminated at the plant. He then set up a plan that would allow this refund to go to the local hospital if the target of zero injuries was achieved. With this community-based incentive, P&G employees met the target, and the hospital received a large donation.[16]

A word of caution should be noted with regard to rewards programs, however: they can provide an incentive for employees not to report safety accidents, as highlighted in Ethics in HRM. Rather than awards, many companies prominently display in their workplaces the number of consecutive days they have operated without an injury. The idea is to motivate employees to keep the injury-free "streak" going and possibly set new records for injury-free performance.

Figure 12.2 provides the steps recommended for launching a successful safety incentive program.

## INVESTIGATING AND RECORDING ACCIDENTS

Every accident, even those considered minor, should be investigated by the supervisor and a member of the safety committee. Such an investigation may

# ETHICS IN HRM

## Bury the Record

A supervisor was instructing a group of new recruits in the cleaning of metal parts in an assembly plant. She was attempting to demonstrate the cleaning technique to two employees at one workstation, while at another workstation, another new employee was trying to clean the parts himself. The cleaning liquid was highly toxic. The employee felt restricted by his safety gloves and so removed them. His eyes started to water, and instinctively he rubbed them with his solution-soaked hands. The pain was overwhelming, and no water was immediately available with which he could rinse his eyes. The employee suffered some temporary vision loss.

Who is to blame? The worker who started to clean without receiving full instructions and without using the issued gloves? The supervisor who could have forbidden the worker to start work until she explained the safety aspects? Or the company that failed to post warning signs about the hazardous nature of the cleaning solvent and did not have an eye-washing facility available?

Because workplace accidents increase workers' compensation premiums and the number of inspections, the company had an interest in not reporting the accident. Furthermore, because the company had instituted a reward program that provided incentives to employees for accident-free days, even the employees did not want to report the accident. Thus, the supervisor and the employees agreed to "bury the record." According to one survey of Canadian workers, 30 percent are afraid to report accidents, 29 percent know someone who reports false claims, and 27 percent know their employers are not reporting accidents. This is illegal. Another company was fined $600,000 for misleading the Workplace Health and Safety Insurance Board after it deliberately chose not to report that injured workers had missed time at work. In a highly publicized case in 2003, a young worker fell five storeys to his death, landing just one metre from the supervisor, who was his uncle. The first thing the supervisor did was call 911, and he was overheard telling workers, "Workers' comp will be here right away, so you get that railing up right now."

Source: Adapted from Ipsos Reid, July 2003, as described in *Canadian HR Reporter* (April 19, 2004): 17.

determine the factors contributing to the accident and reveal what corrections are needed to prevent it from happening again. Correction may require rearranging workstations, installing safety guards or controls, or, more often, giving employees additional safety training and reassessing their motivation for safety.[17]

Employers are required to keep certain records and to compile and post annual summaries of work-related injuries and illnesses. From these records, organizations can compute their incidence rates (i.e., the number of injuries and

## FIGURE 12.2

### STEPS IN A SUCCESSFUL SAFETY INCENTIVE PROGRAM

- Obtain the full support and involvement of management by providing cost benefits.
- Review current injury and health statistics to determine where change is needed.
- Decide on a program of action and set an appropriate budget.
- Select a realistic safety goal such as reducing accidents by a set percentage, improving safety suggestions, or achieving a length of time without a lost-time injury. Communicate your objectives to everyone involved.
- Select incentive rewards on the basis of their attractiveness to employees and their fit with your budget.
- Develop a program that is both interesting and fun. Use kickoff meetings, posters, banners, quizzes, and/or games to spark employee interest. Give all employees a chance to win.
- Communicate continually the success of your program. Provide specific examples of positive changes in behaviour.
- Reward safety gains immediately. Providing rewards shortly after improvements reinforces changed behaviour and encourages additional support for the safety program.

illnesses per 100 full-time employees during a given year). The standard equation for computing the incidence rate is shown below; 200,000 constitutes the base for 100 full-time workers who work 40 hours a week, 50 weeks a year:

$$\text{Incidence rate} = \frac{\text{Number of injuries and illnesses} \times 200{,}000}{\text{Total hours worked by all employees during period covered}}$$

The same formula can be used to compute incidence rates for (1) the number of workdays lost because of injuries and illnesses, (2) the number of nonfatal injuries and illnesses without lost workdays, and (3) cases involving only injuries or only illnesses.

Incidence rates are useful for making comparisons between work groups, between departments, and between similar units in the same organization. They also provide a basis for making comparisons with other organizations doing similar work. The occupational health and safety departments in each province and Human Resources and Social Development Canada compile data that employers can use to measure their safety records against those of other organizations. As noted in Ethics in HRM, organizations that report and investigate their own accidents often face more inspections, higher insurance premiums, and possible lawsuits.

# CONTROLLING AND ELIMINATING HEALTH HAZARDS

| OUTCOME 3 |

From the title alone, occupational health and safety legislation was clearly designed to protect the health and the safety of employees. Because of the dramatic impact of workplace accidents, however, managers and employees alike may pay more attention to these kinds of immediate safety concerns than to job conditions that are dangerous to their health. It is essential, therefore, that health hazards be identified and controlled.[18] Furthermore, pressure from the federal government and unions, as well as increased public concern, has given employers a definite incentive to provide the safest and healthiest work environment possible.

## SAFETY HAZARDS AND ISSUES

Workers face many different safety hazards on the job, which differ depending on their occupations. It is impossible to discuss all of them in this chapter. However, we will discuss a number of hazards that have been getting a great deal of attention from HR managers and firms lately.

### Fatigue

Few safety issues have been in the news more recently than employee fatigue. You have probably heard about air traffic controllers who have fallen asleep on the job and could not be awakened by pilots trying to contact them. Fatigue is more of a problem in organizations that operate around the clock or have night shifts. Studies show that 30 to 50 percent of night-shift workers report falling asleep at least once a week while on the job, according to one expert.[19]

Fatigue may not result in "life or death" consequences for most jobs. Nonetheless, managers, employees, and the public are concerned about how it affects workplace safety and performance. The regulations in certain industries limit the number of hours employees can work per shift. The airline industry is one such industry. However, even with the limits, workers are finding themselves fatigued. Some experts say downsizing may be a factor as fewer workers are being asked to cover more shifts.

### Distracted Driving

Do you know what the leading cause of worker fatalities each year is? Motor vehicle crashes. Moreover, according to a National Highway Traffic Safety Administration

# HIGHLIGHTS IN HRM 12.3

## Texting While Driving: A Sample HR Policy

A survey of more than 2,000 employers conducted by the National Safety Council found that 58 percent had some type of cell-phone use policy in place, and roughly one-quarter of those surveyed prohibit both handheld and hands-free devices while driving for some or all employees. Here is an example of AT&T's policy:

> Employees are required to be familiar with and comply with local laws before using a wireless

device while operating a motor vehicle for business purposes. Safe operation of any vehicle in the performance of company business is the responsibility of the driver and must be given appropriate attention at all times. In every situation, do not use a wireless device while the vehicle is in motion if doing so distracts attention from driving. Additionally, all employees are prohibited from using data services on their wireless devices, such as texting or accessing the Web or other distracting activities, while driving.

Sources: "Texting While Driving Toolkit Sample Company Policy," AT&T, accessed May 20, 2011, http://www.att.com.: J. Ferguson "Distracted driving and Employers Policies" *HR Web Café* November 1, 2009, http://www.hrwebcafe.com

---

study, people who send text messages while driving are three times more likely to crash than other drivers, and distracted driving accounts for 80 percent of all accidents. When it comes to mass transit, the consequences of distracted driving can be catastrophic. For example, in 2008, a Los Angeles commuter train collided head on with another train. Twenty-five people died, including the operator of the train. Another 135 others were injured. A subsequent investigation of the accident found that the operator had sent or received 57 text messages while on the job that day, including one sent 22 seconds before the crash.[20]

To help prevent distracted driving accidents, a growing number of employers are adopting mandatory cell-phone policies for their employees. Highlights in HRM 12.3 shows a template of such a policy developed by AT&T that companies can utilize. Other companies are doing more than establishing policies. They are outfitting their phones with apps such as Phone Guard, which prevents drivers from texting, browsing the Web, or checking email when they are travelling 10 miles per hour or faster. Mobile phones are not the only electronic safety culprit, however. Workers who stop hearing the world around them because they are wired up to MP3 players also create risks.

## Workplace Violence

Many people think of workplace violence as a physical assault. But there are many forms, including

- Threatening behaviour, such as shaking fists or throwing objects
- Verbal or written threats
- Harassment—any behaviour that demeans, embarrasses, or humiliates
- Verbal abuse, including swearing, insults, or condescending language
- Physical attacks, including hitting, shoving, pushing, or kicking[21]

Manon Blanc at Queen's University and Kevin Kelloway, director of the CN Centre for Occupational Health and Safety at Saint Mary's University, have identified the job characteristics that put workers at risk for aggression and violence in the workplace:

- Interacting with the public
- Making decisions that influence other people's lives (e.g., terminating an employee or assigning a failing grade) or denying the public a service or request

- Supervising and/or disciplining others
- Working nights or working alone
- Handling cash, handling or guarding valuables, or collecting or delivering items of value
- Caring for the physical or emotional needs of others or going to clients' homes
- Serving or selling alcohol or dealing with individuals under the influence of mind-altering substances[22]

Exposure to workplace violence results in employees fearing more incidents of violence, leading to personal strains (such as stress) and organizational strains (reduced commitment, neglect of job duties).

The Canadian Centre for Occupational Health and Safety suggests that preventive measures should include

- *Workplace design*, such as locks or physical barriers (pass-through windows or bulletproof enclosures), lighting, and electronic surveillance
- *Administrative practices*, such as keeping cash register funds to a minimum, varying the time of day that cash is emptied, and using a security firm to deliver cash
- *Work practices* (particularly for those working alone away from an office, such as home care workers and real estate agents) that might include having a designated contact kept informed of the employee's schedule and checking the credentials of clients[23]

Employers in all Canadian jurisdictions are bound to take all reasonable precautions to protect the safety and health of their workers. At this time, however, only British Columbia and Saskatchewan have specific laws requiring employers to protect their workers from violence. Ontario has introduced Bill 168, which added new provisions to the province's occupational health and safety act to cover situations of workplace violence and harassment. Under this legislation, workplace harassment is defined as *engaging in a course of vexatious comment or conduct against a worker in a workplace that is known or ought reasonably to be known to be unwelcome.*

However, under common law, an employer may be held liable for the actions of employees. Nurses are victims of violence at a rate that is 16 times higher that of other service workers; almost 70 percent of nurses have been physically assaulted.[24] Managers and supervisors can be trained to recognize violence indicators, such as those given in Figure 12.3. Awareness of these threatening behaviours can provide an opportunity to intervene and prevent disruptive, abusive, or violent acts. Managers must effectively communicate a zero-tolerance policy for violence and encourage employees to report any possible or observed incidents of workplace violence. A meaningful reporting procedure with clear lines of responsibility can ensure that management is promptly notified of potential security risks to take immediate steps to resolve the issues. Finally, organizations have formalized workplace violence prevention policies, informing employees that aggressive employee behaviour will not be tolerated.

## Workplace Emergencies

Because an organization's HR department deals with every employee, it is in an ideal position to spearhead the effort to plan for emergencies, deal with them, and provide assistance to employees afterward. A workplace emergency is an unforeseen situation that threatens employees, customers, or the public; disrupts or shuts down operations; or causes physical or environmental damage. Emergencies can be natural or human-made. In addition to workplace violence, they can include the following.

- Floods
- Hurricanes

**Using the Internet**

The Canadian Initiative on Workplace Violence, a social research firm, offers information at **http://www. workplaceviolence.ca**

FIGURE 12.3

PART 4

## VIOLENCE INDICATORS: KNOW THE WARNING SIGNS

Most people leave a trail of indicators before they become violent. Similarly, disgruntled former employees who commit acts of violence leave warning signs of their intent before and after termination. The following behaviours should be taken seriously when assessing situations of potential violence:

- Direct or veiled threatening statements
- Recent performance declines, including concentration problems and excessive excuses
- Prominent mood or behaviour changes; despondence
- Preoccupation with guns, knives, or other weapons
- Deliberate destruction of workplace equipment; sabotage
- Fascination with stories of violence
- Reckless or antisocial behaviour; evidence of prior assaultive behaviour
- Aggressive behaviour or intimidating statements
- Written messages of violent intent; exaggerated perceptions of injustice
- Serious stress in personal life
- Obsessive desire to harm a specific group or person
- Violence against a family member
- Substance abuse

**Sources:** Adapted from *Violence in the Workplace: Risk Factors and Prevention Strategies*, NIOSH Bulletin #59; Gillian Flynn, "Employers Can't Look Away from Workplace Violence," *Workforce* 79, no. 7 (July 2000): 68–70; Dannie B. Fogleman, "Minimizing the Risk of Violence in the Workplace," *Employment Relations Today* 87, no. 1 (Spring 2000): 83–98.

- Tornadoes
- Fires
- Toxic gas releases
- Chemical spills
- Radiological accidents
- Explosions
- Civil disturbances and terrorism

**emergency action plan**
A plan an organization develops that contains step-by-step procedures for dealing with various emergency situations

Most large organizations have emergency action plans to deal with incidents such as these. An **emergency action plan** must include, among other things, procedures for reporting a fire or other emergency, evacuating a facility, and accounting for employees after an evacuation. The plan must also include procedures for employees who must remain in facilities to ensure that critical plant operations continue, as well as procedures for workers performing rescue and medical duties. A copy of the emergency action plan should either be provided to employees or kept in a convenient location where employees can access it. Highlights in HRM 12.4 shows a readiness assessment checklist organizations can complete to determine how prepared they are for an emergency.

It is also advisable for organizations to have alternative communication centres or backup computer servers they can use if their facilities are destroyed or inaccessible. The off-site physical or Web locations can be used to store originals or duplicate copies of accounting records, legal documents, emergency contact lists, and other essential records. Amazon.com, for example, has a computing service that allows companies to store data on its servers in addition to or in lieu of their own servers. HR managers should also make sure that employees know whom to contact and how during an emergency. A firm's website can also be used to disseminate crisis information to employees, the press, and other entities that need information.

# HIGHLIGHTS IN HRM 12.4

## Emergency Readiness Checklist

| How Prepared Is Your Business for an Emergency? | Yes | No | Unsure |
|---|:---:|:---:|:---:|
| 1. Does your business know what kinds of emergencies might affect it? – both internally and externally? | ❏ | ❏ | ❏ |
| 2. Does your business have a written, comprehensive emergency plan in place to help ensure your safety and take care of employees until help can arrive? | ❏ | ❏ | ❏ |
| 3. Has your business created and practiced procedures to quickly evacuate and find shelter in case of an emergency? | ❏ | ❏ | ❏ |
| 4. Has your business created a communication plan to communicate with employees in an emergency? (Examples include setting up a telephone call tree, a password-protected page on the company website, email alert or call-in voice recording, and a contact list that includes employee emergency contact information.) | ❏ | ❏ | ❏ |
| 5. Has your business talked with utility service providers about potential alternatives and identified back-up options? | ❏ | ❏ | ❏ |
| 6. Has your business determined operations that need to be up and running first after an emergency and how to resume key operations? | ❏ | ❏ | ❏ |
| 7. Has your business created a list of inventory and equipment, including computer hardware, software, and peripherals (such as backed up/protected records and critical data) for business continuity and insurance purposes? | ❏ | ❏ | ❏ |
| 8. Has your business met with your insurance provider to review current coverage in case of an emergency? | ❏ | ❏ | ❏ |
| 9. Does your business promote family and individual preparedness among co-workers (for example, by providing emergency preparedness information during staff meetings, through newsletters, the company intranet, and periodic employee emails, and via other internal communication tools)? | ❏ | ❏ | ❏ |
| 10. Have emergency shutdown procedures been developed for equipment such as boilers, automatic feeds, or other operations that cannot simply be left running in an emergency evacuation? | ❏ | ❏ | ❏ |
| 11. Has your business worked with your community on emergency planning efforts and helped to plan for community recovery? | ❏ | ❏ | ❏ |

Source: Planning for Emergencies © 2007 National Safety Council

## Crisis Management Teams

Most large organizations have formal crisis management teams. These teams, composed of both hourly and managerial employees, conduct initial risk assessment surveys, develop action plans to respond to violent situations, and, importantly, perform crisis intervention during violent, or potentially violent, encounters. For example, a crisis management team would investigate a threat reported by an employee. The team's mandate would be to gather facts about the threat, decide whether the organization should intervene, and, if so, determine the most appropriate method of doing so. Occasionally, a member of the team or an individual manager will be called on to intervene and calm an angry employee.[25] When this occurs, the steps given in Figure 12.4 will help defuse a volatile situation.

FIGURE 12.4

## CALMING AN ANGRY EMPLOYEE

If you try to defuse a tense situation, remember that anger frequently results from a person's feeling of being wronged, misunderstood, or unheard. Keep the following tips in mind to guide you:

- Strive to save the employee's dignity during an angry confrontation. Do not attack a person's rash statements or continue a muddled line of thinking.

- Hold all conversations in private. Do not allow the employee to create an embarrassing public situation for himself or herself, yourself, or other employees.

- Always remain calm. Anger or aggressiveness on your part will trigger a similar response in the employee.

- Listen to the employee with an open mind and nonjudgmental behaviour. Give the employee the benefit of hearing him or her out.

- Recognize the employee's legitimate concerns or feelings. Agree that the employee has a valid point and that you will work to correct the problem.

- If the employee is very emotional or if the engagement seems out of control, schedule a delayed meeting so people can calm down.

- Keep the discussion as objective as possible. Focus on the problem at hand, not the personalities of individuals. A cornerstone of conflict resolution is to "attack the problem, not the personality."

- If the employee appears overly aggressive, withdraw immediately and seek professional help before any further discussion with the employee.

- If your efforts fail to calm the employee, report the incident to your manager, security, or HR personnel.

**Source:** Adapted from professional literature on crisis management and seminars attended by the authors.

When violent incidents, such as the death of a coworker, happen at work, employees can experience shock, guilt, grief, apathy, resentment, cynicism, and a host of other emotions.[26] Such incidents may require the crisis management team to perform crisis intervention through positive counselling techniques.[27]

## CREATING A HEALTHY WORK ENVIRONMENT

As is apparent from its title, the *Occupational Health and Safety Act* was clearly designed to protect the health and safety of employees. However, because of the dramatic impact workplace accidents have, managers and employees sometimes pay more attention to them than health hazards. Accidents happen quickly. The effects of health hazards show up only over time. When they do show up, however, they adversely affect workers, their families, and their companies.

### ERGONOMICS

One way to help eliminate health hazards in the workplace is via ergonomics. Recall that we discussed ergonomics in Chapter 4 when we looked at job design. Ergonomics focuses on ensuring that jobs are designed for safe and efficient work while improving the safety, comfort, and performance of users. Ergonomics can be as simple as rearranging a workstation so that fewer steps are needed to gather items or organizing items so that they are within easier reach. Part of ergonomics involves looking at the design of equipment and the physical abilities of the operators who use it. There is substantial variation in the way people move depending on their physical sizes, genders, ages, and other factors. Designing equipment controls to be compatible with both the physical characteristics and the reaction capabilities of the people who must operate them and the environment in which they work is critically important. Ergonomics also considers the requirements of a diverse workforce, accommodating, for example, women who may lack the strength to operate equipment requiring intense physical force or Asian Canadians who may lack the stature to reach equipment controls.

**FIGURE 12.5**

KEY ELEMENTS FOR A SUCCESSFUL ERGONOMICS PROGRAM

Companies with award-winning ergonomics programs list the following as common elements of success:

- *Provide notice and training for employees.* Implement a well-publicized ergonomics policy or present ergonomic information in safety policies or training programs. Train employees, supervisors, and managers in basic workplace ergonomics.
- *Conduct preinjury hazard assessment.* Survey the workplace and work processes for potential hazards and adopt measures to lessen the exposure to ergonomic risk factors. Answer the question, "Are certain work areas more prone to ergonomic hazards than others?"
- *Involve employees.* Include employees in risk assessment, recognition of musculoskeletal disorder (MSD) symptoms, design of work-specific equipment or tools, and the setting of work performance rules and guidelines.
- *Plan and execute.* Integrate ergonomic responsibilities into the performance plans for all personnel. Demand accountability for program success.
- *File injury reports.* Encourage early reporting of MSD symptoms or injuries. Refer employees to the company's medical facilities or to the employee's personal physician for treatment.
- *Evaluate and assess the ergonomics program.* Periodically review the effectiveness of the ergonomics program. If the program appears to be ineffective, determine the underlying causes for failure and propose corrective changes.

**cumulative trauma disorders**
Injuries involving tendons of the fingers, hands, and arms that become inflamed from repeated stresses and strains

Ergonomics has proven cost-effective at organizations such as Compaq Computer, 3M, and Pratt & Whitney, which eliminated, or at least reduced, many repetitive-motion injuries, particularly those related to the back and wrist. The key elements of successful ergonomic programs are shown in Figure 12.5.

## Cumulative Trauma Disorders

Meat cutters, fish filleters, cooks, dental hygienists, textile workers, violinists, flight attendants, office workers at computer terminals, and others whose jobs require repetitive motion of the fingers, hands, or arms are reporting injuries in growing percentages. Known as **cumulative trauma disorders** or repetitive-motion injuries, these musculoskeletal disorders (MSDs) are injuries of the muscles, nerves, tendons, ligaments, joints, and spinal disks caused by repeated stresses and strains. One of the more common conditions is *carpal tunnel syndrome*, which is characterized by tingling or numbness in the fingers occurring when a tunnel of bones and ligaments in the wrist narrows and pinches nerves that reach the fingers and the base of the thumb. Without proper treatment, employees with carpal tunnel syndrome can lose complete feeling in their hands. Another cumulative trauma disorder prevalent among tennis players is tennis elbow.

## Computer Workstation Issues

Figure 12.6 provides a checklist of potential repetitive-motion problem areas for employees using computers. Video display terminals (VDTs) are a particular concern. The problems that managers have to confront in this area fall into three major groups:

1. *Visual difficulties.* VDT operators frequently complain of blurred vision, sore eyes, burning and itching eyes, and glare.
2. *Muscular aches and pains.* Pains in the back, neck, and shoulders are common complaints of VDT operators.
3. *Job stress.* Eye strain, postural problems, insufficient training, excessive workloads, and monotonous work are complaints reported by three-quarters of VDT users.

## FIGURE 12.6

### COMPUTER WORKSTATION ERGONOMICS CHECKLIST

Use the following list to identify potential problem areas that should receive further investigation. Any "no" response may point to a problem.

1. Does the workstation ensure proper worker posture, such as
   - Thighs in the horizontal position?
   - Lower legs in the vertical position?
   - Feet flat on the floor or on a footrest?
   - Wrists straight and relaxed?

2. Does the chair
   - Adjust easily?
   - Have a padded seat with a rounded front?
   - Have an adjustable backrest?
   - Provide lumbar support?
   - Have casters?

3. Are the height and tilt of the work surface on which the keyboard is located adjustable?
4. Is the keyboard detachable?
5. Do keying actions require minimal force?
6. Is there an adjustable document holder?
7. Are armrests provided where needed?
8. Are glare and reflections minimized?
9. Does the monitor have brightness and contrast controls?
10. Is there sufficient space for knees and feet?
11. Can the workstation be used for either right- or left-handed activity?

**Source:** The National Institute for Occupational Safety and Health (NIOSH), *Elements of Ergonomics Programs: A Primer Based on Workplace Evaluations of Musculoskeletal Disorders* (Washington, DC: U.S. Government Printing Office, March 1997).

To capitalize on the benefits of VDTs while safeguarding employee health, Dr. James Sheedy, a VDT and vision expert, offers these tips on how to minimize the negative effects of computer use on the eyes and body:

- Place the computer screen four to nine inches below eye level.
- Keep the monitor directly in front of you.
- Sit in an adjustable-height chair with lower back support and with feet flat on the floor.
- Use shades or blinds to reduce the computer screen glare created by window lighting.
- Keep elbows close to the body and supported.
- Keep wrists and hands in line with forearms.

## Chemical Hazards

When a boiler maker at Teck Cominco Ltd., a smelter plant in Trail, British Columbia, started to experience symptoms that resembled motion sickness, he never associated it with exposure to poisonous thallium metal. Like many workers, he had limited awareness of the chemicals in the workplace. And not only workers in industrial settings are exposed to chemicals. Many teachers work in prefabricated temporary classrooms, which may contain mouldy material. It is estimated that more than 65,000 different chemicals are currently in use with which humans may come into contact. Many of these chemicals are harmful, lurking for years in the body with no outward symptoms until the disease they cause is well established. Increasingly, employees are complaining of physiological reactions to low-level chemical exposures in the environment, such as headaches, dry nasal passages, and nausea. These complaints have several labels, such as total allergy symptom, 20th-century disease, and multiple chemical sensitivity. (For a full discussion of chemical hazards, read Chapter 5 in *Management of Occupational Health and Safety*, 5th Edition (Nelson Canada, 2011), by Kevin Kelloway and Lori Francis.

In the belief that workers have the right to know about potential workplace hazards, industry, labour, and government have joined forces to develop a

**CHAPTER 12:** PROMOTING SAFETY AND HEALTH

common information system for labelling hazardous substances. The Workplace Hazardous Materials Information System (WHMIS) is based on three elements:

1. *Labels.* Labels are designed to alert the worker that the container holds a potentially hazardous substance. The two types of labels (supplier labels and workplace labels) must contain specified and regulated information, including product identifiers and data on safe handling and material safety.
2. *Material Safety Data Sheets (MSDSs).* An MSDS identifies the product and its potentially hazardous ingredients and suggests procedures for handling the product safely. The MSDS information must be comprehensive, current, and available in English and French.
3. *Training.* Workers must be trained to check for labels and to follow specific procedures for handling spills. Training workers is part of the due diligence required of employers; it also becomes an important factor in the event of a lawsuit. The Peel Board of Education in Ontario has developed a computer-based program to train workers in WHMIS. This program allows illiterate workers to respond to audio commands by touching the screen.

## Smoking and Tobacco Smoke

For the past 10 years, probably the most heated workplace health issue has been smoking. In a study published in the *Journal of the American Medical Association*, findings showed that "in businesses that permitted smoking, more than 60 percent of the office air samples contained nicotine levels above the 'significant risk' level of 6.8 micrograms per cubic metre."[28] Because of findings such as these, smokers have been banned from lighting up on airplanes, at work, and in restaurants and hotels. Furthermore, nonsmokers, fuelled by studies linking "passive smoking" (inhaling other people's smoke) with disease and death and irritated by smoke getting in their eyes, noses, and clothes, have demanded a smoke-free environment. Employers will benefit from this ban. Smokers on average miss 6.16 days of work per year, nearly double the rate of nonsmokers.[29] A Labour Canada study found that employees who smoke cost companies about $2,500 more per year (than nonsmoking employees) in increased absenteeism, lost productivity, and increased health and life insurance premiums.[30] It has been documented that health care costs are higher for smokers; for this reason, some employers are charging smokers more for extended health insurance or are reducing their benefits. Many employers, however, prefer positive reinforcement through wellness programs to encourage employees to stop smoking.

A British Columbia arbitrator has ruled that smoking is as addictive as cocaine and so constitutes a drug dependency.[31] Under human rights legislation, employers may have to allow workers with a substance abuse problem to take a leave of absence to seek treatment. If nicotine addiction is accepted as a disability, companies may have to provide smoking cessation programs and refrain from disciplining addicted employees who smoke.

## BUILDING BETTER PHYSICAL AND EMOTIONAL HEALTH AMONG EMPLOYEES

**OUTCOME 4**

Along with improving working conditions that are hazardous to employee health, employers today are cognizant of the physical and emotional health of their employees and thus provide them with programs to maintain and improve both. Firms are doing so not only to lower their health costs but also because they recognize that employees not distracted by health problems are able to operate more safely. Better health can also reduce absenteeism, increase efficiency and creativity on the part of employees, and lead to better morale and teamwork among them. An organization with a healthy, safe, resilient, and creative workforce is certainly in a better position to compete than an organization with unhealthy workers.

# THE BUSINESS CASE

## Investing in Employee Health

For the 2,800 employees at Husky Injection Molding Systems of Bolton, Ontario, work seems like play as they visit their children over lunch; eat fresh, healthy cafeteria food; play table tennis on their breaks; and receive an extra vacation day for staying fit. Husky spends more than $4 million a year on employee benefits, but this investment more than pays for itself in higher productivity, lower turnover, and lower absenteeism. The voluntary turnover rate is about 8 percent, which is below the industry average of 10 percent. The absenteeism rate is 3.7 days, less than half of the manufacturing industry average of 9.1 days. Injury claims are 1.5 for every 200,000 hours worked, compared to an industry average of 7.2. The annual drug benefit costs are $255 per employee compared to the industry average of $507. The estimated savings are $8.4 million a year.

Husky is not the only company seeing returns on investments in workplace well-being. Organizations in Atlantic Canada found that employees who participated in a three-month wellness program reduced the risk of heart disease and stroke, for an estimated return on the investment of $1.64 for every dollar spent. In one of the largest studies done on return on investment of health care programs, the National Wellness Institute delivered wellness programs consisting of smoking cessation workshops, lifestyle and nutrition counselling, and on-site fitness to 90,000 employees in 30 locations. Those who participated had lower health care costs of between $5 and $16 per month. Even a one-time inexpensive program can show returns. TELUS introduced a flu immunization program and saw absences due to respiratory illness drop from 33 to 22 percent. Overall, studies of wellness programs document cost–benefit ratios of between $3 and $8 for every dollar spent. The benefits to organizations include decreased lost workdays, decreased workers' compensation costs, increased employee morale and productivity, reduced overtime costs, and reduced workplace injuries. Yet only 60 percent of Canadian workplaces offer wellness programs. Why aren't more companies doing it?

Sources: Vera N. Held, "Husky's Andrée Brière on Productivity and Stress Free Employees," *HR Professional* (August/September 2005): 19–25; T. Grant, "Husky Woos Workers with Unique Perks," *The Globe and Mail* (August 20, 2001); S. Kee, "The Bottom Line on Wellness," *Canadian Health Care Manager* 9, no. 1 (Fall 2002): 23; G. Lowe, "The Dollars and Sense of Health Promotion," *Canadian HR Reporter* (September 23, 2002): 7–8.

---

Recall that we discussed employee assistance programs (EAPs) in Chapter 11. As we have indicated, EAPs can help employees with a range of problems. EAPs can also help workers with relationship, marital, and family problems; anger, depression, anxiety, and stress; and eldercare demands. Workplace issues, addiction, and self-improvement are other areas in which EAPs provide workers with help. If an employee's situation necessitates it, the EAP refers the worker to in-house counsellors or outside professionals.

> **depression**
> Negative emotional state marked by feelings of low spirits, gloominess, sadness, and loss of pleasure in ordinary activities

Importantly, wellness programs produce measurable cost savings to employers, as described in the Business Case.

Next, we look at some of the issues employees face in terms of their physical and emotional health that EAPs and other workplace programs can address.

## Depression in the Workplace

Although personal crises are typically fraught with emotion, most of them are resolved in a reasonable period of time, and the troubled individual's equilibrium is restored. Unfortunately, when personal crises linger, stress and tension may cause or intensify a mood disorder, such as depression. **Depression** is a decrease in functional activity accompanied by symptoms of low spirits, gloominess, and sadness. Highlights in HRM 12.5 lists the symptoms of depression.

About 5 percent of Canadians experience depression. With available treatment, however, 70 percent of these individuals will significantly improve, usually within a matter of weeks.

Since depression lowers individual productivity, causes morale problems, increases absenteeism, and contributes to substance abuse, it is important for managers to identify signs of depression on the job and to learn to deal with depressed employees. The more likely workplace signs of depression are

# HIGHLIGHTS IN HRM 12.5

## Depression in the Workplace

When a depressed mood persists for a few weeks, deepens, and eventually starts interfering with work and other aspects of everyday life, it has likely become an illness—or a clinical depression. In the workplace, a person with depression will exhibit many of the following signs:

### Recognizing Depression
**Personal Changes**

- Irritability, hostility
- Hopelessness, despair
- Slowness of speech
- Chronic fatigue

- Withdrawal from or extreme dependency on others
- Alcohol or drug abuse

**Workplace Changes**
- Difficulty in making decisions
- Decreased productivity
- Inability to concentrate
- Decline in dependability
- Unusual increase in errors in work
- Accident proneness
- Frequent tardiness, increased "sick" days
- Lack of enthusiasm for work

Someone who has been experiencing many of these signs for a few weeks or more should seek help immediately.

Source: Reprinted by permission of Canadian Mental Health Association, National.

decreased energy, concentration and memory problems, guilt feelings, irritability, and chronic aches and pains that do not respond to treatment. When confronted with depressed employees, managers and supervisors are encouraged to be concerned with the employee's problem, be an active listener, and—should the depression persist—suggest professional help.[32] Under no circumstances should managers attempt to play amateur psychologist and try to diagnose an employee's condition. Mood disorders such as depression are complex in nature and do not lend themselves to quick diagnoses. Furthermore, in reviewing such cases, the organization should pay particular attention to workplace safety factors because there is general agreement that emotional disturbances are primary or secondary factors in a large portion of industrial accidents and violence.

## Alcoholism

Alcoholism affects workers in every occupational category—blue collar and white collar. In confronting the problem, employers must recognize that alcoholism is a disease that follows a rather predictable course. Thus, they can take specific actions to deal with employees showing symptoms of the disease at particular stages of its progression. Alcoholism typically begins with social drinking getting out of control. As the disease progresses, the alcoholic loses control over how much to drink and eventually cannot keep from drinking, even at inappropriate times. The person uses denial to avoid facing the problems created by the abuse of alcohol and often blames others for these problems. The first step in helping the alcoholic is to awaken the person to the reality of his or her situation.

To identify alcoholism as early as possible, it is essential that supervisors monitor the performance of all personnel regularly and systematically. A supervisor should carefully document evidence of declining performance on the job and then confront the employee with unequivocal proof that the job is suffering. The employee should be assured that help will be made available without penalty. Since the evaluations are made solely with regard to lagging job performance, a supervisor can avoid any mention of alcoholism and allow such employees to seek aid as they would for any other problem.[33]

## Abuse of Illegal Drugs

The abuse of drugs by employees is one of the major employment issues today. Drug abuse is now a national problem and has spread to every industry, occupation, and employee level. Estimates of the costs of substance abuse by employees vary considerably. Besides lost productivity, there are the costs of increased numbers of accidents and injuries and rising rates of employee theft. The costs of substance abuse can have a dramatic impact on the bottom line. In the United States, when random drug testing was introduced, the number of fatal accidents dropped sharply. Drug testing remains a controversial issue. In general, pre-employment drug or alcohol testing or random testing of current employees is prohibited by human rights laws. Furthermore, human rights legislation prohibits discrimination on the basis of disability, and drug and alcohol dependency is generally considered to be a disability.

Although attention is usually focused on the abuse of illegal drugs, it should be noted that the abuse of legal drugs can also pose a problem for employees. Employees who abuse legal drugs—those prescribed by physicians—often do not realize they have become addicted or how their behaviour has changed as a result of their addiction. Also, managers should be aware that some employees may be taking legal sedatives or stimulants as part of their medical treatment and that their behaviour at work may be affected by their use of these drugs.

## JOB STRESS AND BURNOUT

HR professionals are well aware of the negative effects of workplace stress on employees' health and job performance. For example, job stress places both women and men at risk for cardiovascular problems and depression and increases employee susceptibility to infectious diseases. All of these contribute to higher health care costs and can lower productivity, job satisfaction, and retention. Importantly, in a study on the magnitude of stress in the workplace, 54 percent of respondents indicated that they "often" or "always" come home from work in a state of fatigue and nearly 50 percent come in to work tired.[34]

**Stress** is any demand on the individual that requires coping behaviour. Stress comes from two basic sources: physical activity and mental or emotional activity. The physical reaction of the body to both types of stress is the same. Psychologists use two separate terms to distinguish between positive and negative forms of stress, even though reactions to the two forms are the same biochemically. **Eustress** is positive stress that accompanies achievement and exhilaration. Eustress is the stress of meeting challenges such as those found in a managerial, technical, or public-contact job. Eustress is regarded as a beneficial force that helps us forge ahead against obstacles. What is harmful is **distress**. Stress becomes distress when we begin to sense a loss of our feelings of security and adequacy. Helplessness, desperation, and disappointment turn stress into distress.

### JOB-RELATED STRESS

Although the body experiences a certain degree of stress (either eustress or distress) in all situations, here we are primarily concerned with stress related to the work setting. In this setting, management can use some preventive approaches.

### Sources of Job-Related Stress

Causes of workplace stress are many. However, according to a study by Luminari, a national health care company, four factors have a major influence on employee stress:

- *High demand:* having too much to do in too short a time
- *High effort:* having to expend too much mental or physical energy over too long a period

---

**stress**
Any adjustive demand caused by physical, mental, or emotional factors that require coping behaviour

**eustress**
Positive stress that accompanies achievement and exhilaration

**distress**
Harmful stress characterized by a loss of feelings of security and adequacy

**burnout**
The most severe stage of distress, manifesting itself in depression, frustration, and loss of productivity

- *Low control:* having too little influence over the way a job is done on a day-to-day basis
- *Low reward:* receiving inadequate feedback on performance and no recognition for a job well done[35]

Other recognized job stressors include layoffs and organizational restructuring; disagreements with managers or fellow employees; prejudice because of age, gender, race, or religion; inability to voice complaints; and poor working conditions. Even minor irritations such as a lack of privacy, unappealing music, and other conditions can be distressful to one person or another.

## Burnout

**Burnout** is a severe stage of distress. Career burnout generally occurs when a person begins questioning his or her own personal values. Quite simply, the person no longer feels that what he or she is doing is important. Depression, frustration, and a loss of productivity are all symptoms of burnout. Burnout is due primarily to a lack of personal fulfillment in the job or a lack of positive feedback about performance.[36] In organizations that have downsized, the remaining employees can experience burnout because they must perform more work with fewer coworkers. Overachievers can experience burnout when unrealistic work goals are unattainable.[37]

## COPING WITH STRESS

**OUTCOME 5**

Many employers have developed stress management programs to teach employees how to minimize the negative effects of job-related stress. A typical program might include instruction in relaxation techniques, coping skills, listening skills, methods of dealing with difficult people, time management, and assertiveness. All of these techniques are designed to break the pattern of tension that accompanies stress situations and to help participants achieve greater control of their lives. Organizational techniques such as clarifying the employee's work role, redesigning and enriching jobs, correcting physical factors in the environment, and effectively handling interpersonal factors should not be overlooked in the process of teaching employees how to handle stress. Stress management counsellors recommend several ways to resolve job-related stress, as described in Figure 12.7. Reality Check provides a perspective on psychosocial issues in the Canadian workplace.

Before concluding this discussion, we should observe that stress that is harmful to some employees may be healthy for others.[38] Most managers learn to handle distress effectively and find that it actually stimulates better performance. However, there will always be those who are unable to handle stress and need assistance in learning to cope with it. The increased interest of young and old alike in developing habits that will enable them to lead happier and more productive lives will undoubtedly be beneficial to them as individuals, to the organizations where they work, and to a society where people are becoming more and more interdependent.

## FIGURE 12.7

TIPS FOR REDUCING JOB-RELATED STRESS

- Build rewarding relationships with coworkers.
- Talk openly with managers or employees about job or personal concerns.
- Prepare for the future by keeping abreast of likely changes in job demands.
- Do not greatly exceed your skills and abilities.
- Set realistic deadlines; negotiate reasonable deadlines with managers.
- Act now on problems or concerns of importance.
- Designate dedicated work periods during which interruptions are avoided.
- When feeling stressed, find time for detachment or relaxation.
- Do not let trivial items take on importance; handle them quickly or assign them to others.
- Take short breaks from your work area as a change of pace.

Many Canadians report experiencing stress on the job.

Shannon Fagan/Getty Images

# REALITY CHECK

## CN Centre for Occupational Health and Safety

The CN Centre for Occupational Health and Safety is a research institute founded at Saint Mary's University in Halifax, Nova Scotia, through an endowment from CN. According to Kevin Kelloway, the director of the CN Centre, the mandate of the centre is (1) to coordinate and conduct research in occupational health and safety; (2) to build capacity for occupational health and safety research in Nova Scotia; and (3) to provide mechanisms for training and education in occupational health and safety.

Professor Kelloway, as co-author of the book *Managing Occupational Health and Safety*, 5th Edtion (Toronto: Nelson Canada, 2011), says,

> The hottest issue in Canadian occupational health and safety is the recognition of psychosocial issues in the workplace. Although we have known about work stress for years, it is now becoming increasingly clear that work stress is an occupational health and safety issue. Court decisions and new harassment legislation put the onus on employers to manage these issues, and the Canadian Standards Agency is developing a new standard for the management of psychosocial issues in the workplace. For many

organizations, this is a new area, and occupational health and safety departments are being tasked to come up with solutions. Best practice in this area is going to start with surveillance of work stress issues—monitoring the workplace to identify emerging problems or issues. Typically, surveillance will consist of regular assessment using standardized instruments (e.g., a companywide annual survey) as well as more immediate indicators (e.g., complaint-driven processes). Beyond surveillance, companies are going to be expected to actually do something to manage psychosocial risks. Let's take the example of workplace harassment— almost every jurisdiction in Canada now has anti-harassment legislation that puts the onus on employers to establish safe environments for employees. In this case, primary intervention deals with removing the stressor, so we implement programs to reduce workplace aggression, harassment, or incivility (for example). In many public venues, such as hospital waiting rooms or airports, it is now common to see statements that violence and aggression are not tolerated— these are part of the primary prevention program. Secondary intervention deals with the

*continued*

immediate consequence of the stressor, so we might teach individuals how to respond to or deal with workplace harassment, or we teach individuals stress management skills to reduce their level of anxiety. Finally, tertiary intervention deals with more long-term consequences.

So we provide employee and family assistance plans so that individuals can access counselling and therapy in a timely manner. This three-pronged approach is quickly becoming the gold standard for how we deal a wide variety of workplace stress issues.

Source: Interview with Kevin Kelloway.

# SMALL BUSINESS APPLICATION

Although small companies may be too small to justify a designated health and safety officer in their organization, they still must ensure that health and safety practices are adhered to. As such, small companies may draw on outside organizations such as consultants or local workplace safety boards for assistance in the establishment and monitoring of safe workplace practices.

Managers frequently say that dealing with people-related issues, such as sickness, problems at home, problems with other workers, or any other issues impacting the success of team members, takes a significant portion of their time. As such, small companies that are able to have managers address the personal issues of employees help foster an organizational climate conducive to success.

Effective management is a balance between employee needs such as fair, respectful treatment of and communication with employees and sensitivity to individual employees' situations and organizational needs, such as providing direction to employees to ensure the accomplishment of organizational needs. So how does a manager accomplish this? To be successful, managers need to (1) genuinely care about their staff; (2) have a close-enough working relationship to have visibility into each employee's work satisfaction and productivity; (3) have effective dialogue with their staff to know what is important to each employee and what is required to support their individual needs; (4) provide fair counsel to employees regarding their specific needs; (5) have the power to meet individual needs when warranted; and (6) maintain the role of providing support while maintaining organizational fairness and success as the primary goal.

In smaller organizations, managers are able to observe employees more frequently and may be able to detect when these employees are experiencing stress. As a first step in the process of employee assistance, a manager may be able to listen to an employee and provide a supportive work environment. In some cases, of course, a manager may have to refer employees for professional help, through local hospitals or social workers.

# SUMMARY

## SUMMARY

**OUTCOME 1** Occupational health and safety legislation is designed to ensure, so far as possible, safe and healthful working conditions for every working person. In general, these acts extend to all employers and employees. This legislation sets standards, ensures employer and employee compliance, and provides safety and health consultation and training where needed. Both employers and employees have certain responsibilities and rights under these acts. Employers not only are required to provide a hazard-free work environment but also must keep employees informed about legislative requirements and must require their employees to use protective equipment when necessary. Employers are required to keep employees informed of hazardous substances and instruct them in avoiding the dangers presented. Employees, in turn, are required to comply with safety standards, report hazardous conditions, and follow all employer safety and health regulations.

**OUTCOME 2** To provide safe working conditions for their employees, employers typically establish a formal program that, in a large percentage of organizations, is under the direction of the HR manager. The program may have many facets, including providing safety knowledge and motivating employees to use it, making employees aware of the need for safety, and rewarding them for safe behaviour. Incentives such as praise, public recognition, and awards are used to involve employees in the safety program. Maintenance of required records from accident investigations provides a basis for information that can be used to create a safer work environment.

**OUTCOME 3** Job conditions that are dangerous to the health of employees are now receiving much greater attention than in the past. There is special concern for toxic chemicals that proliferate at a rapid rate and may lurk in the body for years without outward symptoms. Health hazards other than those found in manufacturing operations—such as VDTs and cumulative trauma disorders—present special problems many firms are addressing with ergonomic solutions.

**OUTCOME 4** Along with providing safer and healthier work environments, many employers establish programs that encourage employees to improve their health habits. Wellness programs that emphasize exercise, nutrition, weight control, and avoidance of harmful substances serve employees at all organizational levels.

**OUTCOME 5** An important dimension of health and safety is stress that comes from physical activity and mental or emotional activity. Many sources of stress are job related. Employers can develop stress management programs to help employees learn techniques for coping with stress. In addition, organizations need to redesign and enrich jobs, clarify the employee's work role, correct physical factors in the environment, and take any other actions that will help reduce stress on the job. Unchecked, stress can lead to depression, alcoholism, and drug abuse, which, if severe enough, can be regarded as disabilities. Managers need to be aware of the signs of these diseases and be prepared to help employees via EAPs or counselling and by making reasonable accommodations for the employees' treatment.

## KEY TERMS

burnout, 440

cumulative trauma disorders, 434

depression, 437

distress, 439

emergency action plan, 431

eustress, 439

industrial disease, 423

occupational illness, 418

occupational injury, 418

stress, 439

## DISCUSSION QUESTIONS

1. Ergonomics-related injuries now account for over 40 percent of lost-time injuries in the province of Ontario. Prepare a list of the most common types of ergonomics-related injuries and then make suggestions about how employers can reduce these types.

2. Learn about the safety programs at your institution. In what ways do you think they might be similar to safety programs in the workplace? In what ways might they be different?

3. An unhealthy work environment can lower productivity, contribute to low morale, and increase medical and workers' compensation costs. Working individually or in teams, list specific ways managers can

   a. Help individual employees avoid repetitive strain injuries caused by prolonged computer use

   b. Deal with employee complaints about sick building syndrome

   c. Address employee fears caused by pandemics

4. Many students, balancing school, work, and family demands, experience stress. Consult the Canadian Mental Health Association website (http://www.cmha.ca/) to determine your level of stress. What are some coping mechanisms that you use?

5. Both unions and management express concern for the well-being of their employees. However, union reaction to the proposed introduction of wellness initiatives is not always positive. Unions fear that information collected—for example, as part of an EAP—will be kept and used against the employee experiencing performance problems. They also state that the real culprit in any employee health issue is the work context, not employee behaviour or lifestyle. So even if employees exercise and stop smoking, work hazards still remain. Unions also fear reprisals for those employees unwilling to participate in programs, particularly where groups are provided with incentives for achieving program aims. As the HR manager responsible for the introduction of a wellness initiative, how would you deal with these concerns?

# HRM EXPERIENCE

## Reducing Employee Stress

Job stress and its negative effect on both employees and the organization are a growing concern for managers and supervisors. As this text discusses, employee distress costs employers staggering amounts of money in lost productivity, absenteeism, turnover, increased workers' compensation claims, and health care costs. The cost of distress on the personal lives of employees is unmeasurable. Not surprisingly, stress management is an important aspect of any manager's job.

Stress management programs typically focus on three things to reduce workplace stress: (1) they identify factors in jobs that create stress; (2) they discuss specific techniques and managerial practices that help elevate workplace stress; and (3) they help individuals identify personal characteristics that serve to increase or decrease stress for them.

## Assignment

1. Working in groups of four to six, identify personal experiences that caused workplace stress.

Explain exactly why these incidents were stressful. Suggest ways to reduce or eliminate these stressful conditions.

2. Stress management often begins by having individuals identify their skills and abilities and jobs that will help them succeed. Assessing our preferences and skills can help us understand why some tasks or roles are more stressful than others. Identify work-related stress by answering these questions:

- What skills that I enjoy using am I currently using in my job?

- What skills that I enjoy using am I currently not using?

- What specific things about my job do I like?

- What things about my job do I dislike?

- Based on my personal skills and abilities, what would my perfect job be?

Visit the *Managing Human Resources* CourseMate website at http://www.belcourt7e.nelson.com for quizzes, flashcards, videos, games, and more!

# CASE STUDY 1

## WORKPLACE SAFETY AND YOUNG WORKERS

Every year, about 50 young Canadians are killed on the job and about 60,000 more suffer injuries serious enough to be reported to safety officials. Young workers are six times more likely to be killed or have a workplace injury than any other group. About 95 percent of those affected workers are men. This means that 1 in 11 young men can expect to suffer a workplace injury. Typically, these young men are employed at small manufacturing businesses, fast-food restaurants, convenience stores, and warehouses. The accidents usually happen within the first six months on the job. These young men lose fingers while slicing meat at the deli counter, are crushed by equipment they do not know how to operate, are electrocuted on metal ladders that touch hydro poles, or are burned handling chemicals with no protective equipment.

The top five causes of injuries to young workers are slips and falls, overexertion, being struck by an object, exposure to toxic chemicals, and burns. Young workers are more likely to be injured during the first six months on the job because they are not familiar with the work, they are often given tedious and dangerous work that others do not want to do, they may be eager to impress their new supervisors, and they are not aware of their rights.

Less than half receive any job training. Only about 30 percent of teenagers receive instruction in first aid and CPR in their safety training, but most learn nothing about the law, their rights, hazards on the job, or safety management. Young workers are especially vulnerable because they feel invincible and lack experience. They believe the following myths:

- I can take risks; I won't die.
- I can handle anything; I am young and fit.

- Nothing will happen to me; I am safe at work.
- I must do any job my employer tells me to do.
- I am not responsible for workplace safety; this is my employer's responsibility.

Most will not ask for safety training because they are unaware of risks or are fearful of losing their jobs.

Many provinces, recognizing these risks, have added health and safety training to the high school curriculum. Most such programs discuss workplace hazards, employer rights and responsibilities, health and safety laws, and the workers' right of refusal. Alberta has the most advanced training course for young workers in Canada: Job Safety Skills, which consists of 75 hours of instruction, divided into three modules:

- Personal safety management (first aid, back care, safety, and the law)
- Workplace safety practices (ergonomics, confined space entry, transportation of dangerous goods, and farm safety)

- Safety management systems (loss control, accident investigation, and a mock workshop in which students develop an entire safety program)

## Questions

1. Why are there more workplace injuries among those aged 16 to 25?
2. By law, workplace safety is the responsibility of the employer and employee. Why have nearly all provinces created courses in occupational health and safety as part of the high school curriculum? Should these be mandatory courses or electives?
3. Check the website of the Industrial Accident Prevention Association (http://www.iapa.ca), which has excellent information on occupational health and safety training programs. Design a training program that an employer could provide to young workers.

---

**Sources:** Adapted from Peter Cheney, "Focus," *The Globe and Mail* (April 25, 2006): F1 and F8; S. Singh, "HR's Role in Health and Safety for Young Workers," *HR Professional* 18, no. 5 (November 2001): 17–18; L. Ramsay, "Work Can Kill You," *National Post* (September 27, 1999): C12; L. Young, "Young Workers: Changing the Face of Safety," *Occupational Health and Safety* 14, no. 4 (June–July 1998): 24–30; "Workplace Safety," *The Globe and Mail* (Friday, May 12, 2000); Government of Canada, "Youth Path, Health and Wellness," http://www.youth.gc.ca/healsafe.

## CASE STUDY 2

### JOB STRESS

Job fatigue and stress are significant problems faced by employees and their managers. Unfortunately, when a case of depression arises as a result, trying to resolve the problem may be difficult—sometimes leading to conflict—as this case illustrates.

Donald Knolls was an air traffic control supervisor for International Gateway Airport (IGA), an airport serving a major metropolitan area. In 2011, Donald began to experience depression-related problems due largely to severe stress and fatigue on the job. A few months later, he requested and was granted a disability leave for treatment of his illness. After eight months, his personal physician, an expert in depression treatment and a licensed consulting psychologist, agreed that he was sufficiently improved to return to his former position.

IGA then sent Donald to the physician it had used when Donald first requested his disability leave. After an extensive evaluation, the doctor concluded that although Donald had made considerable strides in overcoming his depression, he should not be immediately returned to his former supervisory position because the conditions of the job had not changed and Donald was apt to

find the stress too great. Instead, he recommended that Donald be returned to a nonsupervisory position on a six-month trial basis, with the case to be reviewed at the end of that time. IGA followed the advice of its doctor and did not return Donald to a supervisory position. Donald, angered by management's decision, filed a grievance through IGA's alternative dispute resolution procedure, a procedure that could end in binding arbitration.

During several meetings between Donald and management, the employer maintained that it had the right to rely on the medical opinion of "a fair and impartial" doctor who had determined that Donald should not be returned to the position that was the cause of his original stress-related emotional problems. Additionally, management pointed out to Donald that IGA's disability leave provision states that it "may require appropriate medical documentation if it believes an employee is not fit to return to his or her former position."

Donald responded, through a lawyer he hired to represent his position, that the disability leave provisions were clear but, nevertheless, biased against an employee because they completely disregarded the opinion of his physician and psychologist. According to Donald, "Why bother to get expert medical opinions if they are dismissed?" He further noted, "I have never felt better. I'm really ready to get back to my job." Finally, Donald's lawyer contended that Donald was the victim of discrimination based on his former state of depression: "What happened to Donald would not have happened if his illness had been a more conventional physical injury."

## Questions

1. When conflicting medical opinions are presented, should the advice of a medical expert count more heavily than the opinion of a general physician? Explain your answer.
2. Is the charge of discrimination presented by Donald's lawyer relevant to this case? Explain your answer.
3. If you were presented with this case, what decision would you reach? Explain.

## NOTES AND REFERENCES

1. "Workplace Safety Policies," ttp://atlantic.psac.com/what/healthsafety/documents/BRIEF_Independent%20Review_WHSCC_ENG1.pdf, retrieved August 27, 2009.

2. Adrian Gostick, "Delivering Timely Safety Recognition," *Occupational Safety and Health* 73, no. 9 (September 2004): 94; "Developing Tomorrow's Leaders," *Canadian Business* 78, no. 2 (2005): 59.

3. "Creating Healthy Workplaces," http://www.awcbc.org and http://www.iapa.ca, retrieved November 22, 2011.

4. "Framing the Problem," http://www.lco-cdo.org/en/provincial-offences-call-for-papers-libman-sectionI, retrieved July 17, 2011.

5. "Lear Corporation Canada Ltd Fined $125,000 for Health and Safety Violation," *Canada News Wire*, May 23, 2006; D. Lodd, "GM fined $325,000," *Canadian Press*, July 12, 2009.

6. Rob Stewart, "The Challenge of Creating a Culture of Safety," *Canadian HR Reporter* (March 28, 2005): 11.

7. M. J. Colligan and A. Cohen, "The Role of Training in Promoting Workplace Safety and Health," in M. J. Barling and M. Frone (eds.) *The Psychology of Workplace Safety* (Washington, DC: American Psychological Association, 2003): 223–248.

8. Todd Nighswonger, "Is First-Aid First in Your Workplace?" *Occupational Hazards* 64, no. 4 (April 2002): 45–47.

9. Tim W. McDaniel, "Employee Participation: A Vehicle for Safety by Design," *Occupational Hazards* 6, no. 5 (May 2002): 71–76.

10. John P. Spath, "How to Get Employees Involved in the Safety Program," *Occupational Hazards* 66, no. 9 (September 2004): 63.

11. Craig Miller, "Can the Internet Improve Safety?" *Occupational Safety and Health* 73, no. 6 (June 2004): 98.

12. G. C. Shah, "Five Steps to Digital Safety," *Occupational Safety and Health* 71, no. 3 (March 2002): 22–25.

13. Roger Brooks, "OSHA's E-Tool for Lockout/Tagout," *Occupational Safety and Health* 71, no. 4 (April 2002): 22–24.

14. Larry Hansen, "How Will They Know?" *Occupational Hazards* 66, no. 10 (October 2004): 39.

15. R. Bruce McAffee and Ashley R. Winn, "The Use of Incentives/Feedback to Enhance Work Place Safety: A Critique of the Literature," *Journal of Safety Research* 20 (1989): 7–19. See also Thomas R. Krause, John H. Hidley, and Stanley J. Hodson, "Broad-Based Changes in Behavior Key to Improving Safety Culture," *Occupational Health and Safety* 59, no. 7 (July 1990): 31–37, 50; Matthew P. Weinstock, "Rewarding Safety," *Occupational Hazards* 56, no. 3 (March 1994): 73–76; Susan J. Marks, "Incentives that Really Reward and Motivate," *Workforce* 80, no. 6 (June 2001): 108–113.

16. Tara Neal, "Tools of the Trade," *Occupational Health and Safety* 18, no. 2 (March 2002): 60–68.

17. Diana McCrohan, "Add Impact to Your Program," *Occupational Safety and Health* 73, no. 2 (February 2004): 52.

18. Terese Steinback, "Workplace Strategies for Removing Obstacles to Employee Health," *Employee Benefits Journal* 25, no. 1 (March 2000): 9–10.

19. Randolph, P Schmid, "Odd Work Schedules Pose Health Risk," *ABC News* (April 16, 2011), http://abcnews.go.com.

20. Jennifer Steinhauer and Michael Cieply, "Rail Line Says Train Ran Signal: Death Toll at 25," *New York Times*, September 13, 2008, http://www.nytimes.com/2008/09/14/us/14crash.html?pagewanted=all, retrieved July 19, 2012; "Train Engineer Was Texting Just Before California Crash," http://www.reuters.com/article/2008/10/02/us-usa-train-crash-idUSN0152835520081002, retrieved July 19, 2012.

21. Canadian Centre for Occupational Health and Safety, "Types of Workplace Violence," http://www.ccohs.ca, retrieved July 18, 2006.

22. Kevin Kelloway, "Predictors and Outcomes of Workplace Violence," *HR Professional* 20, no. 1 (February/March 2003): 50.

23. Canadian Centre for Occupational Health and Safety, "Preventative Measures for Violence," http://www.ccohs.ca, retrieved July 19, 2006.

24. Andre Picard, "Remedy Is Needed for Violence against Nurses," *The Globe and Mail*, March 30, 2006, A17.

25. John C. DelBel, "Workplace Aggression," *Nursing Management* 34, no. 9 (July 2003): 30. See also Bruce T. Blythe and Terri Butler Stivarius, "Assessing and Defusing Workplace Threats of Violence," *Occupational Safety and Health* 73, no. 2 (February 2004): 20.

26. Claire Ginther, "A Death in the Family," *HR Magazine* 46, no. 5 (May 2001): 55–58.

27. Bruce T. Blythe, "The Human Side of Crisis Management," *Occupational Hazards* 66, no. 7 (July 2004): 37.

28. "Smoke Gets in Your Lungs," *HRfocus* 73, no. 2 (February 1996): 17.

29. Todd Humber, "Snuffing out Smoking," *Canadian HR Reporter* (April 11, 2005): 19.

30. D. Dyck, "Wrapping Up the Wellness Package," *Benefits Canada* 23, no. 1 (January 1999): 16–20.

31. "British Columbia versus Imperial Tobacco Company," http://www.courts.gov.bc.ca/jdb-txt/ca/04/02/2004bcca0269.htm, retrieved August 27, 2009.

32. Zachary Meyer, "Combating Employee Depression by Integrating Behavioral, Medical, and Pharmaceutical Benefits," *Employee Benefit Plan Review* 59, no. 2 (August 2004): 13.

33. Susan K. McFarlin, William Fals-Stewart, Debra A. Major, and Elaine M. Justice, "Alcohol Use and Workplace Aggression: An Examination of Perpetration and Victimization," *Journal of Substance Abuse* 13, nos. 1–2 (2001): 303–321.

34. "Change Your Culture and Lower Your Benefit Costs," *HRfocus* 81, no. 11 (November 2004): 6.

35. "Change Your Culture and Lower Your Benefit Costs," 6.

36. Max Messmer, "Are You Burning Out Your Best Employees?" *Strategic Finance* 85, no. 11 (May 2004): 12. See also Bob Gunn, "The Antidote to Burnout," *Strategic Finance* 86, no. 3 (September 2004): 8.

37. "Stop Burnout—Before It Stops Your Employees," *HRfocus* 79, no. 2 (February 2002): 3–4.

38. Sora Song, "The Price of Pressure," *Time* (July 19, 2004): 68.

CHAPTER

# 13

# Employee Rights and Discipline

MANAGINGHU
HUMANRESOU
RESOURCESM

## After studying this chapter, you should be able to

| OUTCOME 1 | Explain the different regimes that govern the employment relationship. |

| OUTCOME 2 | Explain the difference between expressed and implied terms of employment contracts. |

| OUTCOME 3 | Explain the rules governing the dismissal of employees. |

| OUTCOME 4 | Identify and explain the privacy rights of employees. |

| OUTCOME 5 | Explain the process of establishing disciplinary policies, including the proper implementation of organizational rules. |

| OUTCOME 6 | Discuss how to investigate a disciplinary problem. |

| OUTCOME 7 | Differentiate between the two approaches to disciplinary action. |

| OUTCOME 8 | Identify the different types of alternative dispute resolution procedures. |

| OUTCOME 9 | Discuss the role of ethics in the management of human resources. |

In this chapter, we discuss employee rights, workplace privacy, and employee discipline. At a general level, the rights of employees are those described in the employment contract. However, that is a very incomplete description. First, many employment contracts are not written down but are oral contracts, so the precise terms may not be obvious to the employee or the employer. Second, many important aspects of the employment relationship appear in the form of customs or practices rather than as noted contract terms. Third, common law judges have long shaped the scope of the employment contract by "implying" contract terms. "Implied" contract terms may not be known to either party to the contract but are nevertheless treated by the courts as enforceable contract terms. Fourth, employment contracts may be limited, altered, or voided by a range of employment legislation through which the government intervenes in the employment relationship. The true scope of employee rights and employer obligations is therefore influenced by all of these factors.

Furthermore, managers are discovering that the right to discipline and discharge employees—a traditional responsibility of management—is more difficult to exercise in light of the growing attention to employee rights. Disciplining employees is a difficult and unpleasant task for most managers and supervisors; many of them report that taking disciplinary action against an employee is the most stressful duty they perform. Balancing employee rights and employee discipline may not be easy, but it is a universal requirement and a critical aspect of good management.

Because the growth of employee rights issues has led to an increase in the number of lawsuits filed by employees, we include in this chapter a discussion of alternative dispute resolution as a way to foster organizational justice. Because disciplinary actions are subject to challenge and possible reversal through governmental agencies or the courts, management should make a positive effort to prevent the need for such action. When disciplinary action becomes impossible to avoid, however, that action should be taken in accordance with carefully developed HR policies and practices. Because ethics is an important element of organizational justice, the chapter concludes with a discussion of organizational ethics in employee relations.

# THE THREE REGIMES OF EMPLOYMENT LAW

**OUTCOME 1**

**common law of employment**
The body of case law in which courts interpret employment contracts and the legal principles taken from those cases that guide the interpretation of employment contracts

**implied contract terms**
Terms judges read into employment contracts when the written contract does not expressly deal with the matter

At the outset of our discussion in this chapter, it is important to understand the different sources of employee rights in the law of employment. Three different legal regimes govern the employment relationship: (1) the common law; (2) statutory regulation; and (3) collective bargaining and arbitration law. This chapter deals primarily with the first two, whereas Chapter 14 considers the third regime in greater detail. However, we will consider all three in this chapter, particularly in regard to how they govern the rules of employee discipline and dismissal.

## THE COMMON LAW OF EMPLOYMENT

The rights and obligations of employers and employees are determined first by the terms of the employment contract. However, often there is no written contract, or the terms of the contract are vague or fail to address a particular situation. As such, it is common for disagreements to arise under employment contracts. Whenever a dispute arises about the meaning and application of an employment contract, either party to the contract may file a lawsuit in the courts and ask a judge (and sometimes a jury) to decide what the contract means or how it was intended to apply in a particular circumstance. The judges' decisions are recorded in law books and, more recently, in electronic legal databases and are considered in future disputes involving similar issues. Over time, a huge body of "case law" has been compiled that considers the meaning and application of employment contracts to an endless array of employment scenarios. This body of law is known as the **common law of employment**.

It is crucial for HR managers to understand how the common law of employment influences the terms and conditions of employment and the interpretation of employment contracts. Common law judges have developed a long list of **implied contract terms** that are incorporated into all employment contracts, unless a written term in the contract overrides the implied term. For example, probably the most well-known implied term is the requirement for both the employer and the employee to give reasonable notice that they are terminating the employment contract. If the written contract includes a clause specifying how much notice of termination is required, then the implied term requiring reasonable notice will not apply (provided that the contractual notice clause complies with the notice provisions in employment standards legislation).

Important terms courts have implied into employment contracts include the following:

- Obligation of the employer and the employee to provide reasonable notice that they are terminating the contract

- Obligation on the employer to maintain a safe workplace

- Obligation on the employer to treat employees with decency, civility, respect, and dignity

- Obligation on the employee to serve the employer with loyalty and fidelity
- Obligation on the employee to perform competently
- Obligation on the employee to advance the employer's economic interests
- Obligation on the employee to avoid insubordination and insolence

Breach of an implied term has the same effect as breach of a written term. Therefore, it is crucial that HR managers are familiar with the scope of implied terms applied by the courts to employment contracts.

## STATUTORY EMPLOYMENT REGULATION

Unhappy with the outcomes of the common law model of employment, governments in Canada have over the past century intervened by passing a large variety of legislation aimed at influencing the employment relationship. As we saw in Chapter 3, employment equity legislation is intended to address systemic discrimination against women, Aboriginal people, people with disabilities, and visible minorities. Human rights legislation prohibits discrimination in employment on certain designated grounds, including sex, age, religion, and skin colour. Pay equity legislation addresses inequities in how men and women are compensated; employment standards legislation regulates the content of employment contracts by imposing minimum contract standards, such as minimum wage, maximum hours of work, and overtime pay; occupational health and safety legislation attempts to ensure safe working conditions; labour relations laws give employees the right to form and belong to unions and to bargain for better working conditions and restricts the right of employers to dismiss or discipline employees for exercising rights protected by the legislation (see Chapter 14). This is only a sampling of the wide range of legislation in Canada that addresses aspects of the employment relationship.

Statutory regulation operates alongside the common law, coexisting with it but also often modifying it. Usually, it is not permissible to contract out of protective employment legislation, with the result that regulation acts as a default minimum amount of protection required. For example, although the common law includes an implied obligation on the parties to provide reasonable notice of termination of the contract, employment standards regulation also imposes an obligation on employers to provide notice of termination. The employment standards' notice requirement is considered a "minimum" that must be provided to an employee, and a contract term providing less notice will be unenforceable (see Highlights in HRM 13.1).

# HIGHLIGHTS IN HRM 13.1

### Take Notice!

What happens if the employment contract includes a notice of termination clause that provides for less notice than required by employment standards legislation? That was the issue in a case called *Machtinger v. HOJ Industries*. The contract included a written term permitting the employer to terminate the contract without notice. At the time of dismissal, the employee was entitled to four weeks' notice under the Ontario *Employment Standards Act*. This was the issue before the Supreme Court of Canada: what happens when a contractual notice of termination clause provides for less notice than the

minimum notice required by employment standards legislation? The employer argued that the statutory minimum notice should be applied, whereas the employee argued that reasonable notice should be applied.

The Supreme Court ruled that reasonable notice applies because the effect of including the illegal notice clause in the contract was to void the contract term altogether. If the contract notice term is void, then it is as if there was no notice term, in which case, the implied term requiring reasonable notice is read into the contract. As a result, rather than receiving the four weeks' statutory notice he was entitled to, the employee was awarded reasonable notice amounting to 7.5 months.

Source: *Machtinger v. HOJ Industries Ltd.*, [1992] 1 S.C.R. 986.

**collective agreement**
An employment contract between an employer and a union that sets out the terms of employment of a group of the employer's employees represented by the union

**labour arbitrator**
A person assigned to interpret and decide disputes ("grievances") about the meaning, interpretation, and application of a collective agreement governing employees in a unionized workplace

Thus, an employee may be entitled to 12 months' notice of termination according to the implied contractual requirement to pay reasonable notice but entitled to only 8 weeks' notice under employment standards legislation. An employer may opt to provide only the minimum notice under the legislation. Although, legally, the employee is contractually entitled to the larger reasonable notice, in practice, recovering it would require the employee to file a lawsuit (known as a "wrongful dismissal" case), which is expensive and time consuming. As a result, many employees simply accept the statutory minimum notice and do not pursue their common law entitlement to reasonable notice.

## COLLECTIVE BARGAINING LEGISLATION AND LABOUR ARBITRATION

Collective bargaining legislation, such as the Ontario *Labour Relations Act*, seeks to improve conditions of work by empowering workers to join together and bargain for a better contract for themselves than is usually possible when an individual employee bargains with his or her employer. It does this by facilitating a right of workers to organize into unions and bargain collectively with the employer with the aid of a professional union bargainer and by permitting workers to strike and employers to "lock out" the employees in limited circumstances to apply pressure to reach an agreement. This process is discussed further in Chapter 14.

For now, it is important to note some crucial differences between the rules that govern unionized and nonunionized workplaces in Canada. The contract that is bargained in a unionized workplace is known as a **collective agreement**. The common law of employment does not apply to a collective agreement. Therefore, for example, the implied term permitting an employer to terminate an employee by giving reasonable notice does not apply when employees are unionized. This is an important difference between unionized and nonunionized workplaces. Whereas a nonunionized employer can terminate an employee for any reason or no reason at all (subject to statutes that prevent discriminatory dismissals) by simply giving the proper notice, a unionized employer usually needs just cause to dismiss a worker, unless the dismissal is due to purely economic reasons (a permanent layoff). In other words, unlike a nonunionized employer, a unionized employer usually needs a valid reason to fire an employee.

Another important difference between a collective agreement and an individual employment contract is the method of enforcement. A nonunion employee must sue the employer in a court for breach of the employment contract. That process is often costly (because the employee will usually retain a lawyer) and very time consuming. A unionized employee, on the other hand, must file a grievance alleging that the collective agreement has been violated, and that grievance, if not settled or resolved, may be referred to a **labour arbitrator** instead of a court. Arbitration is much quicker than a lawsuit, and the costs are covered by the union as part of the benefit paid for by employees in the form of union dues. Labour arbitrators have built up their own form of common law, known as "arbitration law," which helps guide the interpretation and application of collective agreements. Although, on some issues, arbitration law may be the same or similar to the approach of common law judges interpreting individual employment contracts, the two bodies of law should not be confused.

## UNDERSTANDING THE INDIVIDUAL EMPLOYMENT CONTRACT

OUTCOME 2

Since the individual employment contract is a type of contract, the general rules of contract law developed in the common law apply. One important rule of contract law is that a valid contract requires "mutual consideration."

This means that both parties to the contract must receive some benefit in the exchange. This has important implications for HR managers. For example, it means that once an employee has commenced employment, the employer cannot unilaterally change or introduce new terms of employment unless the employee agrees to the change and receives some new benefit in exchange. Employers frequently run into this problem when they permit an employee to start working before presenting the employment contract to the employee for his or her signature. When that happens, the employee has started work under a verbal contract. If the employer later presents a written contract that includes terms beneficial to the employer (such as a notice of termination clause that provides less than reasonable notice), those new terms will not be enforceable, even if the employee signs the contract, if the employee was not also given some new benefit (such as a raise or a new holiday) in exchange for signing the contract.

The fact that the rules of contract law apply to the employment relationship has other important implications. For example, it means that the employee can insist that the employer comply with the terms of the contract. This might seem obvious, yet many HR managers mistakenly believe that the employer has the right to unilaterally make changes to the conditions of employment. If an employer unilaterally changes a term of the employment contract, it will usually have breached the contract, enabling the employee to sue for breach and, if he or she so chooses, to claim that he or she has been constructively dismissed.

A **constructive dismissal** occurs when an employer commits a significant or fundamental breach of the contract, such as eliminating an important benefit enjoyed by the employee, reducing compensation, or demoting an employee. In that case, the employee may treat the contract as having been terminated by the employer, quit, and sue the employer to recover either contractual notice or implied reasonable notice. Highlights in HRM 13.2 illustrates the need for HR managers to be careful when attempting to make a change to employees' terms and conditions of employment.

To make a change to the terms of an employment contract without breaching the contract, the employer should do either of the following:

1. Obtain the employee's agreement to the change and provide the employee with some new consideration (benefit) or
2. Terminate the employment contract in its entirety by giving the required notice of termination and then offer a new contract on the revised terms. See the Business Case.

**constructive dismissal**
When an employer commits a fundamental breach of the contract, such as by unilaterally changing a key term of the contract, the employee can treat the breach as a termination

PART 5

# HIGHLIGHTS IN HRM 13.2

## Caution with Contracts

Employers cannot unilaterally change the contract. For example, the owner of a small business informed his office manager that she would no longer be the office manager but would be the accountant. Other changes to her work included no eligibility for bonuses and no business trips,

and the owner would not honour an agreement to give her shares in the company after five years. When she protested these changes, he told her to quit. The employee sued, and the courts agreed that her contract had been unilaterally changed. The court awarded her the monies owed on the remainder of her five-year contract and gave her shares in the company worth $180,000.

Source: "Changing Terms of a Fixed Term Employment Contract without Employee Consent Proves Costly to Employer," http://www.yorku.ca/ddoorey /lawblog/, retrieved May 24, 2012.

NEL

**CHAPTER 13:** EMPLOYEE RIGHTS AND DISCIPLINE     453

# THE BUSINESS CASE

## The Danger of Changing a Contract Term Without the Employee's Agreement

What if the employee just will not agree to a contract amendment that the employer wants? In *Wronko v. Western Inventory Service*, the employer wanted to change a term in the employment contract that required the employer to pay two years' salary to the employee in the event that the employee was terminated. The employer asked Mr. Wronko to sign a revised contract that reduced the payment required from 2 years to 30 weeks. Wronko refused to sign and indicated that he did not agree to the change. The employer then gave Wronko two years' notice that it was amending the term accordingly. After two years, the employer again gave Wronko a revised contract and told him that this new contract was now "in effect" and that if Wronko did not sign the new contract, then the company did "not have a job for [him]."

Wronko quit and sued the employer for wrongful dismissal, alleging he was entitled to two years' salary as per the original contract. The employer argued that it was permitted to give notice of the change to a term in the contract, which it had done. The Ontario Court of Appeal disagreed. It ruled that when faced with an employee who will not agree to a proposed change to the employment contract, an employer must either withdraw the proposed amendment or terminate the entire contract by giving the required notice and then offer the employee a new contract including the revised terms. The employer here had not given notice that it was terminating the contract; it had only given notice of its intention to make a unilateral change to one term of the contract. Therefore, the court ruled that the employee was entitled to two years' salary (minus money earned by the employee during that period). The employer should seek to make the amendment palatable to the employee by offering some benefit to the employee in exchange for the benefit it seeks to obtain from the amendment. This could avoid the costs associated with having to terminate the contract in its entirety.

HR managers need to understand the terms of employment contracts to appreciate the scope of their managerial authority. For example, does an employer have a contractual right to suspend an employee without pay as a form of progressive discipline or to put an employee on temporary layoff during an economic downturn? In both cases, the employer is essentially preventing the employee from performing his or her end of the bargain. That would be a breach of the contract unless the employer can point to a contract term that empowers it to suspend or lay off. Most contracts do not confer these rights on employers, with the result that suspensions and layoffs are usually contract breaches, and the employees affected could opt to quit and sue for constructive dismissal.

## THE RULES GOVERNING DISMISSAL

### DISMISSAL OF A NONUNION EMPLOYEE: WRONGFUL DISMISSAL

OUTCOME 3

Under the common law of employment, either the employer or the employee can terminate the employment contract by providing the other side with the amount of notice specified in the contract, or if the contract does not include a notice term or includes a term requiring less notice than required by employment standards legislation, with reasonable notice. What amount of notice is "reasonable" is determined by the court, applying a variety of criteria judges have developed over the years, including the employee's age and the availability of alternative similar employment given the employee's experience and training. However, the two most important factors in assessing notice are (1) the length of service with the employer and (2) the nature of the job performed by the employee. Generally, the longer an employee has worked for an employer, the longer the period of notice. In addition, the courts have developed a form of cap on the length of reasonable notice that is tied to the job performed by the employee: nonmanagerial employees are usually not entitled to more than 12 months' notice, whereas managerial employees may be entitled to as much as 24 months' notice.[1]

Notably, a nonunion employer does not need a reason to dismiss an employee. It can dismiss an employee at any time, for any reason (that is not a violation of a statute, such as human rights legislation) or for no reason at all. It just needs to give the employee the proper contractual or reasonable notice. Most dismissals in Canada are done by means of the employer providing the employee with notice, which can be working notice or a payment of wages equal to what the employee would have received for working during the notice period.

However, an employer may also dismiss a nonunion employee without any notice if the employee has committed a serious breach of the contract, such as engaging in significant dishonesty, gross incompetence, sexual harassment, or workplace bullying or violence. When a nonunion employer dismisses an employee for cause, without notice, it is called a **summary dismissal**.

One comprehensive study of summary dismissal cases found that employers won 40 percent of the time when the charge was dishonesty, theft, substance abuse, or abusive behaviour; 54 percent of the time when the charge was insubordination; 65 percent of the time when the charge was conflict of interest or competing with the employer; and just 25 percent of the time when the charge was poor performance.[2]

Whenever an employee believes he or she should have received more notice than that provided, the employee may file a **wrongful dismissal** lawsuit. This is a claim filed in court alleging that the employer breached the employment contract by failing to provide the required notice of termination. Although in a case of summary dismissal the court will have to decide whether the employer had cause sufficient to warrant the employee forfeiting his or her entitlement to notice, it is important to note that the court will not question whether the employer had a legal right to dismiss the employee. The issue in a wrongful dismissal case is whether notice should have been given and, if so, how much. It is not whether the employer had just cause to dismiss the employee, which is the issue usually at stake in a unionized arbitration case. Therefore, the remedy in a successful wrongful dismissal case is usually money; courts do not overturn the decision to dismiss, and they virtually never order the employer to reinstate the employee.

## Statutory Regulation of Dismissal

The common law entitlement of employers to dismiss a nonunion employee for any reason by giving proper notice has been restricted in a number of ways by government intervention. Statutes prohibit employers from dismissing employees for certain reasons. For example, human rights legislation prohibits dismissals based on discriminatory reasons. Labour relations legislation prohibits an employer from dismissing an employee involved in organizing a union. Many types of employment statutes prohibit dismissals and punishment as a reprisal against employees who exercise their **statutory rights.** For example, employment standards and occupational health and safety statutes usually prohibit employers from punishing employees in any way as a reprisal for the employee making claims under the statute. The tribunals responsible for enforcing the statutes usually have the authority to order the employer to reinstate the employee, with full back pay and benefits, if they find that the reason for the dismissal was prohibited by the statute.

As noted earlier, employment standards legislation in Canada imposes a minimum amount of notice of termination required. For example, in Ontario, the amount of notice required in the *Employment Standards Act* is linked directly to years of service: one week's notice per year of service to a maximum of 8 weeks. But that amount goes up in the case of mass layoffs to as much as 18 weeks' when 500 or more employees are terminated. In addition, the legislation imposes

**summary dismissal**
When a nonunion employer terminates an employee without notice because the employee has committed a serious breach of the contract

**wrongful dismissal**
A lawsuit filed in a court by an employee alleging that he or she was dismissed without proper contractual or reasonable notice

**statutory rights**
Legal entitlements that derive from government legislation

a separate obligation to pay "severance pay" when the employer has an annual payroll of $2.5 million or more or when 50 or more employees are being terminated in a 6-month period due to the closure of all or part of a business. Severance pay is one week's pay per year of service to a maximum of 26 weeks. Other provinces have similar requirements with variations. HR managers should be knowledgeable about the statutory provisions that govern the employment contract and dismissals to avoid costly and potentially embarrassing complaints by employees.

## DISMISSAL OF A UNIONIZED EMPLOYEE: JUST CAUSE

Most collective agreements in unionized workplaces confer a right on employers to lay off workers, although they regulate the selection of the employees to be laid off and the order of recalls. Therefore, a unionized employer usually has the option of laying off workers for economic reasons. In addition, collective agreements usually include a "management rights" clause that grants employers the right to impose discipline short of dismissal, such as unpaid suspensions. As we noted previously, since most individual employment contracts do not include expressed management rights to impose temporary layoffs or unpaid suspensions, these actions are usually considered breaches of the individual employment contract amounting to a constructive dismissal.

However, although unionized employers may have these additional managerial rights, they are also significantly more restrained than nonunionized employers in other ways. Most notably, in stark contrast to most individual employment contracts, collective agreements usually include a term requiring that the employer have just cause to impose discipline or dismiss an employee. As a result, unlike a nonunionized employer, a unionized employer usually needs a reason to dismiss an employee. That reason can then be challenged by the employee and the union through the grievance procedure in the collective agreement rather than in the courts. The implied common law right of employers to dismiss employees for any reason by giving them reasonable notice does not apply to unionized employees. Moreover, a labour arbitrator has the statutory power to substitute a lesser penalty than the one imposed by the employer. That means that labour arbitrators can (and often do) reinstate employees when they rule that the employer did not have just cause to dismiss the employee.

As a result, it is particularly crucial in a unionized setting that HR managers keep careful records of employee misconduct. Labour arbitrators expect employers to apply progressive discipline before dismissing a unionized employee, except when the employee's misconduct is particularly serious. It is very common for arbitrators to reinstate dismissed unionized employees and to substitute an unpaid suspension of some duration. In considering the appropriate penalty for employee misconduct, arbitrators consider the entirety of the situation looking for "mitigating" factors, which include the employee's length of service and past disciplinary record, the manner in which the employer treated other similar incidents involving other employees, and even the employee's personal circumstances, such as the impact the dismissal would have on the employee and his or her dependants.

We can see, therefore, that nonunionized employers face challenges similar to those of unionized employers when they attempt to summarily dismiss an employee without providing notice. The nonunionized employer must convince a court that the employee's misconduct was sufficiently serious to warrant forfeiting notice of termination. A unionized employer needs to convince a labour arbitrator that it had just cause to dismiss the employee. In meeting these tests, employers face common challenges; similar advice can therefore be applied to both unionized and nonunionized employers in regard to properly preparing for and implementing discipline, as outlined in Figure 13.1

## FIGURE 13.1

### TIPS TO CONSIDER WHEN DISMISSING A NONUNIONIZED EMPLOYEE WITH CAUSE OR A UNIONIZED EMPLOYEE WITH JUST CAUSE

- *Terminate an employee for cause only if there is a clear and articulated reason.* An employer should have clearly articulated, easily understandable reasons for discharging an employee. The reasons should be stated as objectively as possible and should reflect company rules, policies, and practices.

- *Set and follow termination rules and schedules.* Ensure that every termination follows a documented set of procedures. Procedures can be from an employee handbook, a supervisory manual, or even an intra-office memorandum. Before terminating, give employees notices of unsatisfactory performance and improvement opportunities through a system of warnings and suspensions.

- *Nonunionized employers should consider bargaining a contractual right to suspend an employee.* The right to suspend an employee without pay is a key component of

progressive discipline in unionized workplaces, but that right rarely appears in nonunionized employment contracts. Nonunionized employers could include greater disciplinary rights in the contract language to give them more disciplinary options.

- *Document all performance problems.* A lack of documented problems in an employee's personnel record may be used as circumstantial evidence of pretextual discharge if the employee is "suddenly" discharged.

- *Be consistent with employees in similar situations.* Document reasons given for all disciplinary actions even if they do not lead to termination. Terminated employees may claim that exception-to-the-rule cases are discriminatory. Detailed documentation will help employers explain why these "exceptions" did not warrant termination.

Figure 13.2 describes this process from the employee's perspective. However, it is important to recall that the nonunionized employer always has the option of dismissing the employee with notice (not asserting cause), which is an option not available to a unionized employer. Highlights in HRM 13.3 provides an overview of the laws and regulations regarding dismissals.

## FIGURE 13.2

### FIRING BACK!

Once you have received either verbal or written warnings about performance, a decision has usually been made to fire you. What can you do? If you are a unionized employee, you can file a grievance challenging the discipline. But a nonunion employee will not usually have that option. Writing back to pick holes in the accusations is the least effective defence. Using the same weapons as management, you must prove that the just cause will not hold.

Howard Levitt, a legal expert on dismissal, offers the following advice:

- Establish in writing that you were unaware of the standards of performance or conduct. You can argue that the standards are new or were not part of the initial job offer, position description, performance evaluations, or previous warnings. The company must prove that you were grossly incompetent, so any letters of praise or good performance review should be used. Any aspects of performance that may override the weak areas should be noted. For example, if you are being dismissed for poor communication skills but your productivity figures are increasing, this should be documented. As soon as you commence employment, start a file containing all performance evaluations; letters of praise from customers, coworkers, internal clients,

and supervisors; and all other examples of performance achievements. Establish a paper trail of good performance.

- Argue that the company, while complaining about poor performance, has not stated specifically what is required to improve performance.

- Assert that you were not given the time, training, assistance, or learning opportunities necessary to improve performance.

- Establish, if true, that the employer hired you knowing that you did not possess the necessary skills. Note any understanding that you would receive the appropriate training.

- State, if applicable, that the skills desired now were not part of your original job description.

- Attribute your poor performance to factors outside your control, such as a decline in sales in all regions, or poorly priced products, or a temporary illness. If possible, establish that the company contributed to the performance problem by failing to respond to your (documented) suggestions for improvement.

Levitt further advises that letters and all other documentation be written with the assistance of a specialist. In the end, a nonunion employee will not get his or her job back if dismissed for performance problems, but if successful, they may receive an attractive severance package.

**Source:** Howard Levitt, Counsel, Lang Michener, Toronto, "How Employees Can Fight Firing for Just Cause," *Toronto Star*, August 17, 1992, C1.

# HIGHLIGHTS IN HRM 13.3

## Overview of Regimes Governing Dismissals

HR managers are usually responsible for implementing dismissals of employees. This is a stressful part of the profession. However, it helps significantly to understand the basic legal rules governing the process. Here is a quick summary of the key issues and regimes discussed in this chapter.

### Common Law (Nonunion Employees)

The common law rules of contract govern the employment relationship between individual employees and nonunion employers. Every contract includes a notice of termination clause. The clause is either expressed (written) into the contract, or the courts imply a requirement for both parties to provide reasonable notice of termination. The courts decide how much notice is "reasonable" by applying a list of criteria. An expressed notice term supersedes the implied "reasonable notice" requirement, but courts will not enforce an expressed term if it requires less notice than required under employment standards legislation. A nonunion employer does not need a reason to dismiss an employee provided that it gives proper notice. Summary dismissal—dismissal without notice—is permitted only when the employee has committed a serious breach of the contract. Disputes about contracts in nonunion workplaces are resolved in court after one of the parties files a lawsuit for breach of contract. The usual remedy is lost wages and benefits during the notice period that should have been given (not reinstatement).

### Statutory Regulation (Union and Nonunion Employees)

Employment standards regulation explains the minimal notice of termination required, which usually applies only to the employer. The length of notice in employment standards regulation is often less than the common law reasonable notice. Employment standards regulations also often require "severance" pay in addition to notice when the employer is large or there has been a mass termination. Various pieces of legislation prohibit dismissals for certain public policy reasons, such as for discriminatory reasons or as retaliation for the employee exercising statutory rights. Claims alleging a violation of a statute are decided by administrative tribunals, not courts, and the remedy can include lost wages and benefits and reinstatement.

### Collective Bargaining and Labour Arbitration

Union employees enjoy greater protection from dismissals. They are governed by the rules of collective agreements, not contract law; the common law does not apply to collective agreements. A union employer can usually lay off or dismiss an employee for economic reasons by giving at least the statutory minimum notice or a longer period in the collective agreement. But collective agreements usually require the employer to have just cause in all other situations, so a union employer must have a reason to dismiss someone. A dismissed union employee challenging the employer's decision must file a grievance that may be litigated before a labour arbitrator (not a court). An arbitrator has the power to overturn the employer's decision and impose a lesser penalty (such as suspension) or reinstate the employee.

## EMPLOYEE PRIVACY RIGHTS

**OUTCOME 4**

There are many instances in which the interests of employees can come into conflict with those of the employer. An important example relates to employee privacy rights at work and outside the workplace. To what extent should employees be entitled to privacy in their relationship with the employer?

### PRIVACY ISSUES AT THE WORKPLACE

Employers have a legitimate interest in ensuring that their employees work efficiently and avoid improper conduct at work, such as theft, harassment, or misuse of company computers. Surveillance of the workplace is a common method for managing these challenges. However, employer surveillance can also have the feel of "Big Brother" to employees, who may feel entitled to some measure of privacy at work. Balancing managerial rights and employee expectations about their entitlement to privacy can be a difficult job for HR managers.

A right of privacy at work has been recognized in various degrees under all three regimes of employment law. The strongest protections of employee rights are probably those recognized by labour arbitrators interpreting collective

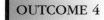

### Using the Internet

Canadian labour laws, both federal and provincial, can be found on this site:

**http://www. canadianlabourrelations.com/ canadian-labour-laws.html**

agreements. Arbitration law usually requires employers to establish both that there is a pressing need for surveillance and that the surveillance is conducted in a reasonable manner that balances the employee's interest in a reasonable amount of privacy with the employer's business concerns. In applying this balancing test, arbitrators have sometimes prohibited surveillance cameras; personal searches of people, bags, and clothing; and employer searches of employee emails and Internet use. However, when the employer can show a strong reason justifying the surveillance and that there was no other reasonable, less intrusive means of obtaining the information, arbitrators have tended to permit surveillance.[3]

Governments have sometimes passed legislation to protect employee privacy rights. For example, the British Columbia *Personal Information Protection Act* applies to the private sector in British Columbia and requires a similar balancing of employer and employee interests in assessing whether an employer can conduct surveillance on employees. An important recent piece of legislation is the federal *Personal Information Protection and Electronic Documents Act* (PIPEDA), which, among other things, regulates an employer's collection and dissemination of information about employees, as well as the right of employees to access their personnel files in some circumstances. It applies to federally regulated workplaces but also to some "commercial activities" engaged in by provincially regulated companies. (Commercial activities include the selling of information, such as employee lists or information about employees.)

Organizations covered by PIPEDA must obtain an individual's consent when they collect, use, or disclose the individual's personal information. The individual has a right to access personal information held by an organization and to challenge its accuracy, if necessary. Any organization that collects personal information can use that information only for the purpose for which it was collected. If an organization wants to use it for another purpose, it must obtain the individual's consent again. Individuals must also be assured by the organization that their information will be protected by adequate safeguards. Recent interpretations of the PIPEDA indicate that the legislation requires a balancing of employer and employee rights similar to that required by labour arbitrators and other privacy legislation, such as that in British Columbia. For example, employers covered by the legislation are now restricted in their ability to secretly monitor employee computer use unless they can prove that less intrusive means of monitoring computer use were used and did not solve the problem.[4]

Because privacy laws often oblige corporations to obtain consent from the individual whose personal information is being gathered, HR professionals should conduct an audit to determine if the organization's practice conforms to the legislation.

## Using the Internet

For further information on PIPEDA, see the federal Privacy Commissions Guide for Businesses and Organizations at **http://laws-lois.justice.gc.ca /eng/acts/P-8.6/index.html**

PART 5

Monitoring employee behaviour is an important deterrent to inappropriate conduct of employees.

© Digital Vision/Getty Images

For example, one organization collected information about the birth country of employees to facilitate international transfers. However, collecting this information for clerks, who will not be transferred, is unnecessary and would not meet the new standards.[5] Sources of information from selection interviews, employee evaluations, and disciplinary reports may have to be made available to employees.[6]

Employers have traditionally enjoyed a greater latitude under the common law to monitor their employees' behaviour. For example, court cases governing email and the Internet have granted employers the right to monitor materials created, received, or sent at work on the premise that the employer owns the computer, the employee is expected to be performing only work-related tasks while at work, and there is no reasonable expectation of privacy when using the employer's computers and equipment. Two recent court cases have made this very clear. In one case, the employee, with 18 years of service, was terminated for using the company Internet for personal purposes, including accessing pornography. In another case, an employee with 15 years of service was found to have been using the company Internet to manage his own unrelated travel business, for up to two hours a day on company time, using the company's computers.[7]

However, even under the common law, an employer's right to monitor its employees' conduct at work is not absolute. In fact, common law judges appear to be slowly recognizing an implied right to privacy at work. In one recent case, an employer installed a hidden camera in the office of one of its employees. When the employee found out, she quit and sued for constructive dismissal. The employer defended its actions by claiming it had a legal right to install surveillance cameras. The court disagreed and found that the employer violated an implied term in the contract that it would treat its employees in good faith and fairly. Installing a hidden camera without any strong justification violated that term. The court ordered 7.5 months of reasonable notice damages.[8]

As you can see, employee surveillance can raise legal concerns. Nevertheless, surveillance of employees in various forms is quite common (see Figure 13.3).

## FIGURE 13.3

### EMPLOYEE MONITORING PRACTICES

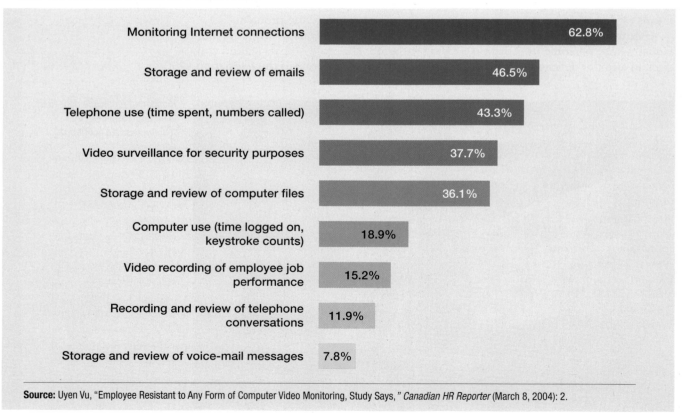

| Practice | Percentage |
|---|---|
| Monitoring Internet connections | 62.8% |
| Storage and review of emails | 46.5% |
| Telephone use (time spent, numbers called) | 43.3% |
| Video surveillance for security purposes | 37.7% |
| Storage and review of computer files | 36.1% |
| Computer use (time logged on, keystroke counts) | 18.9% |
| Video recording of employee job performance | 15.2% |
| Recording and review of telephone conversations | 11.9% |
| Storage and review of voice-mail messages | 7.8% |

**Source:** Uyen Vu, "Employee Resistant to Any Form of Computer Video Monitoring, Study Says," *Canadian HR Reporter* (March 8, 2004): 2.

FIGURE 13.4

## EMAIL, COMPUTER, AND VOICE MAIL: POLICY GUIDELINES

- Ensure compliance with applicable legislation and common law rules.
- Specify the circumstances, if any, under which the system can be used for personal business.
- Specify that confidential information not be sent on the network.
- Set forth the conditions under which monitoring will be done—by whom, how often, and with what notification to employees.

- Specify that email and voice-mail information be sent only to users who need it for business purposes.
- Expressly prohibit use of email or voice mail to harass others or to send anonymous messages.
- Make clear that employees have no privacy rights in any material delivered or received through email or voice mail.
- Specify that employees who violate the policy are subject to discipline, including dismissal.

HR experts and legal authorities strongly encourage employers to develop clear policies and guidelines that explain to employees how email, the Internet, and voice mail are to be used, including when and under what conditions employees can be monitored[9] (see Figure 13.4). As with other employment policies, employees should sign a form indicating that they have read and understand the policy. The employer's surveillance and monitoring practices have a greater chance of being upheld by a court or tribunal if the rules have been clearly explained to the employees and implemented in accordance with the company's own guidelines. Reality Check describes the privacy issues facing the courts, and Ethics in HRM outlines the issues raised through monitoring employees.

# REALITY CHECK

## Privacy Issues with New Technologies

Paul Boniferro, partner, head of the Ontario labour and employment group at McCarthy Tétrault, Canada's largest law firm, with offices in Vancouver, Calgary, London, Ottawa, Montreal, Quebec City, and London, England, describes a case involving the use of biometric scanning: "We have a client in the property management industry. The security officers and building maintenance staff were being asked to no longer use access passes and punch cards, but to have their hands scanned by a biometric system."

The idea of using a biometric scanning device started with 9/11. The problem for landlords was that no one knew who was in the towers of the World Trade Center. Property managers are responsible for knowing who is in the building for security purposes and for emergency events.

Swipe cards can be exchanged or stolen, and so are not reliable methods of identification. Furthermore, the employer had heard that employees were giving each other their punch cards for logging in, and effectively stealing time from the employer.

The employer wanted to install a biometric entry system for security, for emergency contact, and for tracking employee time for payroll purposes. The biometric system scans and reads handprints, which are unique to every individual, and therefore solved both the problems of employee identification and time theft.

The employees refused, saying that it was an invasion of their privacy. They felt that "Big Brother" wanted to control their whereabouts and know where they were at all times. In another case where a unionized employer introduced a similar system, the union filed a grievance alleging a breach of the collective agreement's protection of worker privacy. The case went to a labour arbitrator.

The arbitrator agreed with the union (and the employees) and based her decision on these factors:

1. The employer has to first establish that there is an issue and a problem that needs to be controlled. In this case, the theft of time was not established as an issue that needed to be addressed.

2. The company has to establish that there is no other reasonable and less intrusive method to manage the three issues.

*continued*

3. The employer has to establish that all necessary precautions have been taken to protect the privacy of the employees.

4. Furthermore, the employer must consult with the union about the implementation and the protection of employees' privacy.

The employer was not allowed to use the system. However, in another similar situation, in a manufacturing environment, the current employees were allowed to keep their passes, but all new employees were required to use the biometric system. Existing employees, on a voluntary basis, could use the system. The company also charged $25 to replace lost cards, and over time employees no longer wanted the hassle of the cards. Now, 100 percent of its employees are using the biometric system.

Source: Interview with Paul Boniferro.

## EMPLOYEE CONDUCT OUTSIDE THE WORKPLACE

Consider the following situation. On Monday morning, the owner of ABC Corporation reads in the newspaper that a company employee has been charged with robbery and assault on a local convenience store owner. The employee has been released pending trial. A phone call to the employee's supervisor reveals that the employee has reported to work. What should the owner do? What is the owner legally entitled to do? What can an employer do if it believes that an employee

# ETHICS IN HRM

## Supervising or Super-Spying?

Cameras monitor much of our everyday life, often without our knowledge. Surveillance systems may be monitoring you as you leave the lobby of your apartment building, as you enter the underground garage, as you drive on the highway to work, as you purchase a coffee at the variety store, and even at some workplaces. Pinhole cameras the size of a quarter can fit into a picture on a wall, a telephone, or a ceiling device that looks like a water sprinkler. They can catch an employee loading up on office supplies; they can even determine whether the employee is using chat lines or the Internet for personal reasons. Some employers keep records of the calls employees make and their duration. A standard feature on network management software enables the administrator to pull up the screen of any employee on the network.

Employees who work as customer representatives, handling 60 to 80 calls a day, may have their conversations monitored by supervisors or a trainer to ensure that the information given is accurate and that service standards are maintained. At one firm that raises money for charities, employees are required to make 8,500 keystrokes an hour; failure to achieve this standard is noted electronically. (Distractions are minimized by covering windows, forbidding conversation unrelated to business, and facing all desks in the same direction.) Eight cameras are capable of zooming in on any desk in case any employee is displaying materials unrelated to work.

Even baby sitters and nannies are being targeted for electronic monitoring. Cameras hidden in books watch the children and the baby sitter or nanny while anxious parents are at work. Parents insist that this surveillance enables them to ensure the safety and emotional security of their children; baby sitters and nannies are outraged at the lack of trust and invasion of their privacy.

According to a national director with the Canadian Union of Postal Workers, "Surveillance and monitoring is really about power, and the uneven levels of power in the workplace. If it is abused by employers, then it really becomes a powerful weapon that is used to control the behaviour of workers, or as a source of discipline." A 2000 study found that people consider these electronic monitoring systems highly invasive and unfair.

Sources: David Zwieg, "The Line Between Benign and Invasive Monitoring Technologies," *HR Professional* 19, no. 4 (August/September, 2002): 36–38; J. Powell, "Keeping an Eye on the Workplace," *Financial Post*, September 6, 1997, 24; M. Gooderham, "Rise in Technology Lets Everyone Be a Spy," *The Globe and Mail*, June 7, 1995, A1; A. M. Stewart, "For a Nervous Breakdown, Please Press One," *The Globe and Mail*, June 1, 1994, A25; G. Arnaut, "Electronic Big Brother Is on the Job," *The Globe and Mail*, October 22, 1996, C1; R. Fulford, "Tolerating Electronic Sweatshops," *The Globe and Mail*, December 14, 1994, C1.

is lying about his or her inability to work due to sickness or disability? Can the employer spy on the employee outside the workplace? What if an employee writes damaging things about the company on his or her personal blog?

These are questions that commonly arise. Generally, an employer has no reach over the private lives of its employees; when an employee "punches out," he or she is no longer subject to the employer's control. Thus, both union and nonunion employers have been found to have lacked proper cause to dismiss employees who are arrested for activities unrelated to the workplace. However, when the employer can establish that the employee's off-duty conduct adversely impacts the economic interests of the employer, such as business reputation, or the employee's ability to perform his or her job, then the employer may be justified in taking action in response to that conduct. Therefore, an employee who writes slanderous or damaging comments about the employer, or who discloses confidential information on a personal blog or social networking website such as Facebook, will usually be subject to summary dismissal by a nonunion employer. See Highlights in HRM 13.4.

Employers that wish to conduct secret surveillance on employees during off-hours need to be particularly careful. Both courts and arbitrators have required employers to show a valid business reason that the surveillance is necessary and to establish that the surveillance was conducted in a reasonable manner without violating common law and statutory rules protecting property rights and prohibiting nuisance. For example, recent court cases have suggested that videotaping an employee inside his or her home is an unreasonable invasion of privacy and constitutes the tort of nuisance. Videotaping in a public place was found reasonable in other cases. Labour arbitrators have been more strict in limiting outside employer surveillance than courts, usually requiring the employer to show that there was no other less intrusive means of obtaining the necessary information.[10] Employers covered by privacy legislation discussed earlier are also more restricted in the scope of their right to conduct employee surveillance than those governed solely by the common law.[11]

# HIGHLIGHTS IN HRM 13.4

## The Long Arm of the Employer

Employees usually are not subject to the authority of their employer during nonworking hours. Nor are employers expected to act as morality police. Of course, a nonunion employer can always dismiss an employee whose off-duty conduct it does not like by giving the employee proper notice. However, if the nonunion employer wants to summarily dismiss the employee without notice, or if the employer is covered by a collective agreement, it will need to prove that the off-duty conduct amounts to proper cause for dismissal.

Sometimes off-duty employee behaviour can have an adverse impact on the employer's interests or can directly impede the ability of the worker to perform his or her job. An example of the latter scenario is a case in which an employee is incarcerated and unable to come to work or a truck driver loses his driver's licence. If the employee cannot work as a result of off-duty behaviour, this would usually amount to cause for summary dismissal without notice.

Even if the employee's behaviour does not physically prevent him or her from working, it is possible that the employer's interests are nevertheless adversely effected by the behaviour. For example, in a recent case, a court found that an employer had cause to summarily dismiss an employee without notice who was convicted of possession of child pornography on his personal computer at home. There was no problem with the employee's job performance, and the offensive conduct took place entirely during the employee's nonworking hours. Nevertheless, the court found that the company's very visible public reputation as the largest employer in town and as a prominent contributor to local children's activities had been damaged by its association with the employee's illegal conduct.

Source: *Kelly v. Linamar Corp* (2005, Ontario Superior Court of Justice).

# DISCIPLINARY POLICIES AND PROCEDURES

**OUTCOME 5**

The rights of managers to discipline and discharge employees are increasingly limited. There is thus a great need for managers at all levels to understand discipline procedures. Disciplinary action taken against an employee must be for justifiable reasons, and there must be effective policies and procedures to govern its use. Such policies and procedures assist those responsible for taking disciplinary action and help ensure that employees will receive fair and constructive treatment.

Disciplinary policies and procedures should extend to a number of important areas to ensure thorough coverage. Figure 13.5 presents a disciplinary model that illustrates the areas where provisions should be established. The model also shows the logical sequence in which disciplinary steps must be carried out to ensure enforceable decisions.

A major responsibility of the HR department is to develop, and to have top management approve, its disciplinary policies and procedures. The HR department is also responsible for ensuring that disciplinary policies, as well as the disciplinary action taken against employees, are consistent with the collective agreement (if one exists) and conform to current laws. However, the primary responsibility for preventing or correcting disciplinary problems rests with an employee's immediate supervisor. This person is best able to observe evidence of unsatisfactory behaviour or performance and to discuss the matter with the employee. Should discipline become necessary, the employee's immediate supervisor is the logical person to apply the company's disciplinary procedure and monitor employee improvement.

## THE RESULTS OF INACTION

Figure 13.6 on page 465 lists the more common disciplinary problems identified by managers. Failure to take disciplinary action in any of these areas serves only to aggravate a problem that eventually must be resolved. Failure to act implies that the performance of the employee concerned has been satisfactory. If disciplinary action is eventually taken, the delay will make it more difficult to justify the action if challenged by the employee. A union employee can "grieve" the discipline, and a nonunion employee can treat the discipline as a breach of contract, and perhaps even a constructive dismissal, and sue the employer in a court for wrongful dismissal.

In defending against such a challenge to the employer's discipline, the employer is likely to be asked why an employee who had not been performing or behaving satisfactorily was kept on the payroll. Or an even more damaging question might be, "Why did that employee receive satisfactory performance ratings [or perhaps even merit raises]?"

**FIGURE 13.5**

A DISCIPLINARY MODEL

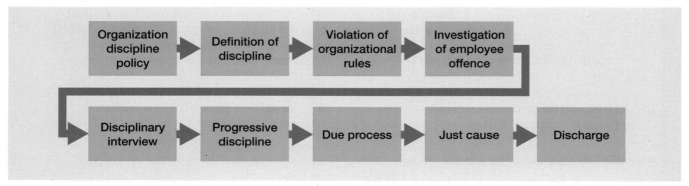

**FIGURE 13.6**

COMMON DISCIPLINARY PROBLEMS

**Attendance Problems**
- Unexcused absence
- Chronic absenteeism
- Unexcused/excessive tardiness
- Leaving without permission

**Dishonesty and Related Problems**
- Theft
- Falsifying employment application
- Willfully damaging organizational property
- Punching another employee's time card
- Falsifying work records

**Work Performance Problems**
- Failure to complete work assignments
- Producing substandard products or services
- Failure to meet established production requirements

**On-the-Job Behaviour Problems**
- Intoxication at work
- Insubordination
- Horseplay
- Smoking in unauthorized places
- Fighting
- Gambling
- Failure to use safety devices
- Failure to report injuries
- Carelessness
- Sleeping on the job
- Using abusive or threatening language with supervisors
- Possession of narcotics or alcohol
- Possession of firearms or other weapons
- Sexual harassment

Such contradictions in practice can only aid employees in successfully challenging management's corrective actions. Unfortunately, some supervisors try to build a case to justify their corrective actions only after they have decided that a particular employee should be discharged. The following are common reasons given by supervisors for their failure to impose a disciplinary penalty:

1. The supervisor had failed to document earlier actions, so no record existed on which to base subsequent disciplinary action.
2. Supervisors believed that they would receive little or no support from higher management for the disciplinary action.
3. The supervisor was uncertain of the facts underlying the situation requiring disciplinary action.
4. Failure by the supervisor to discipline employees in the past for a certain infraction caused the supervisor to forgo current disciplinary action to appear consistent.
5. The supervisor wanted to be seen as a likable person.[12]

## SETTING ORGANIZATIONAL RULES

The setting of organizational rules is the foundation for an effective disciplinary system. These rules govern the type of behaviour expected of employees. Organizations as diverse as Gerber Products, Steelcase, and Pitney Bowes have written policies explaining the type of conduct required of employees. Because employee behaviour standards are established through the setting of organizational rules and regulations, the following suggestions may help reduce problems in this area:

1. Rules should be widely disseminated and known to all employees. It should not be assumed that employees know all the rules.
2. Rules should be reviewed periodically—perhaps annually—especially those rules critical to work success.
3. The reasons for a rule should always be explained. Acceptance of an organizational rule is greater when employees understand the reasons behind it.

4. Rules should always be written. Ambiguity should be avoided as this can result in different interpretations of the rules by different supervisors.

5. Rules must be reasonable and relate to the safe and efficient operation of the organization. Rules should not be made simply because of personal likes or dislikes.

6. If management has been lax in the enforcement of a rule, the rule must be restated, along with the consequences for its violation, before disciplinary action can begin.

7. Employees should sign a document stating that they have read and understand the organizational rules.

When seeking reasons for unsatisfactory behaviour, supervisors must keep in mind that employees may not be aware of certain work rules. Before initiating any disciplinary action, therefore, it is essential that supervisors determine whether they have given their employees careful and thorough orientation in the rules and regulations relating to their jobs. In fact, the proper communication of organizational rules and regulations is so important that arbitrators cite *neglect in communicating rules* as a major reason for reversing the disciplinary action taken against an employee by unionized employers.[13]

## INVESTIGATING THE DISCIPLINARY PROBLEM

**OUTCOME 6**

It is a rare manager who has a good, intuitive sense of how to investigate employee misconduct. Too frequently, investigations are conducted in a haphazard manner; worse, they overlook one or more investigative concerns.[14] In conducting an employee investigation, it is important to be objective and to avoid the assumptions, suppositions, and biases that often surround discipline cases. Figure 13.7 lists seven questions to consider in investigating an employee offence. Attending to each question will help ensure a full and fair investigation while providing reliable information free from personal prejudice.[15]

### FIGURE 13.7

**CONSIDERATIONS IN DISCIPLINARY INVESTIGATIONS**

1. In very specific terms, what is the offence charged?
   - Is management sure it fully understands the charge against the employee?
   - Was the employee terminated for insubordination, or did the employee merely refuse a request by management?

2. Did the employee know he or she was doing something wrong?
   - What rule or provision was violated?
   - How would the employee know of the existence of the rule?
   - Was the employee warned of the consequence?

3. Is the employee guilty?
   - What are the sources of facts?
   - Is there direct or only indirect evidence of guilt?
   - Has anyone talked to the employee to hear his or her side of the situation?

4. Are there extenuating circumstances?
   - Were conflicting orders given by different supervisors?
   - Does anybody have reason to want to "get" this employee?
   - Was the employee provoked by a manager or another employee?

5. Has the rule been uniformly enforced?
   - Have all managers applied this rule consistently?
   - What punishment have previous offenders received?
   - Were any other employees involved in this offence?

6. Is the offence related to the workplace?
   - Is there evidence that the offence hurt the organization?
   - Is management making a moral judgment or a business judgment?

7. What is the employee's past work record?
   - How many years of service has the employee given the organization?
   - How many years or months has the employee held the present job?
   - What is the employee's personnel record as a whole, especially his or her disciplinary record?

## Documenting Misconduct

"It's too complicated." "I just didn't take time to do it." "I have more important things to do." These are some of the frequent excuses used by managers who have failed to document cases of employee misconduct. The most significant cause of inadequate documentation, however, is that managers have no idea of what constitutes good documentation. Unfortunately, the failure of managers to record employee misconduct accurately can result in the reversal of any subsequent disciplinary action. The maintenance of *accurate* and *complete* work records, therefore, is an essential part of an effective disciplinary system. For documentation to be complete, the following eight items should be included:

1. Date, time, and location of the incident(s)
2. Behaviour exhibited by the employee (the problem)
3. Consequences of that action or behaviour on the employee's overall work performance and/or the operation of the employee's work unit
4. Prior discussion(s) with the employee about the problem
5. Disciplinary action to be taken and specific improvement expected
6. Consequences if improvement is not made and a follow-up date
7. Employee's reaction to the supervisor's attempt to change behaviour
8. Names of witnesses to the incident (if appropriate)

When preparing documentation, it is important for a manager to record the incident immediately after the infraction takes place, when the memory of it is still fresh, and to ensure that the record is complete and accurate. Documentation need not be lengthy, but it must include the eight points in the preceding list. Remember, a manager's records of employee misconduct are considered business documents, and as such, they are admissible as evidence in arbitration hearings, administrative proceedings, and courts of law. As noted by one manager at a seminar on discipline, "When taking corrective action against an employee, the importance of compiling a complete and objective disciplinary record simply cannot be overstated."

## The Investigative Interview

Before any disciplinary action is initiated, an investigative interview should be conducted to make sure employees are fully aware of the offence.[16] This interview is necessary because the supervisor's perceptions of the employee's behaviour may

An investigative interview should always be held in private and should elicit the comments and concerns of the employee.

**CHAPTER 13:** EMPLOYEE RIGHTS AND DISCIPLINE

not be entirely accurate.[17] The interview should concentrate on how the offence violated the performance and behaviour standards of the job. It should avoid getting into personalities or areas unrelated to job performance. Most important, the employee must be given a full opportunity to explain his or her side of the issue so that any deficiencies for which the organization may be responsible are revealed.

## APPROACHES TO DISCIPLINARY ACTION

OUTCOME 7

If a thorough investigation shows that an employee has violated an organizational rule, disciplinary action must be imposed. Two approaches to disciplinary action are progressive discipline and positive discipline.

### Progressive Discipline

**progressive discipline**
Application of corrective measures by increasing degrees

**positive, or nonpunitive, discipline**
A system of discipline that focuses on early correction of employee misconduct, with the employee taking total responsibility for correcting the problem

**Progressive discipline** is the application of corrective measures by increasing degrees. Progressive discipline is designed to motivate an employee to correct his or her misconduct voluntarily. The technique is aimed at nipping the problem in the bud, using only enough corrective action to remedy the shortcoming. However, the sequence and severity of the disciplinary action vary with the type of offence and the circumstances surrounding it. Because each situation is unique, a number of factors must be considered in determining how severe a disciplinary action should be.

The typical progressive discipline procedure includes four steps. From an oral warning (or counselling) that subsequent unsatisfactory behaviour or performance will not be tolerated, the action may progress to a written warning, to a suspension with pay, and, ultimately, to discharge. It would usually be a breach of contract and a constructive dismissal for an employer to suspend a nonunion employee without pay, unless the contract includes an expressed term permitting this (and most do not).

The "capital punishment" of discharge is utilized only as a last resort. Organizations normally use lower forms of disciplinary action for less severe performance problems. It is important for managers to remember that three important things occur when progressive discipline is applied properly:

1. Employees always know where they stand regarding offences.
2. Employees know what improvement is expected of them.
3. Employees understand what will happen next if improvement is not made.

### Positive Discipline

Some HR professionals believe that progressive discipline has certain flaws, including its intimidating and adversarial nature, that prevent it from achieving the intended purpose. For these reasons, some organizations are using an approach called **positive, or nonpunitive, discipline**. Positive discipline is based on the concept that employees must assume responsibility for their personal conduct and job performance.[18]

Positive discipline requires a cooperative environment in which the employee and the supervisor engage in joint discussion and problem solving to resolve incidents of employee irresponsibility. The approach focuses on early correction of misconduct, with the employee taking total responsibility for resolving the problem. Nothing is imposed by management; all solutions and affirmations are jointly reached. HR managers often describe positive discipline as "nonpunitive discipline that replaces threats and punishment with encouragement."

Although positive discipline appears similar to progressive discipline, its emphasis is on giving employees reminders rather than reprimands as a way to improve performance. The technique is implemented in three steps. The first is a conference between the employee and the supervisor. The purpose of this meeting is to find a solution to the problem through discussion, with oral agreement by the employee to improve his or her performance. The supervisor refrains from reprimanding the employee or threatening him or her with further disciplinary action. Supervisors may document this conference, but a written record of this meeting is not placed in the employee's file unless the misconduct occurs again.

If improvement is not made after this first step, the supervisor holds a second conference with the employee to determine why the solution agreed to in the first conference did not work. At this stage, however, a written reminder is given to the employee. This document states the new or repeated solution to the problem, with an affirmation that improvement is the responsibility of the employee and a condition of continued employment.

When both conferences fail to produce the desired results, the third step is to give the employee a one-day *decision-making leave* (a paid leave). The purpose of this paid leave is for the employee to decide whether he or she wishes to continue working for the organization. The organization pays for this leave to demonstrate its desire to retain the person. Also, paying for the leave eliminates the negative effects for the employee of losing a day's pay. Employees given a decision-making leave are instructed to return the following day with a decision either to make a total commitment to improve performance or to quit the organization. If a commitment is not made, the employee is dismissed with the assumption that he or she lacked responsibility toward the organization. The fact that the employer goes through this process would not necessarily mean that it has cause to dismiss the employee. There is a strong likelihood that the employer would still be required to give the employee reasonable notice, or such other notice required in the written terms of the contract, because it is very hard to prove common law cause based solely on inadequate performance. Therefore, another strategy might be to give the employee a working notice of termination after the second conference and then offer to reemploy the employee on a new contract if the performance improves over the notice period.

## INFORMING THE EMPLOYEE

Regardless of the reasons for a discharge, it should be done with personal consideration for the employee affected. Every effort should be made to ease the trauma a discharge creates.[19] The employee must be informed honestly, yet tactfully, of the exact reasons for the action. Such candour can help the employee face the problem and adjust to it in a constructive manner.

Managers may wish to discuss, and even rehearse, with their peers the upcoming termination meeting. This practice can ensure that all important points are covered while giving confidence to the manager. Although managers agree that there is no single right way to conduct the discharge meeting, the following guidelines will help make the discussion more effective:

1. Come to the point within the first two or three minutes and list in a logical order all reasons for the termination.
2. Be straightforward and firm, yet tactful, and remain resolute in your decision.
3. Make the discussion private, businesslike, and fairly brief.
4. Do not mix the good with the bad. Trying to sugarcoat the problem sends a mixed message to the employee.
5. Avoid making accusations against the employee and injecting personal feelings into the discussion.
6. Avoid bringing up any personality differences between you and the employee.
7. Provide any information concerning severance pay and the status of benefits and coverage.
8. Explain how you will handle employment inquiries from future employers.[20]

Termination meetings should be held in a neutral location, such as a conference room, to prevent the employee from feeling unfairly treated. When discussing the termination, management must never provoke the employee or allow the employee to become belligerent toward management. Should the employee become agitated or show signs of hostility, the meeting should be stopped immediately, with notification given to security or the HR department.

Finally, when terminated employees are escorted off the premises, the removal must not serve to defame the employee. Managers should not give peers the impression that the terminated employee was dishonest or untrustworthy. Furthermore, managers are advised never to discuss the discharge or "badmouth" the terminated employee with other employees, customers, or other individuals.

## ALTERNATIVE DISPUTE RESOLUTION PROCEDURES

**OUTCOME 8**

In unionized workplaces, grievance procedures are stated in virtually all collective agreements. In nonunionized organizations, however, **alternative dispute resolution (ADR)** procedures are a developing method to address employee complaints.[21] The employer's interest stems from the desire to meet employees' expectations for fair treatment in the workplace while guaranteeing them due process—in the hope of minimizing discrimination claims or wrongful discharge suits.[22]

### Step-Review Systems

As Figure 13.8 illustrates, a **step-review system** is based on a preestablished set of steps—normally four—for the review of an employee complaint by successively higher levels of management. These procedures are patterned after the union grievance systems we will discuss in Chapter 14. For example, they normally require that the employee's complaint be formalized as a written statement. Managers at each step are required to provide a full response to the complaint within a specified time period, perhaps three to five working days.

An employee is sometimes allowed to bypass the meeting with his or her immediate supervisor if the employee fears reprisal from this person. Unlike grievance procedures in unionized organizations, however, nonunionized appeal procedures ordinarily do not provide for a neutral third party—such as an arbitrator—to serve as the judge of last resort. In most step-review systems, the president, chief executive officer (CEO), vice president, or HR director acts as the final authority, and this person's decision is not appealable. Some organizations give employees assistance in preparing their complaint cases. For example, an employee who desires it may be able to get advice and counsel from a designated person in the HR department before discussing the issue with management.

Unfortunately, step-review systems may not yield their intended benefits. Employees may believe that management is slow in responding to complaints and that management's response often does not solve the problem. Furthermore, employees may believe that, regardless of policies forbidding reprisal, supervisors would still hold it against them if they exercised their rights as spelled out in the step-review system. These concerns should not lead to the conclusion that all step-review systems are ineffective but rather that management must take special precautions to ensure that the systems work and provide the benefits intended.

## FIGURE 13.8

CONVENTIONAL STEP-REVIEW APPEAL PROCEDURE

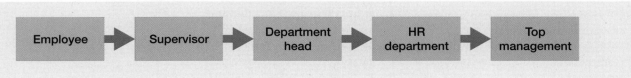

## Peer-Review Systems

A **peer-review system**, also called a complaint committee, is composed of equal numbers of employee representatives and management appointees. Employee representatives are normally elected by secret ballot by their coworkers for a rotating term, whereas management representatives are assigned, also on a rotating basis. A peer-review system functions as a jury because its members weigh evidence, consider arguments, and, after deliberation, vote independently to render a final decision.

Organizations consider one of the benefits of the peer-review system to be the sense of justice that it creates among employees. The peer-review system can be used as the sole method for resolving employee complaints, or it can be used in conjunction with a step-review system. For example, if an employee is not satisfied with management's action at step 1 or 2 in the step-review system, the employee can submit the complaint to the peer-review committee for final resolution.

## Open-Door Policy

The open-door policy is an old standby for settling employee complaints. The traditional **open-door policy** identifies various levels of management above the immediate supervisor that an aggrieved employee may contact; the levels may extend as high as a vice president, president, or CEO. Typically, the person who acts as "the court of last resort" is the HR director or a senior staff official.

The problems with an open-door policy are well documented. Two of its major weaknesses are the unwillingness of managers to listen honestly to employee complaints and worker reluctance to approach managers with their complaints. As an employee once told the authors of this text, "My manager has an open-door policy, but the door is only open one inch." Obviously, this employee felt he had little opportunity to get through to his manager. Other problems are attributed to this system as well. The open-door policy generally fails to guarantee consistent decision making because what is fair to one manager may seem unfair to another. Higher level managers tend to support supervisors for fear of undermining authority. And, as a system of justice, open-door policies may lack credibility with employees. Still, the open-door policy is often successful when it is supported by all levels of management and when management works to maintain a reputation for being fair and open-minded.

A peer-review system can create a sense of justice among employees.

© 2009 Jupiterimages Corporation

## Ombudsperson System

An **ombudsperson** is a designated individual from whom employees may seek counsel for the resolution of their complaints. The ombudsperson listens to an employee's complaint and attempts to resolve it by seeking an equitable solution between the employee and the supervisor. This individual works cooperatively with both sides to reach a settlement, often employing a problem-solving approach to the issue. Because the ombudsperson has no authority to finalize a solution to the problem, compromises are highly possible, and all concerned tend to feel satisfied with the outcome.

To function successfully, ombudspeople must be able to operate in an atmosphere of confidentiality that does not threaten the security of the managers or subordinates who are involved in a complaint. For example, complaints of sexual harassment, abuse of power, or issues that deal with circumstances that violate the law or unethical behaviour (whistle blowing) require high degrees of confidentiality to protect those involved. Although ombudspeople do not have the power to decide employee complaints, it is recommended that they have access to high levels of management to ensure that employee complaints receive fair treatment.

## Mediation

Along with arbitration, mediation is fast becoming a popular way to resolve employee complaints. **Mediation** employs a third-party neutral (called a mediator) to help employees and managers reach voluntary agreement acceptable to both parties. The essence of mediation is compromise. The **mediator** holds a meeting with the employee and management, listens to the position of each side, gathers facts, and then, through discussion, suggestions, and persuasion, obtains an agreement that will satisfy the needs and requirements of both sides. A mediator serves primarily as a fact finder and to open up a channel of communication between the parties. Unlike arbitrators, mediators have no power or authority to force either side toward an agreement. They must use their communication skills and the power of persuasion to help the parties resolve their differences. A cornerstone of mediation is that the parties maintain control over the settlement outcome.

Mediation is a flexible process that can be shaped to meet the demands of the parties. Also, it can be used to resolve a wide range of employee complaints, including discrimination claims or traditional workplace disputes.[23] Employees like the process because of its informality. According to one authority, "Mediation might be described as a private discussion assisted by an impartial third party."[24] Settlements fashioned through mediation are readily acceptable by the parties, thus promoting a favourable working relationship.

## Arbitration

Arbitration, which is fully explained in Chapter 14, works like this: the employee and the employer present their cases, or arguments, to an arbiter, who is typically a retired judge. He or she then makes a decision that the parties have agreed to be bound by. Arbitration can save litigation costs and avoid time delays and unfavourable publicity. However, to ensure that their arbitration policies are legal, employers must

- Have a clear, well-defined, and widely communicated arbitration policy
- Specify those topics subject to arbitration
- Inform employees of the rights they are relinquishing by signing an arbitration agreement
- Provide a procedurally fair arbitration system
- Allow for the nonbiased selection of an arbitrator or arbitration panel[25]

# MANAGERIAL ETHICS IN EMPLOYEE RELATIONS

Throughout this text, we have emphasized the legal requirements of HRM. Laws, agency rulings, and court decisions impact all aspects of the employment process—recruitment, selection, performance appraisal, safety and health, labour relations, and testing. Managers must comply with governmental regulations to promote an environment free from litigation.

However, beyond what is required by the law is the question of organizational ethics and the ethical—or unethical—behaviour engaged in by managers. **Ethics** can be defined as a set of standards of acceptable conduct and moral judgment. Ethics provides cultural guidelines—organizational or societal—that help us decide between proper or improper conduct. Therefore, ethics, like the legal aspects of HR, permeates all aspects of the employment relationship. For example, managers may adhere to the organization's objective of hiring members from the designated groups, but how those employees are supervised and treated once employed gets to the issue of managerial ethics. We have presented Ethics in HRM boxes in each chapter of this book to illustrate the complexity of ethical dilemmas.

Compliance with laws and the behavioural treatment of employees are two completely different aspects of the manager's job. Although ethical dilemmas will always occur in the supervision of employees, how employees are treated largely distinguishes the ethical organization from the unethical one. Interestingly, a recent research study, *Employee Trust and Organizational Loyalty*, sponsored by the Society for Human Resource Management, showed that employee perceptions of ethical behaviour by their organizational leadership may be the most important driver of employee trust and loyalty. According to the study, of critical interest to employees is the consistent and credible communication of information about the organization's ethical standards and its values, the organization's mission, and its workplace policies.[26]

Many organizations have their own code of ethics that governs relations with employees and the public at large.[27] This written code focuses attention on ethical values and provides a basis for the organization, and individual managers, to evaluate their plans and actions. HR departments have been given a greater role in communicating the organization's values and standards, monitoring compliance with its code of ethics, and enforcing standards throughout the organization. Organizations now have ethics committees and ethics ombudspeople to provide training in ethics to employees. The ultimate goal of ethics training is to avoid unethical behaviour and adverse publicity, to gain a strategic advantage, and, most of all, to treat employees in a fair and equitable manner, recognizing them as productive members of the organization.

**OUTCOME 9**

**ethics**
A set of standards of conduct and moral judgments that help determine right and wrong behaviour

**PART 5**

# SMALL BUSINESS APPLICATION

Issues of employee rights and discipline will be discussed in the context of a small advertising business. The company at hand has 75 employees, made up of sales staff, customer service staff, copy staff, and printers. The company produces a weekly free publication and generates revenue through the sale of advertising space. Although the company used to be profitable, currently, it is starting to lose money. If sales continue to decline, the company could be rendered insolvent in two years, putting all employees at risk. There are two reasons the company is losing money. First, advertising sales are down, not just for this company but for all companies in this business.

Second, a key client has reduced its business volume and complained that the service it has been receiving from staff was subpar.

So what is the company to do? First, although this company would like to preserve the employment of all of its staff, if sales volumes have been reduced to the point of incurring losses, the company has no choice but to reduce costs or find ways to increase sales. If work volumes are down with these sales volumes, the company may elect to reduce staff or hours to address this reality.

The second issue here is that of the client raising concerns about staff, which has resulted in

*continued*

business decline. In such a situation, the company will need to investigate the situation thoroughly and identify a remedy. The company would likely ask the client if it has examples of the issues of concern. The company also would likely draw from other sources of interaction between staff and the client, which may include order records. Then the company may discuss the situation with the management responsible for supporting

this client. Finally, if specific staff have been identified and evidence has been produced, a meeting with the staff in question to further explore this situation would be required. If the conduct of staff has been found to be unacceptable, the lessons learned in this chapter regarding discipline of staff should provide guidance on steps to take depending on the magnitude of the offence.

# SUMMARY

## SUMMARY

**OUTCOME 1** There are three regimes of employment law. The common law is a body of rules made by judges in the course of interpreting employment contracts. Employment regulation is legislation enacted by governments to regulate the terms of the employment contract and is enforced by an administrative tribunal. Collective bargaining law includes the rules that govern unionized employees. The employment contract for unionized employees is called a collective agreement, and it is interpreted and enforced by labour arbitrators rather than courts.

**OUTCOME 2** An employment contract between an employee and an employer may comprise expressed, written terms and a series of "implied terms" imposed by common law judges. Sometimes there are no written terms, in which case the contract is an oral one that includes all of the implied terms judges have created over the years. A written term usually supersedes an implied term provided that the written term does not violate a statutory minimum standard.

**OUTCOME 3** A nonunionized employer can dismiss an employee for any reason provided that it gives either the required contractual notice or implied reasonable notice (as long as the reason for the dismissal is not prohibited by a statute). It can also dismiss an employee with no notice if the employee has committed a serious breach of contract. A unionized employer, on the other hand, usually needs to prove it had just cause to dismiss an employee.

**OUTCOME 4** The PIPEDA provides employees with some rights regarding the use of their personal information. Employers should

establish policies regarding privacy issues. Employers have the right, under certain conditions, to monitor the work of employees, including their use of email and the Internet.

**OUTCOME 5** The HR department, in combination with other managers, should establish disciplinary policies. This will help achieve both acceptance of the policy and its consistent application. To reduce the need for discipline, organizational rules and procedures should be widely known, reviewed on a regular basis, and written and explained to employees. The rules must relate to the safe and efficient operation of the organization. When managers overlook the enforcement of rules, they must reemphasize the rule and its enforcement before disciplining an employee.

**OUTCOME 6** In the context of management, discipline does not mean punishment. Rather, discipline is a tool used to correct the practices of employees to help them perform better so that they conform to acceptable standards. Even when it is justified, managers do not generally enjoy disciplining their employees. However, failing to do so generally aggravates a problem that eventually must be resolved. Investigation of employee misconduct begins with proper documentation of wrongdoing. When managers are investigating employee problems, they need to know specifically the infraction of the employee, whether the employee knew of the rule violated, and any extenuating circumstances that might justify the employee's conduct. When employees are to receive discipline, the rule must be uniformly enforced and the past work record of the employee must be considered.

**OUTCOME 7** The two approaches to discipline are progressive discipline and positive discipline. Progressive discipline follows a series of steps based on increasing the degrees of corrective action. The corrective action applied should match the severity of the employee misconduct. Positive discipline, based on reminders, is a cooperative discipline approach in which employees accept responsibility for the desired employee improvement. The focus is on coping with the unsatisfactory performance and dissatisfactions of employees before the problems become major.

**OUTCOME 8** ADR procedures present ways by which employees exercise their due process rights. The most common forms of ADR are step-review systems, peer-review systems, the open-door policy, the ombudsperson, mediation, and arbitration.

**OUTCOME 9** Ethics in HRM extends beyond the legal requirements of managing employees. Managers engage in ethical behaviour when employees are treated in an objective and fair way and when an employee's personal and work-related rights are respected and valued.

## KEY TERMS

alternative dispute resolution (ADR), 470
collective agreement, 452
common law of employment, 450
constructive dismissal, 453
ethics, 473

implied contract terms, 450
labour arbitrator, 452
mediation, 472
mediator, 472
ombudsperson, 472
open-door policy, 471
peer-review system, 471

positive, or nonpunitive, discipline, 468
progressive discipline, 468
statutory rights, 455
step-review system, 470
summary dismissal, 455
wrongful dismissal, 455

## DISCUSSION QUESTIONS

1. Do you have a right to your job? What rights do you have with respect to employment?
2. In what ways, if any, does a unionized employee have greater protection from dismissal than a nonunionized employee in the Canadian model? Do you think that is fair or not? Why?
3. What is the difference between just cause in a unionized environment and cause for summary dismissal in a nonunionized environment?
4. Under what conditions can an employer monitor employees? Ask a group of working students the following questions:
   - Are you monitored at work?
   - What types of monitoring are used?
   - For what purposes does your employer monitor the workplace?
   - Do you object to the monitoring? If so, why? If not, why not?
5. What are the privacy settings on your Facebook page? Do you think that your employer or prospective employer should be allowed to look at it?
6. You have discovered that an employee has not been keeping client files updated, as is required by your company policy. Outline the steps that you would use to deal with this performance problem.
7. Discuss why documentation is so important to the disciplinary process. What constitutes correct documentation?

8. What do you think would constitute an effective ADR system? What benefits would you expect from such a system? If you were asked to rule on a discharge case, what facts would you analyze in deciding whether to uphold or reverse the employer's action?
9. In groups, discuss whether the following situations are fair or not fair:

   a. Zabeen was using the company Internet to locate a nursing home for her increasingly handicapped father. Her supervisor observed this and verified it with the information technology unit. Zabeen was given a written reprimand. Meanwhile, Sonia used the company telephone to do her personal banking and bill paying and was not reprimanded.
   b. Anthony spent his lunch hour at the gym, consisting of a strenuous workout program with a personal trainer. Meanwhile, Nicholas met his friends for lunch, sharing several beers at the local pub. Both employees felt fatigued in the afternoon, and their diminished productivity was noticed by their supervisor. Nicholas was asked to meet with his supervisor to review performance standards and received a verbal warning. Anthony was not.

# HRM EXPERIENCE

## Learning about Employee Rights

In the constantly changing field of HR, it is imperative that both HR managers and supervisors be aware of changes that affect the organization and the process of managing employees. Nowhere is this more true than in the growing field of employee rights. As employees demand more job and employment rights regarding monitoring, unjust dismissals, and off-duty conduct, employers must be knowledgeable about new laws, court rulings, and the policies of other organizations that influence each area. This knowledge will enable managers to respond to these employee concerns in a positive and proactive manner. Failure to provide employees with their rights could lead to costly and embarrassing lawsuits, resulting in diminished employee loyalty or morale. The purpose of this exercise, therefore, is for you to familiarize yourself with issues of employee rights.

## Assignment

Working individually or in teams, for each of the following employee rights topics, identify and discuss the concerns and interests at stake for both employees and employers. Answer the questions pertaining to each topic.

- Wrongful dismissal lawsuits
- Employee searches and monitoring
- Employee conduct away from the workplace
- Email and Internet use at work and at home
  1. What are the employer's interests?
  2. What are the employee's interests?
  3. What do you think is a fair balance between these interests?
  4. What, if any, laws or court cases affect this right?
  5. Generally, how are employers responding to this employee right?

Visit the *Managing Human Resources* CourseMate website at http://www.belcourt7e.nelson.com for quizzes, flashcards, videos, games, and more!

# CASE STUDY 1

## MANAGING CONFIDENTIAL INFORMATION

Emballages Prévost was founded in 1980 by its current president and CEO, Michel Prévost, who set himself the goal of always managing the company the way a good parent would manage a family. The company was able to carve out a specialized niche for itself producing packaging for the pharmaceutical industry. It now has a workforce of 115, composed of 95 production employees, 10 employees in the field, and 10 in management and administration.

Initially, the head of finance and accounting, Paul Demers, was responsible for the company's HR because Mr. Prévost has never felt the need to hire an HR specialist. Although Paul Demers is an extremely thorough and disciplined manager,

he has no interest in HR tasks. As a result, the firm's executive secretary, Sophie Dumouchel, has been in charge of HR for the last seven years. She is an independent, career-oriented, cheerful, and enthusiastic person who has always given senior management the impression that she was on top of her job. Michel Prévost has recently been concerned about the handling of confidential information. He has received a number of formal complaints from key employees who say they have witnessed other employees disclosing confidential information. After a brief inquiry, Mr. Prévost has become convinced that the problem stems from Sophie Dumouchel. She appears to have been using her position to manipulate her coworkers. As well, there are claims that she has sometimes disclosed highly confidential information about some employees and started certain rumours.

Everyone seems to be afraid of her and wants to be in her good books. When questioned on the matter, Ms. Dumouchel categorically denied everything and said that these accusations were due to the fact that some of her coworkers were jealous of her because of her more privileged position. Mr. Prévost has not found sufficient proof to accuse Sophie or anyone else of disclosing confidential information.

Michel Prévost has never had had any problems of this kind before and is now asking himself some serious questions about the company's responsibility in managing its HR records. He remembers that you are a management consultant for small and medium enterprises and sit on a hospital board of directors with him. He thus decides to get in touch with you about the situation. You offer to help him.

## Questions

1. The firm does not have a policy on privacy or the management of confidential information. Develop one. This site on workplace privacy will be helpful: http://www.cippic.ca /workplace-privacy.
2. Using the questions in Figure 13.7, prepare for a meeting with Ms. Dumouchel.

## CASE STUDY 2

### DISMISSING AN EMPLOYEE FOR ABSENTEEISM

Supervisors report that discharging an employee is one of the toughest tasks they perform as managers. Termination for absenteeism can be particularly difficult because if the absenteeism is related to a disability, the employer will need to consider not only the rules governing dismissal with notice and with cause but also requirements in human rights legislation.

Mr. Keays was hired in 1986 by Honda as an assembly-line worker. In 1997, he was diagnosed with chronic fatigue syndrome and consequently went on disability benefits until the insurer declared that he was fit to return to work. When he returned, the employer put him into its disability program, which required him to submit medical reports for every absence from work. The employer began to doubt the veracity of Mr. Keay's doctor's reports and, therefore, in 2000, ordered him to see a doctor it had selected. Mr. Keays obtained legal advice recommending that he not see the employer's doctor unless the employer clearly indicated the purpose of the examination. The employer ignored the lawyer's request and summarily dismissed Mr. Keays for cause (without notice) when he refused to meet with the employer's doctor. The employer claimed that this was insubordination, entitling it to dismiss Mr. Keays without notice.

Mr. Keays sued for wrongful dismissal. He argued that his employer did not have a contractual right to force him to attend a different doctor chosen by the employer simply because the employer did not like the opinion of the employee's own doctor. Therefore, he was not being insubordinate by refusing an order that the employer had no right to make. Moreover, he argued that the requirement to submit medical letters for every absence and to submit to a medical examination by the employer's doctor amounted to harassment and discrimination on the basis of his disability and was part of a conspiracy between the employer and the doctor intended to enable the employer to dismiss him for cause after the doctor issued a report saying Mr. Keays was able to work. Therefore, he argued that in addition to reasonable notice damages, he should be entitled to damages for bad faith in the manner in which he was dismissed and to punitive damages to for the employer's egregious conduct.

## Questions

1. Do you think the employer should be entitled to dismiss Mr. Keays without giving him reasonable notice?
2. Does an employer have a right to insist that employees submit to medical examinations by doctors chosen by the employer?
3. If the doctors inform the employer that Mr. Keays's absences are due to his chronic fatigue syndrome and that they are likely to continue in the future, should the employer be entitled to dismiss Mr. Keays?
4. If Mr. Keays wins his wrongful dismissal case, will the court order Honda to reinstate him to his previous employment? Should it do that?

**Source:** *Honda vs Keays,* http://www.mccarthy.ca/article_detail.aspx?id=4053.

# CASE STUDY 3

## IMPROVING PERFORMANCE THROUGH A PROGRESSIVE DISCIPLINE POLICY

Simon Ouellet, former president of the Human Resources Professionals Association of Ontario, was recruited by Fantom Technologies to be vice president of HR. Fantom is a manufacturer of state-of-the-art floor care products based in southern Ontario.

One of the first issues he faced in his new job was an unacceptable absenteeism rate. There were about 250 employees on the 3 assembly lines, operating 2 shifts a day. The average employee was absent 13 or 14 days a year. The benchmark for other manufacturing sites was 8 or 9 days. Simon calculated that Fantom was employing between 30 and 35 extra people to cover absences. This hurt the bottom line.

A related problem was punctuality. Employees were habitually 5 or 10 minutes late on their shifts. In a white-collar environment with flextime, this would not have been as critical. But tardiness in this situation meant that the assembly line could not operate and that the other employees on the three lines were forced to remain idle.

The solution was to develop a system of progressive discipline. Simon prepared a simple two-page policy. Page 1 dealt with culpable absenteeism—the behaviour in the control of employees, such as arriving late, leaving work without permission, calling in sick but playing golf, and so on. Page 2 dealt with legitimate or innocent absences. Simon met with the unions and notified them that this policy would come into effect as of December 1998. All employees started at zero absences at this time.

The policy assumed that all absences were innocent. However, if an employee was absent 5 times in a 12-month period, the supervisor met with that employee to express concern over the absences and to identify any need for counselling or assistance. The goal of the meeting was to express legitimate concerns, reinforce that the employee was needed, and ensure that the employee accepted responsibility for managing his or her own attendance. Following this meeting, if the employee had fewer than two absences in the ensuing six months, the employee was no longer part of the program. However, if the absence pattern continued, the employee was counselled a second and third time. If no improvements resulted, a level 4 employment status review was conducted. This was done on a case-by-case basis. For example, a frequently absent employee with 28 years of good service would be treated differently from another employee with the same absenteeism record but only 2 years of employment.

The results were impressive. About 70 employees entered the program. Of these, 8 to 10 advanced to step 2, 2 to step 3, and none to step 4. The absenteeism rate dropped to an average of fewer than 10 days, and punctuality was no longer an issue. Labour costs were reduced because it meant that 20 fewer employees were needed.

## Questions

1. "The policy assumed that all absences were innocent." What do you think this means?
2. Do you think the application of the policy would be affected if the absences were due to a disability as defined in the Human Rights Code?
3. The policy was active as of December 1998, and all employees were treated equally from that date, regardless of their previous absenteeism records. Was this fair?
4. Could a policy of this type be developed to manage student punctuality and absenteeism?

**Source:** Interview with Simon Ouellet.

## NOTES AND REFERENCES

1. *Cronk v. Canadian General Insurance* (1995), 19 O.R. (3rd) 515 (Ontario Court of Appeal).

2. T. Wagar, "Wrongful Dismissal: Perception vs. Reality," *Human Resources Professional* 8, no. 10 (1996).

3. *Doman Forest Products Ltd.* (1990), 13 Labour Arbitration Cases (4th) 275.

4. G. England, *Individual Employment Law* (Irwin Law, 2008), 205–208.

5. S. Cohen and A. V. Campell, "It's Time to Face the Inevitable and Comply with Privacy Laws," *Canadian HR Reporter* 15, no. 2 (January 28, 2002): 9–10.

6. David Brown, "10 Months to Get Ready," *Canadian HR Reporter* 16, no. 4 (February 24, 2003): 1, 11.

7. Dan J. Shields and Valerie Jepson, "When Internet Use Turns to Abuse," *HR Professional*, April–May 2006, 28.

8. *Colwell v. Cornerstone Properties* (Ontario Superior Court of Justice, 2008).

9. Gillian Flynn, "Internet Issues at Work," *Workforce-Vendor Directory* 80, no. 10 (2002): 33–34.

10. *Prestressed Systems Inc.* (2005), 137 Labour Arbitration Cases (4th), 193.

11. *Doman Forest Products Ltd.* (1990), 13 Labour Arbitration Cases (4th), 275, considering the impact of the *British Columbia Privacy Act* on the right of employers to conduct surveillance of employees.

12. One of the original studies on this topic can be found at Edward L. Harrison, "Why Supervisors Fail to Discipline," *Supervisory Management* 30, no. 4 (April 1985): 17.

13. George W. Bohlander and Donna Blancero, "A Study of Reversal Determinants in Discipline and Discharge Arbitration Awards: The Impact of Just Cause Standards," *Labor Studies Journal* 21, no. 3 (Fall 1996): 3–18.

14. "Steps to Take before Recommending Disciplinary Action," *PM Public Management* 86, no. 6 (July 2004): 43.

15. "22 Tips for Avoiding Employee Lawsuits," *HRfocus* 80, no. 12 (December 2003): 4.

16. Jathan W. Janove, "Private Eye 101," *HR Magazine* 49, no. 7 (July 2004): 127.

17. Kelly Mollica, "Perceptions of Fairness," *HR Magazine* 49, no. 6 (June 2004): 169.

18. Readers interested in the pioneering work on positive discipline should see James R. Redeker, "Discipline, Part I: Progressive Systems Work Only by Accident," *Personnel* 62, no. 10 (October 1985): 8–12; James R. Redeker, "Discipline, Part 2: The Nonpunitive Approach Works by Design," *Personnel* 62, no. 11 (November 1985): 7–14.

19. Richard Bayer, "Firing: Letting People Go with Dignity Is Good for Business," *HRfocus* 77, no. 1 (January 2000): 10. See also Paul Falcone, "Give Employees the (Gentle) Boot," *HR Magazine* 46, no. 4 (April 2001): 121–128.

20. "The New Rules of Termination," *HRfocus* 78, no. 5 (May 2001): 1, 11–15.

21. Elizabeth Hill, "AAA Employment Arbitration: A Fair Forum at Low Cost," *Dispute Resolution Journal* 58, no. 2 (May–June 2003): 8.

22. Theodore Eisenberg and Elizabeth Hill, "Arbitration and Litigation of Employment Claims," *Dispute Resolution Journal* 58, no. 4 (November 2003–January 2004): 44.

23. Margaret M. Clark, "EEOC's Effort to Expand Mediation Gains Momentum," *HR Magazine* 48, no. 5 (May 2003): 32.

24. "How Best to Avoid Mediation Mistakes," *HRfocus* 77, no. 9 (September 2000): 2. See also Nancy Kauffman and Barbara Davis, "What Type of Mediation Do You Want?" *Dispute Resolution Journal* 53, no. 2 (May 1998): 10.

25. George W. Bohlander, Robert J. Deeny, and Mishka L. Marshall, "Alternative Dispute Resolution Policies: Current Procedural and Administrative Issues," *Labor Law Journal* 47, no. 9 (September 1996): 619–626; Thomas R. Kelly and Danielle L. Berke, "What's New in ADR?" *HRfocus* 73, no. 4 (April 1996): 15.

26. Jennifer Schramm, "Perception on Ethics," *HR Magazine* 49, no. 11 (November 2004): 176.

27. "Ethical Corporate Behavior Begins with a Code of Conduct," *HRfocus* 79, no. 7 (July 2002): 8–9.

# The Dynamics of Labour Relations

## After studying this chapter, you should be able to

OUTCOME 1  Identify and explain the federal and provincial legislation that provides the framework for labour relations.

OUTCOME 2  Explain why employees join unions.

OUTCOME 3  Describe the process by which unions organize employees and gain recognition as their bargaining agent.

OUTCOME 4  Discuss the bargaining process and the bargaining goals and strategies of a union and an employer.

OUTCOME 5  Differentiate the forms of bargaining power that a union and an employer may utilize to enforce their bargaining demands.

OUTCOME 6  Describe a typical union grievance procedure and explain the basis for arbitration awards.

To someone studying industrial relations for the first time, the subject invokes images of workers on strike, picketing exercises, tough negotiators, and public inconvenience. But it is not always this way. Most industrial relations matters do not make it to the press. In fact, more than 90 percent of collective bargaining negotiations are settled between management and unions without strikes or lockouts.[1] There were 2,571 collective bargaining agreements that expired just in Ontario in 2011.[2] The vast majority of these were settled without much acrimony and away from the press.

In terms of the process, the union local will normally meet with its membership and decide on demands for changes to the collective agreement. Management will review the demands and try to reconcile them with the financial situation of the organization. It will then come up with its own demands and counteroffers. The two sides will meet, perhaps over a few weeks or months, and conduct tough bargaining, usually in good faith and respectfully. In the end, both sides will most likely make concessions on their original positions and sign a collective bargaining agreement to cover the workplace, usually over the next 2 to 4 years.

Unions, however, tend to evoke strong opinions, positive or negative, for many people. Unions are workers' associations formed to enhance their power in dealing with employers and improve their pay and working conditions. To some, the word evokes images of labour–management unrest— grievances, strikes, picketing, boycotts. To others, the word represents industrial democracy, fairness, opportunity, equal representation. Many think of unions as simply creating an adversarial relationship between employees and managers.

Regardless of attitudes toward them, since the mid-1800s, unions have been an important force shaping organizational practices, legislation, and political thought in Canada. Today, unions remain of interest because of their influence on organizational productivity and HR policies and practices. Like business organizations themselves, unions are undergoing changes in both operation—such as mergers and coalitions—and philosophy.

In spite of the long history of unions, the intricacies of labour relations are unfamiliar to many individuals. Therefore, this chapter describes government regulation of labour relations, the labour relations process, the reasons that workers join labour organizations, and the structure and leadership of unions. Importantly, according to labour law, once the union is certified to negotiate for bargaining-unit members, it must represent everyone in the unit equally. Therefore, in the latter sections of the chapter, we discuss the important topics of contract administration, particularly the handling of employee grievances and arbitration.

About 30 percent of all employees in Canada are unionized, with rates higher in the public sector (71 percent) than in the private sector (16 percent).[3] Unions and other labour organizations can affect significantly the ability of managers to direct and control the various functions of HRM. For example, pay rates may be determined through union negotiations, or unions may impose restrictions on management's employee appraisal methods. Therefore, it is essential that managers in both the union and the nonunion environment understand how unions operate and be thoroughly familiar with the important body of law governing labour relations. Remember, ignorance of labour legislation is no defence when managers and supervisors violate labour law. Before reading further, test your knowledge of labour relations law by answering the questions in Highlights in HRM 14.1.

# GOVERNMENT REGULATION OF LABOUR RELATIONS

**OUTCOME 1**

Labour relations in Canada are regulated by a multiplicity of federal and provincial laws. There are specific laws, or acts, for different sectors, industries, and workers. The system is highly decentralized. For example, interprovincial

# HIGHLIGHTS IN HRM 14.1

## Test Your Labour Relations Know-How

1. During a labour organizing drive, supervisors questioned individual employees about their union beliefs. Was this questioning permissible?

   Yes _____     No _____

2. While an organizing drive was underway, an employer agreed—as a social gesture—to furnish refreshments at a holiday party. Was the employer acting within the law?

   Yes _____     No _____

3. A company distributed to other anti-union employers in the area a list of job applicants known to be union supporters. Was the distribution unlawful?

   Yes _____     No _____

4. During a union organizing drive, the owner of Servo Pipe promised her employees a wage increase if they would vote against the union. Can the owner legally make this promise to her employees?

   Yes _____     No _____

5. John Green, a maintenance engineer, has a poor work record. Management wishes to terminate his employment; however, Green is a union steward and is highly critical of the company. Can management legally discharge this employee?

   Yes _____     No _____

Answers on page 508

transportation and communications are under federal jurisdiction, whereas manufacturing and mining are under provincial jurisdiction. However, 90 percent of workers are governed by provincial legislation.

## THE *INDUSTRIAL RELATIONS DISPUTES AND INVESTIGATION ACT*

The *Industrial Relations Disputes and Investigation Act* (1948) specified the right of workers to join unions, allowed unions to be certified as bargaining agents by a labour relations board, required management to recognize a certified union as the exclusive bargaining agent for a group of employees, required both unions and management to negotiate in good faith, outlined unfair labour practices by both unions and management, and created a two-stage compulsory conciliation process that was mandatory before strikes or lockouts became legal.[4]

The federal government later incorporated these rights into a more comprehensive piece of legislation known as the *Canada Labour Code*. At the same time, the Canada Industrial Relations Board (CIRB) was established to administer and enforce the code. Similarly, each province has a labour relations board that administers labour law and provincial labour law statutes, such as the Ontario *Labour Relations Act*. (The exception is Quebec, which has a labour court and commissioners.) Members of the labour relations boards are generally government appointees. Labour relations boards are generally autonomous from the federal government and have representatives from both labour and management. The duties of the labour relations board include

- Administering the statutory procedures for the acquisition, transfer, and termination of bargaining rights
- Hearing complaints related to unfair labour practices
- Supervising strikes and lockout votes
- Determining whether bargaining was done in good faith
- Remedying violations of labour legislation[5]

## THE LABOUR RELATIONS PROCESS

Individually, employees may be able to exercise relatively little power in their relationship with employers. Of course, if they believe they are not being treated fairly, they have the option of quitting. However, employees can also correct this situation by organizing and bargaining with the employer collectively. When employees pursue this option, the labour relations process begins. As Figure 14.1 illustrates, the **labour relations process** consists of a logical sequence of four events: (1) workers desire collective representation; (2) the union begins its organizing campaign and, if successful, is certified and recognized; (3) collective negotiations lead to a contract; and (4) the contract is administered. Laws and administrative rulings influence each event by granting special privileges to, or imposing defined constraints on, workers, managers, and union officials.[6]

## WHY EMPLOYEES UNIONIZE

The majority of research on why employees unionize comes from the study of blue-collar employees in the private sector. These studies generally conclude that employees unionize as a result of economic need, and because of a general dissatisfaction with managerial practices, and thereby seek to have a voice in the setting of working conditions and/or to fulfill social and status needs. In short, employees see unionism as a way to achieve results they cannot achieve acting individually. As Highlights in HRM 14.2 illustrates, some segments of the labour force are very difficult to unionize. It should be pointed out that some employees join unions because of the union-shop provisions. A **union shop** is a provision of the collective agreement that requires employees to join as a condition of employment.

**labour relations process**
A logical sequence of four events: (1) workers desire collective representation; (2) the union begins its organizing campaign, which may lead to certification and recognition; (3) collective negotiations lead to a contract; and (4) the contract is administered

**union shop**
Provision of the collective agreement that requires employees to join the union as a condition of their employment

### Using the Internet

For a history of labour, read the article "The Cradle of Collective Bargaining: History of Labour" at

**http://www.humanities. mcmaster.ca/~cradle**

**OUTCOME 2**

**FIGURE 14.1**

THE LABOUR RELATIONS PROCESS

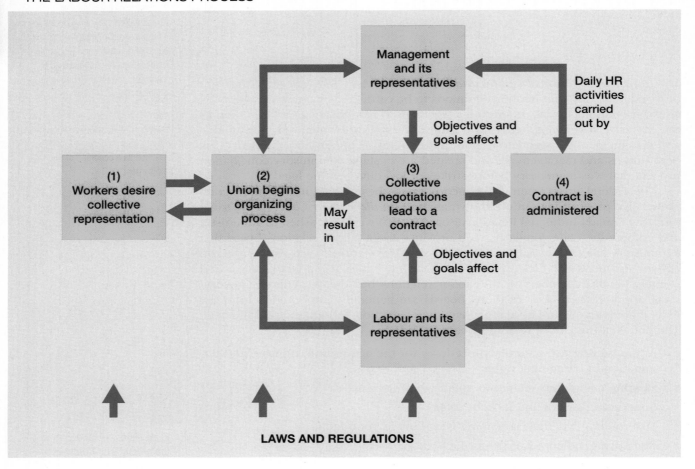

## Economic Needs

Whether employees select unionization will greatly depend on whether the employees perceive the union as likely to be effective in improving various economic conditions of employment—often referred to as the union's instrumentality. Dissatisfaction with wages, benefits, and working conditions appears to provide the strongest reason to join a union. This point is continually supported by research studies that find that both union members and nonmembers have their highest expectations of union performance regarding the "bread-and-butter" issues of collective bargaining.[7] Hourly earnings were $26.40 for those in unions and $21.49 for those not in a union.[8] Unions are built on these traditional issues of wages, benefits, and working conditions.

## Dissatisfaction with Management

Employees may seek unionization when they perceive that managerial practices regarding promotion, transfer, shift assignment, or other job-related policies are administered in an unfair or biased manner. Employees cite favouritism shown by managers as a major reason for joining unions. This is particularly true when the favouritism concerns the HR areas of discipline, promotion, job assignments, and training opportunities.

We have noted throughout this book that today's employees are better educated than those of the past and often express a desire to be more involved in decisions affecting their jobs. Chapter 4 discussed the concept of employee

# HIGHLIGHTS IN HRM 14.2

## Homeworkers: Canada's Invisible Labour Force

Rosanna Gonzalez (not her real name) works in the basement of her home in a small room crowded with industrial sewing machines. Rosanna is in the process of making 410 sweatshirts. To meet her deadline, she will have to put in 40 hours of work in 2 days. There is no natural light in the airless basement room and no way to escape the flying dust and thread particles. Last week, the assignment was T-shirts. Rosanna received 38 cents per shirt. She can churn one out in five minutes, but even at that speed, she still earns only about $4.50 per hour.

In most provinces, the law requires that homeworkers be paid at least one dollar above minimum wage to compensate them for the use of space and equipment in their homes. But enforcement of the law is rare. Canadians are quick to condemn working conditions in developing countries yet are notably silent about abuses in their own country. Joining a union is a traditional response to abysmal working conditions. For homeworkers, unionization is a remote possibility at best. These individuals (most of whom speak no English) work in scattered and unlicensed locations and are usually unaware of their rights. Those who are aware are afraid that if they complain, they will suffer retribution at the hands of the retailers, contractors, and subcontractors with whom they do business. These women have few employment options and are often the sole providers for their children. For them the choice is clear: put up with the exploitation or do not work at all.

empowerment and highlighted various employee involvement techniques. The failure of employers to give employees an opportunity to participate in decisions affecting their welfare may encourage union membership. It is widely believed that one reason managers begin employee involvement programs and seek to empower their employees is to avoid collective action by employees. For example, employers in the auto, semiconductor, and financial industries involve employees in collaborative programs as a means to stifle unionization. In one organizing effort by the United Auto Workers at a Nissan plant, the union lost the election because workers were satisfied with the voice in decision making that Nissan's participatory style of management gave them.

## Social and Leadership Concerns

Employees whose needs for recognition and social affiliation are being frustrated may join unions as a means of satisfying these needs. Through their union, they have an opportunity to fraternize with other employees who have similar desires, interests, problems, and gripes. Simply, employees may join unions for the same reason they would join a civic organization, club, or sports team, namely to enjoy the companionship of others and to benefit in the prestige and value that organization may provide. Additionally, the union also enables them to put leadership talents to use as officers of the union and representatives of fellow employees. One study found that employees became union stewards so that they could be seen as "a fellow your buddies look to" and as a person who "stands up to the boss."[9]

Getty Images

Involving employees in decision making may reduce the desire to seek representation through unionization.

## ORGANIZING CAMPAIGNS

**OUTCOME 3**

Once employees desire to unionize, a formal organizing campaign may be started either by a union organizer or by employees acting on their own behalf.[10] Contrary to popular belief, most organizing campaigns are initiated by employees rather than by union organizers. Large national unions such as the United Auto Workers, the United Brotherhood of Carpenters, the United Steelworkers, and the Teamsters, however, have formal organizing departments whose purpose is to identify organizing opportunities and launch organizing campaigns.

**authorization card**

A statement signed by an employee authorizing a union to act as his or her representative for the purposes of collective bargaining

## Organizing Steps

The organizing process normally includes the following steps:

1. Employee/union contact
2. Initial organizational meeting
3. Formation of an in-house organizing committee
4. Application to a labour relations board
5. Issuance of a certificate by a labour relations board
6. Election of a bargaining committee and contract negotiations

*Step 1.* The first step begins when employees and union officials make contact to explore the possibility of unionization. During these discussions, employees investigate the advantages of representation, and union officials begin to gather information on employee needs, problems, and grievances. Union organizers also seek specific information about the employer's financial health, supervisory styles, and organizational policies and practices. To win employee support, labour organizers must build a case *against* the employer and *for* the union. Note also that most organizing drives take place inside the company.

*Step 2.* As an organizing campaign gathers momentum, the organizer schedules an initial union meeting to attract more supporters. The organizer uses the information gathered in Step 1 to address employee needs and explain how the union can secure these goals. Two additional purposes of organizational meetings are (1) to identify employees who can help the organizer direct the campaign and (2) to establish communication chains that reach all employees.

*Step 3.* The third important step in the organizing drive is to form an in-house organizing committee composed of employees willing to provide leadership to the campaign. The committee's role is to interest other employees in joining the union and in supporting its campaign. An important task of the committee is to have employees sign an **authorization card** indicating their willingness to be represented by a union in collective bargaining with their employer. Union membership cards, once signed, are confidential, and only the labour relations board has access to them. The number of signed authorization cards demonstrates the potential strength of the labour union.[11] Legislation across Canada requires that a union collect authorization cards as a first step in the union certification process.

There are then two different processes for union certification used in Canada. One method is known as a card-check. Under this method, a union is certified to represent the workers if the union submits to the labour board authorization cards on behalf of a majority of workers (such as 55 percent) in an appropriate bargaining unit. The second method, known as a mandatory ballot, is a two-step process. First, the union must obtain authorization cards on behalf of a certain number of workers (in Ontario, it is 40 percent or more) to obtain a vote. Then the labour board orders a vote of employees in the bargaining unit, which the union must win. In other words, those who do not cast ballots are not assumed to be voting against the certification of the union.

*Step 4.* When the union has collected sufficient authorization cards to satisfy the requirements under the applicable certification model, it will file an application for certification. It submits to the labour board its authorization cards, but the employer does not get to see them. The labour board then applies the model, either certifying the union on the basis of a card-check, ordering a vote in provinces that use a mandatory ballot model, or dismissing the application if the union does not submit the required number of authorization cards.

*Step 5.* Once the labour board has applied the process, it will declare whether or not the union has been successful in its application for certification. If the union is successful, the board will "certify" the union. If the union fails to meet the required test, the board will dismiss the application.

*Step 6.* Once the labour relations board determines that the union is certified, the bargaining committee is put in place to start negotiating a collective agreement. If the union is a national union, such as the Canadian Auto Workers (CAW), usually a national representative works with the bargaining committee to negotiate a collective agreement with the company. Labour relations legislation imposes a duty on employers and unions to bargain in good faith and make reasonable efforts to complete a collective agreement.

## Employer Tactics

Employers must not interfere with the labour relations process of certification. They are prohibited by law from dismissing, disciplining, or threatening employees for exercising their right to form a union. Employers cannot promise better conditions, such as increased vacation days, if the employees vote for no union or choose one union over another. Nor can they threaten to close the business, as one company did as workers were voting.[12] They cannot unilaterally change wages and working conditions during certification proceedings or during collective bargaining. Like unions, they must bargain in good faith, meaning that they must demonstrate a commitment to bargain seriously and fairly. In addition, they cannot participate in the formation, selection, or support of unions representing employees (see Figure 14.2).

None of these prohibitions prevents an employer from making the case that the employees have the right not to join a union and that they can deal directly with the employer on any issue. Employer resistance to unionization is the norm in Canada, and opposition has been found to decrease the probability of successfully organizing.[13] When Walmart consolidated its entry into Canada by buying 122 nonunionized Woolco stores, the company was widely viewed as anti-union. However, Walmart spokespeople insist that they are not anti-union but rather "pro-associate" (the Walmart term for the retail salesclerk).[14]

Employers' attempts to influence employees are scrutinized closely by officials of the organizing union and by the labour relations board. In the Walmart case (at the end of the chapter), an unfair labour practice was found to have been committed by a labour board and the union was automatically recognized, even though a minority of the employees had signed authorization cards. Over time, Walmart has developed a reputation for remaining union free, as described in the Reality Check.

## Union Tactics

Unions also have a duty to act in accordance with labour legislation. Unions are prohibited from interfering with the formation of an employer's organization. They cannot intimidate or coerce employees to become or remain members of a union. Nor can they force employers to dismiss, discipline, or discriminate against nonunion

## FIGURE 14.2

### EMPLOYER "DON'TS" DURING UNION ORGANIZING CAMPAIGNS

Union organizing drives are emotionally charged events. Furthermore, labour law, labour relations board rulings, and court decisions greatly affect the behaviour and actions of management and union representatives. During the drive, managers and supervisors should avoid the following:

- Attending union meetings, spying on employee–union gatherings, and questioning employees about the content of union meetings
- Questioning current employees about their union sentiments—especially about how they might vote in a union election
- Threatening or terminating employees for their union support or beliefs
- Changing the working conditions of employees because they actively work for the union or simply support its ideals
- Supplying the names, addresses, and phone numbers of employees to union representatives or other employees sympathetic to or opposed to the union
- Promising employees improvements in working conditions (e.g., wage increases, benefit improvements) if they vote against the union
- Accepting or reviewing union authorization cards or pro-union petitions because employees' names are listed on these documents
- Providing financial or any other support to employees opposed to unionization

# REALITY CHECK

## Walmart Avoiding Unionization at All Costs

Walmart is one of the most well-known household names in North America and is rapidly increasing in popularity around the globe. In 2006, *Forbes* magazine reported that Walmart "operates in 44 countries, has 2,276 stores outside of the U.S., has more than 100,000 employees in Mexico alone, and does $56.3 billion in sales overseas." In 2005, Walmart started to make its move to India. Predictions are that the retail giant will become even more powerful, topping $500 billion by 2010. For decades, Walmart has been fighting to keep unions out of its stores. Some Canadian stores have been successfully unionizing, but Walmart has been relentless in its pursuits to keep its operations nonunionized.

The Saguenay-region store was the first to become unionized, in 2004; however, in 2005, before members could take their first collective bargaining dispute to arbitration, Walmart closed the store, claiming financial difficulties. The workers fought back but lost as Justice Binnie claimed that it was up to them to prove that Walmart acted in bad faith, thus engaging in unfair labour practices. The courts ruled that Walmart's decision could not be legally seen as anti–union motivated, even though

"Walmart has fought unionization in its stores in Quebec in every way imaginable within its legal means," said Gregor Murray, a professor of industrial relations at the Université de Montreal who has followed the Walmart case for years.

Several other Walmart stores were successful in securing union certification since Walmart closed the store in 2005, but only the auto and lube workers at a Gatineau, Quebec, Walmart location were successful at obtaining a collective agreement imposed by arbitration. This operation was, however, also closed in October 2008.

In 2008, Walmart workers at another Gatineau store joined the union, United Food and Commercial Workers Canada. In the summer of 2010, after two years of battling with management, they were successful in achieving an arbitration-ruled collective agreement between the union and Walmart, making them the second group of Walmart employees in North America to have a collective agreement. Ironically, although the store was not closed by Walmart, workers filed for and were officially granted decertification from their union just over a year into their first collective agreement. What this means is that only the Walmart in Weyburn, Saskatchewan, remains unionized in Canada. Obviously, Walmart has been relentless in its pursuit to remain union free.

---

Sources: Robert Malone, "Wal-Mart Takes Over The World," *Forbes*, January 1, 2006, http://www.forbes.com/2006/01/12/walmart-rules-the-world-cx_rm_0113walmart.html; Andrew Chung, "Wal-Mart Workers Hope to Show Their Union the Door," *The Star.com*, March 8, 2011, http://www.thestar.com/news/canada/article/950705–wal-mart-workers-hope-to-show-their-union-the-door; Tonda MacCharles, "Top Court Backs Wal-Mart over Union Store Closing," *The Star.com*, November 27, 2009, http://www.thestar.com/news/canada/article/731668–top-court-backs-wal-mart-over-union -store-closing; "Quebec Wal-Mart Workers Leave Union More than 150 Gatineau Employees Had First Collective Agreement for Just More than a Year," *CBC News*, October 31, 2011, http://www.cbc.ca/news/canada/ottawa/story/2011/10/31/ottawa-gatineau-walmart-workers.html; "Quebec Wal-Mart Workers Get Rare Union Deal: Only One Other North American Wal-Mart Has a Collective Agreement," CBC News, October 8, 2010, http://www.cbc.ca /news/canada/ottawa/story/2010/10/08/ottawa-wal-mart-deal.html.

---

**bargaining unit**
Group of two or more employees who share common employment interests and conditions and may reasonably be grouped together for the purposes of collective bargaining

**unfair labour practices (ULPs)**
Specific employer and union illegal practices that deny employees their rights and benefits under federal and provincial labour law

employees. They must provide fair representation for all employees in the **bargaining unit**, whether in collective bargaining or in grievance procedure cases. Unions cannot engage in activities such as strikes before the expiration of the union contract.

Any of the prohibited activities noted above for both employers and unions are considered **unfair labour practices (ULPs)**. Charges of ULPs are filed with the labour relations board, whose duty it is to enforce labour relations legislation. A summary of ULPs is presented in Highlights in HRM 14.3. See Ethics in HRM as well.

## HOW EMPLOYEES BECOME UNIONIZED

The procedures for union certification vary across Canadian jurisdictions. As mentioned earlier, the common practice is for unions to present documentation to the appropriate labour relations board for certification. The labour relations board must certify a union before it can act as a bargaining unit for a group of employees. As noted, to acquire certification, the union must demonstrate that it has obtained the minimum level of membership support required by the labour relations board. It is also possible for a union to obtain the right to represent workers through voluntary recognition, a process in which the employer simply agrees to recognize the union as the representative of the employees.

# HIGHLIGHTS IN HRM 14.3

## Unfair Labour Practices

Unfair labour practices by employers include

- Helping to establish or administer a union
- Altering the working conditions of the employees while a union is applying for certification without the union's consent
- Using intimidation, coercion, threats, promises, or exercising undue influence while a union is being organized
- Failing to recognize or bargain with the certified union
- Hiring professional strike breakers

Unfair labour practices by unions include

- Contributing financial or other support to an employer's organization
- Not representing fairly the employees in the bargaining unit
- Bargaining or negotiating a collective agreement with an employer while another union represents the employees in the bargaining unit
- Calling or authorizing an unlawful strike or threatening to do so
- Threatening or intimidating workers to influence their support for the union

# ETHICS IN HRM

## Caterpillar Closes Electro-Motive Plant

For over 85 years, Caterpillar Inc. has been one of the world's leading manufacturers. In 2011, with branches all across North America, Caterpillar's sales soared to over $60 billion. Caterpillar's subsidiary, Progress Rail Services, operates Electro-Motive out of London, Ontario. In 2010, Caterpillar purchased Electro-Motive for US$820 million in cash from Berkshire Partners LLC and Greenbriar Equity Group LLC. They inherited some 700 Canadian workers; 450 of them were unionized members represented by the CAW.

Shortly after taking over, the parties sought to hammer out a collective agreement. Caterpillar's Electro-Motive division made a number of tough demands: "pay cuts of 50 per cent in many job categories, elimination of a defined-benefit pension plan, reductions in dental and other benefits and the end of a cost-of-living adjustment." These did not go over well with the union and were not met after a long, drawn-out negotiation process. Although members voted overwhelmingly in favour of a strike, the union assured management that it would continue to work under the current collective agreement until a deal

was reached. Progress Rail (Electro-Motive) responded with a lockout that lasted a month, followed by the announcement that the plant would be closing due to financial constraints.

The CAW dubbed the action of Caterpillar heartless, claiming that it was the company's intention to close the plant from the beginning. If so, then this raises serious ethical concerns for workers whose livelihood and pensions were at risk. National CAW President Ken Lewenza said that in his 21 years in public service, he has never heard of an organization, local, national, or international, blatantly advising an employee group that it is going to cut wages in half and slash pension and benefits, and this is a "take-it-or-leave-it offer." Lewenza further claimed, "I've never had a situation where I've dealt with such an unethical, immoral, disrespectful, highly profitable company like Caterpillar." It may be argued that Caterpillar had an ethical obligation to come to an agreement that would be in the best interests of its employees. But the firm maintained that doing so would have placed it in financial duress.

Sources: John D. Stoll, "CAW Votes in Favour of London Caterpillar Plant Strike," *The National Post*, December 30, 2011, http://business.financialpost.com/2011/12/30/caw-votes-in-favour-of-london-caterpillar-plant-strike/, retrieved May 2012; Tavia Grant, "In the Electro-Motive Shutdown, an Unsettling Message for Canadian Industry," *The Globe and Mail*, February 21, 2012, http://www.theglobeandmail.com/report-on-business/economy/manufacturing/in-the-electro-motive-shutdown-an-unsettling-message-for-canadian-industry/article2345597/; Keith Leslie, "Plant Closure Puts 450 Out of Work in Ontario," *Winnipeg Free Press*, February 4, 2012, http://www.winnipegfreepress.com/business/plant-closure-puts-450-out-of-work-in-ontario-138701674.html.

**management rights**
Decisions regarding organizational operations over which management claims exclusive rights

## Voluntary Recognition

All employers, except those in Quebec, may voluntarily recognize and accept a union. This rarely happens, except in the construction industry, where there is a great reliance on union hiring halls.

## CONTRACT NEGOTIATION

Once a bargaining unit has been certified by the labour relations board, the employer and the union are legally obligated to bargain in good faith over the terms and conditions of a collective agreement. Usually, the terms of a collective agreement apply for a minimum of one year and a maximum of three years, although there is no legally mandated maximum. As the contract expiry date approaches, either party must notify the other of its intention to bargain for a renewal collective agreement or contract negotiation.

## DECERTIFICATION

All legislation allows for the decertification of unions under certain conditions. If the majority of employees indicate that they do not want to be represented by the union or that they want to be represented by another union, or if the union has failed to bargain, an application for decertification can be made to the labour relations board. If a collective agreement has been reached with the employer, this application can be made only at specified times, such as a few months before the agreement expires. Workers at seven Starbucks in Vancouver voted to decertify from the CAW. Employees can initiate an application for decertification if the union fails to bargain.

## IMPACT OF UNIONIZATION ON MANAGERS

Why would employers oppose the unionization of their employees? First, studies from the field of labour economics routinely show that wages and benefits are higher in union organizations compared to similar nonunion organizations. Second, unions can have a significant effect on the rights exercised by management in making decisions about employees. Third, unionization restricts the freedom of management to formulate HR policy unilaterally and can challenge the authority of supervisors.

### Challenges to Management Decisions

Unions typically attempt to achieve greater participation in management decisions that affect their members. Specifically, these decisions may involve such issues as the subcontracting of work, productivity standards, and job content. Employers quite naturally seek to claim many of these decisions as their exclusive **management rights**—decisions over which management claims exclusive rights. However, the union may challenge and erode these prerogatives at the bargaining table, through the grievance procedure, and through strikes.

### Loss of Supervisory Authority

At a recent labour–management conference, a union official commented, "Contract terms covering wages, benefits, job security, and working hours are of major importance to our membership." However, for managers and supervisors, the focal point of the union's impact is at the operating level (the shop floor or office facility), where the terms of the collective agreement are implemented on a daily basis. For example, these terms can determine what corrective action is to be taken in directing and in disciplining employees. When disciplining employees, supervisors must be certain they can demonstrate *just cause* (see Chapter 13) for their actions because these actions can be challenged by the union and the supervisor called as a defendant during a grievance hearing. If the challenge is upheld, the supervisor's effectiveness in coping with subsequent disciplinary problems may be impaired. Specific contract language can also reduce the supervisor's ability to manage in areas such as scheduling, training, transfers, performance evaluation, and promotions. Under provisions of the collective agreement, supervisors may have to promote employees by seniority rather than by individual merit.

# STRUCTURES, FUNCTIONS, AND LEADERSHIP OF LABOUR UNIONS

Unions that represent skilled craft workers, such as carpenters or masons, are called **craft unions**. Craft unions include the International Association of Iron Workers, the United Brotherhood of Carpenters, and the United Association of Plumbers and Pipefitters. Unions that represent unskilled and semiskilled workers employed along industry lines are known as **industrial unions**. The Canadian Union of Postal Workers is an industrial union, as are the United Auto Workers, the United Steelworkers, and the Office and Professional Employees International Union. Although this distinction still exists, technological changes, union mergers, and competition among unions for members have helped reduce it. Today, skilled and unskilled workers, white-collar and blue-collar workers, and professional groups are being represented by both types of unions.

Besides unions, **employee associations** represent various groups of professional and white-collar employees. Examples of employee associations include the Federation of Quebec Nurses and the Alberta Teachers Association. In competing with unions, these associations, for all purposes, may function as unions and become just as aggressive as unions in representing members.

Regardless of their type, labour organizations are diverse organizations. Each will have its own structure, objectives, and methods of governance. When describing labour organizations, most researchers divide them into three levels: (1) central labour congresses, (2) international and national unions, and (3) local unions belonging to a parent national or international union. Each level has its own reason for existence and its own operating policies and procedures.

## THE CANADIAN LABOUR CONGRESS

The Canadian Labour Congress (CLC) is a central federation of unions. In 2011, the total membership of the CLC was over 3.2 million Canadians and represented the majority of all unions in Canada.[15] Because of its size and resources, the CLC is considered the most influential labour federation in Canada. It is mainly a service organization representing over 90 international and national unions; these finance the CLC through dues based on membership size. Like the AFL-CIO in the United States, the CLC attempts to influence legislation and promote programs that are of interest to labour. It does this by lobbying, resolving jurisdictional disputes, maintaining ethical standards, providing education and training to its members, conducting research, and representing Canadian interests in the international labour movement.

## INTERNATIONAL AND NATIONAL UNIONS

International unions tend to be affiliates of American unions, with headquarters in the United States. In Canada, there are 39 international unions (with a membership of 1.2 million workers) and 184 national unions (with a membership of 3.1 million).[16] The large membership base offers a good deal of leverage to local unions engaged in strike action.

Both international and national unions are made up of local unions. The objectives of these "umbrella" unions are to help organize local unions, to provide strike support, and to assist local unions with, among other things, negotiations and grievance procedures. These unions also represent their members' interests with internal and external constituents. By ensuring that all employers pay similar wages to their unionized workers, they also remove higher wages as a competitive disadvantage.

In Canada, most of the decision-making authority in national unions is vested in the local unions or at the bargaining-unit level. This is often referred

**craft unions**
Unions that represent skilled craft workers

**industrial unions**
Unions that represent all workers—skilled, semiskilled, unskilled—employed along industry lines

**employee associations**
Labour organizations that represent various groups of professional and white-collar employees in labour–management relations

**union (shop) steward**
Employee who as a nonpaid union official represents the interests of members in their relations with management

**business agent**
Normally a paid labour official responsible for negotiating and administering the collective agreement and working to resolve union members' problems

---

### Using the Internet

The Canada Industrial Relations Board website is a valuable source of information about unions:

**http://www.cirb-ccri.gc.ca**

---

One of the functions of a union steward is to discuss issues with management as they arise. Here a steward is discussing a safety issue with the site manager.

---

to as bottom-up unionism. However, many international unions, especially craft unions, are more likely to retain a greater degree of control over the affairs of local unions. This is often referred to as top-down unionism.

## LOCAL UNIONS

Employees of any organization can form their own union, with no affiliation to a national or international union. In situations such as this, the local is the union. There are more than 600 independent local unions in Canada. However, most local unions are members of national or international unions or the CLC, which makes financial resources and advice available to them.

Unionized employees pay union dues that finance the operation of the local union. Local unions tend to make their own decisions but turn to the national union for collective bargaining help, research, and assistance when handling certain types of grievances. Many national unions also provide training for local unions on the roles and responsibilities of union officers. The officers of a local union are usually responsible for negotiating the local collective agreement, ensuring that the agreement is adhered to, and investigating and processing member grievances. Most importantly, they help prevent their members from being treated by their employers in ways that run counter to management-established HR policies.[17] They also keep members informed through meetings and newsletters.

### Role of the Union (Shop) Steward

The **union (shop) steward** represents the interests of union members in their relations with immediate supervisors and other members of management. Stewards are usually elected by the union members in their own department and serve without union pay. Since stewards are full-time employees of the organization, they often spend considerable time after working hours investigating and handling members' problems. When stewards represent members during grievance meetings on organizational time, their lost earnings are often paid by the local union.

A union steward can be viewed as a "person in the middle," caught between conflicting interests and groups. The relationship between a manager/supervisor and the union steward can have a major bearing on union–management cooperation and on the efficiency and morale of the workforce.

### Role of the Business Agent

Negotiating and administering the collective agreement and working to resolve problems arising in connection with it are the major responsibilities of the **business agent**. In performing these duties, business agents must be all things to all people in their unions. They are often required to assume the role of counsellor in helping union members with both personal and job-related problems. They are also expected to satisfactorily resolve grievances that cannot be settled by union stewards. Administering the daily affairs of the local union is another significant part of the business agent's job.

## LABOUR RELATIONS IN THE PUBLIC SECTOR

Collective bargaining among federal, provincial, and municipal government employees and among employees in parapublic agencies (private agencies or branches of government acting as extensions of government programs) has been an area of important activity for the union movement. More than 70 percent of public employees are now unionized.

The three largest unions in Canada represent public-sector employees. The Canadian Union of Public Employees (CUPE) is the largest union in Canada, with 548,000 members. The second-largest union, with 340,000 members, is the National Union of Public and General Employees (NUPGE). The largest union representing employees at the federal level is the Public Service Alliance of Canada (PSAC), with 166,000 members. PSAC comprises 17 different unions representing various groups, such as the Professional Institute of the Public Service of Canada

(PIPS), the Social Science Employees Association (SSEA), and air traffic controllers. Growth in these unions is threatened by increased cost-cutting efforts of governments at all levels, resulting in employee reductions.

Although public-sector collective bargaining is quite similar to bargaining in the private sector, a number of differences are worth noting. We explore these differences in two contexts: (1) the political nature of the labour–management relationship and (2) public-sector strikes.

## POLITICAL NATURE OF THE LABOUR–MANAGEMENT RELATIONSHIP

Government employees are not able to negotiate with their employers on the same basis as their counterparts in private organizations. It is doubtful that they will ever be able to do so because of inherent differences between the public and private sectors.

One of the significant differences is that labour relations in the private sector have an economic foundation, whereas in government, the foundation tends to be political. Since private employers must stay in business to sell their goods or services, their employees are not likely to make demands that could bankrupt them. A strike in the private sector is a test of the employer's economic staying power, and, usually, the employer's customers have alternative sources of supply. Governments, on the other hand, must stay in business because alternative services are usually not available.

Another difference between the public and private sectors relates to the source of management authority. In a private organization, authority flows downward from the board of directors and, ultimately, from the shareholders. In contrast, authority in the public sector flows upward from the public at large to their elected representatives and to the appointed or elected managers. It follows that public employees can exert influence not only as union members but also as pressure groups and voting citizens.

## STRIKES IN THE PUBLIC SECTOR

Strikes by government employees create a problem for lawmakers and for the general public. Because many of the services that government employees provide, such as policing and firefighting, are considered essential to the well-being of the public, public policy is opposed to strikes by these people. However, various provincial legislatures have granted public employees the right to strike. Where striking is permitted, the right is limited to specific groups of employees—those performing nonessential services—and the strike cannot endanger the public's health, safety, or welfare. Public-sector unions contend, however, that denying them the same right to strike as employees in the private sector greatly reduces their power during collective bargaining.

Public employees who perform essential services do, in fact, strike. Teachers, sanitation employees, police, transit employees, firefighters, and postal employees have all engaged in strike action. To avoid potentially critical situations, various arbitration methods are used for resolving collective bargaining deadlocks in the public sector. One is **compulsory binding arbitration** for employees such as police officers, firefighters, and others in jobs where strikes cannot be tolerated; in this case, a neutral third party is appointed to resolve the deadlock. Another method is **final offer arbitration**, under which the arbitrator must select one or the other of the final offers submitted by the disputing parties. With this method, the arbitrator's award is more likely to go to the party whose final bargaining offer has moved the closest to a reasonable settlement. The government can also enact back-to-work legislation, an option being used with increasing frequency.

## THE BARGAINING PROCESS

Those unfamiliar with contract negotiations often view the process as an emotional conflict between labour and management, complete with marathon sessions, fist pounding, and smoke-filled rooms. In reality, negotiating a collective agreement entails long hours of extensive preparation combined with diplomatic manoeuvring

**compulsory binding arbitration**
Binding method of resolving collective bargaining deadlocks by a neutral third party

**final offer arbitration**
Method of resolving collective bargaining deadlocks whereby the arbitrator has no power to compromise but must select one or another of the final offers submitted by the two parties

PART 5

**Using the Internet**

The Public Service Labour Relations Board oversees employer–employee relations in the federal public service:

**http://www.pslrb-crtfp.gc.ca**

OUTCOME 4

**collective bargaining process**
Process of negotiating a collective agreement, including the use of economic pressures by both parties

and the development of bargaining strategies. Furthermore, negotiation is only one part of the **collective bargaining process** (see Figure 14.3). Collective bargaining also may include the use of economic pressures in the form of strikes and boycotts by a union. Lockouts, plant closures, and the replacement of strikers are similar pressures used by an employer. In addition, either or both parties may seek support from the general public or from the courts as a means of pressuring the opposing side.

## PREPARING FOR NEGOTIATIONS

Preparing for negotiations includes assembling data to support bargaining proposals and forming the bargaining team. This permits collective bargaining to be conducted on an orderly, factual, and positive basis with a greater likelihood of achieving desired goals. Negotiators often develop a bargaining book that serves as a cross-reference file to determine which contract clauses would be affected by a demand. The bargaining book also contains a general history of contract terms and their relative importance to management.[18] Assuming that the collective agreement is not the first to be negotiated by the parties, preparation for negotiations ideally starts soon after the current agreement has been signed. This practice allows negotiators to review and diagnose weaknesses and mistakes made during the previous negotiations while the experience is still current in their minds.

### Gathering Bargaining Data

Employers gather economic data primarily in the areas of wages and benefits. However, internal data relating to grievances, disciplinary actions, transfers, promotions, overtime, and former arbitration awards are useful in formulating and supporting the employer's bargaining position. The supervisors and managers who must live with and administer the collective agreement can be very important sources of ideas and suggestions concerning changes that are needed in the *next* agreement. Their contact with union members and representatives provides them with firsthand knowledge of the changes that union negotiators are likely to propose.

When negotiating contracts, union bargainers talk about "taking wages out of competition." This term refers to having similar contract provisions—particularly concerning wages and benefits—between different companies to prevent one employer from having a favourable labour cost advantage over another. For example, the United

## FIGURE 14.3

### THE COLLECTIVE BARGAINING PROCESS

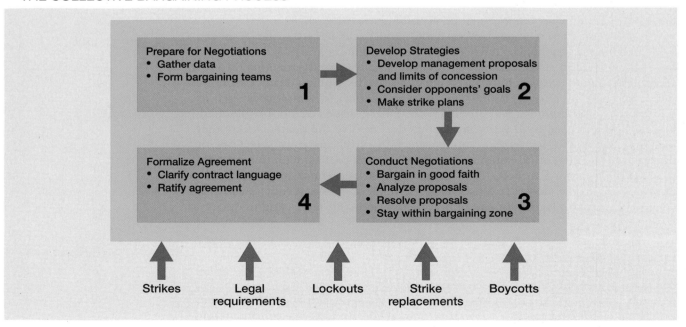

Auto Workers, representing workers at both General Motors and Ford, will seek similar contract provisions. Furthermore, this allows unions to show their members that they are receiving wages and benefits comparable to those of other employees doing similar work. Other negotiated collective agreements, particularly at the local and regional levels, play a significant part in settling the terms of the collective agreement.

## Bargaining Teams

Normally, each side has four to six representatives at the negotiating table. The chief negotiator for management is usually the vice president or manager for labour relations or, most often, a hired labour lawyer; the chief negotiator for the union is usually the local union president, national union representative, or business agent. Others making up management's team may include representatives from accounting or finance, operations, HR, legal, or training. The local union president is likely to be supported by the chief steward, various local union vice presidents, and a representative from the national union.

The initial meeting of the bargaining teams is a particularly important one because it establishes the climate that will prevail during the negotiations that follow. According to one experienced negotiator, "The conduct of negotiations largely depends on the relationship and attitude of negotiators toward one another. If you want conflict in your bargaining sessions, just start off attacking the other side." This *attitudinal structuring* is done to change the attitudes of the parties toward each other, often with the objective of persuading one side to accept the other side's demands.[19]

## DEVELOPING BARGAINING STRATEGIES AND TACTICS

Both management and union negotiators approach bargaining with a defined strategy. In tough economic periods, the employer's strategy might be cost containment or specific reductions in wages or benefits. Conversely, in times of economic growth—when a union strike would harm sales—the employer will be more willing to meet union demands. The employer's strategy should also consider proposals the union is likely to submit, goals the union is striving to achieve, and the extent to which it may be willing to make concessions or to resort to strike action to achieve these goals.

At a minimum, the employer's bargaining strategy must address these points:

- Likely union proposals and management responses to them
- A listing of management demands, limits of concessions, and anticipated union responses
- Development of a database to support management bargaining proposals and to counteract union demands
- A contingency operating plan should employees strike

Certain elements of strategy are common to both the employer and the union. Generally, the initial demands presented by each side are greater than those it may hope to achieve.[20] This is done to provide room for concessions. Moreover, each party usually avoids giving up the maximum it is capable of conceding to allow for further concessions that may be needed to break a bargaining deadlock.

The negotiation of a collective agreement can have some of the characteristics of a poker game, with each side attempting to determine its opponent's position while not revealing its own.[21] Each party normally tries to avoid disclosing the relative importance that it attaches to a proposal so that it will not be forced to pay a higher price than is necessary to have the proposal accepted. As in buying a new car, the buyer and seller employ a lot of strategy to obtain the best outcome possible.

## Negotiating the Collective Agreement

Although there is no "exact" way to negotiate a collective agreement, typically each side focuses on one issue or several related issues until agreement is reached. For each bargaining issue to be resolved satisfactorily, the point at which agreement is

**bargaining zone**
Area within which the union and the employer are willing to concede when bargaining

reached must be within limits that the union and the employer are willing to accept. In a frequently cited bargaining model, Ross Stagner and Hjalmar Rosen call the area within these two limits the **bargaining zone**. In some bargaining situations, such as the one illustrated in Figure 14.4, the solution desired by one party may exceed the limits of the other party. Thus, that solution is outside the bargaining zone. If that party refuses to modify its demands sufficiently to bring them within the bargaining zone or if the opposing party refuses to extend its limit to accommodate the demands of the other party, a bargaining deadlock results.[22] For example, when bargaining a wage increase for employees, if the union's lowest limit is a 4 percent increase and management's top limit is 6 percent, an acceptable range—the bargaining zone—is available to both parties. If management's top limit is only 3 percent, however, a bargaining zone is not available to either side, and a deadlock is likely to occur. Figure 14.4, which is based on the original model by Stagner and Rosen, shows that as bargaining takes place, several important variables influence the negotiators and their ability to reach agreement within the bargaining zone.

An employer is obligated to negotiate in good faith with the union's representatives over conditions of employment (the same obligation applies to the union representatives). Good faith requires meetings to be held at reasonable times and places to discuss employment conditions. It also requires that the proposals submitted by each party be realistic. In discussing the other party's proposals, each side could offer reasonable counterproposals for those it is unwilling to accept. The counterproposal can be "no change" or "we don't agree to that"—there is no requirement to agree to all or part of the other side's proposals. Finally, both parties must sign the written document containing the agreement reached through negotiations.

## FIGURE 14.4

THE BARGAINING ZONE AND NEGOTIATION INFLUENCES

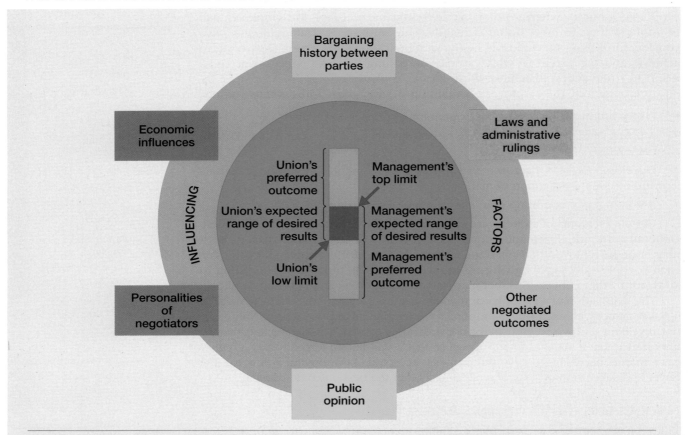

**Source:** From *Psychology of Union–Management Relations*, First Edition, by Stagner/Rosen, © 1996 Wadsworth, a part of Cengage Learning, Inc. Reproduced by permission. http://www.cengage.com/permissions.

# INTEREST-BASED BARGAINING

Sometimes labour–management negotiations are characterized as adversarial. With adversarial bargaining, negotiators start with defined positions and, through deferral, persuasion, trade, or power, the parties work toward the resolution of individual bargaining demands. With adversarial bargaining—and its give-and-take philosophy—the results may or may not be to the complete satisfaction of one or both parties.[23] In fact, when one side feels it received "the short end of the stick," bitter feelings may persist throughout the life of the agreement. As noted by one labour negotiator, "adversarial bargaining does little to establish a long-term positive relationship based on open communications and trust. By its nature, it leads to suspicion and compromise."[24] To overcome these negative feelings, labour and management practitioners may use a nonadversarial approach to negotiating.

**Interest-based bargaining (IBB)** is based on the identification and resolution of mutual interests rather than the resolve of specific bargaining demands.[25] Interest-based bargaining is "a problem-solving process conducted in a principled way that creates effective solutions while improving the bargaining relationship."[26] The focus of bargaining strategy is to discover mutual bargaining interests with the intent of formulating options and solutions for mutual gain.

IBB is novel in both its philosophy and its bargaining process. Also distinct are the bargaining tools used to expedite a successful nonadversarial negotiating experience. Rather than using proposals and counterproposals as a means of reaching agreement (as with adversarial negotiations), participants use brainstorming, consensus decision making, active listening, process checking, and matrix building to facilitate the settlement of issues. An underlying goal of IBB is to create a relationship for the future based on trust, understanding, and mutual respect. The Business Case outlines how IBB can save money.

## MANAGEMENT AND UNION POWER IN COLLECTIVE BARGAINING

Fortunately, the great majority of labour–management negotiations are settled peacefully. However, should negotiations become deadlocked, bargaining can become highly adversarial as each side will now employ its bargaining power to achieve its desired ends. The party's **bargaining power** consists of its economic, political, and social influence to achieve its demands at the expense of the other side.

## Union Bargaining Power

The bargaining power of the union may be exercised by striking, picketing, or boycotting the employer's products or services. A strike is the refusal of a group of employees to perform their jobs. Canadians are often surprised to learn that Canada has the second highest rates of days lost to strikes in the world.[27] It is a legal requirement that unions hold and win a strike vote as a condition of striking lawfully. A strike vote by the members does not mean they actually want or expect to go out on strike. Rather, it is intended as a vote of confidence to strengthen the position of their leaders at the bargaining table.

Of critical importance to the union is the extent, if any, to which the employer will be able to continue operating through the use of supervisory and nonstriking personnel and employees hired to replace the strikers. In some jurisdictions, employers face restrictions to their right to hire replacement workers. In the 1990s, the use of "scabs" at the Royal Oak Mines in Yellowknife so infuriated a striking miner that he blew up the mine, killing nine workers (see Highlights in HRM 14.4). (Employers have the right to dismiss workers who engage in sabotage or violence during a strike.) The violence and strife associated with the use of replacement workers has caused Quebec and British Columbia to forbid their use.

In organizations with high levels of technology and automation, and consequently fewer employees, continuing service with supervisors and managers

**interest-based bargaining (IBB)**
Problem-solving bargaining based on a win–win philosophy and the development of a positive long-term relationship

**bargaining power**
The power of labour and management to achieve their goals through economic, social, or political influence

OUTCOME 5

# THE BUSINESS CASE

## Building Trust and Saving Money at the Same Time: City of Toronto and Toronto Professional Fire Fighters' Association, Local 3888

Toronto Fire Services (TFS) provides a vital service to the citizens of Toronto, from fire response, to vehicle accidents, to medical emergencies and other hazardous and dangerous incidents. TFS responded to over 144,000 emergency calls and roughly 270,000 vehicle incidents in 2010. The Toronto Professional Fire Fighters Association (TPFFA) represents roughly 3,000 employees/firefighters.

Through the use of interest-based bargaining (IBB), Toronto City Council successfully ratified several collective agreements with the TPFFA, Local 3888. The first time IBB was used was back in 2003, and a five-year collective agreement was reached. The collective agreement included wage increases up to 3.5 percent over a 3-year period, as well as seniority-based increases in wages. A deferred implementation schedule was agreed to for paying out recognition pay, which essentially staggered the financial impact on the city of Toronto.

As is customary with IBB, the City of Toronto and the TPFFA sought to achieve a settlement that would balance the goals and objectives of the city—"to negotiate a timely and reasonable settlement without resorting to arbitration, to successfully introduce interest-based bargaining in its relations with its bargaining agents and to reach an agreement based on that approach."

From the beginning, efforts were made by the City of Toronto's Corporate Employee and Labour Relations team to revamp the labour relations approach to that of an IBB style. In that spirit, City Council directed Chief William Steward to make improvements to labour relations within TFS a priority. With a renewed understanding of the issues at hand, both parties understood the need to work toward similar goals. In the end, the "agreement represents a significant change and improvement in labour/management relations at the City of Toronto. The settlement embraces joint problem solving, recognizes the needs of the parties and allows them to continue to build on their relationship within a stable collective agreement." Interestingly, firefighters are part of the city's essential services and cannot strike, so there has to be trust between the two parties to get this kind of respect at the negotiations table. The results of this mutually beneficial contract were adopted by other police and fire services across much of Ontario.

### Some Benefits of IBB

| | Traditional Approach | Interest-Based Bargaining |
| --- | --- | --- |
| Settlement reached | 125 days over several years | 25 days over 4 months |
| Objective of both parties met | No | Yes |
| Grievances—these cost money | Arbitration<br>Backlog of 3,411 | Mediation before to avoid arbitration to avoid fees<br>Backlog reduced |
| Employee outcomes—affect long-term success of the organizations | Decreased employee morale, increased absenteeism, grievances, lack of credibility in leadership | Improved morale, increased credibility of leadership, both management and the association, and a significant reduction in grievances and improvement in attendance |

Sources: William A. Stewart, Fire Chief, *Toronto Fire Department Annual Report*: http://www.toronto.ca/fire/annual_report/pdf/tfs_2010_annual_report.pdf; City of Toronto website: http://wx.toronto.ca/inter/it/newsrel.nsf/0/87fce553996b7ff185256e38007a74e5?OpenDocument; Jeff Gray and Jennifer Lewington. Hush-hush firefighter deal lifts Toronto's unions. *The Globe and Mail* October 26, 2007. http://www.theglobeandmail.com/news/national/hush-hush-firefighter-deal-lifts-torontos-unions/article131195/; http://www.macroberts.org/pages.php/22/

# HIGHLIGHTS IN HRM 14.4

## A Tragic Labour Dispute

Let us go back in time to the strike at Giant Mine in the early 1990s for one of Canada's most tragic industrial relations disputes—with lessons for all. The Giant Mine is located in Yellowknife, Northwest Territories. In 1990, the Royal Oak Mines purchased the Giant Mine, with the owner, Margaret (Peggy) Witte, taking over the top executive position and responsibilities. At that time, the Giant Mine was experiencing financial problems, and there was a very real fear that the mine would close. The miners belonged to the Canadian Association of Smelter and Allied Workers (CASAW), Local 4. The collective agreement that CASAW had with its former employers, covering approximately 240 miners, expired in March 1992. The union wanted better pensions, improved safety standards, and a 5 to 10 percent wage increase. The company wanted wage and benefits cuts.

A lockout by management the day before the union was set to commence a strike followed the failure to reach agreement during collective bargaining. Although replacement workers had not been utilized in labour disputes in Canadian mines for approximately 40 years, Ms. Witte immediately brought them in, many from outside the region. To further complicate matters, Ms. Witte also hired Pinkerton, a security company with a history of anti-union animosities. She also flew in a 50-member RCMP (Royal Canadian Mounted Police) team to protect the replacement workers and some of the workers who wanted to return to work. Crossing a picket line is viewed as very anti-union by activists. As the president of the local CASAW stated: "Once someone crosses that picket line they become sub-f . . . ing

human. A transformation takes place. They go lower than a reptile." In front of the union's office, a picture of a rat represented "scabs on the run" ("scab" is a derogatory term used by trade union activists and others to describe people who replace striking workers during a strike).

The industrial dispute changed the complexion of the town. Yellowknife had been a small, close-knit community, where residents knew each other fairly well. Violence erupted in the community, as well as on the picket line, and "neighbour was pitted against neighbour." People were afraid to take sides. "The guts were torn out of the town. You had fights in the school yards and in the streets, and you didn't dare break up a fight because you might be getting into something big." The company also terminated 45 striking employees due to "alleged acts of personal violence and alleged damage to property." In further collective bargaining, the employer refused to allow these workers to return to work and was unwilling to include a clause that would allow for arbitration on this issue.

Tragedy struck on September 18, 1992, when three replacement workers and six union members who crossed the picket line were killed when their mining car hit a bomb that was taped to one of the rails inside the mine. Roger Warren, a miner who had worked for Giant Mine for 12 years, was convicted for this crime in 1995 and was later sentenced to life in prison. Even after the strike ended, some viewed the replacement workers with scorn and contempt. As one woman stated: "I don't have any sympathy for those bastards who got blown up. If they hadn't been in there scabbing, they wouldn't be dead." In the end, this industrial relations dispute was a tragedy for all parties.

Sources: Adrienne Tanner, "Union reeling over mine blast murder charges." *Toronto Star*, October 18 (1993): p. A3; Lee Selleck, "Royal Oak Mines didn't bargain in good faith, rules CLRB." *Labour Times*, December (1993): p. 3; Peter Cheney, "Murder in a mineshaft pit friends against friends", *Toronto Star*, January 16 (1993): p. A10; P. Simao, "Statement from Reuters News Service," June 13 (1998): p.1; Industrial Inquiry Commission. *Royal Oak Mines and CASAW*, December 13 (1993).

is more likely. Among the highly automated telephone companies, most services can be maintained by supervisors during a strike. According to one authority, "Because of technological change, striking in many industries no longer has the effect of curtailing the employer's operations significantly."[28] Consequently, the greater the ability of the employer to continue operating, the less the union's chances of gaining its demands through a strike.

When a union goes on strike, it often pickets the employer by placing people at business entrances to advertise the dispute and to discourage others from entering the premises. Because unions often refuse to cross another union's picket line, the pickets may serve to prevent the delivery and pickup of goods or performance of other services. For example, a Teamster truck driver may refuse to deliver produce to a food store whose employees are on strike with the United Food and Commercial Workers (UFCW) union. Once a strike has been settled, the workers are entitled to return to their jobs, although not necessarily their previous positions. The right to return to work is often an issue to be negotiated.

Picketing is used by unions to publicize their disputes and discourage people from entering the premises.

© Mark Spowart/Demotix/Demotix/Corbis

Although laws vary, employees are often required to submit in writing their intention to return to their jobs once a strike is finalized.

Another economic weapon of the union is the *boycott*, which is a refusal to patronize the employer. For example, production employees on strike against a hand tool manufacturer might picket a retail store that sells the tools made by the struck employer. Unions will also use handbills, radio announcements, email campaigns, and newspaper ads to discourage the purchase of the employer's product or service.

## Management Bargaining Power

When negotiations become deadlocked, the employer's bargaining power largely rests on being able to continue operations in the face of a strike or to shut down operations entirely.

Another prevalent bargaining strategy is for the employer to continue operations by using managers and supervisors to staff employee jobs. In one case, nearly 30,000 managers left their offices to serve as operators, technicians, and customer service representatives during a strike between Verizon and the Communications Workers of America. As noted previously, technological advances enhance the employer's ability to operate during a strike.

The employer may elect to lock out its employees. The lockout is a bargaining strategy by which the employer denies employees the opportunity to work by closing its operations. In a highly publicized case, during the 2004–2005 National Hockey League season, management locked out players represented by the National Hockey League Players' Association. Besides being used in bargaining impasses, lockouts may be used by employers to combat union slowdowns, damage to their property, or violence within the organization that may occur in connection with a labour dispute.[29] Employers may still be reluctant to resort to a lockout, however, because of their concern that denying work to regular employees (employees who are not members of the union who may be locked out; they may or may not be members of another union) might hurt the organization's image.

## RESOLVING BARGAINING DEADLOCKS

Unions and employers in all types of industries—sports, transportation, entertainment, manufacturing, communication, and health care—have used mediation and arbitration to help resolve their bargaining deadlocks. As discussed in Chapter 13, mediation is a voluntary process that relies on the communication and persuasive skills of a mediator to help the parties resolve their differences. In all Canadian jurisdictions, conciliation is compulsory before a legal strike or lockout. The conciliator, appointed by the provincial or federal ministry of labour, attempts to reach a workable agreement.

Unlike a mediator, an **interest arbitrator** assumes the role of a decision maker and determines what the settlement between the two parties should be. In other words, interest arbitrators write a final contract that the parties *must* accept. Compared to mediation, arbitration is not often used to settle private-sector bargaining disputes. In the public sector, where strikes are often prohibited, the use of *interest arbitration* is a common method to resolve bargaining deadlocks. Generally, one or both parties are reluctant to give a third party the power to make the settlement for them. Consequently, a mediator is typically used to break a deadlock and assist the parties in reaching an agreement. An arbitrator is generally called on to resolve disputes arising in connection with administration of the agreement, called *rights arbitration* or *grievance arbitration*, which will be discussed shortly.

**interest arbitrator**
Third-party neutral who resolves a labour dispute by issuing a final decision in the disagreement

## THE COLLECTIVE AGREEMENT

When negotiations are concluded, the collective agreement becomes a formal *binding* document listing the terms, conditions, and rules under which employees and managers agree to operate. Highlights in HRM 14.5 shows some of the major articles in a collective agreement and provides examples of some new and progressive contract clauses. Two important items in any collective agreement pertain to the issue of management rights and the forms of security afforded the union.

**Using the Internet**

One of the newer forms of mediation is online mediation. Check out how experts can be used by visiting these sites:

**http://www.mediate.com/odr**
and **http://www.adrr.com**

### THE ISSUE OF MANAGEMENT RIGHTS

Management rights have to do with the conditions of employment over which management is able to exercise exclusive control. Almost without exception, the collective agreement contains a *management rights* clause. This clause states that "management's authority is supreme in all matters except those it has expressly conceded in the collective agreement, or in those areas where its authority is restricted by law." Management rights might include the right of management to determine the products to produce, to determine the location of production or service facilities, or to select production equipment and procedures. The following is an example of a clause defining management rights in one collective agreement:

> It is agreed that the company possesses all of the rights, powers, privileges, and authority it had prior to the execution of this agreement; and nothing in this agreement shall be construed to limit the company in any way in

# HIGHLIGHTS IN HRM 14.5

## Items in a Collective Agreement

### Typical clauses will cover

- Wages
- Grievance procedures
- Vacations
- No strike/no lockout clause
- Holidays
- Overtime
- Work schedules
- Safety procedures

- Management rights
- Severance pay
- Union security
- Seniority
- Transfers
- Pensions and benefits
- Discipline
- Outsourcing

### Other clauses will cover

- Employee access to records
- Limitations on use of performance evaluation
- Eldercare leave, childcare, work–family balance provisions
- Flexible medical spending accounts
- Protection against hazards of technology equipment
- Limitations against electronic monitoring
- Bilingual stipends
- Domestic partnership benefits

**grievance procedure**
Formal procedure that provides for the union to represent members and nonmembers in processing a grievance

the exercise of the regular and customary functions of management and the operation of its business, except as it may be specifically relinquished or modified herein by an express provision of this agreement.[30]

## UNION SECURITY AGREEMENTS

As we noted at the beginning of this chapter, unions must represent all bargaining-unit members equally regardless of whether employees join the union. In exchange for this obligation, union officials will seek to negotiate some form of compulsory membership as a condition of employment. Union officials argue that compulsory membership precludes the possibility that some employees will receive the benefits of unionization without paying their fair share of the costs. A standard union security provision is dues checkoff, which gives the employer the responsibility of withholding union dues from the paycheques of union members who agree to such a deduction.

Other common forms of union security found in collective agreements are different types of "shop" agreements. These agreements—in varying degrees—attempt to require employees to join the union. For example, a *union shop* agreement may provide that any employee who is not a union member on employment must join the union within 30 days or be terminated. Another, the *agency shop*, provides for voluntary membership. However, all bargaining-unit members must pay union dues.

## ADMINISTRATION OF THE COLLECTIVE AGREEMENT

Negotiation of the collective agreement, as mentioned earlier, is usually the most publicized and critical aspect of labour relations. Strike deadlines, press conferences, and employee picketing help create this image. Nevertheless, as managers in unionized organizations know, the bulk of labour relations activity comes from the day-to-day administration of the agreement because no agreement could possibly anticipate all the forms that disputes may take. In addition, once the agreement is signed, each side will naturally interpret ambiguous clauses to its own advantage.[31] These differences are traditionally resolved through the grievance procedure.

## NEGOTIATED GRIEVANCE PROCEDURES

OUTCOME 6

The **grievance procedure** typically provides for the union to represent the interests of its members (and nonmembers as well) in processing a grievance. It is considered by some authorities to be the heart of the bargaining agreement or the safety valve that gives flexibility to the whole system of collective bargaining.[32]

The grievance process is normally initiated by the union—or an individual employee—when it feels management has violated some article of the collective agreement. In one case, the union filed a grievance against a supervisor when it believed that the supervisor promoted an employee out of seniority order—called a bypass grievance. A significant benefit of the grievance procedure is that it provides a formal and orderly procedure for the union to challenge the actions of management without resorting to strikes. One authority has noted, "The grievance procedure fosters cooperation, not conflict, between the employer and the union."[33]

The operation of a grievance procedure is unique to each collective bargaining relationship, but the procedure is usually required under Canadian labour relations statutes. For example, grievance procedures normally specify how the grievance is to be initiated, the number and timing of steps that are to compose the procedure, and the identity of representatives from each side who are to be involved in the hearings at each step. When a grievance cannot be resolved at one of the specified steps, most agreements provide for the grievance to be submitted to a third party—usually an arbitrator—whose decision is final. Some collective agreements provide for mediation as a way to resolve employee grievances. When used, *grievance mediation* will be listed as a formal step in the grievance procedure preceding arbitration.[34]

# RIGHTS ARBITRATION

The function of **rights arbitration** is to provide the solution to a grievance that a union and an employer have been unable to resolve by themselves. As mentioned earlier, arbitration is performed by a neutral third party (an arbitrator or impartial umpire). This third party's decision dictates how the grievance is to be settled.[35] Both parties are obligated to comply with the decision.

**rights arbitration**
Arbitration over interpretation of the meaning of contract terms or employee work grievances

**arbitration award**
Final and binding award issued by an arbitrator in a labour–management dispute

## The Decision to Arbitrate

In deciding whether to use arbitration, each party must weigh the costs involved against the importance of the case and the prospects of gaining a favourable award. It would seem logical that neither party would allow a weak case to go to arbitration if there were little possibility of gaining a favourable award. Logic, however, does not always prevail. For example, it is not unusual for a union to take a weak case to arbitration to demonstrate to its members that the union is willing to exhaust every remedy in looking out for their interests. Union officers also are not likely to refuse to take to arbitration the grievances of members who are popular or politically powerful in the union, even though their cases are weak. Moreover, unions have a legal obligation to provide assistance to members who are pursuing grievances. Because members can bring suit against their unions for failing to process their grievances adequately, many union officers are reluctant to refuse taking even weak grievances to arbitration.

Management, on the other hand, may allow a weak case to go to arbitration to demonstrate to union officers that management "cannot be pushed around." Also, managers at lower levels may be reluctant to risk the displeasure of top management by stating that a certain HR policy is unworkable or unsound. Stubbornness and mutual antagonism also may force many grievances into arbitration because neither party is willing to make concessions to reach an agreement, even when it may recognize that it is in the wrong.

## The Arbitration Process

In our experience, employees unfamiliar with arbitration find the process confusing and often stressful. Arbitration hearings have the appearance of a court hearing but without many of the formalities of a court proceeding.

The process begins with the swearing-in of witnesses. The parties then make opening statements, followed by the presentation of facts and evidence and the oral presentation of witnesses. The hearing concludes with each side making summary statements that are arguments in support of its position.

In arbitrating a dispute, it is the responsibility of the arbitrator to ensure that each side receives a fair hearing during which it may present all of the facts it considers pertinent to the case. The primary purpose of the hearing is to assist the arbitrator in obtaining the facts necessary to resolve a human relations problem rather than a legal one. The arbitrator, therefore, has a right to question witnesses or to request additional facts from either party. After conducting the hearing and receiving post-hearing briefs (should the parties choose to submit them), the arbitrator considers the evidence and renders an award. In the majority of cases, the costs of arbitration are shared equally by the parties.

## The Arbitration Award

The **arbitration award** is a formal written document given to both sides. As in grievance procedures, there is no specific format to an arbitration award, but, typically, the award contains five parts: (1) the submission to arbitrate, (2) the facts of the case, (3) the positions of the parties, (4) the opinion of the arbitrator, and (5) the decision rendered. As might be expected, the decision of the arbitrator is of major importance to the parties. However, the reasoning behind the decision—the opinion—is equally important as it can provide guidance concerning the interpretation of the collective agreement and the resolution of future disputes arising from its administration.

# SMALL BUSINESS APPLICATION

Unions impose procedural requirements, just as other regulators do. What is different about unionization is that the legal requirements regarding the behaviour of employers regarding union activity is often not as clear-cut as with other legal compliance. Additionally, and most significantly, is that errors in interpretation can have long-lasting implications as labour relations boards have the power to certify unions without a membership vote if the labour relations board has concerns that the employees' right to union representation has somehow been impeded.

So what is a small employer to do? Assuming that small employers prefer the flexibility associated with being nonunionized, they should provide employees with competitive wages and treat employees fairly and with respect, to have little or no risk of becoming unionized. The fact that a company is small decreases the probability of a union targeting it because in such cases, the cost to the union to certify, bargain, and represent workers would likely be greater than the collected union dues from a small membership. That being said, a small company can still become unionized. For employers in small businesses who sense discontent in the workplace, actions should be taken to understand and address this situation. If this discontent festers to the point where an employer hears of unionization attempts, he or she would be well advised to consult with an HR or labour relations consultant, or labour relations lawyer, to get assistance in establishing an appropriate course of action, as well as review the sections in this text on unfair labour practices.

So far we have spoken from the standpoint of a small company dealing with unionization attempts. But what does a small employer do if it has a union? In this case, it follows the same process as large companies. It must bargain with the union and negotiate a collective agreement that outlines the employment terms and conditions for a period of time. The company must also collect and submit union dues to the union representing employees. Finally, it must follow the legislative requirements set for represented employees, including grievance management and arbitration.

# SUMMARY

**OUTCOME 1** Labour relations legislation in Canada recognizes the right of employees to form and join unions and prohibits both unions and employers from engaging in unfair labour practices. Provincial labour relations laws are administered and enforced by labour relations boards.

**OUTCOME 2** Studies show that workers unionize for different economic, psychological, and social reasons. Although some employees may join unions because they are required to do so, most belong to unions because they are convinced that unions help them improve their wages, benefits, and various working conditions. Employee unionization is largely caused by dissatisfaction with managerial practices and procedures.

**OUTCOME 3** A formal organizing campaign is used to solicit employee support for the union. Once employees demonstrate their desire to unionize, the union will file an application with the labour relations board for approval of the union as the certified bargaining agent.

**OUTCOME 4** Negotiating a collective agreement is a detailed process. Each side prepares a list of proposals it wishes to achieve while additionally trying to anticipate proposals desired by the other side. Bargaining teams must be selected, and all proposals must be analyzed to determine their impact on and cost to the organization. Both employer and union negotiators are sensitive to current bargaining patterns within the industry, general cost-of-living trends, and geographic wage differentials. Managers establish goals that seek to retain control over operations and to minimize costs. Union negotiators focus their demands around improved wages, hours, and working conditions. An agreement is reached when both sides compromise their original positions and final terms fall within the limits of the parties' bargaining zone.

Currently, there is an increased interest in nonadversarial negotiations—negotiations based on mutual gains and a heightened respect between the parties. IBB is one form of nonadversarial negotiations.

**OUTCOME 5** The collective bargaining process includes not only the actual negotiations but also the power tactics used to support negotiating demands. When negotiations become deadlocked, bargaining becomes a power struggle to force from either side the concessions needed to break the deadlock. The union's power in collective bargaining comes from its ability to picket, strike, or boycott the employer. The employer's power during negotiations comes from its ability to lock out employees or to operate during a strike by using managerial or replacement employees.

| OUTCOME 6 | When differences arise between labour and management, they are normally resolved through the grievance procedure. Grievance procedures are negotiated and thus reflect the needs and desires of the parties. The typical grievance procedure consists of three, four, or five steps—each step having specific filing and reply times. Higher

level managers and union officials become involved in disputes at the higher steps of the grievance procedure. The final step of the grievance procedure may be arbitration. Arbitrators render a final decision to problems not resolved at lower grievance steps.

The submission to arbitrate is a statement of the issue to be solved through arbitration. It is simply the problem the parties wish to have settled. The arbitrator must answer the issue by basing the arbitration award on four factors: the contents of the collective agreement (or employment policy), the submission agreement as written, testimony and evidence obtained at the hearing, and various arbitration standards developed over time to assist in the resolution of different types of labour–management disputes. Arbitration is not an exact science because arbitrators give varying degrees of importance to the evidence and criteria by which disputes are resolved.

## KEY TERMS

arbitration award, 503
authorization card, 486
bargaining power, 497
bargaining unit, 488
bargaining zone, 496
business agent, 492
collective bargaining process, 494

compulsory binding arbitration, 493
craft unions, 491
employee associations, 491
final offer arbitration, 493
grievance procedure, 502
industrial unions, 491
interest arbitrator, 501

interest-based bargaining (IBB), 497
labour relations process, 483
management rights, 490
rights arbitration, 503
unfair labour practices (ULPs), 488
union shop, 483
union (shop) steward, 492

## DISCUSSION QUESTIONS

1. Discuss the key reasons why employees form unions. Refer to examples to illustrate your answer.
2. *Fast Food High* is a film produced by CTV and inspired by the real story about how a group of teenage workers tried to organize a union at McDonald's in Orangeville, Ontario. Watch the film and discuss in groups the reasons that these workers want to form a union and the effectiveness of their efforts.
3. Graduate students in many Canadian universities are members of unions, such as CUPE 3903. These students help conduct tutorials, grade student examinations, etc. Do you think university students have different reasons for joining unions versus, for example, workers in a manufacturing firm? Explain your answer.
4. What are unfair labour practices? What are the consequences of unfair labour practices? Use examples to explain your answer.
5. A group of students wants a Burger King fast-food franchise on their university campus.

University administrators want a health-food restaurant. Resources allow for only one food outlet. Divide the class into bargaining teams, with one team representing the students and the other team representing the university administrators. (If there is another issue on your campus, use the real and current issue instead.)
6. The union representing garbage collectors and other outside workers and the municipality are in the middle of tense negotiations. The collective bargaining agreement has expired. What form of bargaining power does each side possess to enhance its bargaining demands? What are the advantages and disadvantages of each form of bargaining power for both the employer and the union?
7. What are the main differences between labour relations in the private versus the public sector? How are disputes involving essential service workers in the public sector usually resolved?

# SUMMARY

# HRM EXPERIENCE

## Learn about Unions

Unions, like business organizations, are dynamic and varied organizations. Some unions are very large, such as the CAW, and represent workers nationally. Others are smaller in size and represent only specific groups of employees or organize only in a designated geographic area. This exercise will help you learn more about unions.

## Assignment

Working individually or in teams, select four or five different unions or employee associations and report on the following. Vary your selections (e.g., large/small, public/private) to widen your understanding of labour organizations.

- History of the union
- Membership size and type of employees represented
- Mission of the union
- Structure of the union, including its major departments
- National officers
- Names of employers with whom they have an agreement
- Special benefits they offer members
- Other interesting or pertinent information

National unions and their locals, along with library research, can also provide information. Be prepared to present your findings during a class discussion.

Visit the *Managing Human Resources* CourseMate website at http://www.belcourt7e.nelson.com for quizzes, flashcards, videos, games, and more!

# CASE STUDY 1

## UNIONIZATION OF FARM WORKERS

There is a long-standing tradition of Canada's federal government to promote free collective bargaining among employee groups. However, in 1994, the Conservative government in Ontario took steps that effectively excluded Ontario farm workers from collective bargaining rights, rendering previous collective agreements invalid. The International Labour Organization's (ILO) Freedom of Association Committee ruled that the Ontario government should make changes to recertify the union representing farm workers as well as reinstate their collective agreements. This did not happen, and the federal government did little to intervene.

In 2001, seven years later, the UFCW, which was trying to organize the farm workers, won a Supreme Court decision. This led to the Ontario government's introduction of the *Agricultural Employees Protection Act* (AEPA) in 2002. But this act, although it allowed farm workers to organize, did not explicitly allow collective bargaining or the right to strike. This also means that not only can a farm worker be fired for striking, but also issues that arise in the workplace cannot be channelled to arbitration for ruling. It appears that these farm workers are able to collectively join a union and bring forth issues, but it is up to employers to act in good faith as they are only required to listen under the AEPA. The legislation was challenged in the courts.

In December 2009, the Supreme Court heard arguments from the UFCW on the matter. A recent decision by the Supreme Court of Canada handed down the ruling that "the Labour Relations Act, 1995 does not apply to employees or employers in agriculture." The case was dismissed without costs, and the AEPA was found to be in line with the *Charter of Rights and Freedoms*. Thus, although the act seems to go against international trade union rights on some level, the courts have ruled that it does not violate Canadian human rights.

## Questions

1. Are farm workers entitled to the same rights as other types of unionized workers? Why? Why not?

2. Are collective bargaining rights also human rights? Refer to ILO conventions and the Canadian *Charter of Human Rights* in your response.

3. Discuss the pros and cons of farm workers having the right to strike.

**Sources:** Roy Adams, *Labour Left Out: Canada's Failure to Protect and Promote Collective Bargaining as a Human Right* (Ottawa: Canadian Centre for Policy Alternatives, 2006); David Doorey, "Ontario Government Repeals Labour Relations Act Replaces It with Model in Agricultural Employees Protection Act!" February 23, 2012, http://www.yorku.ca/ddoorey /lawblog/?p=4856&cpage=1#comment-55733; Supreme Court of Canada Citation: *Ontario (Attorney General) v. Fraser*, 2011 SCC 20, <2011> 2 S.C.R. 3, April 29, 2011, http://scc.lexum.org/en/2011/2011scc20/2011scc20.pdf.

# CASE STUDY 2

## WALMART STORES IN CANADA

In 2006, Walmart was operating more than 6,500 stores with 1.8 million employees around the world. In the early 1990s, Walmart Stores Inc. expanded into Canada, with the purchase of 122 stores from the failing Woolco chain. Walmart had refused to purchase nine Woolco stores that were unionized.

Walmart tries to distinguish itself from other retailers by its culture. For example, it calls its workers "associates," not employees. Every day at 8:45 a.m., a compulsory meeting is held at each store during which company managers share financial information and performance targets and respond to questions. The meeting ends with the Walmart cheer. The company operates an open-door policy, whereby any employee can talk to any member of management about issues and receive answers without being threatened with reprisal. The sundown rule ensures that management responds to the questions before sundown the same day.

The first Walmart store ever to be unionized was in Windsor, Ontario, where the United Steelworkers (Retail and Wholesale Division) was certified by the Ontario Labour Relations Board (OLRB). On April 14, 1997, the United Steelworkers began its organizing drive. On April 26, the store manager became aware that associates were being approached to sign unionization cards. The district manager was told of the organizing drive and the next morning attended the morning meeting. The district manager asked the associates why they would want to join a union and spent the day circulating through the store to discuss their problems or concerns. By April 27, 84 associates had signed cards. On April 29, an associate asked to speak at the morning meeting and there expressed her opposition to the union, ending with the statement, "A union will only cause discontentment in our store, and I assure you as I am standing here, Walmart will not put up with it." (Management did not ask, nor did the associate reveal, why she wanted to speak.) An inside organizer was prevented from responding because it was 9 a.m. and customers were waiting to enter the store.

Between May 4 and May 9, Walmart managers—including managers from outside the store—responded to questions placed in a question-and-answer box and to those raised while they wandered about the store. Most of the questions focused on compensation and hours of work. However, questions were also raised about whether Walmart would close the store and dismiss the employees if the union was successful. Walmart answered that "it would be inappropriate for our company to comment on what it will or will not do if the store is unionized." It repeated that line when employees asked the same question in person. One associate testified that one manager said that things would change if the employees were unionized—for example, the profit-sharing plan would be revoked. On May 9, the union lost the vote, with 151 employees voting against it and 43 voting for it.

The OLRB nonetheless certified the union because the employer violated the *Labour Relations Act* by not disassociating itself from the remarks made by the associate at the meeting; by not allowing the inside organizer to respond; by soliciting questions about the impact of unionization but then refusing to tell employees that they would not all be fired if the union won; and by using senior outside managers to engage employees in frequent and repetitive discussions about the unionization drive in the days leading up to the vote. The OLRB stated that the union had 84 cards signed before the managers' visits, and a week later, this support had dropped. A second vote would not change the outcome because the threat to job security could not be erased from employees' minds. After Walmart's illegal conduct was remedied by a certification order, the Ontario government changed the law to take away that remedial option from the labour board. However, the right to certify a union as a remedy for unfair labour practices has once again been restored in Ontario and exists in other Canadian jurisdictions.

Despite numerous organizing drives, Walmart continues to try to be union free. The UFCW charged Walmart with unfair labour practices in thwarting a union organizing drive in British Columbia by discrediting the key organizer and by advising employees that if he turned up at their homes, they could call the police. The B.C. Labour Board said, "Walmart has an anti-union history . . . and simply cannot resist the temptation to get involved in certification campaigns. While Walmart has tended not to repeat its mistakes, there is no shortage of new ones that it finds ways to make." In the company's view, not being able to answer employee concerns about unionization is not part of its culture of open communication. But two labour relations boards believe that the company has gone too far in communication by, for example, distributing anti-union literature at a store in Quesnel, B.C. Walmart is seeking to change labour laws to allow it to address employee concerns.

## Questions

1. What were the rights of Walmart, the employer, during these two organizing drives?
2. The certification of the first Walmart was hailed by labour as a milestone event. Why?
3. In your opinion, can Walmart remain union free indefinitely? Why or why not?
4. Should foreign companies that operate in Canada use their resources to try to weaken Canadian labour laws or accept the legal culture of the country and comply with those laws?

**Sources:** Adapted from Uyen Vu, "Wal-Mart Seeks to Change Labour Laws," *Canadian HR Reporter*, September 13, 2004, 1; V. Galt, "Wal-Mart Must Give Union Access," *The Globe and Mail*, May 13, 2003, B5; J. Hobel, "Allegation of Union Vote Rigging Investigated at Wal-Mart," *Canadian HR Reporter*, September 20, 1999, 1, 19; "Employer Interference: The Wal-Mart Case," *Worklife Report* 11, no. 2, 1–4.

# ANSWERS TO HIGHLIGHTS IN HRM 14.1

1. No. Individual questioning of employees about their union membership or activities is unlawful.
2. Yes. However, this must be part of normal conduct and cannot be interpreted as a gesture to buy votes.
3. Yes. Blacklisting of job applications or employees is against labour law.
4. No. During an organizing drive, an employer cannot promise improvements in wages or benefits as a means of defeating the union.
5. Yes. Employees can be disciplined or discharged for work-related misconduct but not solely because of their union affiliations or union sentiments.

# NOTES AND REFERENCES

1. See M. Gunderson, D. Hyatt, and A. Ponak, "Strikes and Dispute Resolution," in D. Taras, M. Gunderson, and A. Ponak, editors. *Union–Management Relations in Canada*, 5th ed. (Toronto: Addison Wesley Longman, 2005): 332–370.

2. "Ontario Collective Bargaining Agreements Expirations," http://www.labour.gov.on.ca/english/lr/pdf/11_ae.pdf, retrieved May 2012.

3. "Unionization 2011," http://www.statcan.gc.ca/pub /75-001-x/2011004/article/11579-eng.htm, retrieved May 2012.

4. Bruce E. Kaufman, "Reflections on Six Decades in Industrial Relations: An Interview with John Dunlop," *Industrial and Labor Relations Review* 55, no. 2 (January 2002): 324–348; C. Heron, *The Canadian Labour Movement: A Short History* (Toronto: James Lorimer & Company, 1989); M. Gunderson, A. Ponak, and D. Gottlieb Taras, *Union–Management Relations in Canada*.

5. Gunderson et al., *Union–Management Relations in Canada*, 5th ed.

6. Readers interested in reading more about the labour relations process can consult Gunderson et al.,

*Union–Management Relations in Canada*, 5th ed.; J. Godard, *Industrial Relations: The Economy and Society* (Toronto: McGraw-Hill Ryerson, 1994).

7. Maureen Hannay, "The Unionization of Professionals," *Journal of Labor Research* 23, no. 3 (Summer 2002): 487–498. See also John A. McClendon, Hoyt N. Wheeler, and Roger D. Weikle, "The Individual Decision to Unionize," *Labor Studies Journal* 23, no. 3 (Fall 1998): 34–54.

8. Statistics Canada, "Average Hourly Wages," 2011, http://www.statcan.gc.ca/tables-tableaux/sum-som /l01/cst01/labr69a-eng.htm, retrieved May 2012.

9. For a pioneering study on why workers unionize, see E. Wight Bakke, "Why Workers Join Unions," *Personnel* 22, no. 7 (July 1947): 3.

10. Kate Bronfenbrenner and Robert Hickey, "Successful Union Organizing in the United States—Clear Lessons, Too Few Examples," *Multinational Monitor* 24, no. 6 (June 2003): 9.

11. William H. Holley, Kenneth M. Jennings, and Roger S. Wolters, *The Labor Relations Process*, 8th ed. (Mason, OH: South-Western, 2005).

12. Lorna Harris, "Labour Board Punishes Employer for Heavy Handed Efforts to Block Union," *Canadian HR Reporter* 15, no. 9 (May 6, 2002): 6.

13. K. J. Bentham, "Employer Resistance to Union Certification: A Study of Canadian Jurisdictions," *Relations Industrielles* (Winter 2002): 159–187.

14. J. Heinz, "Union Attempts to Organize Walmart Stores in Ontario," *The Globe and Mail*, June 3, 1995, B3.

15. *Union Coverage in Canada 2011*, Workplace Information Directorate, Labour Program, Human Resources and Skills Development Canada, April 2012, http://www.hrsdc.gc.ca/eng/labour/labour_relations /info_analysis/union_membership/unionmembership2011. pdf, retrieved May 2012.

16. Ibid.

17. E. Kevin Kelloway and Julian Barling, "Members' Participation in Local Union Activities: Measurement, Prediction, and Replication," *Journal of Applied Psychology* 78, no. 2 (April 1993): 262–278.

18. John A. Fossum, *Labor Relations: Development, Structure, Process*, 9th ed. (Homewood, IL: BPI-Irwin, 2005).

19. For the original description of attitudinal structuring, see Richard E. Walton and Robert B. McKersie, *A Behavioral Theory of Labor Negotiations* (New York: McGraw-Hill, 1965). This book is considered a classic in the labour relations field.

20. Leigh Thompson, *The Mind and Heart of the Negotiator*, 3rd ed. (Upper Saddle River, NJ: Prentice Hall, 2004).

21. Thomas R. Colosi, "The Principles of Negotiation," *Dispute Resolution Journal* 57, no. 1 (February–April 2002): 28–31.

22. Ross Stagner and Hjalmar Rosen, *Psychology of Union–Management Relations* (Belmont, CA: Wadsworth, 1965): 95–97. This is another classic in the field of labour–management relations.

23. Nils O. Fonstad, Robert B. McKersie, and Susan C. Eaton, "Interest-Based Negotiations in a Transformed Labor–Management Setting," *Negotiation Journal* 20, no. 1 (January 2004): 5. See also Robert B. McKersie, Susan E. Eaton, and Thomas A. Kochan, "Kaiser Permanente: Using Interest-Based Negotiations to Craft a New Collective Bargaining Agreement," *Negotiation Journal* 20, no. 1 (January 2004): 13.

24. Joe Stanley, interview with author, Phoenix, Arizona, January 5, 2005.

25. The Federal Mediation & Conciliation Service (FMCS) has a complete and comprehensive program to train labour and management negotiators in the art and techniques of IBB. Information on the IBB program can be obtained from the FMCS national headquarters at 2100 K Street, N.W., Washington, DC 20427, or from FMCS district offices.

26. *Interest-Based Negotiations: Participants' Guidebook* (Washington, DC: Federal Mediation and Conciliation Service, 1998): 11.

27. H. Scoffield, "Canada a World Leader in Hitting the Bricks," *The Globe and Mail*, June 4, 2007, B3.

28. Bill McDonough, president of UFCW Local 99, interview with author, January 12, 2005, Phoenix, Arizona.

29. Robert Schwartz, "Everything You Were Afraid to Ask about Lockouts," *Labor Notes*, 397 (April 2012), 13.

30. Labor agreement, Wabash Fibre Box Company and Paperworkers.

31. John B. Larocco, "Ambiguities in Labor Union Contracts: Where Do They Come From?" *Dispute Resolution Journal* 59, no. 1 (February–April 2004): 38.

32. *Grievance Guide*, 11th ed. (Washington, DC: BNA Books, 2003).

33. Vera Riggs, Labor-Management Relations Conference, August 11, 2004, Phoenix, Arizona.

34. Peter J. Conodeca, "Ready ... Set ... Mediate," *Dispute Resolution Journal* 56, no. 4 (November 2001–January 2002): 32–38.

35. Arbitration awards are not final in all cases. Arbitration awards may be overturned through the judicial process if it can be shown that the arbitrator was prejudiced or failed to render an award based on the essence of the agreement.

# International Human Resources Management

# After studying this chapter, you should be able to

**OUTCOME 1**  Explain the economic, political, and cultural factors in different countries that human resources managers need to consider.

**OUTCOME 2**  Identify the types of organizational forms used for competing internationally.

**OUTCOME 3**  Explain how domestic and international human resources management differ.

**OUTCOME 4**  Discuss the staffing process for individuals working internationally.

**OUTCOME 5**  Identify the unique training needs for international assignees and their employees.

**OUTCOME 6**  Identify the characteristics of a good international compensation plan.

**OUTCOME 7**  Reconcile the difficulties of home- and host-country performance appraisals.

**OUTCOME 8**  Explain how labour relations differ around the world.

When you pick up a newspaper or turn on the TV, you will notice that stories are constantly being told about companies competing globally. These stories might include the failed bid by a Chinese company to buy Saskatchewan-based Potash. Or they might highlight companies expanding into other markets, such as Bombardier in Morocco or Scotiabank in the Dominican Republic. Or the stories might focus on international companies gaining dominance here in Canada, such as ING or Target. "No matter what kind of business you run, no matter what size you are, you're suddenly competing against companies you've never heard of all around the world that make a very similar widget or provide a very similar service," as one global manager put it. In fact, nearly three-quarters of HR professionals from companies large and small in a wide range of industries and countries say they expect their company's international business to grow in the coming years.[1] Some of these companies are handling the challenge well. Others are failing miserably as they try to manage across borders. More often than not, the difference boils down to how people are managed, the adaptability of cultures, and the flexibility of organizations.

Up until this point in the book, we have emphasized HRM practices and systems as they exist in Canada. Nonetheless, the topic of international HRM is so important that we wanted to dedicate an entire chapter to its discussion. The first part of this chapter describes some of the environmental factors that affect the work of managers in a global setting. Just as with domestic operations, the dimensions of the environment form a context in which HRM decisions in foreign countries are made. Next, we present a brief introduction to international business firms. In many important respects, the way a company organizes its international operations influences the type of managerial and HR issues it faces. A major portion of this chapter deals with the various HR activities involved in the recruitment, selection, development, and compensation of employees who work in an international setting.

# THE GLOBAL ENVIRONMENT

OUTCOME 1

In Chapter 1, we highlighted some of the global trends affecting HRM. The global environment of today is much different than it was 10 years ago. Because technological, political, cultural, and economic conditions are constantly shifting across the world, how people are managed in those changing environments will shift as well. On the one hand, free trade agreements between countries, technological advances that increase individual productivity, and the development of common platforms for moving knowledge and information will draw more tightly the bonds that connect us, increasing global similarities and the need for HRM to integrate practices. On the other hand, political and cultural differences create global environments that present needs for HRM to adapt practices to the local countries in which they are operating.

## GLOBAL SIMILARITIES

Some key factors that have influenced HRM include increased (1) free trade, (2) service-based business, and (3) integrated technology platforms. Because these factors have increased the economic integration across countries, they have emphasized the need for HRM practices and systems to be more globally integrated and consistent across countries.

*Free trade.* A major economic factor was the creation of free trade zones within Europe, North America, and the Pacific Rim. Twenty-seven member countries now comprise the European Union (EU), whose goal is to facilitate the flow of goods, services, capital, and human resources across national borders in Europe in a manner similar to the way they cross provincial borders in Canada.[2] A similar transition occurred within North America with the passage of the North American Free Trade Agreement (NAFTA) in 1994. NAFTA created the world's largest free market.

Like NAFTA, numerous trade agreements, including the Association of Southeast Asian Nations (ASEAN), East Asia Economic Group, Asia-Pacific Economic Cooperation (APEC), and South Asian Association for Regional Cooperation (SAARC), have significantly facilitated trade among Asian countries, making Asia the fastest growing region in the world. China—its fastest growing country—has emerged as a dominant trade leader since instituting trade reforms in the late 1970s. In the last decade and a half, China's economy has grown dramatically, drastically altering political and trading relations among nations. China's 1.3 billion people represent a massive, largely untapped consumer market for global companies. Today, more cars are sold in China than in Europe, for example. Driving this trend are big multinational corporations such as General Electric (GE), Toyota, and Intel, which are building or expanding their manufacturing units in the country. But many smaller firms are heading to China as well. "It's not so much that [companies] want to go East: They feel that they have no choice," said one international HR staffing consultant. "They must be in China. It's not a question of if, but a question of how." In addition to China, India's economy is also growing very quickly, as is Brazil's.[3]

*Business services versus manufacturing.* Through technological advances, the number of manufacturing jobs is decreasing in proportion to the number of service-based jobs. Companies are increasingly turning to sophisticated machinery that requires fewer workers to produce the same amount of product, such as cars, clothes, and computers. For example, increased automation of manufacturing processes in the auto industry has eliminated the number of workers needed on the shop floor. Even in less developed countries, where manufacturing is typically stronger due to the low cost of labour and high cost of capital-intensive equipment, labour-saving technology is becoming more affordable and accessible. Take, for instance, a textile factory in Vietnam. It is more cost effective for the factory to purchase high-tech threading equipment to spin the cotton into thread than to hire hundreds of people to thread the cotton by hand, even when the average wage for such employees is less than $100 a month.

On the other hand, service-based jobs are much harder to replace with technology than manufacturing jobs. Most people would prefer to talk with a person instead of a computer-generated program regarding wireless Internet connection problems with their computer. Although technology can provide you with the classes you need to graduate, talking with a career counsellor can help you choose the right classes to get a job after graduating.

Services will always be in demand, regardless of whether you are in a developed country such as Canada or a less developed country such as Haiti. Service-based jobs that can be traded across borders range from highly complex to simple, including research and development, consulting, finance and accounting, HRM, tech support, customer service, and basic data entry jobs. Traditionally, during trade negotiations, less developed countries have expressed concern over the advantages that developed countries have over them in the service sectors. Although this is still true in certain areas today, many less developed countries have developed strong capabilities in different service sectors. For example, with companies such as Infosys and thousands of small- and medium-sized information technology (IT) companies, India is often seen as a hub for (IT) services that can be sold anywhere in the world.

***Integrated technology platforms.*** Although the increasing use of technology has resulted in more service-based jobs, technology has also increased the rate at which these services can be traded across countries. Along with the creation of the World Trade Organization, 1995 also signified the beginning of the Internet era. America Online (AOL) went public in 1995 to mark the beginning of integrated technology platforms that could be shared instantaneously across the world. In the words of Thomas Friedman, these events "flattened the world," making many service-based jobs able to be done anywhere in the world.[4] *Integrated technology platforms* represent common operating systems such as Microsoft Windows 7 that can be used across multiple computers connected through the Internet. Through these common platforms, work becomes less specific to particular companies and countries.

In this era, employees become empowered to compete without the need for a large company. For example, many websites, such as guru.com, have developed an online marketplace where individuals can offer various services and compete for business throughout the world. Imagine that you are interested in developing a new website for your company. By going to the Internet, you can select various individuals offering these services. They may be from Manila, Philippines; Mumbai, India; Manhattan, New York; or Munich, Germany.

These three factors of increased trade, service-based business, and integrated technology platforms have shifted the way companies are managing their HR. HR units can no longer operate as separate groups attached only by a common brand and finances. HR managers must integrate their operations to capture the benefits that come from having people all on the same page.

## GLOBAL DIFFERENCES

Although free trade agreements and technological factors may call for a more unified HR system in your company, other global factors can act as major obstacles. These factors consist of political and cultural differences. First, political differences are found in a country's labour laws, property rights, and patents. For example, when the American-based welding company Lincoln Electric started operations in Brazil, it was not able to offer its yearly bonus program based on performance because any bonuses paid for two consecutive years become a legal entitlement.

In many countries, particularly those in Africa, property rights are poorly protected by governments. Whoever has the political power or authority can

**cultural environment**
The communications, religion, values and ideologies, education, and social structure of a country

**host country**
A country in which an international corporation operates

seize others' property with few or no repercussions. Civil unrest can also lead to the poor enforcement of property rights. Companies have less incentive to locate factories or invest in countries experiencing strife. Another issue relates to intellectual property rights: rights related to patents, trademarks, and so forth. Despite the fact that private property rights are now generally enforced in China, intellectual property rights have seen little protection. For example, when General Motors (GM) formed a joint venture with a Chinese company to produce and sell a new automobile in the country, a knockoff version of the car could be seen on China's streets even before GM and its partner were able to manufacture their first car. Environmental restrictions also make some countries more attractive to do business in than others.

Beyond the political issues just mentioned, a country's **cultural environment** (communications, religion, values and ideologies, education, and social structure) also has important implications when it comes to a company's decision about when and how to do business there. Because of language and culture similarities, many Canadian companies are finding the United States, Ireland, and the United Kingdom attractive places to locate their facilities, particularly call centres. Eastern Europe has also begun to attract interest because citizens there are well educated and largely possess English-speaking skills.

Figure 15.1 summarizes the complexity of the cultural environment in which HR must be managed. Culture is an integrated phenomenon. By recognizing and accommodating taboos, rituals, attitudes toward time, social stratification, kinship systems, and the many other components listed in Figure 15.1, managers stand a better chance of understanding the culture of a **host country**—a country in

## FIGURE 15.1

CULTURAL ENVIRONMENT OF INTERNATIONAL BUSINESS

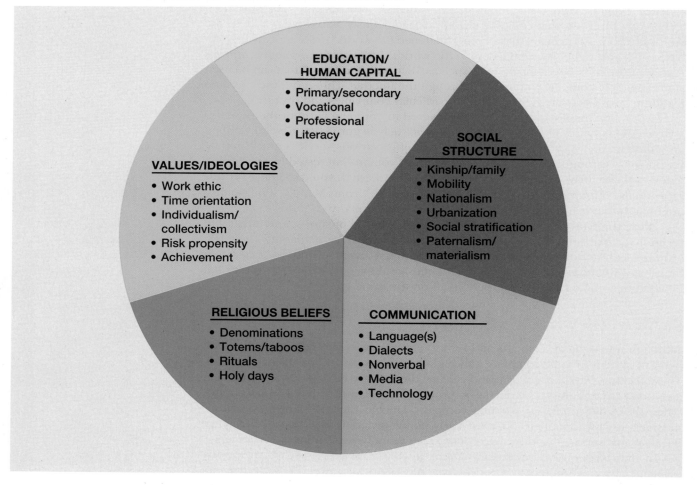

# HIGHLIGHTS IN HRM 15.1

## Understanding the Importance of Cultural Differences

A North American company decided to open an office in Paris and sent the future manager to find office space and hire employees. The manager found a great location at a good price on the outskirts of Paris. Then she advertised the vacant positions in French business magazines. When she interviewed her first candidate, an alumnus of the École Polytechnique de Paris, she asked the candidate for a copy of his transcript and his grade point average. At first, he evaded the request. Then he refused, saying that he was a graduate of the most prestigious Grande école, and added, as he left the office, "Besides, your company's offices are not exactly in the best part of town." That same day, all other alumni of the École Polytechnique who were scheduled for interviews cancelled their appointments.

The manager, from the home country, had failed to understand cultural differences between North Americans and the French. In France, the location of the office is important, and the most desirable locations are the city centres. Only second-rate companies locate offices in the suburbs of Paris. Second, the French educational system is hierarchical and highly selective, and those attending the École Polytechnique de Paris are considered to be the very best graduates. These graduates are in high demand, and a North American company would be very fortunate to hire one. Networking in France is done through alumni associations, so word would spread quickly about this failed interview. The lesson to be learned is that hiring local talent requires sensitivity to local culture and customs.

Source: Adapted from Lionel Laroche "Hiring Abroad" *CMA Management,* 76, 1, March 2002, page 57.

which an international business operates. Different cultural environments require different approaches to HRM. Highlights in HRM 15.1 describes some of these cultural differences. Strategies, structures, and management styles that are appropriate in one cultural setting may lead to failure in another. Even in countries that have close language or cultural links, HR practices can be dramatically different. In some countries, night shifts are taboo. In other countries, employers are expected to provide employees with meals and transportation between home and work. In India, workers generally receive cash bonuses on their wedding anniversaries with which to buy their spouses gifts, and dating allowances are provided to unmarried employees. These are practices that would never occur to Canadian managers and HR practitioners.[5] For example, in many countries, bribes are considered a normal business practice (see Ethics in HRM). Throughout this chapter, we will discuss several HR issues related to adapting to different cultural environments. Reality Check provides more examples of adaptation to a country's context.

# ETHICS IN HRM

## Bribery Abroad

Ikea has refused to open stores in Russia because of continuing concerns about bribery and corruption. Canadian employees sent to other countries to conduct business and negotiate deals are not immune to bribery attempts. SNC-Lavalin has been accused of two mysterious payments of $56 million dollars to foreign agents in the Middle East, where the company has large construction projects.

Although businesses wish to be productive and profitable, it is unacceptable to achieve these goals through unethical behaviour. Transparency International, a global coalition against corruption, estimates that systemic corruption can add 20 to 25 percent

*continued*

to the costs of government procurement and may result in the purchase of inferior goods or unnecessary services. Every organization that does business internationally should have a code of ethics, which should contain specific clauses forbidding bribery.

Experts recommend that any employee sent abroad to negotiate deals should review the *Corruption of Foreign Public Officials Act*. Under this act, any employee caught

bribing foreign officials could face five years in jail and unlimited fines. Last year, NICO Resources was fined 9.5 million dollars for giving a Bangladeshi official a $190,000 vehicle. The chief executive officer could also face jail time, even if he was unaware of the bribe. Knowledge of this act will make it easier for an employee to state to corrupt negotiators that if he gave a bribe, he could go to jail.

Source:  C. Campbell "SNC-Lavalin's murky affair shows need to tighten bribery law" *The Globe and Mail*, March 29, 2012, A. 17. B. Best, "Battling Bribery, Corruption Abroad," *Canadian HR Reporter* (April 9, 2007): 17, 20.

## MANAGING ACROSS BORDERS

**OUTCOME 2**

International business operations can take several different forms. A large percentage carry on their international business with only limited facilities and minimal representation in foreign countries. Others, particularly Fortune 500 corporations, have extensive facilities and personnel in various countries

# REALITY CHECK

## Global versus Local HRM Practices

Gene Lai, B.A., M.H.R.M., has the kind of international experience that many HR professionals would love to have. In Canada, he was vice president of HR for Steelcase Canada for 9 years, and vice president of operations for 11 years. Steelcase Canada is a subsidiary of Steelcase Inc. a manufacturer of office furniture, with headquarters in Grand Rapids, Michigan. Steelcase has factories throughout the world, including one in China with 200 employees. When Steelcase acquired a competitor in China, with a factory employing 1,200 employees, Gene accepted an assignment as project leader for the post-merger integration. His job was to merge the two operations and build a new factory.

Gene had a very flexible mandate and could use HRM practices that would make the most sense for corporate needs as well as regional needs. In some instances, it was necessary to choose the processes used at headquarters. He says, "For example, it made sense to have a consistent global policy around people development because Steelcase is a team-based organization, and we expect employees worldwide to be able to work in teams. Ethics is also a corporate value; how we do business has to be consistent across all countries."

But in other cases, responding to local practices made more sense. As Gene states, "From a regional perspective, I found after spending time in Asia, there are certain

practices that have to be aligned with regional needs. One thing that people in North America would never consider is the flood allowance. Every year, there are floods. Employees are paid a premium during this period to cope with the problems caused by the floods. One of the measures that the Chinese candidates use for judging a company is the generosity of the company flood allowance. The flood allowance is about $30 US ... for a person making about 50 cents per hour. Along the same line, especially in the factory environment, the obligation is for the employer to provide room and board. Eighty percent are migrants and need a dormitory. Likewise, employees compare employers based on how much is spent providing three meals a day. In general, companies provide $1.10 for the three meals, and that is considered generous.

"There are differences in how compensation is perceived. In China, compensation is measured by the amount of take-home pay. The number of hours worked is less of an issue. Unlike North America, the more hours you work beyond the normal 40 hours, the less employees are paid per hour. For example, an employee would make 50 cents an hour for the first 40 hours, and then 40 cents an hour for the next 10 hours, and then 30 cents an hour for the next ten hours. Why would anyone work overtime for less money per hour? But these migrant employees look at how much could be earned in a month, not how many hours. If they work 8 hours, they have 16 hours for leisure, but leisure is less important than money. So they prefer to work more hours."

Source: Gene Lai

of the world. Dell, for example, employs more people outside the United States than within it. Managing these resources effectively and integrating their activities to achieve global advantage is a challenge to the leadership of these companies.

Figure 15.2 shows four basic types of organizations and how they differ in the degree to which international activities are separated to respond to the local regions and integrated to achieve global efficiencies. The **international corporation** is essentially a domestic firm that builds on its existing capabilities to penetrate overseas markets. Companies such as Honda, GE, and Procter & Gamble (P&G) used this approach to gain access to Europe—they essentially adapted existing products for overseas markets without changing much else about their normal operations. (One such adaptation, for example, was P&G's extremely successful introduction of a detergent brick used on washboards in India.)

A **multinational corporation (MNC)** is a more complex form that usually has fully autonomous units operating in multiple countries. Shell, Philips, and ITT are three typical MNCs. These companies have traditionally given their foreign subsidiaries a great deal of latitude to address local issues such as consumer preferences, political pressures, and economic trends in different regions of the world. Frequently, these subsidiaries are run as independent companies, without much integration. The **global corporation**, on the other hand, can be viewed as a multinational firm that maintains control of operations back in the home office. Japanese companies, such as Matsushita and NEC, tend to treat the world market as a unified whole and try to combine activities in each country to maximize efficiency on a global scale. These companies operate much like a domestic firm, except that they view the whole world as their marketplace.

Finally, a **transnational corporation** attempts to achieve the local responsiveness of an MNC while also achieving the efficiencies of a global firm. To balance this "global/local" dilemma, a transnational corporation uses a network structure that coordinates specialized facilities positioned around the world. By using this flexible structure, a transnational corporation provides autonomy to independent country operations but brings these separate activities together

**international corporation**
A domestic firm that uses its existing capabilities to move into overseas markets

**multinational corporation (MNC)**
A firm with independent business units operating in multiple countries

**global corporation**
A firm that has integrated worldwide operations through a centralized home office

**transnational corporation**
A firm that attempts to balance local responsiveness and global scale via a network of specialized operating units

# FIGURE 15.2

## TYPES OF ORGANIZATIONS

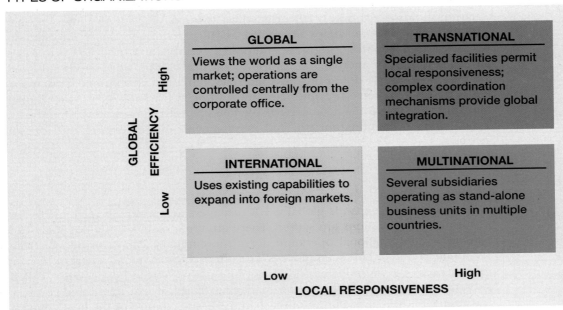

**GLOBAL**
Views the world as a single market; operations are controlled centrally from the corporate office.

**TRANSNATIONAL**
Specialized facilities permit local responsiveness; complex coordination mechanisms provide global integration.

**INTERNATIONAL**
Uses existing capabilities to expand into foreign markets.

**MULTINATIONAL**
Several subsidiaries operating as stand-alone business units in multiple countries.

GLOBAL EFFICIENCY — High / Low

LOCAL RESPONSIVENESS — Low / High

**expatriates, or home-country nationals**
Employees from the home country who are on an international assignment

**host-country nationals**
Employees who are natives of the host country

**third-country nationals**
Employees who are natives of a country other than the home country or the host country

into an integrated whole. For most companies, the transnational form represents an ideal rather than the reality. However, companies such as Ford, Unilever, and Shell have made good progress in restructuring operations to function more transnationally.[6]

Although various forms of organization exist, in this chapter, we will generally refer to any company that conducts business outside its home country as an international business. Canada, of course, has no monopoly on international business. International enterprises are found throughout the world. A number of European and Pacific Rim companies have been conducting business on an international basis much longer than their Canadian counterparts. The close proximity of European countries, for example, has facilitated international trade among them for centuries. More recently, companies from Japan and China have proven to be some of the most powerful companies in the world. A Global Fortune 500 list from 2000 would have revealed that the top 10 companies were all located in the United States. In 2010, only 2 of the top 10 companies came from the United States. The others are based out of Europe and Asia. Many of these companies generate more revenue annually than do entire small nations. Consequently, they are corporations that have a significant impact on the world economy.

With the global environment being filled by companies originating from different countries and operating in multiple cultures, increased pressure is being placed on the HRM function. International HRM is being seen more and more as a key source of competitive advantage for international businesses.

## DOMESTIC VERSUS INTERNATIONAL HRM

**OUTCOME 3**

International HRM differs from domestic HRM in several ways. In the first place, it necessarily places a greater emphasis on functions and activities such as relocation, orientation, and translation services to help employees adapt to new and different environments outside their own countries and to help newly hired employees in foreign countries adapt to working for companies headquartered outside their borders. Today, global HR management has become a front-and-centre issue for a wide variety of firms. Many larger corporations, and even smaller ones doing business in key international markets, now have full-time HR managers devoted solely to assisting with the globalization process. British Airways, for example, has a team of HR directors who travel around the world to help country managers stay updated on international concerns, policies, and programs. Coca-Cola provides support to its army of HR professionals working around the world. A core HR group in the company's Atlanta headquarters holds a two-week HR orientation twice a year for the international HR staff. This program helps international HR practitioners share information about HR philosophies, programs, and policies established either in Coca-Cola's headquarters or in another part of the world that can be successfully adopted by others.[7] Because doing business internationally can be extremely complex, many companies also hire international staffing firms such as Boston Global Consulting. These firms have expertise when it comes to relocating employees, establishing operations abroad, and helping with import/export and foreign tax issues.

## STAFFING INTERNATIONALLY

**OUTCOME 4**

When a company expands globally, HR managers are generally responsible for ensuring that operations are staffed. There are three main ways a company can staff a new international operation. First, the company can send people from its home country. These employees are often referred to as **expatriates, or home-country nationals**. Second, it can hire natives of the host country, called **host-country nationals**, to do the managing. Third, it can hire **third-country nationals**, natives of a country other than the home country or the host country.

Each of these sources of overseas workers provides certain advantages and certain disadvantages. Most corporations use all three sources for staffing their multinational operations, although some companies exhibit a distinct bias for one or another of the three sources.[8]

As shown in Figure 15.3, at early stages of international expansion, organizations often send home-country expatriates to establish activities (particularly in less developed countries) and to work with local governments. This is generally very costly. Traditionally, expatriates have received generous salaries, automobiles, full relocation services, private schooling for their children, trips home, and other perks. These services frequently end up costing more than $300,000 yearly, on average, making the cost of a typical 3-year expatriate assignment more than $1 million. Companies are taking greater pains to outline more clearly the overall goal of the foreign assignment and its timetable for completion. Ingersoll-Rand, an international equipment maker, now carefully documents in detail what should be accomplished during an assignment abroad—whether the assignment is designed to enhance an assignee's leadership skills, improve productivity and sales targets abroad, transfer specific technology to a foreign operation, or staff it with local, expatriate, or third-country nationals.

Nearly 70,000 Canadians are working abroad, mainly in the United States (44 percent), followed by Europe (33 percent), Asia/Pacific (15 percent), and Central and South America (8 percent). Most employees now consider foreign work credentials essential or extremely useful.[9] Figure 15.4 lists the reasons Canadians are sent on global assignments.

In recent years, there has also been a trend to send expatriates on shorter, project-based assignments (2 to 12 months versus 1 to 3 years) and to shift more quickly toward hiring host-country nationals. This has three main advantages:

1. Hiring local citizens is generally less costly than relocating expatriates. Local citizens also know the cultural and political landscape of the country and are often more likely to be able to gain the support of local staff members.
2. Since local governments usually want good jobs for their citizens, foreign employers may be required to hire locally.
3. Most customers want to do business with companies (and people) they perceive to be local versus foreign.

Global companies have the challenge of managing operations and people in many different countries.

## FIGURE 15.3

### CHANGES IN INTERNATIONAL STAFFING OVER TIME

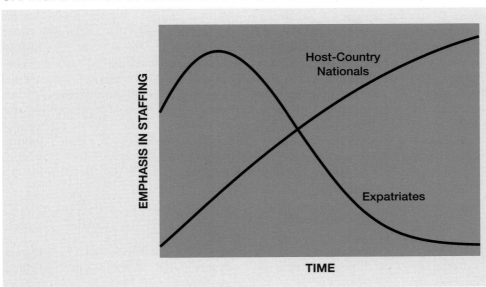

**CHAPTER 15:** INTERNATIONAL HUMAN RESOURCES MANAGEMENT

## FIGURE 15.4

### WHY CANADIANS ARE SENT ON GLOBAL ASSIGNMENTS

HR managers have to consider not only why employees are given international assignments but also how to entice them to accept these assignments. The number one reason employees decline an international assignment is because of family issues, related to housing, a reluctant spouse with a career, schooling, and even repatriation. To deal with these issues, organizations are offering a predecision trip to the foreign country, orientation programs and work permits for spouses, short-term assignments so that the family does not have to move, and extensive vacations, particularly in hardship locations. Compensation is not usually an issue.

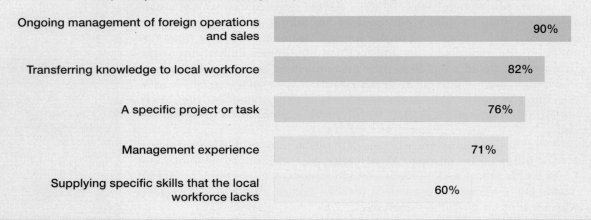

Multiple objectives were cited by companies maintaining an expatriate program.

| | |
|---|---|
| Ongoing management of foreign operations and sales | 90% |
| Transferring knowledge to local workforce | 82% |
| A specific project or task | 76% |
| Management experience | 71% |
| Supplying specific skills that the local workforce lacks | 60% |

**Sources:** S. Dobson, "Enticing Employees to Go on Relocation," *Canadian HR Reporter* (May 18, 2009): 17–18; "Why Canadians Are Sent on Global Assignments," *Canadian HR Reporter* (December 1, 2003): 22.

Because Canadian companies want to be viewed as true international citizens, there has also been a trend away from hiring expatriates to head up operations in foreign countries, especially European countries. Bombardier and Four Seasons, which have strong regional organizations, tend to replace their expatriate managers with local managers as quickly as possible. Highlights in HRM 15.2 describes some of the issues in checking the references of locals. In addition to hiring local managers to head their foreign divisions and plants, more companies are using third-country nationals. Third-country nationals are often multilingual and already acclimated to the host country's culture—perhaps because they live in a nearby region. Thus, they are also less costly to relocate and sometimes better able to cope culturally with the foreign environment.

Companies tend to continue to use expatriates only when a specific set of skills is needed or when individuals in the host country require development. For example, after embarking on a joint venture in China with a formerly state-owned enterprise, Ingersoll-Rand discovered that it had to educate its Chinese employees not only on the company's practices and culture but also on free-market, Western business practices. This required the company's expatriates to stay in China longer than planned.[10] It is important to note, however, that although top managers may prefer one source of employees over another, the host country may place pressure on them that restricts their choices. Such pressure takes the form of sophisticated government persuasion through administrative or legislative decrees designed to employ host-country individuals. Tax incentives, tariffs, and quotas are frequently implemented by the host country to encourage local hiring.

### RECRUITING INTERNATIONALLY

Improved telecommunications and travel have made it easier to match up employers and employees of all kinds worldwide. Rolls-Royce, headquartered in the United Kingdom, hires 25 percent of its 25,000 employees abroad. Because its customers

---

### Using the Internet

Canadian employers wishing to assess the academic credentials of over 15,000 foreign-born employees can consult the not-for-profit World Education Services at

**http://www.wes.org/ca**

# HIGHLIGHTS IN HRM 15.2

## Reference Checking

An American company was very impressed with the 20-page résumé of a candidate for a management position for its new Japanese office. The promising candidate had worked on a wide variety of deals. However, on checking his references, the company learned that he had been involved in all of these deals—as the interpreter!

Those checking references in foreign countries have to be aware of privacy regulations. For example, Canada and the United States have privacy laws that govern what data are and are not allowed to be accessed and used by potential employers. An employee working in the Indian office of a Canadian company is covered by the laws of India, not Canada.

There are also cultural differences in the ways references are checked. If you wanted to know if a candidate had a criminal history in Latin America, you would need to know the name of the applicant's mother. It is also helpful to understand the political context in which reference checking is done. One candidate who had worked in a country that had recently become a democracy supplied the name of his former supervisor as a reference. However, when the supervisor was contacted, he claimed to have never known the candidate. After the call, the supervisor phoned the applicant and said, "A company called asking about you, but don't worry. I told them that I don't know you and that you never worked for us." Based on the practices of the former government, the supervisor was sensitive to any kinds of investigative questions.

Source: Adapted from Traci Canning, "Hiring Global," *HR Professional* (June/July 2006): 34.

---

come from around the globe, Rolls-Royce figures that its workforce should as well. Airbus, the European commercial jet maker, recruits engineers from universities and colleges all over Europe. American-based Boeing's need for engineers is so great that it also recruits internationally and has even opened a design centre in Moscow. The trend is likely to continue as the populations in developed countries age and HR managers search for talent elsewhere.

HR departments must be particularly responsive to the cultural, political, and legal environments both domestically and abroad when recruiting internationally. Companies such as Starbucks, Levi Strauss, and Honeywell have made a special effort to create codes of conduct for employees throughout the world to ensure that standards of ethical and legal behaviour are known and understood. PepsiCo has taken a similar approach to ensuring that company values are reinforced (even while recognizing the need for adapting to local cultures). The company has four core criteria that are viewed as essential in worldwide recruiting efforts: (1) personal integrity, (2) a drive for results, (3) respect for others, and (4) capability. Zurich, a Swiss financial and insurance company with operations in North America and Europe, makes sure that its inbound North American assignees take diversity and sexual harassment courses. This training is rarely provided in other parts of the world.[11]

In general, however, employee recruitment in other countries is subject to more government regulation than it is in Canada. Regulations range from those that cover procedures for recruiting employees to those that govern the employment of foreign labour or require the employment of the physically disabled, war veterans, or displaced people. Many Central American countries, for example, have stringent regulations about the number of foreigners who can be employed as a percentage of the total workforce. Virtually all countries have work permit or visa restrictions that apply to foreigners. A **work permit or visa** is a document issued by a government granting authority to a foreign individual to seek employment in that government's country. Whatever the employee's destination, HR managers need to ensure that work permits and visas are applied for early in the relocation process.[12]

At the executive level, companies use search firms such as Korn/Ferry in North America or Spencer Stuart in the United Kingdom. At lower levels, more informal

**work permit or visa**
A government document granting a foreign individual the right to seek employment

**guest workers**
Foreign workers invited to perform needed labour

**transnational teams**
Teams composed of members of multiple nationalities working on projects that span multiple countries

approaches tend to be useful. At lower levels, companies recruiting abroad often need to advertise their firms and employment "brand" to recruits who are not familiar with it. In countries such as India and China, an employer's reputation is extremely important to candidates' families—sometimes more important than pay.

Many employers have learned that the best way to find workers in these countries is through referrals and radio announcements because many people lack sufficient reading or writing skills. Some countries, in fact, require the employment of locals if adequate numbers of skilled people are available. Specific exceptions are sometimes granted (officially or unofficially) when there is a strong demand for labour, such as the cases for Mexican farm workers in Canada and for Italian, Spanish, Greek, and Turkish workers in Germany and the Benelux countries (Belgium, the Netherlands, and Luxembourg). Foreign workers invited to perform needed labour are usually referred to as guest workers. Although hiring nonnationals may result in lower direct labour costs for a company, the indirect costs—those related to housing, language training, health services, recruitment, transportation, and so on—can be substantial. Some companies competing in industries with acute talent shortages are nonetheless finding the expenditures worthwhile. Nursing is one such industry.[13]

## Apprenticeships

A major source of trained labour in European nations is apprenticeship training programs (described in Chapter 7). On the whole, apprenticeship training in Europe is superior to that in Canada. In Europe, a dual-track system of education directs a large number of youths into vocational training. The German system of apprenticeship training, one of the best in Europe, provides training for office and shop jobs under a three-way responsibility contract between the apprentice, his or her parents, and the organization. At the conclusion of their training, apprentices can work for any employer but generally receive seniority credit with the training firm if they remain in it. France has been able to draw on its "Grandes écoles" for centuries. Created during the Renaissance to fulfill a need that universities were not meeting at the time, the Grandes écoles educate prospective engineers up to the equivalent level of master of engineering. Snecma, an international equipment supplier headquartered in Paris, hires about 80 percent of its employees from the Grandes écoles.[14]

## Staffing Transnational Teams

In addition to focusing on individuals, it is also important to note that companies are increasingly using transnational teams to conduct international business. Transnational teams are composed of members of multiple nationalities working on projects that span multiple countries. GE's LightSpeed VCT, a state-of-the art medical scanner, was designed with input from cardiologists around the world. The machine's innards were designed by GE engineers in four different countries, and the software to run it was written by multiple teams from India, Israel, France, and the United States working together.[15] Aware that many products developed in developed economies will have a limited market in developing economies, companies such as P&G, GE, and Tata Motors have turned to transnational teams to help develop low-cost but high-quality products for the poor. For example, Tata Motors developed the "Tata Nano," a car for nearly $2,000. As the cheapest car in the world, the Tata Nano was developed by a large transnational team, with suppliers in different countries designing specific parts to meet a price-sensitive threshold.

Teams such as these are especially useful for performing tasks that the firm as a whole is not yet structured to accomplish. For example, they may be used to transcend the existing organizational structure to customize a strategy for different geographic regions, transfer technology from one part of the world to another, and communicate between headquarters and subsidiaries in different countries. In GE's case, the company realized its competitors were developing their own medical scanning technology more quickly. GE decided it could no longer afford to duplicate its efforts in different divisions around the world—that these groups would have to work together as a team.

Sometimes companies send employees on temporary assignments abroad as part of transnational teams lasting, say, a few months. This might be done to break down cultural barriers between international divisions or disseminate new ideas and technologies to other regions. In other instances, employees are transferred for extended periods of time. Years ago, Fuji sent 15 of its most experienced engineers from Tokyo to a Xerox facility in Webster, New York. Over a five-year period, the engineers worked with a team of American engineers to develop the "world" copier. The effort led to a joint venture that has lasted for decades. Fuji-Xerox now employs approximately 34,000 people globally at 60 member companies around the world.[16]

The fundamental task in forming a transnational team is assembling the right group of people who can work together effectively to accomplish the goals of the team. For GE's LightSpeed team, this frequently meant holding eight-hour global conference calls encompassing numerous time zones. (The call times were rotated so that no single team had to stay up all night for every call.) Many companies try to build variety into their teams to maximize responsiveness to the special needs of different countries. For example, when Heineken formed a transnational team to consolidate its production facilities, it ensured that team members were drawn from each major region within Europe. Team members tended to have specialized skills, and members were added only if they offered a unique skill that added value to the team.

## SELECTING EMPLOYEES INTERNATIONALLY

Selecting employees in a foreign country environment can be difficult. When embarking on hiring employees in a new country, a firm's international HR managers should get to know the local market and customs in hiring. This will help the firm understand what to look for in an employee. When GE first entered India, it did not realize that much of the effective hiring was done through family ties and friendship networks. Not wanting to appear biased, GE at first did not allow such practices. However, after struggling to select good recruits, GE finally incorporated peer and family referral systems into their selection practices. This led to selection of employees that stayed within the organization much longer.

To better understand the local market, there are a few things firms can do. First, international HR managers should get to know the universities, technical schools, and primary schools in the area. More than ensuring qualifications, schools provide extensive networks to future employees and provide insight on the type of hires managers would want to select. This means taking time to understand how the local schools operate. In many developing countries, higher education systems are underdeveloped and do not provide either enough future employees or employees with suitable skills. For example, Rolls-Royce and Intel have both become involved in the development of school curricula for both managerial and engineering skill development. By partnering with local universities, Rolls-Royce and Intel offer funding and curriculum design to better prepare students for the work environment. At their own expense, these companies see such costs as investments in future employees and a chance to shape the skills they need to run their companies in those countries.

Second, international HR managers should develop networks in the business and government communities. Because many companies' reputations may not precede them, they must use personal networks to develop trust in the company. An international HR manager's job will not be just to select the right people who come to the office but to select the right people within the community. For instance, when Unilever, a large British-Dutch consumer products company, opens up operations in a foreign environment, it often becomes heavily involved

Expatriate employees receive intensive training on their host countries—the cultural differences, negotiation tactics, business practices, everyday living, and other aspects of working and living successfully in a foreign country.

© The Image Bank/Getty Images

in the local community by conducting community feedback meetings, local education programs, and environmental studies. The company's heavy involvement in the local environment helps to rapidly build its local reputation, which increases its knowledge of potential new hires.

Finally, to select employees in a local environment effectively, international HR managers must understand the employees of the firm's competitors. As they map out and get to know key employees in competing organizations, they develop a better understanding of what to look for in other employees while building up a new pool of applicants to recruit in the future. For example, companies such as Exxon and GE, as well as smaller companies, will turn to employees of competing companies because they already know that these employees have the necessary skills and abilities to survive in their company. This is especially important to note as more and more domestic companies are hiring away foreign international firms' employees, with the lure of patriotism and the staying power of a local company.

## Selecting Global Managers

What if an organization cannot find the appropriate talent in the local country? What if a firm is opening up operations in a foreign country but needs managers who know the ins and outs of the company or who have company-specific expertise? In this case, organizations need to select managers from one country and move them to another. Unfortunately, many of these decisions are based primarily on company-specific expertise and not on country- or culture-specific expertise. In other words, little attention is paid to how likely it is that the person will be able to complete the task in a very specific environment.

The demand for expatriate employees is growing rapidly. Selecting a global manager depends on a variety of different employment factors, including the extent of contact the manager will have with local citizens and the government and the degree to which the foreign environment differs from the home environment. For example, if the job involves extensive contacts with the community, as with a chief executive officer, this factor should be given appropriate weight. The magnitude of differences between the political, legal, socioeconomic, and cultural systems of the host country and those of the home country should also be assessed.[17]

Levi Strauss has identified the following six skill categories for the **global manager**, or manager equipped to run an international business:

- Ability to seize strategic opportunities
- Ability to manage highly decentralized organizations
- Awareness of global issues
- Sensitivity to issues of diversity
- Competence in interpersonal relations
- Skill in building community[18]

**global manager**
A manager equipped to run an international business

If a candidate for expatriation is willing to live and work in a foreign environment, an indication of his or her tolerance of cultural differences should be obtained. On the other hand, if local nationals have the technical competence to carry out the job successfully, they should be carefully considered for the job before the firm launches a search (at home) for a candidate to fill the job. As we explained, most corporations realize the advantages to be gained by staffing international operations with host-country nationals wherever possible.

Selecting home-country and third-country nationals requires that more factors be considered than in selecting host-country nationals. Although the latter must possess managerial abilities and the necessary technical skills, they have the advantage of familiarity with the physical and cultural environment and the language of the host country. Figure 15.5 compares the advantages of hiring global managers from these three different groups. The discussion that follows, however, will focus on the selection of expatriate managers from the home country, along with their compensation and performance appraisals.

**FIGURE 15.5**

COMPARISON OF ADVANTAGES IN SOURCES OF OVERSEAS MANAGERS

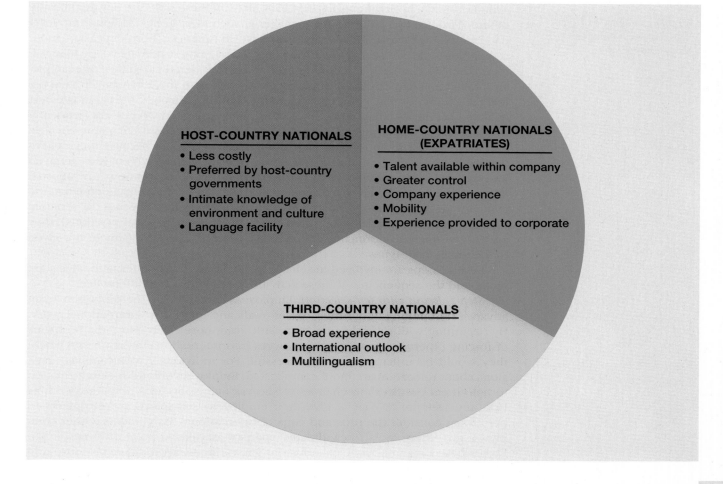

**HOST-COUNTRY NATIONALS**
- Less costly
- Preferred by host-country governments
- Intimate knowledge of environment and culture
- Language facility

**HOME-COUNTRY NATIONALS (EXPATRIATES)**
- Talent available within company
- Greater control
- Company experience
- Mobility
- Experience provided to corporate

**THIRD-COUNTRY NATIONALS**
- Broad experience
- International outlook
- Multilingualism

# HIGHLIGHTS IN HRM 15.3

## Skills of Expatriate Managers

| CORE SKILLS | AUGMENTED SKILLS |
|---|---|
| Experience | Technical skills |
| Decision making | Negotiation skills |
| Resourcefulness | Strategic thinking |
| Adaptability | Delegation skills |
| Cultural sensitivity | Change management |
| Team building | |
| Maturity | |

**core skills**
Skills considered critical to an employee's success abroad

**augmented skills**
Skills helpful in facilitating the efforts of expatriate managers

Colgate-Palmolive, Whirlpool, and Dow Chemical have further identified a set of **core skills** that they view as critical for success abroad and a set of augmented skills that help facilitate the efforts of expatriate managers. These two types of skills are shown in Highlights in HRM 15.3. Many of these skills are not significantly different from those required for managerial success at home. Although in years past, the average expatriate manager was a North American–born Caucasian, more companies today are seeing the advantages of assigning expatriates depending on their ethnicity. But such a decision needs to be considered carefully. For example, an Indian-Canadian candidate applying for a position in India may never have visited the country or may not relate well to the culture. Ultimately, the candidate best qualified for the job should be sent. Unfortunately, talented women are frequently overlooked for global managerial positions—perhaps because companies believe they will fare poorly in foreign, male-dominated societies or because they believe women have less desire to go abroad. However, many women who have been given international assignments have performed well. Because locals know how unusual it is for a woman to be given a foreign assignment, they frequently assume that the company would not have sent a woman unless she was the very best. In addition, because women expatriates are novel (particularly in managerial positions), they are very visible and distinctive and may even receive special treatment not given to their male colleagues.[19]

Several steps are involved in selecting individuals for an international assignment, and the sequencing of these activities can make a big difference:

*Step 1: Begin with self-selection.* Employees should begin the process years in advance by thinking about their career goals and interest in international work. By beginning with self-selection, companies can more easily avoid the problems of forcing otherwise promising employees into international assignments where they would be unhappy and unsuccessful. For individuals with families, decisions about relocation are more complicated. Employees should seek information to help them predict their chances of success living abroad. Companies such as EDS and Deloitte & Touche give their employees self-selection instruments to help them consider the pros and cons of international assignments. Other companies give these tools to candidates' spouses as well. At Solar Turbines, a San Diego–based manufacturer of industrial gas turbines, a candidate's spouse and sometimes his or her children undergo a day of assessment to see how well they are likely to respond to an international assignment.[20]

*Step 2: Create a candidate pool.* After employees have self-selected, organizations can build a database of candidates for international assignments. Information in the database might include availability, languages, country preferences, and skills.

*Step 3: Assess candidate's core skills.* From the short list of potential candidates, managers can assess each candidate on technical and managerial readiness relative to the needs of the assignment. Although many factors determine success abroad, the initial focus should be on the requirements of the job.

*Step 4: Assess augmented skills and attributes.* As shown in Figure 15.6, expatriate selection decisions are driven typically by technical competence and professional and international experience. In addition, however, an increasing number of organizations have also begun considering an individual's ability to adapt to different environments. Satisfactory adjustment depends on flexibility, emotional maturity and stability, empathy for the culture, language and communication skills, resourcefulness and initiative, and diplomatic skills.[21]

Even companies that believe they have selected the best candidates frequently experience high expatriate **failure rates**. Figure 15.7 shows the major causes of assignment failure. Poor cultural fit is a major reason why assignments fail. For example, although China is among the easiest countries to which to attract Western expatriates, it is also one of the hardest places for them to succeed because the country's culture is so different. A lack of expatriate support from headquarters is another major cause. Expatriates often describe themselves as "out of sight and out of mind." This highlights the importance of headquarters maintaining close contact with them to see how they are faring. Yet another big factor is a spouse's inability to adjust to his or her new surroundings. Today, more companies are preparing families by offering them cultural and language training.

For many reasons, women often make very successful expatriates.

## FIGURE 15.6

### EXPATRIATE SELECTION CRITERIA

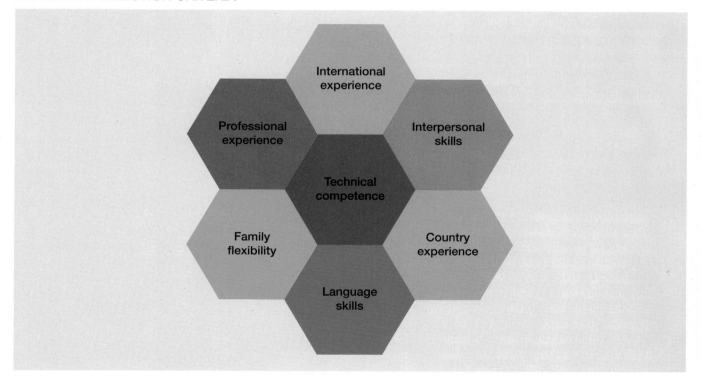

## FIGURE 15.7

### CAUSES OF EXPATRIATE ASSIGNMENT FAILURE

- Family adjustment
- Poor performance
- Lifestyle issues
- Other opportunities arise
- Work adjustment
- Business reasons
- Bad selection
- Repatriation issues

There are a number of ways to improve the success of expatriate assignments. Ultimately, the expatriate must find a way to adjust to the demands of their company, the country environment, and their family needs. Employees who share a common vision with the company are willing to undergo difficulties for the organization. Employees who take time to understand the culture and market in which they are operating will be better able to cope with unexpected changes and demands. Finally, employees who have family members who are supportive and interested in an overseas assignment are much more successful in their international assignments. As a result, expatriates stand a greater chance of being able to successfully adjust to their international positions. See Figure 15.8 to examine how these three factors must be aligned to ensure expatriate adjustment. In addition, training and development for both expatriates and their spouses can have a big impact.

## FIGURE 15.8

### EXPATRIATE ADJUSTMENT FACTORS

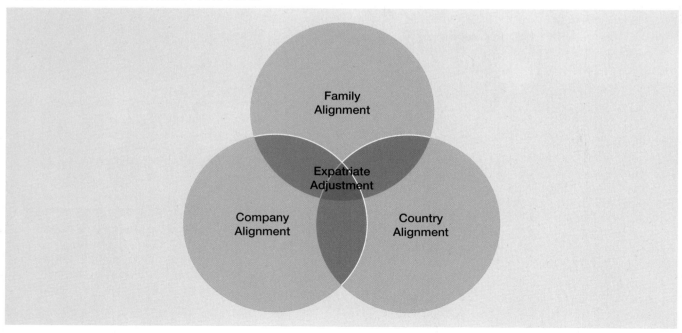

# TRAINING AND DEVELOPMENT

Although companies try to recruit and select the very best people to send abroad, once they are selected, it is often necessary to provide them with some type of training. This type of training is important not only for expatriate managers but also for the foreign employees they will ultimately supervise. For example, to know and understand how the Japanese or Chinese negotiate contracts or how businesspeople from Latin America view the enforcement of meeting times can help expatriate managers and their employees deal with each other more successfully. The biggest mistake managers can make is to assume that people are the same everywhere. Corporations that are serious about succeeding in global business are tackling these problems head-on by providing intensive training. At Motorola, this type of training is conducted at divisions worldwide by Motorola University, the company's educational arm. All employees, including division heads, receive 40 hours of training each year to learn, in part, how to work together as "Motorola People."[22]

Apart from developing talent for overseas assignments, most companies have found that good training programs also help them attract needed employees from the host countries. In less developed countries especially, individuals are quite eager to receive the training they need to improve their work skills. Increasingly, organizations such as the World Bank, ExxonMobil, and Petroleos de Venezuela are entering into partnerships with university executive education programs to customize the training experiences to the specific needs of expatriate managers and foreign nationals.

**OUTCOME 5**

## Using the Internet

The Outpost Expatriate Network is an online information centre for expatriates and their families:

**http://www.outpostexpat.nl**

## CONTENT OF TRAINING PROGRAMS

Lack of training is one of the principal causes of failure among employees working internationally. Those working internationally need to know as much as possible about (1) the country where they are going, (2) that country's culture, and (3) the history, values, and dynamics of their own organizations. Figure 15.9 gives an overview of what one needs to study for an international assignment. In many cases, the employee and his or her family can obtain a great deal of general information about the host country, including its culture, geography, social and political history, climate, and food, via the Internet, books, lectures, videotapes, and DVDs. The knowledge gained will at least help the participants have a better understanding of their assignments. Sensitivity training can also help expatriates overcome ethnic prejudices they might harbour. Expatriates can simulate a field experience in sensitivity training by visiting a nearby subculture in their native countries or by actually visiting the foreign country prior to relocating there.

**FIGURE 15.9**

PREPARING FOR AN INTERNATIONAL ASSIGNMENT

To prepare for an international assignment, individuals should become acquainted with the following aspects of the host country:

1. Social and business etiquette
2. History and folklore
3. Current affairs, including relations between the host country and Canada
4. Cultural values and priorities
5. Geography, especially its major cities
6. Sources of pride and great achievements of the culture
7. Religion and the role of religion in daily life
8. Political structure and current players
9. Practical matters such as currency, transportation, time zones, hours of business
10. The language

However, at least five essential elements of training and development programs prepare employees for working internationally: (1) language training, (2) cultural training, (3) assessing and tracking career development, (4) managing personal and family life, and (5) repatriation—a final, but critical, step.[23]

## Language Training

Communication with individuals who have a different language and a different cultural orientation is extremely difficult. Most executives agree that it is among the biggest problems for the foreign business traveller. Fortunately, for most Canadians, English is almost universally accepted as the primary language for international business. Particularly when many people from different countries are working together, English is usually the designated language for meetings and formal discourse. Many companies provide instruction in English for those who are required to use English in their jobs. Dow Chemical requires that all employees across the globe be fluent in English so that they can communicate more easily with one another. At Volkswagen's Shanghai operation, only after workers pass German language examinations do they become eligible for further training in Germany. Learning the language is only part of communicating in another culture, however. Even with an interpreter, much is missed.

## Cultural Training

Cross-cultural differences represent one of the most elusive aspects of international business, but if cultural training is successfully done, it tends to improve the satisfaction and success of expatriates and their employers. Brazilians tend to perceive North Americans as always in a hurry, serious, reserved, and methodical, whereas the Japanese view North Americans as relaxed, friendly, and impulsive. Why do these different perceptions exist, and how do they affect the way we do business across borders?

People's attitudes and behaviours are influenced, in large part, by the society in which they have received their education and training. Each culture has its expectations for the roles of managers and employees. On her first day on the job abroad, one expatriate manager recalls her boss ordering a bottle of wine to split between the two of them at lunch. Although this is a common practice in Britain, the expatriate manager was initially taken aback. Likewise, what one culture encourages as participative management, another might see as managerial incompetence. An American manager in Asia once complained that meetings held in his foreign place of employment accomplished nothing. He was used to arriving at a final decision during meetings. But to his Asian coworkers, meetings were solely a place in which to share ideas; decisions were to be made later.[24] Being successful depends on one's ability to understand the way things are normally done and to recognize that changes cannot be made abruptly without considerable resistance, and possibly antagonism, on the part of local nationals.

A wealth of data from cross-cultural studies reveal that nations tend to cluster according to similarities in certain cultural dimensions, such as work goals, values, needs, and job attitudes. Using data from eight comprehensive studies of cultural differences, Simcha Ronen and Oded Shenkar have grouped countries into the clusters shown in Figure 15.10.

Ronen and Shenkar point out that although evidence for the grouping of countries into Anglo, Germanic, Nordic, Latin European, and Latin American clusters appears to be quite strong, clusters encompassing the Far Eastern and Arab countries are ill defined and require further research, as do clusters of countries classified as independent. Many areas, such as Africa, have not been studied much at all. It should also be noted that the clusters presented in Figure 15.10 do not include Russia and the former satellites of the Soviet Union. Those countries, if added to the figure, would likely fall between the Near Eastern and Nordic categories. Studying cultural differences can help managers identify and

FIGURE 15.10

A SYNTHESIS OF COUNTRY CLUSTERS

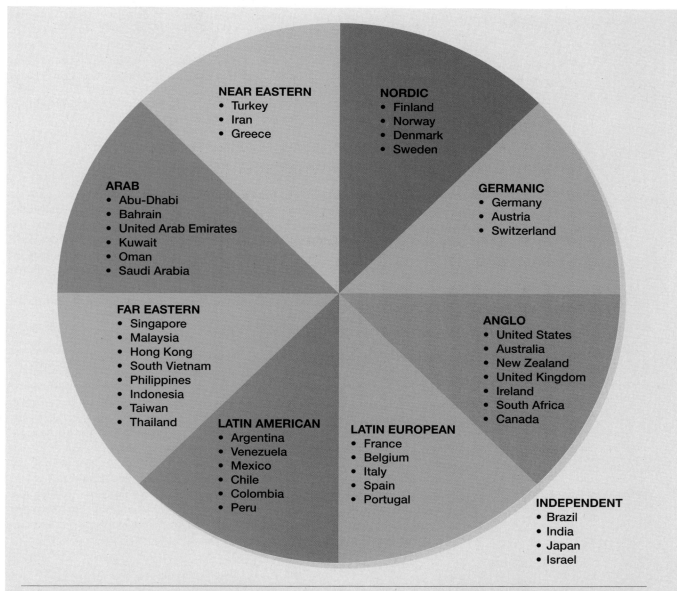

**NEAR EASTERN**
- Turkey
- Iran
- Greece

**NORDIC**
- Finland
- Norway
- Denmark
- Sweden

**ARAB**
- Abu-Dhabi
- Bahrain
- United Arab Emirates
- Kuwait
- Oman
- Saudi Arabia

**GERMANIC**
- Germany
- Austria
- Switzerland

**FAR EASTERN**
- Singapore
- Malaysia
- Hong Kong
- South Vietnam
- Philippines
- Indonesia
- Taiwan
- Thailand

**ANGLO**
- United States
- Australia
- New Zealand
- United Kingdom
- Ireland
- South Africa
- Canada

**LATIN AMERICAN**
- Argentina
- Venezuela
- Mexico
- Chile
- Colombia
- Peru

**LATIN EUROPEAN**
- France
- Belgium
- Italy
- Spain
- Portugal

**INDEPENDENT**
- Brazil
- India
- Japan
- Israel

**Source:** Simcha Ronen and Oded Shenkar, "Clustering Countries on Attitudinal Dimensions: A Review and Synthesis," *Academy of Management Review* 10, no. 3 (July 1985): 435–454. Copyright © 1985 by Academy of Management Review. Reproduced with permission of Academy of Management (NY) in the format Textbook via Copyright Clearance Center.

understand work attitudes and motivation in other cultures. When compared to the Japanese, for example, North Americans may feel little loyalty to their organizations. In Japan, employees are more likely to feel a strong loyalty to their company, although this may be changing. Japanese companies no longer universally guarantee an employee a job for life, and layoff decisions are increasingly being made based on merit, not seniority—a practice unthinkable in the country in the past. Latin Americans tend to view themselves as working not only for a particular company but also for an individual manager. Thus, managers in Latin American countries can encourage performance only by using personal influence and working through individual members of a group. In North America, competition has been the name of the game; in Japan, Taiwan, and other Asian countries, cooperation is more the underlying philosophy.[25]

**culture shock**
Perpetual stress experienced by people who settle overseas

One of the important dimensions of leadership, whether in international or domestic situations, is the degree to which managers invite employee participation in decision making. Alllthough it is difficult to find hard data on employee participation across different countries, careful observers report that Canadian managers are about in the middle on a continuum of autocratic to democratic decision-making styles. Scandinavian and Australian managers also appear to be in the middle. South American and European managers, especially those from France, Germany, and Italy, are toward the autocratic end of the continuum; Japanese managers are at the most participatory end. Because Far Eastern cultures and religions tend to emphasize harmony, group decision making predominates there.[26]

## Assessing and Tracking Career Development

International assignments provide some definite developmental and career advantages. For example, working abroad tends to increase a person's responsibilities and influence within the corporation. In addition, it provides a person with a set of experiences that are uniquely beneficial to both the individual and the firm. In this way, international assignments enhance a person's understanding of the global marketplace and offer the opportunity to work on a project important to the organization.[27]

To maximize the career benefits of a managerial assignment, a candidate should ask two key questions before accepting a foreign post:

1. Do the organization's senior executives view the firm's international business as a critical part of their operation? Research shows that expatriates with clear goals that truly need to be accomplished are likely to find their assignments more rewarding. Realizing this, fewer companies are sending expatriates abroad for career development purposes only.
2. Within top management, how many executives have a foreign-service assignment in their background, and do they feel it is important to have overseas experience? Colgate-Palmolive sees a foreign assignment as part of an extended career track rather than as a one-off assignment. A successful foreign assignment tends to lead to another and another. "Our top priority is to identify, develop, and retain the next two to three generations of leaders," said one Colgate-Palmolive manager. Part of that strategy includes directly using knowledge of the company's current and former expatriates.

## Managing Personal and Family Life

As noted previously, one of the most frequent causes of an employee's failure to complete an international assignment is personal and family stress. **Culture shock**—a disorientation that causes perpetual stress—is experienced by people who settle overseas for extended periods. The stress is caused by hundreds of jarring and disorienting incidents, such as being unable to communicate, having trouble getting the telephone to work, being unable to read the street signs, and a myriad of other everyday matters that are no problem at home. Soon minor frustrations become catastrophic events, and one feels helpless and drained, emotionally and physically.

In Chapter 5, we observed that more and more employers are assisting two-career couples in finding suitable employment in the same location. To accommodate dual-career partnerships, some employers are providing informal help finding jobs for the spouses of international transferees. However, other companies are establishing more formal programs to assist expatriate couples. These include career- and life-planning counselling, continuing education, intercompany networks to identify job openings in other companies, and job-hunting/fact-finding trips. In some cases, a company may even create a job for the spouse, although this is not widely practised. The available evidence suggests that although a spouse's career may create some problems initially, in the long run, it actually may help ease an expatriate's adjustment process.[28]

## Repatriation

An increasing number of companies are developing programs specifically designed to facilitate **repatriation**—that is, helping employees make the transition back home. Coming back is often difficult. An employee recently repatriated from Colombia walked outside his Edmonton office and waited for his driver, not remembering that he had driven his own car to work. Another family, repatriated from Kazakhstan, had to be restrained from purchasing all the fresh vegetables at the supermarket because in Kazakhstan, if there was fresh produce, you hoarded it because it might not be there next week. Repatriation programs are designed to prepare employees for adjusting to life at home (which at times can be more difficult than adjusting to a foreign assignment). ExxonMobil employees are given a general idea of what they can expect following a foreign assignment even before they leave home. Unfortunately, not all companies have career development programs designed for repatriating employees. Several studies have found that the majority of companies do not do an effective job of repatriation. Here are some general findings:

1. About 36 percent of Canadian companies have a repatriation plan.
2. Another one-third have programs to facilitate appropriate career positions on repatriation.
3. Over two-thirds provide career planning assistance toward the end of assignment, whereas 8 percent provide this assistance after repatriation.
4. About one-fifth of companies start planning for repatriation even before the candidate leaves.[29]

Employees often lament that their organizations are vague about repatriation, their new roles within the company, and their career progression. In many cases, employees abroad have learned how to run an entire international operation—or at least significant parts of it. When they return home, however, their responsibilities are often significantly diminished. In fact, the evidence suggests that only a fraction of them are promoted. It is also not uncommon for employees to return home after a few years to find that there is no position for them in the firm and that they no longer know anyone who can help them—their long-time colleagues have moved to different departments or even different companies. This frequently leaves the repatriated employee feeling alienated.

Even when employees are successfully repatriated, their companies often do not fully utilize the knowledge, understanding, and skills developed on their assignments. This hurts the employee, of course, but it also hurts the firm's chances of utilizing the employee's expertise to gain a competitive advantage. Not surprisingly, expatriates frequently leave their companies within a year or two of coming home. Some experts say that the number of expatriates who do so is as high as 50 percent.

At companies with good repatriation processes, employees are given guidance about how much the expatriate experience may have changed them and their families. Some firms introduce former expatriates and their spouses to other former expatriates at special social events. And more companies are making an effort to keep in touch with expatriates while they are abroad, which has been made easier by email, instant messaging, and videoconferencing. Colgate-Palmolive's division executives and other corporate staff members frequently visit international transferees. Dow appoints a high-level manager who serves as a home-country contact for information about organizational changes, job opportunities, and anything related to salary and compensation. Monsanto's repatriation program is designed not only to smooth the employee's return to the home organization but also to ensure that the expatriate's knowledge and experience are fully utilized. To do so, returning expatriates get the chance to showcase their new knowledge in debriefing sessions. Some companies also create databases of expatriates to help other employees who go abroad later.[30] A repatriation checklist is shown in Highlights in HRM 15.4.

# HIGHLIGHTS IN HRM 15.4

## Repatriation Checklist

Before they go:

- Make sure there is a clear need for the international assignment. Do not send someone abroad unnecessarily. Develop a clear set of objectives and expectations and time frames in which they should be met.

- Make sure that your selection procedures are valid. Select the employee and look at and involve the employee's family.

- Provide (or fund) language and cultural training for the employee and the employee's family.

- Offer counselling and career assistance for the spouse.

- Establish career-planning systems that reward international assignments and lead to promotion and knowledge sharing.

While they are away:

- Jointly establish a developmental plan that focuses on the goal to be achieved.

- Tie performance objectives to the achievement of the goal.

- Identify mentors who can be a liaison and support person from home.

- Keep communications open so that the expatriate is aware of job openings and opportunities.

- Arrange for frequent visits back home (for the employee and the family). Make certain they do not lose touch with friends and relatives.

When they come back home:

- Throw a "welcome home" party and arrange for a meeting with other former expatriates.

- Offer counselling to ease the transition.

- Arrange conferences and presentations to make certain that knowledge and skills acquired away from home are identified and disseminated.

- Set up an expatriate database to help other employees who go abroad later.

- Get feedback from the employee and the family about how well the organization handled the repatriation process.

Sources: Adapted from Bennet & Associates, Price Waterhouse, and Charlene Marmer Solomon, "Repatriation Planning Checklist," *Personnel Journal* 14, no. 1 (January 1995): 32; Charlene Marmer Solomon, "Global HR: Repatriation Planning," *Workforce* 2001, special supplement: 22–23.

## COMPENSATION

OUTCOME 6

One of the most complex areas of international HRM is compensation. Different countries have different norms for employee compensation. For North Americans, although nonfinancial incentives such as prestige, independence, and influence may be motivators, money is likely to be the driving force. Other cultures are more likely to emphasize respect, family, job security, a satisfying personal life, social acceptance, advancement, or power. Since there are many alternatives to money, the rule is to match the reward with the values of the culture. In individualistic cultures, such as Canada, pay plans often focus on individual performance and achievement. However, in collectively oriented cultures such as Japan and Taiwan, pay plans focus more on internal equity and personal needs.[31]

In general, a guiding philosophy for designing pay systems might be "think globally and act locally." That is, executives should normally try to create a pay plan that supports the overall strategic intent of the organization but provides enough flexibility to customize particular policies and programs to meet the needs of employees in specific locations. After a brief discussion of compensation practices for host-country employees and managers, we will focus on the problems of compensating expatriates.

### COMPENSATION OF HOST-COUNTRY EMPLOYEES

As shown in Figure 15.11, hourly wages vary dramatically from country to country, from more than $50 on average in Norway to a few dollars in developing

## FIGURE 15.11

HOURLY WAGES IN DIFFERENT COUNTRIES

| Hourly Compensation Costs* in U.S. Dollars | | |
|---|---|---|
| Country or Area | 1997 | 2009 |
| Norway | 26.97 | 53.89 |
| Denmark | 24.64 | 49.56 |
| Belgium | 28.23 | 49.40 |
| Austria | 27.38 | 48.04 |
| Germany | 29.26 | 46.52 |
| Switzerland | 28.33 | 44.29 |
| Finland | 22.17 | 43.77 |
| Netherlands | 23.44 | 43.50 |
| France | 24.99 | 40.08 |
| Sweden | 25.11 | 39.87 |
| Ireland | 17.15 | 39.02 |
| Italy | 19.67 | 34.97 |
| Australia | 19.12 | 34.62 |
| United States | 22.67 | 33.53 |
| United Kingdom | 18.24 | 30.78 |
| Japan | 22.28 | 30.36 |
| Canada | 18.89 | 29.60 |
| Spain | 13.91 | 27.74 |
| Greece | NA | 19.23 |
| Israel | 12.32 | 18.39 |
| Singapore | 12.15 | 17.50 |
| New Zealand | 12.37 | 17.44 |
| Korea, Republic of | 9.42 | 14.20 |
| Portugal | 6.38 | 11.95 |
| Slovakia | 2.86 | 11.24 |
| Czech Republic | 3.24 | 11.21 |
| Argentina | 7.43 | 10.14 |
| Estonia | NA | 9.83 |
| Hungary | 3.05 | 8.62 |
| Brazil | 7.11 | 8.32 |
| Taiwan | 7.04 | 7.76 |
| Poland | 3.13 | 7.50 |
| Mexico | 3.30 | 5.38 |
| Philippines | 1.14 | 1.50 |

NA = data not available.

*Hourly compensation costs in U.S. dollars for production workers in manufacturing.

**Source:** U.S. Department of Labor, Bureau of Labor Statistics, May 2011.

**global compensation system**
A centralized pay system whereby host-country employees are offered a full range of training programs, benefits, and pay comparable to those of a firm's domestic employees but adjusted for local differences

countries. Host-country employees are generally paid on the basis of productivity, time spent on the job, or a combination of these factors. In industrialized countries, pay is generally by the hour; in developing countries, pay is by the day. The piece-rate method is quite common. In some countries, including Japan, seniority is an important element in determining employees' pay rates. When companies commence operations in a foreign country, they usually set their wage rates at or slightly higher than the prevailing wage for local companies. Eventually, however, they are urged by other businesses, government, or even headquarters to reduce costs to conform to local practices to avoid "upsetting" local compensation practices. In Italy, Japan, and some other countries, it is customary to add semiannual or annual lump-sum payments equal to one or two months' pay. These payments are not considered profit sharing but an integral part of the basic pay package. Profit sharing is legally required for certain categories of industry in Mexico, Peru, Pakistan, India, and Egypt among the developing countries and in France among the industrialized countries. Compensation patterns in Eastern Europe are in flux as these countries make the adjustment to more capitalistic systems.

Employee benefits can range dramatically from country to country as well. In France, for example, benefits are about 70 percent, compared to around 30 percent in Canada. Whereas in North America, most benefits are awarded to employees by employers, in other industrialized countries, most of them are legislated or ordered by governments. Some of these plans are changing. Defined contribution plans are on the rise, sex equality is becoming important, and stock ownership is being tried.[32]

Because the largest cost for most companies is labour, it plays a primary role in international HR decision making. However, some people believe that companies are overcapitalizing on worldwide compensation differences. Many firms (Nike included) have generated bad press for charging hundreds of dollars for their individual products while the people who make them—sometimes children in developing countries working under terrible conditions—earn only a few cents. This has led to international political protests and pressure on firms to exercise greater global social responsibility. As Nike discovered, it is pressure companies cannot afford not to take seriously. Starbucks clearly takes good corporate citizenship seriously. Among Starbucks' many initiatives is its association with Fair Trade and Conservation International to help farmers in developing countries get a premium for the coffee they grow. We will discuss more on the fair treatment of workers in developing countries toward the end of the chapter.

## COMPENSATION OF HOST-COUNTRY MANAGERS

In the past, remuneration of host-country managers has been ruled by local salary levels. Today, however, more companies are offering their host-country employees a full range of training programs, benefits, and pay comparable to those of their domestic employees in the country of origin but adjusted for local differences. These programs are known as **global compensation systems**. Among other benefits, the agricultural processing firm Archer Daniels Midland offers its employees abroad an employee assistance program. At first, many employees were suspicious about the program, believing that it was designed to collect private information about them. However, after employees became confident that their information was confidential, the program sent a message that the company is interested in their well-being and values them.

According to a survey by the HR consulting firm Watson Wyatt, companies are split evenly as to whether they have central (global) compensation systems or decentralized (local) systems. Companies with centralized systems report having higher effectiveness and satisfaction levels with their compensation systems, and more companies are saying that they are moving toward centralized systems. Unilever, for example, used to leave the compensation arrangements largely to the boss of a region or a big country. Now brand managers in different countries increasingly compare notes, so they see potential discrepancies based on market differences and expatriate assignments. So the company moved from a narrow grading structure to five global work levels.[33]

# COMPENSATION OF EXPATRIATE MANAGERS

If the assignment is going to be successful, the expatriate's compensation plan must be competitive, cost-effective, motivating, fair, easy to understand, consistent with international financial management, relatively easy to administer, and simple to communicate. To be effective, an international compensation program must do the following

1. Provide an incentive to leave Canada.
2. Allow for maintaining a North American standard of living.
3. Provide for security in countries that are politically unstable or present personal dangers.
4. Include provisions for good health care.
5. Take into account the foreign taxes the employee is likely to have to pay (in addition to domestic taxes) and help him or her with tax forms and filing.
6. Provide for the education of the employee's children abroad, if necessary.
7. Allow for maintaining relationships with family, friends, and business associates via trips home and other communication technologies.
8. Facilitate reentry home.
9. Be in writing.[34]

For short-term assignments, usually those that are project based, expatriates are frequently given per diem (per day) compensation. These managers might reside in hotels and service apartments instead of leasing houses. They are also less likely to bring their family members with them. The assignment becomes more like a commuting assignment in which the expatriate spends the week in the host country and returns home on the weekend.

For longer-term assignments, there are two basic types of compensation systems. The first is **home-based pay**, based on the **balance-sheet approach**, a system designed to equalize the purchasing power of employees at comparable positions living overseas and in the home country and to provide incentives to offset qualitative differences between assignment locations.[35] The balance-sheet approach generally comprises the following steps:

*Step 1: Calculate base pay.* Begin with the home-based gross income, including bonuses. Deduct taxes and pension contributions.

*Step 2: Figure cost-of-living adjustment (COLA).* Add a cost-of-living adjustment to the base pay. Typically, companies do not subtract when the international assignment has a lower cost of living. Instead, they allow the expatriate to benefit from the negative differential. Often a housing allowance is added in here as well.

*Step 3: Add incentive premiums.* General mobility premiums and hardship premiums compensate expatriates for separation from family, friends, and domestic support systems, usually 15 percent of base salary, although in recent years, some companies have reduced this amount. Sometimes incentive premiums are paid for hazardous duty or harsh conditions the expatriate might experience while abroad.

*Step 4: Add assistance programs.* These additions are often used to cover added costs such as moving and storage, automobile, and education expenses.

The differences in compensation paid to those working overseas are intended to correct for the higher costs of overseas goods and services so that in relation to their domestic peers, expatriates neither gain purchasing power nor lose it. A myriad of calculations are required to arrive at a total differential figure, but, in general, as we have said, the cost typically runs between three and five times the home-country salary. Fortunately, employers do not have to do extensive research to find comparative data. They typically rely on data published quarterly by federal government departments, such as External Affairs, for use in establishing allowances to compensate civilian employees for costs and hardships related to assignments abroad. Alternately, they consult international relocation experts to make sure all of the relocation bases are covered. For example, in some countries, expatriates are mandated by local law to participate in host-country programs—whether or not their pay packages are home or host based.[36]

**home-based pay**
Pay based on an expatriate's home country's compensation practices

**balance-sheet approach**
A compensation system designed to match the purchasing power in a person's home country

**host-based pay**
Expatriate pay comparable to that earned by employees in a host country

**localization**
Adapting pay and other compensation benefits to match that of a particular country

**split pay**
A system whereby expatriates are given a portion of their pay in the local currency to cover their day-to-day expenses and a portion of their pay in their home currency to safeguard their earnings from changes in inflation or foreign exchange rates

The second type of compensation system is host-based pay. Companies are under pressure to move expatriates to host-based pay because it is generally less costly. Host-based pay is compensation that is equivalent to that earned by employees in the country where the expatriate is assigned. This process is called localization. When an employee is localized, his or her compensation is set on par with local standards and practices. Incentive premiums are generally phased out, and the employee pays only local taxes and falls under the social benefit programs established by the government of the host country. Some companies localize only certain aspects of the pay package or do so gradually over a course of three to five years.

Usually, the decision to localize an employee depends on whether he or she will ultimately remain abroad or return home. In many companies, the decision depends on whether the employee or the employer is the driving force behind the localization. An expatriate employee with a strong desire to remain in the host country beyond the planned length of assignment (perhaps because he or she married a local or has simply fallen in love with the country) is likely to be more amenable to localization. Localization should not be viewed as a cost-saving panacea, however. There are many countries in which expatriates would refuse to "go local." Forcing an employee to do so can ultimately result in a failed assignment, costing the company much more money than it would have saved by localizing him or her.

Recently, split-pay plans have become popular among companies. Under a split-pay system, expatriates are given a portion of their pay in the local currency to cover their day-to-day expenses. The rest of their pay is distributed in their home currency to safeguard their earnings should changes in foreign exchange rates or inflation adversely affect their pay.

Another serious issue related to expatriate compensation is medical care. Employees are unlikely to consent to go abroad if they cannot get health care comparable to what is available in their home countries. Often Canadian-based plans cannot cover expatriate employees or efficiently deal with claims that need to be reimbursed in foreign currency. One solution is to transfer the employee to a global employment company that can provide these types of benefits. Basically, the employee is transferred to the global employment company, which administers all of his or her benefits as well as those of numerous employees working for other companies. Still another issue is the need to provide expatriates and employees who travel abroad with security. Citigroup hires private drivers for employees doing business in countries such as Mexico—even for employees on extended stays. Companies can also purchase travel-related insurance covering a range of services, such as evacuation and disability or travel-related injuries.[37] HR managers are generally responsible for evaluating and implementing these different types of programs.

# PERFORMANCE APPRAISAL

**OUTCOME 7**

As we noted earlier, individuals frequently accept international assignments because they know that they can acquire skills and experiences that will make them more valuable to their companies. Frequently, however, it can be difficult for the home office to evaluate the performance of employees working abroad. Even the notion of performance evaluation is indicative of a North American management style that focuses on the individual, which can cause problems in Asian countries such as China, Japan, and Korea and Eastern European countries such as Hungary and the Czech Republic. Performance appraisal problems can contribute to failure rates among expatriates and derail an individual's career rather than enhance it.[38]

## WHO SHOULD APPRAISE PERFORMANCE?

In many cases, an individual working internationally has at least two allegiances: one to his or her home country (the office that made the assignment) and the other to the host country in which the employee is currently working. Superiors in each location frequently have different information about the employee's performance and may also have very different expectations about what constitutes good performance. For these reasons, the multiple rater (360-degree) appraisal discussed in Chapter 8 is gaining favour among global firms. There are exceptions, however. Thai workers do not see it as their business to evaluate their bosses, and Thai managers do not think subordinates are in any way qualified to assess them. Before implementing a different appraisal process, HR managers need to understand how the process is likely to be received in the host country.[39]

## HOME- VERSUS HOST-COUNTRY EVALUATIONS

Domestic managers are frequently unable to understand expatriate experiences, value them, or accurately measure their contribution to the organization. Geographic distances create communication problems for expatriates and home-country managers, although email, instant messaging, and other HR information systems technologies have begun to help close the gap.[40] Still, local managers with daily contact with the expatriate are more likely to have an accurate picture of his or her performance. Host-country evaluations can sometimes be problematic, however. First, local cultures may influence one's perception of how well an individual is performing. As noted earlier in the chapter, participative decision making may be viewed either positively or negatively, depending on the culture. Such cultural biases may not have any bearing on an individual's true level of effectiveness. In addition, local managers sometimes do not have enough of a perspective on the entire organization to know how well an individual is contributing to the firm as a whole.

Given the pros and cons of home-country and host-country evaluations, most observers agree that performance evaluations should try to balance the two sources of appraisal information. Although host-country employees are in a good position to view day-to-day activities, in many cases, the individual is still formally tied to the home office. Promotions, pay, and other administrative decisions are connected there, and, as a consequence, the written evaluation is usually handled by the home-country manager. Nevertheless, the appraisal should be completed only after vital input has been gained from the host-country manager. As discussed in Chapter 8, multiple sources of appraisal information can be extremely valuable for providing independent points of view—especially if someone is working as part of a team. If there is much concern about cultural bias, it may be possible to have people of the same nationality as the expatriate conduct the appraisal.

## PERFORMANCE CRITERIA

Because expatriate assignments are so costly, many HR managers are increasingly under pressure to calculate the return on investment (ROI) of these assignments. What did the firm get for the million dollars it spent to send an expatriate abroad? Has the expatriate achieved the goals set forth in the assignment in the appropriate time frame? Obviously, the goals and responsibilities inherent in the job assignment are among the most important criteria used to evaluate an individual's performance, and different goals necessitate measuring different criteria. The criteria are tied to the various reasons employees were sent abroad in the first place—whether the goal was to transfer technical skills or best practices, improve a division's financial performance, or develop managerial talent.[41] The Business Case outlines the costs of employee expatriates and initiatives companies can undertake to improve ROI.

There are five steps related to calculating the ROI of an assignment:

1. Defining the assignment's objectives
2. Agreeing on the quantifiable measurements for the assignment
3. Developing an equation that converts qualitative behaviour into quantifiable measurements

4. Evaluating the expatriate's performance against these measurements
5. Calculating the ROI, which can be a complex cost accounting or a simple calculation to see whether the expatriate covered the cost of keeping him or her on assignment.

The danger with ROI calculations, however, is that there is a temptation to resort to using "easy" criteria such as productivity, profits, and market share to measure an expatriate's performance. These criteria may be valid, but they are still deficient if they do not capture the full range of an expatriate's responsibility. Other, more subtle factors should be considered as well. Leadership development, for example, involves a much longer-term value proposition. In many cases, an expatriate is an ambassador for the company, and a significant part of the job is cultivating relationships with citizens of the host country. As we discussed at the beginning of this chapter, an individual's success or failure is affected by a host

# THE BUSINESS CASE

## The Costs of Employing Expatriates

Organizations typically make selection decisions on the basis of a match between job requirements and the candidates' skills and abilities. But selection decisions in international assignments must always compare the costs of employing locals versus expatriates. The chart below compares the cost of employing a Canadian manager in the United Kingdom to employing a U.K. manager. The case involves a manager, based in Ontario, who earns about $85,000 a year, with a $17,000 bonus, who is to be sent on a three-and-a-half-year assignment to London, England. He is married, with one school-age child who attends private school. This manager receives an automobile allowance and a trip home every year. The company pays for the relocation, household goods storage, and tax return preparations.

Total cost of assignment for 3.5 years:

| Cost Element | $ |
| --- | --- |
| Base salary | 297,500 |
| Bonus | 59,500 |
| Gross income | 357,000 |
| Cost of living allowance | 92,800 |
| Housing allowance | 135,000 |
| Education allowance | 61,500 |
| Automobile allowance | 55,300 |
| Home leaves | 32,400 |
| Relocation, storage, and tax return | 76,300 |
| Additional tax expenses | 175,500 |
| **Total Cost** | **$985,800** |

The costs of sending this manager on an international assignment are nearly a million dollars, compared to the approximately $300,000 it would cost to employ a U.K.-based manager.

Below is a list of initiatives that would improve the ROI of expatriates:

| | |
| --- | --- |
| Better candidate selection | 32% |
| Career-planning skills | 26% |
| Communicating objectives | 24% |
| Assignment preparation | 20% |
| Monitoring program | 17% |
| Cross-cultural training | 10% |
| Developing or expanding intranet | 7% |
| Communication/recognition | 6% |
| Web-based cultural training | 5% |
| Mandating destination support | 4% |
| Other | 17% |

However, the best way to mitigate the costs of international assignments is to make them short-term assignments of 3 to 12 months. The advantages of short-term assignments include lower risk of failure, lower costs, less family disruption, greater ability to set short-term goals, and greater probability that women will accept these assignments.

Sources: L. Dixon and M. Simm, "Short term assignments growing in popularity," *Canadian HR Reporter*, 21, 5, March 10, 2008, P. 7; Andrea Poe, "Selection Savvy," *HR Magazine* 47, no. 4 (April 2002): 77–83; Jeff Bitten, "Compensation Strategies for International Assignments," *Canadian HR Professional* 18, no. 2 (April/May 2001): 29–31.

of technical and personal factors. For example, as one might guess, it is much easier to adjust to similar cultures than to dissimilar ones. A Canadian can usually travel to the United Kingdom or Australia and work with locals almost immediately. Send that same individual to Hungary or Malaysia, and the learning curve is steeper. Moreover, the expatriate's adjustment period may be even longer if the company has not yet established a good base of operations in the region. The first individuals transferred to a country have no one to show them the ropes or to explain local customs. Even relatively simple activities, such as navigating the transit system, can prove to be problematic. The U.S. State Department has developed rating systems that attempt to distinguish the different degrees of difficulty associated with different regional assignments. These difficulty factors need to be considered and built into the appraisal system.[42]

## PROVIDING FEEDBACK

Performance feedback in an international setting is clearly a two-way street. Although the home-country and host-country superiors may tell an expatriate how well he or she is doing, it is also important for expatriates to provide feedback regarding the support they are receiving, the obstacles they face, and the suggestions they have about the assignment. More than in almost any other job situation, expatriates are in the best position to evaluate their own performance.

In addition to ongoing feedback, an expatriate should have a debriefing interview immediately on returning home from an international assignment. These repatriation interviews serve several purposes:

1. They help expatriates reestablish old ties with the home organization and may prove to be important for setting new career paths.
2. The interview can address technical issues related to the job assignment itself.
3. The interview may address general issues regarding the company's overseas commitments, such as how relationships between the home and host countries should be handled.
4. The interview can be very useful for documenting insights an individual has about the region. These insights can then be incorporated into training programs for future expatriates. However, if the learning is not shared, then each new expatriate to a region may have to go through the same cycle of adjustment.[43]

## THE LABOUR ENVIRONMENT WORLDWIDE

A country's labour environment plays a large role in international business and HR decisions. As we have said, wages and benefits vary dramatically across the world, as do safety, child labour, and other legal regulations. Indeed in many countries, working conditions resemble slave labour camps, as outlined in Highlights in HRM 15.5. In many countries, the state's regulation of labour contracts is profound and extensive. Labour unions around the world differ significantly as well. Differences exist not only in the collective bargaining process but also in the political-legal conditions. For example, the EU prohibits discrimination against workers in unions, but in many other countries, including countries in Central America and Asia, labour unions are illegal. China has only one union, the All-China Federation of Trade Unions, an 80-year-old Communist Party institution that for decades has aligned itself more closely with management than workers. In some countries, only workers at larger firms are allowed to organize.[44]

Union strength depends on many factors, such as the level of employee participation, per capita labour income, mobility between management and labour, homogeneity of labour (racial, religious, social class), and unemployment levels. These and other factors determine how well a union will be able to represent labour effectively. Nearly all of Sweden's workers are organized, giving the unions in this country considerable strength and autonomy. By contrast, in countries with

| OUTCOME 8

# HIGHLIGHTS IN HRM 15.5

## Dirty List

The Government of Brazil has established a "dirty list" of employers who subject their workers to slavelike conditions. These include cases where an employee works exhausting hours (no breaks, no days off), is forbidden to leave the company because of a debt, and earns less than the minimum wage of $336. In 2012, 300 employers were on the list, mainly in rural areas, where sugar cane and other crops are grown. The dirty list has the power to stop this abuse. Until employers stop treating employees as slaves, as documented by government inspectors, they will not be able to obtain credit from financial institutions or governments. Previously, employers did not care about the fines, but they do care about access to credit. To be removed from the list, the employer must pay fines and unpaid labour taxes, as well as meet labour standards.

Canada also has a dirty list of employers, which can be found at http://www.yorku.ca/ddoorey/lawblog/?page_id=4176. David Doorey's list is taken from the Ontario government's Sunshine List of Bad Employers. These are employers who are in violation of the *Employment Standards Act*.

Source: S. Lehman, "Brazil employers accused of slave-like conditions" *Associated Press*, January 30, 2012. http://www.businessweek.com/ap/financialnews/D9S1HU600.htm

relatively high unemployment, low pay levels, and no union funds with which to support social welfare systems, unions are driven into alliance with other organizations: political party, church, or government. This is in marked contrast to Canada, where the union selected by the majority of employees bargains only with the employer, not with other institutions. By contrast, the unions in many European countries (such as Sweden) have a great deal of political power and are often allied with a particular political party. When employers in these countries deal with unions, they are, in effect, dealing indirectly with governments.

In a number of countries, however, including Japan, Germany, New Zealand, and the United Kingdom, unions have been losing some of their power. Ironically, the power of the unions to gain high wages and enforce rigid labour rules has been blamed for hurting competitiveness, particularly in European countries. Laws make it difficult to fire European employees, so workers are hired only sparingly. Unemployment benefits are very generous, so people tend to remain unemployed for longer rather than seek work. But because companies are increasingly tempted to offshore jobs to lower labour-cost countries, unionized workers are beginning to make more concessions. For example, at Bosch in France, union bosses opposed management's plan to lengthen the workweek. But fearful workers overruled the union bosses, voting instead for the longer workweek.[45] As the power of unions declines, the trend has been to demand compensation in other ways—through benefits or through greater participation in company decision making. Various approaches to participation will be discussed later.

## COLLECTIVE BARGAINING IN OTHER COUNTRIES

We saw in Chapter 14 how the collective bargaining process is typically carried out in companies operating in Canada. When we look at other countries, we find that the process can vary widely, especially with regard to the role of government. Collective bargaining can take place at the firm, local, or national level. In Australia and New Zealand, for most of the 20th century, labour courts had the authority to impose wages and other employment conditions on a broad range of firms (many of which were not even privy to the suits brought before the courts). In the United Kingdom and France, the government intervenes in all aspects of collective bargaining. Government involvement is only natural where parts of industry are nationalized. Also, in countries with heavy nationalization, government involvement is more likely to be accepted, even in the nonnationalized companies. At Renault, the French government–owned automobile manufacturer, unions use political pressures in their bargaining with managers, who are essentially government employees. The resulting agreements then set the standards for other firms. This is true in spite of the fact that union membership rates in France have declined dramatically since the 1970s. In developing countries, governments commonly have representatives present during bargaining sessions to ensure that unions with relatively uneducated leaders are not disadvantaged in bargaining with skilled management representatives. Still, in these countries, a union may do little more than attempt to increase wages and leave the rest of the employment contract unchanged. In more developed countries, goals related to other aspects of the employment relationship, such as workweek lengths, safety requirements, and grievance procedures, are more likely to be pursued.

## INTERNATIONAL LABOUR ORGANIZATIONS

The most active international union organization has been the International Confederation of Free Trade Unions (ICFTU), which has its headquarters in Brussels. The ICFTU is a confederation of 311 national trade union groups representing 175 million trade union members in 155 countries and territories. Cooperating with the ICFTU are numerous International Trade Secretariats (ITSs), which are international federations of national trade unions operating in the same or related industries. In addition to the ITSs, the ICFTU also cooperates with the European Trade Union Confederation (ETUC). The ETUC represents 60 million trade unionists from 82 trade unions in 36 Western, Central, and Eastern European countries. Another active and influential organization is the International Labour Organization (ILO), a specialized agency of the United Nations created in 1919. The ILO perhaps has had the greatest impact on the rights of workers throughout the world. It promotes the rights of workers to organize, the eradication of forced and child labour, and the elimination of discrimination. Over the decades, 182 countries have voluntarily committed to nearly 200 international conventions proposed by the ILO. The organization has been effective because it involves nation-states as well as workers and their employers. In recent years, the ILO has redefined its mission based on the "Decent Work Agenda." The Decent Work Agenda promotes the idea that there is an ethical dimension of work. This ethical dimension includes decent homes, food, education, the right to organize, and social programs to protect workers when they are elderly, disabled, or unemployed. Moreover, the agenda pertains to workers worldwide, including the self-employed—a situation common in agricultural-based, developing countries. Given the fact that half of the world's population lives on $2 a day or less, that 250 million children around the world are forced to work, and that only 20 percent of people globally are covered by any sort of social insurance programs, these are worthy goals. Some companies, however, oppose the decent pay initiative, believing that it promotes unionization.[46]

## LABOUR PARTICIPATION IN MANAGEMENT

In many European countries, provisions for employee representation are established by law. An employer may be legally required to provide for employee representation on safety and hygiene committees, worker councils, or even boards of directors. Although their responsibilities vary from country to country, worker councils basically provide a communication channel between employers and workers. The legal codes that set forth the functions of worker councils in France are very detailed. Councils are generally concerned with grievances, problems of individual employees, internal regulations, and matters affecting employee welfare.

**codetermination**
Representation of labour on the board of directors of a company

A higher form of worker participation in management is found in Germany, where representation of labour on the board of directors of a company is required by law. This arrangement is known as **codetermination** and often by its German word, *Mitbestimmung*. Although sometimes puzzling to outsiders, the system is fairly simple. Company shareholders and employees are required to be represented in equal numbers on the supervisory boards of large corporations. Power is generally left with the shareholders, and shareholders are generally assured the chairmanship. Other European countries and Japan either have or are considering minority board participation.[47]

Each of these differences makes managing HR in an international context more challenging. But the crux of the issue in designing HR systems is not choosing one approach that will meet all the demands of international business. Instead, organizations facing global competition must balance multiple approaches and make their policies flexible enough to accommodate differences across national borders. Throughout this book, we have noted that different situations call for different approaches to managing people, and nowhere is this point more evident than in international HRM.

# SMALL BUSINESS APPLICATION

At first glance, one might question whether international HRM applies to small business. Certainly, from the standpoint of sending expatriates from a home country to a host country with expatriate allowances and incentives, such practices are unlikely to find their way into small companies. However, international work, whether producing goods or products in one country and selling them in another, is as likely to be embraced by small businesses as by large companies. In fact, recognizing that small business is by its nature more likely to be responsible for only portions of a supply chain, with other suppliers and partners involved, it may be that small companies are more likely to be involved in international business, which may involve dimensions of international work. Accordingly, small business owners must learn to support staff requirements in this international context.

Small businesses support international work requirements through visa compliance, supplier relations, partnership, global delivery, and tariffs and exchange rates. Let us exemplify this through the review of a sporting goods distributor and manufacturer. This company has 30 employees responsible for the distribution of goods across Canada. The products they distribute are manufactured in China and in Europe. As such, on occasion, some staff need to travel to China or Europe and require visitor or work visas depending on the nature of their visit. Employees in this business regularly work with international suppliers. The company also partners with Chinese manufacturers to produce goods abroad for sale in Canada.

This company has some clients whose orders are so large that an entire order is manufactured, packaged, and shipped directly from offshore to the customer, without ever being received in the home country. Finally, with this much international trade, the impact of tariffs, shipping costs, and exchange rates can make the difference between profit and loss.

So how does this company address international HRM? Each employee who is involved in the international supply chain must learn to work with the complexities of international business. This includes business travel into regions with different language, culture, and legal systems, requiring preparation and training to deal with these complexities. This also includes working within a framework of global delivery and the confines of time zone differences that, on occasion, require participating in evening conference calls to accommodate business hours in China. International HRM also involves managing the volatile fluctuations of currency exchange in the timing of ordering, pricing, and paying for goods, as well as adapting business practices to accommodate different business styles in different countries. These adaptations create challenges for employees. However, once employees learn to be interested in and sensitive to the legal, cultural, and language differences in working across geographic boundaries, they quickly appreciate that the world is very small, with people being able to seamlessly collaborate with people around the globe. In this company, the international nature of the business makes the company an interesting place for employees.

# SUMMARY

**OUTCOME 1** Economic, political, and cultural factors in different parts of the world influence the need for global integration of HR practices and the need for local adaptation. These competing forces create a tension for HR managers. The tension is found in how to manage people in a way that complies with cultural and political-legal norms while at the same time taking advantage of globally standardized practices.

**OUTCOME 2** There are four basic ways to organize for global competition: (1) the international corporation is essentially a domestic firm that has leveraged its existing capabilities to penetrate overseas markets; (2) the multinational corporation has fully autonomous units operating in multiple countries to address local issues; (3) the global corporation has a world view but controls all international operations from its home office; and (4) the transnational corporation uses a network structure to balance global and local concerns.

**OUTCOME 3** International HRM places greater emphasis on a number of responsibilities and functions such as relocation, orientation, and translation services to help employees adapt to a new and different environment outside their own country.

**OUTCOME 4** Many factors must be considered in the selection and development of employees. Although hiring host-country nationals or third-country nationals automatically avoids many potential problems, expatriates are preferable, but more costly, in some circumstances. When expatriates are hired, most companies try to minimize their stay. Operations are handed off to host-country nationals as soon as possible.

**OUTCOME 5** Once an expatriate is selected, an intensive training and development program is essential to qualify that person and his or her spouse for the assignment. Wherever possible, development should extend beyond information and orientation training to include sensitivity training and field experiences that will enable the manager to understand cultural differences better. Those in charge of the international program should provide the help needed to protect managers from career development risks, reentry problems, and culture shock. Email, instant messaging, and videoconferencing are making it easier for companies to stay in touch with their expatriates.

**OUTCOME 6** Compensation systems should support the overall strategic intent of the organization but be customized for local conditions. Compensation plans must give expatriates an incentive to leave Canada; meet their standard-of-living, health care, and safety needs; provide for the education of their children, if necessary; and facilitate repatriation.

**OUTCOME 7** Although home-country managers frequently have formal responsibility for appraising individuals on foreign assignments, they may not be able to fully understand expatriate experiences because geographic distances pose communication problems. Host-country managers may be in the best position to observe day-to-day performance but may be biased by cultural factors and may not have a view of the organization as a whole. To balance the pros and cons of home-country and host-country evaluations, one option is performance evaluations that combine the two sources of appraisal information.

**OUTCOME 8** In many European countries—Germany, for one—employee representation is established by law. Organizations typically negotiate the agreement with the union at a national level, frequently with government intervention. In other countries, union activity is prohibited or limited to only large companies. European unions have much more political power than many other unions around the world, although their power has declined somewhat, due to globalization forces. The ICFTU, the ETUC, and the ILO are among the major worldwide organizations endeavouring to improve the conditions of workers.

## KEY TERMS

augmented skills, 526
balance-sheet approach, 537
codetermination, 544
core skills, 526
cultural environment, 514
culture shock, 532
expatriates, or home-country nationals, 518
failure rate, 527

global compensation system, 536
global corporation, 517
global manager, 525
guest workers, 522
home-based pay, 537
host-based pay, 538
host country, 514
host-country nationals, 518
international corporation, 517

localization, 538
multinational corporation (MNC), 517
repatriation, 533
split pay, 538
third-country nationals, 518
transnational corporation, 517
transnational teams, 522
work permit or visa, 521

## DISCUSSION QUESTIONS

1. Identify a Canadian company attempting to open offices in Kuwait, as Quizno's is doing. How do economics, politics, and culture impact the way these companies manage their employees in Kuwait?

2. If you were starting now to plan for a career in international HRM, what steps would you take?

3. What cultural differences exist between North Americans, Asians, and South Americans that would affect HR policies? In which of these regions would it be advisable to send as few Canadian managers as possible to run operations? Why?

4. Scotiabank operates in 50 countries and employs Canadians to staff its New Delhi office. What are the advantages of employing Canadians with roots in the host country? Would you use expatriate managers or host-country nationals to staff Scotiabank offices? Why?

5. If you were going to send a new manager to Bejing, what specific types of training would you provide to her before she left? Try using the information on http://www.canuckabroad.com to help you identify differences between China and Canada.

6. Talk with a foreign student on your campus; ask about his or her experience with culture shock on first arriving in Canada. What did you learn from your discussion?

7. Should compensation packages be equal across the world, or should they be adapted to the local cultures and economies? In teams, debate each position.

8. Assume that you are working for GE in Afghanistan. The power often goes out in your building, business deals take longer than in Canada, and you experience a great deal of stress due to the unstable political environment. Would you want your performance to be assessed in relation to the difficulty of doing business in Afghanistan?

9. Do you think that there should be some international standard for labour rights? If so, what should that standard be, and how should it be enforced?

# HRM EXPERIENCE

### A Canadian (Expatriate) in Paris

Often a great deal of work is involved in setting up expatriate assignments. The administrative requirements can be far ranging and extend beyond the employee to include family issues. Suppose you were faced with the following scenario. What would be the most pressing considerations that you would need to address?

### The Scenario

You are the head of HR for Sarip International, a consulting firm specializing in hotel and restaurant management. Your firm is opening an office in Paris, and Jim Verioti, director of sales and marketing, has been asked to assume responsibilities for the expansion. Jim understands that the expatriate assignment will last two to three years, and although he has travelled to Europe for work on several occasions, this is his first long-term assignment overseas. He has a lot of questions about what he can expect and some personal constraints.

Jim and his wife Betty have just moved into their new home (their mortgage is around $1,500 per month). In addition, Betty is an elementary school teacher and does not know how the move will affect her job security. Their three children, Veronica (14), Reggie (12), and Archie (10), are of ages at which school considerations are very important. A friend told them about the American School in Paris, and this is a consideration. None of the Veriotis speak French.

### Assignment

Working in teams of four to six, put together the package that would allow Jim to move his family to Paris while still maintaining his present lifestyle (his current annual salary is $140,000 plus incentives). Address at least the following issues:

1. Visas and permits
2. Relocation allowance and housing
3. Language and culture training
4. Spousal employment concerns

5. Health/medical/insurance issues

6. Compensation and incentives

7. Education for the children

The following websites may be helpful to you, but other resources may prove valuable as well.

- Canadian Embassy in Paris (http://www.international.gc.ca/canada-europa/France/menu-en.asp)
- French Embassy in Canada (http://www.ambafrance-ca.org)

- Expatica.com (http://www.expatica.com/france.asp)
- The Paris France Guide (http://www.parisfranceguide.com)
- Centers for Disease Control and Prevention (http://www.cdc.gov/travel)
- Travlang (currency calculator) (http://www.travlang.com/money)

Visit the *Managing Human Resources* CourseMate website at http://www.belcourt7e.nelson.com for quizzes, flashcards, videos, games, and more!

## CASE STUDY 1

### CULTURAL CONUNDRUM

Anna has enjoyed great success in the Toronto office of a global company. When she was offered an assignment in Tokyo, she approached the job with the full confidence of her employer that she could oversee the reorganization of the subsidiary. By asking her extensive network of colleagues about Japan, she learned a few tips. For example, she learned that when a Japanese businessman hands you his business card, it is proper to read the card before taking it and to never throw it on the desk. Even with tips like these, however, Anna's assignment was heading toward failure.

After six months, she was very discouraged, and when she returned home for the holidays, she reported the following problems:

- Although everyone spoke English, there were communication problems.
- Everything took too long to complete, with deadlines missed and employees not following schedules.
- Although she asked her employees for feedback and information and received promises that these would be forthcoming, no data arrived.

The company's response was to give her cross-cultural training, in which Anna learned the following:

- In Japanese culture, group identity supersedes individual identity. Loyalty is to the group,

and criticisms of performance are taboo. Group meetings are the norm, and one-on-one meetings designed to facilitate feedback make employees very uncomfortable.

- Japanese culture is based on hierarchy and is organized to recognize the power differentials between superiors and subordinates. Japanese workers do not expect to have input into decisions; their only expectation is to be told what to do. If forced to participate in decision making, the typical Japanese worker will avoid uncertainty by accumulating every possible item of information to support the decision.
- Japan is a masculine society, and women are employed in low-status positions. Anna's credibility as a decision maker would be questioned, and male employees would be uncomfortable working for her.

The communication problems only compounded the difficulty of the situation. Yes, the employees spoke English. But there were cultural differences. To a direct request to meet a deadline that they perceived as impossible, employees would save face (for themselves and the person making the request) by saying that they would do their best. Saying no is not part of Japanese culture.

Anna made the mistake of transferring her management style, which was successful in Toronto, to Tokyo without understanding the cultural differences.

## Questions

1. Exactly what preparation should Anna's company have given her before she started her assignment?
2. In general, what should a candidate for an international assignment do to prepare for a job, in the absence of company orientation and training?

3. Many believe that women on international assignments prove to be very effective because they are both task oriented (a North American cultural imperative) and relationship oriented (an important attribute in Asian and other cultures). Why did these two sets of skills not help Anna?

**Sources:** Adapted from Z. Fedder, "Same Language, Different Meanings," *Canadian HR Reporter* 13, no. 11 (June 5, 2000): 9; S. McKay, "Women Going Global," *Financial Post Magazine* December 1998: 38–54.

# CASE STUDY 2

## RECRUITING AND RETAINING INTERNATIONAL EMPLOYEES

Cambior, based in Longueil, Quebec, is one of Canada's largest gold producers, employing 2,700 people at mines in Quebec, Peru, French Guyana, and Surinam. Of these, over 1,000 are based outside Canada. Their HR policies for managing these international employees are described below.

### STAFFING

Cambior has had no problems recruiting employees for its operations. The company finds that candidates who are attracted to international assignments tend to apply to organizations where these assignments are possible.

Cambior uses three types of postings to staff its mines:

- Short-term assignments that are used for special projects or during construction of the mine
- Home-based assignments where employees will spend periods of time at the mine and then return home for rest and recuperation. The longest period that an employee is on-site is 30 days, followed by 26 days of recuperation.
- Long-term assignments, usually for executives, who move with their families close to the mine. The biggest problems with these assignments are the education of the children and the careers of working spouses.

### COMPENSATION

Cambior uses a tax equalization policy that guarantees that an employee on assignment will be no better or worse off as a result of taxes. If the taxes are higher in the host country, then the company absorbs the costs of these extra payments. If they are lower, the excess reverts to the company. Employees are also given hardship allowances. Cambior has established an Employee Leasing Company that hires the employees for these international secondments, which allows the employee to retain home-based benefits such as pension plans and employment insurance.

### HEALTH AND SAFETY

Cambior has found that safety standards are consistent across their international operations, but health issues are more complex. For example, employees need to be educated about malaria, and special provisions are made for other diseases not normally found in Canada. Employees have to feel assured that if there is a serious health issue, they will receive rapid medical treatment. Each site has a complete medical facility. Medical evacuations are done when the condition is life threatening.

Violence is an issue in developing countries. Special sessions on topics such as kidnap training and emergency evacuation are provided.

### Questions

1. Describe the advantages and limitations of Cambior's staffing policies. How would you compare these to the advantages and limitations of employing host-country nationals?
2. What kinds of hardships would Cambior employees face? What would be appropriate compensation for these conditions?
3. What benefits required by law in Canada would be unlikely to be provided in developing countries?

**Sources:** Adapted from N. Bédard, "Human Resources for a Global Company," *CIM Bulletin* 97, no. 1078 (March 2004): 99–100; Cambio, "About Us," http://www.cambio.com.

# NOTES AND REFERENCES

1. Peter Dowling, Denice E. Welch, and Randall S. Schuler, *International Human Resource Management: Managing People in a Multinational Context*, 3rd ed. (Cincinnati, OH: South-Western, 1999); Nancy J. Adler, *International Dimensions of Organizational Behaviour* (Cincinnati, OH: South-Western, 1997); J. Michael Geringer, Colette Frayne, and John Milliman, "In Search of 'Best Practices' in International Human Resource Management: Research Design and Methodology," *Human Resource Management* 41, no. 1 (Spring 2002): 5–30; "Cendant Mobility Survey Shows Continued Challenges around Repatriation Management; Focus on Cost Control Also Driving New Approaches to Global Assignments, Say Global Mobility Practitioners," *PR Newswire* (April 28, 2004).

2. M. F. Wolff, "Innovation and Competitiveness among EU Goals for Knowledge Economy," *Research Technology Management* 44, no. 6 (November/December 2001): 2–6; Tony Emerson, "The Great Walls: The United States and Europe Are Leading the Race to Carve Up the Trading World," *Newsweek* (April 23, 2001): 40. For more information about the EU online, see the Europa website at http://europa.eu.int.

3. Sadanand Dhume, "Just Quit It," *Far Eastern Economic Review* 165, no. 36 (September 12, 2002): 46–50; George Koo, "Fast Lane to China: Companies That Never Thought of Doing Business Overseas Are Now Looking to the Thriving Chinese Economy," *Computer Technology Review* 24, no. 4 (April 2004): 42.

4. Thomas Friedman, *The World Is Flat* (New York: Farrar, Straus and Giroux, 2005).

5. Interested readers can access this journal online at http://www.tandf.co.uk/journals/online/0958-5192.html; Beth McConnell, "Global Forum Speakers to Share Insights on International HR," *HR Magazine* 48, no. 3 (March 2003): 115–117.

6. Abagail McWilliams, David Van Fleet, and Patrick Wright, "Strategic Management of Human Resources for Global Competitive Advantage," *Journal of Business Strategies* 18, no. 1 (Spring 2001): 1–24.

7. DeeDee Doke, "Perfect Strangers: Cultural and Linguistic Differences between U.S. and U.K. Workers Necessitate Training for Expatriates," *HR Magazine* 49, no. 12 (December 2004): 62.

8. Carla Joinson, "No Returns," *HR Magazine* 47, no. 11 (November 2002): 70–77; Frank Jossi, "Successful Handoff," *HR Magazine* 47, no. 10 (October 2002): 48–52; Steve Bates, "Study Discovers Patterns in Global Executive Mobility," *HR Magazine* 47, no. 10 (October 2002): 14; Morgan McCall and George Hollenbeck, "Global Fatalities: When International Executives Derail," *Ivey Business Journal* 66, no. 5 (May/June 2002): 74–78; Leslie Gross Klass, "Fed Up with High Costs, Companies Thin the Ranks of Career Expats," *Workforce Management* 83, no. 10 (October 1, 2004): 84.

9. Wallace Immen, "Going Abroad to Get Ahead," *The Globe and Mail*, February 22, 2006, C1.

10. David Lipschultz, "Bosses from Abroad," *Chief Executive* 174 (January 2002): 18–21.

11. Readers interested in codes of conduct and other ethical issues pertaining to international business might read Nadar Asgary and Mark Mitschow, "Toward a Model for International Business Ethics," *Journal of Business Ethics* 36, no. 3 (March 2002): 238–246; Diana Winstanley and Jean Woodall, "The Adolescence of Ethics in Human Resource Management," *Human Resource Management Journal* 10, no. 4 (2000): 45; J. Brooke Hamilton and Stephen Knouse, "Multinational Enterprise Decision Principles for Dealing with Cross-Cultural Ethical Conflicts," *Journal of Business Ethics* 31, no. 1 (May 2001): 77–94; Michael Maynard, "Policing Transnational Commerce: Global Awareness in the Margins of Morality," *Journal of Business Ethics* 30, no. 1 (March 2001): 17–27.

12. Keeping Out the Wrong People: Tightened Visa Rules Are Slowing the Vital Flow of Professionals into the U.S.," *Business Week*, no. 3902 (October 4, 2004): 90; "Security Delays Hurt U.S. Business," *Legal Times*, August 23, 2004.

13. Anne E. Kornblut, "Bush Cites Political Hurdles in Plan for 'Guest Workers,'" *The New York Times*, March 24, 2005, A6.

14. "Society: Affirmative Action? Oui! At Long Last, France Takes a Page from America in Order to Manage Diversity—and Bring Minorities into Elite Schools," *Newsweek International*, April 12, 2004, 30.

15. Scott A . Snell, Charles E. Snow, Sue Canney Davison, and Donald C. Hambrick, "Designing and Supporting Transnational Teams: The Human Resource Agenda," *Human Resource Management* 37, no. 2: 147–158; Debra Shapiro, Stacie Furst, Gretchen Spreitzer, and Mary Ann Von Glinow, "Transnational Teams in the Electronic Age: Are Team Identity and High Performance at Risk?" *Journal of Organizational Behaviour*, 23 (June 2002): 455–467; Claude Philipps, Harold Sirkin, Duane Filtz, and Scott Kirsner, "Time [Zone] Travelers: They Bounce from Beijing to Bangalore at a Moment's Notice," *Fast Company*, no. 85 (August 2004): 60–67.

16. Snell et al., "Designing and Supporting Transnational Teams," 147–158; Leslie Gross Klass, "Fed Up with High Costs, Companies Thin the Ranks of Career Expats," *Workforce Management* 83, no. 10 (October 1, 2004): 84.

17. Andrea Poe, "Selection Savvy," *HR Magazine* 47, no. 4 (April 2002): 77–83; "Exploiting Opportunity: Executives Trade Stories on Challenges of Doing Business in Global Economy," *Business Mexico* 15, no. 2 (February 2005): 54–58.

18. Yehuda Baruch, "No Such Thing as a Global Manager," *Business Horizons* 45, no. 1 (January/February 2002): 36–42.

19. Sheree R. Curry, "Offshoring Swells Ranks of 'Returnees' Working Back in Their Native Countries," *Workforce Management* 84, no. 2 (February 1, 2005): 59; Margaret Linehan and Hugh Scullion, "Selection, Training, and Development for Female International Executives," *Career Development International* 6, no. 6 (2001): 318–323; Nancy Lockwood, "The Glass Ceiling: Domestic and International Perspectives," *HR Magazine* 49, no. 6 (June 2004): S1–S11.

20. Nancy Wong, "Mark Your Calendar! Important Tasks for International HR," *Workforce* 79, no. 4 (April 2000): 72–74; Robert O'Connor, "Plug the Expat Knowledge Drain," *HR Magazine* 47, no. 10 (October 2002): 101–107; Andrea Graf and Lynn K. Harland, "Expatriate Selection: Evaluating the Discriminant, Convergent, and Predictive Validity of Five Measures of Interpersonal and Intercultural Competence," *Journal of Leadership & Organizational Studies* 11, no. 2 (Winter 2005): 46–63.

21. McCall and Hollenbeck, "Global Fatalities: When International Executives Derail," 74–78; Poe, "Selection Savvy," 77–83; Juan Sanchez, Paul Spector, and Cary Cooper, "Adapting to a Boundaryless World: A Developmental Expatriate Model," *Academy of Management Executive* 14, no. 2 (May 2000): 96–106; Eric Krell, "Evaluating Returns on Expatriates: Though Difficult to Ascertain, Measuring the Return on the Cost of Expatriate Assignments Is Necessary to Justify the Expensive Investment," *HR Magazine* (March 2005): 12.

22. "Motorola to Increase Operations in China," *The New York Times*, November 8, 2001, C4; Peter J. Buckley, Jeremy Clegg, and Hui Tan, "Knowledge Transfer to China: Policy Lessons from Foreign Affiliates," *Transnational Corporations* 13, no. 1 (April 2004): 31–73.

23. Lionel Laroche, John Bing, and Catherine Mercer Bing, "Beyond Translation," *Training & Development* 54, no. 12 (December 2000): 72–73; Sabrina Hicks, "Successful Global Training," *Training & Development* 54, no. 5 (May 2000): 95.

24. Jared Wade, "The Pitfalls of Cross-Cultural Business," *Risk Management* 51, no. 3 (March 2004): 38–43.

25. Vipin Gupta, Paul Hanges, and Peter Dorman, "Cultural Clusters: Methodology and Findings," *Journal of World Business* 37, no. 1 (Spring 2002): 11–15; Jane Terpstra-Yong and David Ralston, "Moving toward a Global Understanding of Upward Influence Strategies: An Asian Perspective with Directions for Cross-Cultural Research," *Asia Pacific Journal of Management* 19, no. 2 (August 2002): 373–404.

26. Ping Ping Fu et al., "The Impact of Societal Cultural Values and Individual Social Beliefs on the Perceived Effectiveness of Managerial Influence Strategies: A Meso Approach," *Journal of International Business Studies* 35, no. 4 (July 2004): 33; Geert Hofstede, *Culture's Consequences: Comparing Values, Behaviors, Institutions, and Organizations across Nations* (Thousand Oaks, CA: Sage, 2001).

27. Lisa Bohannon, "Going Global," *Career World* 29, no. 6 (April/May 2001): 28–30; Aimin Yan, Guorgong Zhu, and Douglas T. Hall, "International Assignments for Career Building: A Model of Agency Relationships and Psychological Contracts," *Academy of Management Review* 27, no. 3 (July 2002): 373–391; Justin Martin, "The Global CEO: Overseas Experience Is Becoming a Must on Top Executives' Resumes, According to This Year's Route to the Top," *Chief Executive* no. 195 (January–February 2004): 24–31.

28. "Prudential Relocation Survey Finds Spouses' Experiences a Key Factor in the Success of International Work Assignments," *Canadian Corporate News*, December 7, 2004.

29. Virginia Galt, "It's Not Easy to Come Home Again," *The Globe and Mail*, February 22, 2006, C6.

30. Mila Lazarova and Paula Caligiuri, "Retaining Repatriates: The Role of Organizational Support Practices," *Journal of World Business* 36, no. 4 (Winter 2001): 389–401; "Expatriate Administration: New Realities and HR Challenges," *Employee Benefit News* (March 1, 2005); "For Those Working Abroad, Moving Home Can Be Jarring," *The Kansas City (Missouri) Star* (via Knight-Ridder/Tribune Business News), February 22, 2005.

31. Calvin Reynolds, *Guide to Global Compensation and Benefits* (New York: Harcourt, 2001); Gary Parker, "Establishing Remuneration Practices across Culturally Diverse Environments," *Compensation & Benefits Management* 17, no. 2 (Spring 2001): 23–27; Timothy Dwyer, "Localization's Hidden Costs," *HR Magazine* 49, no. 6 (June 2004): 135–141.

32. Caroline Fisher, "Reward Strategy Linked to Financial Success: Europe," *Benefits & Compensation International* 32, no. 2 (September 2002): 34–35; "Comparative Analysis of Remuneration: Europe," *Benefits & Compensation International* 31, no. 10 (June 2002): 27–28; Fay Hansen, "Currents in Compensation and Benefits: International Trends," *Compensation and Benefits Review* 34, no. 2 (March/April 2002): 20–21.

33. Chao Chen, Jaepil Choi, and Shu-Cheng Chi, "Making Justice Sense of Local-Expatriate Compensation Disparity: Mitigation by Local Referents, Ideological Explanations, and Interpersonal Sensitivity in China-Foreign Joint Ventures," *Academy of Management Journal* 45, no. 4 (August 2002): 807–817.

34. Patricia Zingheim and Jay Schuster, "How You Pay Is What You Get," *Across the Board* 38, no. 5 (September/October 2001): 41–44; "Benefits for Expatriate Employees: International," *Benefits & Compensation International* 31, no. 10 (June 2002): 26–27; Steven P. Nurney, "The Long and Short of It: When Transitioning from a Short-Term to a Long-Term Expatriate Assignment, Consider the Financial Implications," *HR Magazine* 50, no. 3 (March 2005): 91–95.

35. Stephan Kolbe, "Putting Together an Expat Package: As More and More Companies Adopt an International Outlook, They Are Increasingly Sending Staff on Overseas Assignments—Usually Involving a Complex Relocation Package," *International Money Marketing* (September 2004): 33.

36. The U.S. State Department Index of Living Costs Abroad can be found at http://www.state.gov/travel/.

37. Barbara Hanrehan and Donald R. Bentivoglio, "Safe Haven: Accommodating the Needs of Employees and Families in Hostile Environments Can Increase Expenses and Alter Tax Liability," *HR Magazine* 47, no. 2 (February 2002): 52–54.

38. Paul Hempel, "Differences between Chinese and Western Managerial Views of Performance," *Personnel Review* 30, no. 2 (2001): 203–215.

39. "Cross-Cultural Lessons in Leadership: Data from a Decade-Long Research Project Puts Advice to Managers in Context, Country by Country," *MIT Sloan Management Review* 45, no. 1 (Fall 2003): 5–7.

40. Paula Caligiuri, "The Big Five Personality Characteristics as Predictors of Expatriate's Desire to Terminate the Assignment and Supervisor-Rated Performance," *Personnel Psychology* 53, no. 1 (Spring 2000): 67–88; Calvin Reynolds, "Global Compensation and Benefits in Transition," *Compensation and Benefits Review* 32, no. 1 (January/February 2000): 28–38; Charlene Marmer Solomon, "The World Stops Shrinking," *Workforce* 79, no. 1 (January 2000): 48–51; Stephenie Overman, "Mentors without Borders: Global Mentors Can Give Employees a Different Perspective on Business Matters," *HR Magazine* 49, no. 3 (March 2004): 83–87.

41. Frank Jossi, "Successful Handoff," *HR Magazine* 47, no. 10 (October 2002): 48–52; Paula Caligiuri and David Day, "Effects of Self-Monitoring on Technical, Contextual, and Assignment-Specific Performance," *Group & Organization Management* 25, no. 2 (June 2000): 154–174.

42. Mark Mendenhall and Gary Oddou (eds.), *Readings and Cases in International Human Resource Management* (Cincinnati, OH: South-Western, 1999).

43. Ariane Berthoin, "Expatriates' Contributions to Organizational Learning," *Journal of General Management* 26, no. 4 (Summer 2001): 62–84; Peter J. Buckley, Jeremy Clegg, and Hui Tan, "Knowledge Transfer to China: Policy Lessons from Foreign Affiliates," *Transnational Corporations* 13, no. 1 (April 2004): 31–73.

44. Bernhard Ebbinghaus and Jelle Visser, *The Societies of Europe: Trade Unions in Western Europe since 1945* (London, England: Palgrave Macmillan, 2000); John Pencavel, "Unionism Viewed Internationally," *Journal of Labor Research* 26, no. 1 (Winter 2005): 65–98.

45. Christopher Rhoads, "Germany Faces Storm over Tech Staffing—Labor Groups Are Enraged by Proposal to Import Badly Needed Workers," *The Wall Street Journal*, March 7, 2000, A23; "European Workplaces Tighten Policies as Countries Struggle to Compete Worldwide," *Pittsburgh (Pennsylvania) Post-Gazette* (via Knight-Ridder/Tribune Business News), November 28, 2004.

46. Dharam Gahi, "Decent Work: Universality and Diversity" (discussion paper, International Institute for Labour Studies, 2005), 1–22; Jean-Michael Servais, "Globalization and Decent Work Policy: Reflections upon a New Legal Approach," *International Labour Review* 143, no. 1–2 (Spring–Summer 2004): 104–108; "Philosophical and Spiritual Perspectives on Decent Work," *International Labour Review* 143, no. 3 (Autumn 2004): 290–292. Interested readers can find more information about international trade unions by checking out the websites of the ICFTU (http://www.icftu.org) and the ILO (http://www.ilo.org).

47. Dirk Kolvenbach and Ute Spiegel, "The Reform of the Works Council Constitution Act in Germany and Its Effects on the Co-Determination Rights of the Works Council," *International Financial Law Review* (2001): 59–65; Pencavel, "Unionism Viewed Internationally," 65–98.

# GLOSSARY

**9-box grid**
A comparative diagram that includes appraisal and assessment data to allow managers to easily see an employee's actual and potential performance (page 158)

## A

**alternative dispute resolution (ADR)**
A term applied to different types of employee complaint or dispute resolution procedures (page 470)

**applicant tracking system (ATS)**
A software application recruiters use to post job openings, screen résumés, contact potential candidates for interviews via email, and track the time and costs related to hiring people (page 170)

**apprenticeship training**
A system of training in which a worker entering the skilled trades is given thorough instruction and experience, both on and off the job, in the practical and theoretical aspects of the work (page 249)

**arbitration award**
Final and binding award issued by an arbitrator in a labour–management dispute (page 503)

**assessment centre**
A process by which individuals are evaluated as they participate in a series of situations that resemble what they might need to handle the job (page 215)

**attrition**
A natural departure of employees from organizations through quits, retirements, and deaths (page 67)

**augmented skills**
Skills helpful in facilitating the efforts of expatriate managers (page 526)

**authorization card**
A statement signed by an employee authorizing a union to act as his or her representative for the purposes of collective bargaining (page 486)

## B

**balanced scorecard (BSC)**
A measurement framework that helps managers translate strategic goals into operational objectives (page 69)

**balance-sheet approach**
A compensation system designed to match the purchasing power in a person's home country (page 537)

**bargaining power**
The power of labour and management to achieve their goals through economic, social, or political influence (page 497)

**bargaining unit**
Group of two or more employees who share common employment interests and conditions and may reasonably be grouped together for purposes of collective bargaining (page 488)

**bargaining zone**
Area within which the union and the employer are willing to concede when bargaining (page 496)

**behaviour modelling**
An approach that demonstrates desired behaviour and gives trainees the chance to practise and role-play those behaviours and receive feedback (page 258)

**behaviour modification**
A technique that operates on the principle that behaviour that is rewarded, or positively reinforced, will be exhibited more frequently in the future, whereas behaviour that is penalized or unrewarded will decrease in frequency (page 248)

**behaviour observation scale (BOS)**
A behavioural approach to performance appraisal that measures the frequency of observed behaviour (page 305)

**behavioural description interview (BDI)**
An interview in which an applicant is asked questions about what he or she did in a given situation (page 205)

**behaviourally anchored rating scale (BARS)**
A behavioural approach to performance appraisal that consists of a series of vertical scales, one for each important dimension of job performance (page 304)

**benchmarking**
The process of comparing the organization's processes and practices to those of other companies (page 68)

**benchmarking**
The process of measuring one's own services and practice against the recognized leaders to identify areas for improvement (page 263)

**blended learning**
The use of multiple training methods to achieve optimal learning on the part of trainees (page 252)

**bona fide occupational qualification (BFOQ)**
A justifiable reason for discrimination based on business reasons of safety or effectiveness (page 90)

**bonus**
An incentive payment that is supplemental to the base wage (page 365)

**branding**
A company's efforts to help existing and prospective workers understand why it is a desirable place to work (page 156)

**burnout**
The most severe stage of distress, manifesting itself in depression, frustration, and loss of productivity (page 440)

**business agent**
Normally a paid labour official responsible for negotiating and administering the collective agreement and working to resolve union members' problems (page 492)

## C

**calibration**
A process whereby managers meet to discuss the performance of individual employees to ensure that their employee appraisals are in line with one another (page 289)

**career counselling**
The process of discussing with employees their current job activities and performance, personal and career interests and goals, personal skills, and suitable career development objectives (page 178)

**career networking**
The process of establishing mutually beneficial relationships with other businesspeople, including potential clients and customers (page 181)

**career paths**
Lines of advancement in an occupational field within an organization (page 173)

**career plateau**
A situation in which, for either organizational or personal reasons, the probability of moving up the career ladder is low (page 176)

**change management**
Change management is a systematic way of bringing about and managing both organizational changes and changes on the individual level (page 6)

**chief ethics officer**
A high-ranking manager directly responsible for fostering the ethical climate within the firm (page 269)

**chief learning officer**
A high-ranking manager directly responsible for fostering employee learning and development within the organization (page 239)

**codetermination**
Representation of labour on the board of directors of a company (page 544)

**collaborative software**
Software that allows workers to interface and share information with one another electronically (page 10)

**collective agreement**
An employment contract between an employer and a union that sets out the terms of employment of a group of the employer's employees represented by the union (page 452)

**collective bargaining process**
Process of negotiating a collective agreement, including the use of economic pressures by both parties (page 494)

**combined salary and commission plan**
A compensation plan that includes a straight salary and a commission (page 369)

**common law of employment**
The body of case law in which courts interpret employment contracts and the legal principles taken from those cases that guide the interpretation of employment contracts (page 450)

**compensatory model**
A selection decision model in which a high score in one area can make up for a low score in another area (page 224)

**competence-based pay**
Pay based on an employee's skill level, variety of skills possessed, or increased job knowledge (page 346)

**competency assessment**
Analysis of the sets of skills and knowledge needed for decision-oriented and knowledge-intensive jobs (page 241)

**compulsory binding arbitration**
Binding method of resolving collective bargaining deadlocks by a neutral third party (page 493)

**concentration**
Term applied to designated groups whose numbers in a particular occupation or level are high relative to their numbers in the labour market (page 100)

**concurrent validity**
The extent to which test scores (or other predictor information) match criterion obtained at about the same time from current employees (page 220)

**construct validity**
The extent to which a selection tool measures a theoretical construct or trait (page 221)

**constructive dismissal**
When an employer commits a fundamental breach of the contract, such as by unilaterally changing a key term of the contract, the employee can treat the breach as a termination (page 453)

**consumer price index (CPI)**
A measure of the average change in prices over time in a fixed "market basket" of goods and services (page 337)

**content validity**
The extent to which a selection instrument, such as a test, adequately samples the knowledge and skills needed to perform a particular job (page 220)

**contrast error**
A performance rating error in which an employee's evaluation is biased either upward or downward because of comparison with another employee just previously evaluated (page 298)

**contributory plan**
A pension plan in which contributions are made jointly by employees and employers (page 404)

**cooperative training**
Training program that combines practical on-the-job experience with formal educational classes (page 250)

**core capabilities**
Integrated knowledge sets within an organization that distinguish it from its competitors and deliver value to customers (page 47)

**core skills**
Skills considered critical to an employee's success abroad (page 526)

**core values**
The strong and enduring beliefs and principles that the company uses as a foundation for its decisions (page 42)

**corporate social responsibility**
The responsibility of the firm to act in the best interests of the people and communities affected by its activities (page 10)

**craft unions**
Unions that represent skilled craft workers (page 491)

**criterion-related validity**
The extent to which a selection tool predicts, or significantly correlates with, important elements of work behaviour (page 220)

**critical incident**
An unusual event that denotes superior or inferior employee performance in some part of the job (page 303)

**critical incident method**
A job analysis method by which important job tasks are identified for job success (page 127)

**cross-training**
The process of training employees to do multiple jobs within an organization (page 268)

**cross-validation**
Verifying the results obtained from a validation study by administering a test or test battery to a different sample (drawn from the same population) (page 220)

**cultural audits**
Audits of the culture and quality of work life in an organization (page 51)

**cultural environment**
The communications, religion, values and ideologies, education, and social structure of a country (page 514)

**culture shock**
Perpetual stress experienced by people who settle overseas (page 532)

**cumulative trauma disorders**
Injuries involving tendons of the fingers, hands, and arms that become inflamed from repeated stresses and strains (page 434)

**customer appraisal**
A performance appraisal that, like team appraisal, is based on total quality management concepts and seeks evaluation from both external and internal customers (page 293)

# D

**defined-benefit plan**
A pension plan in which the amount an employee is to receive on retirement is specifically set forth (page 404)

# GLOSSARY

**defined-contribution plan**
A pension plan that establishes the basis on which an employer will contribute to the pension fund (page 404)

**depression**
Negative emotional state marked by feelings of low spirits, gloominess, sadness, and loss of pleasure in ordinary activities (page 437)

**designated groups**
Women, visible minorities, Aboriginal people, and persons with disabilities who have been disadvantaged in employment (page 84)

**differential piece rate**
A compensation rate under which employees whose production exceeds the standard amount of output receive a higher rate for all of their work than the rate paid to those who do not exceed the standard amount (page 363)

**distress**
Harmful stress characterized by a loss of feelings of security and adequacy (page 439)

**diversity management**
The optimization of an organization's multicultural workforce to reach business objectives (page 107)

**downsizing**
Planned elimination of jobs (page 6)

## E

**eldercare**
Care provided to an elderly relative by an employee who remains actively at work (page 408)

**e-learning**
Learning that takes place via electronic media (page 254)

**emergency action plan**
A plan an organization develops that contains step-by-step procedures for dealing with various emergency situations (page 431)

**employee assistance programs (EAPs)**
Services provided by employers to help workers cope with a wide variety of problems that interfere with the way they perform their jobs (page 406)

**employee associations**
Labour organizations that represent various groups of professional and white-collar employees in labour–management relations (page 491)

**employee empowerment**
Granting employees power to initiate change, thereby encouraging them to take charge of what they do (page 135)

**employee involvement groups (EIs)**
Groups of employees who meet to resolve problems or offer suggestions for organizational improvement (page 138)

**employee leasing**
The process of dismissing employees who are then hired by a leasing company (which handles all HR-related activities) and contracting with that company to lease back the employees (pages 17)

**employee profile**
A profile of a worker developed by studying an organization's top performers to recruit similar types of people (page 154)

**employee stock ownership plans (ESOPs)**
Stock plans in which an organization contributes shares of its stock to an established trust for the purpose of stock purchases by employees (page 379)

**employee teams**
An employee contributions technique whereby work functions are structured for groups rather than for individuals and team members are given discretion in matters traditionally considered management prerogatives, such as process improvements, product or service development, and individual work assignments (page 139)

**employment equity**
The employment of individuals in a fair and nonbiased manner (page 84)

**entrepreneur**
Someone who starts, organizes, manages, and assumes responsibility for a business or other enterprise (page 192)

**environmental scanning**
Systematic monitoring of the major external forces influencing the organization (page 43)

**ergonomics**
An interdisciplinary approach to designing equipment and systems that can be easily and efficiently used by human beings (page 136)

**error of central tendency**
A performance rating error in which all employees are rated about average (page 298)

**escalator clauses**
Clauses in collective agreements that provide for quarterly cost-of-living adjustments in wages, basing the adjustments on changes in the consumer price index (page 338)

**essay method**
A trait approach to performance appraisal that requires the rater to compose a statement describing employee behaviour (page 303)

**ethics**
A set of standards of conduct and moral judgments that help determine right and wrong behaviour (page 473)

**eustress**
Positive stress that accompanies achievement and exhilaration (page 439)

**expatriates, or home-country nationals**
Employees from the home country who are on an international assignment (page 518)

## F

**failure rate**
The percentage of expatriates who do not perform satisfactorily (page 527)

**fast-track program**
A program that encourages new managers with high potential to remain with an organization by enabling them to advance more rapidly than those with less potential (page 178)

**final offer arbitration**
Method of resolving collective bargaining deadlocks whereby the arbitrator has no power to compromise but must select one or another of the final offers submitted by the two parties (page 493)

**flexible benefits plans (cafeteria plans)**
Benefits plans that enable individual employees to choose the benefits that are best suited to their particular needs (page 391)

**flextime**
Flexible working hours that permit employees the option of choosing daily starting and quitting times provided that they work a set number of hours per day or week (page 143)

**flow data**
Data that provide a profile of the employment decisions affecting designated groups (page 99)

**focal performance appraisal**
An appraisal system in which all of an organization's employees are reviewed at the same time of the year rather than on the anniversaries of the individual hire dates (page 283)

**forced-choice method**
A trait approach to performance appraisal that requires the rater to choose from statements designed to distinguish between successful and unsuccessful performance (page 302)

**furloughing**
A situation in which an organization asks or requires employees to take time off for either no pay or reduced pay (page 15)

## G

**gainsharing plans**
Programs under which both employees and the organization share financial gains according to a predetermined formula that reflects improved productivity and profitability (page 376)

**global compensation system**
A centralized pay system whereby host-country employees are offered a full range of training programs, benefits, and pay comparable to those of a firm's domestic employees but adjusted for local differences (page 536)

**global corporation**
A firm that has integrated worldwide operations through a centralized home office (page 517)

**global manager**
A manager equipped to run an international business (page 525)

**global sourcing**
The business practice of searching for and utilizing goods sources from around the world (page 156)

**globalization**
The trend to opening up foreign markets to international trade and investment (page 8)

**graphic rating scale method**
A trait approach to performance appraisal whereby each employee is rated according to a scale of characteristics (page 301)

**grievance procedure**
Formal procedure that provides for the union to represent members and nonmembers in processing a grievance (page 502)

**guest workers**
Foreign workers invited to perform needed labour (page 522)

## H

**Hay profile method**
A job evaluation technique using three factors— knowledge, mental activity, and accountability—to evaluate executive and managerial positions (page 341)

**hiring freeze**
A practice whereby new workers are not hired as planned or workers who have left the organization are not replaced (page 67)

**home-based pay**
Pay based on an expatriate's home country's compensation practices (page 537)

**host-based pay**
Expatriate pay comparable to that earned by employees in a host country (page 538)

**host country**
A country in which an international corporation operates (page 514)

**host-country nationals**
Employees who are natives of the host country (page 518)

**hourly work**
Work paid on an hourly basis (page 333)

**human capital**
The knowledge, skills, and capabilities of individuals that have economic value to an organization (page 4)

**human capital readiness**
The process of evaluating the availability of critical talent in a company and comparing it to the firm's supply (page 59)

**human resources information system (HRIS)**
A computerized system that provides current and accurate data for purposes of control and decision making (page 12)

**human resources management (HRM)**
The process of managing human talent to achieve an organization's objectives (page 4)

**human resources planning (HRP)**
The process of anticipating and providing for the movement of people into, within, and out of an organization (page 40)

## I

**implied contract terms**
Terms judges read into employment contracts when the written contract does not expressly deal with the matter (page 450)

**industrial disease**
A disease resulting from exposure to a substance relating to a particular process, trade, or occupation in industry (page 423)

**industrial engineering**
A field of study concerned with analyzing work methods and establishing time standards (page 136)

**industrial unions**
Unions that represent all workers—skilled, semiskilled, unskilled—employed along industry lines (page 491)

**informational interview**
An informal meeting with someone in an occupation that interests you (page 191)

**instructional objectives**
Desired outcomes of a training program (page 244)

**interest arbitrator**
Third-party neutral who resolves a labour dispute by issuing a final decision in the disagreement (page 501)

**interest-based bargaining (IBB)**
Problem-solving bargaining based on a win–win philosophy and the development of a positive long-term relationship (page 497)

**internal labour market**
Labour market in which workers are hired into entry-level jobs and higher levels are filled from within (page 155)

**international corporation**
A domestic firm that uses its existing capabilities to move into overseas markets (page 517)

**internship programs**
Programs jointly sponsored by colleges, universities, and other organizations that offer students the opportunity to gain real-life experience while allowing them to find out how they will perform in work organizations (page 251)

## J

**job**
A group of related activities and duties (page 122)

**job analysis**
The process of obtaining information about jobs by determining the duties, tasks, or activities of jobs (page 124)

**job characteristics model**
A job design theory that purports that three psychological states (experiencing meaningfulness of the work performed, responsibility for work outcomes, and knowledge of the results of the work performed) of a jobholder result in improved work performance, internal motivation, and lower absenteeism and turnover (page 134)

**job classification system**
A system of job evaluation in which jobs are classified and grouped according to a series of predetermined wage grades (page 339)

**job description**
A statement of the tasks, duties, and responsibilities of a job to be performed (page 122)

**job design**
An outgrowth of job analysis that improves jobs through technological and human

considerations to enhance organization efficiency and employee job satisfaction (page 133)

**job enrichment**
Enhancing a job by adding more meaningful tasks and duties to make the work more rewarding or satisfying (page 134)

**job evaluation**
A systematic process of determining the relative worth of jobs to establish which jobs should be paid more than others within an organization (page 338)

**job family**
A group of individual jobs with similar characteristics (page 122)

**job progressions**
The hierarchy of jobs a new employee might experience, ranging from a starting job to jobs that successively require more knowledge and/or skill (page 173)

**job ranking system**
The simplest and oldest system of job evaluation by which jobs are arrayed on the basis of their relative worth (page 338)

**job shadowing**
The process of observing an employee in his or her work environment to obtain a better understanding of what the employee does (page 191)

**job sharing**
The arrangement whereby two part-time employees perform a job that otherwise would be held by one full-time employee (page 143)

**job specification**
A statement of the needed knowledge, skills, and abilities of the person who is to perform the job (page 122)

**just-in-time training**
Training delivered to trainees when and where they need it to do their jobs, usually via computer or the Internet (page 254)

## K

**knowledge workers**
Workers whose responsibilities extend beyond the physical execution of work to include planning, decision making, and problem solving (page 11)

## L

**labour arbitrator**
A person assigned to interpret and decide disputes ("grievances") about the meaning, interpretation, and application of a collective agreement governing

employees in a unionized workplace (page 452)

**labour relations process**
Logical sequence of four events: (1) workers desire collective representation; (2) the union begins its organizing campaign, which may lead to certification and recognition; (3) collective negotiations lead to a contract; and (4) the contract is administered (page 483)

**learning management system (LMS)**
Online system that provides a variety of assessment, communication, teaching, and learning opportunities (page 254)

**leniency or strictness error**
A performance rating error in which the appraiser tends to give employees either unusually high or unusually low ratings (page 298)

**line managers**
Non-HR managers who are responsible for overseeing the work of other employees (page 25)

**localization**
Adapting pay and other compensation benefits to match those of a particular country (page 538)

**lump-sum merit program**
Program under which employees receive a year-end merit payment, which is not added to their base pay (page 366)

## M

**management by objectives (MBO)**
A philosophy of management that rates performance on the basis of employee achievement of goals set by mutual agreement of employee and manager (page 306)

**management forecasts**
The opinions (judgments) of supervisors, department managers, experts, or others knowledgeable about the organization's future employment needs (page 55)

**management rights**
Decisions regarding organizational operations over which management claims exclusive rights (page 490)

**manager and/or supervisor appraisal**
A performance appraisal done by an employee's manager and often reviewed by a manager one level higher (page 291)

**Markov analysis**
A method for tracking the pattern of employee movements through various jobs (page 56)

**mediation**
The use of an impartial neutral to reach a compromise decision in employment disputes (page 472)

**mediator**
A third party in an employment dispute who meets with one party and then the other to suggest compromise solutions or to recommend concessions from each side that will lead to an agreement (page 472)

**mentors**
Individuals who coach, advise, and encourage individuals of lesser rank (page 179)

**merit guidelines**
Guidelines for awarding merit raises that are tied to performance objectives (page 366)

**mission**
The basic purpose of the organization as well as its scope of operations (page 41)

**mixed-standard scale method**
A trait approach to performance appraisal similar to other scale methods but based on comparison with (better than, equal to, or worse than) a standard (page 302)

**multinational corporation (MNC)**
A firm with independent business units operating in multiple countries (page 517)

**multiple cutoff model**
A selection-decision model that requires an applicant to achieve some minimum level of proficiency on all selection dimensions (page 224)

**multiple hurdle model**
A sequential strategy in which only the applicants with the highest scores at an initial test stage go on to subsequent stages (page 224)

## N

**nearshoring**
The process of moving jobs closer to one's home country (page 16)

**nepotism**
A preference for hiring relatives of current employees (page 163)

**noncontributory plan**
A pension plan in which contributions are made solely by the employer (page 404)

**nondirective interview**
An interview in which the applicant is allowed the maximum amount of freedom in determining the course of the

discussion, while the interviewer carefully refrains from influencing the applicant's remarks (page 204)

## O

**occupational illness**
Any abnormal condition or disorder, other than one resulting from an occupational injury, caused by exposure to environmental factors associated with employment (page 418)

**occupational injury**
Any cut, fracture, sprain, or amputation resulting from a workplace accident or from an exposure involving an accident in the work environment (page 418)

**offshoring**
The business practice of sending jobs to other countries (page 16)

**ombudsperson**
A designated individual from whom employees may seek counsel for resolution of their complaints (page 472)

**onboarding**
The process of systematically socializing new employees to help them go "on board" with an organization (page 266)

**on-the-job training (OJT)**
A method by which employees are given hands-on experience with instructions from their supervisor or other trainer (page 249)

**open-door policy**
A policy of settling grievances that identifies various levels of management above the immediate supervisor for employee contact (page 471)

**organization analysis**
Examination of the environment, strategies, and resources of the organization to determine where training emphasis should be placed (page 239)

**organizational capability**
The capacity of the organization to act and change in pursuit of sustainable competitive advantage (page 71)

**orientation**
The formal process of familiarizing new employees with the organization, their jobs, and their work units (page 264)

**outplacement services**
Services provided by organizations to help terminated employees find a new job (page 175)

**outsourcing**
Contracting out work that was formerly done by employees (page 6)

## P

**panel interview**
An interview in which a board of interviewers questions and observes a single candidate (page 206)

**passive job seekers**
People who are not looking for jobs but could be persuaded to take new ones given the right opportunity (page 161)

**pay equity**
Equal pay for work of equal value (page 348)

**pay grades**
Groups of jobs within a particular class that are paid the same rate (page 344)

**peer appraisal**
A performance appraisal done by one's fellow employees, generally on forms that are compiled into a single profile for use in the performance interview conducted by the employee's manager (page 292)

**peer-review system**
A system for reviewing employee complaints that utilizes a group composed of equal numbers of employee representatives and management appointees, which functions as a jury because its members weigh evidence, consider arguments, and, after deliberation, vote independently to render a final decision (page 471)

**performance appraisal**
The result of an annual or biannual process in which a manager evaluates an employee's performance relative to the requirements of his or her job and uses the information to show the person where improvements are needed and why (page 282)

**performance management**
The process of creating a work environment in which people can perform to the best of their abilities (page 282)

**perquisites**
Special nonmonetary benefits given to executives; often referred to as perks (page 373)

**person analysis**
Determination of the specific individuals who need training (page 243)

**piecework**
Work paid according to the number of units produced (page 333)

**point system**
A quantitative job evaluation procedure that determines the relative value of a job by the total points assigned to it (page 339)

**position**
The different duties and responsibilities performed by only one employee (page 122)

**position analysis questionnaire (PAQ)**
A questionnaire covering 194 different tasks that, by means of a five-point scale, seeks to determine the degree to which different tasks are involved in performing a particular job (page 127)

**positive, or nonpunitive, discipline**
A system of discipline that focuses on early correction of employee misconduct, with the employee taking total responsibility for correcting the problem (page 468)

**predictive validity**
The extent to which applicants' test scores match criterion data obtained from those applicants/employees after they have been on the job for an indefinite period (page 220)

**preemployment test**
An objective and standardized measure of a sample of behaviour that is used to gauge a person's knowledge, skills, abilities, and other characteristics (KSAOs) relative to other individuals (page 214)

**proactive change**
Change initiated to take advantage of targeted opportunities (page 7)

**profit sharing**
Any procedure by which an employer pays, or makes available to all regular employees, in addition to base pay, special current or deferred sums based on the profits of the enterprise (page 376)

**progressive discipline**
Application of corrective measures by increasing degrees (page 468)

**promotion**
A change of assignment to a job at a higher level in the organization (page 175)

## Q

**quality of fill**
A metric designed to assess how well new hires are performing on the job (page 56)

## R

**reactive change**
Change that occurs after external forces have already affected performance (page 7)

**real wages**
Wage increases larger than rises in the consumer price index; that is, the real earning power of wages (page 338)

**realistic job preview (RJP)**
Informing applicants about all aspects of the job, including both its desirable and undesirable facets (page 167)

**reasonable accommodation**
Attempt by employers to adjust the working conditions or schedules of employees with disabilities or religious preferences (page 103)

**recency error**
A performance rating error in which the appraisal is based largely on the employee's most recent behaviour rather than on behaviour throughout the appraisal period (page 298)

**recruiting process outsourcing (RPO)**
The practice of outsourcing an organization's recruiting function to an outside firm (page 154)

**red circle rates**
Payment rates above the maximum of the pay range (page 345)

**reengineering**
The fundamental rethinking and radical redesign of business processes to achieve dramatic improvements in cost, quality, service, and speed (page 6)

**reliability**
The degree to which interviews, tests, and other selection procedures yield comparable data over time (page 199)

**relocation services**
Services provided to an employee who is transferred to a new location, which might include help in moving, selling a home, orienting to a new culture, and/or learning a new language (page 175)

**repatriation**
The process of employee transition home from an international assignment (page 533)

**replacement charts**
Listings of current jobholders and people who are potential replacements if an opening occurs (page 57)

**rerecruiting**
The process of keeping track of and maintaining relationships with former employees to see if they would be willing to return to the firm (page 163)

**rights arbitration**
Arbitration over interpretation of the meaning of contract terms or employee work grievances (page 503)

## S

**sabbatical**
An extended period of time in which an employee leaves an organization to pursue other activities and later returns to his or her job (page 177)

**salary plus bonus plan**
A compensation plan that pays a salary plus a bonus achieved by reaching targeted sales goals (page 370)

**selection**
The process of choosing individuals who have relevant qualifications to fill existing or projected job openings (page 198)

**selection ratio**
The number of applicants compared to the number of people to be hired (page 225)

**self-appraisal**
A performance appraisal done by the employee being evaluated, generally on an appraisal form completed by the employee prior to the performance interview (page 291)

**sequential interview**
A format in which a candidate is interviewed by multiple people, one right after another (page 206)

**severance pay**
A lump-sum payment given to terminated employees (page 67)

**severance pay**
A lump-sum payment given to terminated employees by an employer at the time of an employer-initiated termination (page 402)

**sexual harassment**
Unwelcome advances, requests for sexual favours, and other verbal or physical conduct of a sexual nature in the working environment (page 105)

**silver handshake**
An early retirement incentive in the form of increased pension benefits for several years or a cash bonus (page 403)

**similar-to-me error**
A performance rating error in which an appraiser inflates the evaluation of an employee because of a mutual personal connection (page 299)

**situational interview**
An interview in which an applicant is given a hypothetical incident and asked how he or she would respond to it (page 204)

**Six Sigma**
A set of principles and practices whose core ideas include understanding customer needs, doing things right the first time, and striving for continuous improvement (page 6)

**skill inventories**
Files of personnel education, experience, interests, and skills that allow managers to quickly match job openings with employee backgrounds (page 56)

**split pay**
A system whereby expatriates are given a portion of their pay in the local currency to cover their day-to-day expenses and a portion of their pay in their home currency to safeguard their earnings from changes in inflation or foreign exchange rates (page 538)

**spot bonus**
An unplanned bonus given for employee effort unrelated to an established performance measure (page 365)

**spot rewards**
Programs that award employees "on the spot" when they do something particularly well during training or on the job (page 248)

**staffing tables**
Graphic representations of all organizational jobs, along with the numbers of employees currently occupying those jobs and future (monthly or yearly) employment requirements (page 56)

**standard hour plan**
An incentive plan that sets rates based on the completion of a job in a predetermined standard time (page 364)

**statutory rights**
Legal entitlements that derive from government legislation (page 455)

**step-review system**
A system for reviewing employee complaints and disputes by successively higher levels of management (page 470)

**stock data**
Data showing the status of designated groups in occupational categories and compensation levels (page 99)

**straight commission plan**
A compensation plan based on a percentage of sales (page 368)

**straight piecework**
An incentive plan under which employees receive a certain rate for each unit produced (page 363)

**straight salary plan**
A compensation plan that permits salespeople to be paid for performing various duties that are not reflected immediately in their sales volume (page 368)

**strategic human resources management (SHRM)**
The pattern of human resources deployments and activities that enable an organization to achieve its strategic goals (page 40)

**strategic planning**
Procedures for making decisions about the organization's long-term goals and strategies (page 40)

**strategic vision**
A statement about where the company is going and what it can become in the future; clarifies the long-term direction of the company and its strategic intent (page 41)

**stress**
Any adjustive demand caused by physical, mental, or emotional factors that require coping behaviour (page 439)

**structured interview**
An interview in which a set of standardized questions with an established set of answers is used (page 204)

**subordinate appraisal**
A performance appraisal of a superior by an employee, which is more appropriate for developmental than for administrative purposes (page 291)

**succession planning**
The process of identifying, developing, and tracking key individuals for executive positions (page 57)

**summary dismissal**
When a nonunion employer terminates an employee without notice because the employee has committed a serious breach of the contract (page 455)

**SWOT analysis**
A comparison of strengths, weaknesses, opportunities, and threats for strategy formulation purposes (page 60)

**systemic discrimination**
The exclusion of members of certain groups through the application of employment policies or practices based on criteria that are not job related (page 101)

## T

**task analysis**
The process of determining what the content of a training program should be on the basis of a study of the tasks and duties involved in the job (page 241)

**task inventory analysis**
An organization-specific list of tasks and their descriptions used as a basis to identify components of jobs (page 129)

**team appraisal**
A performance appraisal, based on total quality management concepts, that recognizes team accomplishment rather than individual performance (page 292)

**team incentive plan**
A compensation plan in which all team members receive an incentive bonus payment when production or service standards are met or exceeded (page 374)

**telecommuting**
Use of personal computers, networks, and other communications technology to do work in the home that is traditionally done in the workplace (page 144)

**termination**
Practice initiated by an employer to separate an employee from the organization permanently (page 67)

**third-country nationals**
Employees who are natives of a country other than the home country or the host country (page 518)

**time-to-fill metric**
The number of days from when a job opening is approved to the date the candidate is selected (page 169)

**transfer**
Placement of an individual in another job for which the duties, responsibilities, status, and remuneration are approximately equal to those of the previous job (page 175)

**transfer of training**
Effective application of principles learned to what is required on the job (page 261)

**transnational corporation**
A firm that attempts to balance local responsiveness and global scale via a network of specialized operating units (page 517)

**transnational teams**
Teams composed of members of multiple nationalities working on projects that span multiple countries (page 522)

**trend analysis**
A quantitative approach to forecasting labour demand based on an organizational index such as sales (page 53)

## U

**underutilization**
Term applied to designated groups that are not utilized or represented in the employer's workforce proportional to their numbers in the labour market (page 100)

**unfair labour practices (ULPs)**
Specific employer and union illegal practices that deny employees their rights and benefits under federal and provincial labour law (page 488)

**union shop**
Provision of the collective agreement that requires employees to join the union as a condition of their employment (page 483)

**union (shop) steward**
Employee who as a nonpaid union official represents the interests of members in their relations with management (page 492)

## V

**validity**
The degree to which a test or selection procedure measures a person's attributes (page 199)

**value creation**
What the firm adds to a product or service by virtue of making it; the amount of benefits provided by the product or service once the costs of making it are subtracted (page 62)

**values-based hiring**
The process of outlining the behaviours that exemplify a firm's corporate culture and then hiring people who are a fit for them (page 52)

**variable pay**
Tying pay to some measure of individual, group, or organizational performance (page 360)

**vesting**
A guarantee of accrued benefits to participants at retirement age, regardless of their employment status at the time (page 405)

**video résumés**
Short video clips that highlight applicants' qualifications beyond what they can communicate on their résumé (page 201)

**virtual team**
A team with widely dispersed members linked together through computer and telecommunications technology (page 141)

## W

**wage and salary survey**
A survey of the wages paid to employees of other employers in the surveying organization's relevant labour market (page 342)

**wage curve**
A curve in a scattergram representing the relationship between the relative worth of jobs and wage rates (page 343)

**wage-rate compression**
Compression of differentials between job classes, particularly the differential between hourly workers and their managers (page 350)

**work permit or visa**
A government document granting a foreign individual the right to seek employment (page 521)

**work valuation**
A job evaluation system that seeks to measure a job's worth through its value to the organization (page 341)

**workers' compensation insurance**
Insurance provided to workers to defray the loss of income and cost of treatment resulting from work-related injuries or illness (page 399)

**wrongful dismissal**
A lawsuit filed in a court by an employee alleging that he or she was dismissed without proper contractual or "reasonable" notice (page 455)

**Y**

**yield ratio**
The percentage of applicants from a recruitment source that make it to the next stage of the selection process (page 169)

# NAME INDEX

# ORGANIZATION INDEX

## A

Ability Edge, 174
About.com, 190–191
Accenture, 15, 45, 57, 59, 141
Aetna Life and Casualty, 25
Air Canada, 42, 398
Airbus, 253, 521
Alberta Teachers Association, 491
All-China Federation of Trade
    Unions, 541
AltaGas, 406
Amazon.com, 40, 155, 431
America Online (AOL), 513
American Airlines, 135
American Association of Industrial
    Management, 339–340
American Association of Retired
    Persons (AARP), 299
American Society for Training and
    Development, 239
American Society of Training, 263
Aon-Hewitt, 396
Apple Computer, 63, 377
Asia-Pacific Economic Cooperation
    (APEC), 512
Association of Southeast Asian Nations
    (ASEAN), 512
Association of Universities and
    Colleges of Canada, 21
Association of Workers' Compensation
    Boards of Canada, 418
AT&T, 208, 409, 429
Avenor, 299
Aviva, 4
Avon Foods, 267

## B

BAE Systems, 250
Bank of Montreal, 107
The Bay, 53, 222
B.C. Hydro, 106
Bell Canada, 257, 349–350
Berkshire Partners LLC, 489
Best Buy, 285, 399
BHP Ekati Diamond Mine, 21
Black & Decker, 291
BMO Financial Group, 206
BMW, 9
BMW Canada, 293
Boeing, 11, 521
Bombardier, 511, 520
Bonneville Power
    Administration, 250
Bosch, 542
Boston Global Consulting, 518
Bow Valley College, 21

British Airways, 518
British Columbia Civil Liberties
    Union, 218
British Columbia, Office of the
    Auditor, 48
British Columbia, Province of, 48
Budweiser, 9
Bureau of Apprenticeship and
    Training (U.S.), 250
Burger King, 330
Business Development Bank
    of Canada (BSC), 410

## C

Calgary Health Region, 393
Cameco Corporation, 99
Canada Post, 350
Canadian Armed Forces, 106
Canadian Association of Smelter
    and Allied Workers (CASAW), 499
Canadian Auto Workers (CAW),
    486–487, 489, 490
Canadian Centre for Occupational
    Health and Safety, 425, 430
Canadian Civil Liberties
    Association, 220
Canadian Coalition for Good
    Governance, 372
Canadian Forces, 253
Canadian Human Rights Commission
    (CHRC), 94, 96, 103, 218, 219
Canadian Human Rights Tribunal,
    106, 350
Canadian Labour Congress (CLC), 491
Canadian Nurses Association, 53
Canadian Pacific Hotels, 207
Canadian Tire, 53, 295–297, 379
Canadian Union of Postal
    Workers, 462, 491
Canadian Union of Public Employees
    (CUPE), 492
Career Edge, 174
CareerBuilder, 190, 202, 208
CareerPath, 191
Caterpillar, 256, 489
Caterpillar University of
    Leadership, 256
Center for Corporate Citizenship, 10
Centre de recherche industrielle du
    Québec (CRIQ), 98
Charles Schwab and Company, 64
Chemico, 59–60
Chrysler, 6, 62, 336
Church of Scientology, 237
Cigna, 291
Cisco Canada, 389
Cisco Systems, 12, 15, 254

Citigroup, 538
City of Ancaster, 103
City of Chartlottetown, 267
City of Mississauga, 336
City of Richmond, 105
City of Toronto, 103, 107, 498
City of Waterloo, 213
CityMax.com, 267
CN, 107
CN Centre for Occupational Health
    and Safety, 441–442
CNA Financial Corp., 40
Coca-Cola, 8, 9, 377, 518
Coca-Cola's Fountain Manufacturing
    Operation, 267–268
Cold Metal Products, 406
Colgate-Palmolive, 526, 532, 533
Communications Workers of
    America, 500
Comp Analyst, 343
Compaq Computer, 136, 434
Compass Group, 97
Conexus, 260, 389
Conference Board of Canada, 9, 25,
    108, 109, 236, 252, 337, 342,
    398, 409
Connaught Laboratories, 110
The Container Store, 153, 171
Continental Airlines, 62
Coopers & Lybrand, 257, 373, 393–394
Cornell University, 136
Corning, Inc., 12, 55

## D

Daimler-Benz, 62
Dell Computer, 208, 293, 517
Deloitte, 6, 39, 157, 163–164
Deloitte & Touche, 18, 526
Department of National Defence, 110
Deutsche Bank, 402
Dexter, 66
Digital Equipment of Canada, 108–109
Disney, 47, 291
Diversity Leadership Council,
    RBC, 109
Dow Chemical, 526, 530
Drake Beam Morin (DBM), 177, 182
Durham College, 251

## E

East Asia Economic Group, 512
Ebco, 108
École Polytechnique de Paris, 515
The Economical Insurance Group
    (TEIG), 401
Economy Carriers, 426

# SUBJECT INDEX

# SUBJECT INDEX

## C